10 the BEST of EVERYTHING

Nathaniel Lande & Andrew Lande

PASSPORT *to the* BEST

10 *the* BEST
of EVERYTHING

An ULTIMATE GUIDE *for* TRAVELERS

NATIONAL GEOGRAPHIC

WASHINGTON, D.C.

For Natalya, Just the Best
& For Michelle

f or Edison Marshall, Jean deWitt Fitz, and Papa Hemingway, whose storytelling, heroic adventure, and friendship to one author as a child, enriched a life threefold, with wonderment, adventure, and discovery.

— . —

And for the courageous men and woman of the International Committee of the Red Cross, an organization whose humanitarian mission is to protect the lives and dignity of victims of war and internal violence and to provide them with assistance. A portion of the authors' royalties are donated to its mission.

~FOREWORD~

"It's what you discover after you know it all that counts".

—John Wooden

Visit the Guggenheim museum in Bilbao, a modern building that shimmers with light, whose stunning proportion and sense of space make the soul soar.

In St. Petersburg, promenade the wide boulevards of Peter the Great's Venice of the North, the city that inspired Pushkin and Tolstoy. In early summer, beneath a dusty blue sky that never darkens, join revelers enjoying the fleeting magic of White Nights.

Through perpetual springtime lush with oleander, roses, lemons, and mangos, walk on top of the world along the island of Madeira's mountain aqueducts, built five centuries ago by Moorish slaves. In the evenings sip Madeira wine to make you smile as you listen to Fado music that will make you weep.

Cruise the Svalbard and Spitsbergen Islands of northern Norway and experience the enchantment of a polar wilderness,

where the sky is impossibly clear and the midnight sun imperially bright.

Sail a felucca down the Nile by night, when the sky is sprinkled with stars and the banks with neon-lit minarets. In the day disembark to visit the pharaonic temples that lie between Luxor and Aswan.

Spend an evening in the Foreign Correspondents' Club in Phnom Penh, Cambodia, where, at the back—a splendid conversion of two three-story shop houses—you can look out onto the Royal Palace. Walk through the bar and dining room to an open fronted veranda overlooking the brilliant confluence of the Mekong and Tongle Sap Rivers, one of Asia's best views. The next day, clamber through the temple courts of Angkor Wat, where giant Buddhas doze in a green gloom among the strangler figs. A silent place at the center of a spinning world.

Journey on.

TABLE OF
~CONTENTS~

🚢 **Bon Voyage** 🚢

~Introductions~

I was a young boy when I discovered the other half of the world, with my father, an Oxford classicist, my guide though China and India. As we crossed the Khyber Pass into Burma, I began making copious notes—lists of what I had seen grouped into categories of man-made places and the natural world.

Years later, as director of TIME World News Service, my job took me all over the world, giving me an opportunity to expand my growing file of special places and exceptional experiences. This file became a resource for my colleagues, who were always asking me for places to shop, a good hotel, or a great restaurant. From this I developed a "passport to the best," which you hold in your hands. It includes lists of favorites in many categories, a trove of extraordinary

historical and literary excursions, and Lande's List, a compendium of the best hotels and restaurants, compiled from fellow correspondents and first-hand experience.

Once, returning from an assignment in the Far East, I stopped at the Bristol Hotel in Paris, on the Faubourg St.-Honoré. After shedding my clothes, I took a shower and forgot them. Six months later, when I returned to Paris, I opened my armoire and there, starched crisp and fresh, was my correspondent's kit, now lavender scented. My shoes gleamed like mirrors. For me, that experience embodies the governing philosophy of this book: Each selection, whether a hotel, restaurant, or expedition, exceeds expectations.

In the last century, wealthy European and American families traditionally sent their sons and daughters on a Grand Tour. Journeys often included London, Paris, Rome, Florence, and Athens, and these cities were first-hand introductions to the classical world they had long studied. They sought out literary landmarks, lingered over historical sights, and pursued extraordinary experiences. They went on to become sophisticated and worldly, and, indeed, to complete their education. Now, international travel is more widespread and accessible, but the impetus remains constant. Our curiosity and imagination are drawn to people and places vastly different from ourselves; we will always look beyond our own borders to the unfamiliar.

Nobody needed Mozart's concertos before he wrote them, or Monet's studies before he painted them. But I cannot imagine the world without these riches. The same holds true for my travels. In this book, I invite readers to join me on the journeys that have expanded my vision, delighted my senses, and refreshed my spirit.

— *Nathaniel Lande*

My father instilled in me the joy of discovery and the difference between being a well-heeled tourist and a well-seasoned traveler. Like my grandfather, he had studied at Oxford, and when I was young, he introduced me to Europe.

As a director at TIME, my father was once invited to write a speech for a friend who was head of an international airline. He refused to accept a fee for his work, and so, in gratitude, a gift of two first-class tickets—to anywhere in the world—arrived at his office.

I had just returned home for Easter break, complaining of boarding school food and the term paper I had to write on French history. *"Billet de faveur,"* my father exclaimed, holding up the tickets. "Let's go to Paris!"

A few hours later we were dining at the Bristol Hotel, an old favorite of his. The restaurant had just won its first Michelin star and was very proud. The waiters in their black tails and white ties introduced me to the best meal I had ever eaten, topped with chocolate soufflé, *tart tatin,* and crème brûlée. As the French have always known, and as I was beginning to learn, it is at the dining table that people are most civilized, conversation brightest, optimism strongest. Later, my father was amused when I announced how much I liked Paris, as he was signing the $300 bill for lunch without wine.

That afternoon I swam in the pool on top of the Bristol, fashioned in teak like a Spanish galleon, and for a few minutes I became Captain Kidd in search of a pirate's booty. Then I discovered other treasure. We took an aimless stroll to the left bank, across boulevard St.-Germain, and down to rue de Buci. There I had my first plunge into that garden of delight, an open-air market. In the street everyone was part performer and part spectator. Nowhere in Paris was the show better.

Then as now, Paris taught me a few things; one of the most useful is that the best way to know a country's people is through its markets. In Buenos Aires or Barcelona, go where the locals are buying their oranges and lettuces, and you'll learn more about them than you would in all of the best libraries and museums.

Later, my worldview was enhanced when I studied at Trinity College, Dublin. I remember the dampness that winter and how early in the morning the steam heat clanked for just a few minutes before falling silent. I heard the heat but never felt it. But soon I warmed to my new home. I discovered the glories of Dublin and Ireland, with excursions to the west coast, and the beauty of the country.

In my travels, I have recorded mental snapshots: Paris, Dublin, and other great cities of the world; crossing continents and channels; sailing from Barcelona to Lisbon to the China Sea. Along the way, I assembled material for this album of special experiences and places, which I am very happy to share with you.

— Andrew Lande

PART JUST -THE- BEST ONE

In Part One, experts and bon vivants help us determine the Ten Best of Everything, from watches to alpine climbs, lake crossings to intimate hideaways, food halls to flea markets, before arriving in ten favorite cities to enjoy the ten best things to do on a Sunday afternoon.

While the definition of "the best" is necessarily subjective, the ten best lists assembled here are diverse, informative, and, best of all, full of surprises. Essentially, we have selected what we, based on our experiences, believe represent the best. We list our selections in no special order. In a few instances, a selection may be found in more than one category, and that is because it possesses specific characteristics that make it deserving of a double or triple listing.

Not long ago, we interviewed master chef Ferrán Adrià at his celebrated El Bulli restaurant north of Barcelona. El Bulli is noted for its cutting-edge culinary technology, preparation, and sophisticated food presentation. Each guest is presented with an overwhelming 35 courses at one sitting, with a menu created for each patron. Over dinner, Adrià confided to Andrew that when he travels, he longs for nothing so much as an old-fashioned, American-style burger. For all those who feel the same, we have included the world's ten best burger joints.

I have always been keenly particular about getting a good night's sleep. Standing six foot six with a problematic back, I have become a scholar of the mattress, and my supine studies have resulted in our list of the world's ten best mattresses—including Beauty Rest, Serta's Perfect Night, and London's Savoy Hotel's custom-made mattresses available for special order.

In this section, readers will discover Arnold Palmer's favorite golf courses, Philippe de Rothschild's advice on wines, techniques for preparing a proper English tea, and Fortnum and Mason's ten best brews. You'll learn the best places to cruise and to walk, the world's best swimming pools (the most exotic may be La Mamounia's in Marrakesh), and much, much more. In short, here is Just the Best.

~GOLF COURSES~

Arnold Palmer is synonymous with golf. He's won a whopping 92 championships and has gained much acclaim as a course designer. He was four years old when his father, Milfred J. "Deacon" Palmer, gave the boy his first set of clubs. Then the boy was off to the links, playing and caddying at the Latrobe (Pa.) Country Club, where Deacon worked as the pro. In a neat twist of fate, Palmer now owns the club.

"I can't tell you how much I appreciate what the game has done for me," Palmer says on the website for his golf academy. "I look at the people I've met and the associations I've made through golf. I can't give enough to golf. If I had more, I'd give more. Everything I have I owe to golf.

"My views on the game aren't ones that have been molded slowly through the years of playing and practicing. They are based on simple fundamentals taught to me by my father, Deacon.

"He taught me the game of golf. A great deal of the success I've enjoyed in my career, I owe to him. He believed golf is really pretty simple and a whole lot of fun … if you rely on two vital aspects, fundamentals and attitude. I totally agree.

"Pap believed in keeping the game as simple as possible. He felt that if a player mastered basic fundamentals, then his swing and his entire game would develop naturally.

"The one thing my father always stressed, though, was practice. To him, the brain could learn the basics of golf from reading or watching, but practice taught the body what they were. He'd be the first to point out that nothing could take the place of getting out and hitting golf balls. It's how I learned, and how you should as well.

"If you possess the burning desire to play great golf, along with a willingness to work hard at your game, you'll discover the secrets that I learned from Pap long ago, that playing great golf is not as difficult as it might appear, and that the game is a lifelong joy to play when you find out how easy it actually can be."

Since Palmer has designed some of the best fairways in the world, we asked him to tell us what goes into making a challenging, enjoyable golf course. Below is his list. And based on these requirements, we've tried to shoot below par for the Ten Best courses.

THE MAKING OF A GREAT GOLF COURSE:

1 - Budget	**7** - Vegetation
2 - Style or Type	**8** - Environmentally
3 - Terrain Features	Sensitive Areas
4 - Water Source	**9** - Safety
5 - Soil	**10** - Variety of Holes
6 - Prevailing Winds	[most important]

GOLF COURSES

1 – PINE VALLEY GOLF CLUB
Clementon, New Jersey
Crump/Colt (1918), Par 70—6,183 m (6,765 yd)
Tel: 856-309-3203

Pine Valley is somewhat mysterious in golfing circles because it is hard to find and extremely private. Those who have found the club located in New Jersey's lonesome Pine Barrens say the course is one of the world's finest. The founders started the club in 1913, with the purchase of 75 hectares (184 acres) of scruffy pinelands. The later addition of 168 hectares (416 acres) of picturesque virgin woodlands enhanced the remote beauty of the place.

2 – CYPRESS POINT CLUB
Pebble Beach, California
Mackenzie (1929), Par 72—5,974 m (6,536 yd)
Tel: 831-624-2223

The late great duffer Bob Hope once quipped that during a membership drive at this exclusive club, they drove away 20 members. Cypress Point is indeed a private place, which explains why you won't see casual players chipping away on the Pacific coastline. Located south of Pebble Beach in California's gorgeous Big Sur country, the club has an 18-hole course of rolling fairways. Dr. Alister Mackenzie, architect of Augusta National Golf Club (number 8 in this list) designed Cypress also.

3 – MUIRFIELD VILLAGE GOLF CLUB
Gullane, Scotland, United Kingdom
T. Morris (1889), Par 71—6,600 m (7,221 yd)
Tel: 44-(0)-16-2084-2123

Home to the world's oldest golfing society, Muirfield opened in 1744. More than 200 years later, Jack Nicklaus won his first British Open here on the storied greens near Edinburgh. Most golfers consider Muirfield to be a particularly demanding test of ability.

4 – ST. ANDREWS (OLD COURSE)
St. Andrews, Scotland, United Kingdom
Tel: 44-(0)-133-446-6666, www.standrews.org.uk
Par 72—6,653 m (7,279 yd)

Any golfer worth his or her weight in golf clubs wants to play the Old Course at St. Andrews, the most famous one in the world. Golf has been played on this heathery patch of land on Scotland's east coast since the 15th century. In addition to the Old Course, there are four more excellent 18-hole courses, one 9-hole course, and a practice center to accommodate golfers of all skill levels. All are public, but reservations are a must.

The Old Course is embedded in the stormy North Sea dunes and is challenging to even the best of golfers. For people who aren't even pretending to be Tiger Woods, Strathtyrum Course is ideal. The nine-hole Balgove is best for children and beginners.

5 – PEBBLE BEACH GOLF LINKS
Pebble Beach, California
Neville/Grant (1919), Par 72—6,158 m (6,737 yd)
Tel: 800-654-9300, www.pebblebeach.com

Pebble Beach Golf Links may be the best known course in the United States. As you work your way over the narrow fairways, make sure you pause to drink in the outstanding views of the rocky shores that make up this part of California's Pacific coast. There's an especially good vista at the 18th hole, a 501-meter (548-yard) par 5.

Since the wind can be a big factor here, be sure to select the proper club if you want to score well.

6 – ROYAL MELBOURNE GOLF CLUB
Melbourne, Australia
Mackenzie/Russell (1926), Par 72—6,031 m
(6,598 yd) (East) and 6,022 m (6,589 yd) (West)
Tel: 61-3-9598-6755, www.royalmelbourne.com.au

Located in eastern Australia, this lovely private club has two 18-hole courses, East and West. For tournaments and special members' events, the club forms the Composite Course of 12 holes from the West and 6 from the East. This first was created in 1959 when Royal Melbourne was the site of the Canada Cup, now called the World Cup.

7 – SHINNECOCK HILLS GOLF CLUB
Southampton, New York
Toomey/Flynn (1931), Par 70—6,394 m (6,996 yd)
Tel: 631-283-3525

Shinnecock Hills boasts a few notable firsts. It has the first clubhouse in the United States, built in 1893 from a design by Stanford White. It was also the first club that admitted women as members. The rolling terrain of Long Island's south shore gives the course plenty of variety. And winds off the Atlantic Ocean can make playing this private course quite challenging.

8 – AUGUSTA NATIONAL GOLF CLUB
Augusta, Georgia
Mackenzie/Jones (1932). Par 72—6,311 m (6,905 yd)
Tel: 706-667-6719

Each spring, the venerable club in central Georgia is the site of the Masters, maybe the most revered tournament in the United States. Hot-pink azaleas bloom near the championship 18-hole and 9-hole courses. Three of the

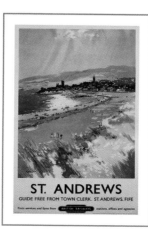

ST. ANDREWS
GUIDE FREE FROM TOWN CLERK, ST. ANDREWS, FIFE

sport's toughest and most famous holes are here: the 11th, 12th, and 13th holes together are known as "Amen Corner." Winners are easy to spot, because they are given special green blazers.

9 – PINEHURST COUNTRY CLUB
Pinehurst, North Carolina
D. Ross (1903-35), Par 72—6,445 m (7,051 yd)
Tel: 910-235-8507, www.pinehurst.com

Established in 1894 in the Sand Hills region of North Carolina, Pinehurst has eight outstanding courses and more holes than any other resort. Course No. 1 is the most scenic and picturesque in terms of design. However, all the courses have tree-lined fairways and numerous bunkers. Payne Stewart won the 1999 U.S. Open here with a dramatic 15-foot putt at the 18th hole. Sadly, it was his last major tournament; he died in an airplane crash that fall.

10 – ROYAL COUNTY DOWN GOLF CLUB
Newcastle, N. Ireland, United Kingdom
T. Morris (1889) Dunn/Vardon, Par 72—6,369 m (6,968 yd)
Tel: 44-28-4372-3314, www.royalcountydown.org

The more than 100-year-old Royal County Down Golf Club has two 18-hole courses: the Championship and the less formidable Annesley. Located about 48 kilometers (30 miles) south of Belfast and 145 kilometers (90 miles) from Dublin, the club is stunningly set between the mountains of Mourne and the Irish Sea. However, it is as tough a place to play as it is beautiful to see. The fairways are lined with masses of native plants such as heather and gorse. Wild tussocks cover the bunkers. And the wind off the sea can add to the tension.

TEN BEST
~TENNIS VENUES~

O n the courts at Wimbledon, we serve our ten favorites.

1 – ROD LAVER ARENA
Melbourne, Australia
Tel: 61-3-9286-1600, www.mopt.com.au

Completed in 1988, this mammoth structure can seat up to 15,000. It was named after Australia's own Rod "the Rockhampton Rocket" Laver, the only tennis player in history to win two Grand Slams (1962 and 1969). Appropriately, the arena is used for Grand Slam matches, as well as a number of other events in sports and entertainment.

2 – ROLAND-GARROS
Paris, France
Tel: 33-(0)-1-47-43-48-00, www.rolandgarros.com

Roland-Garros is one of four tournaments in the Grand Slam circuit (the others are Wimbledon and the U.S. and Australian Opens). Here, the contestants play on clay courts. Built in 1928, the stadium has been renovated many times. It recently opened to the general public year round.

3 – ALLIANZ SUISSE OPEN
Gstaad, Switzerland
Tel: 41-31-952-5577, www.swissopengstaad.com

Some of the world's best tennis players have been coming to this Alpine resort village each summer since 1915 to play

in the Allianz Suisse Open Gstaad. Perhaps no other tournament outside of the Grand Slam is so clearly a part of tennis history.

4 – MONTE-CARLO COUNTRY CLUB
Monte-Carlo, France
Tel: 33-(0)-4-93-41-30-15, www.mccc.mc

The Monte-Carlo Country Club's sumptuous setting between mountain and sea makes it an especially lovely spot to play tennis. It is home to the Monte-Carlo tournament, established in 1897. The club itself opened several decades later as Prince Louis II of Monaco's ploy to capitalize on the tourists who were discovering the charms of the French Riviera. The courts are clay, and there are more than 1,800 changing rooms.

5 – U.S. OPEN
Flushing Meadows, New York
Tel: 718-760-6200, www.usopen.org

The U.S. Open began life in 1881 as a purely entertaining men's singles tournament in Newport, R.I. Gradually, the event expanded to include women's singles, men's and women's doubles, and mixed doubles. By the late 1960s, the tournament settled permanently in Queens, N.Y. Today the open takes place in the Louis Armstrong Stadium/Arthur Ashe Stadium. There, more than 600 amateurs and professionals gather each summer. The prize coffers are worth almost $18 million.

6 – ALL ENGLAND LAWN TENNIS & CROQUET CLUB

Wimbledon, United Kingdom
Tel: 44-(0)-2-8946-2244, www.wimbledon.org

They still play the game on grass courts here in this club south of London. There are others kinds: five shale, three continental clay, one American clay, and five indoor courts. But it is the grass ones that are famous, befitting the genteel image that this venerable British sporting event evokes. What began as a garden party in 1877 is now a major spectacle that millions of people look forward to watching every summer.

7 – NEWPORT CASINO & INTERNATIONAL TENNIS HALL OF FAME

Newport, Rhode Island
Tel: 401-846-0642, www.tennisfame.com

The famous architectural firm McKim, Mead & White designed this imposing club in 1880, where members could play lawn or court tennis. The glorious grass courts are the oldest continuously used competitive courts, as well as the only ones open to the public. If you're more interested in the history of the sport than playing a round, check out the hall of fame's comprehensive collections.

8 – LA QUINTA RESORT & CLUB

Palm Springs, California
Tel: 800-598-3828, www.laquintaresort.com

The sunken court within this posh resort is bordered by terraced beds of flowers and trees. If it's being used, relax; La Quinta has 22 others with clay, hard, and grass surfaces. Ten of the courts are lit for night-time games.

9 – PALAIS OMNISPORTS DE PARIS BERCY

Paris, France
Tel: 33-(0)-1-40-02-60-60, www.bercy.fr

The Bercy, as the Palais Omnisports de Paris Bercy is called, was modeled after New York City's Madison Square Garden. The pyramid-shaped structure and its surrounding lawns are on the Seine's Right Bank. In addition to tennis events, the Bercy—with seating for about 17,000—is a popular venue for sporting events, operas, and concerts.

10 – GENERALI OPEN PROFESSIONAL MEN'S TENNIS TOURNAMENT

Kitzbühel, Austria
Tel: 43-5356-72076, www.generaliopen.at

Home to the Generali Open Professional Men's Tennis Tournament, Kitzbühel's spectacular clay courts along with the beautiful surroundings in the Tyrolean Alps make this a very special venue. The Kitzbühel Tennis Club opened in 1925 as a place mainly for the foreign tourists who came to the mountains in the summer. As the sport of tennis caught on, the club expanded with indoor courts. In the 1990s, a new stadium opened.

Ten Best
~Polo Clubs~

World-famous polo teacher, coach, and player Rege Ludwig rates the top ten polo clubs in the world.

1 – The International Polo Club Palm Beach
Wellington, Florida
Tel: 561-204-5687, www.internationalpoloclub.com/home.htm

Located in the heart of South Florida's tony horse country, this club provides an elegant setting for players and fans. The main road lined with stately palms rolls past lush grounds punctuated by tropical plants.

The season kicks off in January and ends in April. Thousands of people gather to watch some of the best players and ponies in the world show off their mastery of the ancient sport. The arenas of play include three playing fields and a stick and ball field.

The club is quickly overtaking its rival, the Palm Beach Polo & Country Club, as the place to see and be seen on Sunday afternoons. Built in 2004, the posh International has a state-of-the-art stadium, restaurant, and bar.

2 – Santa María Polo Club
Sotogrande, Spain
Tel: 34-956-610-012 or 134, www.santamariapoloclub.com

Located in the Costa del Sol region of Spain, this club is one of the most highly reputed sports complexes in the world. The Santa María Polo Club offers its members nine grounds spread out across four gaming areas. It organizes more than 30 tournaments a year in high, medium, and low handicap. The club's polo school has developed an excellent reputation under the capable hands of five polo instructors and assisted by Tito Gómez, an experienced player.

3 – Guards Polo Club
Smith's Lawn at Windsor Great Park, Surrey, United Kingdom
Tel: 44-(0)-178-443-4212 or 44-(0)-208-795-2222
www.guardspoloclub.com

In terms of members and grounds, Guards is the largest polo club in Europe; the 10 playing grounds are spread out over about 53 hectares (130 acres).

Situated south of London in the center of Windsor Great Park, the club was established in 1955. Polo season here goes from April to mid-September. The three main tournaments—the Queen's Cup, Royal Windsor, and Archie David—take place in June. However, the biggest crowds come in the following month for the Hurlingham Polo Association's International Day.

The club offers "The Polo Experience," in which you spend a day in the care of a pro, learning to play polo under the tutelage of John Horswell, coach to England's polo team.

4 – Cowdray Park Polo Club
Midhurst, West Sussex, United Kingdom
Tel: 44-(0)-173-081-3257, www.cowdraypolo.co.uk

Combine a day out in the beautiful Sussex countryside with the opportunity to watch top-notch polo. At Cowdray Park,

LUDWIG POLO CLINICS

74-350 Primrose Drive, Palm Desert, California
Tel: 760-773-3558

The great Rege Ludwig, world-renowned polo instructor, conducts his famous clinics at the Eldorado Polo Club in Southern California. These three-day clinics, held on the grass polo fields, are tailored for beginning and experienced polo players.

"The best and fastest way to learn a sport is to watch and imitate a champion."

—Rege Ludwig

coaches are on hand also to teach rookies or help experienced players improve.

5 – ELDORADO POLO CLUB

Indio, California
Tel: 760-342-2223, www.eldoradopolo.com

Located about two hours east of Los Angeles, the Eldorado covers 73 hectares (180 acres) of the east side of the Coachella Valley. It is the perfect place to play polo, desert-style. There are 14 fields and stables for 1,000 horses. Eldorado prides itself on sponsoring two women's-only tournaments each year.

6 – WILL ROGERS POLO CLUB

Pacific Palisades, California
Tel: 310-573-5000, www.willrogerspolo.org

In the 1930s, there were more than 25 polo fields in the Los Angeles area. Today, the Will Rogers field is the only one. The humorist created and landscaped the field in 1926 on the grounds of what later became his home. Rogers, an avid polo fan, used to play here with his friends. David Niven, Spencer Tracy, Hal Roach, Walt Disney, and Clark Gable played on the fields. After Rogers died, his widow gave the grounds as a gift to the state of California. People can watch matches here free of charge on weekends from April through October.

7 – THE CHANTILLY POLO CLUB

Apremont, France
Tel: 33-(0)-3-44 64 04 30, www.poloclubchantilly.com

Equestrian sports have long been popular in Picardie. It was here, on the grounds in front of the glorious château de Chantilly, that the first thoroughbred horse race took place in France during the reign of Louis XIV, the Sun King. So it is appropriate that this region should be home to the country's largest polo club. Located just west of Paris, the club has 250 players competing in various tournaments and some 3,500 horses in training.

The famous Rothschild family built a polo field in 1920 on one of the three farms that surrounded the chateau. Seventy-five years later, Patrick Guerrand-Hermès and a group of friends turned the field into the club. It now encompasses ten fields, two of which can be used year-round. The chalky soil is an excellent surface for polo.

8 – WHITFIELD COURT POLO CLUB

Whitfield Court, Waterford, Ireland
Tel: 353-51-384216, www.whitfieldcourtpoloclub.com

Major Hugh Dawnay started the Whitfield Court Polo Club and International Polo School in 1976. Since then, players from more than 30 countries have visited this place in southern Ireland to learn the sport. There are two fields, one full-size and the other all-weather. Members play three days a week from May to September. The club's major tournament takes place in August.

Accommodations at the residential polo school are in the Dawnays' home. Dawnay himself has had coaching stints outside of Ireland, notably in Palm Beach, Fla., and Costa Careyes, Mex.

EL METEJÓN POLO RANCH

Buenos Aires, Argentina
Tel: 54-222-643-2227
http://021wap.md5.com.ar/elmetejonpolo.html

Argentina's El Metejón Polo Ranch is becoming a hip spot for international polo players since it opened in 1998. Not far from the country's very chic capital of Buenos Aires, the ranch has the atmosphere of a traditional Argentine *estancia*. The facilities are outstanding and the quality of the game is top-notch.

Many come here to learn or improve their game. Hundreds of good ponies are available. Good players also relish the chance to play with or against some of the finest players in the world. There are three fields and 122 hectares (300 acres).

An excellent time to visit El Metejón is in late November/early December, when the Argentine Polo Championship takes place in Palermo. You will have the opportunity to watch the best teams in Argentina compete for the title.

9 – ROYAL PALM POLO SPORTS CLUB

Boca Raton, Florida
Tel: 561-734-7656, www.boca-polo.com

This state-of-the-art club has a stadium, 350 stalls, and seven fields spread out across 65 hectares (160 acres) in South Florida. It was the creation of Arthur Vining Davis, one of the founders of Alcoa. He wanted to bring high-goal polo to the area, so he laid the fields out in 1955 next to his hotel. (The hotel is now the Royal Palm Yacht and Country Club.) John T. Oxley purchased the club, which was not doing well financially, 13 years later and rebuilt it in 1977.

Oxley died in 1996, leaving the management of his legacy to his sons Tom and Jack. Polo season starts in January and ends in May.

10 – SANTA BARBARA POLO & RACQUET CLUB

Carpinteria, California
Tel: 805-745-5959, www.sbpolo.com

The Santa Barbara Polo & Racquet Club is the third oldest continuously operating polo club in the United States. It was established in Southern California's wine country in 1911. Since then, it has gained a great following among the international polo set. Matches take place every Sunday in the spring, summer, and fall. Spread across 12 ocean-front hectares (30 acres), the club has three polo fields and stabling for more than 300 horses. There's an indoor arena for instruction and intercollegiate games. Not a true equestrian? Never fear. You can try your hand at Golf Cart Polo, a twist on the sport of kings in which guests can swing mallets from the comfort of golf carts, all expertly driven by club employees. For those less keen on actually playing polo, the club has tennis courts, a swimming pool, and a spa.

FOR the LOVE of the GAME

Polo was always a way to meet terrific people. Like Elizabeth. But somehow, something happened between chukkers. In the beginning, I thought there was no more exciting pastime than playing the fastest ball sport in the world. However, I finally took polo up for the wrong reasons. My handicap was that I had not so much fallen off my horse, but fallen for Elizabeth. There she was, on that May afternoon, in her British Racing Green Land Rover, admiring the game, knowing it was fast, dangerous, and handsome, like polo players themselves.

That's when Elizabeth tailgated into my life. She was a sports writer for the *Los Angeles Times.* "You must be a polo player," she called out to me as I swaggered on the sidelines. The introduction startled me. After all, I was a spectator … who longed to play. I was just posing. "You are very tall for a polo player," she added, admiringly.

Secretly, I liked the thought of how I might look in brown polished boots made of soft leather in Argentina, smartly tailored white cord breeches, and a blue Locke helmet. I fantasized about galloping past this pretty polo girl in her summer dress and wide-brimmed hat, those big eyes smiling underneath.

"I must admit I have a thing for polo," I answered.

"How long have you been playing? You must be from the Argentine?"

From Argentina … music to my ears! Was it my brown hair and dark eyes? Did I really have an *estancia* in South America?

"Yes, I do spend some time there."

"I'd like to see you play. I'm Elizabeth," she said, offering her hand. "I adore polo players." "Nathaniel," I responded, accenting each syllable to a more continental, "Nat-tan-yel." I was in deep trouble.

I took up the sport in earnest.

I didn't know it at the time, but after the rush and accomplishment of adding just one goal to my handicap, I would find the sport is addictive. When I counted up the expenses—a string of ponies, saddles, grooms, boarding, vet fees, club dues—the sport had consequences indeed. The most dangerous handicap was bankruptcy. But not so in the game of love. I wanted to play the game and, through it, to impress Elizabeth.

My learning curve took me to some of the best places in the world for the sport: Westbury, N.Y.; Palm Beach, Fla.; Buenos Aires. Then, having heard that the action on the polo front was in the Dominican Republic, I flew down to take a look for myself. What I found on this island of beautiful beaches was a haven for polo. The island's most unique vacation property is the Casa de Campo golf and country club complex. This is on the southeast coast at

Punta La Romana, a reconstructed Italian village complete with stone buildings covered in red tiles. A creation of the Gulf and Western sugar empire, Casa has five polo fields and 200 ponies.

My instruction began with a maharajah from India, who brilliantly coached me for two weeks. I continued my odyssey to Palm Beach Polo. There, on 891 hectares (2,200 acres) I found 15 emerald fields. The club has the finest high-goal tournaments where players vie for prestige and power.

From Palm Beach, I journeyed across the country to Southern California to take some clinics at the Eldorado Polo Club near Palm Springs. The world-famous Rege Ludwig took pity on me there. He instructed me to hold the reins high above my belt and lead the pony by using my legs and my weight.

Onto Whitfield in Ireland, where the famed Major Hugh Dawnay held court.

The major is the author of *Polo Vision*, a guide whose strength lies in the simplicity and clarity of the tactical explanations and innovative riding drills. These instructions impart effective methods and techniques for striking the ball and winning. The mantra was "stay focused on the place you are going and follow your lead."

And I was certainly heading toward Elizabeth.

For a final polish, I settled to the championship season in Buenos Aires at Palermo, where teams like La Dolfina and Ellerstina, players such as Alberto Pedro Heguy Sr. and Adolpho Cambiaso held polo currency. Could I ever play with them?

At Diego Richini's famed polo ranch, El Metejón, I advanced under the careful tutelage of María Chavanne. The first day, after a light breakfast, the horses were ready to be mounted. There were 12 horses for every rider for each game. All morning was devoted to stick-and-balling. In the afternoon we played 4-chukker games with Chavanne and some of the other best polo players in the world.

"It takes three days before you are really fit and then you will be better as the week progresses," she promised as she smacked the ball. "Then, when you feel the adrenaline in your veins over this sport, you will start to really feel polo. That is when there's no turning back."

"Elizabeth," I thought, "I am on my way!"

That afternoon, playing a hard-won match against the Brits, I was called to the game. Sore, tired, and exhausted, I nonetheless thought that polo was the most important thing in my life.

That revelation was followed by a new problem to ponder: whether I had lost sight of my goal. Was I attracted to Elizabeth or truly to polo?

It seemed perfectly reasonable at the time. After all, Elizabeth would understand; she was a sports writer. Had the adrenaline rush restricted the flow of male hormones? No, it couldn't be. After all, I lectured myself, why did I take up the sport in the first place, if not to win Elizabeth? I wanted her adoring approval. I was a polo player. She had made me an honest man.

Still I played on until a broken collarbone, two broken ribs, and sprained wrists made it clear that the game had certain undeniable risks. Were plaster casts and bandages hallmarks of courage or signs of stupidity? I had learned to play on polo fields around the world, and I was finally playing a respectable game. But after yet another painful injury, compounded by the prospect of bankruptcy, I realized that there was something missing.

Elizabeth! There was more to life than polo. It was time to turn in my mallet. So I went home to find her, in hopes of kindling a relationship that far exceeded the bounds of the game.

But she was gone. Appropriately enough, she had run off with a polo player from Argentina.

Ten Best
~Swimming Pools~

We dive into the good life.

1 – La Mamounia
Marrakech, Morocco
Tel : 212-44-38-86-00, www.mamounia.com

The azure pool within Marrakech's most prestigious hotel feels like a desert oasis. Towering palms surround the water, which is kept at 24°C (75°F). Guests can lounge about on teak furniture outfitted with soft cushions. For lunch, the poolside Restaurant Les Trois Palmiers serves a buffet with dozens of exotic treats. Waiters supply cool drinks.

The hotel was built in 1923 in a blend of ornate Moroccan and art deco styles. This was one of the places for foreign dignitaries to stay at that time. Sir Winston Churchill, an avid artist as well as a statesman, set up his easel and painted here on the grounds.

2 – Gran Hotel La Florida
Barcelona, Spain
Tel: 34-93-259-30-00
www.hotellaflorida.com

Overlooking the city below is the hotel's 37-meter (121-foot) indoor-outdoor swimming pool. It is made of stainless steel. There's a spa here as well.

3 – Hotel du Cap-Eden-Roc
Cap d'Antibes, France
Tel: 33-(0)-4-93-61-39-01, www.edenroc-hotel.fr

The Hotel du Cap-Eden-Roc's saltwater infinity pool is carved into the edge of the French Riviera's rocky coastline; sunbathers have their choice of terraces nearby. Since the hotel opened in 1870, it has been practically a synonym for glamour. F. Scott Fitzgerald based his descriptions of the Hotel des Étrangers in *Tender Is the Night* on it. The list of other famous guests here includes Sophia Loren, Johnny Depp, Naomi Campbell, Fred Astaire, and Cher.

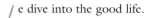

4 – The Bristol
Paris, France
Tel: 33-(0)-53-43-43-00
www.hotelbristol.com

Nobody expects to find an indoor pool built to look as though it is inside a teak yacht on the roof of a hotel in the center of Paris. Yet, here it is, an architectural original. In case you're not really feeling it, one wall is covered with a mural of nattily attired people on the deck of a 19th-century yacht sailing along a rocky coastline.

5 – Copacabana
Playa La Habana, Cuba
Tel: 537-204-1037

A small wall buffers this seawater pool from the breaking waves of the Caribbean just 12 steps away.

Swimming Paradise

The pool itself was built in the sea and has been enveloped by a structured formation.

6 – BEVERLY HILLS HOTEL
Beverly Hills, California
Tel: 310-276-2251, www.thebeverlyhillshotel.com

Stars, agents, and other movie types have been lounging and making deals here for years. Within the green-striped cabanas, you'll find fax and phone service. And there are butlers available to attend every whim.

7 – THE DATAI, LANGKAWI
Kedah Darul Aman, Malaysia
Tel : 603-7840-5537, www.thedatai.com

Guests can choose between two pools at this resort on the island of Langkawi. The larger one is at the top of a hill surrounded by the jungle. The second is close to the beach and the turquoise waters of the Andaman Sea.

8 – PALAZZO SASSO
Ravello, Italy
Tel: 39-089-81-81-81, www.palazzosasso.com

The swimming options are seemingly endless at this stunning old hotel on the Amalfi coast. The main pool, which is heated, is outfitted with underwater windows that overlook the Mediterranean. Guests can also swim in one of the many plunge pools.

9 – LAS VENTANAS AL PARAÍSO
Los Cabos, Mexico
Tel: 52-624-144-2800, www.lasventanas.com

The infinity pool at this resort on the tip of the Baja Peninsula seems truly to melt into the Pacific Ocean. At night, light from within the pool itself and from torches nearby creates a magical atmosphere.

10 – CIRAGAN PALACE KEMPINSKI
Istanbul, Turkey
Tel: 90-212-326-46-46, www.ciraganpalace.com

Landscaped by a palace, the two pools here are stunning and exotic, befitting the legacy of the Ottoman Empire. One is indoors; the other, outdoors.

THE WATER'S FINE! TWO MORE SWIM SETTINGS:

HOTEL CIPRIANI
Venice, Italy
Tel: 39-041-520-7744, www.hotelcipriani.com

This venerable luxury hotel has the only swimming pool in central Venice. Because of that, the Cipriani leads a double life in summer when it becomes a "country" club for wealthy Venetians. The filtered saltwater pool is kept at 26°C (78°F) in the spring and fall, thus extending the swimming season beautifully. For food, the poolside restaurant is outstanding.

THE CORAL CASINO
Santa Barbara, California
Tel: 805-565-8285

Don't despair because this club is private; the doors open for guests of the Four Seasons Biltmore hotel. Once you've gained admittance, you'll be treated to an Olympic-size pool that overlooks the rich blue Pacific Ocean. You'll also find multitiered cabanas, a delightful staff, a restaurant, and a café with poolside service. So don your shades and pretend you're a movie star like those who used to come here.

Ten Best
~Sporting Events~

Antonio Fins is an award-winning journalist and a member of the *South Florida Sun-Sentinel* editorial board. He has written for *BusinessWeek* magazine and other publications. A sports enthusiast, we asked him to describe his ten favorite sporting events.

1 – The 24 Hours of Le Mans, France
www.lemans.org

Skill, speed, and stamina are the three *s*'s that mark the world's best automobile race, the 24 Hours of Le Mans. The race, organized by Automobile Club de L'Ouest, bridges past and present on the automotive circuit.

The competition is set on a non-permanent track at Circuit de la Sarthe near the city of Le Mans on the Sarthe River. Roughly 46 cars start the race, in a series of classes that include prototype high-performance vehicles, dedicated race cars, and street cars. The diversity of autos gives the race a mix of old-fashioned and modern competitors. The winner is the car, driven by a team of three drivers, that covers the greatest distance in 24 hours.

The first Le Mans contest took place in May 1923; today it is held every June. The race begins at 4 p.m., and for 24 hours the sound of roaring engines fills 13 kilometers (8 mi) of French countryside.

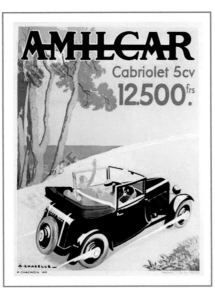

2 – The Olympic Games
www.olympic.org

It's hard to imagine that Zeus and the other gods lording over ancient Greece ever envisioned the global event the modern Olympiad has become. For a two-week span, athletes from dozens of countries compete against each other in scores of different sports. And that's just the summer games, which began their modern run in the late 1800s. The winter games, featuring sports that largely require snow and ice, draw a smaller field of competitors. But the competition for the gold, silver, and bronze is just as intense. Remember Tonya Harding and Nancy Kerrigan?

National rivalries are varied. Consider the United States hockey team winning the gold over the favored Soviets in 1980; Jamaica's jubilant 1988 bobsled team overcoming long odds to win hearts, not medals; or Argentina beating America's 2004 "Dream Team" and going on to capture the gold in basketball. Even the competition among national Olympic committees to host the games is fierce, with bribery accusations and investigations becoming, sadly, the norm in sports news over the last several years.

Still the games must go on; to be sure that they do, the International Olympic Committee decided to stagger the winter and summer games. So during every even-numbered year, runners will bear the torch that eventually lights the Olympic flame somewhere in the world.

¡SOY CANALLA SOY!

The first thing you hear is the singing. "¡Soy canalla! ¡Soy canalla soy! ¡Canalla yo soy!" In Argentina, where soccer is a religion, the best-known soccer clubs are Boca Juniors and River Plate. But its most passionate fans are found among Rosario's *canallas,* about 298 kilometers (185 miles) northwest of Buenos Aires.

The game at El Gigante stadium in Rosario hasn't started yet, but fans are already singing. You hear the music long before you reach your seat, the serenade of thousands, blended with heavy, steady drums. There's no better place to experience a game than at the El Gigante stadium. Fans gather with friends for *fútbol* talk and picnic on barbecue and wine.

When the players finally step onto the field, El Gigante explodes. Confetti falls, white streamers and flares fly, and the chanting intensifies to surround-sound. The singing continues: "¡Soy canalla! ¡Soy canalla soy! ¡Canalla yo soy!"

— Melina I. De Rose

3 – WORLD CUP SOCCER
www.worldcup.com

Thirty nations play, but billions of people in countries all around the world drop everything they're doing for a month every four years to see who claims the title of World Cup soccer champion.

The teams that compete in the World Cup finals are those that emerge from a series of qualifying rounds played out over the prior three years. The tournament of tournaments is therefore a showcase of the finest squads from across the continents and hemispheres.

It's during the finals that the intense challenge begins. First, in a series of first-round games, each team plays the three rivals in its opening bracket. Teams get three points for each win, one point for a tie, and zero for a loss. The top two teams in the bracket then move on to the single-game elimination rounds, with victorious teams proceeding though quarterfinal and semifinal rounds before the final championship match.

All the while the world's gaze is squarely fixed on the matches and the festival atmosphere in the stands. Chanting, singing, flag-waving, and superstitions are all part of the carnival that ensues.

Since the first World Cup tournament took place in 1930, the most dominant team has been Brazil. Winner of five championships since 1958, the greatest Brazilian teams were led by perhaps the most famous soccer player ever, Pele.

Rivalries are often fierce and deeply rooted: Two of the many in the sport are between England and Argentina, and one that has recently emerged between neighbors—Mexico and the United States.

4 – THE SUPER BOWL, UNITED STATES
www.superbowl.com

The Super Bowl is so big that even the commercials are worth watching. The first Super Bowl (held in January 1967) was played to plenty of empty seats and a waning TV audience. But now Super Bowl Sundays, progressively marked with Roman numerals, are the most celebrated one-game professional championship on the 12-month Gregorian calendar.

The Super Bowl concludes a 16-game regular season, and three postseason play-off rounds. It pits the top team from the American Football Conference against the top team from the National Football Conference for the coveted Vince Lombardi Trophy (not to mention diamond-studded rings for players, coaches, and front office "suits"). The Sunday evening spectacle is preceded by two weeks of parties and pre-game hype.

5 – THE NATIONAL BASKETBALL ASSOCIATION FINALS, UNITED STATES
www.nba.com

The NBA Finals. Showtime and the "Ghosts of the Garden." Rockets and Knicks, Spurs and Pistons. The National Basketball Association's finals are a showdown of stars and teams for the ages. It takes four games to win, but at least 93 games to get there. And the teams that do bring a lot of glitter with them. Movie stars in front-row seats. Cheerleaders that resemble Las Vegas show girls in high-energy dance routines. The see-and-be-seen spectacle ringing the court is as intriguing as the game itself.

Pro basketball has changed radically over the last four decades. The three-point shot, the slam-dunk, a pendulum swing against defense makes NBA ball a high-scoring, acrobatic affair. What hasn't changed is the prize, the right to be crowned world champion.

A "HANDS ON" EXPERIENCE:

SAIL NZ
Auckland, New Zealand
Tel: 64-9-359-5987, www.sailnz.co.nz

If you've ever had the desire to sail aboard an America's Cup racing yacht, Sail NZ can oblige. The sailing operator based in Auckland takes sailors and landlubbers alike aboard the *NZL 40* and *NZL 41,* two grand prix yachts used in the 1995 race. They go out for two-hour cruises or three-hour match races. Passengers can either help sail the boats or drink in the views of the harbor.

NZL 40 was built for the 1995 America's Cup in San Diego, California, and was brought to New Zealand as a trial boat for the 1999-2000 America's Cup in Auckland. *NZL 40* is the 40th America's Cup yacht built to the current America's Cup Class.

THE 18TH MAN

In Louis Vuitton Cup yacht racing, the privileged 17th man aboard observes and says nothing. However, Bruno Trouble is different. He is Vuitton's 18th man, navigating nine syndicates for the America's Cup. This is no easy task. The elegant man from France is everywhere, at the helm, conducting press conferences at the company's comprehensive Media Center, mediating, fixing, smoothly supervising, and navigating changing and choppy waters for the cup. He is a captain's captain, a man with compass-like precision.

The Louis Vuitton Cup is both prelude and passport. Without it, no challenger can set sail against the defending champion for the America's Cup, a race that's taken place for more than 150 years. Billionaires and bankers, spinnakers and sailors whose currency is just pure passion, cross the currents with sweat and spit as they did in 2003 over Auckland's Hauraki Gulf, most every day, in round-robins, and semifinals.

Boats like *Alinghi, Oracle, Prada,* and *One World* are some of the sleekest sailing ships the world has yet seen. Names like Dickson and Conner winch new meaning to the commanding sailing lexicon. At a cost of a hundred million dollars just to sail in these waters, designers, crews, and skippers carry on, blending seamanship with the most modern computer technology. The Kelvar-laminated sails alone (made in Arizona) cost eighty thousand dollars; during a season, no less than thirty sets might be used. Skipping over the waves, always searching for the cutting edge, each team is allowed two boats. The America's Cup is a race challenged by changing winds, where winning is often decided by strategic starts and victory is measured in seconds.

Since its very inception, Louis Vuitton and the America's Cup have shared the same values: a taste for excellence and accomplishment, and the determination to lead in research and design—but always with a deep commitment to tradition. Their initial meeting in 1983 caused an international sensation.

Solidly bolted to its plinth on the floor of the New York Yacht Club since 1851, the America's Cup trophy captivated generations of British yachtsmen as they tried to win it back over a long century of competition. The America's Cup became a symbol of the supremacy of American technology. Then the priceless silver trophy began to attract other nations, but it wasn't until the 1960s that any of them actually raced the Americans. Switzerland, for now, retains the trophy and the bragging rights.

6 – THE MASTERS, UNITED STATES

www.masters.org

The green jacket. That's all one has to say. The brainchild of legends Bobby Jones and Clifford Roberts, the first Masters was held in 1934. It was called Augusta National Invitation Tournament for the first five years of its existence before the name changed to what it is today. Unlike other sports championships and showcase events, the Masters remains steeped in tradition and continuity. The four-day stroke playing of 18 holes each day instead of the formerly customary 36 holes on the third day is still the rule.

Jones and Roberts left indelible images on the sport. But it was in the 1950s that legends and superstars took over the game. A pair of victories by Ben Hogan, and the first of four for Arnold Palmer made those two players the best known in America. The 1960s marked the arrival of the "Golden Bear," Jack Nicklaus, who became the first Masters champion to repeat in consecutive years. Today, the average winning score is eight under par. The setting at the Augusta National Golf Club in Augusta, Georgia, provides a lush, southern scenery that is unmatched at courses around the world.

7 – POLO AT PALERMO, ARGENTINA

www.aapolo.com or www.pololine.com

Argentine polo is considered the best in the world, and it's no wonder the Argentine Open Championship is the top draw for the sport's best players and most knowledgeable fans. The

tournament, first known as the River Plata Polo Championship, takes place between late November and early December. First held in 1893, the tournament is older than the tango.

In 1923, the new Argentine Polo Association moved to the field in Palermo, where polo has been played ever since. The host country usually dominates, given that Argentines have dominated the sport since the end of World War II.

The Argentine Open is played in the "Catedral," the grounds in the chic Palermo neighborhood of the capital city. The sport was introduced in Argentina by English ranchers, but it soon became the domain of the Argentine "gauchos," cowboys, who were expert and skilled in a similar game called "pato." Observers of modern global sport competitions insist that true polo aficionados must attend the Argentine Polo Open at least once in their lives.

8 – WIMBLEDON, ENGLAND

www.wimbledon.org

Center court. Grass surfaces. Strawberries and cream. What better way to spend a fortnight in old London Town? Wimbledon at the All England Lawn Tennis & Croquet Club. Located in southwest London, this grand spectacle is one of the four tennis tournaments that make up the grand slam.

Wimbledon is considered to be the most prestigious, largely because of its setting and surrounding pomp. It's the only major tournament played on a natural turf surface.

Wimbledon has figured prominently in the history of tennis and in its development into the egalitarian and highly skilled sport that so many millions enjoy. Originally created in France during the 12th century, the sport took its modern form in Britain during the 1800s. In 1874, Walter Clopton Wingfield patented his game of lawn tennis in London, and three years later, Wimbledon, the first of the major tournaments, was created.

The setting at Wimbledon and its history only magnifies the match-ups on the grass courts. Connors versus Borg. Evert and Navratilova. Agassi and Sampras. Venus versus Serena. The winner on center court holds a trophy to show who has reached the mountaintop, and perhaps a number one ranking in the world tennis order.

9 – WORLD SERIES, UNITED STATES
www.mlb.com

Home runs and chilly nights. Pitching duels and seventh-game thrillers. A century's worth of the World Series has seen all that and much, much more. The Fall Classic is more than a sporting event; it's a fixture on the American cultural landscape. Grandfathers and grandmothers remember Don Larsen's perfect game in 1956. Fathers and mothers recall the amazing Mets of 1969. And sons and daughters have grown up with another New York Yankees dynasty.

To get to the series, each of the 32 teams in the major leagues must endure a 162-game season, followed by three playoff rounds. The first is a best-of-five series, followed by two best-of-seven series. The World Series engenders nostalgia, too, stretching from the hopeful days of April and spring, through the doggedly hot days of summer, before reaching the apex in the autumn winds of October, when heroics on the mound and in the batter's box prove decisive.

10 – THE GRAND NATIONAL, ENGLAND
www.thegrandnational.net or www.aintree.co.uk

Stamina and speed make the Grand National's steeplechase the world's most renowned horse race. First held in 1839, the three-day meet is held in Britain's Aintree Racecourse in Liverpool. The Grand National pits as many as 40 horses against each other on a 7-kilometer (4.5-mile) course replete with obstacles.

The challenges presented by the steeplechase require the competing horses and jockeys to demonstrate a variety of riding skills. The horses and riders have to successfully jump a total of 30 fences, made more difficult by a six-foot wide ditch on the take-off side. After the final fence is cleared, the first horse to reach the finish line in a 451-meter (494-yard) sprint wins the race.

The Grand National takes place every April, and captures the attention of Britain like no other event in the country's sporting calendar. The first event, Opening Day, brings a crowd of 26,000 spectators to Aintree for the start of the racing cycle. The second day, known as Ladies Day, combines sport with fashion and is considered the highlight of northern England's social season. The Grand National is held on the final day, completing the three-day extravaganza of sport and culture.

Ten Best
~Climbs~

n Auckland, we visited with Sir Edmund Hillary, who took us to the heights in mountain climbing. Here are a few peaks that meet the challenge.

1 – Mount Khuiten, Mongolia

In Mongolia, it's easy for a traveler to be quickly swept away by the endless green steppes, the heartiness of the Kazakh nomads, and the rolling landscapes that define the Altai Mountains. This makes the trek to Mount Khuiten as enjoyable and scenic as the climb itself.

The mountain straddles the corners of Russia, China and Mongolia. To reach it, trekkers must cross a golden, vast, and barren landscape that is one of the last remote regions on Earth. This remarkable journey is enhanced by the gentle hospitality of the Kazakh nomads.

2 – Kilimanjaro, Tanzania

Flat-topped Kilimanjaro is Africa's highest mountain. Located on Tanzania's northern border with Kenya, the mountain is composed of three extinct volcanoes, Kibo, Mawenzi, and Shira. The highest peak, Uhuru, is 5,899 meters (19,340 feet) high.

Reaching the top of Kilimanjaro is exhilarating. Take the Machame Route up so you can see the region's wonderful animals and birds. Then you'll begin the trek across the Shira Plateau through the Grand Barranco Canyon and on to the top. If all goes as planned, you'll reach Stella Point with a chance to continue around Kibo's rim to Uhuru.

CLIMBING & TREKKING

INTERNATIONAL MOUNTAIN GUIDES
Ashford, Washington
360-569-2609, www.mountainguides.com

International Mountain Guides directors Phil Ershler, George Dunn, and Eric Simonson organize and lead climbing, trekking, and mountaineering expeditions to the highest places on Earth, from the classic Swiss Alps to the forbidding Himalaya to the Andes. (Closer to home, they regularly ascend Mount Rainier and Denali.) Since the climbers founded the company in 1975, they have taken groups on more than 500 expeditions. All three have their alpine certification from the American Mountain Guides Association.

3 – THE ANDES, PERU

The Inca Trail is an in-depth journey through a variety of ecosystems, from plains to desert to tropical cloud forests. You'll pass views of snowcapped mountains and rushing rivers. The highlight is Machu Picchu, the famed lost city of the Incas that was discovered in 1911 by Hiram Bingham. Then continue your trek to what was the heart and soul of the Inca Empire, Cuzco.

4 – MOUNT EVEREST, NEPAL

Rising 8,856 meters (29,035 feet) above sea level, Everest is the highest mountain on Earth. For decades, reaching the top of this giant has been considered one of the greatest mountaineering achievements. Sir Edmund Hillary and Tensing Norgay accomplished this feat in 1953 when they approached the peak along the South Col route. Since then, more than 2,000 others have made ascents through South Col. It is, by far, the most successfully climbed route on the mountain.

5 – THE MATTERHORN, SWITZERLAND

Nestled in the Swiss Alps, the Matterhorn is the most recognized mountain on the European continent. In the shape of a roughly chiseled rock pyramid, this peak serves as a defining geographical landmark. For many climbers, ascending the Matterhorn, the birthplace of the sport of mountaineering, represents a return to the purist traditions of climbing.

6 – MOUNT ELBRUS, RUSSIA

Dynamic in both region and terrain, Mount Elbrus stands as a watchtower in the Caucasus Mountains between Europe and Asia. Elbrus is a large, double-coned volcano, whose summits vary by about 20 meters (65 feet). For the climber with moderate skills, the highest mountain in Europe has great appeal because it presents a strenuous, yet rewarding climb. The mountain's location affords visitors excellent opportunities to see the region's large melting pot of ethnic groups, such as Turkish, Georgian, Azeri, and Russian.

7 – CITLALTÉPETL AND IZTACCÍHUATL, MEXICO

In the heart of Mexico, about 1,287 kilometers (800 miles) south of the United States border, Citlaltépetl and and Iztaccíhuatl are the third and seventh highest mountains respectively in North America. The first is 5,614 meters (18,406 feet) tall, while the second is 5,233 meters (17,159 feet) tall. Ascents of these two volcanoes are by far the most attractive climbs in Mexico. From a distance, it's easy to see how Iztaccíhuatl or "white woman" got its name; the snowcapped peaks look like the head, breasts, and feet of a sleeping woman.

8 – DENALI, ALASKA

Mount McKinley, also called Denali in Athabascan, in Denali National Park, Alaska, at 6,194 meters (20,320 feet) is the highest mountain in North America. This massif needs

CLIMBS

"First I saw the mountains in the painting and then I saw the painting in the mountains."

— Chinese Proverb

THE ULTIMATE EXPERIENCE

THE BRIDGE CLIMB
Sydney, Australia
Tel: 61-(0)-2-8274-7777, www.bridgeclimb.com

The ascent of the Sydney Harbor Bridge is a terrific adventure in urban climbing. You can scale this modern wonder several times from dawn to night, when the lights below twinkle on the glassy surface of the water. Not an accomplished climber? Don't fret. A local company called BridgeClimb has been preparing and leading thousands of people to the "summit" since 1998.

The bridge over Sydney Harbor is the largest of its kind in the world. It opened officially in 1932. It is open from 7 a.m. to 7 p.m. daily.

no explanation as to why it should be climbed. From its base to its apex, it rises nearly 5,490 meters (18,000 feet), an elevation gain unsurpassed anywhere in the world. No other mountain offers such breathtaking and diverse views each day of an ascent.

Mount McKinley's tremendous size and beauty create a magnetism that continually draws climbers from around the world. Choice months for attempting Denali are May and June, before the threats of avalanches and open crevasses become too severe. The mountain provides an unforgettable experience, touching the psyche of all mountaineers who have undertaken its challenges.

9 – ANNAPURNA, NEPAL
In terms of sheer geological and cultural diversity, a trek to Nepal's Annapurna region is unbeatable. By circumnavigating the giant Himalaya, you'll see everything from lush bamboo forests to arid high mountain landscapes. Most visitors here climb over the famous Thorung La (5,368 meters; 17,599 feet). The hike into this glorious mountain pass rewards one with spectacular blazes of orange as the sun rises, casting the white Himalayan peaks in a fiery glow.

10 – DAMAVAND, IRAN
The Elburz Mountains stand huge and stunning as they lean against the Caspian Sea northeast of Tehran. Damavand's peaks range in altitude from 5,612 meters (18,400 feet) to more than 5,795 meters (19,000 feet). Steam rises from the hot springs and fumaroles that pockmark this dormant volcano, and two small glaciers provide dazzling views.

Although Damavand is not particularly challenging as a technical climb, mountaineers appreciate its beauty and its position in Persian mythology as possibly the resting place of Noah's ark.

TEN BEST
~HORSEBACK RIDES~

Bayard Fox, the owner of Bitterroot Ranch in Wyoming and a director of Equitours, rounds up ten amazing rides. These include excursions through the Loire Valley, Tuscany, and the west coast of Ireland. "I have greatly enjoyed nearly all of the hundred or so riding trips I have taken in the last 25 years. Each one has its own unique attractions. The trips listed are my favorites though it is very hard to choose. Travel on horseback has many advantages. It opens doors to people and places because most of the world loves horses and those who ride them. I think it is entirely appropriate that horses were the means of travel at the time that most of the history one sees on our trips was created."

1 – VALLE DE BRAVO, MEXICO

The ride circles the beautiful lake of Valle de Bravo. The route takes one high into the surrounding mountains, through a magnificent forest of Montezuma pines, with spectacular views of the azure lake far below. Guests stay in a lovely villa with charming hosts. The horses and tack compare well with the best European rides.

2 – MASAI MARA, KENYA

For sheer excitement and adventure, this ride through the Masai Mara in Kenya wins hands down. Flat-out gallops on excellent polo ponies, alongside zebras and wildebeests, past elephants, giraffes, lions, and dozens of other animals is a thrilling experience that one could never get from inside a Land Rover. Hemingway-style camping and superb service are other pluses. Close contact with the proud Masai in remote areas adds to the fascination.

3 – LOIRE VALLEY, FRANCE

To me, the great castles of the Loire Valley are among the finest legacies history has left us. Chenonceau, Cheverny, and Chaumont are outstanding examples of the tremendous flowering of French culture of the period. The history is brought alive by staying each night in real castles still in private hands and riding into courtyards over drawbridges like knights of old. I especially treasure the memory of a long, wild gallop along the lovely, tree-lined banks of the Cher River heading for Chenonceau.

4 – TUSCANY, ITALY

A ride that we run through this stunning part of Italy is a happy combination of idyllic Tuscan landscape seen from the backs of fine horses and a chance to study some of the world's great art treasures in Florence and Siena. The renovated castle (Castello di Tocchi) where guests stay keeps the ancient charm while providing modern comfort. The host, who also runs a cooking school, is marvelously entertaining, and the preparation of food and choice of wine are celebrated here with near religious fervor.

Horseback Riding Tours

WORLDWIDE HORSEBACK RIDING ADVENTURES:

EQUITOURS
Dubois, Wyoming
Tel: 307-455-3363
www.equitours.com or www.ridingtours.com

Bayard Fox is an authority on horseback riding vacations. This company has been offering equine vacations all over the world for more than three decades. Each tour exceeds a standard of perfection, meeting Bayard's personal criteria, including courtesy, enjoyment, and a once-in-a-lifetime riding experience.

5 – QUEBEC, CANADA

We often forget that Quebec is something of a foreign country within Canada itself, with a different language and culture that is basically French. The Inn to Inn Ride on the Gaspé Peninsula on the Gulf of St. Lawrence passes through magnificent forests, skirts the seashore, and overnights in a string of inns. The fall foliage season with the blazing maples is one of nature's wonders.

6 – JEREZ AND SEVILLE, SPAIN

Visiting a riding center near Seville in Andalusia combines excellent riding with fascinating introductions to the rich culture of this area of southern Spain.

Guests on this trip enjoy performances of some of the best flamenco dancers and visit the breathtaking show at the Royal Riding School in Jerez, which is such a tribute to the beauty and athleticism of the horse. Riders take lessons in dressage and jumping, and can also ride through the countryside.

7 – RAJASTHAN, INDIA

The palace-to-palace ride in Rajasthan on fine Marwari endurance horses is considered an exotic tour. The palaces themselves are impressive architectural gems. The food and service are exquisite.

8 – CAPPADOCIA, TURKEY

Of all rides, the one through Cappadocia wins the prize for richest in history: Greek, Roman, early Christian, and Ottoman. The horses perform extremely well, taking riders over fascinating terrain and through interesting villages. Part of the trip includes a stop in Istanbul, which gets my vote as the world's most beautiful city.

9 – THE ANDES, PERU

Our ride through the sacred valley of the Incas, from Cuzco to Machu Picchu was a haunting, spiritual experience for me. I cannot imagine a more dramatic setting than the Andes with their sheer cliffs and lush valleys. The Peruvian Pasos we rode were beautifully gaited and well mannered.

10 – ESTANCIA, ARGENTINA

The horse still plays a vital role in Argentine country life; the nation has one of the world's great equestrian traditions. The self-sufficient Estancia Huechahue at the foothills of the Andes enables guests to see how gauchos actually live and to ride with them, providing an unusual chance to understand this powerful culture. The ranch is a base for pack trips high into the Andes.

Ten Best
~Ski Runs & Lodges~

1 – Whistler/Blackcomb
British Columbia, Canada
www.whistlerblackcomb.com

These two towering mountains provide excellent skiing with a huge vertical drop. Several decades ago, the mountains were mainly the domain of courageous hikers. Today, Whistler's village offers everything snowboarders and skiers crave: cafés, international stores, and more than a hundred restaurants that cater to all tastes.

Fairmont Chateau Whistler
Whistler, British Columbia, Canada
Tel: 604-938-8000,
www.fairmont.com/whistler

The spectacular Fairmont Chateau Whistler resort rests at the base of breathtaking Blackcomb Mountain. Non-skiers can relish the Vida Wellness Spa and the Chateau Whistler Golf Club.

2 – Kitzbühel, Austria
www.skiaustria.com

In the pantheon of European ski resorts, Kitzbühel is considered the "Pearl of the Alps." It is the most famous holiday resort in the Tyrol; 54 cable cars are available to ferry downhillers to the slopes, and miles of trails are constantly groomed for cross-country skiers. This 700-year-old village offers skiers the history of an alpine community where skiing began in the winter of 1892.

Hotel Goldener Greif
Kitzbühel, Austria
Tel: 43-(0)-53-566-4311, www.hotel-goldener-greif.at

In the heart of the cozy village of Kitzbühel stands this beautifully restored hotel, which dates back to 1271. After a long day on the slopes, there's no cozier place to sit than in front of a blaze in the large fireplace. Or snuggle down in the charming Tyrolean-style guest rooms. There's a casino in the building, as well as a restaurant and a bar.

3 – Zermatt, Switzerland
www.zermatt.com

To me, picturesque Zermatt is Switzerland's best ski resort, better than the neighboring Gstaad or St. Moritz. A remarkably peaceful car-free getaway, Zermatt holds the world's second biggest lift-served vertical drop and has huge snowfalls, thanks to its altitude.

Riffelalp Resort
Zermatt, Switzerland
Tel: 41-27-966-05-55

The Riffelalp Resort is the highest Alpine resort in Europe. Just above Zermatt, the hotel offers 65 double rooms, five suites, plus two apartments with all conveniences. Most rooms have balconies with breathtaking views of the Matterhorn.

4 – PARK CITY, UTAH

Park City's reputation for great skiing helped make the area a host venue for the 2002 Olympic Winter Games. The resort, with 19 lifts, limits lift-ticket sales to avoid long waits in line. There are runs for all levels with 709 hectares (1,750 acres) of Rocky Mountain powder.

DEER VALLEY RESORT
Park City, Utah
Tel: 435-649-1000, www.deervalley.com

The plush lodge is a full-service, four-diamond hotel with a health spa, ski valets, heated outdoor pool, hot tub, steam room, sauna, fitness center, and award-winning restaurants.

5 – BANFF/LAKE LOUISE
Alberta, Canada

Canada's oldest national park, Banff, offers some of the best downhill skiing in the heart of the North American Rockies. The four areas are Mount Norquay, Sunshine Village, Lake Louise Ski Area, and Nakiska, which was designed for the alpine events of the 1988 Winter Olympics.

THE FAIRMONT BANFF SPRINGS
Banff National Park, Alberta, Canada
Tel: 403-762-2211, www.fairmont.com/banffsprings

Styled after a Scottish castle, this hotel packs a punch in terms of hospitality and scenery. It has been a symbol of Rocky Mountain magnificence for more than a century. And it's within driving distance of the four skiing areas within the park. In addition, guests can try cross-country skiing, play golf, and unwind in Willow Stream, a world class European-style spa.

6 – CHAMONIX MONT-BLANC, FRANCE
www.chamonix.com

Host to the world's first Winter Olympic games in 1924, Chamonix ranks among the top contenders for the title of "world's most famous ski resort." It is at the foot of Mont-Blanc, the highest peak in the Alps and the second highest in Europe (4,810 meters; 15,771 feet). The resort town is renowned for having a lift-served vertical drop of 2,809 meters (9,209 feet), as well as having one of the world's longest ski runs: the 22-kilometers (13.7-miles) long Vallée Blanche.

LE HAMEAU-ALBERT
Chamonix, Mont-Blanc, France
Tel: 33-(0)-04-50-53-05-09

Le Hameau-Albert is a terrific place to go after working up an appetite on the slopes, because the elegant hotel offers amazing food. It is located within a few minutes of the center of town. The architecture is a fun fusion of Old World tradition and modern style.

7 – STOWE, VERMONT
www.stowe.com

One of the most renowned resorts on the ski map, Stowe sports a New England tradition and the biggest vertical drop in the area. The two ski areas are Mount Mansfield and Spruce Peak. The latter actually backs onto Smugglers' Notch's terrain.

GREEN MOUNTAIN INN
Stowe, Vermont
Tel: 802-253-7301, www.greenmountaininn.com

For more than 150 years, the Green Mountain Inn has offered lovely accommodations. Guests now have their choice of lodgings in the inn itself or in townhouses. There is a heated pool and health club, as well as two restaurants. Every afternoon the innkeepers provide hot tea and freshly baked cookies for guests.

8 – MONT TREMBLANT,
Quebec, Canada
www.tremblant.ca

Tremblant is one of the better known resorts in eastern Canada, about an hour from Montreal. Open since 1939, the mountain has four distinct slopes laced with 94 runs. The resort operates 19 lifts.

THE ULTIMATE TOBOGGAN

Okay, so an ice run isn't the same as skiing. Don't think for a minute that it's not as scary. In fact, it may be a far more hair-raising way to get down a mountainside in the winter.

Take the one in St. Moritz, Switzerland. The famous Cresta ice run is three-quarters of a mile long down a steep gully through ten testing corners, past the tiny hamlet of Cresta, to the village of Celerina. The total drop is 157 meters (514 feet).

The first Cresta ice run was built over nine weeks in the winter of 1884–85. Since then, it's been rebuilt every year with fresh snow. The run usually opens two or three days before Christmas and continues operation for nine weeks until the end of February.

The overseer is the St. Moritz Tobogganing Club, an English organization that has had a partnership with the Swiss for decades. Members come from all over the world; non-members are also welcome to try the run.

The first Lord Brabazon of Tara wrote, "The Cresta is like a woman with this cynical difference: to love her once is to love her always."

For more information, go to www.crestarun.com.

—

THE PALACE HOTEL
St. Moritz, Switzerland
Tel: 41-81-837-10-00,
www.badruttspalace.com/home.asp

Here's the place to stay if you're going to try the Cresta ice run. The Palace Hotel is a landmark in town, overlooking breathtaking, unspoiled scenery. A favorite of celebrities since 1896, the hotel is elegant in every detail.

FAIRMONT TREMBLANT

Mont Tremblant, Quebec, Canada
Tel: 819-681-7000, www.fairmont.com/tremblant

With a ski lift right at the door, it's clear that the Fairmont intends to serve skiers. The hotel has 314 guest rooms and 62 suites. There is a spa, several restaurants, and an arcade of shops and boutiques in the pedestrian-only village.

9 – CORTINA, ITALY

www.skiitaly.com

Cortina was the site of the Olympic Games in 1956. Cortina d'Ampezzo, surrounded by the craggy Dolomite Mountains, is a prime run on any thrill seeker's European winter itinerary. The central village has 52 lifts and 140 kilometers (87 miles) of groomed runs. The Cortina Center can arrange bobsledding, snow rafting and high-speed tobogganing. The crowd in this stylish old resort dresses impeccably well.

MIRAMONTI MAJESTIC GRAND HOTEL

Cortina d'Ampezzo, Italy
Tel: 39-0471-849500

The Miramonti has expanding views over the Cristallo. Situated within parklike grounds not far from Cortina, the five-star hotel has elegantly appointed rooms and a restaurant that specializes in outstanding regional cuisine. A courtesy shuttle ferries guests between the hotel and the village.

10 – ASPEN, COLORADO

www.aspensnowmass.com

Aspen's four mountains are world-famous, with terrains that can accommodate skiers of all abilities. The resort is also a great choice for experts, who can access hundreds of acres of terrain off the backside of the mountain.

THE ST. REGIS RESORT

Aspen, Colorado
Tel: 970-920-3300

In true St. Regis fashion, this resort is a perfect place for winter skiing, summer sports, and the arts. The hotel has 179 guest rooms and suites, a heated outdoor pool, and a fitness center. The new Remède Spa offers 15 separate rooms and an exquisite menu of massage therapy and other body treatments.

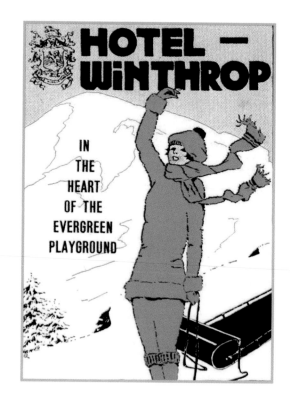

TEN BEST
~BEACHES~

Henry David Thoreau writes, "The seashore is a most advantageous point from which to comprehend the world. The waves forever rolling to the land are far traveled coming home and leaving again." Here are ten beaches to sit back on and comprehend the world.

1 – SEYCHELLES
www.seychelles.com

One of the most photographed beaches in the world, the pale pink

sands of Anse Source d'Argent unfurls across the island of La Digue, one of the 115 components of this archipelago in the Indian Ocean. The sands sparkle against a backdrop of towering granite boulders, worn by time and weather. The turquoise water is relatively shallow and protected from the ocean's waves by a reef.

2 – MALDIVES
www.visitmaldives.com

Whether your dream beach trip consists of spending a few pampered nights in a four-star resort or swimming among tropical fish some 24 meters (80 feet) underwater, the Maldives are the sort of islands where either—or both—can come true. Straddling the equator southwest of Sri Lanka, the 1,102 islands that make up the Maldives form 26 atolls. The soft air enveloping the archipelago blends into a beautiful palm-fringed haze.

3 – BORA BORA, TAHITI
www.boraboraisland.com

This is one of the magical islands that make up French Polynesia in the South Pacific. Just 29 kilometers (18 miles) long, this lush little slip of land lies in a protected lagoon edged by white sandy shores, the best being at Matira Point. Bora Bora boasts the nickname the "Romantic Island," a moniker easy to appreciate with its isolated beaches, intimate hotels, and quiet atmosphere.

4 – THE HAMPTONS, NEW YORK
www.hamptons.com

One of the hip spots for the air-kissing, well-heeled set, the Hamptons boast some of the prettiest beaches on Long Island. The unspoiled shoreline begins around Southampton and runs east to the end of the island at Montauk. Wind-swept dunes and waving grasses border the Atlantic Ocean.

5 – LANIKAI BEACH, HAWAII
www.hawaii.com

Half a mile of sparkling sand, palm trees swaying over a white beach, lush tropical plants, and endless sunshine make Lanikai one of Hawaii's most scenic beaches. The shore is protected by a nearby coral reef, which keeps the surf relatively calm. The water is always deep green and postcard-perfect.

BEACHES

PINK SANDS OF BERMUDA

www.bermuda.com

Bermuda has both magnificently large and refreshingly small beaches. Some are private, reserved for resort guests, but are never a problem to visit.

Bermuda's finely pulverized sand takes on its characteristic pink hue from the calcium carbonate remains of coral reefs and the beautiful turquoise waters. For a glorious walk, stroll between South Shore Park and Horseshoe Bay in Southampton Parish.

6 – NANTUCKET ISLAND, MASSACHUSETTS
www.nantucket.net

The most popular beaches on this island in the North Atlantic are Surfside and Children's. The waters here are relatively calm, and there's plenty of sand to use for sunbathing or castle-building. Madaket Beach is known for its rougher surf and not-to-be-missed sunsets. Quidnet Beach provides great views of Sankaty Head lighthouse.

7 – FRASER ISLAND, AUSTRALIA
www.seefraserisland.com

Perched on the sunny Queensland coast 259 kilometers (161 miles) northeast of Brisbane, Fraser Island is the world's largest sand island and home to a wonderful beach. This World Heritage Site is an ecologist's dream, with 1,664 square kilometers (640 square miles) of unspoiled natural paradise. Rain forests with 1,000-year-old trees sprout from the sand. Lodgings here accommodate a wide range of tourists, from the backpacking ecology lover to pampered resort fans.

8 – ST. BART'S
www.st-barths.com

One of many islands in the Caribbean Sea, St. Bart's stands out with its blend of French chic and island relaxation. With beautiful secluded beaches, fine French cuisine, and gracious hotels, this tropical playground is popular with the Jet Set. The 13-kilometer (8-mile)-long island is edged by 20 beaches and small coves for swimmers and sunbathers, with sparkling water and white sand.

9 – LANGKAWI, MALAYSIA
www.langkawi.com.my

The name "Langkawi" translates into "the land of one's wishes," a welcoming concept that somewhat belies the island's historic origins as a reputed refuge for pirates. Langkawi has since become a modern hideaway for the traveler seeking an escape. If your vacation wishes extend from uncrowded white sands and clear waters to lush green forests, you will find yourself content here. Datai Bay, located on Pulau Langkawi, is a heavenly retreat on the Andaman Sea.

10 – KAUNA'OA BAY, HAWAII

Located on the Kohala Coast of the Aloha State's Big Island, Kauna'oa Bay is the quintessential Hawaiian spot. The .4- kilometer (.25-mile)-long, crescent-shaped beach has plenty of white sand, palm trees, and calm, clear, blue water. In addition to swimming and sunbathing, beachgoers here can snorkel or ride boogie boards. (Be careful swimming, however, because there are no lifeguards on this public beach.) At night, nestle into the sands and peer out into the water to see if you can catch a glimpse of manta rays swimming.

TEN BEST
~WALKS & HIKING TOURS~

There is something very special and spiritual about walking: fresh air, unlimited discovery, and ever finer views taking you as far as the eye can see. At a slower pace, there is the opportunity to enjoy nature's wonders, the hidden treats the world has to offer, which become sharper and focused far away from the blur of speed tours. We asked Bob Ellsasser, head of Country Walkers, to write about his favorite strolls.

1 – GREAT SMOKY MOUNTAINS

The Great Smoky Mountains, long regarded as the ancestral homeland of the Cherokee Indians, is a region rich in natural diversity and pioneer history. Named by the Cherokee for the mysterious wisps of blue-gray smoke that often shroud the highest peaks, this majestic mountain range marks the southern climax of the Appalachian chain. Established as a national park in 1934, the area today spans a magnificent 202,500 hectares (500,000 acres), making it the largest wilderness area of the eastern United States. Within proximity of its extensive 1,448 kilometers (900 miles) of walking trails lies an abundant reserve of both natural and historic interests. The Smokies are home to more than 130 species of trees, 1,500 varieties of flowering plants, and 200 types of birds. Nestled within this haven of cascading waterfalls and fantastic mountain vistas stand the preserved remnants of pioneer heritage: the log cabins, farmhouses, grist mills, and barns built in the 18th and 19th centuries by European settlers. Entering into this immense and abundant forest, walkers can retrace a pioneer past that follows the footsteps first marked by the Cherokee Indians.

2 – QUEBEC, CANADA

A walking tour throughout this northern wonderland—not far from the region's hub of Québec City—reveals natural and cultural treasures. The Saguenay Fjord estuary is a unique ecosystem where fresh water blends with sea tide, creating this journey's special environment. Granite cliffs plunge into the St. Lawrence River, where villages cluster by the water's edge. There is an extensive trail network in the Saguenay National Park, a UNESCO World Heritage Site. Granite peaks, brilliant lakes, high gorges, hanging waterfalls, eagles, and snow geese—all are common sights. Nearby are authentic auberge inns to relax in French-Canadian comfort.

3 – CINQUE TERRE, ITALY

Imagine walking a spectacular coastal path with the Mediterranean on one side, mountains on the other, and Italian fishing villages just ahead. Now multiply that experience by five. Welcome to the captivating region linking the "five villages" of the Cinque Terre. Footpaths

Ireland's Southwest

"Wandering re-establishes the original harmony which once existed between man and the universe."

— Anatole France

cross the terraced slopes of the Riviera di Levante to hamlets with pastel-colored buildings and contrasting shutters and lead to brightly painted boats in small harbors. Walk past trattorias and a solitary abbey to a rocky promontory with the sea always in full view and a clear sky overhead. Then continue on to the wooded hills, descending into fashionable Portofino and sail across the Gulf of Poets.

Along the route, there's Ligurian cuisine, including characteristic Italian pesto made from locally grown basil— a source of particular pride among chefs and restaurateurs from these neighboring villages, each one claiming the best recipe. Sciacchetrà is a rare, crisp, fragrant white wine, a specialty harvested from the Cinque Terre's terraced vineyards. Stop in at the Splendido, one of my favorite hotels in Portofino.

4 – CLOUD FORESTS OF COSTA RICA

A cloud forest is a tropical forest that's usually found near the top of coastal mountains and is covered in clouds throughout most of the year. Walks through those of Costa Rica represent the ultimate encounters with nature's boundless variety. Traveling on foot, you'll explore rugged craters and lagoon waterfalls, freshwater ponds and tranquil sea coves. Cloud forest trees tower above, and wide rivers run through lush floral lanes. One part of the adventure provides a lofty perspective on the area's abundant natural wonders, as you cross bridges suspended high above the forest. Brilliant colors and wild sounds create a vibrant and exotic sensory experience. You'll find a variety of lodgings in Costa Rica to renew your enthusiasm for another day's discoveries in this striking land.

5 – SOUTHWEST IRELAND

Timeworn paths invite walkers into a world of splendor and captivating legends here at the British Isles' westernmost point. Ireland's historic past comes alive in the southwest region, where ancient abbeys and castles stand alongside quaint country homes. Walk the Dingle Peninsula, past stone cottages set against dramatic cliffs on one side of the route, with small islands far away to sea on the other. Discover ancient Iron Age ruins on the western tip of the peninsula at Slea Head. Follow a path through the moss-carpeted forests in Killarney National Park. Set out by boat to explore historic Inisfallen Island on Lough Leane. And stroll along County Kerry's spectacular sand dunes.

The walk is also rich in wildlife discoveries; you might see red deer, otter, and great crested grebe, especially around the Lakes of Killarney.

Lively pub lunches with a pint of Guinness close at hand in small farming villages offer a sweet taste of local culture. Evenings find the warm embrace of Irish hospitality at splendid village hotels—a highlight is the Cahernane Hotel in Killarney, a former estate of the Earl of Pembroke.

6 – THE OREGON TRAIL

This adventure in the Pacific Northwest follows in the footsteps of explorers Meriwether Lewis and William Clark, who traversed this rugged terrain on their epic westward expedition. The walking tour begins at the base of volcanic Mount Hood, along the mighty Columbia River, past waterfalls leading to spectacular mountain views and meadows filled with wildflowers. A walk on Mount St. Helens, famous for its historic 1980 eruption, has bold, stark beauty. Near Mount Adams, on the forest plateau, deer and elk play beneath a fir canopy that leads to hidden lakes and marshes. Rushing rivers give this destination boundless vitality, and towns with nearby fruit orchards dot the landscape. The Oregon Trail is also rich in the history of Native Americans, whose civilizations in this region reach back thousands of years. This environment also yields a culinary bounty; fine wines, sweet herbs, and fresh salmon all complement the splendor.

7 – CRETE

Faraway enclaves reachable only by foot or boat distinguish this island destination. You'll walk past hidden coves, descend into little-known gorges, and follow cobbled pathways to Venetian castles and snow-white beaches on a deep blue sea. These walking days can be stretched with swims, taverna lunches, and picnics under a canopy of olive trees within full view of the Mediterranean. Crete holds the distinction of being home to Europe's earliest civilization, the Minoan, and its legends and natural treasures run so deep that historians, archaeologists, and travelers alike continue to make bold, new finds. From the old harbor in the fortified town of Chania, to forays into the remote southern coastal reaches of the island, and walks into the palace of King Minos, only Crete's astonishing natural beauty could possibly rival the region's historic importance. It is no wonder that fable and fact meet in the Greek islands.

8 – BHUTAN

Ancient citadels rise on the horizon. Buddhist temples and carved wood farmhouses are discovered along fertile valleys. Swiftly flowing rivers dash across an open landscape, the snowcapped Himalaya towering in the distance. The journey in the Kingdom of Bhutan leads into the heart of a modern-day Shangri-La. Exploring temples and elegant fortresses, called *dzongs,* on foot helps one experience the serenity that characterizes the Bhutanese way of life. Surrounded by gorgeous mountain vistas, paths lead to hillsides forested with rhododendron and blue pine, golden farm fields with mustard and buckwheat, and rustic villages.

Travelers have only recently been allowed to visit Bhutan, and tourists to the country are still limited to a fortunate few. There is a warmth and hospitality to experience in local culture, customs, and ceremonies. From vistas overlooking the Punakha Valley to the intricately patterned Thimphu weavings, the walk has beauty in this peaceful realm.

Lodgings in Bhutan are ideally situated for natural scenery—in a forest, overlooking a river, or perched on the rim of a valley. Local cuisine is a unique blend of unusual and piquant tastes.

9 – SWITZERLAND

Spirits soar at the sight of the alpine landscape; and what better place to walk than over breathtaking mountains. The average altitude of 1,351 kilometers (4,428 feet) exceeds many of the highest peaks elsewhere. Venturing into two culturally distinct regions and hearing three languages along the way, you can experience variety, wilderness, and Swiss hospitality. Beginning in Kandersteg, chairlifts and gondolas take you to flower-strewn paths, pristine lakes, and waterfalls. Look over the Lauterbrunnen Valley, framed by five summits, ancient glaciers, and mountain ranges that seem to extend forever. There is no better way to end the day than by sharing a fondue and cornichons, topped off with a bite of chocolate.

10 – NOVA SCOTIA, CANADA

Dark green hills and rugged shorelines create a superb setting for walking adventures in this maritime gem. Paths lead through the heart of the spectacular Cape Breton Highlands National Park. From Cheticamp, an Acadian fishing village famous for its music and rug-hooking, explore headland cliffs where bald eagles soar above. The Gulf of St. Lawrence is 305 meters (1,000 feet) below and leads to an expanse near North Harbour Beach, where there are opportunities to set out to sea on whale-watching tours. Walk through fishing communities with deep Scottish roots, in isolated meadows, along craggy coasts, and on cobblestone beaches.

COUNTRY WALKERS

Waterbury, Vermont
Tel: 802-244-1387
www.countrywalkers.com

HADRIAN'S WALL

Cross Country International
Milbrook, New York
Tel: 800-828-8768, www.walkingvacations.com

The 140-km (84-m) National Trail along Hadrian's Wall opened in May 2003.

A World Heritage Site since 1987, Hadrian's Wall is a great feat of Roman engineering. It runs across northern England at the narrowest part of the country, from the banks of the Tyne in the east to the Solway Firth in the west.

It marked the northern boundary of the Roman Empire under the rule of Emperor Hadrian, who ordered its construction in A.D. 122. His main intent was to protect Britain from the warring tribes of the north. Plenty of the Roman wall remains, in the form of turrets, forts, and civilian settlements.

Long after the Romans left, the wall and the boundary it represented figured in English and Scottish history. Walk past Thirlwall Castle where Edward I (Edward Longshanks of the movie *Braveheart*) stayed in 1306 during his campaign against the Scots. Continue on to Sewingshields where King Arthur is said to have hidden Queen Guinevere.

This walk across the Pennines mountains slices through some of the prettiest country in Great Britain. You'll pass through towns and villages where you'll be tempted to browse in the quaint shops or take tea. You'll trudge past farms and forests. Whatever you do, don't rush this wonderful adventure. The weather is best in July and August, but autumn can be spectacular, albeit brisk.

JUST THE
PLACES
BEST

TEN BEST
~ISLANDS~

Leslie Thomas is a successful writer in England who's been in the business for almost 40 years. During that time, he has written 25 novels and several travel books, such as *Some Lovely Islands, My World of Islands, The Hidden Places of Britain,* and the newly released *Dover Beach.* Given his interest in islands, we thought he was the natural source for naming the ten best islands.

1 – NANTUCKET, MASSACHUSETTS
Nantucket was once one of the richest places in America, built on the profits of the whale oil industry. Even today in the delectable old town there are fine brick houses with silver mailboxes.

Old time sailors used to call Nantucket "The Little Grey Lady of the Sea." On the misty morning I first arrived there, I could understand why. A woman was riding a horse along the beach to the utter delight of her family aboard my ferry, and she bore a banner that said "Crazy Aunt Rides Again." It is a unique place.

2 – ISLES OF SCILLY, BRITAIN
These are the out-riders of England, a clutch of tiny islands off Lands End, Cornwall, awash in the Atlantic, and in a world of their own. Five are sparsely inhabited and there are hundreds of islets, skerries, and rocks stretching out to the Bishop Rock Lighthouse. The next stop is America.

Balmy Atlantic air supports the spring flower industry. Part of the duchy of Cornwall, the isles are owned by Prince Charles.

3 – SABA, NETHERLANDS WEST INDIES
During my years of island finding, I have been to most places in the Caribbean— Barbados, Antigua, Jamaica, and many islands much smaller. But the most unusual is Saba, east of the U.S. Virgin Islands, rising almost 914 meters (3,000 feet) above the sea. It is home to 1,500 inhabitants, many of whom have the same family name: Hassell.

4 – CANARY ISLANDS, SPAIN
Europeans flock to the Canary Islands in winter in search of a little sun. Temperatures range between 21°C and 24°C (70°F–75°F) through January and February.

On Tenerife stands one of Europe's loftiest peaks, Mount Teide, snowcapped in winter against a deep blue sky. You can watch whales or sail over to Gomera, which was the final stop Columbus made before setting out to discover America.

5 – FAIR ISLE, SCOTLAND
Fair Isle is the most isolated inhabited island in Britain. It is home to only 60 people, but hundreds of thousands of birds reside here as well. Most of the visitors to this wild and wonderful place are bird-watchers. Sheep placidly graze on the steeply angled meadows.

ISLANDS

"We may run, walk, stumble, drive, or fly, but let us never lose sight of the reason for the journey, or miss a chance to see a rainbow on the way."

—An Unknown Traveler

6 – LORD HOWE ISLAND, AUSTRALIA

Lord Howe is way out in the middle of the Tasman Sea, a two-and-a-half-hour plane ride from Sydney. It takes days by boat. However you go, it is worth it.

Named after a British admiral, Lord Howe is the world's most southerly coral island. Two hundred or so people call it home, many descended from families who settled there in the 18th century.

7 – CAPRI, ITALY

Capri is the only island I have ever visited that is just as I imagined it would be. The lyrical songs are only too true. The town square itself takes some believing. It's like a stage, and not not much bigger either. There are colored balconies all around and a lovely campanile where the clock divertingly chimes, not to mark the time but whenever it feels like it. From the highest point on the island, you can look across to the volcano of Vesuvius with the Italian coast stretched out over a shining sea.

8 – CHANNEL ISLANDS, UNITED STATES

People rarely venture out to the Channel Islands from the California mainland, although it seems just a stone's throw away. The most accessible, and famous, is Santa Catalina, which I reached in two hours by ferry from the port of Los Angeles. There I found a placid village called Avalon, a calm bay, and a famous prewar dance hall—round like a fortress—where the big bands once played.

9 – TAHITI, FRENCH POLYNESIA

These days, travelers will tell you that Tahiti is no longer a dream. True, it has an international airport, and smart hotels rise within sight of the coral reef. I have seen the changes over the years, yet the island is still beautiful and still rises suddenly green to the cloud-touched mountain tops. At least from the sea, before you come too close, you can still see Tahiti as Paul Gauguin saw it—in all its extravagance and romance—when he voyaged there from France to paint.

10 – ISLANDS OF THE ANDAMAN SEA, THAILAND

The joy is to watch how these islands are transformed by changing distances, by sunlight, by clouds. On some, there is a sliver of beach, just enough from which to swim; others are edged with little villages built on boards, the houses tied together. All are tropical paradises: Koh Phi Phi, Koh He, Koh Racha, Koh Surin, Koh Dok Mai, to name some of the favorites. Koh Phuket serves as a good jumping-off point. Devastated by the 2004 tsunami, these islands are slowly making a comeback.

 *Island Dreaming*

TEN BEST
~OPERA HOUSES~

We have selected the best opera houses in the world, each as special as an aria, and we hope you have the opportunity to experience every one.

1 – LA SCALA
Milan, Italy
Tel: 39-02-72-003-744, www.teatroallascala.org

Milan's Teatro alla Scala is perhaps the most famous opera house in the world, the one most associated with "opera." Built in 1778 with four tiers with separate loges, it is the home of Rossini, Belling, Donizetti, and Verdi. One of the most ingenious features of La Scala is the concave channel under the wooden floor of the orchestra; this is credited for giving the theater superb acoustics.

2 – TEATRO DI SAN CARLO
Naples, Italy
Tel: 39-(0)-81-7972-331
www.teatrosancarlo.it

Built by King Charles of Bourbon and inaugurated in 1737, the magnificent red-and-gold theater is the world's oldest working theater, and, until La Scala, it was the most prestigious in Italy. Giaochino Rossini's most popular operas premiered on its stage.

3 – TEATRO COLON
Buenos Aires, Argentina
Tel: 54-11-4378-7132, www.teatrocolon.org.ar

Not to be outdone by wealthy U.S. industrialists, opera-loving Argentines completed the Teatro Colon in 1908. With so many architects involved, it is not surprising that the building has a great many styles associated with European theaters.

This opera house's outstanding record of great performances is matched only by the famous artists who have graced its stage. Teatro Colon has its own elaborate costume and scenic construction departments.

4 – THE ROYAL OPERA HOUSE
London, England
Tel: 44-(0)-20-7240-1200,
www.royalopera.org

An opera house has stood in the present location of the Royal Opera House at Covent Garden since the early 18th century; the current building is the third.

TI ADORO

Dear Friends,

I hope to be remembered, of course, as a singer of opera, that sublime art form which reached its greatest expression in my country, and for the love of opera which will remain central to my life. But life, thankfully, has its different moments and, like many of my predecessors—including the great Caruso, I have the diverse multitude of music written for the tenor voice. The musical literature for a tenor is the most varied of all in any language and the tenor writing always covers the widest range of emotion. I grew up loving all kinds of music and the great opera arias themselves are really the best pop songs ever written as their melodies have been reflected in so much popular repertoire.

I very much hope that you will enjoy sharing the journey with me.

— Luciano Pavarotti

George Handel's operas were the first ever to be performed here, and he wrote many of his operas and oratorios for this place in particular. From 1735 until his death in 1759 he gave regular seasonal performances here.

5 – THE BOLSHOI

Moscow, Russia
Tel: 7-(095)-250-73-17, www.bolshoi.ru

One of Russia's premier theaters, coupled with one of the best symphony orchestras in the world, the Bolshoi in Moscow has survived fire, war, and revolution. Its stunning neoclassic portico, topped by a statue of Apollo in his chariot, is a precursor to the magnificent splendor visitors will find inside.

Four balconies and a top gallery surround the orchestra, where the seats are Chippendale chairs upholstered in red damask. The great stage is known for its celebrated ballet company. Here, Yuri Grigorovich choreographed memorable productions of *Swan Lake, The Golden Age*, and *Romanda*.

6 – SYDNEY OPERA HOUSE

Sydney, Australia
Tel: 61-2-9250-7111, www.sydneyoperahouse.com

Situated on a spit of land that juts out into Sydney's harbor, the spectacularly contemporary Sydney Opera House has wonderful views of the sailboat-dotted water.

Even if attending a performance doesn't suit your plans, you might want to visit the opera house just to see the building; tours are offered frequently. The structure was designed by Joern Utzon to suggest a series of overlapping shells and sails. The grand opening took place in 1973; the first public performance was Prokofiev's *War and Peace*.

Inside, each theater is paneled in different types of wood to enhance the venue's acoustic qualities as well as offer pleasing aesthetics. All major performance areas have their own foyers.

OPERA HOUSES

7 – PARIS OPÉRA
Paris, France
Tel: 33-(0)-1-72-29-35-35, www.opera-de-paris.fr

The main facade of the Paris Opéra is an imposing sight, even in a city filled with architectural marvels like Paris. The highly ornamented building with it crowning dome was built in 1875. It is a theater house suitable for both ballet and opera. Some of the greatest ceremonial spaces in the world are here at the Paris Opera, lending their sublimity to lofty occasions.

The rich and striking interiors capture the tastes and attitudes of France's Second Empire. In 1962, Marc Chagall created new frescoes on the center of the Palais Garnier's ceiling. The result, nothing short of spectacular, is all the more special for not conflicting with the formal character of the interior decor.

8 – OPÉRA ROYAL
Versailles Court Theater, France
www.chateauversailles.fr

The interior of the Opéra Royal in the famously opulent palace of Versailles is a clever creation. The wooden walls were actually painted to resemble marble, which they do quite perfectly. Gold is harmoniously blended with the pinks and greens of the marbling and the sky-blue curtain and upholstery. Breaking with traditional Italian-style theaters, two balconies ring the house, topped by an ample colonnade that seems to extend into infinity thanks to a play of mirrors.

Ange-Jacques Gabrielle built the theater in 1769 in preparation for the marriage of the dauphin, the future King Louis XVI, to the Austrian princess Marie-Antoinette. After the French Revolution, the theater was used just

occasionally for various events. Today, special gala performances are often held there.

9 – VIENNA STAATSOPER
Vienna, Austria
Tel: 43-1-514-44-0, www.wiener-staatsoper.at

Built in 1869, the Staatsoper was inaugurated with a performance of Mozart's *Don Giovanni*. Its reputation as the center of Viennese musical life has long been established, and the Staatsoper remains one of the world's top opera houses. Although much of it was destroyed when the Allies bombed the city toward the end of World War II, on March 12, 1945, the grand staircase and some of the other public areas miraculously survived. For an idea of how things looked before the air raid, walk through the main doors into the box office foyer. The theater you see now reopened after the Russian occupation of Austria ended, and the first piece performed there was Ludwig von Beethoven's *Fidelio*, a hymn to freedom.

10 – TEATRO AMAZONAS
Manaus, Brazil
www.teatroamazonas.com.br

When rich planters decided to build an opera house in the heart of the Amazon, they spared no expense on details and construction. With the perseverance of these rubber barons, Teatro Amazonas is a glorious rival to Europe's best opera houses. Artists associated with the theater include Crispim Do Amaral, who painted the drop curtain, and Domenica de Angelis, who decorated the Noble Room.

The Chair: Backstage at the Bolshoi

A few years ago, I was working on a documentary, *Backstage at the Bolshoi,* with the famed ballet company. I am very partial to dancers, whom I find nimble, lithe, delicate, hardworking, and beautiful.

On this assignment, my 6-foot, 6-inch frame seemed to be out of sorts and out of place. During a rehearsal break, being a tap dancer, I could not resist showing off with time steps, so some day I could announce that I had danced on stage at the Bolshoi.

I was a guest of the great ballet master and choreographer Yuri Grigorovich, who was apparently amused by me. Each day, he greeted me as "The Great Lande-da." Then I became a curious study in his gaze. I was not sure why. Was it that we were frustrated hoofers? Or did he like my Buffalo shuffle?

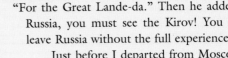

In between filming, I visited the Kremlin, Leo Tolstoy's house, and Aleksandr Pushkin's museum. Moscow held great fascination for me. I loved Russia for its literature, its music, its people, but most of all for its great contribution to dance. Soon my assignment came to an end.

I had admired the chairs in the orchestra at the Bolshoi, since they were not like concert seats at all, but crafted Chippendale chairs, upholstered in silk brocade, as elegant as the beautiful house itself. Grigorovich presented me with one.

A chair from the Bolshoi! It was too generous.

"For the Great Lande-da." Then he added, "In Russia, you must see the Kirov! You cannot leave Russia without the full experience."

Just before I departed from Moscow, the great master of the Bolshoi presented me with a letter of introduction written in Cyrillic, dotted with official seals above the letterhead, and addressed to the head of the Kirov, his archrival, the famed ballet company in St. Petersburg. "Good-bye, my friend. I will see you again," he said.

Journeying to St. Petersburg, with the letter of introduction in hand, I arrived at the Kirov. Reading the letter, the ballet master looked at me in amazement. Much to my delight, I was welcomed to the Royal Box each evening, entertained with dinners and toasts, and the entire *corps de ballet* held me in admiration. Russian hospitality was on parade. But it seemed that my reception was a little excessive. Why? I had not even done a soft shoe or a buck and wing. I later learned the reason.

The founder of the Kirov was a Frenchman, Jean Pierre Batiste Lande, who had been invited by Catherine the Great to come to Russia to give Russian officers dancing lessons. He stayed on, introducing the court to ballet, and voilà, a Russian ballet school was born.

By way of historical background: It was in 1698, when Peter the Great returned to Russia after an extended tour in the West, that he commissioned artists to come to his country. Peter and Catherine the Great were so impressed by a recital of Monsieur Lande's students that the St. Petersburg Imperial Ballet School was established. Lande's productions were performed at the St. Petersburg Theatre, later called the Maryinsky, and finally the Kirov. Many international artists performed, and the Kirov became a premier center for ballet. European dancers returned from their Russian tours with stories of the beautiful theater, the tremendous experience, and the generous salaries paid to guest artists.

This history put me in the limelight. Lande was the founder of Russian ballet. I was much too shy to deny this heritage. I was having too much fun. In truth, Grigorovich had played a masterful joke on his friends by introducing me as the great-grandson of Jean Pierre.

Sent as his personal tribute, as I learned the scheme, I could only bow my head sheepishly. The less said the better. Surely Grigorovich had choreographed the charade for the amusement of the entire Bolshoi. "There was that dunce, Lande, showing off."

How could I tell the truth? Or betray Gregorovich? My silence was interpreted as modesty; and modesty, rewarded with admiration. I wish I could say the story ended here. But there is the matter of the treasured chair that Gregorovich had bestowed to my custody.

True to form, I soon discovered that no one is allowed to take any antique out of Russia, especially a treasure from the Bolshoi. I supposed he thought he would soon be getting postcards from me, stamped by the KGB from a gulag in Siberia. What to do?

The Kirov became the mother of invention. I explained my dilemma of the chair, and the Kirov took pity. Surely the Bolshoi had given me the chair out of respect. How could they refuse Lande?

The solution they created was that I buy a ticket to Helsinski, and the Kirov would arrange the rest, with an introduction to a furniture expert in Finland.

To the Kirov's scenery shop went the chair. In short time, it was dismantled, painted with a washable watercolor paint, and the sum of its parts deposited in a burlap bag. In addition, the prop shop supplied me with documentation, handsomely stamped with seals, announcing that I was a poor furniture manufacturer, having come to Russia with a template in search of a company to reproduce chairs. Alas, I was being recommended to a sister company in Finland, the Finnish-Russian Cooperative Furniture Exchange.

Taking the night train to Helsinski, I felt like James Bond undercover, through customs with my unassuming burlap bag without a hitch. Arriving in Finland, I found the cooperative, and the people there beautifully restored my prized possession.

Today, I sit in my chair. My lovely Russian wife, Natalya, is in awe. A dancer herself, she is not sure if I am a descendant of the great Jean Pierre Batiste Lande or not. Neither am I, but it was sure worth the experience.

TEN BEST
~GARDENS~

1 – CHÂTEAU DE VERSAILLES
Versailles, France
Tel: 33-(0)-1-30-83-77-88, www.chateauversailles.fr

The famous French landscape designer André Le Nôtre laid out these gardens southwest of Paris in the 17th century at the behest of Louis XIV. The Sun King wanted them to magnify the glory of his palace at Versailles, which was itself a monument to his absolute rule.

The 101 hectares (250 acres) are riddled with paths that lead to flower beds, quiet corners decorated with classical statuary, ornamental lakes, and a canal that King Louis used for gondola rides.

2 – SINGAPORE BOTANIC GARDEN
Singapore
Tel: 65-6471-7361, www.sbg.org.sg

Considered one of the world's prettiest botanical gardens, the Singapore Botanic Garden was established in 1859. Its 52 hectares (128 acres) are divided into three "cores." Bukit Timah Core is geared for educational and recreational use. In Tanglin Core, visitors can find a bandstand and many statues sprinkled among favorite native plants and trees. The most popular core for tourists is Centre. The National Orchid Garden is in this section, atop the park's highest point, where more than 60,000 colorful orchids bloom.

3 – DESCANSO GARDENS
La Canada Flintridge, California
Tel: 818-949-4200, www.descanso.com

A mere 20-minute drive outside of Los Angeles you'll find a bucolic paradise with more than 100,000 plants and one of the world's largest collections of camellias. The gardens and woods of Descanso ("rest" or "repose" in Spanish) unfold over 65 hectares (160 acres) of the San Rafael Hills. Don't miss the Japanese garden and the International Rosarium that is home to thousands of roses. Children particularly enjoy riding the Descanso Gardens Enchanted Railroad, a mini-diesel train.

4 – BUTCHART GARDENS
Vancouver Island, British Columbia
Tel: 250-652-4422, www.butchartgardens.com

The Butchart Gardens are a dazzling example of a successful reclamation project. The land, used for years by Portland Cement, by 1904 had exhausted its value as a quarry. That's when Jennie Butcher, the wife of Portland Cement's owner, filled the space with soil from nearby farms. Her vision expanded into a 22-hectare (55-acre) tract filled with 700 varieties of plants that bloom from March to October.

CAPABILITY BROWN

Lancelot "Capability" Brown was the man to see if you were an 18th-century English aristocrat desiring to create a magnificent garden. By some estimates, Brown designed about 170 gardens that still exist—in some shape or form—around the stately homes and estates of Great Britain. So trustworthy and professional was he that he got his nickname from telling his clients that their grounds had "great capabilities."

Some of the key elements of a Brown creation are wide, rolling lawns with rows or groves of trees. The trees then often lead to scenes straight out of Greek or Roman mythology, replete with temples, monuments, and bridges. He carved out lakes as well. Of course, the end results looked as though the scene had been placed there by Mother Nature, an Arcadia in England.

Brown was born in 1715 in Northumberland, in the northernmost reaches of the country. He started out as a gardener's assistant, then worked his way up to designing gardens himself; to ensure his creations' success, Brown took up architecture and became quite accomplished in that field, too.

By 1753, Brown was much sought after as a designer. His acclaim did not escape the notice of the royal family. He was made head gardener at Hampton Court Palace in 1761. He kept his private practice going, also. He died on February 6, 1783, in London.

Two of Brown's most stunning projects are Petworth House in West Sussex and Blenheim Palace at Woodstock.

5 – VILLA D'ESTE
Tivoli, Italy
Tel: 39-07-743-12070

A Renaissance cardinal decided to make life in Tivoli bearable by turning a dilapidated Benedictine monastery into a lovely villa, the Villa d'Este. This was embellished by one of the most fascinating garden and fountain complexes in the world, recently listed by UNESCO as one of Italy's 31 major historical/artistic sites. Among the most bewitching of the mossy fountains are: the Fontana del Bicchierone (water pours out from a large shell-shaped basin); the Rometta fountain, which is a miniature Rome complete with a wolf-suckling Romulus and Remus; and the Avenue of the Hundred Fountains, where animal heads, lilies, a small boat, basins, and so on all spurt water.

6 – DUMBARTON OAKS
Washington, D.C.
Tel: 202-339-6410, www.doaks.org

You might feel as though you've stepped into a Merchant-Ivory set in any of the gardens that make up this estate at the north end of Georgetown, one of Washington's poshest neighborhoods. Vines tumble down stone walls enclosing the Fountain Terrace. Lovers' Lane meanders past a Roman-style amphitheater built around a small deep-blue pool. And what used to be a simple cow path leading away from the pool is now called Melisande's Allée, perhaps as a nod to the haunting opera *Pelleas et Melisande*.

7 – GARDENS OF THE VILLA ÉPHRUSSI DE ROTHSCHILD
St.-Jean-Cap-Ferrat, France
Tel: 33-(0)-4-93-01-33-09, www.villa-ephrussi.com

In the early 1900s, Béatrice Éphrussi, a Rothschild baroness, built a pink-confection, Venice-style villa surrounded by

Grand Gardens

GARDENS

"Though we travel the world over to find the beautiful, we must carry it with us or we don't find it at all."

— Ralph Waldo Emerson

breathtaking gardens, with the sparkling sea beyond. Pathways meander through the seven themed gardens, the focal point being the French gardens, with a lily-pad-dotted pool, dancing fountains, and a Temple of Love replicating the Trianon at Versailles. There are also a Provençal garden, filled with olive trees and lavender; a lapidary garden, with sculptures too large to be displayed in the villa; and Spanish, Japanese, Florentine, and exotic gardens.

8 – STOURHEAD
Warminster, England
Tel: 44-(0)-1-747-841152, www.nationaltrust.org.uk

To the English gentry of the 18th century, the more classical something could be, the better. Stourhead is a grand example of genteel fascination with the past. Henry Hoare II punctuated the gardens of his Wiltshire estate with re-created ruins and classical buildings such as the Pantheon and Temple of Apollo.

9 – THE MASTER-OF-NETS GARDEN
Suzhou, China
www.suzhou.gov.cn/English/Travel/7.shtml

This residential garden in southeast China, called Wangshiyuan in Chinese, was designed during the Song dynasty (A.D. 960–1270). The arrangement of pavilions, halls, music rooms, winsome bamboo groves, and waterside perches is an exercise in natural harmony. The central section is a small world within itself; piles of yellow stones form "mountains" complete with caverns, and a tiny arched bridge called the "leading to quietude" crosses a pond to a small pavilion in the center.

10 – SANS SOUCI
Potsdam, Germany
Tel: 49-331-969-4190, www.spsg.de

Frederick the Great of Prussia built this splendid rococo palace as his summer place, where he could live without a care, *sans souci*. Busts of Roman emperors, decorative statues, and a Chinese teahouse dot the lavish grounds.

CHELSEA FLOWER SHOW

London, England
www.rhs.org.uk

Each May for five days, garden designers and aficionados from around the world come to London to attend the Chelsea Flower Show. The event began in 1862 as the Great Spring Show in Kensington; in 1913 it moved to its current location at the Royal Chelsea Hospital. This is the place to see the latest trends and developments in horticulture. Hundreds of exhibitors show off their skills in creating gardens for city homes and country estates. New plants often make their debuts here. The show is open to the public for the last three days.

English Gardens

England's romantic gardens, with their billowing masses of roses and rustic cottages, are emblematic of the country itself. Many visitors come with the express purpose of seeing the country's famous garden sights.

Early in the 1700s, English gardens resembled the formal classical gardens of Italy and France. Then began a movement, spurred on first by romantically inclined writers and poets, for more "natural" gardens. Alexander Pope, a poet and essayist, lobbied for a return to the "amicable simplicity of unadorned nature" in an essay on gardening in the 1713 *Guardian*. In his *Epistle to Burlington,* he proclaimed: "In all, let nature never be forgot ... Consult the genius of the place." The English landscape style went on to be finessed by three designers: William Kent, Lancelot (Capability) Brown, and Humphrey Repton. You'll see their work at many of England's historic homes.

Not all gardens are residential. You'll find some enchanting ones in the cloisters of cathedrals. Monks and nuns carefully tended these peaceful green spaces, growing the food they needed, as well as medicinal herbs.

For comprehensive information on English public gardens, the National Trust is the best place to start. The agency also suggests itineraries. The Web site is www.nationaltrust.org.uk.

Below is a list of gardens cited by www.gardenvisit.com as being outstanding examples of garden design. They provide the perfect skeleton for a garden lover's trip to England.

Biddulph Grange, Blenheim Palace, Castle Howard, Chatsworth, Great Dixter, Hampton Court Garden, Harewood House, Wisley, Rousham Landscape Garden, Royal Botanic Garden, Edinburgh, Sissinghurst Castle Garden, Stowe Landscape Gardens, Studley Royal, Hidcote Garden, Royal Botanic Garden, Kew, Leonardslee Gardens, and Levens Hall Garden.

THE MOSS ROSE

It's hard to imagine a greater honor for a horticulturist than having a plant named after you. Such is the case for the noted horticulturist Nancy Moss, whose family has carefully perfected the Moss rose. Portulaca grandiflora is a hardy, drought-resistant flowering plant that comes in an array of bright colors.

TEN BEST
~LONDON PUBS~

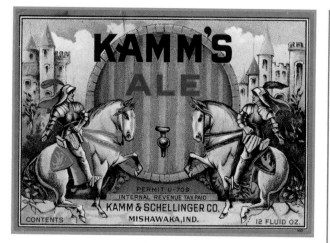

3 – GRENADIER
Wilton Row, tel: 44-(0)-207-235-3074

Tucked away in the city's Belgravia section, this pub has been around for many years. Early in the 19th century, it was a favorite of officers who served the Duke of Wellington in the Napoleonic wars; they used it basically as their mess. The front room is decorated with Wellington memorabilia, including swords and paintings. It's entirely appropriate to order the beef Wellington while you're here, accompanied by a hearty stout.

4 – THE OLD BELL
95 Fleet Street, tel: 44-(0)-207-583-0216

They've been hoisting pints at the Old Bell for more than 300 years. Built after the Great London Fire of 1666, the Bell first was popular with the workers and masons rebuilding the city. Printers from the famous Fleet Street papers also congregated within the dark paneled walls.

Although the printing industry has changed dramatically, the pub remains and still thrives as a cozy afterwork spot.

1 – FOX & HOUNDS
29 Passmore Street, tel: 44-(0)-207-730-6367

This small pub in the center of Chelsea has the dark, classic atmosphere one would expect in a London pub. It was built in the 1860s and has developed a sterling reputation with beer aficionados. The chef posts the daily menu on a blackboard, and the food is rarely disappointing.

2 – THE GRAPES
76 Narrow Street, tel: 44-(0)-207-987-4396

I was worried about the fate of this beloved pub when the Docklands started to develop in the 1980s. Thankfully, the Grapes has survived and continues to go strong. You'd be hard pressed to find a more traditional pub along the banks of the Thames.

THE UNIQUE ENGLISH PUB

Peter Hayden is regarded as the world's leading authority on pubs. Here he shares his thoughts on England's pub scene.

The pub is more than just a shop where drinks are sold and consumed. For centuries it has been a place where friends meet, colleagues "talk shop," and business people negotiate deals. Many pubs provide affordable accommodation, particularly in rural areas. In remote communities pubs often serve a dual role, such as church or post office. 'Pub' was invented by the Victorians, an abbreviation of 'public house.' It was the Romans who gave England its first 'pubs' almost 2,000 years ago.

Over the next few centuries, invaders came and went, and occasionally settled. One thing they all had in common was their fondness for drinking, with a particular thirst for ale, brewed using malted barley, water, and yeast. The spread of Christianity did nothing to lessen the English thirst for ale, and the church adopted many pagan rituals that involved drinking.

Then pilgrims who made pilgrimages to various shrines all over Britain put a tremendous strain on the resources of the monasteries, which had provided sustenance and lodging. A new type of establishment was needed to accommodate all the people. Such an establishment became known as an inn.

The earliest inns were run by monks who offered travelers shelter, food, and drink. Many of these old inns are around today still offering hospitality to travelers. Probably the most famous of all the inns was the Tabard, in Southwark, London. Here, in 1388, Chaucer began his *Canterbury Tales:* "In Southwark, at The Tabard, as I lay ready to go on pilgrimage and start for Canterbury ..."

During the reign of Elizabeth I (1558–1603), England began to assert herself in the world through exploration and military might. Population growth and a changing economy saw the expansion and creation of towns. Professionals, such as lawyers, bankers, writers, and civil servants, prospered most from urban society. Inns evolved into taverns. The image of the cozy tavern with a large open fire, customers gathered round in lively conversation, smoking pipes and quaffing ale, hangs in many modern pubs.

London was famous for its taverns. Seventeenth-century literati Ben Jonson, Samuel Pepys, and Dr. Samuel Johnson were pillars of tavern society, and many claim them as patrons. Samuel Johnson's biographer, James Boswell, made famous Johnson's quote that appears in many a pub to this day: "No, Sir, there is nothing which has yet been contrived by man, by which so much happiness is produced as by a good pub or inn."

5 – THE GUINEA GRILL
30 Bruton Place
Tel: 44-(0)-207-499-1210

Located in the posh neighborhood of Mayfair, the Guinea is a splendid restaurant set in a traditional London pub. Its lamb, steak, and fresh seafood come highly recommended. For a light snack, try a sandwich at the bustling bar: The Guinea is a regular winner or finalist in the Pub Sandwich of the Year awards. It has a terrific beer menu, too, of course.

6 – THE PRINCE ALFRED
5a Formosa Street, Maida Vale
Tel: 44-(0)-207-286-3287

Named after Queen Victoria's second son, this is an unusually pretty pub with handpainted designs on the walls and ceilings and a stunning bow window. It opened in 1863, at the height of the British Empire, at a time when men and women drank in different sections—wooden partitions between those sections still stand, dividing the area into five separate snugs, ideal for good conversation.

7 – THE COLTON ARMS
187 Greyhound Road
Tel: 44-(0)-207-385-6956

If you're looking for a *Cheers* scene where everyone seems to know everyone else's name, this wee place near the Barons Court tube stop is it. The Colton Arms, with its traditional oak furniture and well-handled pint glasses, is the epitome of a traditional London pub, serving as a second living room, of sorts, for locals.

8 – THE SALISBURY
90 St. Martin's Lane
Tel: 44-(0)-207-836-5863

Built in the heyday of Victorian pubs, the Salisbury is a beauty with huge mirrors, art nouveau light fixtures, and a polished mahogany bar. It's been well-maintained, too; the owners gave it a recent facelift.

This place draws a steady crowd. To catch it during quieter times, come in mid-morning or mid-afternoon.

9 – THE OLD CHESHIRE
Wine Office Court, 145 Fleet Street
Tel: 44-(0)-207-353-6170

If you're a writer or reader, you really must come here; this was the haunt of Dr. Samuel Johnson, William Makepeace Thackery, and Charles Dickens. (Mark Twain also came here during a visit.) Need more convincing? They serve some of the best Welsh rarebit in the area. The melted cheese-and-ale concoction over toast is often called Welsh "rabbit."

10 – THE KINGS ARMS
Two Shepherd Market
Tel: 44-(0)-207-629-0416

This Mayfair pub, with its warm, cozy atmosphere, is within walking distance to many of London's most famous attractions and shops, making it a very popular place with locals and tourists alike. In addition to serving the sort of hearty, simple fare one would expect, the chefs also also prepare very tasty vegetarian dishes.

TEN BEST
~U. S. NATIONAL PARKS~

In April 2000, at the opening of Giant Sequoia National Monument, U.S. President Bill Clinton sang the praises of U. S. national parks and historic sites. In doing so, he invoked the name of Theodore Roosevelt, the president who essentially created the National Park System in the early 1900s. In Roosevelt's words: "The ages have been at work on the [national landscape], and man can only mar it. What you can do is keep it for your children and your children's children."

The national park system comprises more than 370 areas of special importance in the U.S.—a system that includes exceptional natural, historical, scientific, and recreational sites, including lakeshores, battlefields, monuments, and seashores. Here are what we feel are the ten best of the system.

1 – SEQUOIA & KINGS CANYON NATIONAL PARKS
Three Rivers, California
Tel: 559-565-3341, www.nps.gov/seki

While both of these parks have groves of giant sequoias, Sequoia—the southernmost of the two—is more accessible for casual visitors. To appreciate the rugged splendor, you should hike a trail; we recommend Congress, River, Zumwalt Meadow, and the Moro Rock Trails. If you have

time only to drive, then follow the Generals Highway for 27 kilometers (17 miles) from the Ash Mountain Entrance to the General Sherman Tree, the world's largest sequoia. Named for a Civil War general, William Tecumseh Sherman, the tree is 275 feet (84 meters) tall.

2 – GETTYSBURG NATIONAL MILITARY PARK
Gettysburg, Pennsylvania
Tel: 717-334-1124, www.nps.gov/gett

Only cannon, stone walls, and countless monuments recall the horrors that unfolded on these bucolic fields on July 1, 1863. Here Union and Confederate soldiers fought the bloodiest battle of the Civil War. Three days later, 51,000 men were dead, wounded, or missing. Take the 30-kilometer (18-mile) self-guided battlefield driving tour; you'll pass McPherson Ridge, where the fighting began; and Little Round Top, strategic high ground. Don't miss seeing Evergreen Cemetery, where President Abraham Lincoln gave his stirring Gettysburg address on Nov. 19, 1863.

3 – ALAGNAK WILD AND SCENIC RIVER
King Salmon, Alaska
Tel: 907-246-3305, www.nps.gov/rivers/wsr-alagnak.html

This pristine river begins within the Katmai National Preserve at the head of the Aleutian Peninsula. From there,

Visit Our National Parks

it rushes along for 108 kilometers (67 miles) past boreal forests and wet sedge tundra before joining the Pacific Ocean. Otters, moose, brown bears, and ospreys are just a few of the creatures that call this wilderness home.

4 – SANTA FE NATIONAL HISTORIC TRAIL

Colorado, Kansas, Missouri, New Mexico, and Oklahoma
Tel: 505-988-6888, www.nps.gov/safe

Between 1821 and 1880, the Santa Fe Trail was the main link between St. Louis, the gateway to the West, and Santa Fe, one of the West's most prosperous cities. Families in covered wagons, soldiers, and prospectors bound for glorious gold (they hoped) all took the trail. When the railroad came to Santa Fe in 1880, the trail became obsolete. About 15 percent of the original trail

CHIEF SEATTLE

A 19th-century West Coast Indian Chief named Seattle is credited for one of the most eloquent speeches about environmental preservation ever delivered. Whether the words were his or those of his translator, they have great significance for national parks.

"Every part of this Earth is sacred to my people. Every shining pine needle, every sandy shore. Every mist in the dark woods, every clearing and humming insect is holy in the memory and experience of my people. We are part of the Earth and it is part of us."

remains. Parts are on privately owned land, but you can still carve a trip out of it and drive past the forts and stores those early pioneers passed. Fort Osage in Missouri is a must-see, as is the quaint Last Chance Store in Council Grove, Kansas. Cyclists, hikers, and equestrians can follow the course of the trail for 30 kilometers (19 miles) in the Cimarron National Grassland in Kansas.

5 – STATUE OF LIBERTY NATIONAL MONUMENT

New York
Tel: 212-363-7621, www.nps.gov/stli

The 46-meter-tall (151-foot) green woman who stands as a graceful sentinel of Upper New York Bay has become an international symbol of freedom. Given to the United States in 1886 from the people of France, Lady Liberty has been one of the first—and certainly the most welcoming—sites in the United States for millions of immigrants. Frédéric-Auguste Bartholdi sculpted her, perhaps in the image of his mother, and Gustave Eiffel (of Eiffel Tower fame) devised an iron frame for the enormous copper sheets.

Visitors take ferries from Battery Park to Liberty Island. From there, the best way to truly get a feel for this marvelous piece of art is to take the elevator to the top of the pedestal and then climb the 354 steps to the top of her crown. The views are breathtaking, well worth every step.

6 – BLUE RIDGE PARKWAY

North Carolina, Virginia
Tel: 828-271-4799, www.nps.gov/blri

Showcasing the age-old beauty of the southern Appalachians, the Blue Ridge Parkway is the most visited unit within the National Park System. The 755-kilometer

(469-mile), two-lane road connects Shenandoah National Park in the north to Great Smoky Mountains National Park in the south. You'll ride along the crest of the Blue Ridge, as well as other mountains, dipping into deep hollows then rising up above the trees as high as 1,829 meters (6,000 feet). Plenty of remnants of the region's mountain people who once lived here exist along the way.

7 – NEW ORLEANS JAZZ HISTORICAL PARK
Louisiana
Tel: 504-589-4806, www.nps.gov/jazz

When Congress passed legislation that created the park in 1994, the intention was "to preserve the origins, early history, development, and progression of jazz." And what better place to do this than New Orleans, in the heart of the Mississippi Delta, where the uniquely American art form was born.

This young park is evolving, and how it will emerge from 2005's devastating Hurricane Katrina remains to be seen. According to the original plans, the park eventually will consist of four buildings in Louis Armstrong Memorial Park. Until those buildings are restored, the park's headquarters is located at 916 North Peters Street in the famous French Quarter.

8 – YOSEMITE NATIONAL PARK
California
Tel: 209-372-0200, www.nps.gov/yose

The work of giant glaciers during the ice age, Yosemite is a famous natural wonderland in the Sierra Nevada showcasing waterfalls, meadows, and forests of giant sequoia. Half Dome and El Capitan, rock formations towering above Yosemite Valley, are virtually American icons. Try to visit Yosemite Falls, the tallest in North America; hike to Mirror Lake; kayak along the Merced River; visit the giant sequoias in Mariposa Grove; then relax at the Ahwahnee, the parks' grand old Arts and Crafts-style lodge.

9 – HAWAII VOLCANOES NATIONAL PARK
Hawaii
Tel: 808-967-7311, www.nps.gov/havo

This is the place for anyone eager to get close to an active volcano. Located on the Big Island (as the island of Hawaii is often called), Kilauea and Mauna Loa are two of the most active volcanoes in the world. The first is more than 1,219 meters (4,000 feet) high and still growing. It abuts the second, a monster mountain that towers some 4,169 meters (13,680 feet) above the sea. The park stretches from sea level to Mauna Loa's snowy summit.

10 – GRAND CANYON NATIONAL PARK
Arizona
Tel: 928-638-7888
www.nps.gov/grca

Stand on the edge of this immense gorge—more than 1.5 kilometers (one mile) deep and up to 29 kilometers (18 miles) wide—and you will experience nature's grandeur. The Colorado River carved the chasm over millennia. Hiking, rafting, and driving opportunities are outstanding.

~WORLD HERITAGE SITES~

1 – VENICE AND ITS LAGOON
Italy

One of the world's most romantic cities, Venice seduces with its 118 tiny islands bedecked with baroque palaces and linked by more than 400 bridges. Founded in the 5th century and reigning as a major maritime power by the 10th, the entire city is an architectural wonder built on centuries of wealth, with extraordinary buildings showcasing exquisite style—including the Basilica di San Marco, the Palazzo Ducale, and the church of Santa Maria della Salute.

2 – ANGKOR ARCHAEOLOGICAL PARK
Siem Reap, Cambodia

This magnificent park stretches out over 400 square kilometers (154 square miles) of northwestern Cambodia. From here, the Khmer empire ruled the region between the 9th and 15th centuries. Perhaps the most famous part of the park is Angkor Wat, a 12th-century temple complex dedicated to Lord Vishnu. After the Siamese conquered the Khmers in 1220, Angkor disappeared into the surrounding jungles until the mid-19th century, when the colonizing French rediscovered them.

3 – VATICAN CITY
Rome, Italy
www.vatican.va

The Vatican may be the world's smallest independent state, but its importance is immense. The historical seat of Roman Catholicism, it is, with St. Peter's Basilica and the Vatican Museums, the repository of some of mankind's major artistic treasures. Michelangelo's Pietà, his Sistine Chapel, and the Rooms of Raphael are just some of the magnificent splendors found here.

FCC PHNOM PENH

363 Sisowath Quay, Phnom Penh, Cambodia
Tel: 855-23-210-142,
www.fcccambodia.com/phnom_penh

The Foreign Correspondents Club Phnom Penh is not exactly a UNESCO World Heritage site. But, to the weary, thirsty, hungry foreign correspondent, this club is a sight for sore eyes. The hotel, restaurant, and bar represent some of the best accommodations available in the Cambodian capital. Opened in 1993 by a British investment group, the FCC is in a nicely renovated French-colonial building that overlooks the Mekong River and the National Museum. Each of the seven rooms is named after a temple. The restaurant serves homemade ice cream, and the bar is renowned for its stiff drinks.

VENICE ON VIEW

Lady Carla Thorneycroft has played a major role in the restoration of Venice. Born to an American mother and an Italian father, she has lived in London most of her life.

She fell in love with Venice while visiting her grandmother when she was six years old; her grandfather was keeper of the state archives there. And the magical city has been a major part of her life. Since 1966, Lady Thorneycroft has chaired the Venice in Peril Fund, a project providing money to help preserve Venice's rich culture and intellectual life. It was created that year after a major flood washed over the city, once again threatening to ruin its charms and landmarks.

It seems only logical, therefore, that we asked her to expand on our No. 1 World Heritage site. In her own words:

"Venice marked out a position as a world power from the 12th to the 14th centuries. After falling to Napoléon in 1797, she joined the kingdom of Italy in 1866. Today her palazzos have become museums, shops, hotels, and convents that are in continuous architectural restoration.

Little has changed in 200 years. Bridges, clock towers, and squares evidence a glorious past. The city sounds are footsteps and bells and a slow ebbing tide along canals. The waterway is on exhibit to a magical past at every turn.

"Ever since the 10th century, Venice has endowed the world with extraordinary buildings and works of art from Tiepolo to Canaletto."

In closing, we asked Lady Thorneycroft to name her ten favorite structures in Venice:

1 – Andrea Palladios's facade of the church of San Francesco della Vigna
2 – The Accademia Gallery
3 – The Porta della Carta to the Doge's Palace
4 – Sansovino's loggetta at the base of St. Mark's Campanile
5 – The Madonna dell'Orto, Tintoretto's Parish Church
6 – San Nicolò dei Mendicoli
7 – The Great Window of SS. Giovanni e Paolo
8 – S. Giorgio Maggiore
9 – Scuola di San Rocco
10 – Piazzetta San Marco

4 – PALACE AND GARDENS OF SCHÖNBRUNN
Vienna, Austria
www.schoenbrunn.at/de/publicdir

This was the favorite palace of Empress Maria Theresa, who spent summers here while she ruled the Habsburg Empire in the 18th century. Her husband, Franz Stephen, designed the lush gardens and founded the world's first zoo on the grounds here in 1752.

5 – LORD HOWE ISLAND
New South Wales, Australia
Tel: 61-2-6563-2114, www.lordhoweisland.info

Out at sea east of Sydney, Lord Howe is a 7-million-year-old volcanic island that has the southernmost coral reef in the world. About 90 species of coral and 500 kinds of fish inhabit the pristine waters around the island. On land, you'll find about 350 people, lush forests, and all sorts of wonderful birds.

6 – HISTORIC CENTER OF CESKY KRUMLOV
Czech Republic
www.ckrumlov.cz/uk/i_index.htm

A beautifully preserved medieval village in the Czech Republic, Cesky Krumlov was built on a meander of the Vltava River. Towering above the town's refined Renaissance and baroque burgher architecture, the castle, begun in the 13th century, combines Gothic, Renaissance, and baroque styles. It's one of the largest in central Europe, with 40 buildings and palaces situated around five castle courts.

UNESCO

United National Scientific, Educational, and Cultural Organization World Heritage Centre
7, Place de Fontenoy, 75352 Paris 07 SP, France
Tel: 33-(01)-45-6816-60,
http://whc.unesco.org/en/home

In 1972, UNESCO passed the World Heritage Convention, an international treaty designed to preserve the world's great cultural and natural sites. Places that are approved are called World Heritage sites; currently there are 812 on the list: 628 are from the cultural world, 160 are from the natural world, and 24 are a mixture of both. The sites are found in 137 nations, from the coral reefs of Australia to Old Town Lunenburg in Canada. Between 25 and 30 new sites are considered every year and evaluated on the basis of their cultural significance, uniqueness, and other criteria.

7 – DROTTNINGHOLM THEATRE, PALACE, AND THE CHINESE PAVILION
Drottningholm, Sweden
46-8-556-931-00 (theater), www.raa.se/varveng/drotte.asp

These three charming 18th-century structures are located outside of Stockholm on an island in Lake Malar. The castle, which shows the influence of Versailles, is the residence of the Swedish royal family, but parts are open to the public. The baroque theater is considered one of the best of its kind in Europe. The pavilion was designed in French baroque style with Chinese elements.

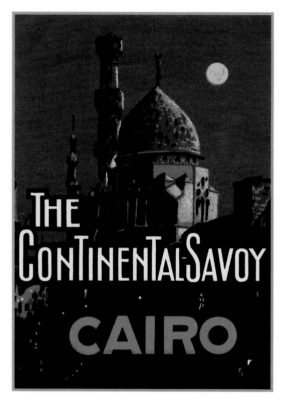

9 – PALACE AND PARK OF FONTAINEBLEAU

Fontainebleau, France
Tel: 33-(0)-1-60-71-50-70
www.musee-chateau-fontainebleau.fr

François I (1454-1547) turned what had been a medieval hunting lodge into a mammoth Italianate palace, importing Italian artists to design the interior. Many French monarchs were born and several died at this luxe palace, located in an immense forest south of Paris. Napoléon abdicated as Emperor of the French here in 1814.

10 – OLD CITY OF JERUSALEM

Israel

The Wailing Wall. The Dome of the Rock. The Church of the Holy Sepulcher. Each of these iconic religious sites—and some 200 more—are within the walls of Jerusalem. The ancient city is a crucible of sorts for three of the world's major faiths: Judaism, Christianity, and Islam. And for that reason, it has been the site of violent clashes among adherents of each.

8 – ABU SIMBEL

Aswan, Egypt
http://touregypt.net/aswan4.htm

If UNESCO had not intervened when Egypt was building the Aswan Dam in the 1960s, the two ancient temples at Abu Simbel constructed during the reign of Ramses II and his wife, Nefertari, would be underwater today. The two temples at Abu Simbel were taken apart and then reassembled about 60 meters (200 feet) above the place where they had been built some 3,000 years before.

PRINCE OF WALES

"At last, people are beginning to see that what I can only call 'living traditions' can help create lasting sustainability and enjoyable social exchange. I hope we will endeavor to integrate the best of the past with the best of the new. Architecture, as Jefferson realized, is the pre-eminent embodiment of a nation's values. It never lies about where our priorities are."

— Charles, Prince of Wales

Waiting for MacPherson

His directive to me was powered and inspired: "Egypt is history in the making. For God and TIME Magazine. I'll meet you in Aswan. Wait for me." I had been on assignment, following the journey of St. Paul through the Mediterranean. In Crete, the call came. I was being diverted to Egypt, to the ancient land of the pharaohs and pyramids.

The dispatch continued: "Meet MacPherson in Cairo."

I was a young underqualified correspondent, reporting and filming the opening of the Aswan Dam, with its attending Nubian surroundings. The day's history would soon bring understanding and change. Underneath the stars of Aswan, I give testament to this file.

Arriving in Africa's largest city, Cairo, whose foundation was laid in A.D. 969, I admired a mixture of villas and neoclassic multicolored mansions aged by a sprinkling of architectural mischief from *Arabian Nights* and third-world realities.

Taxis always speed in Cairo, past the Citadel of Saladin, the tombs of the Mamelukes, rolling lawns, stables, formal gardens—once the garrisons of British officers—to the remnants of a flourishing culture where sultans built their magnificent mosques in honor of their prophet. The very same mosques also served as holy bribes to guarantee their benefactors ascension to Islamic Heaven. The French Institute on Kasr el Nil was a reminder of Napoléon's invasion in 1798-1799. French and English were spoken by most educated Egyptians. Despite Middle East turmoil, the city stood in silent testimony of an eloquent and civilized past.

Now, archaeological scholars in search of history and jet setters in search of bargains rubbed elbows in the old city. The Khan at Khalili Bazaar was a first stop to sample an array of merchandise. Each street had a theme. The street of gold and the streets of leather goods, carpets and silver blended with the aroma of Turkish coffee and honey-flavored tobacco. On the street of Fate, Omi Amina, a reader of leaves and palms, offered me her words: "Patience. Allah is Good. You will find your way but you must wait."

Gallabiyas have been the traditional garb of Egyptians for ages, and the village of Kerdesa, on the road to Cairo, manufactures the best. Silky Egyptian cotton of 380 thread count can be bought in the bazaar, and a gallabiya for those wanting to blend in easily by wearing local dress can be tailored in a day. The camera crew took advantage of this opportunity.

I was anxious to meet my chief, the seasoned and experienced MacPherson, to learn the details of my assignment, but we were a few days early. Maybe Omi Amina knew something. We took advantage of fortune: "Be patient; you must wait." A weekend in Luxor was just the ticket. The modern wing of the Winter Palace hosted our visit to Egypt's pharonic past. The temples of Thebes, Karnak, and Luxor were fabled charms sitting on the east bank of the Nile near the Valley of the Kings.

Two hours by car from Cairo is the garden city of Ismailia, with overflowing bougainvillea and wooden balconies. It was oppressively hot, and we took refuge at the Number Six Beach, a private club open to foreigners for a nominal fee. At this welcomed oasis, we sipped iced jasmine tea and enjoyed delicious food as we sat underneath a beach umbrella and gazed across the astonishingly blue canal to the bright yellow Sinai Desert. We swam in the cooling water's salty depths while ships sailed past with exotic cargo destined for the world.

MacPherson, the bureau chief, was a Scotsman who stayed at the Cairo Hilton. At this exclusive retreat, MacPherson held Highland reminiscences of a cooler place far away. Along with telephone, typewriter, and writing pad, he kept in his room a tartan bag, his pipes. He never left home without them, should he be called upon to credit some ceremonial occasion.

The hotel was home to the favored Naga Fuad and Auberge aux Pyramids, with two dozen belly-shaking dancers and a clientele consisting of Saudi sheiks. The Belvedere Room was for quiet dinners and têtes-à-têtes; and the cozy Aberdeen Pub 28 was headquarters. The chief liked the good life and commandeered this touch of Caledonia. Glenlivet on the rocks, stocked specially for him, went a long way in this climate.

Presenting me with a card from Mr. Zein Nagoti, my chief assured me, "He's our man. I've made the arrangements. For you and the crew. And Aswan is surprisingly historic. I'm glad you are here for the betterment of humanity." Then he fell back into his single malt reverie, mumbling something about world peace. World peace?

So to change the world, I had arrived with a crew that consisted of a cameraman, a sound recorder, and me. We three shepherds slaved in the facilities of Mr. Zein Nagoti, head of the Mid-Eastern News Service. Fat and wrinkled with perspiration, Nagoti could get things done in Egypt. His services—for the enormous fee charged for press credentials—included the No. 1 Special. A red and gold card reading PRESS gave us permission to cover President Gamal Abdel Nasser and the great patriarch from the east, Comrade Nikita Khrushev. The Aswan Dam was a joint venture.

The Mid-Eastern News Service headquarters was operated and owned by Nagoti. Part of the service was to allow accommodations for members of the foreign press. As landlord, his building not only had humming offices and slumming apartments, but an active brothel on its top floor. My camera crew adapted quickly to their new digs, as well as to the local custom of taking apple hashish with water pipes. Through the wisps of veils and the dancers' gentle gyrations, the crew was lured into happyland. Despite the moments when they had to return to the 49°C (120°F) climate of Aswan, the crew, living their dream, had found their place in the sun.

I left for Aswan alone, to meet the chief, and arrived in a desert washed in humidity. Aswan is 150 kilometers (93 miles) up the Nile, where Abu Simbel's monument to the empire's glorious past was relocated stone by stone above the High Dam to save the temples from total submersion. The town hit 57°C (135°F) before noon. Hoards of cheering spectators were bussed in for the occasion. But not the chief.

The fortune teller's words haunted me: "Be patient. Allah is good. You will find your way, but you must wait."

Officials were in place to dynamite a portion of bank that would soon open the gates to the dam followed by an explosion of rushing water. The chief never showed. I reasoned he had progressed to his personal happyland with a double malt Macallan. Waiting for three hours in the heat, I was parched. When I went to the well to supply my empty canteen with water, leaving my bag in the custody of my guide, a decision I would soon regret, my cameras and guide disappeared. A BBC colleague saved me, shooting a few frames of film, adding to my collective mirage that Allah was good.

Returning with a roll of film to Cairo a few days later, I collected the rest of my equipment, but not my crew. They were weekending on the coast in Alexandria with their harem. Alexandria is most famous for Lawrence Durrel's *Alexandria Quartet* and the ruins of the lighthouse on Pharos, one of the Seven Wonders of the Ancient World. Now there was another wonder, my crew from TIME magazine.

I checked in at the airport at the assigned time, hoping to meet my chief. The flight was announced, and at customs, each distinguished official looked very much like Omar Sharif. Dressed in shades of khaki, they all sported gold medals and multicolored campaign ribbons. Swollen with baksheesh, gratuities slipped to them in khaki envelopes by returning incoming passengers, they were positive that in the belongings of this non-returning outgoing passenger lay a national treasure. Open sesame! Their prize was an American-made Kodak 35, a French-produced Éclair, a German-manufactured Arriflex, and a Japanese Nikon. "These were made in Egypt," they said. "As antiquities, they cannot leave the country." Being a non-antiquity, I could.

I think that Nagoti was in on the booty, having learned in my last hours that I was neither Muslim nor Christian, Arab nor Palestinian. I suspect a store of resentment erupted. But not the $1,500 from the pockets of the Mid-Eastern News Service for my press credentials.

Could there be something to learn from the Great Sphinx or the Great Pyramids? Or my fortune teller?

Or from my chief, back at the air-conditioned Cairo Hilton on the Nile? No such luck. Now immersed into triple malts, the chief was detained to play the bagpipes by some sheik in a turban tunic left over from Faruk.

Cairo had been like hot curry. Enjoyable in the beginning, but finishing with repercussion. Arriving in Israel via Athens, I dispatched a note to my chief saying that if he should find a used German Arriflex, American-made Kodak 35, French-made Éclair, or a Japanese Nikon, to please know that, at the very least, I had made a contribution to world peace.

The chief was a vaguely eclectic man. I appreciated his love of country. I heard that when he finally ventured out into Cairo's summer heat, he was dressed in a kilt, parading along the banks of the Nile. I'm sure the pipes would inspire Moses from the bulrushes and, in no time at all, lead my faithful crew across the Red Sea to the promised land of Sinai, where I would be patiently waiting for them all.

Ten Best
~Travel Tips From a High-minded, Impecunious Architecture Buff~

each conveys a sense of discovery. The hotels and restaurants have great architectural bones.

"If real estate speculation is your motive, follow the footsteps of artists, who discover places ahead of everyone else (the Hamptons, SoHo, and Red Hook). Pay careful attention to exchange rates; they create great buying opportunities. Latin America is a better value than Europe, with its overpriced euro.

"Where to stay in international cities? Clubs provide an economical and elegant solution, e.g. River, Union, Colony, Cosmopolitan, Harvard in New York; the Racquet Club in Chicago; and the Garrick or Reform in London.

"If the Costa Smeralda, Nantucket, the Hamptons, Palm Beach, and St. Bart's push your buttons, read no further. My suggestions will disappoint you."

Andrew and I met Stephen Lash while sailing on the *Sea Cloud*. Every night at dinner, we discovered we had many travel experiences in common. We became fast friends. As chairman of Christie's, the noted auction house, Lash travels the world and has developed a keen taste. His architectural perspective for all things beautiful is boundless. We recruited him for our list of correspondents. He writes:

"The criteria are random, personal, and quirky, but

1 – Cap d'Antibes in the South of France

Cap d'Antibes remains one of the truly exclusive hideaways of the Côte d'Azur, its exotic belle-époque and modernist villas and fabulous hotels discreetly veiled by vegetation, through which paths lead to private beaches. There's only one hotel in which to stay here, the Hotel du Cap, a grand Edwardian villa in a private park on a promontory overlooking the Mediterranean. Adjoining is the legendary Pavillon Eden Roc, where one can dine and swim. There is a lovely pool set into the rocks overlooking the sea and charming, quirky trapezes and ropes from which one can swing like Tarzan into the water.

I discovered the hotel in 1961 as a student traveler, while staying in a cheap pension in nearby Juan-les-Pins. I found that I could have swimming privileges for the day at Eden-Roc for a mere five francs (then $1). These privileges still exist but at the more elevated price of $20 a day (and well worth it).

Where to stay: **Hotel du Cap-Eden-Roc,** Boulevard Kennedy, tel: 33-(0)-4 93-61-39-01, www.edenroc-hotel.fr

2 – GENOA, ITALY

An unsung destination! Once prosperous, it is a city with a medieval core of tangled passageways surmounted by grand boulevards lined with Renaissance palaces. The late Brendan Gill of *The New Yorker* said, "Poverty is preservation's greatest ally." Such is the case in Genoa, where much survives from centuries of economic downturn. The city is easy to navigate on foot. The regional cuisine—*cucina di Liguria*—is superb, with lots of good local seafood. I know of no grand hotel but recommend the Jolly Hotel Marina, a satisfactory new venture on the waterfront, the latter having been redesigned by Genoa's very own Renzo Piano.

Finally, Genoa is a great spot from which to begin an exploration of the Ligurian coast, including the charming Cinque Terre (Five Towns), and Portofino, all of which

cling precariously to steep cliffs overlooking the sea. You can get to all of these by taking high-speed hydrofoils from the Genoa waterfront.

Where to stay: **Jolly Hotel Marina,** Molo Ponte Calvi, 5, tel: 39-010-25391

3 – OAXACA, MEXICO

This colonial city still bears traces of previous civilizations. There is a colorful market full of fruits, vegetables, and handicrafts. The town explodes with celebration at Christmastime, when the streets come alive with pageantry, and nightly *posadas* recall the Holy Family's search for lodging in Bethlehem. Nearby are the archaeological sites of Monte Alban and Mitlan. A good place to stay is the charming Hotel Camino Real, which occupies a converted convent.

Where to stay: **Hotel Camino Real Oaxaca,** Calle 5 de Mayo 300, tel: 52-9-51-501-6100, www.caminoreal.com/oaxaca

4 – ACAPULCO, MEXICO

I also have a fascination with Acapulco (perhaps the next South Beach), with its neglected art deco neighborhood so often bypassed by tourists who go instead to the big developments closer to the airport. My Mexican friends have encouraged me to try Hotel Los Flamingos, which is perched on a cliff overlooking the Pacific and was once owned by Hollywood's very own Errol Flynn.

Where to stay: **Hotel Los Flamingos,** Av. Lopez Mateos, Tel: 52-744-482-0690, www.flamingosacapulco.com

Ligurian Coast

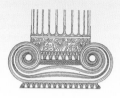

5 – PARIS FAVORITES

There are many great luxury hotels in Paris, of course. However, the one I like is the Hôtel de Crillon on the Place de la Concorde. Sometimes overlooked, it has great architectural merit. Try to get a room that faces the Place de la Concorde.

To eat, I recommend Le Grand Véfour, an extraordinary three-star restaurant in a spectacular 18th-century setting overlooking the gardens of the Palais-Royal. For less pricey ambience, I always enjoy the Brasseries Lipp, Flo, Coupole, and Dôme. Don't neglect the bistros like Chez Allard.

Where to stay: **Hôtel de Crillon,** 10 Place de la Concorde
Tel: 33-(0)-1-44-71-15-00, www.crillon.com

Where to eat: **Le Grand Véfour,** 17 rue de Beaujolais (1er)
Tel: 33-(0)-1-42-96-56-27
Brasserie Lipp, 151 Boulevard St.-Germain (6e)
Tel: 33-(0)-1-45-48-53-91
La Coupole, 102 Boulevard du Montparnasse (14e)
Tel: 33-(0)-1-43-20-14-20
Brasserie Flo, 7 Cour des Petites Ecuries (10e)
Tel: 33-(0)-1-47-70-13-59
Le Dôme, 108 Boulevard du Montparnasse (14e)
Tel: 33-(0)-1-43-35-25-81

6 – POINT REYES NATIONAL SEASHORE

This is a seashore of extraordinary beauty, with sheep grazing in meadows, cliffs overlooking the crashing Pacific, bushy hillsides, and forested ridges, all intertwined with hiking trails. Blackthorne Inn, near the village of Inverness, is a rustic B&B resembling a giant treehouse.

Where to stay: **Blackthorne Inn,** 266 Vallejo Ave.,
Inverness, tel: 415-663-8621, www.blackthorneinn.com

7 – THE NORTHEAST OF BRAZIL

I highly recommend a visit to the extraordinary new beach resort of Txai, where sophisticated Brazilians are investing in real estate. If you want to add more to your itinerary, you can also see the extraordinary city of Salvador, an early capital of Brazil, with a charming colonial core of decaying pastel houses and gilded baroque churches.

8 – CAPE TOWN, SOUTH AFRICA

This is a glorious city, full of British colonial architecture and expansive views. Wine buffs will make great discoveries in the vineyards of nearby Constantia. The Mount Nelson Hotel, a lovely pink-and-white building, is practically a second home to the first-class passengers traveling to and from the United Kingdom on the Union Castle Line. Drive to the Cape of Good Hope for thrilling views of the Atlantic meeting the Indian Ocean, outdoor bistros, and penguins.

Where to stay: **Mount Nelson Hotel,** 76 Orange Street
Tel: 27-21-483-1000, www.mountnelson.co.za

9 – MIAMI, FLORIDA

South Beach is hot, discovered, and worth the visit. I have nostalgia for the "newer" hotels of the 1950s, such as the legendary Fontainebleau Hilton Resort. This was the choice of many stars, including Elvis Presley and Frank Sinatra, and every president since Eisenhower has stayed here when in the South Florida area. Ask for an ocean-front room with a balcony in the old curved building designed by the legendary Morris Lapidus.

Downtown Miami is also a happening place. The city vibrates with life. I particularly like the nearby town of Coral Gables designed by George Merrick, with its art deco re-creations of European architecture and a sublime Venetian Pool to which the public is granted admission. Nearby are the wonderful Fairchild Tropical Gardens and the 1925 Biltmore Hotel with its lagoon of a pool, straight out Seville.

Where to stay:
The Fontainebleau, 4441 Collins
   Avenue, Miami
Tel: 305-538-2000,
   www.fontainebleau.hilton.com
Biltmore Hotel, 1200 Anastasia Avenue,
   Coral Gables
Tel: 305-445-1926, www.biltmorehotel.com

10 – JERUSALEM, ISRAEL

One feels a direct link to the Bible in this city built of Jerusalem stone. While the Intifada has put a damper on tourism, I recently enjoyed a guided tour through the old city, both the Jewish and Muslim quarters, where I felt safe. Stay at the wonderful King David Hotel and ask for a room overlooking the old city. A visit provides the opportunity to walk in the footsteps of King David and Jesus. Don't neglect the wonderful architecture of the British Protectorate, Eric Mendelsohn's YMCA, and the Rockefeller Museum. The Israel Museum is a national gallery with superb collections.

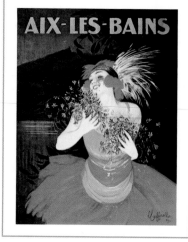

Where to stay: **King David Hotel,** 23 King David Street
Tel: 972-2-620-8882, www.danhotels.com

11 – SKIING FAVORITES

I have been an enthusiastic skier for decades, but resist going to even outstanding modern ski resorts like Vail in Colorado and Meribel in France because they have no sense of history. Instead, I favor the following, all of which are loaded with ambience of the past.

Cortina d'Ampezzo, Italy: A charming Italian town built around a square and campanile. The Hotel Corona is decorated with wonderful works by 20th-century Italian artists. (Hotel Corona, val di Sotto, 20, Tel: 39-(0)-436-3251, www.hotelcoroncortina.it)

St. Moritz, Switzerland: If you can afford it, try the ultra chic Suvretta House that is just outside of town. Bring black-tie attire. (Hotel Suvretta House, Via Chasellas 1, tel: 41-0-818-36-36-36, www.suvrettahouse.ch)

Klosters, Switzerland: An Old World village with a particularly charming hotel, the Chesa Grischuna. (Chesa Grischuna Hotel, Bahnhofstrasse 12, tel: 41-81-422-22-22, www.chesagrischuna.ch)

~FLEA & ANTIQUE MARKETS~

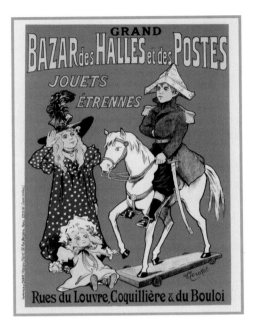

One person's trash is another person's treasure, the saying goes, and so people flock to flea markets in the hopes of finding that precious bargain. Here we have listed the world's ten best places for treasure-hunting.

1 – BERMONDSEY (NEW CALEDONIAN) MARKET

Long Lane and Bermondsey Street, London

There is a saying in London that anything stolen and sold before sunrise is legal. With this tradition, Bermondsey Market, one of London's main antiques markets, attracts dealers from all over and is a mecca for serious collectors. Each Friday the dealers set up their stalls at dawn. Be there early, for by 9 a.m. most of the best bargains have long gone. The area also has several antique shops that remain open all week. A row of old warehouses on Tower Bridge Road houses the best of these.

2 – SAN TELMO FLEA MARKET

Buenos Aires, Argentina

The frenetic San Telmo Flea Market centers on Calle Defensa between Avenue Independecia and Avenue San Juan, with most of the action on Plaza Dorrego. You'll join throngs of people searching for a deal among the many stalls overflowing with antiques, trinkets, costume jewelry, vintage movie posters, and artwork.

One of the delights of this market is the fact that the neighborhood of San Telmo is world-famous for its tango music, so you'll come across street bands and dancers performing impromptu numbers.

The market, open on Sundays only, begins at 4 a.m. and closes about noon.

3 – ROSE BOWL FLEA MARKET

Pasadena, California
Tel: 626-577-3100

The Rose Bowl Flea Market, featuring more than 2,000 vendors, is hands-down Los Angeles's largest secondhand marketplace. This is the place to find pop culture artifacts—a Monkees lunch box, Barbie camper, or Wheel of Fortune pillow, perhaps, along with surfboards, record collections,

MARKETVILLE IN BANGKOK

Bangkok is one of the world's great market capitals. To navigate the dozens of markets in this lovely city, we turned to www.into-asia.com. Here is what the folks there have to say about the best places for shopping:

Markets are generally the cheapest places to shop. This doesn't necessarily reflect on the quality of the goods sold, but some excellent bargains are for the taking in Bangkok. **Chatuchak Weekend Market,** in north Bangkok, is the largest (there are 15,000 shops and stalls here) and probably the best of the lot: a busy bustling maze where you'll shop until your feet are sore—and you still won't have covered half of it! The range of products on sale is phenomenal: handicrafts, religious artifacts, antiques, live animals, music, clothing, plants, flowers, and anything else you can imagine.

Pak Khlong market is a very large and busy wholesale market for fresh flowers and vegetables. It's best to go between 2 a.m. and 4 a.m., when boats on the Chao Phraya River and trucks from nearby provinces arrive with large quantities of flowers, vegetables, spices, and fruits. The market takes place where Khlong Lawt meets the Chao Phraya River, next to the Memorial Bridge on the northeastern edge of Chinatown.

Sampeng Lane, running from Paruhat market through the heart of Chinatown, is a narrow walkway lined with market stalls and tiny local shops jostling for room, specializing in costume jewelry, cutlery, fabrics, and Chinese lanterns. Inside the maze of lanes and alleys within Chinatown is Nakhon Kasem, formerly the Thieves Market, with an eclectic range of items from auto parts to antiques, coffee grinders to ice-cream makers, and finally a selection of Chinese gongs.

The 24-hour **Pratunam market** is notable as the best place in Bangkok to buy cheap clothes, fabrics, and textiles. There are also great bargains in young ready-to-wear fashions, jewelry, and leather goods. Hot and colorful, this is one of Bangkok's oldest established markets. It's located at the intersection of Ratchaprarop and Phetburi Roads.

Patpong night market, located between Silom and Surawong Roads in the infamous go-go-bar district, is well known among tourists. You'll find the same combination of souvenirs, fake brand-name items, and cheap clothes as any tourist area in the city, and it's hard to get a good deal here. You'll have to fend off all the touts.

lawn art, and who knows what else. This huge market unofficially opens its doors at 6 a.m. These early birds pay $10 to $15 admission as opposed to the usual $5. The rest of the crowd can enter at 9 a.m., and the fun continues until 3 p.m. or so. The flea market takes place the second Sunday of every month.

4 – BRIMFIELD OUTDOOR ANTIQUES SHOW
Brimfield, Massachusetts
Tel: 413-283-6149

More than 5,000 antiques and collectibles dealers sprawl across 23 former farm fields at Brimfield's popular flea market, making it the largest in New England. You name it, this place has it: furniture, pictures, new and secondhand clothes—all at rock-bottom prices (especially if you're adept at haggling). There's a jovial atmosphere, with the aroma of food wafting through the air and people crowding round the stalls in the hopes of picking up a 1970s leather jacket or a rare Louis XV chest of drawers. Make sure to bring cash, as stallholders seldom accept credit cards, and the nearest available ATM always has a line. The show takes place a week at a time three times a year, usually around Memorial Day, July 4th, and Labor Day.

5 – SAN JOSE FLEA MARKET
San Jose, California
Tel: 408-453-1110

The San Jose Flea Market, in existence since 1960, is one of the world's largest. Nearly 13 kilometers (8 miles) of treasure-filled alleys and corridors showcase arts and crafts, comic books, jewelry, shoes, fishing supplies, tools, auto accessories, furniture, and antiques. Expect lots of food carts and snack bars. The quarter-mile Produce Row Farmer's Market is legendary. The flea market takes place Wednesday through Sunday.

6 – THE ALL NIGHT FLEA MARKET
Wheaton, Illinois
Tel: 715-526-9769

One night a year, after the sun sets, thousands of flashlight-toting bargain hunters descend upon the town of Wheaton to search hundreds of stalls purveying old and new merchandise. They have only until morning to find their bargains, when they go home bleary-eyed and shopped out. Some say it's the most fun they've ever have at a flea market. It always takes place the third weekend of August.

7 – SHIPSHEWANA FLEA MARKET
Shipshewana, Indiana
Tel: 260-768-4129

In the heart of Indiana's Amish country, hundreds of vendors sell everything from fresh fruit to locally handcrafted furniture. The market began in 1922 when farmers participating in the town's livestock auction sold miscellaneous items out in the parking lot on auction days. The flea market takes place on Tuesdays and Wednesdays between May and October.

ANTIQUES FAIRS IN NEW YORK CITY

Perhaps the most respected antiques fair in the United States is the Winter Antiques Show that takes place every January in New York City at the Seventh Regiment Armory. For years, this veritable museum has been the one that collectors attend so they can find the really good stuff. Don't be stunned if you see Egyptian and Greek vases mixed in with homey, but pricey, American goods, including quilts. The armory is on Manhattan's Upper East Side on Park Avenue at 67th Street.

   Tel: 718-292-7392
   www.winterantiquesshow.com

The other great antiques show held in the armory is the International Fine Art and Antique Dealers Show. Also featuring exquisite works of art dating from antiquity to the present, it takes place in the fall. "Outside the Metropolitan Museum of Art," wrote *The New York Times*, "there is probably not a more awesome collection of beautiful, rare, valuable, exotic and weird objects gathered together under one Manhattan roof ... the term 'museum-quality' seems too modest."

   Tel: 212-642-8572
   www.haughton.com/iads

8 – MARCHÉ AUX PUCES DE CLIGNANCOURT
Les Puces de Saint-Ouen at Clignancourt 48, rue Jules Vallès (Marché des Antiquaires), Saint-Ouen, Paris

Paris is flea market heaven, and the mother of all flea markets is Marché aux Puces de Clignancourt. Dating back to 1920 and boasting up to 3,000 stalls, this daily flea market purveys everything from jewelry, chandeliers, fabric, and paintings to musical instruments, vintage postcards, and eclectic French collections. For antique aficionados, this is pure bliss.

9 – DAYTONA FLEA MARKET
Daytona, Florida
Tel: 904-252-1999

Florida is renowned for its flea markets, but Daytona stands out among the rest. More than a thousand booths vend all kinds of interesting things: Among the expected flea market items you may spot alligator heads, concrete garden statues, high-tech golf equipment, and neon fountains. At one booth, you can get tattooed and pierced. The flea market is in full-swing Friday, Saturday, and Sunday year-round.

10 – 127 CORRIDOR
Jamestown, Tennessee, www.127sale.com

Deemed the world's longest yardsale, the 127 Corridor flea market stretches along hundreds of miles on the highway between Jamestown, Tennessee, and Gadsden, Alabama. More than 2,000 vendors—ranging from families selling goods on their front lawns to professional vendors who rent an empty lot, park, or field—sell antiques and oddities. Folks come from near and far, many in a Winnebego or pulling a trailer behind their truck to stash their goods. The flea market takes place over three weeks every August.

TEN BEST
~MUSEUMS & GALLERIES~

1 – SMITHSONIAN INSTITUTION
Washington, D.C.
www.si.edu/museums

The Smithsonian is the world's largest research and museum complex, with 16 museums and galleries, the National Zoological Park, and various research stations. More than 142 million objects detailing America's story are housed here, so you'd better prepare for a long week of walking. There's so much to see that, if you spent one minute day and night looking at each object on exhibit, in ten years you'd see only ten percent of the whole. Therefore, head out with a plan. Focus on only one or two exhibits at two or three different museums.

Main attractions: Dorothy's ruby red slippers, the dresses of the First Ladies, and the original Star-Spangled Banner at the National Museum of American History; the Gem Hall (including the Hope Diamond) at the National Museum of Natural History; and the Wright brothers' 1903 *Flyer, Spirit of St. Louis,* and *Apollo 11* command module at the National Air and Space Museum.

2 – LE LOUVRE
Paris, France
www.louvre.fr

The Louvre was a medieval fortress and the palace of the kings of France before becoming a museum two centuries ago. The addition of I. M. Pei's pyramid shocked many when it was unveiled in 1989 as the new main entrance, yet it somehow works, integrating the palace's disparate elements. The museum's collections, which range from antiquity to the first half of the 19th century, are among the most important in the world. A good place to start is the Sully Wing, at the foundations of Philippe-Auguste's medieval keep—it's in the heart of the Louvre, kids love it, and it leads straight to the Egyptian rooms.

Main attractions: "Venus de Milo," "Winged Victory of Samothrace," and Leonardo da Vinci's "Mona Lisa."

3 – EGYPTIAN MUSEUM
Cairo, Egypt
www.egyptianmuseum.gov.eg

Though many Western museums contain impressive collections of ancient Egyptian antiquities, none begins to rival the riches on display at Cairo's Egyptian Museum. Devoted entirely to the legacy of the pharaohs, the museum has more than 120,000 items of antiquity on display, ranging from delicately crafted jewelry to towering granite colossi of kings.

Main attractions: Treasures from the tombs of kings and royal families, particularly those belonging to King Tutankhamun. Another big draw is the Royal Mummy Room, which brings you face to face with several of the greatest of the pharaohs, including Seti I and Ramses II.

4 – STATE HERMITAGE
St. Petersburg, Russia
www.hermitagemuseum.org

Russia may be isolated from the artistic centers of Paris, Rome, and London, but the Hermitage has managed to acquire a spectacular collection of world art—more than three million items—spanning the years from the Stone Age to the early 20th century. The museum occupies six buildings along the Neva River, the leading structure being the confection-like Winter Palace. This gloriously baroque, blue-and-white structure was finished in 1764 and over the next several centuries was the main residence of the czars. Catherine the Great founded the museum that same year

when she purchased 255 paintings from Berlin. The museum's focal point is Western Europe art—120 rooms in 4 buildings ranging from the Middle Ages to the present day. Rembrandt, Rubens, Tiepolo, Titian, da Vinci, Picasso, Gauguin, Cézanne, van Gogh, and Goya are all represented here.

Main attractions: The Treasure Gallery's Gold Rooms showcase golden masterpieces from Eurasia, Black Sea Littoral in antiquity, and the Orient. The museum also houses pieces from Nicolas II's private collection, including paintings, drawings, and medals created to commemorate his coronation.

5 – THE BRITISH MUSEUM
London, England
www.thebritishmuseum.ac.uk

Britain's largest museum looks after the national collection of archaeology and ethnography—more than four million objects ranging from prehistoric bones to chunks of Athens' Parthenon, from whole Assyrian palace rooms to exquisite gold jewels.

Main attractions: The Egyptian gallery boasts the world's second finest collection of Egyptian antiquities outside Egypt, including the Rosetta Stone, carved in 196 B.C.

6 – THE PRADO
Madrid, Spain
museoprado.mcu.es

The Spanish royal family is responsible for the Prado's bounty of classical masterpieces. Over centuries, kings and queens collected

and commissioned art with passion and good taste. In addition to stars of Spanish painting such as Velázquez, Goya, Ribera, and Zurbarán, the Prado has big collections of Italian (including Titian and Raphael) and Flemish artists. Fernando VII opened the collection to the public in 1819, in the same neoclassic building it's housed today, designed by Juan de Villanueva.

Main attraction: *The Three Graces* by Rubens.

7 – THE METROPOLITAN MUSEUM OF ART
New York City, New York
www.metmuseum.org

The Metropolitan Museum of Art is the largest museum in the Western Hemisphere. Its collection, some 142 million items, is not only broad—the entire world, from antiquity to the present—but deep, with holdings so large in a number of areas that some collections might be considered museums unto themselves. Its European paintings are stunning: works by Botticelli, Rembrandt, Vermeer, Degas, Rodin .... The Egyptian Collection showcases the tomb of Perneb (circa 2440 B.C.) and the exquisite Temple of Dendur (circa 23-10 B.C.). The American Wing contains American arts and crafts, including a room from a Frank Lloyd Wright Prairie House. And the list goes on and on.

Main attractions: *Adam and Eve,* the well-known engraving by Albrecht Dürer, is only one of the impressive pieces you will discover at the Met.

8 – THE VATICAN MUSEUMS
Vatican City, Italy
mv.vatican.va

Twenty-two separate collections comprise the Musei Vaticani, each one more spectacular than the next. The most famous are probably the Museo Pio-Clementino, with its

MUSÉE DE JACQUEMART-ANDRÉ

Paris, France
Tel: 33-(0)-1-45-62-11-59, www.musee-jacquemart-andre.com/jandre/home_en.htm

We had to include this little gem, as recommended by www.linkparis.com.

The Musée Jacquemart-André was once the residence of Edouard André and his wife, Parisian painter Nellie Jacquemart, and houses a wonderful collection of fine objects. Nellie's fine artistic eye enabled the couple to acquire a splendid collection of treasures: tapestries, rugs, furniture, and manuscripts, but principally paintings and sculpture from India, Egypt, and Greece.

The collection is showcased in the couple's magnificent mansion, a baroque structure built in 1869 and worth a trip in itself. At the foot of the double staircase, decorated with a fresco by Tiepolo, for example, a Winter Garden filled with lush plants appears just as it did in the time of Napoléon III.

The collection contains several Canaleno and Rembrandts, and best of all, 15th- and 16th-century Italian genius in the works of Botticelli, Donatello, Mantegna, Della Robbia, and Ucello; Flemish work by Memling, Massys, and Van Dyck; Dutch paintings by Ruisdael; and French paintings by Lancret, Chardin, Boucher, Fragonard, and David.

The Café Jacquemart-André, open daily, offers light and lovely food in the splendid setting of the former dining room from lunchtime to closing time (11:45 a.m. to 6 p.m.).

GUGGENHEIM MUSEUM BILBAO

Bilbao, Spain
Tel: 34-94-435-90-80
www.guggenheim.org

North American architect Frank Gehry designed this museum of contemporary art in the center of Bilbao near the banks of the Nervión River. It opened in 1997, as part of the city's revitalization plan and overall plan to energize the Basque region.

The 19 galleries cover thousands of square meters (square yards), with airy, sculpted spaces that blend well with the contemporary pieces displayed. The permanent collection includes works by Jeff Koons, Louise Bourgeois, and Richard Serra.

The building itself is as much a work of art as the pieces inside, and made quite a splash in the architectural world upon its opening. Gehry combined different shapes and materials, then used a computer to weave the mathematical aspects together. In this sculpture of a building, you'll see octagonal blocks made of limestone, entire walls of glass, and titanium-coated sinuous forms throughout.

splendid classical sculpture; the Raphael Rooms, entire rooms painted by Raphael; the Pinacoteca (picture gallery), which contains the cream of the Vatican's collection of medieval and Renaissance paintings; and, of course, Michelangelo's Sistine Chapel. But there's also the ancient Egyptian exhibits of the Museo Gregoriano Egizio and the Etruscan offerings of the Museo Gregoriano Etrusco. And that's just a start.

Main attraction: The renowned Sistine Chapel and the Raphael Rooms are not to be missed.

9 – THE UFFIZI GALLERY
Florence, Italy
www.polomuseale.firenze.it

"Great" is an overworked adjective in Italy, where so many of the country's monuments and works of art command the highest praise. In the case of the Galleria degli Uffizi, it barely does justice to a gallery that holds the world's finest collection of Renaissance paintings. All the famous names of Italian art are here, not only the Renaissance masters, but also painters from the early medieval, baroque, and Mannerist heyday.

Main attraction: *The Birth of Venus* by Botticelli is one.

10 – RIJKSMUSEUM
Amsterdam, the Netherlands
www.rijksmuseum.nl

Nearly one million objects fill the Rijksmuseum, the largest collection of art and history in the Netherlands. It is most famous for its paintings by 17th-century Dutch masters, including van Ruysdael, Frans Hals, Johannes Vermeer, and 20 works by Rembrandt van Rijn. Established in 1800 to exhibit the collections of the Dutch *stadtholders*, the Rijksmuseum also displays art from the Middle Ages.

Main attraction: *The Night Watch* by Rembrandt.

TEN BEST
~HIDEAWAYS & INNS~

We have selected one-stop destinations that are great for anyone in need of a vacation—and some serious pampering.

1 – AUBERGE DU SOLEIL
Rutherford, California
Tel: 707-963-1211 or 800-348-5406 (U.S. only) www.aubergedusoleil.com

Napa Valley's magical wine country is the backdrop for this elegant hotel, opened in 1985. The accommodations feature Mediterranean decor; guests have their choice of rooms in the main building or several private cottages on the hillside. The restaurant offers a wine list that reflects the best of the area. At the spa, therapists use special herb-infused oils made from plants and herbs growing the garden. There's a heated pool here, as well as a sun deck.

2 – THE INN AT LITTLE WASHINGTON
Washington, Virginia
Tel: 540-675-3800, www.theinnatlittlewashington.com

For two decades, Patrick O'Connell and Reinhardt Lynch have run this renowned hotel in the foothills of the Blue Ridge. Its 15 charming rooms and suites are meticulous in their details, including one decorated in the exotic style and color of the Far East, and another with its sun-drenched reading room. The luxurious, highly decorated restaurant—one of the top in the world, its cuisine a delectable mix of classical French and modern—is *the* place to take anyone you want to impress.

VENICE SIMPLON ORIENT-EXPRESS

3 – ASHFORD CASTLE
Cong, Ireland
Tel: 353-94-954-6003, www.ashford.ie

Located in the heart of County Mayo in western Ireland, this luxurious castle, dating from the 12th century, is as romantic a place as one could desire. Rooms are decorated in cheerful pastels. The hotel has two dining rooms and three bars; a very traditional afternoon tea is served in the drawing room. An interesting array of activities is offered outdoors; there are three running trails, two tennis courts, archery and falconry lessons, and a tour boat that docks at the castle's jetty twice a day to ferry guests across Lake Corrib. The resort also provides tours led by pony-drawn carriages or traps around the grounds.

4 – PANGKOR LAUT RESORT
Pangkor Laut, Malaysia
www.pangkorlautresort.com

Truly isolated in the middle of the Straits of Malacca, where the only noise comes from clacking palms and the gentle surf, Pangkor Laut is the true definition of paradise. A collection of Malaysian-style luxury villas dot this privately owned island located 5 kilometers (3 miles) off Malaysia's west coast.

PANGKOR LAUT RESORT

Only 250 guests reside at Pangkor Laut at any given time. These lucky few are served by 400 staff, including 50 gardeners who make sure that every flower looks its best on the perfectly manicured grounds. This is the place to lounge in complete bliss.

5 – FEARRINGTON HOUSE
Pittsboro, North Carolina
Tel: 919-542-2121, www.fearringtonhouse.com

Located south of the University of North Carolina at Chapel Hill, Fearrington House represents old-fashioned Southern hospitality. Built around a white clapboard farmhouse constructed in 1927, the inn has 33 rooms and suites, each individually decorated with antiques, original artwork, and fresh flowers. Afternoon tea and a full breakfast are included in the room rates.

6 – LE MANOIR AUX QUAT' SAISONS
Great Milton, Oxford, England
Tel: 44-(0)-1844-278881, www.manoir.com

One reason many people come to this contemporary hotel is to take classes at the Raymond Blanc Cookery School. The chef has established a reputation as the maker of amazing dishes; many of the ingredients are grown right in the Manoir's magnificent gardens, where Blanc grows more than 90 varieties of vegetables and 70 types of herbs. The 32 rooms and suites are in the main house and garden wing; those in the main house are furnished in a more traditional style; those in the garden wing look more contemporary.

7 – THE POINT
Saranac Lake, New York
Tel: 518-891-5674, http://thepointresort.com

This rambling lodge used to be a country estate for the

SHIP WRECKED FOR A WEEKEND

Oscars Waterfront Boutique Hotel
41b Gipps Street, Port Fairy, Australia
Tel: 61-3-5568-3022
www.oscarswaterfront.com

You'll find this charming French provincial-style inn about three-and-a-half hours southwest of Melbourne in the historic village of Port Fairy, a best-kept secret that you dare not tell too many people for fear that the word will get out and the hoards will descend. The grandest place in a town of charming historic edifices, the hotel's cheery riverfront rooms overlook brightly colored fishing boats on the Moyne River. The gourmet breakfasts can be taken on the riverside veranda in warmer weather—some of the reasons guests keep returning are berry hotcakes and tomato bruschetta spread with basil butter.

There's plenty to do in Port Ferry itself, with a vibrant arts and music scene—a well-known folk festival takes place in March—unspoiled beaches, and an 18-hole golf course. Farther down Gipps Street you can walk across a footbridge to Griffiths Island and follow a trail to a mutton bird viewing point and a lighthouse.

"The finest landscape in the world is improved by a good inn in the foreground."

— Samuel Johnson

Rockefeller family. Located on a lake in New York's wild Adirondack Mountains, the resort is the perfect combination of wilderness and civilization. The 11 rooms—spread out in four buildings—have stone fireplaces and eclectic mixes of antique and (of course) Adirondack furniture. Guests can hike or swim in warm weather and tackle winter sports such as cross-country skiing in the cold.

8 – HOTEL SPLENDIDO
Portofino, Italy
Tel: 39-(0)-185-267-801, www.hotelsplendido.com

Situated in possibly one of the prettiest spots in Italy, Hotel Splendido overlooks the sparkling blue Mediterranean Sea. Most of the 65 rooms have water views. The restaurants' cuisine is top-notch; chefs use products from the hotel's olive grove. Eat outside on the terraces or inside in elegantly decorated rooms.

9 – LAS VENTANAS AL PARAÍSO
Los Cabos, Mexico
Tel: 52-624-144-2800
www.lasventanas.com

The name of this ultraprivate, luxury resort means "window to paradise," which is right on in this case. Tucked in between desert and ocean, its white hacienda-style *casitas* descend toward

the beach and feature, Jacuzzis, terra-cotta fireplaces, and rough-hewn wood accents. The dazzling windows of each suite are fashioned from rainbow glass created by local artisans; each balcony comes equipped with telescope to scan for whales or stars; and each minibar is personalized according to a questionnaire guests fill out before arrival. There's also a spa (one treatment uses gems and crystals), plenty of excellent food (including a separate pet menu), and infinity pools that seem to disappear into the ocean.

10 – HÔTEL GUANAHANI & SPA
St. Barts

Tel: 0-590-276-660
www.leguanahani.com

Here is a romantic tropical hideaway, where guests settle into cottages painted in bright shades of yellow, blue, purple, and green. Each one is outfitted in refreshingly simple wooden furniture, and all have their own terraces and gardens. The resort rests on a swath of land that runs between the Caribbean and a lagoon. Water sports are big here, from windsurfing to jet skiing. Scuba diving classes are taught too, so guests can explore the colorful underwater world around then. Guanahani also has a posh spa that carries Clarins products and treatments.

SPLENDIDE HÔTEL
ÉVIAN-les-BAINS

TRAVEL SAFETY & USEFUL TIPS

Here is a good summary of sensible precautions that every traveler should take.

1 – Travel jackets and vests, with their many pockets to store important and useful items, are versatile and practical.

2 – Familiarize yourself with local laws and customs. While in a foreign country, you are subject to its laws.

3 – Make two copies of your passport identification page. Leave one copy at home with friends or relatives. Carry the other with you in a separate place from your passport.

4 – Leave a copy of your itinerary with family or friends at home in case of an emergency.

5 – Carry all medications, important documents, and even essential toiletries in a carry-on bag.

6 – Pack comfortable shoes for walking and travel.

7 – To avoid being a target of crime, do not wear expensive jewelry or obviously expensive clothes.

8 – Baby wipes are useful to carry for quick clean-ups.

9 – A travel first-aid kit complete with an assortment of medications, sterile dressings, and preparations is essential.

10 – Stay healthy. This means, among other things, the following: Take preventive vaccinations before you leave home, wash your hands frequently, and bring antidiarrhea medications. For appropriate destinations, consult a travel doctor for necessary advice, vaccinations, and prescriptions.

IDENTITY THEFT

Identity theft is on the rise, so remember that you may have more to lose than what you are carrying with you.

Before leaving, register your credit cards with a service that will cancel and replace them if they are lost or stolen.

Traveling with extra checks, bank deposit slips, unnecessary credit cards, or a list of your bank account numbers is almost an invitation to identity thieves.

Make sure your credit card is protected by a liability limit on unauthorized purchases.

Never carry your Social Security card or a copy of your Social Security account number.

Always use the hotel safe to store extra cash, identification papers, and the credit cards you will not be using on any given day. If you think you've hidden these things adequately in your room, chances are you haven't.

If the hotel safe does not require two keys to open, one of which is given to you, insist on a receipt for all the items you deposit.

JUST THE
PRODUCTS
BEST

Ten Best
~Watches~

They say Swiss trains always run on time. Dr. Patrick Chourgnoz, world class timekeeper and consultant to European railways, times the best. Not only do the watchmakers we've chosen create timepieces that keep perfect time, they design pieces with great style and grace.

1 – PATEK PHILIPPE
Geneva, Switzerland
www.patekphilippe.com

Complicated watchmaking is the supreme test of a designer's expertise and a watchmaker's skills. At Patek Philippe, they've been been passing the test with flying colors since 1839. The Swiss company has tackled any and all horological complications to create complex portable timepieces for the ages. If you're a fan of watches and find yourself in Geneva, a visit to Philippe's museum is in order.

2 – IWC
Schaffhausan, Switzerland
www.iwc.ch

Since 1868, IWC watches have been legendary among true

timepiece connoisseurs. Ironically, the founder of the company was an American, Florentine Ariosto Jones. He knew that Swiss watchmakers were incredibly skilled—and relatively low paid. So Jones had the parts made in his factory in northeast Switzerland and shipped back to the United States to be finished.

The company has changed hands a few times since then. Perfection of craft, rigorous training of specialists, and refusal to succumb to the lure of mass market are well established principles of IWC. The company makes watches in limited quantities, but they are always of the highest quality.

WATCHES

Log onto the website's virtual factory tour to see how the pieces are made.

3 – VACHERON CONSTANTIN
Geneva, Switzerland
www.Vacheron-Constantin.com

Switzerland's oldest continuously active watchmaker, Vacheron Constantin has been synonymous with fine watchmaking since 1755. The women's Kalla collection consists of watches made with gemstones. For men, we like the Malte collection, with sweeping sword-shaped hands and a Maltese cross on the face.

4 – BREITLING
Grenchen, Switzerland
www.breitling.com

In business since 1884, Breitling watches are known as high performance instruments for professionals. These watches utilize innovative technologies that make them conversation pieces as well as useful timekeepers.

5 – ROLEX
Geneva, Switzerland
www.rolex.com

The name alone conjures up an impression of luxury and cost. Refined to the last detail, Rolex watches follow a meticulous design. The individual parts work in complete harmony, resulting in a superb timepiece.

6 – BREGUET
Valée de Joux, Switzerland
www.breguet.ch

Want to have something in common with Sir Winston Churchill, Queen Victoria, and Arthur Rubenstein? Keep time with a Breguet. Whether it's a watch or a clock, you're assured of owning a distinctive and elegant piece.

7 – OMEGA
Bienne, Switzerland
www.omegawatches.com

This Swiss watchmaker has made special timepieces for astronauts. And if they're good enough to survive space, they should be good enough to wear on Earth.

8 – CARTIER
Paris, France
www.cartier.com

In 1904 Louis Cartier introduced his first watch, the Santos. It was named for his friend, the dashing Brazilian aviator Alberto Santos-Dumont, so he could tell time without taking his hands off the controls of an airplane. It was the beginning of a beautiful marriage between jewelry and timepiece.

9 – BLANCPAIN
Le Brassus, Switzerland
www.blancpain.ch

For more than 250 years, 13 generations of watchmakers have passed down their tradition of creativity. It is an integral part of every Blancpain timepiece.

10 – TAG HEUER
Marin, Switzerland
www.tagheuer.com

TAG Heuer does big business in sports watches and chronographs. From the Olympic Games to competitive Alpine skiing to Formula 1 racing, these watches perform.

TEN BEST
~MATTRESSES~

Research to identify the ten best constructed mattresses began in London. I have always been keenly particular about getting a good night's sleep, in part because I have a problematic back. I was thrilled to discover that London's Savoy Hotel gave their guests an opportunity to order their own custom-made mattresses. So I bought one, and, yes, it is wonderful.

There are differences between mattresses for hotels and homes, mass-produced and custom-made, natural and synthetic. The best way to determine those differences and see what works best for you is to physically test the mattress. Pleasant dreams.

1 – SLEEPEEZEE LTD.
London, England
Tel 44-(0)-20-854-9171
www.sleepeezee.co.uk

This manufacturer has been hired over the years to make beds for several finer international hotels, including the Savoy in London. Sleepeezee also has a royal warrant to supply mattresses to Queen Elizabeth II.

What's so special? For starters, these beds don't use synthetics, latex, or foam. The particular mattress we like is the Hotel BeautyRest Deluxe, which features the company's special BeautyRest coil technology, 1,200 individual springs, and a cotton/wool surface that's hand-stitched with a tailored finished.

2 – SAVOIR BEDS LTD.
London, England
Tel 44-(0)-20-8838-4838, www.savoirbeds.co.uk

"You spend a third of your life asleep," proclaims the website for Savoir Beds. "Sleep well, and your waking life can be physically active and mentally energetic. Sleep badly, and you never catch up with the day."

We couldn't have said it better ourselves. These guys know what they're doing. They only make two models, No. 2 and No. 4, which tie each other for a spot on the ten best list. Each mattress takes at least 60 hours to make. Savoir can tailor the product to antique or specially designed beds. It also makes headboards in a variety of styles and fabrics. And if you're not sleeping like a baby within the first six weeks, Savoir will make the mattress softer or firmer.

Savoir fans have included Emma Thompson, Liza Minelli, and Morocco's late King Hassan. After he slept on a Savoir (not sure if it was a 2 or 4) in a London hotel, the king purchased 24. Prices start at $8,000 for singles and $11,820 for full-size mattress-and-box-spring sets.

At Home in the USA

From Apple to Xerox, some of the great marketing concepts began in the USA. Following are Ten Best companies that give value and quality.

1 – Home Depot
(www.homedepot.com)

Tools, lumber, flowers, plants, gazebos, paint, and even contractors on hand for installation. Literally all supplies to build a house or remodel a home, all at fair, competitive prices. Home Depot carries more than a million products. Take for example:

– Dal-tile (www.dal-tile.com)
From terra-cotta to ceramic, this company offers beautiful tiles made all over the world.

– Kraft Maid (www.kraftmaid.com)
The world's best producer of new generation cabinetry.

– SileStone (www.silestone.com)
Natural quartz for stunning countertops.

– Grohe (www.grohe.com)
The world's finest faucets.

– Kindred (www.homecenter.com)
Works of art in stainless steel sinks.

2 – Apple Computers
www.apple.com

For design, reliability, and style. A truly elegant product.

3 – Staples
www.staples.com

One-stop shopping for office supplies.

4 – Burpee
www.burpee.com

Has been selling everything for your garden since 1876.

5 – Ornella Muth, Inc.
Tel: 201-739-4191

Premier artist for faux painting, murals, and decorative art.

6 – Trader Joe's Markets
www.traderjoes.com

An international selection of high quality wines and foods at reasonable prices.

7 – iExplore
www.iexplore.com

An innovative online travel agency specializing in adventure trips.

8 – Cruisedealership
www.cruisedealership.com
Tel: 888-604-0279

Deeply discounted cruises with great activities, superb dining, new ports of call. Cruise specialists provide personal service.

9 – Amazon
www.amazon.com

The huge online bookstore offering current titles and out-of-print books, reviews, descriptions, sample chapters.

10 – Costco
www.costco.com

Low-cost household goods, electronics, hardware, foodstuffs.

3 – SIMMONS PALACE BED
Marne La Vallée, France
Tel 33-(0)-1-64-62-80-00, www.simmons.fr

Made by Simmons' French operation, the Palace Bed is extremely comfortable. We found it in the Hotel Meurice in Paris. (Guests have actually bought the beds from Simmons through the hotel.) The mattress features the company's famous BeautyRest pocketed coil technology, as well as all natural materials, and hand-stitched ticking. For winter, one side is made extra warm with white wool, while the summer side has pure cotton.

4 – SIMMONS BEAUTYREST WORLD CLASS
Atlanta, Georgia
www.simmons.com

The Simmons Bedding Company has offered some fine beds since it began in the late 19th century. The Beautyrest World Class is no exception. It features 850 coil springs that are designed to minimize motion. The special pocketed cable coil edging that runs along the perimeter of the mattress adds support and makes the bed more durable.

Covered in embroidered suede fabric, the World Class mattress uses memory foam, which NASA developed for the space program several decades ago. The special materials conform to your body's shape and then revert back when you've changed position. Tiny holes allow air to circulate, thereby keeping the bed fresher.

5 – SIMMONS BACKCARE ADVANCED WITH 3-2-1 DESIGN
Atlanta, Georgia
www.simmons.com

For our last Simmons product, we've found a great mattress in the BackCare line. Evidently, this line is tried and true. In 2004 the company asked 100 people sleep on BackCares for two weeks; 92 of them said they slept better than they did on their regular mattresses.

The 3-2-1 has some special features. The first is a panel on top that you can wash along with your sheets, for a fresher mattress top. Then inside the mattress are two channels of coil springs that run beneath the lower back and upper thigh areas, to add support. A wide border of foam rings the edges, also for support. This anatomically correct design supports your body's natural contours.

6 – SERTA PERFECT NIGHT
Hoffman Estates, Illinois
Tel 847-645-0200, www.serta.com

We love this company's Perfect Night mattress, a plush rectangle with five zones of convoluted foam. Don't be taken aback by the word "convoluted" either. According to Serta, "convoluted foam...helps to further relieve pressure and disperse weight in the specific zones of the body." Throw in some fancy inner springs to maintain proper spinal alignment and lots of coils that conform to your body, and you'll never need to count sheep again. We feel sleepy just writing about the Perfect Night.

7 – SEALY
Trinity, North Carolina
Tel 800-MY-SEALY, www.sealy.com

To design Sealy's famous Posturepedic mattress, the company consulted orthopedic surgeons on precisely how the mattress and springs should be constructed to best support the human back. The UniCased Edge is key to this design, because it locks into the innerspring to give stability. Each Posturepedic comes with a special Shock Absorber Plus box spring with steel modules and a solid steel spine for increased durability.

8 – AERO BED
Wauconda, Illinois
Tel 888-462-4468, www.thinkaero.com

There is actually such a thing as a comfortable, adjustable, portable air bed. Aero Products International makes several types that inflate in less than 60 seconds; you can adjust for firmness and comfort.

We're partial to the pillowtop and IntelliWarmth varieties. The latter has tiny heating fibers that can be set at six temperatures.

These beds pack up into fairly lightweight bags.

9 – STEARNS & FOSTER TRIPLECASED
Lockland, Ohio
Tel 866-Bedding, www.stearnsandfoster.com

Now owned by Sealy, Stearns & Foster got into the sleep business in 1846. It has maintained its reputation for using fine materials and paying lots of attention to detail.

The TripLCased is the company's hallmark, a veritable layer cake of foam, coils, and springs that practically cries out for children to jump up and down on. It's available in the full range of S&F's mattress types: firm, plush, pillowtop, EuroTop, and Euro BoxTop.

10 – MCROSKEY AIRFLEX
San Francisco, California
Tel 800-760-9600, www.mcroskey.com

Since 1899, McRoskey has been making some pretty cool mattress-and-box-spring sets. The "air" part of the name refers to a border that lets fresh air inside the mattress to keep it fresh, flexible, and resilient.

Other details McRoskey takes into account are choice of firmness, ticking, materials, specially shaped corners, shaped sides or ends, and recessed box springs.

If the Airflex feels right for you, why not get a mini version for your dog or cat? The pet beds have the same flexible innersprings as the human beds. The mattresses are filled with cotton and polyester only. And they're covered with striped ticking, too.

Ten Best
~Cameras~

To help us come up with a list of the ten best cameras, we've asked professional photographers to tell us what they think are the best available now from the film and digital worlds. We've compiled our list below, based on their advice. So shoot away with confidence.

1 – Leica 35mm
Solms, Germany
www.leica.com

The LEICA M system can be found in the bags of many a top-notch photographer. The German company tries to streamline its cameras so they are limited to features that help create a great picture. The philosophy here is to make sure the person holding the camera is in control, not vice-versa.

Leica is an old company, dating back to 1849 when a young mathematician named Carl Kellner opened an institute to develop lenses and microscopes. It gradually expanded into the new world of cameras early in the 20th century.

2 – Contax 35mm
Reading, England
www.contaxcameras.co.uk

Contax's professional cameras put what you need where you need it. They are straightforward cameras that were first made in Germany in the 1930s; the company then formed a partnership with Japan's Yaschica. Contax's cameras get high marks as easy to use and capable of turning out some very artful photographs.

3 – Nikon 35mm
Tokyo, Japan
www.nikon.com

Nikon's F6 is one of the most advanced SLR cameras available, thanks in part to its auto focus that can shoot up to eight frames per second. There are five sensors inside and a light meter that divides the frame into 1,005 discrete units. Professional photographers often use Nikon lenses.

4 – Canon 35mm
Tokyo, Japan
www.canon.com

The Canon IV is our favorite in the company's pantheon of good cameras. With its speedy auto focus, the camera can be customized to the needs of the user. There are seven cross sensors tucked inside this little gem, and they can detect vertical as well as horizontal lines in all subjects.

5 – Hasselblad large and medium format film
Gothenburg, Sweden
www.hasselblad.com

When Arvid Hasselblad started a photography division within his father's export-import company, he said, "I certainly don't think that we will earn much money on this, but at least it will allow us to take pictures for free."

More than a hundred years later, his outlet for free photographs has become a major player in the photography market. The company produces excellent

FLASHTRAX & SANDISK

For the traveler with digital photographic needs, we like SmartDisk's FlashTrax mass storage and viewing devices (www.smartdisk.com). Based in Fort Lauderdale, Florida, the company makes two types of multimedia players. The FlashTrax XT can send thousands of images to its hard drive, so you can use your flash media cards repeatedly.

No digital camera is complete without memory. We use cards made by SanDisk (www.sandisk.com, based in Sunnyvale, California). It makes a reliable one gigabyte card that can hold up to 400 high-resolution images.

equipment in three separate systems, all of which professionals regularly rely on.

6 – LEICA DIGITAL
(See information for Leica 35 mm)
The new Leica digital cameras are in a class of their own with their classic form and extraordinary lens. The handy Leica D-Lux 2 has unparalleled brilliance in three formats. With its optics, image stabilizer and 8.4 megapixels, and aluminum body, it meets the company's highest standards. The new Leica Digilux 2 combines the best of two worlds: digital technology and traditional analog photography.

7 – PANASONIC LUMIX DIGITAL
Osaka, Japan
www.panasonic.com

The DMC-LC1 has the features and feel of a 35mm camera. The LEICA-VARIO-SUMMICRON lens captures subjects in crisp, clear detail. It is a superb camera and costs less than a Leica, with the same features. The 3.2x optical zoom lens renders sharp images and has a focal distance equivalent to a 28mm-to-90mm lens on a 35mm camera. The exquisite rendering of this lens, heir to the Leica AG's optical technology, makes the DMC-LC1 an expressive tool.

8 – CANON DIGITAL
(see information for Canon 35 mm)
The Japanese company makes a number of good digital cameras, any of which we would include as one of the ten best. Start small and check out the tiny point-and-shoot ELPH series. Not satisfied? Go to the EOD 20D SLR, which has proven to be a popular line. Users give Canon thumbs-up for constructing a solid camera that consistently delivers.

9 – NIKON DIGITAL
(See information on Nikon 35mm)
We think that the D70 combines the best of digital technology with efficient use. No surprise here, given Nikon's stellar reputation.

10 – SONY DSC T33
Tokyo, Japan
www.sony.com

We traditionally associate Sony with stereos and TVs, but if we were skeptical, this little guy was all we needed to see. Less than an inch thick, the T33 has a large screen that covers about 60 percent of the camera's back. This means we don't have to squint to see a picture's details.

104 ❦ PART ONE: JUST THE BEST

TEN BEST
~BEERS~

1 – WESTVLETEREN
Belgium

Westvleteren has the smallest output of the Trappist breweries, with only a limited portion of their production going for export. Brown with a fine white head, the beer's smooth, caramel taste is spiced up with a tinge of pear, raisin, and plum. The epitome of a Belgian brew, it has a very full mouth feel and a high alcohol content.

2 – ALESMITH BARREL AGED SPEEDWAY STOUT
United States

AleSmith Barrel Aged Speedway Stout has great balance that hides its amazing power. A mouthful of fun, whether out of keg, cask, or bottle. It has an aroma of heavy chocolate and alcohol and an extremely rich thick taste combining chocolate, smoke, coffee, and bourbon flavors.

3 – THREE FLOYDS DARK LORD RUSSIAN IMPERIAL STOUT
United States

This beer has a truly opaque color with a very good creamy tan head. The aroma hints of figs, burned chocolate malts, leathery and earthy yeast esters, molasses, and espresso. The taste mixes heavy malt with pungent bitter hops. It attacks the palate with brutal effectiveness and feels thick and long-lasting in the mouth. Smoke, coffee, and fruit notes round out the flavor.

4 – DIEU DU CIEL PÉCHÉ MORTEL
Canada

Pouring in a rich, thick, black stream, Dieu du Ciel Péché  Mortel develops a creamy nitro dark tan head. The body seems to have a certain shine to it. The aroma is complex, but subdued slightly. Thick dark chocolate, plum, molasses, plenty of bittersweet coffee and even strawberries are all present in the nose. The body is rich and robust and has an almost gritty, sugary, yet viscous texture. Good complexity and nice balance of a lot of malty sweetness and coffee bitterness. The finish is a more subtle contin-uation of the body. A near sensory overload and very enjoyable.

5 – ROCHEFORT TRAPPISTES
Belgium

The appearance of this beer is dark brown with a tan head; the taste is a little nutty, with dark fruit flavors, most notably fig. It also exhibits coffee, chocolate, and toffee flavors. The sweet aroma of this brew has a light hint of alcohol in the taste and finish. It is full bodied and possibly the best of the Rochefort.

6 – NØRREBRO BRYGHUS NORTH BRIDGE EXTREME
Denmark

With a dark amber body, this beer has a medium creamy white head. It has a strong and flowery hops aroma; the hops are balanced out by a nice malt background with some aromas of caramel and darker malts. The beer explodes in the mouth, hops and bitterness everywhere, but it fades into some nice maltiness. Extreme, but then again nicely balanced by the malts.

7 – ALESMITH SPEEDWAY STOUT
United States

Good dark appearance balanced by its bitterness and malt flavors, this brew finishes with an alcoholic rush that's dry to the tongue. The color is deep black with a tan

colored head. It has a huge coffee aroma, along with chocolate, malt, and a nice roastiness.

8 – THREE FLOYDS DREADNAUGHT IMPERIAL
United States

A very soft brew that is quite strong, dry, and alcoholic. This beer is golden in color with a colossal body. It has great hop character with texture and balance and a very citrusy overtone. It is creamy and frothy with an incredible finish.

9 – WESTVLETEREN EXTRA
Belgium

With its brown color, heavy sweet yeasty fruity aroma, sweet fruity spicy taste, full body, light sweet alcoholic warm finish, this is a great beer with beautiful woody, leathery, and doughy aroma; date-raisin and toffee flavor; tremendous complexity. Well balanced with no strong overtones yet very complex, it's a world-class beer that has to be savored.

10 – DOGFISH HEAD WORLD WIDE STOUT
United States

This beer has a deep, dark mahogany color with a small tan head. It is rich with dark fruit, dried banana, malt, floral, rum, and alcohol aroma. Its hick mouth feel of sweet malt, dark fruit, banana, and rum flavors give it full body and flavor with a nice balance.

TEN BEST
~ CIGARS ~

My son and co-author, Andrew, knows a lot about cigars; in fact, several years ago we collaborated on a book about them, *The Cigar Connoisseur.* Here are the ten best gleaned from research he conducted for that.

1 – COHIBA
Cuba

The Cohiba cigar brand was introduced in 1968 and soon became the flagship brand of the Cuban cigar industry. Developed initially as a medium-bodied cigar for presentation only by officials of the Cuban government, Cohiba was marketed widely beginning in 1982. The initial sizes were the Lancero, the Corona Especiale, and the Panetela, with the Esplendido, Robusto, and Exquisito added in 1989. In 1992, in honor of the 500th anniversary of Columbus's discovery of the Caribbean, the Siglo series was introduced. The Cohiba cigar has become one of the most coveted cigars in the world. The tobacco used for Cohibas is grown only on certain plantations in the Vuelta Abajo province of Pinar del Río.

2 – TRINIDAD
Cuba

This cigar was marketed for the first time in February 1998,

when it was presented in Havana during the annual gala in which the "Hombre Habano del Año" awards are bestowed. But it was already well known to connoisseurs everywhere because a variation of it had been around since 1969. Named after one of Cuba's prettiest cities, the Trinidad had been produced exclusively for Fidel Castro himself. It's a medium- to full-bodied smoke.

3 – ARTURO FUENTE OPUS X SERIES
Dominican Republic

The Fuente family has been making cigars for three generations. They manufacture a wide range of cigars, but we like those in the Opus X series, especially the double Corona, Robusto, and Perfection #2.

4 – MONTECRISTO
Cuba

Montecristo started in 1935 as a new brand from the Menendez and Garcia families. We've been told that it was named after Alexandre Dumas's novel, *The Count of Montecristo.* Whatever the source, we enjoy the "monties" for their colorado claro wrapper, superb aroma, medium to full flavor, and tangy taste.

Smoke Less but
the Best

CIGARS

"A true connoisseur loves cigars just as he loves music, wine, and life."

— Ernst Schneider, CEO of Davidoff

5 – SANCHO PANZA
Cuba

Named after a character in the famous Spanish novel *Don Quixote,* these subtle cigars are popular in Spain. We recommend them to beginners or to anyone who wants a cigar in the daytime.

6 – PADRÓN ANNIVERSARY SERIES
Nicaragua

The Padrón anniversary series came out in 1994 to commemorate the company's 30th anniversary. There are nine sizes, available with natural or maduro wrappers. Using four-year-old tobacco, these are dark, rich, box-pressed, and in our estimation, absolutely delicious.

7 – H. UPMANN
Cuba

Herman Upmann, a German banker who moved to Cuba in the 1840s, liked cigars so much that he switched businesses. And he did it well. The brand won seven gold medals in seven international exhibitions between 1862 and 1893. (You can see copies of the medals inside every box.) When you purchase these, be sure you get the handmade ones instead of those manufactured in a machine. Classified as mild to medium flavored, the cigars are very smooth.

8 – ASHTON VSG
Dominican Republic

This brand was founded in the mid 1980s by Philadelphia tobacco retailer Robert Levin. The cigars are made at the Fuentes family's factory in Santiago and pack a lot more wallop than most Dominican cigars. The VSG (Virgin Sun Grown) is a blend of tobacco that's been aged for four to five years. The results provide a rich smoke.

9 – GRAYCLIFF
Bahamas

The Graycliff Cigar Company is the brainchild of Enrico Garzaroli, owner of a resort in Nassau, Bahamas; and Avelino Lara, a Cuban cigar expert who used to make Cohibas for Fidel Castro. They're refined and flavorful.

10 – HOYO DE MONTERREY EXCALIBUR
Honduras

This popular and well made cigar is a rich medium-to-full-bodied Cuban-style smoke that is somewhat lighter in both body and appearance than its sister brands, Punch and El Rey del Mundo. This is due to the lighter Connecticut wrapper, as opposed to the Havana-seed or Ecuadoran Sumatra wrapper. The brand was initiated by Lew Rothman and Frank Llaneza in the late 1970s and is considered an excellent non-Cuban cigar. We like Nos. I through V, all available in your choice of natural or maduro wrapper.

TEN BEST
~LUGGAGE, ORGANIZERS, & TRAVEL GEAR~

Filofax or Palm Pilot? The Ten Best team tests the cutting edge and the tried and true.

1 – FILOFAX
www.filofax.com

Filofax has been the first name in organization since 1921. Now, with a full range of Filofax organizers to suit every lifestyle, keeping up with your hectic life has never been easier. Choose from a range of sizes—from wallet-size to desk-size—and a wealth of styles. Filofax organizers come complete with the essential pages you need to get started.

2 – BLACKBERRY
www.blackberry.com

BlackBerry is a leading wireless connectivity company, providing access to a wide range of applications on a variety of wireless devices around the world. It combines award winning hardware, software, and services to keep mobile professionals connected to the people, data, and resources that drive their day. BlackBerry keeps you in-the-loop while you're on the go with push-based technology that automatically delivers e-mail and other data to your BlackBerry device.

3 – PALMONE
www.palmone.com

Beginning with the original PalmPilot organizer, palmOne products have always been designed to keep people organized. Straight out of the box, all palmOne handhelds and smart phones can make your life easier with built-in organizer software to keep track of appointments, addresses, and phone numbers or manage your daily tasks. With over 20,000 titles available for purchase or free download, there's something here for everyone.

4 – TUMI
www.tumi.com

If this company has one true, signature piece, it's the Tumi garment bag. Introduced in the 1980s, this bag was an exciting "first" for the luggage industry. It incorporated the all-black color concept, wide openings, and easy-access pockets. And it was constructed of hard-wearing ballistic nylon. In 2000 Tumi re-engineered the ballistic nylon to make a highly durable abrasion-proof fabric. Then along came a new zipper system in 2001, which reduced the amount of damage from wear and tear to that critical part of the luggage.

Get Organized

3 – LOUIS VUITTON

www.vuitton.com

The crème de la crème of luggage, Louis Vuitton luggage is among the best money can buy. Exquisitely designed and constructed to meet the highest standards, a Louis Vuitton luggage set makes a statement of wealth and luxury.

6. VICTORINOX

www.victorinox.com

Better known for its extensive line of multi-functional pocketknives, Victorinox Swiss Army has been around for more than 100 years. The company now extends their wealth of design knowledge to its luggage line. Victorinox Swiss Army brand has expanded to great heights over the years. The company, a global entity, manufactures and markets a wide range of products including cutlery, apparel, watches, and, of course, luggage.

7. OLIVER PEOPLES

www.oliverpeoples.com

This company offers a premiere collection of retro-inspired spectacles, which has gained its founder, Leight, an optician by trade, international exposure and has transformed the perception of glasses in the 20th century.

8 – WALKING SHOES: MEPHISTO, CAMPER, AND ROCKPORT

www.mephisto.com, www.rockport.com, www.camper.com

Mephisto has set the standard for quality, comfort and durability for almost 40 years. A personal favorite is the Rockport Walking shoe, perhaps the lightest shoe made, with Vibram soles which, unlike those of other walkers, can be reconditioned. It has built in cushions and arch support, and comes in plain or capped toe styles. The Camper brand, from Spain, is comfortable and in vogue.

9 – CARRY-ALL PHOTOGRAPHERS TRAVEL VEST

These cotton vests can be found at Hammacher Schlemmer in New York, at most Army and Navy Surplus Stores, and from the online catalog of the National Geographic (www.shopNG.org). For photographers and the knowing traveler, this vest provides a variety of 19 pockets that hold just about anything—from rolls of film and a cell phone to a personal stereo or a water bottle.

10. SAMSONITE

www.samsonite.com

One of the major players in the luggage industry, Samsonite luggage boasts a history that spans nearly a whole century of catering to the needs of travelers worldwide. When travelers are searching to buy a Samsonite luggage set, they can be reassured that they will find just the right set to meet their traveling needs. The range of products has something to appeal to almost anyone, regardless of budgetary constraints, and their quality ensures that the products will last for many adventures of travel.

Ten Best
~Writing Instruments~

Sir Francis Bacon said, "Reading maketh a full man, conference a ready man, and writing an exact man." We couldn't agree more. Whether an individual prefers fountain, ball, felt, or rollerball pens—or mechanical or wooden pencils—the following companies produce exquisite selections in all variations. If you're looking for one-stop shopping for these, we recommend Fahrney's Pens in Upper Marlboro, Maryland; the website is www.fahrneyspens.com.

1 – Aurora
www.pens.it/aurora

"Since 1919, when the first Italian fountain pen factory was founded in the heart of Turin, beauty and reliability have distinguished Aurora pens," according to Fahrney's. "Expert craftsmanship, technological innovation, and creative style are the enduring factors that have maintained Aurora's success through the years for both their important collector's editions and their everyday writing instruments."

2 – Dunhill
www.dunhill.com

The name "Dunhill" conjures up images of cigarettes in elegant boxes trimmed with gold. But the company makes a fine pen, too.

3 – Cross
www.cross.com

They've been making fine pens and pencils at the A. T. Cross Company's headquarters in Lincoln, Rhode Island, for more than 150 years. For years, a Cross pen has been a classic gift for college or high-school graduates.

4 – Montblanc
www.montblanc.com

"Montblanc has been known for almost 100 years as a maker of distinctive, high-quality writing instruments," according to Fahrney's Pens. "In the past few years, the German-made product line has been expanded to include luxury leather goods and jewelry items. The unmistakable hallmark of every Montblanc design, the signature star, is testament to the superior quality of this remarkable collection."

5 – Waterman
www.waterman. com

These pretty creations are made near Nantes, France. Here's what the experts at Fahrney's say about Waterman's. "They are famous for their balance of functionality and pleasing aesthetics. Of particular note is the Waterman 18K gold, handcrafted nibs for the discerning

PAUL HANKAR
ARCHITECTE
RUE DEFACQZ 63

fountain pen user. Waterman is still an industry leader, with a broad range of fine writing instruments that combine quality and elegance just as they did a hundred years ago, in modern and traditional styles."

6 – CARTIER
www.cartier.com

Finding lovely writing instruments made by the craftsmen at one of the world's finest jewelers doesn't surprise us one bit. Two we really admire are the special mini ballpoint in pink lacquer and platinum topped with a Tonneau watch and the stunning 18-carat yellow gold Louis Cartier studded with 823 tiny diamonds. Now, that's style.

7 – S. T. DUPONT
www.st-dupont.com

According to the experts at Fahrney's, S. T. Dupont is the French luxury goods company whose name is synonymous with quality. "When you purchase an S. T. Dupont pen, you become the owner of a unique, individually numbered item of jewelry, crafted in the finest metals and rigorously tested. The most valuable substance that decorates the pens is the authentic Chinese lacquer made from the sap of the Asian *Rhus vernicifera* tree. Meticulously applied by Dupont's master lacquerers, this living substance has a unique character that ensures no two lacquers are quite the same."

8 – PARKER
www.parkerpen.com

When we think of Parker pens, we think of fine writing instruments. Whether we're using one from the flagship Duofold line or one from the less pricey Insignia one, we enjoy writing with these—even if it's only to pay bills. George Safford Parker established the company in 1888 to find a fountain pen that didn't leak or spill. He figured out

how to make one, and his innovations went on to include a button-filler contraption that did away with the messy job of having to fill the pen by means of an eyedropper.

9 – FABER-CASTELL
www.faber-castell.com

The same family has run Faber-Castell for eight generations, finessing their products through the centuries. The folks at Fahrney's state: "Since 1761, Faber-Castell has developed from a small-scale pencil maker outside Nuremberg, Germany, into the world's leading brand-name pencil. The Graf von Faber-Castell line of fine writing instruments offers quality, prestige, precision, and performance."

10 – NAMIKI
www.namiki.com

From a culture that has revered the art of writing for more than a thousand years comes the Namiki writing instrument collection. Skilled Japanese artisans use the finest materials to create writing instruments that look beautiful and perform flawlessly.

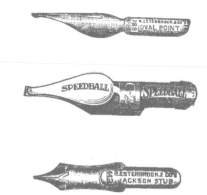

TEN BEST
~TAILORS~

At 6-feet, 6-inches, I've had to visit many a tailor in my time. And when I find a good one, I keep his particulars handy.

1 – JAMES FASHION
Bangkok, Thailand
Tel: 66-2-668-6990-3

James Fashion is arguably one of Bangkok's most popular and best tailors. The staff is very friendly and knowledgeable, and you can't help but feel special at the way they treat you from the moment you step inside the store. They have an enormous range of fabrics and styles. Bolts of beautiful Thai silks, English and Italian wools, and Egyptian cottons fill both floors of the bustling establishment.

2 – ERMENEGILDO ZEGNA
www.zegna.com

In its fourth generation of family ownership, Ermenegildo Zegna, in business since 1910, has focused on really good quality menswear, tailored with impeccable style and personal attention. These are the sort of tailors who will leave their shops for a fitting in a valued customer's home or office. This doesn't come cheaply, but isn't it worth it to get the perfect fit?

3 – CHARVET
Paris, France
Tel: 33-(0)-1-42-60-30-70

The Duke of Windsor made this Parisian tailor famous. Long before he arrived, however, sartorial Frenchmen were getting clothes made here. The selection of fabrics is exquisite and beautiful.

4 – WILLIAM FIORAVANTI
New York, New York
Tel: 212-355-1540

A lingering proponent of the "power look," William Fioravanti's store in midtown Manhattan has been turning out the appropriate suit for more than 40 years. They're all made on site, and the shop can show you a large selection of fine fabric. This is where one goes to get the outfit you'll need when you make partner or take your company public (or just want to show that you are primed for either).

5 – ASCOT CHANG
Hong Kong, New York, Beverly Hills
www.ascotchang.com

Ascot Chang—"Gentleman's Shirtmaker"—has been a winner since its first store opened on Kimberley Road in Hong Kong in 1949, offering custom-made shirts in a plethora of designs and the finest fabrics; as well as formalware. The tailor describes its customers as "some of the world's most demanding and distinguished men—the likes of Mr. George Bush." (They neglect to say if it's Bush junior or Bush senior.)

TAILORS

5 – WORLD GROUP TAILORS
Bangkok, Thailand
Tel: 66-2-234-4799 or 237-5274

I discovered World Tailors in Bangkok years ago. They have quality woolen, linen, and cashmere fabrics and workrooms fit for the King of Thailand—uniforms for the royal household are made here too. They also fit several Thai film stars and members of Thai and European high society. Their custom-made suits cost $300, with three fittings. A kingly savings indeed. They also make suits for women, duplicating any detail and design with attention and accuracy.

6 – ANDERSON & SHEPPARD
London, England
Tel: 44-(0)-20-7734-1420

This venerable Savile Row original is the tailor Prince Charles frequents, and we can see why. The tailors here have been making elegantly draped, slightly wide-shouldered, and high-arm-holed suits since 1873. The latest news is that they're moving around the corner off Savile Row, but there's no doubt in our minds that their reputation will remain one of the best.

7 – RALPH LAUREN
Worldwide services (headquarters in New York, New York)
www.polo.com

Ralph Lauren's Purple Label suits are "made to measure," according to the website. And the tailors in the shops do a fantastic job. (Our personal favorite is the ornate flagship store on the southeast corner of Madison Avenue and 72nd Street in Manhattan's Upper East Side.) Corduroy jackets for a day in the country or broadcloth shirts with French cuffs and collars for the office, Purple Label has it all.

8 – JON GREEN
New York, New York
Tel: 212-861-9611

Jon Green likes to chat a little bit with his clients before he takes measurements and goes over fabric choices. That way, the former musician develops a better idea of what suit best fits the client. His clientele typically turns out in clothes that reflect classic English, Italian, and American style with slightly sloped, slightly roped shoulders and a sound chest. No wonder Mr. Green has developed an almost cult following.

9 – LIANA LEE
New York, New York
Tel: 212-588-9289

Korean-born, New York-based, and a self-admitted "old-fashioned" suitmaker, Liana Lee has a fondness for British styling. Located in the Upper East Side, she makes clothes that are fitted, but not too tight. She is lauded for her attention to detail, and her customers love the fact that she provides an honest woman's perspective on how women want them to look.

10 – CARACENI
Milan, Italy
Tel: 39-(0)-2-76-00-28-24

Established in 1913, this Milanese tailor has not changed its style or technique much since. Nor do they make many suits; they average about 700 a year. But what exquisite results! Such sartorial souls as Humphrey Bogart and Cary Grant have worn Caraceni suits, not to mention generations of kings in Greece and Italy, the Prince of Wales, Prince Rainier of Monaco, and Aristotle Onassis That's all we need to know.

TEN BEST
~WINES~

I know very little about wine, as my vignette "Dining with Rothschild" (page 121) will attest. But Andrew is an expert, having authored wine newsletters and consulted for the Wine Warehouse, a company that distributes premium wines. Here is his list of the ten best.

1 – CHÂTEAU PÉTRUS
Bordeaux, France

Founded by the Arnaud family in the 19th century, the domain's wine receives the care of a pampered child. The grapes are picked only in the afternoon, when the morning dew has evaporated, so as not to risk even the slightest dilution of quality. The unusually old vines are grown in soil that's nearly all clay (whereas in adjacent properties the soil is a mixture of gravel-sand or clay-sand), an ideal condition for making Merlot (95 percent of Pétrus's production). They are replanted plot by plot only after reaching 70 years of age to guarantee the average age of the vines. Fermented in cement vats, the wine ages in new oak barrels for 22 to 28 months and is clarified with 5 fresh egg whites per barrel. Never filtered, Château Pétrus wine is rich and smooth.

2 – ROMANÉE CONTI
Burgundy, France

In Burgundy, between Gevrey and Vougeot, the plot called Romanée-Conti has at first glance nothing extraordinary. But beginning in the 15th century, the Saint-Viviant monks who started the vineyard were especially fastidious in selecting their grapes. They established a subtle balance between grape, soil, climate, orientation, and watering. The legend holds that until 1945, a good vine plant would be buried, leaving just two shoots to properly grow. When the vineyard was reconstituted, workers discovered intricate roots more than a meter (3 feet) deep. It was from that mulch that Romanée-Conti drew its distinctiveness. "We are the keeper of a certain philosophy of wine, and, mainly, we

are concerned by the perfection in details," asserts Aubert de Vilaine, one of the domain's owners.

3 – PENFOLDS GRANGE
Barossa Valley, Australia

From humble beginnings in the 1950's, Grange has maintained its place as Australia's most prestigious red wine. Now internationally renowned, each new vintage is keenly awaited the world over. Richly textured, intensely concentrated, and packed with fruit sweetness, Penfolds Grange wines, regardless of vintage, require medium- to long-term cellaring to develop into immensely complex, beguiling wines that seduce the senses.

4 – HARLAN ESTATE
Napa Valley, California

H. William Harlan, the founder of Harlan Estate, had a vision. Simply put, he was determined to produce a California "First Growth." An entrepreneur with a strong background in real estate and hotel development, Harlan fully understood the importance of "location." His estate is the result of a 20-year search for prime hillside vineyards, culminating in the patchwork acquisition of 93 hectares (230 acres) above the fabled Rutherford-Oakville beachlands. The land is magnificent oak-studded knolls and valleys, only ten percent of which are now under vine.

5 – MARCASSIN
Sonoma Valley, California

Helen Turley and John Wetlaufer purchased a 16-hectare (40-acre) parcel in 1985 and planted just over 3.5 hectares

(8.5 acres) of vines in 1991. The first commercial release of Marcassin Vineyard's estate Chardonnay and Pinot Noir was the 1996 vintage. Both wines were outstanding, and subsequent vintages are showing even greater complexity. Since 1990 Helen Turley has produced a string of profound vineyard-designated Chardonnays from select cool-climate Sonoma sites. Dealing with growers is not the same as owning a vineyard and controlling all aspects of viticulture and winemaking

6 – TURLEY WINE CELLARS
Napa Valley, California

Larry Turley is pursuing his true passion: old-vine Zinfandel and Petite Sirah. He calls them "Big Reds," a phrase that aptly describes their sheer magnitude. But his love of wine runs in the family: His sister, winemaker Helen Turley, is proprietor of Marcassin, California's hottest new Chardonnay brand. Larry Turley, a bearded 49-year-old emergency room physician, has long loved Zinfandels made from California's old vines.

A surprising number of the old-vine vineyards at Turley are still producing, many a century old. Turley believes that older vines offer more character and a better, naturally achieved balance than their younger Zinfandel counterparts, which tend to be more prodigious producers.

7 – CHÂTEAU MARGAUX
Bordeaux, France

Château Margaux was founded in the 1400s. Once the residence of Edward III, King of England, it was one of the most stately fortified châteaux in Guyenne. Over the centuries, the property changed ownership several times. In 1804, the Marquis of La Colonilla acquired it, razed the old Gothic manor house and built in its place the château that still stands today. In 1977, Laura and André Mentzelopoulos purchased the property and lavished money on the vineyards and the winemaking facilities. Emile Peynaud was retained as a consultant to oversee the vinification of the grape juice. Observers expected it would take several vintages before all the improvements would show up, but it took just one vintage, 1978, for the world to see the greatness of Château Margaux.

8 – CAYMUS CABERNET SAUVIGNON
Napa Valley, California

Cabernet Sauvignon has long reigned supreme at Caymus. This is one winery where you can open a 1974, 1975, or 1976 with confidence, knowing the wine will still be loaded with ripe fruit. The 1992 Cabernet Sauvignon exhibits gobs of toasty oak and cassis fruit in a ripe, opulent, full-bodied, round, generous style that is ideal for drinking. The Caymus Special Selection is one of the most renowned luxury specimens of Cabernet Sauvignon in California.

9 – MARTINELLI
Sonoma Valley, California

The Martinelli family has long been prominent among the growers in the Russian River Valley. They have more than 142 hectares (350 acres) of vineyards planted and have been the

DINING WITH ROTHSCHILD

I was part of the TIME team invited by Baron Philip de Rothschild to write about his vineyard, Mouton Rothschild in the Pauillac. The Baron was a man who brought a new vision to the art. Over the course of the assignment as his new friend, I confessed that I knew little about wine.

Later in Paris, at his home for Sunday brunch, the Baron selected a bottle, but my palate was too inexperienced to appreciate a fine vintage. Swirling a decanted wine in a crystal glass, the Baron waxed euphoric, "Ah, it has a dense, deep color with lively, brilliant highlights. Hmmmm, red fruit, smoky notes combining complexity that attacks, indeed a bold balance."

"Nathaniel," he confided, "it has a finish and confirmation."

I asked Philip if he would help me with a list so that I might order wine with authority when entertaining my smart friends back in New York. Without hesitation he summoned his *aide-de-camp*. After poetic praise for Cote de Rhône and Romanée Conti, Mouton and Lafitte, Cuvee and Chardonnay, the Baron uncapped his silver Montblanc pen and memorialized some of the best vintages to his stationery.

Eyeing me with a wink and a twinkle, he handed me his list. "Nathaniel," he intoned, "if you really want to make a good impression, order a bottle of my brother Guy's favorite wine, Lafitte Rothschild 1947. There are only 40 bottles left."

Holding his glass to the sunlight, the Baron smiled, "One of which you are having right now."

A CASE FOR THE 20TH CENTURY

1 – Château Margaux 1900
1900 was a good year for all of the *premier cru*.
Hard to imagine any finer wine.

2 – Quinta do Noval Vintage Port Nacional 1931
A rare and perfect vintage.

3 – Romanée Conti 1937
The 1937 vintage is legend.

**4 – Inglenook Cabernet Sauvignon
Napa Valley 1941**
Largely contributed to the recognition the Cabernet
gained in the Napa Valley. Astonishing richness worthy
of aging in the '30s and '40s.

5 – Château Mouton-Rothschild 1945
Nothing is really comparable to a Mouton '45. The
Château Latour 1990 is par.

6 – Château Cheval Blanc 1947
For many, Château Cheval Blanc 1947 is the greatest
wine ever produced.

**7 – Biondi-Santi Brunello di Montalcino
Riserva 1955**
A fabulous wine.

8 – Penfolds Grange Hermitage 1955
The first commercial vintage that proved Australia could
produce greatness.

**9 – Hermitage La Chapelle
Paul Jaboulet Aîné 1961**
A monument to the glory of the Syrah.

10 – Château Pétrus 1961
Pétrus worthy of the '21, '45, '47 vintages.

**11 – Heitz Cabernet Sauvignon Napa Valley
Martha's Vineyard 1974**
For many collectors, the '74 is the best, its sensuality
extraordinary.

12 – Château d'Yquem 1921
Comes close to a mystical experience.

source for many top wines from other producers. Several years
ago, Steve Martinelli began to estate bottle 4,000 cases, a
relatively small percentage of the Martinelli Vineyards' total
production. However, he had the luxury of choosing the best
parcels. Beginning in 1993, with the help of consultant and
winemaker Helen Turley, he has bottled all the Martinelli
wines without filtration. The results are some of the most
complex and exciting wines being made in California.

10 – CHÂTEAU D'YQUEM
Bordeaux, France
Château d'Yquem is a *Grand Premier Cru* (French, "Great
First Growth" or "Great First Vintage") wine from the
Sauternes region in the southern part of Bordeaux. In the
Bordeaux Wine Official Classification of 1855, Château
d'Yquem was the only Sauternes given this rating, indicating
its perceived superiority over all other wines of its type.
Wines from Château d'Yquem are characterized by their
complexity, concentration, and sweetness. Each d'Yquem
vine produces only about a single glass of wine.

MADEIRA, MY DEAR?

Odds are good that the Founding Fathers of the
United States toasted the signing of the Declaration of
Independence with glasses of Madeira. The fortified
wine was made from grapes grown in the volcanic soils
of the Portuguese island of Madeira, a major stopping
point for ships sailing across the Atlantic from the Old
World to the New. It was also popular because the
wine held up well in oaken barrels. Some bottles hold
their own for up to a hundred years. But we see no
reason anyone should wait that long.

TEN BEST
~PERFUMERS~

Perfumer and historian Pauline Thomas says that women now rely on fragrance wardrobes, rather than a single signature scent. Here we detail the essentials. Hold the Shalimar!

1 – ANNICK GOUTAL
France
Tel: 33-(0)-1-42-60-52-82
www.annickgoutal.nl

Movie stars and royals adore Annick Goutal's wonderful perfumes for women and men. Their packaging—in handcrafted bottles—matches the beauty of their scents. Prince, Madonna, and Queen Noor favor Eau d'Hadrien, and Tina Turner and Steve Spielberg like Gardenia Passion. Goutal's personal fragrance was Passion, one of the first she made.

A former fashion model and pianist, Goutal got into the business in the mid-1980s after she spent several years learning how to make perfume. She'd grown up in her father's confectionary store, so she was very aware of the power of good-smelling things in pretty packages.

After she died, Goutal's daughter, Camille, took over the business. As a child, she asked her mother for her own special scent. That is the charming Eau de Camille, an intoxicating blend of honeysuckle, privet, and freshly mowed grass.

2 – GUERLAIN
France
www.guerlain.com

The venerable house of Guerlain has been making perfume since 1828 (it also made vinegars then). During its time, it has created more than 626 fragrances. Perhaps the most famous is Shalimar, a spicy scent in the equally famous fan-shaped bottle. We like the classic Eau de Cologne Imperiale, inspired by the beauty of Empress Eugenie more than a century ago. She liked it, too, apparently, because she dubbed perfumer Pierre-Francois-Pascal Guerlain "her majesty's official perfumer." Another favorite is Mitsouko, made in 1919 and named after the heroine of the popular novel *La Bataille*. For sheer shape alone, Ode's bottle is a sleek piece of glass, a reflection of the skyscrapers that were rising all over the United States in the 1950s.

3 – LANVIN
France
Tel: 33-(0)-1-44-71-31-73 and 31-83, www.lanvin.com

"Give her anything, but give her Arpege" was a memorable ad campaign slogan for a memorable scent. Created in 1927, Jeanne Lanvin's rich, yellow-gold perfume is still going strong, we're pleased to note. She had Arpege made to commemorate the 30th birthday of her daughter, Marie Blanche. The charming silhouette of a woman reaching to a child on every bottle was based on a photo taken in 1907 of Lanvin and Marie Blanche going to a ball. The bottle itself was designed by Armand-Albert Rateau, a famous decorator of the art deco era. For men, Lanvin Vetyver smells fresh and spicy. It's destined to be a classic like Arpege.

4 – ACQUA DI PARMA
Italy
Tel: 39-(0)-2-552-2881, 3www.acquadiparma.it

Acqua di Parma began turning the smells of the sunny Mediterranean into perfumes in 1916. Bottled in an attractive but straightforward fashion, the scents have an Old-World look that is very sought-after today. (Acqua also has a line of nicely scented candles.) Profumo is a woman's

scent made in the 1930s. It's a heady mix of more than 300 ingredients; the ones most noticeable are ylang ylang and Florentine iris. Less complicated but enjoyable is Lavender Tonic, a cooling herbal scent that has a little bergamot, lemon, and orange blossom added to make it unusual.

5 – CHANEL
France
Tel: 33-(0)-1-42-60-30-70, www.chanel.com

"Chanel No. 5" is a virtual synonym for "perfume." Ernest Beaux developed the perfume in the early 1920s for designer Coco Chanel. It was his fifth concoction for the French couturier, and she considered five to be her lucky number. In an interview with the Fragrance Foundation, Chanel's master perfumer Jacques Polge said that the simple bottle was unusual at the time and has since been photographed more than any other in the perfume business. Other Chanel scents worth trying are Cristalle, a fresh, slick scent, and the dainty floral No. 19.

6 – FLORIS
Great Britain
Tel: 44-(0)-1-845-702-3239, www.florislondon.com

It's tough to beat Floris for longevity. The English perfumer has been working out of 89 Jermyn Street since 1730. Founder Juan Famenias Floris hung out his shingle there shortly after he moved to England from his native Minorca. Eight generations later, his descendants are still in charge. Among the classics are Limes and Special 127 (originally created for a Russian duke and a favorite of Eva Perón). A new one we like, Zinnia, smells faintly of violets and mandarin oranges. Then, to make sure we're thoroughly doused in good smells, we love Rose Mouthwash; a few drops of this mixture in warm water makes breath as sweet as can be.

Essences   Perfumes

The History of Perfume

Perfume was first used by the Egyptians as part of their religious rituals. The two principal uses were the burning of incense, myrrh, and frankincense, followed by applications of balms and ointments. Perfumed oils were applied to the skin for either cosmetic or medicinal purposes and as preludes to lovemaking. With trade routes, perfume spread to Greece, Rome, and the Islamic world.

Perfume enjoyed huge success during the 17th century. Perfumed gloves became popular in France, and, in 1656, the Guild of Glove and Perfume-Makers was established. The use of perfume in France grew steadily. The court of Louis XV was even named "the perfumed court" due to the scents that were applied daily not only to the skin but also to clothing, fans, and furniture.

The 18th century saw a revolutionary advance in perfumery with the invention of eau de cologne. This refreshing blend of rosemary, neroli, bergamot, and lemon was used in a multitude of different ways, especially diluted in bath water. The variety of 18th-century perfume containers was as wide as that of the fragrances and their uses. Many came in beautiful Louis XIV-style pear-shaped bottles. Glass became increasingly popular, particularly in France with the opening of the Baccarat factory in 1765.

As with industry and the arts, perfume changed in the 19th century. Changing tastes and the development of modern chemistry laid the foundations of perfumery as we know it today.

With its abundance of jasmine, roses, and orange trees, the town of Grasse in Provence established itself as the largest production center for raw materials. Soon, Paris became the commercial counterpart to Grasse and the world center of perfume.

Perfumemaker François Coty formed a partnership with René Lalique. Lalique producing bottles for D'Orsay and Roger & Gallet. Baccarat created for Guerlain. Brosse glassworks made the memorable bottle for Arpege and Chanel No. 5.

The 1930s scented the arrival of the leather fragrances and florals with Worth's Je Reviens, Caron's Fleurs de Rocaille, and Jean Patou's Joy. With French perfumery so popular in the 1950's, Christian Dior, Hermès, Jacques Fath, Nina Ricci, and Pierre Balmain created their own scents.

Today, there are over 20,000 fragrances from an industry adding creativity and romance to our lives through fabulous fragrances.

(Courtesy of www.parfumsraffy.com)

PERFUMES

7 – VERA WANG
New York
www.verawang.com

Because clothing designer Vera Wang makes only two scents, she's not a perfumer like the others on our list. But what scents they are! For women, there's Vera Wang—the fragrance combines Bulgarian roses, calla lilies, gardenias, and musk. It was launched at Harrod's in 2002.

For the guys, there's simply Vera Wang for Men. This smells of a bit of nutmeg and is a refreshingly woody scent.

8 – YVES SAINT LAURENT
France
www.ysl.com

The late great French designer made several fragrances. Our favorites are Rive Gauche in its signature blue, silver, and black wrapping; and Opium, the rich, spicy scent that every woman seemed to be wearing after it was introduced in 1977. Women also love seductive YSL Paris, with a base of rose intermingled with bergamot and sandalwood; Baby Doll, floral and fruity; and In Love Again, exploding with grapefruit, grape, tulip tree flower, and blackberry.

9 – CREED
France
Tel: 33-(0)-1-4720-5802

Creed is another old-timer that continues to please. James Henry Creed opened his shop in London in 1760; the company moved to Paris in 1854, where it remains. Oliver Creed is at the helm, picking the best essences available from the world over. Fleurissimo is a sublime choice, commissioned by Prince Rainier of Monaco for his bride, film star Grace Kelly, on their wedding day. Olivier Creed carries on the family tradition by getting his rose essences from Bulgaria, Turkey, and Morocco; jasmine and irises from Florence; and tuberoses from India.

EAU DE COLOGNE SUPÉRIEURE

10 – L'OCCITANE
France
www.loccitane.com

Company founder Olivier Baussane said his goal was to share with the world the wonderful things that grow beneath the warm Provençal sun. Everything indeed has a fresh, delicious scent. Try L'Oranger, a breezy eau de cologne mixing mandarin and mint; and Eau de la Recolte Bleue, capturing the pungent aroma of lavender for which Provence is so famous.

VERBENA HARVEST

One of the most popular flowers used in perfumes is verbena. There are about 250 species of the plant, and most of them come from the Americas. Two types are native to Europe. The ancient Romans revered verbena, because it allegedly could be used to rekindle old flames of passion.

Perfumers and herbalists harvest verbena between May and July before it blooms. They then dry the leaves and soak them in an alcohol mixture to make an extract that has an irresistible lemon fragrance.

JUST THE

TRAVEL

BEST

TEN BEST
~TRAINS~

Great trains include the *Al-Andalus*, a restored classic that tours southern Spain; the *Royal Scotsman* that winds though the Scottish highlands; South Africa's legendary *Blue Train;* and the spartan *Trans-Siberian Express* between Moscow and Vladivostok. Many of the world's luxury trains, including the *Al-Andalus* and the storied *Orient-Express,* are often described as grand hotels on wheels. Each of the trains on our list of Ten Best has its own distinctive personality.

1 – VENICE SIMPLON–ORIENT-EXPRESS
Tel: 866-674-3689 (U.S.)
www.orient-express.com

The *Venice Simplon–Orient-Express* is sophistication and splendid comfort. The classic midnight blue carriages were decorated by celebrated interior designers such as René Lalique (Dining Car 4141). As the world's most celebrated train, the *Venice Simplon–Orient-Express* carries passengers across Europe in the style of a bygone era. The memory of the glamorous carriages, sumptuous cuisine, and personal service will stay with you forever.

Bombed, shot at, and marooned in snow drifts, the history of the *Orient-Express* dates back to October 4, 1883, with the inaugural run steaming from Paris to Guirgi, Romania; and passing through Strasbourg, Vienna, Budapest, and Bucharest. The carriages have histories and individual characters of their own that may date back even farther: Each spent long years of service criss-crossing the frontiers of Europe, operating for a variety of prominent railway companies. Each retains its unique identifying number from its previous incarnation; for instance, Dining Car 4141 was originally a first-class Pullman.

The *Venice Simplon–Orient-Express*'s fabled Paris–Istanbul run was inaugurated in 1921. Today the Orient-Express usually makes only one run to Istanbul, in September, when the Venice-to-Istanbul segment is added to the more frequently scheduled Paris-to-Venice route. Lunch and dinner are served at pre-arranged seatings in three plush dining cars, with white linens and glittering china and silver. Evening dress is black tie or dark suit. In the morning, stewards deliver a continental breakfast.

The carriages recently were completely refurbished to emulate the original features, but modern amenities have been added.

2 – THALYS
www.thalys.com

The striking red-and-gray *Thalys* is Europe's newest high-speed international train. It is regarded as the best

ALL ABOARD!
EUROPE'S
HIGH-SPEED TRAINS

EUROSTAR
www.eurostar.com

The outstanding and convenient *Eurostar* is a high-speed rail service that directly links the United Kingdom to France and Belgium via the Channel Tunnel. From London, *Eurostar* schedules up to 16 services to Paris (2.5 hours) and 9 to Brussels (2.25 hours) daily and also trains to northern France (the journey to Lille takes just 1.75 hours).

TGV
www.tgv.com

TGV stands for *"train à grand vitesse"*—high-speed train—and the trains certainly live up to the name. The French-owned *TGV* ranks second in the world for fastest train behind Japan's *Nozomi*.

TALGO
www.raileurope.com

Talgo is the maker of Spain's high-speed trains. The *Talgo 200* connects major cities in Spain. Equipped with smooth, streamlined cars, these trains average 225 kilometers an hour (140 miles an hour). The *Catalan Talgo* travels between Barcelona and Montpellier.

THALYS
www.thalys.com

Thalys trains, Europe's newest high-speed trains, are covered in greater detail, starting on page 129.

link between Paris and Low Countries cities such as Brussels (1.5 hours), Bruges (2.5 hours), and Antwerp (2.2 hours). Once new lines have been laid in the Netherlands, the run to Amsterdam (4.25 hours) should be cut to 3 hours.

Thalys trains are a Franco-Belgian operation, with cooperation from Dutch and German railways. Operating at an average speed of 242 kilometers an hour (150 miles an hour), they are the world's fourth fastest trains (after Shanghai's *Magrev*, Japan's *Bullet Train*, and France's *TGV*). Moreover, your trip will be incredibly comfortable. Seats in first and second class are deep and spacious. A first-class ticket includes the price of meals—delicious breakfasts, cold plate lunches, and dinners with wine—all served at your seat on trays.

The *Thalys* service has become so popular that many trains are fully booked, despite the fact that there are 18 Paris–Brussels and 5 Paris–Amsterdam departures daily from the Gare du Nord. Service is being extended to additional cities as the network grows.

3 – THE BLUE TRAIN
Tel: 27-12-334-8459, www.bluetrain.co.za

The famous *Blue Train* makes the 1,600-kilometer (994-mile) run from Cape Town to Johannesburg (24 hours) three times a week in high season (summer) and once a week each way in the off-season. The train travels only at speeds up to 110 kilometers an hour (68 miles an hour); the slow, smooth ride allows you plenty of time to soak in the spectacular scenery.

There are two kinds of accommodations on the train: the deluxe suites with a lounge and full-tub bathroom and the luxury suites with a private shower and toilet. Each carriage has only four suites. Food and service are outstanding. When you first board, champagne awaits you in your compartment.

4 – ROYAL SCOTSMAN

Tel: 44-(0)-131-555-1021
www.royalscotsman.com

A red carpet literally is rolled out for travelers on the Royal Scotsman. At the station, a kilt-clad bagpiper wheezes a maximum of 36 passengers on board, where the first order of business is a champagne toast in the lounge/observation car.

Trips depart from either London or Edinburgh for one- to seven-day tours of England's west country, Scotland's highlands, or specialty destinations. A guidebook in each compartment describes the tour's itinerary, which might include visits to castles, museums, homes, golf courses, or gardens. These private visits usually are scheduled before or after regular hours; many owners or operators of the attractions conduct the visits. A special bus follows the rail route to ferry travelers between the train and the excursion sites.

On board, the most comfortable place to spend leisure time is in the beautiful 1908 observation car. The armchairs and sofas are plush, and newspapers are brought aboard daily. In the evening, travelers may partake of cocktails and hors d'oeuvres here before heading to the dining car, and occasionally a trio stages classical musical performances.

Dinners are either black tie or black suit events, with sittings in two dining cars that date from 1945 to 1960. The chef prepares four-star-quality meals with fresh ingredients purchased en route. Well-chosen premium wines complement the menu.

5 – AL ANDALUS EXPRESS

Tel: 34-91-570-1621
www.alandalusexpreso.com

The luxurious *Al Andalus* offers a relaxed way to explore southern Spain's beautiful Andalusian region. Distances covered on the seven-day round-trip from either Madrid or Seville are short, and the train generally travels from town to town during breakfast hours, leaving most of the day free for touring and the night undisturbed for comfortable sleeping.

The emphasis of the train journey is on scenic areas and historic or cultural attractions—the Alhambra in Granada; the eighth-century Mezquita, a huge mosque turned cathedral, in Cordoba; Spain's oldest bullring in Ronda; sherry cellars in Jerez; and much more. The train runs only during the relatively less-crowded spring and fall months, so your experiences at the attractions will be less hectic. These are also the seasons of somewhat milder temperatures than in summer, although the train itself is fully air-conditioned.

One of the prettiest luxury trains, with exquisite marquetry and soft colors, the *Al Andalus* has five special cars that the French built in 1929 to take the King of England on a journey to the French Riviera. The train's superbly restored vintage mahogany-paneled compartments accommodate 80 passengers. Passengers bathe in two unique cars, completely fitted out with spacious private shower/dressing rooms. Attendants clean the rooms after every bather, and the wait is never

FIRST IMPRESSIONS: THE PASHA

While traveling on the *Orient-Express* from Paris to Venice, I had a first impression to add to my travel files. When I first boarded, the train manager suggested that the passengers dress for dinner, which would be served in a beautiful, restored dining car, fitted with walnut panels, Lalique crystal, silver service, freshly cut flowers, and white linen tablecloths.

That evening in the dining car, an interesting dark man appeared, catching my eye. Passing by my table in his flowing afghan and headdress of many colors, he radiated confidence. As he was traveling with two equally exotic ladies, I dubbed him "the pasha." His ladies were also dressed in brocaded tunics with colorful geometric patterned headbands.

I assumed the pasha with his commanding elegance and easy smile was the leader of an African nation. He enjoyed himself. I was curious to learn about him. At dinner the following night, I waited for him. I convinced my tablemates that he was a leader of importance to be reckoned with. He probably had a whole car for himself. Just who was the mystery man? When the passengers left the train in Venice, I thought I would never see him again. But a few days later at the Hotel Cipriani, sitting in the fabled garden, I saw the pasha having lunch.

What luck. The same winning smile. The same lovely ladies. I still wanted to know who he was. What government did he head? Did he make his fortune in Sierra Leone in the diamond trade, or was it gold in Nairobi? I mustered up an introduction, after we nodded recognition. After all, we had much in common. We had been on the same journey. He spoke perfect English. Ah, maybe he was educated in England. We exchanged impressions about the train.

"The very best of my life," he said.

"Where are you from?" I asked, expecting some faraway address.

"I'm from L.A."

"Los Angeles?" He had me. "You mean you're not a king or a pasha?"

"Oh, wow, thanks. No, man. I'm a musician from Sherman Oaks; and this trip, well, it's like music, taking my imagination with me. I've always dreamed about taking a grand tour, going to places I always dreamed of, pretending to be somebody I always wanted to be. So after reading about the *Orient Express*, especially the part about dressing up and all for dinner, I fell right in. After all, travel is music for the soul and appetite for the imagination!"

Something stayed with me that summer afternoon. We all travel from time to time, meeting extraordinary people and stepping into adventure, to curious places, where memories are made, with first and lasting impressions.

more than a few minutes. Terry robes and slippers and a bag for carrying toiletries are provided.

6 – TRANS-SIBERIAN EXPRESS

Thoughts of the *Trans-Siberian Express* conjure up romantic images from *Dr. Zhivago*. In reality, the train is a vital lifeline that links Moscow to Vladivostok on Russia's Far East coast, crossing the Ural Mountains and Siberia's taiga and steppes along the way. The railway's long stretch across Russia makes it the world's longest train route.

As the train travels the railway's incredible length—more than 9,000 kilometers (5,625 miles)—it passes through a huge diversity of landscapes and cultures. You may wish to hop off the train at a few points to meet locals or dip your toes into magnificent Siberian Baikal Lake, or you may just want to sit back and enjoy the train ride.

It takes more than six days to travel the length of the Trans-Siberian railway. Accommodations are spartan by western standards, but it is still an amazing adventure.

A good way to plan a trip is with a Western tour agency. A couple of suggestions include Express to Russia (www.expresstorussia.com) and Russian Experience (www.trans-siberian.co.uk).

7 – THE ROYAL CANADIAN PACIFIC

Tel: 403-508-1400, www.cprtours.com

Introduced in 2000, the *Royal Canadian Pacific* ranks as North America's finest touring train, offering passengers an unparalleled six-day journey through the Canadian Rockies.

The train travels 1,015 kilometers (635 miles) round-trip from Calgary, making stops so passengers can visit Emerald Lake in Yoho National Park, the re-created gold rush town of Fort Steele, the Head-Smashed-In Buffalo Jump World Heritage site, and other lovely attractions. The train accommodates only 23 passengers in its five handsome walnut- and mahogany-paneled carriages drawn from the Canadian Pacific Railway's fleet of fully restored 1940s business cars. The "Mount Stephen"—the train's social hub—includes a reading room that was once a smoking room used by Winston Churchill. The "Royal Wentworth" served as part of King George VI and Queen Elizabeth's Royal Train.

The dining experience is first-rate. Meals are served in two dining rooms at tables that seat either ten or twelve people. The menu features sumptuous repasts. Live music highlights evening entertainment, just right for the stop on the serene banks of Crowsnest Lake.

HEATHROW EXPRESS & GATWICK EXPRESS

www.heathrowexpress.com / www.gatwickexpress.co.uk

The *Heathrow Express* and *Gatwick Express* offer fast and efficient service to and from their respective airports and central London. The journey to Heathrow from Paddington Station takes 15 minutes; the journey to Gatwick from Victoria Station takes 30 minutes.

8 – THE SIERRA MADRE EXPRESS
Tel: 520-747-0346, www.sierramadreexpress.com

The casual and comfortable *Sierra Madre Express* travels through Mexico's breathtaking Copper Canyon. The only other way you can experience the canyon's wild, untouched natural beauty is by hiking in. Peter Robbins, Arizona-based owner of the *Sierra Madre Express,* provisions his 56-passenger train with American food and water for eight-day tours running round-trip out of Tucson. Passengers first bus to Nogales to cross the border. Only two nights are actually spent on board the train. Double compartments have private toilets; the extremely small singles must share facilities. There are no showers.

RAIL EUROPE

www.raileurope.com

Rail Europe is a one-stop source for European travel. It offers a wide range of services and products to fit every traveler's needs—from competitively priced transatlantic air tickets, to hotels and car rentals, to vacation packages. But first and foremost, Rail Europe provides rail travel, selling point-to-point tickets on any route in Europe—including the high-speed *Eurostar* and *TGV* trains—as well as the famous Eurailpass and Eurail Selectpass, for travel in continental Europe.

9 – THE ROCKY MOUNTAINEER
Tel: 604-606-7245, www.rockymountaineer.com

The *Rocky Mountaineer* pioneered daylight-only rail touring through the Canadian Rockies. Its two-day, all-inclusive trip between Vancouver and either Banff or Jasper proved so successful that two trains, each carrying about 500 passengers, now cover the route from mid-April to mid-October and again in snowy December. The train overnights in the mining town of Kamloops, where passengers are treated to dinner and hotel accommodations. In the morning, one section of the train goes to Banff and the other goes to Jasper. Whether you start or finish in Vancouver, you should definitely take a few days to explore the national parks.

10 – THE GHAN: AUSTRALIA
Tel: 13-21-47 (within Australia) or 61-8-8213-4592 (international), www.railaustralia.com.au

The *Ghan* is a living legend in Australia. It takes the ultimate journey through the very heart of the continent. When the *Ghan* first departed Adelaide for Alice Springs in 1929, it was always intended that the train would someday travel through to Darwin. In 2004 the dream became reality.

Traveling through endless vistas of dry Outback, the overnight trip from Adelaide to Alice Springs covers 1,559 kilometers (969 miles). Darwin is another night and 1,419 kilometers (882 miles) down the tracks. The train crosses the Macdonnell Ranges, the Great Victoria Desert, and sheep and cattle stations. You can take off-train excursions to learn about desert flora and fauna. As the train heads much farther north into the Northern Territory, the landscape changes, becoming more mountainous and lush.

Accommodations include berth compartments and reclining seats. Meals are served in the dining car.

Eastern & Oriental Express
Singapore • Kuala Lumpur • Butterworth • Kwai • Bangkok

Venice Simplon–
Orient-Express

BRIENZER
ROTHORN

TEN BEST
~CATHEDRALS~

Regardless of your own spirituality, the great cathedrals are historic and architectural achievements you'll find fascinating to explore.

1 – ST. PAUL'S CATHEDRAL
London, England

Designed by Sir Christopher Wren to replace a church destroyed in the Great Fire of 1666, St. Paul's is one of the world's most famous cathedrals. Built in a mere 35 years, the baroque-syle church reveals inspiration and craftsmanship on a grand scale. Among its many treasures are mosaics from the Victorian Age, the Whispering Gallery, and numerous carvings and statues.

2 – NOTRE-DAME DE PARIS
Paris, France

Notre-Dame de Paris, a spectacular example of Gothic architecture, is another of the world's finest cathedrals. Begun in 1163, the cathedral took more than 200 years to complete. No expense was spared to create an edifice that reflected the Church's rising power—from the spectacular rose windows to the soaring flying buttresses to the intricately carved gargoyles.

3 – HAGIA SOPHIA
Istanbul, Turkey

Originally a Byzantine church built in the sixth century, the Hagia Sophia served as a mosque for more than four centuries after the Ottoman conquest in 1453. Many people consider Hagia Sophia the supreme masterpiece of Byzantine architecture. Much of the gilding has faded, but the original church's grandeur still remains in its vast proportions, wall paintings, and mosaics.

4 – ROUEN CATHEDRAL
Rouen, France

Begun in the 12th century and finished several centuries later, Rouen's Cathedral displays with great majesty the evolution of Gothic architecture. Nineteenth-century Impressionist Claude Monet immortalized the West Facade, a confection of stone detailing and 70 statues, in several of his works.

5 – CHARTRES CATHEDRAL
Chartres, France

Chartres Cathedral (1194–1260) is quite possibly the most beautiful expression of Gothic architecture in all of Europe. This masterpiece contains superb stained-glass windows—many of which are original to the 12th and 13th centuries—and wonderfully preserved statuary. Built on the site of a Romanesque church, the cathedral incorporates elements of the earlier church in the west portal. The mismatched towers on the west facade resulted after the north tower burned down. The banks of the Eure River provide magnificent views of the copper-roofed cathedral.

CATHEDRALS

6 – REIMS CATHEDRAL
Reims, France

Harmonious, monumental, and richly adorned, the Cathédrale Notre-Dame (1211–1311) in Reims is magnificent. Taking its cue from a contemporary, Notre-Dame exhibits the same quadripartite rib vaulting, three-story elevation, and pier structure found in Chartres Cathedral. The cathedral witnessed and ordained the coronation of several kings. The last, that of Charles X, was in 1825.

7 – SANTA MARIA DEL FIORE
Florence, Italy

Although more commonly known as the Duomo, the cathedral in Florence formally bears the name Santa Maria del Fiore—Saint Mary of the Flower, which refers to the lily, the symbol of Florence. The cathedral, designed by Arnolfo di Cambio in 1294 to rival the magnificence of the new cathedrals in Pisa and Siena, is unquestionably beautiful. Brunelleschi, a master of Renaissance architecture, designed and oversaw the construction of the famed dome.

8 – CANTERBURY CATHEDRAL
Canterbury, England

St. Augustine founded the first Canterbury Cathedral in 597; however, the oldest part of the present cathedral—the crypt—dates back only to the 11th century. Over time the cathedral acquired a 12th-century Gothic quire, a 14th- to 15th-century nave, and additions constructed in the uniquely English perpendicular Gothic style. In medieval times, the cathedral was an important pilgrimage site. Notable tombs within the cathedral include King Henry IV and Edward the Black Prince. Trinity Chapel memorializes Thomas Becket, the archbishop who was killed here in 1170. The cathedral sits amid the remains of a monastery, cloisters, a chapter house, and a Norman water tower.

9 – ST. SOPHIA CATHEDRAL
Novgorod, Russia

Dedicated in 1037, St. Sophia Cathedral was commissioned by Prince Yaroslav the Wise. Byzantine in layout and design, St. Sophia sits inside Novgorod's Kremlin walls; it was the spiritual heart of the early Rus state and is still regarded as a treasure and a symbol of Novgorod. The cathedral's gold dome denotes its importance. None of the other cathedrals in Novgorod have gold domes. The exquisite 12th-century bronze gate of the west entrance, used only on select occasions, was brought back from Sigtuna, then the capital of Sweden.

10 – ST. JOHN THE DIVINE
New York City, New York

Rising above Morningside Heights just north of Central Park, the Cathedral Church of St. John the Divine is a stunning masterpiece of medieval-style architecture against the backdrop of one of the world's most modern cities. The interior is Romanesque with Byzantine overtones; the exterior has Gothic touches. The spectacular nave is 86.5 meters (284 feet) long and 39 meters (124 feet) high. Work began in 1892 and is ongoing to this day.

Ten Best
~Landmarks~

1 – Great Wall of China, China

Built about 2000 years ago, the Great Wall zigzags 6,700 kilometers (4,163 miles) across northern China, dotting mountains, plains, grasslands, deserts, and plateaus like the spines on a dragon's back. Many sections are now in ruins or have completely disappeared (pieces are often carted off as a source of stone for local houses and roads), but enough exists to remain a formidable sight.

The wall began as a series of independent walls erected within different states in northern China—notably Yan and Zhao—to protect themselves against warring factions. Great armies of soldiers, prisoners, and local people were conscripted to build the walls, with repairing and extensions carried out as needed. After China became unified under the Qin dynasty in 256 B.C., Emperor Qin Shihuang ordered that the separate walls be joined together as one defensive battlement against the Huns, invading from the north. Ever since, the Great Wall has been been a symbol of Chinese unity and architecture.

The crenellated wall averages 8 meters (25 feet) high and 6 meters (18 feet) wide. Guard houses and signal towers are located at regular intervals. The most accessible section is at Badaling, a 2-hour trip from Beijing. If you have the time, the Mutianyu section, 70 kilometers (45 miles) northeast of Beijing, is even better preserved.

2 – Taj Mahal, India

Most travelers call the Taj Mahal the world's most beautiful building. It has perfect symmetry, and the hue of its white marble varies from hour to hour, season to season. Two of the most sublime times to view the Taj Mahal are at sunset and during a full moon.

Shah Jahan, fifth Mughal emperor, commissioned the Taj Mahal in 1631 in memory of his second wife, Mumtaz Mahal, a Persian princess, as a tribute to his enduring love. A tree-lined reflecting pool fronts the monument, and tall minarets at the four corners of the raised terrace help complete this work of architectural and artistic genius.

3 – Eiffel Tower, France

The all-metal Eiffel Tower, bearing the name of its designer, Gustave Eiffel, was erected for the Paris Exhibition of 1889. Soaring 300 meters (984 feet) high, this masterpiece of engineering instantly became the world's tallest man-made structure, breaking the record held for more than 40 centuries by the Pyramid of Khufu at Giza in Egypt. Critics deplored the tower, declaring it a blight on the Parisian skyline, but the general public loved it. Today, millions of people visit the Eiffel Tower each year to enjoy the 360-degree view it affords of Paris. An elevator takes visitors to the top; on a clear day, the countryside can be seen 64 kilometers (40 miles) away.

4 – THE KREMLIN, RUSSIA

This historic fortress-palace, from which the tsars ruled the expanse of Russia, is matched in size only by the Forbidden City in China. High defensive walls punctuated with a series of 17 strategic towers completely enclose the Kremlin ("citadel"), encompassing 27.5 hectares (68 acres). The 70-meter (230-feet) Savior Tower, built in 1491, dominates the Kremlin skyline. Inside, ornate buildings—palaces, government centers, churches—collectively make the Kremlin an architectural masterpiece. Three cathedrals, including St. Sophia, a fine example of Byzantine architecture, cluster around the Kremlin's main square.

5 – ACROPOLIS, GREECE

The Acropolis ("high city") is a mammoth, steep-sided rock outcropping overlooking Athens, Greece, that is home to the ruins of a complex conceived and built by Athenian statesman Pericles in the fifth century B.C. Open-air theaters line the base and slopes of the Acropolis; on its summit, temples and statues are found. The focal point of the Acropolis, however, is the stunning Parthenon ("a virgin's dwelling"), a temple dedicated to Athena, the city's protecting goddess.

6 – POMPEII, ITALY

The ancient Roman city of Pompeii lay hidden and forgotten under volcanic waste for more than 1,500 years before archaeological excavations slowly began to unearth it. On August 24, A.D. 79, Mt. Vesuvius erupted in a cataclysm so violent that the mountain literally blew up. The explosions sent billowing columns of volcanic steam, cinders, and ash high into the sky, then showered and buried the once thriving city. Most of the 20,000 citizens escaped with their lives. However, a few thousand lingered too long and did not survive the toxic fumes. Archaeologists have revealed many of Pompeii's streets, temples, theaters, homes, public baths, wall murals, and floor mosaics, reconstructing a fascinating history of Roman life.

7 – YELLOWSTONE NATIONAL PARK, UNITED STATES

Some 600,000 years ago a massive volcanic eruption from the center of what is now Yellowstone National Park spewed an immense volume of ash over the western United States, much of the Midwest, northern Mexico, and some areas of the eastern Pacific. The eruption left a caldera, a collapsed crater, 48 kilometers (30 miles) wide by 72.5 kilometers (45 miles) long.

In 1872, President Ulysses S. Grant signed a law declaring that Yellowstone would forever be "dedicated and set apart as a public park or pleasuring ground for the benefit and enjoyment of the people." It became the world's first national park.

The park has hundreds of geysers. Old Faithful, named for its regularity, erupts approximately every hour. Other Yellowstone geothermal features include bubbling mud

pools, hot springs, colorful limestone terraces, and steam spouting fumaroles. The national park also protects a unique ecosystem that is home to a wealth of flora and fauna, including iconic Rocky Mountain wildlife such as grizzly bears, buffalo, wolves, and elk.

8 – STONEHENGE, ENGLAND

Stonehenge is a prehistoric site of megaliths arranged in concentric circles—the largest being 33 meters (108 feet) in diameter—and horseshoe patterns. These standing stones measure up to 6 meters (21 feet) high and weigh as much as 50,000 kilograms (110,231 pounds). Studies reveal that the stones came from faraway mountains. Latest scientific estimates say Stonehenge was built in stages between 3000 and 1500 B.C. Why and how the stones came to be erected on Salisbury Plain remains a mystery. Some speculate Stonehenge was an astronomical calendar; others believe it was used for religious ceremonies. The once popular theory that Stonehenge was created by the Druids, the Celtic priesthood, was disproved when science found that it had been built at least a thousand years before the Druids.

9 – THE PYRAMIDS OF GIZA, EGYPT

The question of who built the pyramids, and how, has long been debated by Egyptologists and historians. Standing at the base of the pyramids at Giza, it is hard to believe that any of these monuments could have been built in one pharaoh's lifetime. The accounts of Herodotus, the fifth century B.C. Greek historian, suggest that the labor force totaled more than 100,000 people. Modern Egyptologists believe the real number is closer to 20,000.

The three great pyramids—tombs for Pharaohs Khufu, Khefre, and Menkaure—are massive (the pyramid of Khufu ranked as the tallest man-made structure for more than 40 centuries). Each stone in the pyramids weighs more than

two tons. The Sphinx, which embodies the body of a lion and the head of a pharaoh, is believed to be the head of Khefre and the guardian spirit for his entire burial complex.

The 1908 edition of *Baedeker's Egypt* warns: "Travelers who are in the slightest degree predisposed to apoplectic or fainting fits, and ladies travelling alone, should not attempt to penetrate into these stifling recesses."

10 – PETRONAS TWIN TOWERS, MALAYSIA

Although no longer the titleholder to "world's tallest building," the Petronas Twin Towers, completed in 1997 and measuring 452 meters (1,483 feet) high, still retain their visually dramatic design, courtesy of U. S. architect Cesar Pelli. They can be appreciated easily from all directions. Halfway up the buildings, a 58-meter (192-feet) twin-tier sky bridge dramatically connects the structures on the 41st and 42nd floors.

TEN BEST
~CRUISES~

With hundreds of cruises to choose from, selecting ten favorite itineraries or cruise lines was difficult. Our list contains both the expected and the unexpected—from tranquil river journeys to open sea voyages, from sailing ships to giant ocean liners.

1 – NILE CRUISES IN EGYPT
www.sonesta.com

As you cruise down the storied Nile in Egypt, you pass tiny minaretted villages, fields tended by white-galabiya-dressed farmers, groves of date palms, and feluccas sailing into

the sunset. The dreamlike reality of the cruise is all that you had imagined, presenting a timeless picture of Egypt's culture and history.

More than 200 "floating hotels" operate on the Nile, offering cruises that range in length from four to eight days. Each has multilingual guides to provide informative commentary on the history, religion, and social customs of ancient Egypt. The itineraries vary, but many stop at the temples of Karnak and Luxor on the east bank and the great complex of temples and tombs that includes the Valley of the Kings on the west bank. Additional stops may include the Aswan High Dam, the submerged Temple of Philae, the austere tomb of the Aga Khan, and the Ptolemaic temples of Esna, Edfu, and Kom Omb.

2 – SEA CLOUD
Tel: 201-884-0407
www.seacloud.com

When all sails are unfurled, the four-masted *Sea Cloud* is a wonder to behold on the open sea. This elegant windjammer sails the Caribbean in winter and the Mediterranean in summer, offering enthusiasts the opportunity to experience the same ambiance that Franklin D. Roosevelt, Winston Churchill, the Duke and Duchess of York, and numerous other royals and moguls once did.

Fully restored to its original 1930s grandeur—handcrafted details, antique furnishings, marble appointments, wood paneling, and more—the ship is exquisite from bow to stern. In the lounge, a six-armed chandelier and wall sconces crowned by eagles illuminate comfortable seats, a bar, well-stocked bookcases, and a grand piano. Passengers may stay in one of the eight original cabins, luxurious staterooms with breathtaking facilities and decor, or in one of the new cabins, equally comfortable but not as spacious.

While on board, guests may sunbathe, rest and relax, and attend lectures and yoga classes during the day, and watch live entertainment in the lounge in the evening. While in port, guests may sightsee, swim, snorkel, water ski, and windsurf.

Dress is elegantly casual, although the welcome dinner and the captain's farewell dinner are dressier affairs. Meals are four-star events prepared by gourmet chefs. Lunch and dinner come with complimentary wines.

The smart and stunning new *Sea Cloud II,* equally elegant but without the sense of history, sails the same routes.

3 – ROAD TO MANDALAY

Orient-Express: Trains & Cruises
Tel: 800-237-1236, www.orient-express.com

Few places on Earth remain untouched in their natural beauty and charm from one century to the next. The ancient land of Burma, however, now known as Myanmar, is an exception to the rule; and the *Road To Mandalay Orient-Express* brings you the best of this fascinating, unspoiled country. A three-, four-, or seven-day journey along the Ayeyarwady River is a voyage of a lifetime. From this mighty river, which runs the length of the country,

treasures can be admired that have for so long been hidden from the world's gaze.

With the comfort and personality for which the original *Orient-Express* is famous, the *Road To Mandalay* provides the most comfortable vantage point from which to absorb the surrounding serene beauty, taking in its golden-spired pagodas, ancient temples, sleepy riverside settlements, and saffron-clad monks.

Originally a Rhine cruiser built in 1964, the ship was completely stripped and refurbished in an elegant style that harmoniously combines modern design with traditional Burmese craftwork.

4 – THREE GORGES IN CHINA
Tel: 86-10-8152-8702
www.china-business-travel.com/packages

A cruise through the Three Gorges of the Yangzi River, the proper name for only the central part of China's longest river (third longest in the world), is an unforgettable journey of mist-shrouded mountains, terraced hillsides, and timeless beauty. In its entirety the river is called the Chang Jiang, which simply means "long river"; it rises in Tibet and flows all the way to Shanghai.

The Three Gorges Dam, scheduled to be completed in 2009, will almost completely inundate the famous gorges, turning them into shallow canyons in the hills just above the river. The water level has already risen some 130 meters

---

NORWEGIAN CRUISE LINE

Norwegian Cruise Line is a leader in the cruise boat industry. Its latest innovation is freestyle cruising—a revolutionary level of service that eases the disembarkation process, decreases the steward-to-passenger-ratio, and provides guests the luxury of ten restaurants to choose from, Broadway style theaters, 24-hour fitness centers, world-class spas, Internet cafés, and casinos with the newest slots and table games afloat. The *Norwegian Dawn, Norwegian Spirit, Norwegian Star,* and *Norwegian Sun* all meet NCL's criteria for freestyle cruising. Destinations include Bermuda, Alaska, the Caribbean, the Hawaiian Islands, and the New England and Canadian coasts.

CRUISES

"The great difference between voyages rests not with the ships, but with the people you meet on them."

—Amelia E. Barr

(426 feet), and is expected to rise another 45 meters (147 feet), but the trip is still a fabulous experience. The M.S. *East King* and *East Queen* are two of the best cruise ships operating the run.

5 – CRYSTAL CRUISES
Tel: 800-446-6620, www.crystalcruises.com

The cruise ships *Crystal Harmony, Crystal Symphony,* and *Crystal Serenity* are virtual resort hotels at sea, amply fulfilling Crystal Cruises' mission to provide the best and most elegant large cruise-ship experience possible.

The ships are among the most spacious in their class and offer distinctive accommodations that bring to mind well-furnished luxury penthouses, complete with European-trained butlers and complimentary daily hors d'oeuvres. The newer *Symphony* features all-outside staterooms and was the first large luxury ship to have private verandas or large picture windows in every cabin. Both ships provide guests with a choice of dining options: Asian and Italian restaurants as well as the fine Crystal Dining Rooms.

The *Harmony* cruises around South America, the Caribbean, the Mexican Riviera, Alaska, New England, and Canada, among many destinations; the *Symphony's*

itineraries include a world cruise, Europe, Africa, and the Panama Canal; and the *Serenity* makes trans-oceanic crossings and cruises the South Pacific.

6 – SEABOURN CRUISE LINE
Tel: 800-929-9391, www.seabourn.com

Seabourn Cruise Line sets a very high standard. Its three full-size vessels—*Seabourn Pride, Seabourn Legend,* and *Seabourn Spirit*—carry 200 guests in elegant onboard cabins, providing them with memorable service. The staff quickly learns your likes and dislikes by keeping a dossier of information on each passenger. Seabourn's little touches keep guests returning year after year. The ships call at ports around the world. A professional golf escort accompanies the Signature Golf cruises.

7 – STAR CLIPPERS
Tel: 800-442-0551, www.starclippers.com

Of all the many fine ships cruising the oceans, we've had some of our most memorable experiences sailing the three ships of the Star Clipper line. On these four- to five-masted vessels, which operate under the flag of Luxembourg, you cruise under sail virtually all the time. On deck, the only concession to the 21st century is the electric winch that

Sail Away

helps hoist the sails. Watching the ship leave her anchorage and silently unfurl as many as 20 sails from her masts soaring more than 200 feet into the sky is an awesome sight.

There are three Star Clipper ships. *Star Flyer* and *Star Clipper* are identical and carry 170 passengers each; the *Royal Clipper* carries 227 passengers and is the largest fully rigged sailing ship in the world. The smaller ships offer an experience closer in feeling to Clipper history.

The air-conditioned public rooms and cabins have nautical art and fixtures and are resplendent in brass, mahogany, and teak. Cabins are small, but as the cruises are very informal, little storage space is needed. Bathrooms are spotless. The ships' officers and enthusiastic young crews from around the world are thoughtful and professional. The food and food service are surprisingly good. All meals are open seating; breakfast and lunch is buffet style, and there's an à la carte menu.

Star Clippers sail to destinations in the Caribbean, Mediterranean, and Far East. If the winds are right, the ship spends each day under sail; at anchor passengers can sightsee, water ski, windsurf, snorkel, and scuba dive.

8 – WINDSTAR CRUISES
Tel: 800-544-0443, www.windstar.com

With the best crew and nicest staff around, the Windstar luxury yachts sail under the appropriate tag line "180° From Ordinary." Officially designated motor-sail-yachts, the vessels' unique rigging allows the sails to furl and unfurl at the touch of a button.

Windstar's unique concept in sailing—casual yet elegant, traditional yet modern—has has catapulted it to the top of the cruise industry in the luxury small ship, casual attire, and alternative dining arenas.

Elegant touches include teak decking and intimate surroundings adorned with rich wood paneling and eclectic

QUEEN MARY 2

Tel: 800-728-6273, www.cunard.com

With the maiden voyage of *Queen Mary 2* on January 12, 2004, Cunard further obscured the already fuzzy distinction between crossing and cruising; it has launched the largest ship that does both. If you long to relive the days when people "crossed the pond" on a proper ocean liner, find a different ship. If it's uncompromising luxury you seek, the *Queen Mary 2* is the ship for you. It is a handsome $800-million hybrid leviathan that is more floating resort than liner or cruise ship.

The gleaming white ship is 345 meters (1,132 feet) in length and is capable of carrying 2,620 passengers. The British Cunard officers, headed by white-bearded Commodore Ronald Warwick, epaulets and all, are a vestige of the golden age of ocean crossings. The 1,253 staff and crew provide exceptional service.

artwork. The attentive service staff and conscientious crew are consummate professionals.

Gourmet chefs prepare sumptuous repasts that include light and vegetarian menu selections and are accompanied by an extensive wine list. And unusually, passengers are invited to visit the bridge whenever they please.

When it comes to accommodations, comfort is the name of the game: All staterooms and suites offer ocean views, sitting area, new LCD flat screen TV, DVD, CD player, safe, mini-bar/refrigerator, international direct-dial phones, bathroom with luxurious pampering toiletries, hair dryer, plush terrycloth robes, and an abundance of closet space. The relatively intimate size of the three Windstar ships—they carry just 148 to 308 guests—creates a casual private-yacht-like atmosphere, encouraging passengers to meet their fellow sailors and establish lasting friendships.

At each port of call, passengers may join a shore excursion—visiting an archaeological dig, a winery, a local market—or partake of complimentary water sports activities off the Water Sports Platform: water skiing, windsurfing, snorkeling, kayaking.

Windstar sailing yachts cruise to more than 47 countries worldwide.

9 – SILVERSEA CRUISES
Tel: 800-774-9996 or 44-(0)-870-333-7030
www.silversea.com

The outstanding *Silver Wind* and *Silver Cloud* are tops in their class. These first two ships in Silversea Cruises' fleet are classified as "small" ships, which means that they can get into harbors that are inaccessible to larger vessels. Twin images of each other, *Silver Wind* and *Silver Cloud* each has a maximum capacity of 296 passengers in double accommodations (the newer *Silver Shadow* and *Silver Whisper* carry 388 passengers).

The smallest accommodation on either *Silver Cloud* or *Silver Wind* is a spacious suite with a large window. Other suites have at least one private veranda, and the five largest suites have double balconies and whirlpool tubs in the bathrooms. The dining room has no fixed seating arrangement. Lunch and breakfast are also served in the Terrace Café, where you can

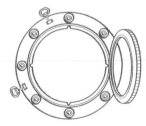

enjoy the view over the aft end of the ship. In addition, 24-hour room service is available. The food is excellent. The ships, built in Genoa, are Italian-owned, and the maritime staff is Italian. Service staff is mainly European, with many Scandinavian and British crew members.

On each cruise, Silversea management invites its passengers to participate in a complimentary "Silversea Experience," the idea being to provide guests with various entertainments they could not find or obtain for themselves. In Mykonos, a village street was blocked off and a street party held that included a buffet, dancing, and music. In Norway, guests were invited aboard deep-sea boats for fishing well above the Arctic Circle. And in St. Petersburg, they sipped champagne and ate caviar in beautiful turn-of-the-century rooms of the Army Palace and were entertained by a private performance of *Giselle*.

10 – RADISSON SEVEN SEAS
Tel: 800-477-7500 or 800-285-1835
www.rssc.com

The result of a 1994 merger between Radisson Cruises and Seven Seas Cruise Line, Radisson Seven Seas historically had one of the most interesting mixes of ships in the luxury cruise market and is the only luxury line to visit all of the continents and both polar regions.

The *Seven Seas Navigator, Seven Seas Mariner,* and *Seven Seas Voyager* offer a luxury cruise with enough different touches that each has its own personality. The *Explorer II* is noteworthy for its biannual visit to Antarctica.

THE ROYAL YACHT BRITANNIA

The *Royal Yacht Britannia* is one of the world's most famous ships. The *Royal Yacht* proudly served Queen and country for 44 years. During that time *Britannia* carried the Queen and the Royal Family on 968 official voyages, from the remotest regions of the South Seas to the deepest divides of Antarctica.

The yacht is now moored in Edinburgh's historic port of Leith, and visitors can wander its five decks.

– The Royal Apartments

Hundreds of original items from the Royal Collection are on display. These include prints and paintings, the baby grand piano, furniture, silverware, and gifts given to the Queen from nations around the world.

– The Royal Bedrooms

The Queen and Duke of Edinburgh's sleeping quarters consist of two suites with an interconnecting door. Also open for view is the bedroom where Prince Charles, Princess Anne, Prince Andrew, and Princess Margaret all honeymooned.

– The Drawing Room

The elegant drawing room, with its chintz-covered sofas, deep armchairs, and luxurious Persian rugs, was used both for official functions and for private entertaining. The baby grand piano, sitting in the corner of the room, was firmly bolted to the deck and was regularly played by Princess

Diana, Princess Margaret, and Princess Alexandra.

– The State Dining Room

The state dining room is the largest and grandest room on the *Royal Yacht*. Throughout the 44 years of *Britannia*'s life it witnessed some spectacular banquets and played host to the rich, the famous, and the powerful. Sir Winston Churchill, Rajiv Ghandi, Nelson Mandela, Bill Clinton, Boris Yeltsin, Ronald Reagan, and Margaret Thatcher have all accepted the ultimate honor to dine at the table of Her Majesty the Queen aboard the *Royal Yacht*.

– The Bridge

Britannia's nerve centre was the bridge, which still retains its original 1950s appearance. As the command point of the *Royal Yacht*, it was one of the most important places on the ship. It was from the bridge that the officers navigated, issued orders, kept the log books, and planned and plotted every mile of the ship's progress.

Britannia is berthed at Ocean Terminal, Edinburgh's stylish new waterfront retail and leisure development. Majestic Tours depart regularly from Waverley Bridge in the center of Edinburgh. This tour will take you via the Modern Art Galleries and the Royal Botanic Gardens before arriving at Ocean Terminal for your tour of *Britannia*. Scot Rail offers an all-inclusive ticket to visit *Britannia*.

Ten Best
~Lakes, Canals, & Watery Wonders~

1 – Victoria Falls, Zimbabwe–Zambia

When the calm flowing water of the Zambezi River encounters the 1,700-meter-wide (5,578-foot) edge of the Victoria Falls gorge, it abruptly plunges 100 meters (328 feet) to the bottom. The impact generates soaring mists and thunderous sounds that can be seen and heard for great distances. During the rainy season—mid-November through late April—the falls virtually disappear behind a thick wall of mist; at other times, the water volume noticeably eases.

2 – Canals of Venice, Italy

Best enjoyed outside the heat of summer, the Venetian canals and their gondolas provide one of the world's most romantic experiences: gliding slowly down narrow palazzo-lined canals on a moonlit night. Venice is a city built on water. The canals—some 150 of them—link nearly 700 tiny islands to make what seems a floating city. Everyone must travel by foot or boat, visitors and locals alike. The 3-kilometer-long (nearly 2-mile-) Grand Canal, the main water thoroughfare, is lined by luxurious, centuries-old palazzos with ornate Renaissance-style facades and is spanned by the elaborately designed Rialto Bridge. When the distance is far, the swift vaporettos (water taxis or busses) are handy.

The Victoria Falls Hotel

KNOWN TO TRAVELLERS OF THE WORLD

3 – Great Barrier Reef, Australia

The Great Barrier Reef stretches 2,000 kilometers (1,200 miles) through the Coral Sea along Australia's northeastern coast. The reef, which in actuality is a collection of thousands of distinct coral reefs, has been designated a World Heritage site for its sheer beauty and uniquely complex and delicate ecosystem. More than 10,000 species, including 1,500 types of fish and 200 kinds of birds, live on the reef's cays, atolls, and islands. The beauty of the fish and coral waterscapes annually draws hundreds of thousands of visitors who come to see the spectacle by diving, snorkeling, and glass-bottom boating. Conservationists fear that the large influx of visitors and their collateral effect on pollution are damaging the very natural wonder that people come to celebrate.

4 – Li River, China

The 83-kilometer (51-mile) stretch of the Li River between Guilin and Yangshuo cities in China has inspired writers and artists for thousands of years. Here the Li River snakes through a fairy-tale landscape of conical limestone peaks, its smooth waters exquisitely mirroring the magical scenery. The vistas are particularly enchanting when flowing mists weave themselves around the peaks, hiding them and then exposing them in moments of surprise. The mountains are vestiges of ancient eroded seabeds that support graceful bamboo groves and terraced rice paddies. Each bend of the river reveals something new and interesting to see, from lumbering water buffalo pulling carts or cooling off in the river to fishermen gliding on narrow bamboo rafts.

5 – SUEZ CANAL, EGYPT

An idea born of the British Empire's colonial interests, the 160-kilometer-long (100-mile-) Suez Canal connects the Mediterranean Sea with the Red Sea. Thousands of men labored ten years (1859–1869) to build this shortcut from the Mediterranean to the vast waters of Asia, and vice versa. Without it, a cargo ship sailing from Italy to Singapore had to go around the southern tip of Africa, doubling the time and distance. Today, an endless parade of supertankers, container ships, and other large oceangoing vessels stream along this blue ribbon that cuts through barren desert. If you stand back far enough from the canal banks, it appears as though the giant ships are gliding through dry desert sands in the middle of nowhere.

THRILL THERAPY IN NEW ZEALAND

SHOTOVER JET
Tel: 64-3-442-9361

The *Shotover Jet* in Queenstown provides the most famous jet boat ride in New Zealand. It races through the spectacular deep canyons of the Shotover River at speeds designed to take your breath away.

As the *Shotover Jet* skims around crags, boulders blur in your peripheral vision and water sprays up with every turn. Occasionally the driver spins the boat around its own length for the trademark *Shotover Jet* 360-degree spin! The thrilling ride fills you with a sense of euphoria and well being, your brain receiving a welcome cocktail of oxygen and endorphins.

DART RIVER JET
Tel: 64-3-442-9992

The Dart River Jet Boat Safari combines thrill-seeking with rich local history. It travels through a stunning World Heritage area, past towering peaks, glaciers, and ancient forests. There are two options: a two-hour boat ride that includes a short walk through the greenest land on Earth, or a boat ride plus a four-wheel-drive ride. The guides are knowledgeable about this area, which is revered by Maori.

Except in summer, all boat rides can be extremely chilly. Bring warm clothing and sunglasses that fit well.

6 – LAKE COMO, ITALY

Thousands and thousands of years ago, glaciers carved the peaks and valley of the Alps. Those same glaciers formed the pre-Alpine lakes of the Lombard region some 48 kilometers (30 miles) north of Milan. Scenic Lake Como, with its deep blue waters, has long been known as "the looking glass of Venus." Vistas of the lake reveal a serene scene surrounded by palatial villas, tree-clad mountains, and quaint villages. A major lake of the country, Lake Como covers 146 square kilometers (56 square miles) and reaches a depth of 414 meters (1,358 feet) between Careno and Argegno.

7 – LAKE BAIKAL, RUSSIA

Home to 20 percent of the world's total unfrozen freshwater reserves, Lake Baikal in southeast Siberia is the largest and oldest (25 million years old) lake in the world. At 1,700 meters (5,578 feet) it is also the deepest. Its age and isolation have produced one of the world's richest and most unusual environments for freshwater fauna, earning it the nickname "Galapagos of Russia." Scientists study Lake Baikal to better understand evolutionary science.

Surrounded by forested shores and the jagged and snow-clad peaks of the Barguzin Mountains, Lake Baikal presents a picture of supreme beauty. In the winter, it freezes over with ice so thick that the Trans-Siberian Railway briefly run trains over its surface. In the summer, its ice-cold, crystalline blue waters are transparent to a depth of 40 meters (131 feet), and colorful wildflowers bloom along its shores.

8 – NILE RIVER, EGYPT

The storied past of the longest river in the world entices many people to cruise its length as it winds through Egypt. "Floating hotels," some reminiscent of dhows, glide smoothly past timeless Egyptian life-scenes unfolding along the date-palm-tree-dotted riverbanks.

9 – BORA BORA, SOUTH PACIFIC

The Polynesian island of Bora Bora in the South Pacific is widely suggested as the world's most beautiful island. A tropical blue lagoon ringed by coral reefs encircles the island, which is crowned by a rugged 727-meter-high (2,385-feet) volcano core draped with tropical foliage. Snorkelers and skin divers love Bora Bora for its warm waters and plentiful sea fauna. Sunbathers delight in the white-sand beaches.

10 – DEAD SEA, ISRAEL

The Dead Sea, shared by Israel and Jordan, is the lowest spot on Earth. Its shoreline is about 400 meters (1,300 feet) below sea level. As the world's saltiest large body of water, averaging a salt content six times higher than that of the ocean, it supports no life. With no outlet, the water that flows into the Dead Sea evaporates in the hot, arid air, leaving the minerals. The Jordan River is the chief source of the incoming water, but since the 1960s much of its water has been diverted for irrigation. Its length has already shrunk by more than a third, and, while the sea will never entirely disappear, because evaporation slows down as surface area decreases and saltiness increases, the Dead Sea as we know it could become a thing of the past.

TEN BEST
~DRIVES~

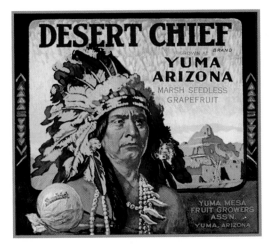

The Big Sur coast in California, the Pyrenees from San Sebastian to Madrid, and other delightful excursions make our top ten drives. Harry Marks of Askmen.com searched out the best of the North American drives, while other correspondents reported on exhilarating and romantic drives in Europe.

1 – PACIFIC HIGHWAY 1, CALIFORNIA
San Luis Obispo to Monterey

California's Route 1 runs nearly the entire length of the state's west coast. The section between San Luis Obispo and Monterey ranks among the best scenic drives in the world. The twists and turns high above the Pacific Ocean make for fun, albeit dangerous, driving. The highway enters dark redwood-forested canyons and passes through sunny grasslands and oak woodlands, with view after dramatic view of land meeting sea. Appealing stops include the Museum of Natural History in Morro Bay State Park and William Randolph Hearst's mansion near San Simeon; romantic inns abound, beckoning you to stay the night in this enchanted land.

2 – ROUTE 93, CANADA AND UNITED STATES
Jasper National Park, Alberta, Canada to Sonora Desert, Arizona

For a truly unforgettable journey, follow Route 93 south out of Jasper National Park in the heart of the Canadian Rockies and head all the way to its terminus deep in the Arizona desert. There's no shortage of spectacular panoramas and roadside stops on this trek. The Canadian mountains and ice fields give way to the Montana valleys before the road meets the harsh terrain of Idaho's Sun Valley and Nevada's desert landscape. This isolated stretch of the highway takes an abrupt shift into Las Vegas before crossing the Hoover Dam into Arizona. Some highlights: Snake River Canyon, Bonneville Salt Flats, the bright lights of Las Vegas.

3 – HIGHWAY 362, QUEBEC, CANADA
Quebec City to Charlevoix

Most people driving east out of Quebec City will take Highway 138, but those in the know will opt for 362. This route is significantly slower, but the astounding scenery along the way will make the drive seem all too brief. The 59-kilometer (37 mile) trip to Charlevoix witnesses a dramatic metamorphosis in terrain as the Laurentian Mountains slope to meet the St. Lawrence River, and there are several parks where you can inspect the geography up close. Just outside Quebec City are the Montmorency Falls, and a bit farther east you'll find the enormous Shrine of Saint-Anne-de-Beaupré. Try to coordinate this trip with the changing of the autumn leaves, but make sure it's still warm enough to take advantage of the whale-watching trips that are offered in Charlevoix.

4 – DALTON HIGHWAY, ALASKA
Fairbanks to the Arctic Ocean

At Milepost 175 of the Dalton Highway (Alaska 11) lays the town of Coldfoot—your last glimpse of civilization before you hit Deadhorse, another 384 kilometers (240 miles) away. In addition to grabbing a hot meal and a few winks here, be sure to prepare an emergency kit that includes a toolbox, extra fuel, and at least two spare tires. The panoramas of the Arctic tundra and boreal forest can't be found anywhere else in the world.

5 – KANCAMAGUS HIGHWAY, NEW HAMPSHIRE
Lincoln to Conway

This east–west route through the White Mountains National Forest is only 54 kilometers (34 miles) long. The first ten miles rise 247 meters (811 feet) in elevation,

presenting visitors with a number of challenging curves and switchbacks along the way. The route's descent parallels the Swift River and leads to the historic towns of Albany and Conway, where picnic stops and hiking trails offer an opportunity to get out and stretch your legs. Anglers may want to stop a bit earlier at the Upper Greeley Pond, a fishing hole renowned for its abundance of speckled trout.

6 – ROUTE 100, VERMONT
Stamford to Newport

With only three stoplights over its 320 kilometers (200 miles) of curved concrete, Vermont 100 is a driver's paradise set within the beauty of the Green Mountain National Forest. This route was designed to hug the natural inclinations of the region's eastern valleys, and it is meticulously maintained year-round to keep traffic flowing to the many adjoining ski areas. Along with the lack of stoplights, there's another surprising absence along this route: fast-food franchises. Antique stores, inns, and fruit stands crop up along the roadside, and the towns of Plymouth and Stowe provide pleasant accommodations.

7 – NORTHERN SPAIN
A loop drive beginning in San Sebastian

From the spurs of the Pyrenees to the Galician Rias, the north of Spain offers the widest variety of scenery and culture in Iberia. The combination of its mild, humid climate, areas of untouched natural beauty, and historic villages, each with its own personality, makes for a romantic drive. A leisurely week-long excursion will allow you to discover rugged mountain scenery in the Picos de Europa and rural scenery, relaxing silence, and abundance of attractions in Cantabria, Asturias, and Galicia. The northern coast consists of magnificent beaches with cliffs of wild, breathtaking beauty.

Scenic Drives

DEUTSCHE BUNDESPOST BERLIN · FÜR DIE JUGEND 1982
60+30
ADLER-LIMOUSINE 1910

HOTEL DEL MONTE
Del·Monte·California

DEUTSCHE BUNDESPOST BERLIN · FÜR DIE JUGEND 1982
90+45
DKW F1 1931

DRIVES

8 – RHINE RIVER VALLEY, GERMANY
Mainz to Cologne

The 192-kilometer (120-mile) stretch of the beautiful, forested Rhine River Valley from Mainz to Cologne showcases the romance, lushness, and rich cultural offerings of a magical land. A network of small roads parallels the river; crisscrossing from side to side allows you to explore fairy-tale castles, magnificent cities, walled towns, medieval cobblestoned villages, vineyards, and the majestic Rhine.

Most of the castles—there are more than 35 along this stretch—date back to the 12th or 13th centuries. Their founders were feudal overlords, who built them with one aim in mind: to protect their lands. Medieval towns still encircled by turreted walls line the banks of the river, while church spires of small villages peek out above the forested slopes of the valley. History takes center stage at Remagen, where a fierce battle was fought for control of the bridge, and at Cologne, where the centuries-old cathedral stands as a magnificent example of High Gothic architecture.

9 – SOUTHERN HILLS OF ITALY
Bari to Roggiano

Rent a Ferrari and motor an east-to-west odyssey across the arch of Italy's boot, from the Adriatic coast to the Tyrrhenian coast, through Apulia, Basilicata, and Calabria—beautiful regions untrammeled by hordes of tourists. This journey of some 250 kilometers (155 miles) begins in Bari, a seaside resort, and then passes through a landscape dotted with ancient beehive-domed limestone dwellings, or *trulli*. The drive continues across rolling countryside to the troglodyte city of Matera, a World Heritage site. After visiting Greek, Roman, Byzantine, and Norman ruins, discover the wilds of Pollino Park and wander the beaches of Cilento Peninsula, which juts into the Tyrrhenian Sea. Make the journey as short or as long as you like.

10 – THE RING OF KERRY, IRELAND
A loop drive beginning in Killarney

Ten thousand years ago, during the last ice age, glaciers carved the spectacular landscape of County Kerry. The Ring of Kerry, a 176-kilometer (110-mile) loop around Ireland's famous Iveragh Peninsula, offers vistas to stir the soul.

The loop is made up of narrow, twisty roads that are used by tour buses, cars, tractors, and donkey carts alike. Sights along the way include Killorglin, a pretty little town on the River Laune, peat bogs, Dingle Bay, flocks of sheep, breathtaking views from Coomakesta Pass, and the Gap of Dunloe. In the middle of the ring stand the mountains of MacGillycuddy's Reeks.

TEN BEST
~AIRLINES~

Around-the-world pass on American Airlines or straight to Singapore? Our correspondents, logging in over a million miles a year, have chosen whose skies are friendliest. We list them in random order.

1 – BRITISH AIRWAYS
www.britishairways.com

British Airways, the second largest international airline, carries more than 34 million passengers annually. As one of the world's longest established airlines, it has always been regarded as an industry-leader. British Airways realizes that a journey is more than just a flight. They aim to provide the best travel experience, from booking to boarding, take-off to landing. British Airways consistently serves the best of world cuisine, finding inspiration from culinary circles, trends, fashion, and art and then adapts these for delivery and presentation in an aircraft environment. The airline's main operating bases are both outside of London: Heathrow, the world's largest international airport, and Gatwick.

2 – CATHAY PACIFIC AIRWAYS
www.cathaypacific.com

Based in Hong Kong, one of the world's most dynamic cities, Cathay Pacific impressively offers service to more than 85 destinations worldwide. Cathay Pacific pays attention to every little detail—from the ground to 9,150 meters (30,000 feet) in the air—to make your flight as enjoyable as possible. The airline has won many awards, including those for service, safety, and business innovation. It was named Airline of the Year in 2005, and ranked No. 1 first-class lounge and business lounge that same year.

3 – THAI AIRWAYS INTERNATIONAL
www.thaiairways.com

From the fabled efficient and friendly service on the ground and in the air to the clean airplanes, flying on Thai Airways International always exceeds one's expectations. The national carrier of the Kingdom of Thailand, Thai Airways operates domestic, regional, and intercontinental flights from its home base in Bangkok. A jury of 300 selected travel consultants worldwide awarded Thai Airways the "Grand Travel Award 2005," for meeting the criteria of "best full-service product and service before, during, and after travel."

4 – VIRGIN ATLANTIC AIRWAYS
www.virgin-atlantic.com

Richard Branson announced to the world in 1984 that a high-quality, value-for-money airline would begin operating within three months. He pulled it off: Three months, some licenses, staff, and an aircraft packed with celebrities later, Virgin Atlantic Airways was born. By 1990 the airline had flown more than a million passengers and was the first airline to offer individual TVs to their business-class passengers. Today, the company continues to be an innovator in airline amenities, offering a super economy service and introducing the longest flat beds in its upper class sections for long-haul flights. The carrier now offers regular service to 25 destinations worldwide.

5 – MALAYSIA AIRLINES

www.malaysiaairlines.com

The award-winning Malaysia Airlines has a fleet of more than a hundred aircraft. It spreads its wings across six continents, servicing more than a hundred different destinations. Malaysia Airlines aims to provide a service that ranks among the best in terms of safety, comfort, and punctuality. It continues to set new world standards with their enhanced in-flight services, reliable ground support, and excellent infrastructure. Moreover, the warmth and friendliness of its staff distinguishes this above most other airlines, the satay appetizers are legendary, and the new reclining beds in business class are a perfect way to travel, not only trans-Pacific, but within Asia.

6 – JAPAN AIRLINES
www.jal.co.jp/en

As one has come to expect of a world-class airline, Japan Airlines (JAL) has embraced

the world's advancements in modern technology, launching interactive websites, introducing e-ticketing, and installing convenient self-service check-in systems at many airports, all in an effort to make flying with JAL a very convenient, efficient, and professional option. In the comfort arena, JAL has awarding-winning bed-style seats in first class and new 170-degree reclining seats in business class. JAL also invested 30 million dollars in state-of-the-art in-flight entertainment features, affording passengers an even more enjoyable travel experience. Although JAL epitomizes modern technology, the airline has never lost sight of two important assets: gracious service and a tradition of excellence.

7 – MIDWEST AIRLINES
www.midwestairlines.com

A small airline that flies only within the United States, Midwest Airlines offers its passengers wide leather seats, superior service, chocolate chip cookies baked onboard, and competitive fares. Their commitment to passenger service and comfort has earned them the reputation as "the best care in the air." Midwest Airlines doesn't neglect the budget-conscious either. Their Saver Service features low fares and extra legroom to some of your favorite vacation destinations. From its hub in Milwaukee, the airline offers nonstop jet service to major destinations in the Midwest and to select cities on the East and West Coasts.

FLYING THE CORAL ROUTE

The fondest memories of air travel come from the Coral Route, a journey that hopped across the islands of the South Pacific from Auckland, New Zealand, to Fiji, Samoa, Tahiti, and the Cook Islands. All those who flew it consider it the most romantic route in the world.

The Coral Route was established as a mail service flown by Tasman Empire Airways Limited (TEAL) in the 1930s. After World War II, thousands of superbly trained military pilots gave civilian aviation a new global experience. During the war, pilots from New Zealand had mastered the tide charts, currents, coral reefs, and lagoons of the South Pacific, as well as the art of aeronautical island-hopping. They saw an opportunity to capitalize on the new craze for luxury air travel. Eventually TEAL renamed itself Air New Zealand and in 1951 began offering a commercial service on the Coral Route to passengers, flying luxury Solent flying boats.

Each flying boat could carry about 45 passengers and had two decks, catered first-rate restaurants with silver service, and powder rooms. Travelers were mostly from the United States and Europe with the occasional celebrity, and the trips were considered very glamorous.

Travelers were accommodated in elegant colonial hotels, and were advised to carry their bathing suits as hand luggage so they could swim in a lagoon while the plane refueled. Flying over the boundless blue Pacific had a touch of daring, swashbuckling allure. Pilots were demigods. The attending hostesses were angels in nifty uniforms.

The service left Auckland in the morning, arriving mid-afternoon in Fiji. A fleet of stately black Daimlers and war-surplus Jeeps with surrey tops were on hand to ferry passengers to the Grand Pacific Hotel, a refined and elegant British colonial building on the waterfront. Passengers enjoyed afternoon tea, a nap, pink gin, and dinner, followed by billiards, with the ghost of Somerset Maugham in the saloon bar.

The next day they flew northeast to Samoa, to Aggie Grey's Hotel, met by Aggie herself, a woman who made her fortune cooking hamburgers for American troops and providing the model for Broadway's "Bloody Mary." Refreshed by a night of dancing and fine food, the passengers continued on to Tahiti, a stopover for artists and writers for centuries.

Another destination was Aitutaki in the Cook Islands. Occasionally, the flying boat was met by a small flotilla of canoes and boats that sailed passengers to an island feast.

Today, Air New Zealand is one of the finest airlines in the world, with aircraft jetting all around the globe, and of course, still flying the Coral Route.

8 – AMERICAN AIRLINES
www.aa.com

We like American Airlines and American Eagle, which strive to provide safe and dependable air transportation to their customers. They are dedicated to making every flight, taken for business or pleasure, something special. American is the largest scheduled passenger airline in the world and provides jet service to destinations throughout North America, the Caribbean, Latin America, Europe, and the Pacific, serving 172 cities with a fleet of 840 aircraft. In 2001, American carried more than 80 million passengers. Sundae May, AA's special service executive in Dallas-Ft. Worth, is the best in the business.

9 – JETBLUE AIRWAYS
www.jetblue.com

JetBlue, a successful low-fare airline based in New York City and offering service to a growing number of destinations, is known for providing a different kind of air travel experience. When JetBlue first began, just after the turn of the 21st century, it was met with the usual critics and their skepticism. Its goal: to bring a human touch back to air travel and to make flying more enjoyable. JetBlue screens employees rigorously, trains them well, and gives them the best tools, all of which together creates a staff of motivated and service-oriented people. JetBlue's fleet of new Airbus A320s, equipped with leather seats and DirectTV programming for every passenger, comes with a host of advantages, including reliability and efficiency.

10 – HAWAIIAN AIRLINES
www.hawaiianair.com

Delivering superior service since 1929, Hawaiian Airlines has made air travel an easy and positive experience. Customer comfort is of utmost importance, second only to its concern for passenger safety. In fact, this airline's reputation for safety and hospitality has few equals. Hawaiian Airlines employees receive rigorous training that reflects the company's commitment to service, both on the ground and in the air. Passengers laud the local cuisine, new aircraft, and overall value.

SIGN OF THE KANGAROO
www.Qantas.com

The Qantas story is inextricably linked with the development of civil aviation in Australia. It began with biplanes carrying one or two passengers in open cockpits.

In 1920 a few determined individuals overcame formidable obstacles to establish the Queensland and Northern Territory Aerial Services Ltd (Qantas). Supported by committed staff and customers, the airline continued to serve the nation during wartime and persevered to build an enterprise.

Today, Qantas is an outstanding long-distance carrier with a long roster of loyal passengers, and it holds an extraordinary safety record that is the envy of most other airlines.

TEN BEST
~SHOPPING AVENUES~

1 – BAHNHOFSTRASSE
Zürich, Switzerland

The Bahnhofstrasse, Zürich's resplendent, tree-lined exclusive shopping avenue, stretches 1.4 kilometers (1 mile). You'll find some of Switzerland's top shopping along its length, from top clothing designers to high-end options for shoes, furs, accessories, china, and jewelry. And, of course, Swiss watches.

2 – RODEO DRIVE
Beverly Hills, California

Rodeo Drive manages to pack in enough audacious glitz to qualify as one of the world's most glamorous and expensive shopping stretches. Just off Rodeo lies Two Rodeo, a strip of boutiques modeled after European boutiques, with cobblestones, fountains, and bistros. Perhaps its least-known amenity is the free two-hour valet parking.

3 – LAUGAVEGUR
Reykjavík, Iceland

Reykjavík's main shopping street hosts numerous clothing boutiques and an assortment of shops offering accessories, leather goods, cosmetics, lingerie, books, music, and the finest handmade knitwear and woolen goods. If you buy an outfit from one of the local fashion houses, rest assured it will be original.

4 – THE GINZA
Tokyo, Japan

The Ginza, comprising eight blocks, is Tokyo's most exclusive shopping area. It boasts some of the most expensive real estate on Earth. Known luxury and exclusive retailers stand side by side with Tokyo's landmark department stores, Mitsukoshi, Wako (whose clock is a landmark unto itself), and the 14-story Marion. The latter actually houses seven movie theaters and two department stores. Many store windows feature elaborate displays that showcase typical Japanese culture. At night colorful neon and fluorescent lights flood the Ginza with light, bringing the otherwise gray city to life.

5 – FIFTH AVENUE
New York City, New York

Large landmark department stores (Saks Fifth Avenue, Bergdorf Goodman, Macy's) and small high-end designer name boutiques (Ferragamo, Harry Winston, Versace, Emanuel Ungaro, Gucci, Henri Bendel, Tiffany, Steuben, Christian Dior) make New York's Fifth Avenue a shopper's paradise.

In December, the stores mount elaborate displays—doormen dressed as toy soldiers at FAO Schwarz, an 8-meter (27-foot) sparkling snowflake floating over the street outside Tiffany, winter wonderland scenes in Macy's windows—that attract holiday shoppers

and sightseers. Strolling the crowded sidewalks of Fifth Avenue at this time of year is a special treat.

6 – MAGNIFICENT MILE
Chicago, Illinois

Just a few blocks off Lake Michigan, North Michigan Avenue is home to such shopping greats as Brooks Brothers, Gucci, Lord & Taylor, Neiman Marcus, and Hermès, as well as Bigsby and Kruthers, both renowned local retailers. The crowds on the Magnificent Mile can be overwhelming on weekends.

7 – AVENUE MONTAIGNE
Paris, France

Avenue Montaigne, located in the "golden triangle" between the Champs Elysées and the Seine River, is the fanciest avenue in Paris. The fashionable and the well-monied shop in the myriad luxury boutiques—Bulgari and Louis Vuitton among them—and haute-couture houses—Emmanuel Ungaro, Guy Laroche, Christian Dior, Nina Ricci, and Chanel—that lie within the avenue's elegant buildings.

8 – AVINGUDA DIAGONAL
Barcelona, Spain

World-famous fashion houses, jewelers, and art galleries line the sweeping Avinguda Diagonal, which forms part of Barcelona's five-kilometer (3-mile) shopping line. Some of the finer shops are found on Passeig de Gràcia, Via Augusta, Carrer de Tuset, and the exclusive Avinguda Pau Casals—small, elegant streets just off Avinguda Diagonal. You will stroll through a mix of Gothic and modern architecture. The avenue has a pick of fun and fine cafés to stop in for tapas.

9 – VIA MONTE NAPOLEONE, VIA DELLA SPIGA, & GALLERIA VITTORIO EMANUELE
Milan, Italy

Milan is a fashion paradise and the center of style, with matching high price tags. In the Duomo area, Via Monte Napoleone, Via della Spiga, and the Galleria Vittorio Emanuele house elegant boutiques and posh cafés inside romantic landmark Victorian buildings.

In addition to the internationally known fine fashion names, the area has inside favorites, such as La Rinascente, Milan's most famous department store, 9 Peck, a renowned food store, and Provera, a favorite for its vintage wine selection. In the streets, there's always a parade of well-heeled Italians casually modeling the latest fashions.

10 – BOND STREET
London, England

Bond Street is home to the most elegant and expensive shops in London. You will find designer clothing, perfume, art and antiques, jewelers, and more Royal Warrant holders (suppliers to the royal family) here than anywhere else in London. Old Bond Street, the short section at the southern end of Bond Street that joins Piccadilly, has been distinguished by the very most posh since the 1850s. Asprey and Agnew, Sotheby's, and Phillips, to name but a few, all appear against a backdrop of elegant houses turned shops that once were home to a host of distinguished politicians, artists, and writers.

TEN BEST
~VISTAS~

1 – GRAND CANYON, ARIZONA

Our friend, noted photographer Gordon Parks, gives this advice when viewing the Grand Canyon: "Leave your binoculars at home." The biggest, most spectacular canyon on Earth, the Grand Canyon is 1.6 kilometers (1 mile) deep, 16 kilometers (10 miles) wide and covers 405,000 hectares (1 million acres). For starters, you'll find staggering views along the South Rim; take the Park Loop Drive, which has a number of exceptional lookout points.

2 – NIAGARA FALLS, UNITED STATES AND CANADA

Niagara Falls—actually three different falls flowing from the Niagara River— is one of the mightiest waterfalls on Earth, with 2,648,800 liters (700,000 gallons) of water washing over 56-meter (184-foot) cliffs each second. The best views are from the Canadian side, which takes in Horseshoe Falls and the smaller American Falls. After dark, the falls are illuminated with colored lights. The "Maid of the Mist" boat takes you right up to the base of the falls.

3 – SAN FRANCISCO BAY, CALIFORNIA

Beautiful San Francisco Bay is the world's largest deep-water harbor. The 60-story-high Golden Gate Bridge, the city's most famous landmark, guards the bay's Pacific Ocean entrance. A walkway offers easy access to the world-famous view back to the city, with the sailboat-dotted bay sparkling far below. An even better view awaits on the other side of the bridge, if you drive into the Marin Headlands and, from the Civil War fort, look out over the top of the giant, fog-swathed towers to the seemingly tiny city beyond.

4 – FLORENCE CITYSCAPE, ITALY

The Florence of Renaissance masters Leonardo da Vinci and Michelangelo remains much the same to this day. The massive yet refined 15th-century dome of the Duomo (the cathedral) dominates the tower-dotted skyline. The 360-degree view from the top of its dome is breathtaking. Other city-defining structures include the Palazzo Vecchio tower and the 14th-century shop-lined Ponte Vecchio. The hillside Piazzale Michelangelo lookout, across the Arno River, provides a splendidly classic view of Florence.

5 – THE WEST COAST OF IRELAND

Ireland's wild west coast, where the Atlantic crashes against high rugged cliffs, appears to stand outside of time. Eire's fabled green hills run right up to the cliffs, edged with fence rows and blooming lilacs and dotted with centuries-old keeps and thatch-roofed homes. Chances are, you'll probably spot a rainbow or two arcing over the land. You will discover one vista more spectacular than the next as you drive along the narrow country roads lacing this magical land.

6 – VERSAILLES, FRANCE

Louis XIV, the Sun King, nearly bankrupted France in adorning Versailles with the finest furnishings to impress his subjects and foreign dignitaries. Versailles was once home to thousands of nobles, bureaucrats, soldiers, and servants. The stables alone held 2,000 horses. Versailles's most renowned chamber is the Hall of Mirrors, so named because the light from the tall arched windows on one side of the room is reflected by the corresponding mirrors opposite. Fine art and chandeliers embellish the hall. The royal chapel and living quarters also define grandeur, as do the immense formal gardens adorned with statues and fountains.

7 – AMALFI COAST, ITALY

You'll find endless breathtaking coastal views on a visit to the Amalfi coast of southern Italy. Picturesque villages cling precariously to steep sea cliffs. During spring and summer bright-hued wildflowers bloom in profusion. The narrow and twisting 50-kilometer (30-mile) Amalfi Drive between Sorrento and Amalfi is inarguably the world's most beautiful and thrilling sightseeing road. Take care as you drive: The road has only occasional railings to keep your car from plunging onto the breaker-washed boulders far below. If you're a faint-hearted driver, you'll probably want to motor north, along the road's inner lane.

8 – THE SERENGETI, TANZANIA

Africa's Serengeti Migration is known as the greatest animal show on Earth. More than a million wild animals—gazelles, zebras, and other ungulates—blanket the Tanzanian landscape as far as the eye can see. When a seasonal drought dries up grass and water supplies in one area, the grazing animals move to the next area where seasonal rains are falling. Although lions and other carnivores do not migrate with the grazing animals, they feast on them when their paths cross. To fully appreciate the magnitude of this animal spectacle, hire a small plane and soar high above.

9 – MANHATTAN SKYLINE, NEW YORK

New York City probably has the world's most recognized skyline. The buildings soar upward in two Manhattan clusters, midtown and downtown, with a "valley" of low buildings in between. The most sensational daytime views occur in the morning, looking west, and late afternoon, looking east. At night the lights of the buildings make the skyline glitter. The best skyline vantage points are from the observation areas on the 86th and 102nd floors of the Empire State Building and from a boat in the harbor.

10 – HONG KONG HARBOUR

Hong Kong Harbour teems with all kinds of boats, from tiny fishing skiffs to great ocean liners, with sparkling skyscrapers rising beyond. From a boat you can study the harbor activity up-close, and the promenade along the Kowloon side provides a good vantage as well. But for a truly spectacular view, head to the top of 552-meter-high (1,800-foot-) Victoria Peak. From here you take in not only the city but the South China Sea and some of the outlying islands as well. In the evening, boat lights sparkle and lights dance across the water, joining in the frenzy of electric activity produced by one of the world's greatest cities.

GUEST-HOUSE
BUTEMBO

KIVU
CONGO BELGE

Drive the Amalfi Coast

HONG
KONG
HOTEL

HONG KONG, CHINA

JUST THE

THINGS TO DO ON A
SUNDAY AFTERNOON

Best

1 – PALAZZO MASSIMO ALLE TERME
Largo di Villa Peretti 1; Tel: 39-06-399-67700

If you have time to visit only one museum (other than the Vatican's), make it this dazzling collection of ancient treasures. One of the four outposts of the recently revitalized National Museum of Rome, the *palazzo* harbors Greek and Roman statuary, mosaics, and frescoes. Entire rooms from the late first century to late Roman villas, with their original palatial decoration, have been reconstructed on the top floor. The building itself is amazing—a beautifully restored Jesuit high school in the style of a very early Roman baroque noble residence. You will be awestruck by the wealth of history here. All objects are labeled in Italian and faultless English.

2 – DISCOVER LA PACE
Just west of Piazza Navona you'll find Rome's hottest new neighborhood, named after the 15th-century church of Santa Maria della Pace. Along the narrow cluster of lanes, stop for a coffee or cocktail at one of the many outdoor cafés, where you might spot an Italian movie star or two.

3 – OVER ROME AT SUNSET
Tel: 39-06-321-11511

Just as the sun sends golden shadows on ancient cupolas and spires, hop into a hot-air balloon and glide over the Eternal City at its most magical moment. Balloons lift off every 15 minutes between 9:30 a.m. and sundown from a fixed platform in the lovely Villa Borghese park off Via Veneto. You can choose a flight accompanied by an art historian who points out the city's major monuments and provides a running commentary.

4 – VISIT THE CATACOMBS
As Christianity took root and spread in the first century A.D., catacombs were carved in the soft tufa rock outside the city walls. The damp, underground galleries, which sometimes ran for miles, have interesting Greek and Latin inscriptions, faded frescoes, imperial seals, and sarcophagi that document the rites and customs of the Church's first centuries. The best known are the Catacombs of San Callisto (Via Appia Antica 126; Tel: 39-06-513-01580,

closed Wed.), the first official underground burial site for early Christians, including many second- and third-century martyrs. A major attraction on the 40-minute guided tour is the papal crypt, with the remains of several martyred early popes.

5 – STROLL AROUND TRASTEVERE

In this ancient quarter where artisans, housewives, yuppies, and ex-pats congregate, you'll find one of the last remaining enclaves of the "real Rome." Begin at Piazza di Santa Maria in Trastevere, where you might want to sip a coffee at the Café de Marzio, a local favorite. Exit the piazza by the newsstand and take Via della Lungaretta. Don't miss the cosmatesque pavement (of geometric mosaic inlay) at San Crisogono, which you'll pass on the right. Proceed along Via della Lungaretta to charming Piazza in Piscinula and turn right at the hilly Arco dei Tolomei, which brings you to a medieval archway. Turn left on Via dei Salumi, right on Via dei Vascellari (which soon becomes Via di Santa Cecilia), and duck into the lovely church of Santa Cecilia in Trastevere. Beyond, check out Piazza dei Mercanti, between Piazza Santa Cecilia and the river, but avoid the touristy restaurants there. Continue along Via di Santa Cecilia to Via Madonna dell'Orto. The facade at the end of the street, curiously decorated with obelisks, was once the headquarters for many guilds of the more humble occupations, such as fruit vendors and chicken keepers. Make a brief detour right on Via Anicia and ring

the bell at No. 12. The custodian will let you into the magnificent, hidden 15th-century cloister of San Giovanni dei Genovesi. Retracing your steps, continue along Via Anicia to Piazza San Francesco d'Assisi and the church of San Francesco a Ripa, where one of Bernini's three "Ecstasies" is displayed. Via San Francesco a Ripa brings you back to the start.

6 – A DRINK AT THE EXCELSIOR
Via Veneto 125; Tel: 39-06-470-81

Built in sumptuous turn-of-the-20th-century style, the venerable Excelsior Hotel for decades has been the gathering place for high society and beautiful people. Take a coffee or cocktail in the luxurious, chandelier-dripping lobby. Afterward, stroll the famous Via Veneto, cradle of la dolce vita immortalized by Fellini, and explore the exquisite boutiques along its bustling side streets.

7 - GALLERIA BORGHESE
Piazzale Scipione Borghese 5; Tel: 39-06-328-10

If the exterior of this 17th-century summerhouse appears attractive, the inside is simply remarkable. Frescoed ceilings, sumptuous wall coverings, faux marble wall decoration, gilded moldings, and marble inlay all vie for your attention. But all this pales in comparison to the artwork on display. The sculpture collection, on the ground floor, contains some of the most famous pieces in the world, including

The Spanish Steps

LIVING HISTORY: ON TOUR IN ROME

Sir John Ward, a respected artist and trustee of London's Royal Academy of Arts between 1975 and 1993, writes about his long-lasting love of Rome.

I first visited Rome 45 years ago. My wife drove us there in an old army jeep. At the time, there were few cars in Italy and we drove right into the city, parked, and walked round the corner to find the Trevi Fountain gushing in all its verdigris glory. And from there, with my small box of watercolors, tin of pencil and chalks, water bottle, and sketching stool, I was swept from one treasure to the next.

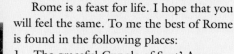

One unravels Rome. It's not a clearly defined affair; it unfolds unexpectedly. Palazzo faces palazzo with but a few feet of separation; stumps of ruins lie like great old boots discarded by the gods while they go off to make love on the grasses of the Palatine. Such extravagance and exuberance will invigorate me until my dying day.

Rome gets the priorities of the visual arts right: Architecture dominates everything, then sculpture, then paintings. To attempt to draw Rome's architecture and to capture some of its life is to explore its wonders in a special way. To sit through a morning and watch the light move gently across domes, porticoes, windows, and shutters, brightening the colors that wash the buildings, is a breathtaking privilege. In Rome, the early bird gets the finest light, as good as the gilding which comes in the evening. (Afternoons, I discovered, were good for siestas.)

The best way to experience Rome is on foot; the pedestrian is always respected, and you are bound to meet courteous, enthusiastic people—one of Italy's greatest joys.

Rome is a feast for life. I hope that you will feel the same. To me the best of Rome is found in the following places:

1 – The graceful Cupola of Sant' Agnese.
2 – Caffè del Greco, on Via dei Condotti: for decades Rome's best-known café, where writers and artists gathered to discuss cultural trends and gossip.
3 – The 15th-century church of Santa Maria della Pace.
4 – Piazza Navona's bustling café life.
5 – The Campidoglio: An astounding combination of architecture and history.
6 – Looking down the Forum toward Trajan's Column.
7 – Piazza della Rotonda, with the Pantheon and cafés.
8 – Villa Farnesina: Built in the early 1500s as a country villa and considered a gem of Renaissance architecture.
9 – The Spanish Steps: The heart of nonarchaeological Rome for more than four centuries.
10 – Magnificent Galleria Borghese and its sculptures.

Bernini's amazing "Apollo and Daphne." Upstairs is the painting gallery, with one marvelous painting after another by many of the best painters in Western history—Bellini, Bronzino, Correggio, Fra Bartolomeo, Raphael, Rubens, Titian. Room IX is particularly thrilling with Botticelli's richly colored "Madonna con Bambino S. Giovanino e Angelo" and Raphael's "Rittrato di Giovane Donna con Unicorn." Remember: You are limited to a two-hour visit. You'll want to return again on another day.

8 – PASTA MUSEUM
Piazza Scanderbeg 117; Tel: 39-06-699-1119

Despite common belief, Marco Polo did not bring the first spaghetti from China to Italy in the 13th century. At this little known museum, located near the Trevi Fountain, you'll discover that the ancient Etruscans and Romans ate pastalike food long before Mr. Polo traveled the Silk Road. You'll see photographs of celebrities eating pasta, examples of pasta art, pastamaking tools, recipes, and books.

THE COLOSSEUM

The largest amphitheater in the Roman world, Rome's Colosseum is truly colossal. When inaugurated in A.D. 80, 50,000 roaring spectators crammed into its seats. The name, however, derives from a giant bronze statue that stood nearby.

9 – LUNCH AT THE ROMAN GARDEN
Via Bocca di Leone 14; Tel: 39-06-69-981

Just steps from Piazza di Spagna, you'll find the enchanting Hotel d'Inghilterra, housed in an ancient palazzo. Established in 1845, this hotel was beloved by many Englishmen on their Grand Tour; it still has a British-club feel to it. People in the know meet at its Roman Garden restaurant, delightful with a frescoed vaulted ceiling. The acclaimed cosmopolitan menu changes with the seasons.

10 – REFRESH AT SPA'DEUS SPA
Centro Benessere Spa'Deus, Via Le Piane 35, Chianciano
Tel: 30-05-78-63-232

With so much to see and do in Rome, the fatigue factor is likely to overtake you at some point. A two-hour drive from the capital city through rolling Tuscan hills brings you to this splendid California-style retreat. The afternoon begins with a stroll through cypress-shaded countryside, after which you can join a Pilates class, work out in the aqua-gym (the pool has an underwater exercise circuit), or perhaps take a mud treatment or a hot bath.

TEN BEST
~BERLIN~

More than a decade after reunification, the prosperity and modernity built up in West Germany since World War II continues to spread slowly to the east. The country's ever more cosmopolitan cities are crammed with galleries, museums, historic buildings, and entertainment of all kinds. Nowhere is change more apparent than in the rapidly developing capital of Berlin, a city on its way to becoming a focal point of 21st-century Europe.

For much of its history, Berlin has been addicted to change. Even before its roller-coaster ride through the 20th century, a early observer remarked that the city was constantly on the verge of becoming, never in a state of being. Its latest transformation has yielded some impressive attractions. Still, with 30 percent of the city devoted to green space, Berlin air is among the best in urban Europe.

1 – LUNCH AT THE HOTEL ADLON
Unter den Linden 77; Tel: 49-(0)-30-2261-1111

A legend reborn. From its 1907 opening until it was destroyed in 1945, the Hotel Adlon was a symbol of Berlin, a lavish host for royalty, heads of government, stage and screen stars, and the greats of literature and science. Facing the Brandenburg Gate, it is virtually a replica of the original and the epitome of a smart hotel, with a first-rate restaurant.

2 – STROLL IN THE TIERGARTEN

The 255-hectare (630-acre) Tiergarten, in the center of Berlin, was once a royal hunting preserve and is the city's oldest public park. The park has been re-wooded and is a lovely place for an afternoon walk.

3 – A VISIT TO GRUNEWALD FOREST

The 302-hectare (745-acre) Grunewald Forest, in the western part of the city, is Berlin's second largest park. Built in 1542, the Grunewald Hunting Lodge was used by the Hohenzollern rulers. It retains its Renaissance great hall and displays paintings and furniture from the royal collection. Its courtyard is the site of summer concerts.

4 – CHARLOTTENBURG PALACE
43-45 Friedrichstrasse; Tel: 49-(0)-30-253-7250

This magnificent former residence of Prussian royalty dates from 1694. A regal entrance court gives way to a series of stunning interiors containing glittering decorations and masterworks by French artist Antoine Watteau, a favorite of Frederick the Great. The palace's extensive grounds are a favorite place for Berliners to relax and stroll.

5 – WANDER PEACOCK ISLAND

Reached by ferry, this mile-long island in the middle of the River Havel near Potsdam has an idyllic 18th-century English-style garden with peacocks, temples, and ponds. Don't miss the delightful 1796 mock castle built by King Frederick William II for his mistress.

6 – ENJOY THE CHAMÄLEON VARIETÉ
Rosenthalerstrasse 40-41, Tel: 49-(0)-30-4000-3935

A lovely old theater where you can sit comfortably at tables, have drinks, and watch performances by talented musicians, dancers, singers, comedians, and acrobats.

7 – KOMISCHE OPER BERLIN
Behrenstrasse 55-57, Tel: 49-(0)-30-4799-7400

The Komische Oper, just off Unter den Linden, is a musical comedy and variety house featuring experimental works. The ensemble was made famous by Bertolt Brecht.

FAVORITE RESTAURANTS

THE BORCHARDT
47 Franzosische Strasse, Tel: 49-(0)-30-2038-7150

A favorite in the days of the Kaiser, the Borchardt has been rebuilt at its original location with all of its turn-of-the-20th-century extravagance. Serves nouvelle cuisine as well as solid German food.

BRECHT
Chausseestrasse 125, Tel: 49-(0)-30-282-3843

Enjoy a drink at the small, intimate Brecht, or a good, hardy Viennese meal. The restaurant is decorated with photos of Brecht's family, friends, and productions.

8 – SEE THE FILM MUSEUM BERLIN
Sony Center, Potsdamer Platz, Tel: 49-(0)-30-300-9030

This museum honors many of Berlin's most famous directors and stars, who were responsible for the city's fame as the hub of Europe's film industry in the 1920s. The museum's collection includes numerous film clips and exhibits of personal memorabilia. Three rooms are devoted to Marlene Dietrich display jewelry, letters, and mannequins wearing her costumes.

9 – MUSICAL INSTRUMENT MUSEUM
Tiergartenstrasse 1, Tel: 49-(0)-30-254-810

In the Tiergarten, next to the tentlike home of the Berlin Philharmonic, this superlative collection of 3,000 musical instruments dates back to the 16th century. Included are Frederick the Great's flute and Edvard Grieg's piano.

10 – SAVOR THE PICTURE GALLERY (GEMALDEGALERIE)
Stauffenbergstrasse 40, Tel: 49-(0)-30-266-2101

This gallery displays about 1,000 paintings, including 26 Rembrandts (don't miss the famous "Man with a Helmet"), 14 Rubens, and works by Botticelli, Dürer, Holbein, Giotto, Titian, Vermeer, and many other old masters. Includes a tremendous range of German Renaissance art.

~LONDON~

London is like a maze: You can't hurry your way through. Around nearly every bend in the road you'll find stately homes, castles, magnificent gardens, carriage houses, cozy pubs, and beautiful churches.

Its 2,000 years of history comprise Roman legions, Saxons and Vikings, kings and queens, plagues, a Great Fire, a splendid architectural heritage dating from the Georgian era, Victoria's great age of railways and imperialism, and the World War II bombs of the Blitz.

The city has an endless ability to entertain, surprise, and reward. Its theaters, opera houses, and concert halls stand comparison with any in the world; its 150 museums and 600 galleries are practically without equal; its entertainment is as innovative as it is cosmopolitan and diverse. And London pubs are a social experience not to be missed. As Dr. Johnson sagely observed, "When a man is tired of London, he is tired of life."

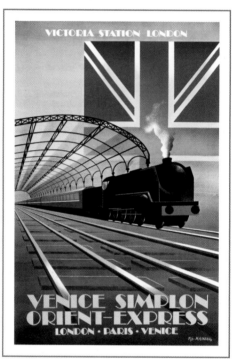

1 – ENJOY TEA AT CLARIDGE'S
Brook Street, Mayfair, Tel: 44-(0)-20-7-629-8860

Take afternoon tea at Claridge's. Everything about this hotel is elegant, and tea is impeccably served, with a quartet playing every afternoon. Nicely located on Brook Street, it is favored by the Queen for social occasions. Notice the beautiful art deco public rooms.

2 – TAKE IN A MATINEE AT THE PALACE THEATRE
Cambridge Circus, Shaftesbury Ave. Tel: 44-(0)-870-895-5579

This wonderfully ornate building, opened in 1891, once housed the Royal English Opera House. It became a music hall for many of England's best loved performers and survived the London air raids during World War II. Pavlova and Nijinsky both danced here. It remains a premier site for popular musicals.

3 – VISIT CHELSEA
Chelsea is known for its Georgian houses and squares, whose inhabitants have enriched the intellectual and cultural life of England. James Whistler, Henry James, Oscar Wilde, Agatha Christie, Bertrand Russell, Peter Ustinov, and Margaret Thatcher have been some of its famous residents. Hundreds of fashionable boutiques line the streets from Sloane Square to the King's Road, and the area is home to the spectacular Chelsea Flower Show each May. Just off Cheyne Walk, which borders the river, you can visit the house of Thomas Carlyle, one of Britain's foremost men of letters. Nearby, the Chelsea

Physic Garden is a botanic center founded in 1673 by the Society of Apothecaries to grow plants for medical study.

4 – SEE SIR JOHN SOANE'S MUSEUM
13 Lincoln's Inn Fields, Tel: 44-(0)-20-7-405-2107
www.soane.org

One of the most remarkable museums in London is the former home of the architect Sir John Soane (1813–1837). Influenced by the Romantic Movement, Soane collected carvings and casts and designed some of the most illustrious buildings in London. Be sure to see his model room, which contains many scaled buildings, and the much admired Adam library. At every turn there are surprises.

5 – ROYAL BOTANIC GARDENS, KEW
Kew, Richmond, Tel: 44-(0)-20-8332-5655, rbgkew.org.uk

A living museum of plants, landscapes, buildings, and statuary, this 122-hectare (300-acre) garden of perfect specimen trees and plants is part of an institute of botanical research. Visitors revel in the more than 50,000 species of flora and explore glasshouses full of lilies and orchids. Whatever the season, Kew has something to see. Don't miss the 18th-century Orangery, now the Tea House, and the extraordinary Chinese pagoda, Kew's 10-story landmark. The great House at Kew was designed by Robert Adam, and is a lovely place to spend a few hours.

6 – DRIVE TO YE OLDE BELL AT HURLEY
High Street, Hurley,
Near Maidenhead, Berkshire
Tel: 44-(0)-162-8-825-881

The Bell is a perfect place for roast beef and Yorkshire pudding on a Sunday afternoon in an old

CABINET WAR ROOMS

Clive Steps, King Charles St., Tel: 44 (0) 20 7-930-6961

This maze of underground rooms served as headquarters for the government's War Cabinet from August 1939 to September 1945. You can imagine Prime Minister Winston Churchill catching some sleep in the small bedroom.

village just 40 minutes from London. Afterward, take a delightful ramble over to Marlow or Henley-on-Thames for a pint on the river.

7 – IMPERIAL WAR MUSEUM
Lambeth Road
Tel: 44 (0)20-7-416-5000 or 44-(0)-20-7-416-5320
www.iwm.org.uk

On the South Bank, Britain's museum of 20th-century war encourages study and understanding of modern warfare and how it affects our lives. Tanks and guns form just a tiny fraction of a fascinating collection that covers every aspect of war—civil and military, social and cultural. Exhibits include photographs, personal letters, film, sound recordings, posters, and paintings.

8 – NATIONAL GALLERY
Trafalgar Square, Tel: 44-(0)-20-7-747-2885

Established in 1824 when the government purchased 38 masterpieces for 57,000 pounds, the gallery now holds 2,000 paintings that tell the story of European art from the 13th to the 18th centuries. You will see the finest collection of Italian art found outside Italy.

London Walking Tours

Bloomsbury St., LONDON, W.C.1.

9 – STROLL FROM PALL MALL TO BUCKINGHAM PALACE

The 18th-century coffeehouses and gaming clubs of Mayfair and St. James's evolved into mostly exclusive gentlemen's clubs along Pall Mall. One of the most famous, the Athenaeum at the corner of Waterloo Place, has long been a preserve of Britain's culturally elite. Members have included Rudyard Kipling, Joseph Conrad, Charles Darwin, and Charles Dickens. A smile and a request to the hall porter will sometimes gain you entry for a look around. In 2002 the club voted to admit women.

A block away is the Mall, a tree-lined road bordering St. James's Park, one of the oldest royal parks in England with one of England's finest gardens. Take a right toward Buckingham Palace, passing Clarence House built by John Nash and home to the late Queen Mother.

The best view of Buckingham Palace is from the Mall, near the Queen Victoria Memorial. Straight ahead is the parade ground where the Changing of the Guard ceremony takes place. In the mid-18th century, King George III bought Buckingham House for his wife, retaining its private character; in 1820, George IV commissioned John Nash to transform the royal house into a palace. In the summer, by booking in advance, you can visit some of the State Rooms and the Queen's Gallery to view one of the world's best private art collections, with works by Van Dyck, Rembrandt, and Vermeer. Tel: 44-(0)-20-7-321-2233.

10 – THAMES BOAT RIDE

citycruises.com or westminsterpier.co.uk

A Thames boat ride is a delightful way to appreciate the role of the river in the development of this great city. From Westminster Pier you can take a short trip downriver, passing the City of Westminster and the City of London, stopping at the Tower of London, and continuing, beyond the revived Docklands, to Greenwich. The trip upstream takes longer and gets you into the country, stopping at Kew, Richmond, and finally Hampton Court Palace. From here a short train ride brings you back into town.

LONDON PASS

www.londonpass.com

The reasonably priced London Pass permits entry to an amazing number of attractions, with the bonus of special offers for the user. The pass includes admission to more than 50 landmarks, galleries, and museums, as well as a public transport option on buses, tubes, and trains. The pass a comprehensive guidebook in five languages. You can have a 1-to-6-day pass sent to you or pick it up at the Britain Visitors Center, 1 Regent Street.

TEA FOR TWO

No doubt you've enjoyed an afternoon tea many times over. But a visit to England is incomplete without taking part in the ritual of "Afternoon Tea." Enjoying tea is as indigenous to the English way of life as the habit of carrying an umbrella 364 days of the year. It is a palliative for stress. The English drink it strong with milk and, usually, sugar. Lump sugar is "correct"; granulated sugar is "working class." Victorian English grandmothers used to tell their marriageable granddaughters that if a suitor requests one lump he is mean. If he requests three lumps he is greedy. If he asks for two lumps he is marriageable.

The English sit down for a cup of tea when they are under stress: when they have heard bad news (Uncle William died and left nothing to the family) and when they have heard good news (the will is being contested). If one's spouse wants a divorce, one needs a cup of tea; if it is raining, one needs a cup of tea; and, if there is simply nothing else to do, then one should have a cup of tea. Tea is drunk at breakfast, in the middle of the morning, and at tea time or bedtime.

MAKING TEA

First, how does one make a cup of tea? Correct technique is very important. To begin, warm the tea pot with hot water. This has nothing to do with the quality of the tea to come but helps prevent your best porcelain teapot from crazing or even cracking when filled with boiling hot water. Secondly, when tea is over, rinse out the teapot but do not wash it with soap or detergents. Let the tannin from the tea leaves rest within the pores of the porcelain.

Put one heaping teaspoon of fresh tea into the warmed pot for each cup to be served plus one "for the pot." Add freshly boiled water. It is best to use filtered tap water as mineral waters can be too strong in flavor and the fluoridation and chlorination of ordinary tap water adversely affect the taste of the tea. Remember, too, the advice given by Charles Laughton in the movie *Ruggles of Red Gap:* "Always bring the pot to the kettle, never the kettle to the pot." Stir with a spoon and let the tea steep for about five minutes. (Some people prefer less steeping, some prefer more; it's up to you to determine the strength of flavor you like.) Then, pour the tea through a strainer and into a second pre-warmed tea pot, and your tea is ready to serve. In many cases, however, the tea is allowed to continue steeping in the first pot, and when it becomes too strong, or when more is needed, additional hot water is added. A shameful practice!

Tea can be and is, of course, drunk from any type of cup or mug. But for esthetic reasons, it should be served in a cup of thin bone china. And tea bags? My dear, it simply

> *"Another novelty is the tea-party, an extraordinary meal in that, being offered to persons that have already dined well, it supposes neither appetite nor thirst, and has no object but distraction, no basis but delicate enjoyment."*
>
> —Anthelme Brillat-Savarin

isn't done! Another critical element is the milk. When serving, it is no small matter whether the milk or the tea is poured first. If the tea comes first, and then the milk, you can see how much milk you require. Eminently sensible. However, hot tea can damage delicate porcelain, so if you pour the milk first and add the tea, you protect the cup.

TEA ROOMS

Afternoon tea is sometimes served at home but is best found in hotels and restaurants, often served with crumpets in winter or scones topped with clotted cream and strawberries in summer, when it is called a "cream tea." The best cream teas are to be had in the western counties of Devon and Cornwall. For the visitor with a day's schedule of shopping, museums, and theater in the evening, a full English breakfast, a large afternoon tea, and a light after-theater supper is ideal.

Throughout England you can indulge in a full afternoon tea at virtually any top hotel. You can expect a choice of teas, almost always properly prepared, together with all the accoutrements—sandwiches, pastries, cakes, tarts, crumpets, and scones. The best hotel in whatever town you happen to be in is probably your best bet, but it's fun to try the local tea rooms as well.

Central London is replete with notable afternoon teas. At Brown's Hotel (30 Albermarle Street) afternoon tea is an institution and about as elegant as it gets. At the Beaufort (33 Beaufort Gardens), near Harrods, you will find a delicious cream tea with hot scones. Tea in the glassed-wall gardens of the conservatory rooms at the Four Seasons (Hamilton Place, Park Lane) is memorable. At the Ritz (150 Piccadilly), reservations are absolutely essential if you want to have tea in the famous allée that leads to the dining room. And, of course, you can expect thoroughly satisfying afternoon teas at Claridge's, the Savoy, the Berkeley, the Connaught, the Athenaeum, the Mandarin Oriental, and the Lanesborough. At Fortnum and Mason (181 Piccadilly) you can have tea in the restaurant, then browse among their more than 40 varieties of tea before making a purchase of your favorites.

TEA OUTPOSTS

In Rome, Babington's English Tea Rooms on the Spanish Square has been catering to British expats and tea lovers of all nations since 1893, when Miss Anna Maria Babington and Miss Isabel Cargill first opened their British outpost.

Vienna, the home of the coffeehouse, is also a great place to take tea, even if only as an excuse to indulge in the pastries that accompany it. The tea is usually quite good in itself, and you cannot do better than the pear-and-poppy seed cake at Café Bräunerhof at Stallburggasse.

Melbourne. There is no more enchanting place to have tea than in the Block Arcade, a Victorian setting for the Hopetoun Tea Rooms, 282 Collins Street.

TEN BEST

~MADRID~

1 – ROW A BOAT AT THE PARQUE DEL RETIRO

Madrid is not by any means a green city, but it does have a lovely breathing space in this 142-hectare (350-acre) park. Rowboats dot Etanque Lake, perfect for lolling away an afternoon. You can also take a carriage ride, watch street theater, hear a concert, visit an exhibition, or just stroll.

2 – LUNCH AT LA TERRAZA DEL CASINO

Alcalá 15
Tel: 34-91-532-12-75

One of Spain's star chefs, Ferrán Adrià, has opened this controversial café in the heart of Madrid. Here he combines sweet and salty flavors in a single dish, as in strawberries with aged Parmesan, grilled watermelon with tomatoes, and foie gras sandwiched between potato chips. Sometimes it works, sometimes it doesn't; nevertheless, you'll find it intriguing. Service is solicitous, the setting sumptuous.

3 – A STROLL AROUND OLD MADRID

Delve into Old Madrid, where winding, centuries-old streets lead past churches and tapas bars, in a quarter steeped in royal history. Begin at 17th-century Plaza Mayor, with its majestic porticos. Leave the square through the arch in the northeast corner leading to Calle de Ciudad Rodrigo. Turn left into the busy Calle Mayor and you soon reach charming Plaza de la Villa. Facing you is the Casa de Cisneros, a reconstruction of a 16th-century palace. Retrace your steps to Calle Mayor, turn left, and continue to the end. The massive white forms of the Catedral de Nuestra Señora de la Almudena appear ahead, with the Palacio Real to the right. Once the royal residence, today the royal palace is used only for state ceremonial purposes. Tours showcase the opulent Throne Room, topped by Tiepolo's ceiling painting "Apotheosis of the Spanish Monarchy"; the tapestry-lined Yellow Room, where ladies once sat on marquetry chairs by Dugourc and ate chocolates; and the Music Room, which contains a rare collection of Stradivari stringed instruments. For a bite to eat, stop by Lhardy (Carrera de San Jerónimo 8), which had been open seven years when Alexandre Dumas dropped by in 1846. The consommé, tea sandwiches, tapas, and sherry are a local tradition. If you prefer to pack a picnic, you can pick up cold meats, cheeses, pastries, and cakes.

PALACE HOTEL

4 – SHOP IN THE SALAMANCA DISTRICT

Need a new outfit for dinner or a show? Chic and sophisticated designer shops line the streets of the exclusive Salamanca district, north of Gran Vía. Among the fashion gurus: Giorgio Armani, Yves St. Laurent, Ralph

Shopping Madrid

Madrid is a "shop stocked with every kind of merchandise," trilled 17th-century playwright Tirso de Molina. He would still be right—the city is packed with shops offering everything from high fashion to leather goods to flamenco guitars to fabulous antiques.

Leather goods are particularly good buys here. You'll find tiny leather shops in the streets radiating off Plaza Major and Puerto del Sol. One of the best is Sanatoria Tenor (Plaza de la Provincial 6), which, for more than 150 years, has supplied boots to an international clientele. Each pair takes about three months to complete. Many customers, including Franklin Roosevelt and Ernest Hemingway, have left their "footprints" on file.

If you're a man who wears a hat, Casa Yustas (Plaza Mayor 30) carries a seemingly endless variety of hats, caps, and berets. And to go with your beret, what better than a dashing, custom-made woolen cape from Serena Capas (Calle de la Cruz 23), a Madrid tradition since 1901.

Manuel Gonzalez Contreras (Calle Mayor 80) and Felix Manzanero (Calle Santa Ana 12) are known for top-quality, custom-made classical and flamenco guitars. If it's a Spanish fan you're after, or an umbrella or a walking stick, the best can be found at Casa de Diego (Puerta del Sol 12), which opened in 1858.

Three antiques galleries, each with about 30 shops, are located along Ribera de Curtidores: Nuevas Galerias at No. 12, Galerias Ribera at No. 15, and Galerias Piquer at No. 20. Finding a lost Goya is unlikely, but the fun is in the quest.

Don't miss Madrid's open-air markets, where you'll find everything from pottery to clothes to food. They usually start early in the morning and last until about 2 p.m. A lot of the produce on sale is grown locally: almonds, strawberries, avocados, and wonderful red and green tomatoes. Look also for cheeses, honey, olives, dried peppers and tomatoes, hams, and herbs.

The best markets: El Rastrillo (Marqués de Viana; Sun.); Mercado Filatélico de la Plaza Mayor (Plaza Mayor; Sun.); and Mercado de San Miguel (Plaza de San Miguel; Mon.-Sat.), a permanent covered food market.

The king of markets, however, is the famous El Rastro flea market, which revs up early Sunday morning. Its open-air stalls and tables center on Calle Ribera de Curtidores and extend along the side streets all the way down to the Manzanares River. You'll find everything from paintings to lamps, T-shirts to music, used furniture to kitchen utensils. There are few bargains, but the scene is too much fun to be missed. If you buy, bargaining is expected. Be very careful of your wallet at the Rastro—it's a pickpocket's heaven.

Lauren, Hermès, along with Madrid's best fashion designers. It's fun just to browse.

5 – WATCH A BULLFIGHT

Long reviled by sensitive foreigners and many Spaniards, the bullfight is nonetheless the most perfect expression of Spanishness: pomp and ceremony, *sol y sombra* (sun and shade), a deep sense of drama, tragedy, and fatalism, all orchestrated by the fearless *furia española*—the legendary fury that made Spain's enemies tremble. *Corridas* are staged at 6 or 7 p.m. every Sunday between March and December at the fabled Las Ventas arena in east Madrid.

6 – MUSEO DEL PRADO

Paseo del Prado; Tel: 34-91-330-28-00

One of the world's most important art museums, the Prado for many people is the main reason for visiting Spain's capital city. Its vast collection is full of masterpieces—stars of Spanish painting such as Velázquez, Goya, Zurbarán, and Ribera, along with big collections of Italian (including Titian and Raphael) and Flemish artists.

Tip: It's best to visit on a sunny day, when the natural lighting in some of the rooms is better. A pleasant café for lunch or a snack is on the lower level of the building.

Top off the afternoon with tea at the nearby Ritz. Built in 1910 by royal appointment of King Alfonso XIII, this luxurious hotel bears an air of classical elegance with its belle epoque interior. Worth a visit for its own sake.

7 – VISIT EL ESCORIAL

San Lorenzo de El Escorial
Tel: 34-91-890-59-02

Felipe II's 16th-century palace-monastery, overlooking the town of San Lorenzo de El Escorial, an hour's drive from Madrid, is one of the most stunning structures ever built. It has 2,673 windows (with sublime views of the mountains beyond) and more than 8 kilometers (12 miles) of passageways. Among its treasures are works by El Greco and Flemish masters and a library collection that rivals the Vatican.

8 – EXCURSION TO ARANJUEZ

This genteel royal town, located 18 kilometers (30 miles) south of Madrid, has endless gardens, shady parks, and a 200-year-old bullring. But most people come to see the luxurious Palacio Real (Royal Palace; Tel: 34-01-891-14-51), with its grand staircase, rococo Throne Room, and Hall of Mirrors.

9 – WANDER ALCALÁ DE HERNARES

The world's first planned university town lies 33 kilometers (20 miles) east of Madrid. See the Monasterio de Religiosas Bernardas, with its baroque extravaganza of a church; the birthplace of Cervantes; and the illustrious university, centering on the fine plateresque college of San Ildefonso.

10 – SEE PICTURESQUE SEGOVIA

This seductive town rising a thousand meters (3,300 feet) above the plain of Old Castile features a Roman aqueduct with 118 arches, a magnificent cathedral, and the fantasy palace of the Alcázar. But there's more than monuments here: Segovia has a healthy cultural life and a meat-and-game (including suckling pig) gastronomy produced in capacious brick ovens. Semi-porticoed Plaza Mayor, with its lovely cafés, is the place to find a refreshing drink.

TEN BEST
~NEW YORK~

Sunday afternoon in the Big Apple has a lot to offer, after a lazy morning in bed with the *New York Times,* a Sunday tradition. You can usually find blockbuster exhibitions, street fairs, and parades at all times of the year.

1 – TEA AT THE MORGAN LIBRARY
29 East 36th Street, Tel: 212-685-0610
www.morganlibrary.org

The great financier J. Pierpont Morgan (1837–1913) commissioned this one-story neoclassic building when his trove of books and manuscripts grew too large for his mansion. Today the library houses one of the world's outstanding collections. Wander amid the many artistic and literary treasures on view. There is also a gift shop and a delightful café with a fine array of tiny sandwiches, scones, and cakes that will be more than enough to carry you through to a late dinner or after-theater snack. Flowers and charming china teapots add to the delightful experience.

2 – METROPOLITAN MUSEUM OF ART
1000 Fifth Avenue, Tel: 212-535-7710, www.met.org

The finest collection of American art in the world, extensive Greek and Roman galleries, a selection of ancient Egyptian art that rivals any outside of Cairo, and an astounding array of European painting and sculpture—these are just some of the reasons why the Met remains the cultural touchstone of this arts-dense city. Its collection, some two million items, is not only broad, ranging worldwide from antiquity to the present, but also deep. In most every artistic field, the holdings are outstanding and often superlative. To avoid feeling overwhelmed, take time to understand the museum's arrangement and then select a limited number of areas to see.

THE BEST HOT DOG!

Papaya King
179 East 86th Street, Tel: 212-369-0648

Every New Yorker will tell you that there is only one hot dog, and even Julia Child confirmed that it is the best hot dog in New York. Line up at the counter and order two grilled dogs topped with relish and enjoy a companion coconut, papaya, orange, or banana drink. It is a fulfilling and essential New York City experience.

3 – VISIT MoMA (MUSEUM OF MODERN ART)

11 West 53rd Street, Tel: 212-708-9400
www.moma.org

The most striking feature of the newly renovated MoMA is the entrance: A 34-meter (110-foot) atrium towers over an indoor walkway, which extends from 53rd Street to a new entryway on 54th Street. Reopened in 2005, this sense of space continues throughout the institution, now almost double its previous size and spread out among six floors, with an additional 3,680 square meters (40,000 square feet) in exhibition space. More of the museum's superlative permanent collection, which ranges from Cezanne to Chuck Close, from the earliest daguerreotypes to interactive electronic art, is now on view, and there are welcome common areas for reading and reflection. The restored and extended Abby Aldrich Rockefeller Sculpture Garden features more than 30 masterworks of modern sculpture. The new Philip Johnson Architecture and Design gallery exhibits iconic artifacts of everyday modern life, ranging from Eames chairs to iPods.

4 – THE FRICK COLLECTION

1 East 70th Street, Tel: 212-288-0700
www.frick.org

New Yorkers tend to think of the Frick as their little secret, perhaps because it still looks more like a very grand private residence from the Gilded Age than an institution open to the public. But don't be put off—inside this French neoclassic building is one of the world's great

art collections. For 15 dollars you can spend the afternoon imagining you've been invited to a turn-of-the-20th-century salon in the home of industrialist Henry Clay Frick. Many of the rooms are arranged almost precisely the way Frick wanted them: Old Master, Impressionist, Italian Renaissance, and French baroque works organized around thematic content and decorative harmony rather than the usual boundaries of style and date. The treasures found here include major works by such greats as Bellini, El Greco, Vermeer, Velázquez, Boucher, Goya, Turner, Van Dyck, Renoir, and Holbein, as well as complete cycles of painted wall panels by Fragonard and Boucher—and numerous decorative pieces including priceless timepieces and bronze statuary.

5 – BRUNCH AT THE RAINBOW ROOM

49 West 49th Street, Tel: 212-632-5100
www.rainbowroom.com

Rockefeller Center is an architectural experience, and any visit to New York should include Sunday brunch at the Rainbow Room on the 65th floor. The Rainbow Room remains a relic from a long-gone age of romance, and it is still among the most opulent settings in the city. This grand room offers spectacular city views, good food, and polished service. The highlight of the sprawling space is the Rainbow Room itself, a stunning gold- and silver-draped ballroom situated around a slowly revolving dance floor.

6 – STROLL SOUTH STREET SEAPORT
19 Fulton Street, Tel: 212-732-7678

A historic trading port that dates back to the 1600s, the "street of ships" is now home to more than 120 shops, restaurants, eateries, and pushcarts filled with the gifts, tastes, and styles of New York City. Old cobblestone streets and scenic views of the Brooklyn Bridge offer a peaceful respite from the urban bustle. Since its restoration in the late '60s, South Street Seaport has grown tremendously. The last few decades of the 20th century saw the openings of the South Street Seaport Museum, the Pier 17 Pavilion, the Fulton Market, and numerous high-end shops. But if you don't want to shop or pay a fee at the museum, it doesn't cost anything to just hang out with friends and family—there are always street performances or live music going on.

7 – VENTURE TO ELLIS ISLAND
Statue of Liberty National Monument and Ellis Island
Tel: 212-363-3206, www.ellisisland.com

Today's visitors to Ellis Island, although unencumbered by bundled possessions and the harrowing memory of a transatlantic journey, retrace the steps of twelve million immigrants who approached America's "front doors to freedom" in the early 20th century. Ellis Island receives today's arriving ferry passengers (Circle Line from Battery Park) as it did hundreds of thousands of new arrivals between 1892 and 1938. In place of immigration inspection, the restored Main Hall now houses the Ellis Island Immigration Museum, dedicated to commemorating the immigrants' stories of trepidation and triumph, courage and rejection, and the lasting image of the American dream.

During its peak years, 1892 to 1924, Ellis Island received thousands of immigrants a day. Each was scrutinized for disease or disability as the long line of hopeful new arrivals made their way up the steep stairs to the great, echoing Registry Room. Over 100 million Americans can trace their ancestry in the United States to a man, woman, or child whose name passed from a steamship manifest sheet to an inspector's record book in the Registry Room.

Over the years, the grand brick and limestone buildings gradually deteriorated in the fierce weather of New York Harbor. Concern about this vital part of America's immigrant history led to the inclusion of Ellis Island as part of the Statue of Liberty National Monument in 1965.

Private citizens mounted a campaign to preserve the Island, one of the most ambitious restoration projects in American history.

Housed in the island's main building, the Ellis Island Immigration Museum is devoted to the history of Ellis Island and the story of immigration to America from the arrival of the first immigrants there to the present day. (Courtesy of www.ellisisland.com)

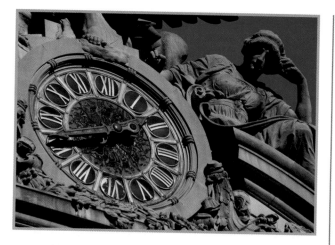

8 – WALK IN CENTRAL PARK

Fifth Avenue to Central Park West and 59th St. to 110th St.
Info. center tel: 212-794-6564, www.centralparknyc.org

With 341 lush hectares (843 acres) in the center of Manhattan, Central Park is an oasis. Besides offering a glimpse of green amid the city, Central Park also provides a wide array of facilities and attractions, including the Central Park Carousel, the Marionette Theater, Summer Stage, the Central Park Wildlife Center, the Charles A. Dana Discovery Center, the Delacorte Theater, the Great Lawn, the Henry Luce Nature Observatory, the Loeb Boathouse, and the North Meadow. The full loop within Central Park covers a distance of 10 kilometers (6 miles). If you walked all the pedestrian paths within the park, you would cover a total of 93 kilometers (58 miles). Of special note is Conservatory Garden with an entrance at Fifth Ave. and 105th St., 212-360-2766. This part of the park has almost 2.5 hectares (6 acres) of New York City's only formal European-style garden, with the most varied collection of flora in Manhattan.

9 – LUNCH AT BALTHAZAR

80 Spring Street, Tel: 212-965-1785

This antiqued brasserie has a style that gets better with age. Since its 1997 debut, Keith McNally's SoHo bistro has retained its buzz and irresistible allure, and even the most abbreviated survey of the New York restaurant world would be incomplete without a visit. Two-thirds of the appeal is atmospheric, and the look is that of an airy, aged brasserie—faded saffron yellow walls, oversize mirrors. The years of cosmopolitans, iced shellfish towers, and celebrity-studded brunches have only given a comfortable wear to the red leather banquettes. Classic bistro standards include a house salad with baby greens, fennel, asparagus, and haricots verts napped in white-truffle oil; textbook duck confit with wild mushrooms; excellent skate with raisins and capers; and the requisite steak frites. Weekend brunches draw an equally bustling scene for savory crepes, puff pastry stuffed with scrambled eggs and doused with hollandaise sauce, and French toast made with homemade brioche.

10 – MEANDER IN GREENWICH VILLAGE

East and west beginning on 5th Avenue and 8th Street

Block for block, the legendary Village is still one of the most vibrant parts of the city. Well-heeled professionals occupy high-rent apartments and town houses side by side with poets and artists and other longtime residents who pay low rents thanks to rent control laws, as well as New York University students. Locals and visitors rub elbows at dozens of small restaurants, cafés spill out onto sidewalks, and an endless variety of small shops entice everyone to buy. Except for a scattering of adult-entertainment shops and questionable bars, the Village is as scrubbed as any posh neighborhood. Greenwich Village lends itself to a leisurely pace, so allow yourself most of a day to explore its back streets and to stop at shops and cafés.

Ten Best
—St. Petersburg—

Peter the Great founded St. Petersburg on the Neva River in the early 18th century as a showcase for Russia's imperial might and as his "window on the West." He invited non-Russians to settle here, and their influence is still seen in the city's diverse culture and history, in its celebration of literature, art, and song. Despite three revolutions and three name changes, Venice of the North, as the city is often called, lives on gloriously.

1 – Enjoy a Caviar Brunch
Nevsky Prospect, Mikhailovskaya Ulitsa 1/7
Tel: 7-812-329-6000

Walk into the 19th-century Grand Hotel Europe, with its marvelous art deco decor, and you feel as if you have entered the court of Czar Nicholas II. The highlight here is brunch local style in L'Europe restaurant—that is, caviar and champagne, enjoyed to the strains of live jazz. Brunch is served Sundays between 12:30 and 4 p.m. Reservations are recommended.

2 – Or lunch at Cafe Literatournoe
Nevsky Prospect 18
Tel: 7-812-312-7137

For nearly two centuries, writers and poets have congregated at the elegant "Literature Café" to share stories over a bite to eat. Its classical decor

remains more or less just as A. S. Pushkin saw it, when he dined here on January 27, 1837, before his fatal duel. The unforgettable luncheon includes blinies and juniper berries, accompanied by live chamber music.

3 – Attend Mass at St. Nicholas
Nikolskaya Pl.

A masterpiece of Russian baroque architecture, the 18th-century church of St. Nicholas is the perfect place to take in a Russian Orthodox mass. The service lasts for hours, providing plenty of time to admire the priests dressed in magnificently embroidered cloaks, the choir singing beautiful a cappella, and the revered icons decorating the walls. Dedicated to the Russian Navy, its exterior is covered with plaques honoring soldiers lost at sea.

4 – A Ballet at the Kirov Mariinsky Theatre
1 Teatralnaya Square
Tel: 114-1211, 114-5924

Home to one of the world's most famous ballet and opera companies, this historic theater was founded by Empress Catherine II in 1783. The theater's sumptuous interior alone is worth a visit. Graceful, elegant classics are the specialty here; perhaps you'll catch Tchaikovsky's *Eugene*

Onegin or *Swan Lake;* or an opera such as Prokofiev's *War and Peace.*

5 – TEA AT THE HOTEL ASTORIA
Bolshaya Morskaya 39
Tel: 7-812-313-5757

Since tea was introduced from China in the 1600s, the brew has been a Russian tradition, served strong and black and favored by tsars and peasants alike. Enjoy some of the best in the luxury of the Hotel Astoria's lobby café. It's served between 3 and 6 p.m. from gleaming samovars, to the strains of harp music—an experience truly fit for a tsar.

6 – VISIT PETERHOF
Tel: 7-812-420-0073

Peter the Great's most famous royal complex is 18 miles from St. Petersburg, on the Gulf of Finland, and in summer you can take a hydrofoil there from the pier outside the Winter Palace. Called the "Russian Versailles," the imperial estate consists of several ornate palaces and 147 fountains, all set in a beautifully landscaped park. Three of the palaces are open to the public, with the magnificent Grand Palace and Peter's summer residence, Monplaisir, not to be missed.

7 – EXCURSION TO THE CATHERINE PALACE
Tel: 7-812-466-6669

In Pushkin, about 16 miles from St. Petersburg, is another impressive ensemble of palaces and parks, including this 18th-century baroque palace, where Empress Catherine the Great lived and died. You'll enjoy wandering through the numerous pavilions and admiring the ponds and sculptures. On a hill in nearby Pavlovsk sits the

residence of Emperor Paul I, a gift from Catherine, his mother. Meticulously restored, it is maintained as if the royal family had just gone away for the day.

8 – WALK PALACE SQUARE

The heart of St. Petersburg is itself a vast monument that you can enjoy with a lot of walking, especially along the Neva River and the canals. The city's main square, Palace Square, best seen in the late afternoon, is flanked by the blue, gold, and white facade of the Winter Palace. The square's focal point is the impressive 156-foot Alexander column.

9 – THE STATE HERMITAGE MUSEUM
Dvortsovaya Naberezhnaya 34
Tel: 7-812-311-3465 or 7-812-219-8625

One of the world's greatest museums, the Hermitage requires more than a Sunday afternoon. Founded on Catherine the Great's original 18th-century collection, it now consists of more than 2.7 million works, a diverse range of art and artifacts from all over the world and from ancient Egypt to 20th-century Europe. The Winter Palace, originally inhabited by the royal family, is part of the complex. Consider taking the overview tour and then returning on your own to explore.

10 – ST. ISAAC'S CATHEDRAL
Isaakievskaya Pl. 1
Tel: 7-812-315-9732

Once the main church of St. Petersburg and the largest in Russia, St. Isaac's gilded dome still dominates the skyline. Begun in 1818, the dazzling interior contains icons, paintings, and massive columns of malachite and lapus lazuli.

The Neva River

TEN BEST
~ISTANBUL~

The only city in the world to have played capital to both Christian and Islamic empires, Istanbul is a mystical, magical mix of East and West. This increasingly popular destination is being touted as Europe's latest hot spot, with its world-class hotels, sophisticated restaurants, and fashionable night clubs. But, in this quixotic land, you're never far away from turrets and belvederes, a smoky bazaar where the ancient tradition of haggling lives on, or the evocative cry of the muezzin from the minaret of a nearby mosque.

1 – BLUE MOSQUE
Hippodrome, Sultanahmet
Tel: 90-212-518-1319

You walk into the imposing, light-filled Blue Mosque (Sultan Ahmet Camii) and are immediately struck by the shimmering brilliance of 20,000-plus blue Iznik tiles. Completed in 1616, this six-minareted place of worship is nearly always filled with the faithful. Don't miss the carpet museum in the Royal Pavilion, where priceless carpets are treated as works of art. You can practice your bargaining at the bazaar.

2 – AYNALIKAVAK SUMMER PAVILION
Aynalikavak Caddesi, Hasköy, Tel: 90-212-250-4094

ISTANBUL
PERA PALACE HOTEL
S. A. RICHTER & Cᵒ - NAPLES   RÉPRODUCTION INTERDITE

Perched on the Pera side of the Golden Horn, where Ottoman sultans once came for country excursions, this gorgeous building is all that remains of a large palace dating from the 17th century. Built in Ottoman rococo style, it's most famous for serving as a sanctuary for Sultan Selim III, a respected composer who wrote music here. In the basement you'll find an exhibit of Turkish musical instruments, but most people come to stroll in the pretty summer-time gardens.

3 – BRUNCH AT THE FOUR SEASONS ISTANBUL
Tevkifhani Sok No. 1, Sultanahmet
Tel: 90-212-638-8200

In the glass-enclosed, saffron-painted inner courtyard of the Four Seasons, you'll enjoy sophisticated Mediterranean and Turkish specialties and impeccable service. Part of the attraction is that this sumptuous hotel, located in the heart of Sultanahmet, was converted from a prison where dissident journalists and politicians were once sent to cool their heels.

4 – SEE TOPKAPI PALACE
Sultanahmet, Tel: 90-212-512-0480

For more than four centuries, the Ottoman sultans ruled their vast domains from this imperial palace. From afar, the maze of buildings, completed in 1479, is a striking sight with its medley of minarets, belvederes, domes, and turrets. Up close, the complex, which incorporates 70 hectares (173 acres) of gardens, courtyards, living quarters, palace quarters, and armories, is overwhelming. Tours can only take in a small part. Among the highlights: the sultan's private court and the 400-room harem quarter, where the sultan's wives and concubines resided in seclusion. And don't miss the sultan's famous jewels—including the Topkapi dagger and the Spoonmakers' Diamond—in the Imperial Treasury.

5 – Lunch at Park Samdan
Mim Kemal Oke Caddesi 18; Tel: 90-212-225-0710
Ring the bell and you are ushered into Park Samdan's stately dining room, sensing right away that you have discovered a favorite local secret. Indeed, tucked away in the fashionable Nisantasi neighborhood, on the European side of the Bosporus, Park Samdan has been a favorite among locals since it opened in 1982. The menu serves up an intriguing mix of Turkish and French cuisine; the meze selection is outstanding. Be sure to try the incomparable ice cream with meringue and a savory, grainy chocolate sauce. The city's trendy elite favor the cozy little second bar at the rear.

6 – An Afternoon on the Bosporus
There are two ways to explore the Bosporus, the strait that divides Europe and Asia: Take a cruise from Quay 3 at Eminönü, which will zigzag north, stop near the Black Sea for lunch, and return; or hop on and off commuter ferries. Either way, you'll see fashionable suburbs such as Bebek, summer residences built by the city's richest families during Ottoman rule, 19th-century wooden villas, and ancient fortresses and palaces. Include a stop at Kanlica on the Asian shore to sample the delicious yogurt served at little restaurants around the plane-shaded square by the quay.

AN AFTERNOON TREAT

Yogurt has a special place in Turkish cuisine. Although often made of cows' milk, the best Turkish yogurts are made of a mixture of cow, sheep, and/or water-buffalo milk. Many traditional dishes are prepared with a yogurt-based sauce, but for the ultimate yogurt experience, taste it in spring after the animals have been browsing on wild herbs and greens. Many connoisseurs prefer to sweeten their yogurt with just a little powdered sugar.

Here are a few of the best places to sample this local specialty:

1 – Ozkonak Muhallebicisi is a neighborhood restaurant famous for its dairy dishes. Also try the clotted cream (*kaymak*) and milk puddings. Akarsu Caddesi, 60. Cihangir, Taksim. Tel: 90-212-249-1307.
2 – An outstanding temple of Ottoman cuisine, Hunkar serves many wonderful dishes. The yogurt is good throughout the year, but best during May. Mim Kemal Oke Cadesi, 21. Nisantasi. Tel: 90-212-296-3811.
3 – You can count on Kanaat Lokantasi, another full-menu restaurant, for first-rate yogurt throughout the year. Selmanipak Caddesi, 25. Uskudar. Tel: 90-216-333-3791.
4 – Asirlik Kanlica Yogurdu is a very old company that produces a very light and delicious yogurt. You can enjoy it in their attractive café on the Bosporus shore. Kanlica Iskele Yani, 2. Ismail Aga Gazinosu, Kanlica. Tel: 90-216-413-4469.

If you can't make it to any of these places, look for packs of Tikvesle Altin Kaymak Yogurdu at any Istanbul market.

Painting on Water

arbling is the exquisite process of capturing on paper the swirling designs of colorful paints floating on oily water. It's called marbling because the abstract patterns resemble the delicate veins that appear in marble.

When marbling began is not precisely known, but the technique probably originated in Central Asia during the Tang dynasty. It traveled along the Silk Road to Iran and then Turkey sometime in the 14th century. There, Islamic monastics seeking to express divine beauty through the arts perfected the art form. The Koran was decorated with marbled paper, and official documents were written on marbled paper to make erasure and forgery nearly impossible.

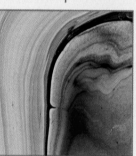

At the end of the 16th century, European tradesmen, diplomats, and travelers brought marbled paper back home to Italy, Germany, France, and England, where it became known as Turkish paper and fetched high prices. There it was popularly used for book bindings and wall coverings. While the technique traditionally uses abstract patterns, in more recent times experiments have been made with figurative designs, especially flowers.

Turkish artist Hikmet Barutcugil has revolutionized marbling art by extending its application to include wood, glass, ceramic, fabrics, and candles. His endpapers are exhibited in museums around the world, including London's British Museum. I visited this great artist one Sunday afternoon at his studio across the Bosporus and learned the craft of marbled papermaking.

"It is called *ebru* in Turkish," Hikmet said, "meaning veined fabric used for covering holy books." I watched Hikmet load his brush with paint and splatter it onto the water surface. He took a metal stylus and zigzagged it through the paint to create different patterns. He then ran a fine comb across the length of the design. He added pools of green and red paint, through which he moved the stylus to create stems, leaves, and flowers.

What remained in effect was a floating picture on the water surface. Hikmet carefully placed a piece of paper and captured the design. Once transferred, he lay the paper out to dry. "Each painting is an original," he said. His secret? "To obtain beautiful results, you need a light hand, a refined taste, and an open mind to appreciate the unexpected patterns forming on the water," he said.

Hikmet conducts workshops that are open to the public. Address: Hikmet and Fusan Barutcugil, EBRI STAN SALACAK, Hafiz Mehmet Bey Sok. No: 8 I hsaniye Üsküdar I. Tel: (0)-216-478-4787 or 90-216-334-59-34.

SHOPPING IN ISTANBUL

Everyone knows about the Grand Bazaar, with its 4,000 shops purveying beautiful carpets, leather ware, alabaster bowls, and other local treasures. But don't forget about the Egyptian (Spice) Market, overflowing with fragrant spices, nuts, and dried fruits. Or the trendy Beyoglu district, with its array of posh shops. Istiklal Caddesi is a popular pedestrian shopping avenue. There are also a number of modern shopping complexes that are fun to browse. On Sunday, head for the flea market in Beyazit Square, a delightful feast of trinkets, unique handmade goods, and antiques. Remember: You'll need your bargaining skills.

7 – TAKE A HELICOPTER TOUR

For a different perspective, hop aboard a helicopter and view Istanbul from high above. You'll be amazed at the extent of the covered bazaar, and see how Topkapi, Hagia Sophia, Blue Mosque, and Suleyman Mosque relate to the Golden Horn, the Bosporus, and the Sea of Marmara—a view ancient invaders surely would have appreciated. Sancak Air (Tel: 90-212-541-4141) offers half-hour and hour tours.

8 – LUNCH AT CAFÉ DU LEVANT

Hasköy Caddesi 27, Hasköy; Tel: 90-212-235-6328

The wealthy Koc family owns this chic French bistro situated midway up the eastern side of the Golden Horn. Its antique Left Bank furniture and vintage ladies' purses on the walls make you feel as if you have entered turn-of-the-20th-century Paris. The menu is full of classic French cuisine, including a fine array of meat and fish dishes. On the dessert menu is *pain perdu*, which deifies French toast. The wine list offers French vintages, but go with one of the Turkish varieties; the whites are good. The place is crowded on weekends, so be sure to make a reservation.

9 – SAMPLE KEBABS AT TIKE

Haciadil Caddesi 4 Aralik, No. 1, 2nd Levent
Tel: 90-212-281-8871

A good place to experience the ultimate Turkish specialty is this sleek, trendy, upmarket joint located in the heart of Istanbul. The big attraction here are the amazingly tender lamb kebabs. Before you order, you'll be offered thin, warm bread with Turkish goat cheese and fresh greens such as rocket, mint, and turnip. In summer, ask to dine in the terraced garden. (There's also a branch in Suadiye on the Asian side.)

10 – SEE THE ARCHAEOLOGICAL MUSEUM

Osman Hamdi Bey Yokusu, Sultanahmet
Tel: 90-212-520-7740

Antiquities from all over the country are showcased in this extensive collection. You'll see Greek, Roman, and Byzantine sculpture, earthenware, bronze, glassware, coins, and medallions. Look for the fourth-century Alexander Sarcophagus, with its fabulous battle scenes; and the Sarcophagus of the Mourning Women, depicting the ancient tradition of hiring women to grieve for loved ones.

Ten Best
~San Francisco~

1 – Ride a Cable car on the Powell Lines

After exploring Fisherman's Wharf with its tourist shops, fish stands, and street performers, hop aboard a cable car. These colorful Victorian cars, with their Bombay roofs and clanging bells, replaced horse-drawn streetcars in 1873 and have been a San Francisco icon ever since. Sights along the Powell-Hyde line include Russian Hill, Nob Hill, and Union Square. Cable cars descend the city's steepest slope (on Hyde Street between Chestnut and Bay Streets). The Powell-Mason line takes in North Beach and Nob Hill. Both lines provide views of the bay, Alcatraz, and the Golden Gate Bridge. Tip: Board along the route rather than waiting with a crowd at the terminus.

2 – Cross Golden Gate Bridge

This beautiful, red-orange bridge, with its art deco towers reaching high above the entrance to San Francisco Bay, has become the defining symbol of the Bay Area. For the best vistas from the San Francisco side, head to Vista Point (at the toll station); Fort Point (off Lincoln Blvd.); and Lands End (U.S.S. *San Francisco* parking lot, off El Camino del Mar). But the greatest experience is to walk across the bridge itself, taking in splendid views over the sailboat-dotted bay, the city glistening far beyond. If it feels as if the bridge is moving, it is: Golden Gate was built to sway 27.7 feet side to side as protection against powerful winds and earthquakes.

IN THE HEART OF THE CITY
POWELL AT ELLIS STREET
SAN FRANCISCO CALIFORNIA
GOLDEN STATE HOTEL
WORTHY OF THE NAME

3 – Shop at Union Square

San Francisco's traditional heart is Union Square, a lively hub of elegant stores, high-end hotels, bell-clanging cable cars, and flower stalls. Stores range from vast Macy's and Neiman Marcus to Tiffany and Chanel. Dominating the square's eastern side is the Westin St. Francis Hotel, its marble and gilt reflecting the opulent vision of railroad magnate Charles T. Crocker. For a thrill, go to the rear lobby and ride a glass elevator up the outside of the tower. Union Square Park has received a 25-million-dollar makeover that includes a granite plaza with a terraced stage, a café, and grassy terraces where weary shoppers relax.

4 – Visit the San Francisco Museum of Modern Art

151 3rd Street; Tel: 415-357-4000; www.sfmoma.org

Spend the afternoon perusing this fabulous collection of 20th-century art. The museum's most renowned work is Henri Matisse's "Femme au Chapeau" ("Woman Wearing a Hat," 1905), a classic example of Fauvism. But many other famous artists are represented here, including Cézanne, Picasso, Rivera, Warhol, Koons, Rauschenberg, and Mondrian, to name a few. The museum also serves as a frequent stopping-off point for prestigious traveling blockbuster shows. The building itself is impressive, a powerful mass of geometric forms. Inside, light pours through a central atrium, and a steel catwalk crosses beneath a skylight 23 terrifying meters (75 feet) above the floor.

5 – TAKE THE FERRY TO SAUSALITO
Tel: 415-455-2000; www.goldengateferry.org

The Golden Gate Ferry departs from the historic San Francisco Ferry building at the foot of Market Street, taking you on the bay amid sailboats and gulls. Thirty minutes later you're in the heart of Sausalito, a Mediterranean-style village clinging to steep hills above a picturesque, yacht-filled harbor. You can spend a pleasant afternoon perusing quaint shops, fine boutiques, and art galleries and dining along the waterfront before catching the ferry back to the city.

6 – LUNCH AT POSTRIO
545 Post Street; Tel: 415-776-7825; www.postrio.com

Opened in 1989 as one of chef Wolfgang Puck's flagship endeavors, this posh institution features striking modern decor. Colorful patterns, whimsical light fixtures, and mirrored art are accented by the works of such world renowned modern artists as Rauschenberg, Rosenquist, and others. As for dining, you're in for a special treat, whether you order one of Wolfgang's gourmet pizzas or a four-course meal with champagne.

VICTORIAN HOME WALK

Contact Jay Gifford at 415-252-9485
E-mail: jay@victorianwalk.com

Get to know the Painted Ladies of San Francisco along the Victorian Home Walk. You'll learn why they feature so many bay windows (to collect light on foggy days) and to identify a wide range of architectural styles, including Queen Anne, Edwardian, and Italianate. Because the city's hills can be daunting, tours are self-paced and low-impact, making them appropriate for young and old.

7 – FERRY BUILDING MARKETPLACE
Foot of Market Street along the Embarcadero
Tel: 415-693-0996; www.ferrybuildingmarketplace.com

The San Francisco Bay Area's culinary traditions and agricultural resources are celebrated at the Ferry Building Marketplace, housed in the historic Ferry Building. Food shops, cafés, and restaurants line its 201-meter (660-foot) skylighted nave. You'll find (and smell) meat, fish, wine, coffee, cheese, chocolate, pastries, olive oil, fresh produce. Of special note are the oysters at Hog Island Oyster Company, where you sit at at the U-shaped bar and watch staff expertly shuck glistening bivalves over mounds of crushed ice. A mixed dozen might include Hog Island's signature plump Sweetwaters, briny Atlantics, and sweet kumamotos. For a special treat, try Charles Phan's nationally acclaimed Vietnamese restaurant, the Slanted Door (415-861-8032), which anchors the Marketplace's northwest corner. Outside, a farmers market—a national showcase of organic and artisanal foods—unfurls Tuesdays, Thursdays, Saturdays, and Sundays.

8 – WANDER WAVERLY PLACE

You'll find this picturesque lane in the heart of Chinatown, parallel to Grant Avenue and Stockton Street between Washington and Sacramento Streets. It's known as the Street of Painted Balconies—look up to see the iron balconies painted red, yellow, and green to understand why. Commercial enterprises generally occupy a building's bottom floor, associations or dwellings the middle floors, and temples are on top, closest to heaven. Don't miss Tin How Temple (125 Waverly Place), the oldest Chinese temple in the United States, founded in 1852. For lunch, the modest Potsticker restaurant (150 Waverly Place) is a good choice. Nearby, on tiny Ross Alley, you can watch fortune cookies being made by hand at the Golden Gate Fortune Cookie Factory.

9 – DRIVE THROUGH NAPA VALLEY

Eighty kilometers (50 miles) north of San Francisco awaits the world-famous Napa Valley, bordered by the Coast Range and dotted with picturesque wineries. The valley's main road, California Route 29, links the main towns: Napa, Yountville, St. Helena, and Calistoga. This two-lane highway is often jammed with cars; a quieter route is the parallel Silverado Trail to the east. The best plan of attack is simply to wander and stop at will. For starters: Charles Krug is the valley's oldest wine producer; tastings at Beringer Vineyards are conducted in a German mansion with stained-glass windows; Domaine Chandon produces sparkling wine; and the fabulous Niebaum-Coppola Estate focuses on the 1882 stone winery known as Inglenook, now belonging to filmmaker Francis Ford Coppola. Dining choices are endless. French Laundry is one of the top restaurants in the country, serving contemporary American cuisine with French influences (reserve at least two months in advance); while Brix prepares excellent seasonal California fare.

10 – EXPLORE NORTH BEACH

In North Beach the good things—music, art, talk, and especially food—are prized. For this zest for life, we owe the Old World Italians, who brought an appreciation of wine, food, and good company. To pretend you're in Italy, just inhale the aromas from the neighborhood's trattorias, cafés, bakeries, and coffeehouses. Bask in the warm Mediterranean mood at Caffé Trieste, or buy picnic supplies at famous Molinari's deli and lay out a blanket in Washington Square. To this Italian love of life, North Beach adds a live-and-let-live philosophy inherited from the Beats—Jack Kerouac, Lawrence Ferlinghetti, Gary Snyder, et al.—who hung out here in the 1950s. Their greatest legacy is City Lights, "a kind of library where books are sold," according to a sign in the window. A place where North Beach's various pasts blend is Mario's Bohemian Cigar Store, one of the oldest and best original cappuccino cafés in North Beach. Try a baked focaccia sandwich and soak in the authentic ambience.

TEN BEST
~PARIS~

1–STROLL THE FIRST ARRONDISSEMENT

The monarchy may be long gone, but almost everything in this neighborhood is a reminder of centuries of royal rule. For a pleasant amble, begin at the Place de la Concorde (where Louis XVI and Marie-Antoinette met their fate at the guillotine in 1793), with its famous view up the Champs-Elysées to the Arc de Triomphe. Stroll the opposite way, through the Jardin des Tuileries, the royal garden designed by André Le Nôtre in 1666. Replanting has restored Le Nôtre's original design, and cafés, pony rides, and a summer "funfair" give a pleasure garden atmosphere. On the garden's opposite end you'll come to the Louvre, originally constructed as a fortress to protect Paris. Kings lived here for 600 years, until it was converted into a museum of royal treasures. It would take weeks to explore this vast space, which has been expanded through the centuries. A good place to start is in the Sully Wing, which leads straight to the fascinating Egyptian rooms containing the largest collection of Egyptian antiquities after the Cairo Museum. If time is limited, pick up one of the free maps or the guidebook "Louvre First Visit" in the main hall and choose a few works of art or periods before setting out (for example, the "Winged Victory of Samothrace" and the "Mona Lisa").

2 – RELAX AT THE RITZ

15 place Vendôme (1st)
Tel: 33-(01)-43-16-30-70;
www.ritzparis.com

A great way to spend a rainy winter Sunday afternoon is in the lavish health club of the Hôtel Ritz, edging the venerable place Vendôme. There's a gorgeous pool, sauna, Jacuzzi and steam room, exercise equipment, and a full range of spa and beauty treatments (by appointment). The center is open from 7 a.m. to 10 p.m., and lunch is available at pool side.

Afterward, stop in at the Hemingway Bar (15 place Vendôme), where the great writer whiled away many a drinking hour. Beyond classics such as a martini or brandy Manhattan, try barman Colin Field's Midnight Moon, made of cognac, Amaretto, cocoa, and champagne.

3 – BRUNCH AT LE GAVROCHE

19 rue St.-Marc (2nd)
Tel: 33-(01)-42-96-89-70

This wine-oriented bistro near the Bourse calms on Sunday afternoons. Start with the duck foie gras followed by the superb roast lamb. Lovely cheeses, good traditional desserts, and great Beaujolais. Book a late lunch, and you'll be able to study the posters on the walls at leisure, an interesting gallery unto itself.

AIR FRANCE

The Left Bank

4 – Visit Place des Vosges

Métro: Bastille, Chemin Vert, St.-Paul, (4th)

Tucked away in the Marais quarter, this square is Paris's oldest, built by Henri IV in 1605. Ancient *hôtels particuliers* resembling tiny, individual castles surround the open-air space, each with its own story. The famous literary hostess Madame de Sévigné, for example, was born in 1626 at number 1B. Victor Hugo lived at number 6 between 1832 and 1848, writing *Les Chants du Crépuscule* and *Ruy Blas;* it has been converted into a museum. Cardinal Richelieu lived at number 21 between 1615 and 1623. Walk through beautiful gardens to the Renaissance-style Hôtel de Sully at number 7, which mounts regular photography exhibitions. History aside, you can stretch out on the square's grass (a rare opportunity in Paris), stroll around the arcades, and browse the small stores.

5 – Monet's House & Gardens

84 rue Claude Monet, Giverny
Tel: 33-(02)-32-51-28-21; www.fondation-monet.com

Claude Monet's famous gardens, located 78 kilometers (50 miles) northwest of Paris, are a national monument. Averse to formality in gardens, the painter created patterns of symmetrical designs and perspectives by planting clumps and shapes of color that change with every month. The lily pond is a lovely sight, surrounded by flowers and weeping willows. Monet's house, with its pink, roughcast facade and green shutters and decorated as he left it, was the scene of frequent entertaining for his many friends.

6 – Luncheon on a Vintage Barge

Symbols of another era, the *guingettes*—moored barges—along the Marne River offer a perfect Sunday escape, if you're so inclined. Guingettes thrived in the thirties and forties, with a rather roguish reputation, when workers spent

ARRONDISSEMENTS GUIDE

Here's a handy list of neighborhood descriptions for the arrondissements of Paris. Note that we classify Paris restaurants by arrondissement to help you to find dining options near your hotel.

1st	Île de la Cité, Louvre, Place de la Concorde
2nd	Opéra, Bourse
3rd	Sentier, Paris garment district
4th	Le Marais
5th	The Latin Quarter
6th	St.-Germain-des-Prés
7th	Les Invalides, Champs-de-Mars
8th	Champs-Elysées, "Golden Triangle" (luxury shopping along the Avenue Montaigne)
9th	Grands Magasins, Opéra, Pigalle
10th	Canal Saint-Martin, Gare du Nord, Gare de l'Est
11th	La Bastille, Place de la République
12th	Gare de Lyon
13th	La Bibliothèque Nationale, Gobelins, Place d'Italie
14th	Montparnasse
15th	Vaugirard, Porte de Versailles
16th	Passy, Auteuil, Bois de Boulogne
17th	Batignolles, Parc Monceau
18th	Montmartre
19th	Belleville, La Villette
20th	Père La Chaise cemetery

PARIS

Sundays drinking, eating, swimming, boating, and dancing to accordion music. The ambience is tamer now, but you'll still revel in serious eating and dancing along the riverside. The traditional cuisine is *moûles frites*—fried oysters—with chilled wine. There are several guingettes in Joinville-le-Pont, 25 minutes on the RER from Paris's Châtelet station.

7 – TAKE IN A BALLET AT THE OPÉRA GARNIER
Place de l'Opéra (1st)
Tel: 33-(01) 40-01-22-63 (tours and museum), 33-(01) 72-29-35-35 (tickets and reservations); Métro: Opéra

The Opéra Garnier, built under Napoléon III, features gold leaf, precious stones, frescoes, and marble in the flamboyant style typical of the era. An enjoyable way to spend an afternoon is to catch a matinée at this opulent venue. While operas are now mostly staged at the Opéra de Paris-Bastille, the thing to see here is ballet.

Afterwards, trundle over to the legendary Harry's Bar (5 rue Daunou), birthplace of the Bloody Mary and always packed with a cheery crowd. Nostalgic Yanks will enjoy the collection of vintage college pennants. If you're brave, try the aptly named house cocktail, *Le Pétrifiant*.

8 – COFFEE OR A DRINK AT LE BALZAR
49 rue des Écoles (5th); Tel: 33-(01)-43-54-13-67
Intellectuals, writers, and students have talked politics at this old-fashioned brasserie near the Sorbonne since it opened in 1898. Jean-Paul Sartre and Albert Camus used to argue here over lunch. The art deco decor—wood paneling and vast wall mirrors, moleskin banquettes, green-and-white tiling—hasn't changed since the 1930s, and neither has the engraved marble menu—fried calves' liver, Fontainebleau cheese, and sauerkraut with ham and sausage are mainstays.

9 – DINNER AT LASSERRE
17 avenue Franklin Roosevelt (8th)
Tel: 33-(01)-43-59-53-43

One of the city's most glamorous and delightfully old-fashioned restaurants is Lasserre, with its silk draperies, fine porcelain, and crystal glasses. The ceiling, painted with clouds and blue sky, slides back on a sunny day. Chef Jean-Louis Nomicos is lauded for bringing new life to this classic place. A friendly and fairly priced wine list and impeccable service make a meal here memorable.

10 – ST.-GERMAIN WALK
A delightful way to pass an afternoon or early evening is to stroll around St.-Germain-des-Prés, roughly bounded by the Seine, boulevard St.-Michel, boulevard St.-Germain, and rue des Sts.-Pères. This was the Paris of the "Lost Generation" of the 1920s, and at one time or another home to Ernest Hemingway (44 rue Jacob), Gertrude Stein (5 rue Christine), Henry Miller (24 rue Bonaparte), Thomas Wolfe (13 rue des Beaux-Arts), Colette (28 rue Jacob), and Anatole France (15 quai Malaquais). Shops, galleries, and bookstores abound. Stop by the legendary Café aux Deux Magots (place St.-Germain-des-Prés), which attracted key figures of a whole postwar generation of philosophers and writers, including Ernest Hemingway, André Breton, and André Gide.

TEN BEST
~SYDNEY~

1 – LUNCH AT THE ROCKS

The land west of Circular Quay between Sydney Cove and Darling Harbour is called The Rocks, where early Sydney began. Today, the former working-class area bustles with shops, cafés, hotels, and restaurants to suit every taste. Foremost among them is the Park Hyatt (7 Hickson Road, 61-2-9241-1234), where you can lunch at the No. 7 at the Park restaurant. The Australian fare is fine, but it's the view that's memorable: the Sydney Opera House and the world-famous harbor in a single window frame.

The Opera House is one of the world's greatest 20th-century architectural statements, with its billowing sails covered with a million ceramic tiles. It's open all year, and opera performances are given monthly, except December. Orchestral music, ballet, chamber music, and plays are ongoing throughout the year. You can book tickets by phone. Caveat: Box seats have poor views of the stage. Tel: 61-2-9250-7777.

2 – BRIDGE CLIMB
5 Cumberland Street
61-2-8274-7777

The extremely popular Bridge Climb provides participants with the gear and guidance to climb to the top of the Sydney Harbor Bridge. The views to the Opera House and the harbor are fabulous, with ferries, paddle steamers, and water taxis passing on the waters far beneath you. If you don't want to climb, take a ferry around Sydney Harbor. Then walk to Kirribilli, where you can have a well-earned espresso in one of the many trendy cafés. To return to the city, walk around the corner to the Luna Park ferry terminal.

3 – TETSUYA'S
529 Kent Street
Tel: 61-2-9267-2900

Many of the dining cognoscenti will tell you that Tetsuya's is the city's finest restaurant. Its low-key entrance and minimalist surroundings contrast sharply with its stunning food. There are no menus. Lunch consists of five courses and dinner six. But rest assured, the individual selections and the overall experience could not be better. The food is Japanese/French fusion, with simple starters such as crab on sushi rice with wasabi mayonnaise. Selections vary regularly, but one of the standout specialties is Tasmanian ocean trout served with fresh trout roe, capsicum peppers, leeks, and crushed capers.

4 – THE NORTHERN BEACHES

The wide, beautiful beaches along the 30-kilometer (18-mile) stretch of coastline north of Sydney are still relatively uncrowded. Buses run regularly from Wynyard Station in the city, offering lovely views of craggy cliffs, wild seas, quiet suburbs, fabulous houses, and lots of chances to get off and explore.

Or continue all the way to Palm Beach, the northernmost beach and a favorite hideaway for local film stars. Here you can hike the well-signed but demanding trail to historic Barrenjoey Lighthouse. The wide expanses of ocean, the misty cliffs, and the views along Pittwater, the Hawkesbury River, and Patonga are breathtaking. To return to the beach, scramble down the steep, rocky Smuggler's route and walk back along the Pittwater side of Palm Beach. For refreshment on the beach, be sure to stop at the shabby but satisfying Carmel's. If you still have the energy, hire a tin dinghy there for an hour or two and pilot yourself around the bends.

5 – CHURCH POINT

Take the bus to Church Point, along the southern shore of Pittwater north of Sydney, and watch the locals at their favorite pastime—sailing in anything that floats. A good vantage point is the fish-and-chips stand on the jetty. Then take the old ferry around Scotland Island, where no cars are allowed. The ferry delivers the milk and mail and takes residents to and from their private jetties.

6 – FERRY RIDE TO MANLY

No trip to Sydney is complete without a ride on the famous Manly Ferry to the seaside resort of Manly. The ferry departs from Circular Quay and takes you on the 11-kilometer (7-mile), 30-minute jaunt across the harbor and into the open sea. At Manly, walk down the Corso to the beachfront, then veer right, past tidal pools, along the outdoor Sculpture Walk all the way to Shelley Beach, where you can swim in the Pacific. Later, top up at one of the many cafés before catching a ferry back to the city.

7 – TARONGA ZOO

Bradleys Head Road, Mosman
Tel: 61-2-9969-2777; www.zoo.nsw.gov.au

One of the quickest and easiest ways to get acquainted with

Australia's wildlife is to visit Taronga Zoo. An added bonus: It's superbly located at Bradleys Head in Mosman, on a hilltop with great views of the city and harbor. Take the ferry from Circular Quay. Once there, a cable car whisks you up the hill to the zoo's highest point, from which you can gradually make your way down past re-created habitats. Don't miss the koala enclosure, with its walkway that winds up to the treetops. You'll also see kangaroos, wombats, and other indigenous creatures.

8 – DARLING HARBOUR

One of the most enjoyable ferry destinations is Darling Harbour, where ships unloaded in the early 19th century. Today, the area is abuzz with activity, thanks to its promenade of restaurants and shops flanked by old sailing ships and private boats of all kinds. The Powerhouse Museum, the country's largest museum, is here, as is the immensely popular Sydney Aquarium and the Sydney Fish Market. You're likely to enjoy street performances by acrobats, mime artists, fire-eaters, and musicians.

9 – ROYAL BOTANIC GARDENS & AROUND

Mrs. Macquarie's Road
Tel: 61-2-9231-8125

An ideal Sunday afternoon activity is wandering through the Royal Botanic Gardens. Stunning examples of flora of Sydney and the surrounding region are set against enchanting views of the Opera House, the city, and the water. Take Mrs. Macquarie's Bushland Walk, where a patch

of Sydney bushland has been re-created circa 1816 using remnant bush. The Palm Grove is a cool summer haven.

The adjacent Art Gallery of New South Wales (Art Gallery Road, The Domain) is the repository of beautiful Asian and South Asian pieces, as well as high-quality works by Australian artists. Nearby, the old wool wharf has been transformed into a trendy playground called Woolloomooloo, busy with shops and upscale restaurants. If you're looking for the really big yachts, this is where to find them. And here you'll also find Harry's Cafe De Wheels, an all-night culinary icon famous for its meat pies—most notably, the Tiger, with mashed green peas and brown gravy.

10 – BONDI BEACH

No beach in Australia is better known by name to overseas visitors than Bondi. To Australians, this kilometer-(.6-mile-) long stretch of sand is a symbol of the relaxed outdoor lifestyle they cherish. It's the most accessible beach from the city, a mere 8 kilometers (5 miles) away. Surrounded by apartments on all but the ocean side, Bondi has been described as "Venice with a swell." If you swim, do so between the pairs of yellow-and-red flags placed at intervals along the beach. Note that there are protected swimming areas at both ends of the beach that are suitable for children. You'll find some good-quality hotels, and eateries on the whole are basic and cheap.

JUST THE
GLORIOUS FOOD
BEST

TEN BEST
~TEA & COFFEE~

When describing tea and coffee, the English poet George Gordon, Lord Byron gave us words to ponder, "'Tis pity wine should be so deleterious, For tea and coffee leave us much more serious."

TEN BEST TEAS

1 – REPUBLIC OF TEA
Worldwide
Tel: 618-478-2100
www.republicoftea.com

With a mission to foment a "Tea Revolution," the Republic of Tea offers a delectable range of full-leaf teas—from black to white and everything in between—that will satisfy even the most discerning sipper. Their online "embassy" will inspire you to expand the horizons of your tea adventures.

2 – TEN REN TEA COMPANY
Worldwide
Tel: 650-583-1047, www.tenren.com

Since 1953, Ten Ren has produced and distributed some of the finest Chinese teas. Combining traditional processing methods and modern technology, Ten Ren ensures that each tea—whether Oolong, Jasmine, Pouchong, Pu-Erh, or Green—will be as fresh as can be.

3 – PEET'S
California
Tel: 510-594-2950, www.peets.com

Peet's offers more than 45 specialty teas that are hand-selected and blended from the freshest and highest quality tea harvests from India and China. Customers return time and time again, enamored of the distinctive flavors and freshness. This retailer's highly informative Web site even recommends which teas are good with milk and which are best for making iced tea.

4 – CHADO
California
Tel: 877-832-5263, www.chadotea.com

Once available only at the Chado Tea Room in Los Angeles, Chado teas are now sold worldwide. The selection is mind-boggling—more than 300 teas!—and the quality is always top rate.

5 – LE PALAIS DES THÉS
Worldwide
Tel: 33-(0)-1-43-56-9090, www.le-palais-des-thes.fr

Le Palais des Thés prides itself on its humanist spirit, regularly visiting tea estates, maintaining long-term relationships with its suppliers, ensuring fair-trade practices, and addressing environmental concerns. The result? Teas of exceptional quality and freshness that are a joy to drink.

6 – IMPERIAL TEA COURT
California
Tel: 415-788-6080, www.imperialtea.com

Founded in 1993, the Imperial Tea Court was the first traditional Chinese teahouse in the United States. It is now renowned as the exclusive purveyor of some of the world's most highly acclaimed and sought-after teas. The Imperial's dedication to the "way of tea" is evident in each delicious cup.

7 – FAUCHON
New York & Paris
Tel: 866-784-7001, www.fauchon.com

Fauchon, a leading gourmet food and specialty company, offers a line of quality teas and coffees. Sipping a cup of "Afternoon in Paris" tea will transport you to the City of Lights and renew your love of tea.

8 – COFFEE BEAN & TEA LEAF
United States
Tel: 805-987-2805, www.coffeebean.com

Established in 1963, the Coffee Bean & Tea Leaf ("the Bean") is a testament to founder Herbert B. Hynam's dedication to excellence and quality. The Bean specializes in whole-bean coffee and loose-leaf teas and continues to be an innovator in blended drinks.

9 – TEANCE
Northern California
Tel: 510-524-1696, www.celadontea.com

If you desire rare and exotic Far East teas, look no further than Teance. Devoted to reviving the art of preparing, drinking, and appreciating traditional, whole-leaf teas, the company features more than a hundred blends and specializes in competition winners and limited-edition teas.

10 – FORTNUM AND MASON
181 Piccadilly, London, England
Tel: 44-(0)-2-077-348-040, www.fortnumandmason.com

Fortnum and Mason, London's venerable gourmet specialty store, has been selling high-quality teas since 1707. The more than 60 blends include teas from Ceylon, India, Nepal, China, and Japan. When in London, experience the fine art of afternoon tea at the store's St. James's Tearoom and enjoy a cup of a traditional tea, such as Earl Grey, a black tea infused with oil of bergamot. Or try a fruit-flavored blend or a green tea rich in antioxidants.

FORTNUM & MASON'S 10 BEST TEAS

1 – Earl Grey
2 – English Breakfast
3 – Ceylon Orange Pekoe
4 – Assam Superb
5 – Queen Anne Tea
6 – Royal Blends
7 – Darjeeling Broken Orange Classic
8 – Lapsong Souchong
9 – Gunpowder Tea
10 – Prince of Wales Blend

TEA FACTS

The world's tea supply comes primarily from six countries: India, Sri Lanka, China, Japan, Kenya, and Indonesia.

A huge variety of teas is readily available, and one of the small pleasures of life is exploring different ones. While nearly all true teas contain caffeine, many teas are now available in a decaffeinated form. Most Westerners prefer black tea from India and Sri Lanka. Indian Assam teas have strong, refreshing flavors and are best drunk with a little cold milk. Sri Lankan teas, such as Orange Pekoe, are very similar to the Assam: strong, hearty, and flavorsome. Chinese semi-fermented teas, with a smokey flavor, are next in popularity, followed by Chinese and Japanese green teas.

Darjeeling is considered the finest of Indian black teas. Currently there are about 80 plantations growing Darjeeling, and they vie for selection as "the best" at numerous competitions. Connoisseurs have come to identify what are called spring, summer, and autumn teas, ranging in taste and aroma from light and floral to deep and complex. India's Assam teas are best in the morning, as they provide a definite kick. Darjeelings lack the "punch" of morning teas and are best enjoyed in the afternoon. Alternative afternoon teas are the Formosa Oolongs, which have an almost sweet taste. Oolong Imperial, for example, has distinctive honey and chestnut undertones. Chinese green teas are less popular in the West.

There are many blended teas known only by trade names, such as Earl Grey, which exude the distinct sweet aroma of bergamot. Russian Caravan is said to have been so named because it was brought from India to St. Petersburg for Catherine the Great. A number of teas have been named after British royals, including the Prince of Wales and Queen Mary.

Flavored teas are fine teas selected and blended with herbs, spices, and fruits. There are old favorites and intriguing new ones. Bitter Lemon, a delightful black tea blended with lemon peel, hibiscus flowers, pineapple pieces, and papaya, has a refreshing taste. Jasmine tea is made from Chung green tea from China, layered with fresh jasmine blossoms. Moroccan Mint is a blend of the finest gunpowder tea and spearmint leaves. Cinnamon Star is a green tea with cinnamon and cloves. Rose hip and Hibiscus blend is a sharp and fruity tisane that makes an excellent afternoon cup.

A natural chamomile gives Chamomile Herb Tea the luscious golden tone and delicate flavor that make it a traditional favorite. In centuries past, the English valued no plant in their gardens more than this herb, which they treasured as a domestic remedy for comforting the soul.

TEN BEST COFFEES

1 – PEET'S COFFEE

Tel: 510-594-2950, www.peets.com

Each day, Peet's hand-roasts its 32 varieties of coffee in small batches, then ships them within 24 hours to give you the freshest, most deeply flavorful cup of coffee possible. Many variables—from where the bean was grown to the way it was processed, from the length and temperature of the roast to every nuance of the weather—affect the roasting process. To guarantee quality, Peet's samples each batch to make sure the roast tastes just right.

2 – TERROIR

Tel: 866-444-5282

www.terroircoffee.com

Specializing in medium-roast styles that bring out the character of the green coffee, this recently established micro-roaster sells only single-origin coffees—no blends. To ensure freshness, Terroir freezes its green coffee in nitrogen-flushed containers. A cup of Terroir's coffee is truly a unique experience.

3 – GREATCOFFEE.COM

Tel: 801-571-8866

This mail-order coffee company, owned and operated by Great Coffees of America, is an offshoot of "The Coffee Review," the most respected and widely read online coffee buying guide. In GreatCoffee.com coffee lovers find a convenient, one-stop shopping outlet for fresh, top-rated coffees from the finest roasters and farms—not to mention a

wealth of information on coffee types and origins. You can treat a friend to a sampler of top-rated coffees or espressos.

4 – THE ROASTERIE

Tel: 800-376-0245, www.theroasterie.com

The Roasterie lovingly "air roasts" its coffee beans, claiming the technique produces a superior outcome: A column of hot air, rather than a conventional turning drum, agitates the roasting beans. Company president Danny O'Neill travels the world over to find the best coffees. Adventuresome coffee lovers slowly make their way through the Roasterie's selection of more than a hundred blends.

5 – DEAN & DELUCA

Tel: 800-221-7714

www.deandeluca.com

Joel Dean and Giorgio DeLuca opened their flagship specialty food store in SoHo, New York City, in 1977. The store has been synonymous with high-quality coffees from around the world.

6 – STARBUCKS

www.starbucks.com

Found now in numerous locations in most U.S. cities and around the world, Starbucks has not allowed ubiquity to diminish its quality. It offers a great selection of the world's best coffees. The company prides itself on locating and purchasing the best coffee from the Americas, Africa, and Southeast Asia. Each coffee is chosen for the qualities that distinguish its origin, thus offering customers defining regional coffees.

A Coffee Review

Kenneth Davids is a coffee expert, an author, and a co-founder of "The Coffee Review," an Internet site (www.coffeereview.com) that serves as a coffee buying guide. Davids conducts blind, expert cuppings of coffees and reports the findings in 100-point reviews, much like those that exist in the wine industry.

Some of the advice Davids gives is basic but bears repeating: When evaluating coffee, first smell it. Begin by sniffing the coffee after it is freshly ground, then smell the brewed coffee to compare the two aromas. Next, taste the coffee. To get the fullest flavor, slurp it, taking the liquid into your mouth so that it spreads evenly over the entire surface of your tongue and reaches all of your taste buds at once. Take your time, and enjoy the process. The more you taste, the better you get at it.

Every fine coffee has particular characteristics that make it unique; however, there are taste generalizations for the three major coffee-growing regions that can be helpful to keep in mind when tasting coffee:

Latin American coffees are known for their clean "mouth feel" and slightly sweet, lively acidity. In some coffees, the acidity sparkles clearly above the other flavor components; in others, it provides a subtle but crisp accent.

African and Arabian coffees often have sweet flavors reminiscent of the aroma of a bowl of fresh fruit. Flavors from these regions range from mellow and winelike to zesty and citrusy.

Coffees from the Pacific region are generally rich and full-bodied, with nutty and earthy flavors. Most can be described as smooth in acidity with a slightly dry finish.

JAMAICAN BLUE MOUNTAIN

Jamaican Blue Mountain coffee has long been considered one of the rarest and most expensive of all coffees. Grown in fog-shrouded mountains at relatively modest elevations, the bean is dense, producing a rich taste and a very distinct aroma.

EAST AFRICAN

Remarkable. Distinctive. Delicious. These adjectives apply to a plethora of coffees grown along a north–south axis that stretches from East Africa down to Zimbabwe. Coffees from Kenya exhibit berry tones, those from Ethiopia have citrus and floral tones, and those from Zambia are medium-bodied and wine-toned.

ARABIAN

The celebrated Arabian Mocha bean grows in mountains at

the southwestern tip of the Arabian Peninsula. Cultivated and processed in the same fashion for more than 500 years, the Arabian bean produces a coffee that is acidic, fruity, and highly fragrant.

CENTRAL AMERICA
Grown along the spine of mountains that runs from southern Mexico to Panama, coffee from Central America is widely diverse in nature. The classic coffees are bright, lively, and robust. The very highest elevation coffees of Guatemala and Costa Rica tend to be bold and full-bodied. Lower elevation coffees are softer and have a more rounded flavor. Nicaraguan coffees are truly hearty.

HAWAIIAN KONA
Hawaii's Big Island possesses that rare combination of ideal growing conditions: high elevation, volcanic soils, cool mornings, warm afternoons, and natural shading. The result is a superior, rich-tasting coffee. The Kona bean grows on the lower slopes of Mount Hualalai and Mauna Loa. A typical Kona cup is gently acidic, fragrant, and wine- or fruit-toned. Not to be missed!

PACIFIC RIM
The best-known and most distinctive Pacific coffees are grown in the Malay Archipelago, a chain of islands that include the nations of Indonesia, Timor, and Papua New Guinea. Deep-toned, traditionally processed coffees from Sumatra, Sulawesi, and Timor exhibit complex fruity, earthy, and musty notes. The wet-processed coffees of Sumatra, Java, and Papua New Guinea are bright and floral. The Indian subcontinent produces Arabica coffees that are sweet, floral, and low in acidity.

SOUTH AMERICAN
South American coffees grow in a mountainous region that stretches from the north—Colombia and Ecuador—down to the high plateaus of Brazil. Robust and flavorful, the classic South American cup is the product of wet processing. Brazil produces the heralded Brazil Santos coffee.

DARK ROASTS
The style of roasting is the single most important factor influencing a coffee's flavor. The longer the roast and the higher the temperature, the darker the bean becomes. The darkest beans are the most flavorful, with a tangy and bittersweet taste.

ESPRESSOS
Espresso is both a unique method of brewing and a style of roast. In brewing, only a cup or two of water is forced through tightly packed ground coffee beans, making an extremely strong cup, or rather shot, of coffee. The espresso roast is dark, but not exceptionally so. The best espresso blends comprise at least three varieties of coffee. The roast can vary from medium to very dark. Italians are famously espresso drinkers, but espresso is popular in many other countries as well.

ORGANICS
Organic coffee must meet exacting standards. It must be propagated, grown, processed, transported, stored, and roasted without the use of synthetic chemicals (e.g., pesticides and herbicides). These coffees are typically more expensive than nonorganic ones as they are more labor intensive and are produced in smaller quantities. However, for many people, the healthful qualities and the distinctive flavors of organic coffee are worth the additional costs.

STARBUCKS' FUNDAMENTALS FOR A GREAT CUP OF COFFEE

The factors that determine a great cup of coffee are Proportion, Grind, Water, and Freshness.

Proportion: Use the right proportion of coffee to water. This is the most important step in making great coffee. For the most flavorful cup of coffee, Starbucks recommends using 10 grams (2 tablespoons) of ground coffee for each 180 milliliters (6 fluid ounces) of water.

Grind: The shorter the brewing process, the finer the grind must be. Different brewing methods have different grind requirements, so grind your coffee accordingly. The amount of time the coffee and water spend together affects the flavor elements that end up in your cup, and the design of your coffeemaker dictates how long the coffee and water are in direct contact during the brewing process.

Water: Use fresh, cold water heated to just below boiling. A cup of coffee is 98 percent water. Therefore, the water you use for making coffee should have a pleasing taste: clean, fresh, and free of impurities.

Freshness: Use freshly ground coffee. Think of coffee as fresh produce. To keep coffee fresh, store it in an opaque, airtight container at room temperature. For the best results, coffee should be ground just before brewing and used or stored immediately.

7 – GRAFFEO COFFEE
Tel: 800-367-9499, www.graffeo.com

For more than 55 years, Graffeo has specialized in only one thing: roasting coffee. This singular focus has resulted in flavorful, delicious blends and a devoted clientele. The finest, freshest Arabica beans from Colombia, Costa Rica, and New Guinea are the basis for all of Graffeo's premium blends.

8 – BUCKS COUNTY COFFEE
Tel: 800-844-8790, www.buckscountycoffee.com

Rodger Owen founded this company in his garage in 1982, originally roasting only nuts. Since adding coffee to its roster in 1988, the company has grown into one of the leading specialty coffee micro-roasters in the United States. The coffees are unique and flavorful.

9 – GREEN MOUNTAIN COFFEE ROASTERS
Tel: 888-879-4627, www.gmcr.com

This specialty roaster offers a wide-ranging variety of coffees and roast styles. Each bean has a distinct story, its flavor speaking of its origin, selection, and quality of roast.

10 – PARADISE ROASTERS
Tel: 763-433-0626, www.paradiseroasters.com

Offering beans from Central America, East Africa, Indonesia, and Hawaii, Paradise Roasters aims to provide its customers with the freshest and highest quality coffee at reasonable prices.

TEN BEST
─DELICATESSENS─

1 – BEN'S
990 blvd. de Maisonneuve, Montréal, Canada
Tel: 514-844-1000

Montréal smoked meat—a blend of corned beef and pastrami—is tender, moist, and flavorful. The smoked meat sandwiches at Ben's rival any New York City corned beef sandwich for taste and are guaranteed to make you a convert. The menu also features cheese blintzes, potato latkes, corned beef and cabbage, and other traditional delicatessen fare. When you dine here, you experience a true deli meal.

2 – LANGER'S DELI
704 S. Alvarado Street, Los Angeles, California
Tel: 213-483-8050

An institution in Los Angeles since 1947, Langer's Deli is heralded for its pastrami sandwiches served on crusty seeded rye. Among the many variations, the No. 19 stands out: thickly sliced, hand-cut pastrami with Swiss cheese and coleslaw. Legions of fans can't be wrong.

3 – ART'S DELI
12224 Ventura Boulevard, Studio City, California
Tel: 818-762-1221

This California establishment looks as if it had been transplanted whole from New York City—right down to the Naugahyde, Formica, and linoleum. The menu fare is

true New York deli as well. Popular items include the chicken and matzo ball soup and hot pastrami and corned beef sandwiches. Portions are generous; come with an empty stomach.

4 – MANNY'S
1141 S. Jefferson Street, Chicago, Illinois
Tel: 312-939-2855, www.mannysdeli.com

Although the corned beef and pastrami sandwiches are consistent crowd-pleasers, this cafeteria-style deli also serves up heaping plates of hash. Laced with bits of pepper, onion, and potatoes and served with two eggs on top, this breakfast dish will have you coming back for more. Other deli fare includes cheese blintzes and potato pancakes.

5 – SECOND AVENUE DELI
156 2nd Avenue, New York, New York
Tel: 212-677-0606, www.2ndavedeli.com

Consistently rated one of the best delicatessens in New York City, Second Avenue Deli exhibits all the hustle and bustle one expects of a New York deli. Second Avenue never fails to satisfy: The hot corned beef, pastrami, and chicken soup feed the soul as well as the stomach, and long-time customers rave about the baked knish. Hint: Go during the day when the corned beef is fresh out of the oven.

Italian  Sandwiches

DELICATESSENS

6 – CARNEGIE DELI

854 7th Avenue, New York, New York

Tel: 212-757-2245, www.carnegiedeli.com

The Carnegie is known as much for its New York scene as its delicious fare. Patrons sit shoulder to shoulder at too-small tables while waiters buzz nimbly through the crowded deli. The corned beef and pastrami are home-cured and rich; the sandwiches come piled high with mountain-size portions. Just try wrapping your hands around one! You'll also enjoy the cheese blintzes, stuffed cabbage with sweet and sour sauce, and the Nova Scotia salmon omelet.

7 – CENTRE STREET DELI

1136 Centre, Thornhill, Ontario, Canada

Tel: 905-731-8037, www.centrestreetdeli.com

This old-fashioned deli serves Jewish soul food that warms the heart. The Montreal smoked meat is juicy, tender, and hand-cut. The thick sandwiches come with coleslaw and fries. Other menu items include perogies, latkes, knishes, cabbage rolls, and chicken soup.

8 – KATZ'S DELI

205 E. Houston Street, New York, New York
Tel: 212-254-2246, www.katzdeli.com

In business since the 1890s, Katz's kosher deli attracts locals, celebrities, and tourists alike. Despite its popularity, the deli has retained its neighborhood diner feel. The corned beef, salami, and hot dogs are all made on the premises. The pastrami and Reuben sandwiches draw the biggest raves.

9 – ZAFTIGS DELICATESSEN

335 Harvard Street, Brookline, Massachusetts
Tel: 617-975-0075, www.zaftigs.com

Zaftigs raises the bar for deli dining. It is a wonderful place with plenty of natural lighting, wooden floors, brightly colored paintings, and comfortable banquettes. The menu features traditional Jewish favorites, such as chopped liver and stuffed cabbage, as well as some new twists to old favorites such as banana-stuffed challah French toast and Cheddar-apple omelettes.

10 – BRENT'S DELI

19565 Parthenia Street, Northridge, California
Tel: 818-886-5679, brentsdeli.com

This deli serves classic deli food, from lean pastrami on rye to cabbage soup, from an egg cream to a four-decker chocolate cake. Nothing on the menu disappoints. The pickle plate brought to the table is an added bonus.

Ten Best
~Bar~B~Que Joints~

1 – Corky's
5259 Poplar Avenue, Memphis, Tennessee
Tel: 901-685-9744, www.corkysbbq.com

This no-frills restaurant is a barbecue landmark in Memphis. Slow-cooked to perfection in open and closed pits and served with tangy sauces, the hickory-smoked meats are so tender they fall off the bone. Try the hand-pulled pork shoulder—it is cooked for more than 22 hours!

2 – The Skylight Inn
1501 S. Lee Street, Ayden, North Carolina
Tel: 252-746-4113

At the Skylight Inn you can order only two things: a pulled pork sandwich topped with coleslaw or a pulled pork dish with cornbread and coleslaw. Whole pigs are slow-roasted over oak fires in open-air pits. Despite the short menu, the Skylight doesn't want for customers.

3 – Dillsboro Smokehouse
403 Haywood Street, Dillsboro, North Carolina
Tel: 828-586-9556, www.dillsborosmokehousebbq.com

Step into the Dillsboro Smokehouse and step into barbecue heaven. The smell of hickory-smoked meats hangs in the air of this friendly, down-home establishment, making your mouth water. Whether you try the house specialty—baby back ribs dripping in a peach-flavored sauce—or opt for barbecued beef, chicken, or pork, your dinner comes with four generous side dishes. Leave room for one of the scrumptious homemade desserts.

4 – Jim Neely's Interstate Barbecue
2265 S. Third Street, Memphis, Tennessee
Tel: 901-775-2304 or 901-775-1045

The sauce recipe might be a secret, but the word is out about Jim Neely's. Each day brings new and repeat customers to this family-owned business that dishes up some of the country's best barbecue. Slow-cooked in closed pits, the meat is incredibly moist and unbelievably good. It's so popular that Jim has installed a drive-thru window!

5 – Arthur Bryant's
1727 Brooklyn Avenue, Kansas City, Missouri
Tel: 816-231-1123, www.arthurbryantsbbq.com

Bryant's has been touted as "the business that gave Kansas City its renown as a barbecue capital." Simple on décor but high on taste, Bryant's has been serving hickory- and-oak-smoked barbecue since the 1920s, counting presidents and celebrities as devotees. Its two sauces—Original and Rich & Spicy—justly deserve the accolades heaped upon them.

TWO MORE B-B-Q TREATS!

NEW ZION MISSIONARY BAPTIST CHURCH
2601 Montgomery Street, Huntsville, Texas

To a Texan, barbecue is sacred. Welcome to New Zion Missionary Baptist Church, where Annie Ward serves up "Holy Barbecue." After one visit you'll be singing the praises of this delicious meat.

— · —

VIRGIL'S REAL B-B-Q
152 W. 44th Street, New York, New York
Tel: 212-921-9494

A massive roadhouse in New York City! Buttermilk onion rings with blue-cheese dip. Hush Puppies with honey butter, rack of pork ribs, Texas hot links, pulled pork, New Orleans-style barbecued shrimp—everything tasty. There is also a good list of top beers.

6 – TENNESSEE RED'S
2133 S.E. 11th Avenue, Portland, Oregon
Tel: 503-231-1710

Laid-back Tennessee Red's serves up some of the tastiest barbecue outside the South. Generous side dishes and no less than five sauces accompany each entrée. The cornbread melts in your mouth.

7 – K.C. MASTERPIECE
4747 Wyandotte Street, Kansas City, Missouri
Tel: 816-531-3332

Known around the world for its barbecue sauce, K.C. Masterpiece has elevated barbecuing to an art. The brisket sandwich and the baby back ribs bespeak authentic Kansas City barbecue.

8 – BBQ & RIBS CO.
North Carolina and Chesapeake, Virginia
Tel: 866-766-5467, www.bbqandribs.com

People in eastern North Carolina have exacting barbecue standards, and BBQ & Ribs meets them. The ribs are cooked St. Louis style for 11 hours over a hickory fire, then chopped and seasoned with a unique "Pigwyzz" vinegar. The taste is unbeatable.

9 – FIREFLY'S
350 E. Main Street, Marlborough, Massachusetts
Tel: 508-357-8883

This award-winning barbecue joint dishes up ribs, brisket, and pulled chicken. Devotees rave about Firefly's Memphis B-B-Q sauce that has a hint of brown sugar molasses and chocolate. Wash it all down with a glass of sweet tea straight out of the South.

10 – THE SALT LICK
18001 FM 1826, Driftwood, Texas
Tel: 512-858-4959, www.saltlickbbq.com

Featuring an indoor open pit where you can see your meal being cooked, the Salt Lick is a warm and friendly establishment that excels at barbecue. Customers sit at picnic tables and dig into mouthwatering platters of ribs, brisket, sausages, and plentiful side dishes.

TEN BEST
~PATISSERIES~

1 – SWEET LADY JANE
8360 Melrose Avenue
Los Angeles, California
Tel: 323-653-7145
www.sweetladyjane.com

This upscale bakery makes some of the best lemon meringue tarts, flourless chocolate cake, and cheesebread in the country. The decorated cakes are both visual and culinary masterpieces. Grab a seat and enjoy a croissant and coffee, a sandwich, or a scone with a cup of tea.

2 – BOULE
420 N. La Cienega Boulevard, Los Angeles, California
Tel: 310-289-9977, www.boulela.com

Treating her pastries as the works of art they are, owner Michelle Myers showcases her desserts in a setting reminiscent of a jewelry store, with high ceilings and a color scheme similar to that of a blue Tiffany box. She uses only the freshest seasonal ingredients to prepare such delicacies as champagne-chocolate truffles, *pain au chocolat,* rose water macaroons, Chino strawberry ice cream, various cakes, and candy also.

3 – MIETTE
One Ferry Building, Shop No. 10, San Francisco, California
Tel: 415-837-0300, www.miettecakes.com

This small pastry shop, inspired by the patisseries of Paris, packs a delectable wallop. With an emphasis on quality, Miette makes only limited amounts of its goods each day from local and organic ingredients. Some favorite items available at Miette's are Parisian macaroons, chocolate éclairs, gingerbread cupcakes, and scrumptious morning buns.

4 – PANELLA
Corso Rinascimento 72
Rome, Italy
Tel: 39-06-6880-2783

The Panella Bakery has been producing bread since 1920. The family owners make more than 80 varieties. Some of the breads and pastries take inspiration from the Far East and Arabia; others are based on old Roman, Greek, and Sicilian recipes. The bakery has expanded and now includes a café offering an excellent selection of sorbets and juices as well as traditional pastries that are made nowhere else.

5 – POILÂNE
8 Rue du Cherche-Midi, Paris, France
Tel: 33-(0)-1-45-48-42-59, www.poilane.fr

Poilâne hasn't changed much since it opened in 1932. The beautiful loaves of bread decorated with simple designs of leaves and flowers will make you yearn for an all-but-vanished Paris. The apple tarts, butter cookies, and sourdough bread cooked in a wood-burning oven are just some of the heavenly items made here.

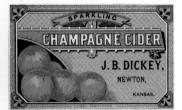

Freshly Baked Bread

6 – FAUCHON
Paris, France
Tel: 33-(0)-1-866-784-7001, www.fauchon.com

Fauchon is a long-respected food emporium in Paris that is renowned for its high-quality gourmet foods. Its patisserie section surpasses all expectations. The classic Megève marries a satiny mousse with a crispy vanilla meringue. Toasted hazelnuts top lemon cream tarts. And as a pièce de resistance, the Douceur has no equal: It is a three-tiered confection of macerated cherries, mascarpone cream thickened with honey, and milk-chocolate sponge cake flecked with nougat.

7 – PAYARD
1032 Lexington Avenue, New York, New York
Tel: 212-717-5252, www.payard.com

Pastry chef François Payard became one of the most famous dessert men in America when he opened his patisserie. Upper East Siders and tourists alike flock to sample the delectable confections—cakes, tarts, truffles, and more—in a belle epoque-inspired setting.

8 – GÉRARD MULOT PATISSERIE
76, rue de Seine, Paris, France
Tel: 33-(0)-1-43-26-85-77

The elegant Gérard Mulot Patisserie is as central to the life of the St.-Germain neighborhood as are the fabled cafés. Mulot bakes many of his pastries fresh every few hours, and regulars stop by as many as four times a day. The flaky pastries melt in your mouth, and the cakes and tarts are sinfully rich.

9 – LADURÉE
2, place de la Gare, Paris, France
www.pladuree.com

Considered by many to be "the quintessential Paris tea salon," the original 1862 Ladurée near the Place de la Madeleine is acclaimed as much for its atmosphere as for its pastries. The walls are hung with elaborately gilt-framed mirrors beneath a ceiling gaily painted with ribbons, bows, and rosy cherubs in a dreamy cloudscape. Everything from the black-aproned wait staff to the silver plated flatware bespeaks old Paris—except for the food. The lush, chewy macaroons are second to none; the Royal Chocolats, a treat made from rum-soaked almond sponge cake and chocolate ganache, is simply divine.

10 – LA BREA BAKERY
United States
818-742-4242, www.labreabakery.com

Chef Nancy Silverton discovered there were no shortcuts to a tasty, dignified handmade loaf. Made from flour, water, and organic grapes, her starter became her prized possession, allowing her to develop breads with deep, complex flavors, chewy textures, and unique cream-colored interiors. Sold wholesale, La Brea breads can be found in markets countrywide.

Ten Best
~Chocolates~

Each chocolatier on our list produces signature melt-in-your-mouth chocolates, be it a single-source dark chocolate bar, a cream- or liqueur-filled bonbon, a praline, fruit dipped in chocolate, a truffle, fudge, or some other sinfully delicious treat. You'll never regret indulging yourself with the confections produced by these premier chocolate-makers.

1 – Teuscher
Zurich, Switzerland
www.teuscher.com

The Teuscher chocolate tradition began more than 60 years ago in a small town in the Swiss Alps. Dolf Teuscher scoured the world to find the finest cocoa, marzipan, fruits, nuts, and other ingredients with which to make his confectionary. After years of experimenting, he skillfully blended these ingredients into his now famous recipes.

Today the Teuscher kitchens in Zürich make more than one hundred varieties of chocolates using these original recipes, which have been handed down from father to son. Only the finest and most expensive natural ingredients are used and absolutely no chemicals, additives, or preservatives are added. The house specialty is a champagne truffles, a blend of fresh cream, butter, and chocolate with a champagne cream center, dusted with confectioner's sugar.

2 – Bodega
Costa Mesa, California
Tel: 888-3-BODEGA,
www.bodegachocolates.com

Bodega chocolates are made from only the finest ingredients, without the benefit of artificial flavors, compounds, or wax. Since each piece is hand-cut, dipped, and wrapped, Bodega offers only a limited variety of goods. But what a delicious selection! The extremely popular fudge truffle bars are rich and buttery and come in five flavors. Try the truly decadent dulce de leche.

3 – Scharffen Berger Chocolate Maker, Inc.
Berkeley, California
Tel: 510-981-4050, www.scharffenberger.com

Specializing in dark chocolate, Scharffen Berger Chocolate Maker is a premier chocolate manufacturer. It executes each step of the manufacturing process itself, all the way from bean to bar to ensure that its finished chocolate delivers a flavor like no other. The chocolate-makers first find the finest cacao available, then carefully taste and blend beans of different origins to create a unique flavor profile. All the chocolate is made in small batches using artisanal manufacturing methods. In addition to its ready-to-eat bars, Scharffen Berger makes a variety of baking chocolates.

CHOCOLATES

4 – JACQUES TORRES CHOCOLATE
350 Hudson Street, New York, New York
Tel: 212-414-2462, www.mrchocolate.com

When you step into Jacques Torres Chocolate, you feel as though you've stepped into a small European specialty store. Many customers compare the experience to the movie *Chocolat*. Jacques specializes in fresh, hand-crafted chocolates. Eat them there, where café tables encourage you to sit, sip hot chocolate, and enjoy a freshly baked *pain au chocolat*—or take a selection home. Visitors often can see the chocolate goodies being prepared behind large glass windows. A second Jacques Torres Chocolate shop is located in Brooklyn.

5 – NORMAN LOVE CONFECTIONS
Ft. Myers, Florida
Tel: 239-561-7215
normanloveconfections.com

"Chocolate is my passion," says Norman Love, who dreamed of making a chocolate candy that was visually stunning as well as delicious. Love and a partner perfected a technique in which the colored designs for each candy are hand-painted or airbrushed into chocolate molds, which are then filled with the finest chocolate imported from Belgium, France, and Switzerland. The pumpkin white chocolate bonbon is almost too gorgeous to eat. Using only the freshest ingredients, his recipes call for pureed raspberries, bananas, ginger, caramel, passionfruit, and hazelnuts, to name a few.

6 – VALRHONA
France
Tel: 33-1-04-75-07-90-90, www.valrhona.com

Valrhona has been creating exceptional gourmet chocolate since 1922, with cocoa beans purchased directly from premier plantations in South America, the Caribbean, and Pacific regions. The chocolate, made in the French style, comes in a variety of bars. Valrhona was one of the first chocolatiers to describe its chocolate like wine, labeling creations as grand cru, single origin, single estate, and vintage chocolate from bean to bar.

7 – GODIVA CHOCOLATIER
Tel: 800-9GODIVA, www.godiva.com

The beginning of Godiva chocolates traces back to a 1920s chocolate- and sweet-making workshop owned and operated by the Draps family in Brussels, Belgium. Their "pralines," typical Belgian filled chocolates, were sold in the large, highly fashionable shops. At the age of 14, Joseph Draps went into the family business. Over the years, he developed both his ability and creative talent as a master chocolate-maker as well as his business sense. He decided to create a prestige range of chocolates and to give it an evocative name. He chose "Godiva" and marketed his chocolates in instantly recognizable gold boxes. In recognition of its excellence, Godiva has been rewarded with an appointment as supplier to the Court of Belgium. Godiva continues to be an innovator in gourmet chocolate, having introduced a new platinum

CHOCOLATES

"Research tells us fourteen out of any ten individuals like chocolate."

— Sandra Boynton

collection. The Mokalata, a sweet cream, cappucino, and milk chocolate confection, is smooth with a bit of a kick.

8 – RICHARD DONNELLY FINE CHOCOLATES
Santa Cruz, California
Tel: 888-685-1871, www.donnellychocolates.com

These chocolates are unusual, to say the least. Richard Donnelly likes to push the chocolate experience by combining its rich tones—he uses Belgian and French chocolate—with ingredients such as lavender, chipotle, saffron, cardamom, and Earl Grey tea. Such innovation helped Donnelly win the Best Artisan award at the prestigious Euro Chocolate Festival in Perugia, Italy, just ten years after he opened his shop. To maintain quality and ensure freshness, Donnelly produces no more than 50 pounds of chocolate a day. If you need a break from the exotic and unusual flavors, try Donnelly's white chocolate macadamia nut or a honey vanilla caramel.

9 – RICHART
Tel: 888-RICHART, www.richart-chocolates.com

Committed to quality, the French chocolate-maker Richart guarantees you the most refined chocolates from the most refined ingredients. Richart recipes, developed and tested by the Richart family, have won France's most prestigious confectioner's honor, the Ruban Bleu, seven times. Having perfected the art of chocolate making, Richart now focuses on enhanced flavors and distinctive designs and colors. A box of assorted chocolates is visually stunning.

10 – PUCCINI BOMBONI
Staalstraat 21, Amsterdam, Netherlands
Tel: 31-(0)-20-620-8458, www.puccini.nl

You'll have to visit Amsterdam to sample what may be the best chocolates in the Netherlands. The proprietors of Puccini Bomboni, a delightful café/restaurant, hand-make each chocolate on the premises and do not deliver. Exotic combinations of chocolate and spices, concocted from the freshest ingredients, are a specialty. The variety isn't enormous, but the quality is amazing.

Ten Best
~Hamburgers~

In the words of Charles Kuralt, "You can find your way across this country [U.S.] using burger joints the way a navigator uses stars."

1 – The Apple Pan
10801 W. Pico Boulevard
Los Angeles, California
Tel: 310-475-3585

Counter seating is the only kind available at this Westside joint. The signature steak burger is a juicy, medium-thick patty on a seedless bun piled high with all the fixings—mayo, sweet relish, crunchy dill pickles, crisp iceberg lettuce, and a slice of half-melted Tillamook Cheddar. For an extra wallop, the hickory burger comes drenched in barbecue sauce. Come prepared to get messy. And leave room for apple pie.

2 – In-n-Out Burger
California, Arizona, Nevada
Tel: 800-786-1000, www.in-n-out.com

In-n-Out franchises—a California institution—are known for their eye-catching yellow-arrow logo and spic-and-span red and white interiors. Bucking the diversification trend of many fast-food chains, In-n-Out serves only fries, beverages, and three types of hamburgers. These all-beef burgers are topped with fresh vegetables and Thousand Island-like dressing and served on griddled buns with optional American cheese. Fries are freshly cut on the spot.

3 – Big Nick's Burgers and Pizza
2175 Broadway, New York, New York
Tel: 212-362-9238

This wildly popular Upper West Side burger and pizza joint is a New York classic: loud, fast-paced, and full of character. The big, juicy hamburgers are among the best in New York.

4 – Lotaburger
1300 San Mateo S.E.
Albuquerque, New Mexico
Tel: 505-255-5601

On July 9, 1952, Blake Chanslor opened a simple little hamburger place in Albuquerque, New Mexico. Serving excellent food at reasonable prices, the restaurant soon expanded into 75 locations in New Mexico. The green chile cheeseburger is the best in the world.

5 – Jury's
4337 N. Lincoln Avenue, Chicago, Illinois
Tel: 773-935-2255

Although it may look like another corner watering hole, this place is actually much more of a restaurant than a bar. White-clothed tables with emerald-green chairs evoke the

ANOTHER FINE BURGER

P. J. CLARKE'S
915 Third Ave., New York, New York
Tel: 212-759-1650

This classic joint on Third Avenue serves up great food. For 120 years this venerable New York institution has entertained the famous, the infamous, and everyone in between. Its hamburgers are the best in town.

old Ireland of Jury's Hotel in Dublin. Bar food is the specialty, with cheese sticks, onion rings, and "the best burger in the city" on the menu.

6 – TAYLOR'S REFRESHER
St. Helena and San Francisco, California
www.taylorsrefresher.com

Taylor's Refresher offers a slice of roadside heaven for burger aficionados. It's a classic burger-and-fries stand, with shady picnic tables out back, screened-in windows for ordering, and parking. The juicy burgers here are messy affairs, complete with lettuce, tomato, and lots of Russian dressing-style sauce. The French fries and onion rings are fresh-cut and golden fried. For a twist, try the Ahi tuna burger or the garlic fries.

7 – BURGERMEISTER
759 Columbus Avenue, San Francisco, California
Tel: 415-296-9907, www.burgermeisters.com
This family-owned and -operated business in the San Francisco Bay area uses only local ingredients, including the finest quality organic beef, to make its hamburgers. One taste of the avocado cheeseburger and you'll be a fan for life.

8 – RARE
303 Lexington Avenue, New York, New York
Tel: 212-481-1999

This favorite haunt of the office crowd serves up a flavorful beef patty on a toasted brioche. Upscale burgers include the pesto-mozzarella burger or the Mexican topped with black-bean spread and guacamole. Experiment with a basket of "frickles"—deep-fried pickles.

9 – MCHALE'S
750 Eighth Avenue, New York, New York
Tel: 212-997-8885

Decorated with wooden Venetian blinds, ceiling fans, and a bar of dark wood, McHale's seems to be straight out of 1950s film noir. The burgers rank among the best.

10 – FUDDRUCKERS
United States
www.fuddruckers.com

At this chain restaurant with locations countrywide, the hamburgers can weigh as much as nearly half a kilogram (one pound). The sides are also generous. Made from freshly ground beef, the burgers are served on fresh-baked buns. Top the burgers yourself at the condiment bar, which has a good selection of jalapenos and a variety of sauces.

TEN BEST
~MARKETS & FOOD HALLS~

Los Angeles's famed Farmer's Market, Harrod's Food Hall, Fortnum & Mason's gourmet counters, Melbourne's Queen Victoria Market, Barcelona's Boqueria, the Saturday village market in St. Tropez ... these great food markets and halls serve the best in fresh fruits, organic vegetables, and gourmet food items. Your shopping list will engorge with goodies.

1 – DEAN & DELUCA
United States and Japan
Tel: 800-221-7714, www.deandeluca.com

First established in Manhattan's posh SoHo neighborhood, this purveyor of pricey gourmet food, wine, and high-end kitchen wares now operates more than a dozen specialty markets and cafés in the United States and Japan. It also sells on line and through mail order catalogs.

But shopping at the flagship store is still the wondrous experience that made it, in the beginning, a requisite visit for out-of-towners looking for "that something special" to take back home from the Big Apple, or New York City.

Dean & DeLuca sells items from around the world, including exotic produce and hard-to-find teas and condiments. The fresh cheeses and prepared food counters are a gastronome's delight, while the pastries and baked goods will appeal to everyone. The selection of coffees—each one unique and flavorful—is fabulous.

2 – FERRY BUILDING MARKETPLACE
One Ferry Building, San Francisco, California
Tel: 415-693-0996, www.ferrybuildingmarketplace.com

The magnificent Ferry Building houses a diverse assortment of small, independently owned and operated businesses that focus on quality artisan food. Each business specializes. You'll find meat and poultry shops, fishmongers, greengrocers, bakeries, cheese emporiums, ice cream parlors, and many others. Each business is noted for its commitment to supporting local and regional products, traditional farming practices, and artisanal methods of preparation. You'll not want to miss the popular farmers' market outside on the plaza Tuesdays, Thursdays, Saturdays, and Sundays.

3 – FORTNUM & MASON

181 Piccadilly, London, England
Tel: 44-(0)-20-7734-8040
www.fortnumandmason.com

Fortnum & Mason was established in 1707 as an upscale green grocer. In its service and goods it came to represent the very essence of Englishness, mixing English goods with products and produce from all over the expanding British Empire. Today, throughout the United Kingdom, that tradition of excellence continues, and nowhere is it more evident than in the ground-floor food hall of Fortnum & Mason. Here you'll find biscuits and cakes; cheese, *charcuterie,* and pies; caviar, salmon, and *foie gras;* chocolates and sweets; coffee and tea; fruits and flowers; preserves, marmalade, and honey; chutneys, pickles, mustards, olives, nuts; and much more. Everything is guaranteed to be top-notch, from the vintage wines to the handmade English chocolates. Luxury prepared foods are also available.

4 – HARRODS FOOD HALL

87-135 Brompton Road, London, England
Tel: 44-(0)-20-7730-1234, www.harrods.com

The food hall at Harrods, London's famous luxury department store, meets all expectations. The hall, or rather halls, is so large you'll no doubt pick up a little something to tide you over while you explore the opulent setting. While many tourists leave with only a souvenir tin of tea or sweets, stamped with the famous Harrods label, locals shop at the

impressive meat and fish counters and pick up crusty loaves of bread, delicious flaky pastries, vintage wines, and exotic chutneys. The selection of goods is unparalleled, as is the service.

5 – QUEEN VICTORIA MARKET

Melbourne, Australia
www.qvm.com.au

A large food market, with an adjoining general merchandise market, Queen Victoria Market is a Melbourne institution. This working market caters to locals and visitors alike. You'll find delicious Greek, Italian, and Polish foods in the delicatessen section, crusty artisanal breads in the bakery section, the freshest fruits and vegetables in the produce section, farm fresh eggs and cheeses in the dairy section, and the finest cuts of beef, whole chickens, and salamis in the meat section. Go early for the best selection. On weekends the market expands to include several hundred stalls of general merchandise, ranging from aromatherapy candles to kitchen wares to pet supplies to souvenirs.

6 – LA BOQUERIA

Rambla 91, Barcelona, Spain

Fish is an essential component of Catalonian fare. At this outstanding fresh food market in Barcelona, Spain, fishmongers have place of honor under the central rotunda. They hawk an amazing variety of fish and other seafood—from shrimp, cuttlefish, and tuna

FARMERS MARKET

to some creatures you may not even recognize. Surrounding the rotunda are stalls selling the freshest fruits, vegetables, breads, olive oils, and many other delicious foods. Even if you're not in the market for a basketful of food, the Boqueria is an entertaining place to visit.

7 – FARMERS MARKET

6333 West Third Street, Los Angeles, California
Tel: 323-933-9211, www.farmersmarketla.com

This open-air Los Angeles market has been serving the city since the 1930s. Originally a meeting place for local farmers selling goods out of their trucks, the Farmers Market has grown into a must-see attraction with more than 70 shops, most of them owner-operated. You will find the freshest meats, seafood, produce, and flowers here, and even dinosaur-shaped doughnuts! Head there on a Sunday morning and just enjoy walking through the stalls and sitting down for breakfast and a cup of coffee.

8 – BALDUCCI'S

155 A W. 66th Street
New York, New York
Tel: 212-653-8320, www.balduccis.com

From its humble beginnings as a fruit-and-vegetable stand in Brooklyn, Balducci's has grown into one of the leading upscale grocery stores in the United States. Balducci's prides itself on providing its customers with the best and the freshest—from olives and cheeses to roasted meats and smoked fish. Chefs work 'round the clock preparing a plethora of ready-made foods—potato and goat cheese timbale, Veracruz-style seafood quesadillas, lemon mustard chicken breast—that are a feast for the eyes as well as the stomach. You will also find fanciful pastries that will melt in your mouth, rustic artisan breads, and an excellent beer and wine selection. There are now nine stores on the East Coast.

9 – BRISTOL FARMS

Southern California
Tel: 310-233-4700
www.bristolfarms.com

Bristol Farms describes itself as an "extraordinary food store." We'd have to concur. Using a supermarket-style approach, complete with wide, well-stocked aisles, Bristol Farms has 11 stores, purveying the finest assortment and highest quality of fresh and specialty foods from around the world.

10 – ZABAR'S

2245 Broadway, New York, New York
Tel: 212-787-2000, www.zabars.com

Louis Zabar began his business more than 75 years ago by selling the best smoked fish at unmatched low prices. The store now is a wonderful warren of fresh baked goods, deli meats, roasted coffee beans, cheeses, prepared foods, and "homemade" style cakes and desserts. You'll also find eclectic kitchen wares and gourmet items from around the world. It's no wonder that if you visit New York, friends in the know will ask you to stop by Zabar's and pick up their favorite items for them.

TEN BEST
~ICE CREAMS~

1 – HANDEL'S HOMEMADE ICE CREAM & YOGURT

Ohio, Pennsylvania, Indiana, Virginia, California
Tel: 330-702-8270, www.handelsicecream.com

This Ohio-based ice creamery uses marshmallows, caramel, strawberries, and real vanilla beans among other high quality ingredients to make its fine ice creams, sherbets, low-fat yogurts, and ices. In addition to its full roster of year-round flavors, Handel's prepares special seasonal or occasional ice creams: Try the peppermint stick or eggnog flavors during the winter holiday season or the pumpkin ripple around Thanksgiving.

2 – DR. BOB'S HANDCRAFTED ICE CREAM

Pomona, California
Tel: 909-865-1956, www.drbobsicecream.com

Winner of more than 30 gold medals, Dr. Bob's HandCrafted Ice Cream is a high butterfat, intensely flavorful treat. Dr. Robert Small invented his particular recipes for ice cream, using only the finest ingredients, including Scharffen Berger chocolate, Tahitian vanilla, and Argentinean caramel. His nine chocolate flavors are perhaps his signature ice creams.

3 – RON'S GOURMET ICE CREAM

1231 Hyde Park Avenue, Hyde Park, Massachusetts
Tel: 617-364-5274

This unique family-owned combination bowling alley and ice cream parlor offers up to 32 flavors each day, plus seasonal variations. The brownie nut ice cream—homemade vanilla ice cream mixed with freshly baked brownies—is a customer favorite.

4 – BERTHILLON

31, rue St.-Louis-en-l'Ile, Paris, France
Tel: 33-(0)-1-4354-3161

Any ice cream connoisseur in Paris must visit Berthillon, home to more than 50 stunning ice cream flavors. Although branches are all over the city, try to visit the chain's flagship parlor on Ile. St.-Louis. Parisians queue around the block for Berthillon's sinfully rich ice creams and sorbets. The sorbets—luscious fruit ices (made without cream or milk)— are divine. Two favorites are the sharp, tangy lemon and the kicky strawberry.

ICE CREAMS

5 – BIM BOM

Infanta esquina 23, Vedado, La Habana, Cuba

This well-loved ice cream parlor serves about 18 different flavors, which you can choose to have in a cone or in a sundae. You can add fruit, nuts, or candies as toppings. The parlor is a delightful place to pass the time.

6 – COPPELIA

23 esquina L, Vedado, La Habana, Cuba

Coppelia is *the* national ice cream of Cuba. There is a Coppelia ice cream parlor in nearly every town. The large spaceship-shaped Havana parlor on L Street was featured in the film *Strawberries and Chocolate*. The tropical fruit ice cream is excellent. Expect long lines on weekends.

7 – COLD STONE CREAMERY

United States
866-464-9467, www.coldstonecreamery.com

Cold Stone not only produces smooth and creamy ice cream each day but also excels at presentation. Each scoop is custom blended to your specifications with mix-ins—candies, nuts, fruit, and more—on a frozen granite stone and served in a freshly baked waffle cone.

8 – CRESCENT RIDGE DAIRY

355 Bay Rd., Sharon, Massachusetts
Tel: 781-784-2740, www.crescentridge.com

With 35 uniquely fresh flavors, Crescent Ridge is a traditional ice cream stand. It will even consider adding to its list of ice creams your suggestion for a new taste delight. Offering old fashioned favorites, Crescent Ridge is surrounded by acres of rolling farmland, a herd of cows, and fresh air. It delivers a lot of good things, including morning milk in glass bottles and ice cream to more than 80 towns near Boston.

9 – VIVOLI GELATO

7, via Isole delle Stinche, Florence, Italy
Tel: 39-5529-2334

The Vivoli family has been making gelato—a soft, rich ice cream—since 1930. Each flavor is made on site with the freshest ingredients. The ice cream melts in your mouth and explodes with flavors that range from refreshing lemon to rich amaretto mousse. The presentation in the display case is so artful that you almost hesitate to ask the server to disturb it by scooping out your favorite ice cream flavor.

10 – HÄAGEN-DAZS

Worldwide
Tel: 800-767-0120, www.haagen-dazs.com

Häagen-Dazs has discovered a way to combine excellent quality and mass production. Its ice cream, found in nearly every supermarket and corner store, is consistently rated one of the best. Founder Reuben Mattus revolutionized ice cream in the United States when he founded the company in the 1920s. Häagen-Dazs sets the standard for innovative flavors and, in the process, has become a household name.

TEN BEST
~DESTINATION & SPECIAL RESTAURANTS~

Entertainer W. C. Fields puts it best, "Never eat at a place called 'Moms,' but if the only other place in town has a sign that says 'Eats,' go back to Moms." These restaurants definitely are not "Mom's."

DESTINATION RESTAURANTS

1 – THE HERBFARM
Woodinville, Washington
Tel: 425-485-5300,
www.theherbfarm.com

Each evening the Herbfarm offers a nine-course meal, served with matching wines to suit the courses. The Herbfarm's commitment to excellence shows in each finely crafted dish, displaying to perfection the best ingredients that the Pacific Northwest has to offer. Local growers and suppliers keep the Herbfarm stocked with both common and unusual produce—wild mushrooms, heritage fruits, handmade cheeses, and fresh-caught fish, to name but a few. Each night's menu is a new creation that draws inspiration from the season.

2 – THE FRENCH LAUNDRY
6640 Washington Street, Yountville, California
Tel: 707-944-2380, www.frenchlaundry.com

This intimate, residence-style restaurant offers an unmatched dining experience. Chef Thomas Keller oversees the artful preparation of three prix-fixe menus that change daily. There is the renowned nine-course Chef's Tasting Menu, the nine-course Vegetable Tasting Menu, and the seven-course menu. Each showcases the best seasonal ingredients available. Reservations are required.

3 – CHEZ PANISSE
1517 Shattuck Avenue, Berkeley, California
Tel: 510-548-5525
www.chezpanisse.com

Chez Panisse has come to symbolize excellence in organic cuisine. Chef Alice Waters has elevated the art of fine cooking to a new level by insisting upon environmental harmony. Each night a prix fixe menu of three or four courses is served that is entirely dependent upon the availability of fresh, organic vegetables, fruits, meats, poultry, and fish from nearby suppliers.

4 – EL BULLI
Cala Montjoi, Roses, Girona, Spain
Tel: 34-97-215-0457, www.elbulli.com

At El Bulli you must give yourself over to the innovative creations of its adulated chef, Ferrán Adrià. Between the artful presentation, the exquisite dishes, and the superb service, you will walk away feeling you've had a truly amazing experience. The degustation menu allows you to try some 25 memorable tastes.

5 – THE INN AT LITTLE WASHINGTON
Middle and Main Streets, Washington, Virginia
Tel: 540-675-3800, www.theinnatlittlewashington.com

Inspired by great French culinary masters, chef Patrick O'Connell has created his own signature style. He artfully pushes the boundaries of classical cooking to come up with such masterpieces as marinated, pan-seared squab on garlic polenta with blackberry sauce. Each standard meal is a four-course affair that includes dessert. And, to top it all off, the setting is pure romance.

6 – FEARRINGTON HOUSE
2000 Fearrington Village, Pittsboro, North Carolina
Tel: 919-542-2121, www.fearrington.com

Set in a charming 1927 farmhouse, Fearrington is known for its sophisticated Southern cuisine, graciously served in a warm, romantic atmosphere. The restaurant features a seven-course prix fixe tasting menu and an a la carte menu. A meal at the Fearrington is one of the truly unforgettable dining experiences.

7 – LE JARDIN DU RUSSIE
Hotel de Russie, Via del Babuino 9, Rome, Italy
Tel: 39-06-32-88-88-70

Located in the Hotel de Russie in the heart of Rome, surrounded by terraced gardens, Le Jardin du Russie serves exquisite food in a setting that transports you to another time and place. The chef emphasizes the use of fresh, local produce and the very best Italian ingredients. Dinner features a four-course set menu and a tasting menu.

8 – GAMBERO ROSSO
Piazza della Vittoria, 13, San Vincenzo, Tuscany, Italy
Tel: 39-05-6570-1021

This top-rated Italian restaurant with a view of the Tyrrhenian Sea serves a tasting menu filled with sophisticated dishes that will make you sigh with pleasure.

9 – WHAMPOA CLUB
Fifth floor, Three on the Bund, Shanghai, China
Tel: 86-21-6321-3737

Under the guidance of master chef Jereme Leung, the Whampoa Club serves some of the finest Shanghainese and Cantonese cuisine in Shanghai. His classical dishes have a contemporary flair, both in taste and presentation. The prawns with wasabi mayonnaise, drunken chicken with

TWO MORE TO TRY

PANE E VINO
1482 East Valley Road, Montecito, California
Tel: 805-969-9274

With an open kitchen, this Tuscan trattoria near Santa Barbara, California, has an intimate atmosphere, as well as some of the best Italian cuisine outside Italy. The menu is outstanding.

— · —

O'NEAL'S
49 W. 64th Street, New York, New York
Tel: 212-717-5940

Owner Michael O'Neal, a great restaurateur and raconteur for more than 20 years, is warmly attentive to his patrons. O'Neal's still retains its homey, traditional character. The onion soup gratinee, chicken pot pie, green salad with Maytag Roquefort dressing, crusty bread, freshly cut french fries, and chocolate sundae are delicious. The coterie of waiters assures fine service.

white shaved ice, and white fish with spicy red pepper sauce are impeccable. Traditional Chinese tea ceremonies are performed tableside; a tea sommelier hovers nearby to answer any questions and make recommendations.

10 – WILDFIRE RESTAURANT
Circular Quay West, Sydney, Australia
Tel: 61-2-8273-1222

Wildfire's incredible menu can hold its own against the restaurant's fabulous views of Sydney Harbor and the Opera House. Dishes from the large open kitchens and wood-fired grills include crisp-fried arrancini balls with crabmeat in saffron and mascarpone, wood-roasted quails wrapped in proscuitto with white bean puree, Mudgee grass-fed-lamb cutlets, and Angus marbled sirloin.

SPECIAL RESTAURANTS

1 – JEAN GEORGES
1 Central Park West, New York, New York
Tel: 212-299-3900, www.jean-georges.com

The spare, elegant decor of Jean Georges focuses attention on exquisite contemporary French cuisine. The food reveals itself to the diner first by appearance, then by scent, and finally by taste. Each step is mesmerizing. Signature dishes created by chef Jean Georges Vongerichten include young-garlic soup with sautéed frog legs and parsley; sea scallops with cauliflower and a capers–raisin emulsion; and sweetbreads en cocotte with baby carrots, ginger, and licorice. Each dish receives its finishing touch tableside, with waiters ladling fragrant soup into bowls, carving succulent slices of Muscovy duck, or pouring a caramel sauce over poached foie gras. The wait staff is courteous, attentive, and always discreet.

2 – PATSY'S
236 W. 56th Street, New York, New York
Tel: 212-247-3491, www.patsys.com

Patsy's, a traditional, family-owned and operated restaurant, is celebrated for its classic Neopolitan cuisine. This well-heeled establishment in the theater district on Manhattan's West Side has entertained a loyal following and has attracted a roster of high-profile personalities, from actors and musicians to authors and politicians. Signature dishes include veal rollatine marsala, chicken cacciatora, and linguine marechiare; the fried zucchini strips and eggplant parmigiana are consistent crowd favorites. The tiramisu topped with fresh raspberries is heavenly. The demand for Patsy's uniquely delicious tomato-based pasta sauces was so great that in 1994 the restaurant began to bottle its marinara sauce. It and other classic Patsy's sauces are available at gourmet food retailers and on line.

3 – L'ATELIER DE JOEL ROBUCHON
7, rue de Montalembert
Paris, France
Tel: 33-(0)-1 4222-5656

This is a relaxing haven in the Hotel Port Royal in the 7th Arrondissement. The red-and-black decor and the absence of traditional restaurant seating reflect Robuchon's long association with all things Japanese. A U-shape bar with high-backed stools rings the kitchen, giving all diners a good view of the arena where young,

highly focused chefs engage in preparation. The menu lists over 20 small dishes and a number of main dishes. Although the menu changes frequently, you won't be disappointed. Favorites include chestnut soup with foie gras and pork served on a toasted baguette with herbs, truffles, and parmesan. Professional, knowledgeable, and helpful service complements the spectacular dishes. The restaurant takes only a limited number of reservations, so be prepared to wait.

4 – SONA
401 N. La Cienega Boulevard, Los Angeles, California
Tel: 310-659-7708, www.sonarestaurant.com

Don't be fooled by Sona's minimalist decor. The atmosphere, service, and food here are all top-notch. The menu is a masterful offering of classically trained chef David Myers' culinary expertise. He creatively meshes seasonal ingredients and innovation, blending textures and flavors in un-expected, delicious ways—such as creamy macaroni with crispy, succulent sweetbreads and foie gras terrine with apple butter and pine nut vinaigrette that's simultaneously savory and buttery. His Kobe steak paired with a bundle of smoky, melt-in-your-mouth short ribs, will transport you. Myers' creativity extends to desserts as well: The chocolate brioche pudding topped with caramelized bananas and macadamia malted ice cream is simply outstanding.

5 – LUCAS CARTON
9, place de la Madeleine, Paris, France
Tel: 33-(0)-1-4265-2290, lucascarton.com

In this magnificent art nouveau dining room, master chef Alain Senderens serves a host of celebrated creations—canard Apicius, foie gras de canard steamed in a cabbage leaf, red-mullet fillets with olives, lemon, and capers—as well as ever-changing new inventions. Every preparation reveals the attention to detail that is the hallmark of Carton.

6 – LE BERNARDIN

155 W. 51st Street, New York, New York
Tel: 212-554-1515, www.le-bernardin.com

This sophisticated seafood establishment is consistently rated one of the top restaurants in New York. Chef Eric Ripert, at the helm in the kitchen since the early 1990s, specializes in preparing dishes with as little fuss as possible. There are several tasting menus as well as a prix-fixe menu that offers choices from both the "simply raw" and "lightly cooked" categories. Highlights include a yellowfin tuna on a mint, watercress, and peanut salad; a deceptively simple-sounding smoked salmon gravlax; and the lightly spiced ceviche of scallops, a wonderful burst of smooth, tangy, and refreshing sensations.

7 – MOLLIES

Coast Village Road, Montecito, California
Tel: 805-565-9381

This charming, unassuming restaurant in Montecito serves Italian dishes made with talent and quality. Mollie Ahestrand trained and learned from masters in Rome and specializes in foods from four Italian regions—Padua, Umbria, Bologna, and Rome. Invited to cook all over the

FLOWER DRUM

17 Market Lane, Melbourne, Australia
Tel: 61-(0)-3-9662-3655

Although renowned chef Gilbert Lau now serves only as a consultant to the Flower Drum, he left the restaurant in the hands of several of the staff who had been employed there for more than 20 years. They continue its tradition of commitment to excellence. The Flower Drum has blossomed into one of the world's truly great Chinese restaurants, serving superb Cantonese cuisine. The restaurant is impeccable in every detail, from the exceptional service...to the creativity of the chefs...to the quality of the ingredients. Several key goods are imported directly from small, quality suppliers in China, particularly for the Chinese New Year celebrations, a time when the Flower Drum especially caters to its many loyal customers.

The waiters know and can recommend the day's specials—be they crisp-skinned Cantonese roast duck served with plum gravy; succulent dumplings of prawn and flying fish roe; a perfectly steamed Murray cod; or huge Pacific oysters with black bean sauce. You'll have no complaint, whatever you choose.

The décor exhibits an understated elegance, the service is deft and professional, and the breadth of the wine list is rarely matched elsewhere. In addition, tea waiters stand ready, so your cup is never empty and any request is met with immediate attention.

A VERY NICE RESTAURANT

SIMPSON'S-IN-THE-STRAND
100 Strand, London, England
Tel: 44-(0)-20-7836-9112

A fabled haunt dating back to 1828, complete with dark paneling and crystal chandeliers, Simpson's is steeped in English tradition, serving the best of English fare tableside from silver-domed carver trolleys. A world apart from nouvelle cuisine and fusion food, Simpson's still finds there are new generations that appreciate exceptional English food.

world for the culinary elite, she makes wonderful rustic lentil and minestrone soups, tender grilled lamb chops, exquisite grilled Atlantic sea bass, and sinfully rich home-made ice creams. The convivial atmosphere is as close as you can get to Tuscany and still be at home.

8 – RESTAURANT GARY DANKO
800 N. Point Street, San Francisco, California
Tel: 415-749-2060, www.garydanko.com

The understated decor of Restaurant Gary Danko shows off to perfection the elegantly prepared and presented dishes that make this restaurant a San Francisco favorite. From juniper-spiced venison medallions with cranberry–onion compote to snapper with saffron, tarragon, and fennel puree, every dish is a feast for the senses. The ever changing menu always features some signature creations, but the meat and game dishes truly excel—the herb-rubbed slices of duck breast and the wild

mushroom-stuffed roasted quail will make converts of non-gamebird diners. Save room for artisan cheeses and delightful desserts such as frozen almond soufflé with blood orange sauce.

9 – CAFÉ JACQUELINE
1454 Grant Avenue, San Francisco, California
Tel: 415-981-5565

Sharing light-as-air soufflés at this romantic, intimate restaurant is a memorable treat. The menu at Café Jacqueline is made up almost entirely of soufflés, though a few non-soufflé starters, such as fresh baked warm bread, hearty French onion soup baked with Gruyère, or endive with Roquefort cheese, slip in. A number of the savory soufflés are generous enough to share, from the classical Gruyère cheese soufflé to the prosciutto and mushroom soufflé. The dessert soufflés are so delicate and delicious you'll probably want one all to yourself.

10 – CHARLIE TROTTER
816 W. Armitage, Chicago, Illinois
Tel: 773-248-6228, www.charlietrotters.com

A master of flavor, texture, and temperature, chef Charlie Trotter challenges the palate as he satisfies it. His widely acclaimed restaurant (named "America's Best Restaurant" in 2000 by the Wine Spectator) combines seemingly disparate ingredients into harmonious creations that delight and tempt the appetite: black buck venison with Japanese *kumai* (jasmine rice cake and red-wine Kalamata olive emulsion), vegetable ragoût with légumes purée, red wine-black trumpet emulsion, and rosemary, for example. Chef Trotter uses only organic and free-range products.

Ten Best
~Steak Houses~

1 – MORTON'S
Worldwide
www.mortons.com

Dark wood details, hushed tones, and tuxedo-clad waiters give each Morton's restaurant in this upscale steakhouse chain the air of a exclusive club. The service is professional and discreet, with bartenders making a mean martini and knowing regulars by name. The dining experience begins when your waiter wheels over a cart laden with fresh vegetables, live lobster, and cuts of steak—porterhouse, rib eye, bone-in prime rib, and more—from which to choose. Cooked to perfection, the steaks are the tenderest cuts available. Each entrée is served with enormous portions of traditional side dishes such as baked potato, creamed spinach, and steamed broccoli with Hollandaise.

2 – THE HITCHING POST
406 E. Highway 246, Buellton, California
Tel: 805-688-0676, www.hitchingpost2.com

This restaurant is famed for its California-style barbecue that has nothing to do with sauce and everything to do with grilling. From the appetizers—perhaps the artichoke starter, a smoky yet juicy treat that wears the secret Hitching Post seasoning like a glove—to the entrées—perhaps filet mignon, New York strip, or even fresh ostrich or California quail—everything is cooked to your specifications over an oak wood fire. All meals come with a relish tray; crackers and butter; soup or shrimp cocktail; salad; baked potato, rice pilaf, or fries; and garlic bread. The restaurant was featured in the acclaimed movie *Sideways*.

3 – OLD HOMESTEAD STEAKHOUSE
56 Ninth Avenue, New York, New York
Tel: 212-242-9040, www.oldhomesteadsteakhouse.com

A large cow still advertises the location of this Meatpacking District icon, the Old Homestead, that opened in 1868. Holding on to a bygone era, the restaurant has walls lined with black-and-white photographs of New York. Middle-aged, aproned waiters man the tables, and male customers outnumber women customers. Appetizers are enormous and refreshingly simple—a half a head of iceberg lettuce drenched in blue cheese, for instance, or a plate of tomatoes and onions so large that it almost takes over the table. Dry-aged steak entrées range from about half a kilogram (18-ounces) of boneless sirloin to about a kilogram (two-pounds) of rib eye to a very large porterhouse that will feed two people. At Old Homestead you'll be treated to an experience you'll not soon forget.

"They dined on mince, and slices of quince, Which they ate with a runcible spoon; And hand in hand, on the edge of the sand, They danced by the light of the moon."

— Edward Lear

4 – Ruth's Chris

United States
www.ruthschris.com

This chain of sophisticated steak houses began as an offshoot of a popular New Orleans hangout for politicians. The décor features dark woods and comfortable booths, with a separate bar scene. You will be pampered here. The signature custom-aged cuts of beef arrive in sizzling butter on 260°C (500°F) plates. And although known for its steaks, the restaurant also features delicious chicken, pork, and seafood entrées as well as Creole appetizers—the shrimp remoulade should not be missed. The menu includes traditional side dishes—onion rings, creamed spinach, various styles of potatoes—and desserts such as cheesecake and bread pudding—all of exceptional taste.

5 – Prime

Bellagio Hotel, 3680 Las Vegas Blvd. S., Las Vegas, Nevada
Tel: 702-693-7223

Prime might be the grandest, most romantic steak house around. Located at the Bellagio Hotel, the restaurant features views of the fountains and lights of Las Vegas, Baccarat chandeliers, plush furnishings, lots of gilt, and excellent service. And the food carries the innovative stamp of master chef Jean-Georges Vongerichten. Customers assemble their own meals, selecting the cut of meat or fish and any of ten different sauces and potatoes. For instance, you might choose the roasted rib eye with herbe de Provence mustard, roasted wild mushrooms, and chick pea fries.

6 – La Cabaña

Rodríguez Peña 1967, Buenos Aires, Argentina
Tel: 54-11-4814-0001

Opened in October 2003, La Cabaña faithfully re-creates the famous Buenos Aires steak house. For decades, the original La Cabaña welcomed VIPs, celebrities, and the famous and infamous from all over the world to dine on what is considered the best steak on Earth. Its visitor book contains signatures of every Argentine president, Charles de Gaulle, Henry Kissinger, Richard Nixon, King Juan Carlos, Maurice Chevalier, Joan Crawford, Arturo Toscanini, Walt Disney, and countless others attracted to La Cabaña's ambience and food, notably the "Grand

Baby Beef," about 100-millimeters-wide (4-inch) and 1.5-kilogram (3.3-pound) steak that has no equal. This smart and elegant new version of La Cabaña honors its namesake's fabled atmosphere and continues the tradition of grilling the best steaks in the world.

7 – BOA STEAKHOUSE
Los Angeles and Las Vegas
www.boasteak.com/balboa

Boa serves up traditional steakhouse dishes with innovative twists. The prawn cocktail is steeped in a vodka-spiked cocktail sauce; the BLT salad is a fanciful construction of apple wood bacon bits, chopped endive, and chunks of tomato. The steaks, which include a deeply flavorful 35-day, dry-aged New York strip and a tender Kansas City filet, can be doctored with eight sauces and four rubs on the menu, among them a sweet, homemade Worcester-shire, an earthy cider-sage sauce, and a tangy blue cheese crust.

8 – SMITH & WOLLENSKY
New York and 10 other U.S. cities
www.smithandwollensky.com

Twenty years after Smith & Wollensky opened its doors in 1977 in New York City, the celebrated steak house began expanding into major metropolitan cities across the United States. Today its superior food and standards of excellence can be found in 11 restaurants, each with its own unique flair. The exquisite dining experience includes an

award-winning list of American wines and USDA prime dry-aged beef. Highest quality seafood, veal, lamb, and poultry are also on the menus, as are first-rate desserts including such classics New York cheesecake and carrot cake.

9 – SPARKS
210 E. 46th Street, New York, New York
Tel: 212-687-4855, www.sparkssteakhouse.com

Sparks is a classic New York steak house that features an abundance of dark wood, long-time career waiters, and pastoral paintings. Catering to a largely male clientele, it serves signature steakhouse dishes—lobster, filet mignon, prime sirloin—with traditional sides and starters that include sauteed mushrooms, creamed spinach, and tomato and onion salad. The cheesecake is one of the best in the city.

10 – GALLAGHER'S STEAK HOUSE
228 W. 52nd Street, New York, New York
Tel: 212-245-5336

This speakeasy-turned-steak house has been drawing customers in since 1927 for its steaks basted with a secretly formulated Gallagher's sauce. The meat is nicely aged and grilled over hickory logs. The roast prime rib of beef and lamb chops are good bets as well. For dessert, a slice of cheesecake is big enough for two, but after one bite you may not want to share. The small wine list accents mostly good California wines.

PART
-THE- NEW GRAND TOUR
TWO

ot long ago, the traditional "Grand Tour" completed every well-to-do European's education. We have created 20 classic adventures for the 21st-century traveler—some literary, some historical. All are remarkable.

Samuel Johnson and James Boswell walked through England, Jules Verne imagined traveling around the world in 80 days, and Somerset Maugham kept copious notes about his travels.

Diarists and writers have long recorded their experiences—people met, destinations remembered. Here is a modern list of special places for the armchair and active traveler. If Jacques Offenbach's "Baracolle" could be the theme for each of these excursions, it would magically and musically carry you in glorious harmony, there and back again.

We have suggested ten literary and ten historical journeys. Included among them are prime selections. Some have stars to indicate our favorites.

"Lande's List" follows, a file that has been held over many years from assignments, when I was director of TIME World News Service. Along with Andrew, colleagues, and correspondents, I have selected the tried and true, plus new additions.

All selections in "Lande's List," meet a very high standard that qualifies them for Passport to the Best.

~Ten Best~
Historical & Literary Journeys

① Unexpected Turns and Culinary Pleasures of the Amalfi Coast

Years ago, as a young man just out of the army, author Gore Vidal was looking for a place to write until at least the end of the century. On a bright, cold day in March, he came to Ravello. Standing on a limestone cliff overlooking the Gulf of Salerno, he thought it the most beautiful spot on Earth. In due course, he made it his own.

The Amalfi Coast waits for the next lucky person to claim his place among the cypresses, citrus groves, and vineyards of Magna Graecia. Nowhere are colors so luminous. The sea and sky are so intensely blue that it is impossible to tell where one begins and the other ends. Scattered along the coast like a rare jeweled necklace, villages of white, pink, and yellow cottages curl around dark blue harbors, enchanting travelers with rich history. We found some of the finest churches, villas, and monasteries Italy has to offer, along with fabulous hotels and cuisine, making a one-of-a-kind journey in a land where "poets go to die."

Below a series of steep rocky promontories draping into the Mediterranean, one can easily believe that all the purest blue in the world resides in this body of water. It is a color all its own. White-washed stone houses with red tiled roofs are stacked along mountains reaching toward the horizon, creating the most beautiful coastline in the world. André Gide remarked passionately, "It is so beautiful that nothing more beautiful can be seen on earth." Below, bobbing in the sea, are yellow and orange fishing boats, adding eye-catching color to the palette.

Many writers have put pen to paper and scribed that the Amalfi Coast is a place to remember. Longfellow, Ibsen, Vidal, William Styron, Richard Wagner, Paul Klee, Tennessee Williams, and D. H. Lawrence, among many others, were inspired by this watercolor canvas. John Steinbeck summed it up best: "It is not quite real when you are there but becomes very real after you are gone." Homer's sirens have been luring travelers here for centuries.

Beyond Pompeii, where the Salentine Peninsula curves seaward, the Amalfi Coast begins. The town of Amalfi itself is on the southern shore of the long peninsular coastline. From the coast's northernmost town, Sorrento, leading to Positano, the road called the Nastro Azzuro (Blue Ribbon), rises over the magnificent crest of land on top of the peninsula. Then in a moment, there is a long view north toward Naples unfolding southward toward Ravello.

This is one of the most spectacular roads in the world. Curving along towering cliffs terraced at intervals with vineyards and lemon groves, it is bordered by a rocky shore far below, with fortress towers that once defended its towns from sea raiders. The sea views are splashed with pine and cactus and brightened by wild roses and bougainvillea.

The coastal drive leaves you well positioned to visit several other famed Italian sites. If the Isle of Capri sounds like a romantic destination, it is easy to reach from Sorrento, Amalfi, or Positano for a day's excursion.

POSITANO

Over the Tyrrhenian Sea, near the Sirenuse Islands and weeping olive trees, Positano opens the stage to the Amalfi Coast. The English first appreciated this ribbon of terraces, steps, and alleys at the beginning of the 20th century. Later the town was revisited first by the Germans and then by American and British troops, when it became a rest camp in the last months of World War II.

Capri and Sorrento have long been on the Grand Tour for international travelers, and Almafi adds dimension.

A GOOD RESTAURANT

LA CAMBUSA
Piazza Vespucci, Positano
Tel: 39-08-987-5432

Luigi Russo, the owner, offers seafood from the day's catch, pasta with eggplant or zucchini, fresh figs, Neapolitan pastry, and local red and white wine. All cooking is done with locally pressed extra-virgin olive oil. Dinner for two, without wine, about $110.

While the climate is temperate most of the year, the best times to go are May and September.

Formerly a fishermen's village, the town located 35 miles south of Naples has long been a fashionable summer resort. Lately it has also developed as an off-season destination, with visitors attracted by the promise of sunshine even during the cool months, the splendor of the blue Tyrrhenian Sea, and the lure of three tiny offshore islands called Li Galli.

LE SIRENUSE
Via Colombo 30
Tel: 39-08-987-5066

This hotel is one of the top hotels in town. Its 19th-century core is the former seaside villa of the aristocratic Sersale family of Naples, and Marchese Paolo Sersale, a co-owner of the hotel and former mayor of Positano, is in charge. Through modern additions, the Sirenuse now has 62 rooms, most of them with balconies looking out on the sea. Many bathrooms are equipped with Jacuzzis, and there is a large, heated outdoor swimming pool. Positano's pebbly public beach is nearby.

HOTEL SAN PIETRO
Via Laurito 2
Tel: 39-08-987-5455

Taking its name from a 500-year-old chapel nearby, the Hotel San Pietro is perched high upon a rock spur that juts out into the sea a little more than a mile from Positano on the road to the village of Praiano.

Built on a terraced cliff, it is linked by its own elevator to a private beach in a cove 270 feet below and to a tennis court in another nearby cove. The 59-room house is managed by a brother-and-sister team, Salvatore and Virginia Attanasio, the nephew and niece of the late Carlino

Cinque, the hotel's designer and founder. With white-gloved service, antiques, and reproductions, guests are pampered and protected. Each room has its own vast terrace, bathrooms are opulent, and service is exemplary. An elevator drops down the mountain to one room with postcard views, a Roman tub, and a glorious and comfortable bed. There are some less-than-desirable rooms at the lower end of the price scale; No. 34 is particularly one to avoid. Doubles from about $400; suites are as high as $1,700, breakfast included.

ALBERGO MIRAMARE
Via Trara Genoino 31
Tel: 39-08-987-5002

One of the most delightful and reasonable accommodations in Positano is the intimate Miramare, owned by the same family as the San Pietro. Smaller, the staff is nevertheless friendly and hospitable. Chambermaids keep rooms spotless with clean towels, polished tiles, and laundry service that compares with the best French laundries. The inn is suspended over the sea in a setting of flamboyant bougainvillea. From the hotel, you can walk down 239 steps, past coach lamps at every turn, to the square, the church, and the seashore.

After a breakfast of croissants and cappuccino, the Miramare offers guests a sail on its private boat to coastal villages. This is a hard place to leave, but trips are offered to Capri, where you can shop, take lunch at the Grand Hotel Quisisana, or have a quick swim from your own cabana at the very private Marina Piccola, away from the crowds.

RAVELLO

"Ravello is nearer the sky than it is to the stars."
— Henry Wadsworth Longfellow

Founded in the fourth century by the Romans, Ravello is more elevated than the other towns along the coast. Just past Atani, the smallest city in Italy, no more than a large plaza, we take a quick turn up the mountain, where drivers of small SITA buses maneuver with agility. The drivers deserve gold medals for courage and patience. Traveling higher, past olive and citrus trees, climbing and negotiating the narrow road, we arrive at a palace that was once the residence of kings and popes. From its terraces, there are privileged views of gardens and the sea.

Fronting the small square of the village is the cathedral built in 1179 by Barisano da Trani. Two Tiglia trees generously give a lime fragrance to the rarefied air.

Traveling east from Positano and north (leaving the Amalfi Drive after passing the town of Amalfi), you're on a winding road that eventually arrives at Ravello. Compared to Positano, this town is not built on as many terraced levels, and the views, though lovely, are not as spectacular from the hotel rooms. However, the town itself is exceptionally attractive, a very peaceful and restful place. Park your car and explore on foot; there is much to appreciate.

Start at the cobblestoned town square, with its old Duomo, and proceed to the nearby shops with beautiful hand-painted ceramics by local artists. Visit the various churches, the monasteries, and the gardens of the villas Cimbrone and Rufolo.

From June to September, during the world-class music festival in Ravello, there are the attractions in the clustered cities and the ruins of Pompeii. By all means, you should take advantage of this opportunity to visit Pompeii, one of the world's great archaeological sites. It is easily reached from Ravello over a good, albeit twisty, road that takes you north over the mountains to the A-3 Autostrada. The drive takes about one and a quarter hours. The best way to see Pompeii is with a guide. If you haven't arranged for one in advance, there will be many offering their services.

HOTEL PALUMBO
Via San Giovanni del Toro 16
Tel: 39-08-985-7244

Originally a 15th-century palace, the Hotel Palumbo has retained its Old World elegance in every way. Each of its 22 bedrooms is different: Some have high ceilings with chandeliers, some have balconies and views. To reach the private bathroom of one room, you must walk down ten steps! Obviously, room selection is important, so ask for a brief description when booking, and also be aware of the fact that the Palumbo has an additional "Residence" nearby. The hotel has a lovely courtyard and terraces, an elegant dining room, and antique-

filled lounges. Staying here is very pleasant. Doubles from $275, including breakfast.

PALAZZO MURAT
Via dei Mulini 23
Tel: 39-08-987-5177

A little farther down Ravello's cobbled street is a jasmine arbor opening to the Palazzo Murat. Once a villa of the King of Naples, shell-capped Palladian windows with wrought-iron-gated balconies overlook the gardens. The villa has 19 guest rooms. Inside, the hotel's near-perfect restaurant offers guests an unexpected delight. The fruit menu is spectacular, offering up to 40 different varieties, each individually prepared and presented.

★ THE CARUSO
Piazza San Giovanni del Toro 2
Tel: 39-08-985-8801
Tel: 39-08-985-7111

This charming hotel set in spacious terraced grounds was a favorite haunt of the Bloomsbury Group, including Virginia Woolf and Lord Keynes. It also helped Graham Greene and William Styron to find the way, respectively, to *The Third Man* and *Set This House On Fire*. Last but not least to fall to Ravello's charms was Gore Vidal, who was introduced to Ravello by Tennessee Williams and who wrote his *Myra Breckinridge* in room No. 9.

Over years, the Hungarian royal family, soprano Toti Dal Monte, the Savoy family, Italian playwright Eduardo De Filippo, Rosalind Russell, Max Reinhart,

AMALFI COAST

Nobel laureate Alexander Fleming, John Huston, Margot Fonteyn, Gina Lollobrigida, Humphrey Bogart, Jackie Kennedy, and any number of other prominent personalities have been guests between and after the world wars.

There are excellent views and many antiques, with Orient-Express elegance and appeal. 48 rooms.

☆ VILLA RUFOLO
Piazza Vescovado
Tel: 39-08-985-7657

The Villa Rufolo, built in the 12th century by one of Italy's patrician families, is Arabic-Norman in style. A lovely hotel with acres of gardens hang over the sea. The rooms are comfortable and accommodating. Every year in July, an orchestra of 112 musicians celebrates Richard Wagner in a music festival there. A specially constructed stage is actually built several thousand feet over the water, giving the most dramatic and amazing illusion of the musicians suspended in air. The concerts are often exceptional. Dramatic lighting creates a visual landscape that enhances the music.

PALAZZO SASSO
Via San Giovanni del Toro
Tel: 39-08-981-8181 or 800-225-4255
www.palazzosasso.com

Palazzo Sasso is a sumptuous five-star hotel in a 12th-century Italian villa hidden in the hilltop village of Ravello. It's perched high on the cliffs, 300 meters (1,000 feet) above the blue Mediterranean and overlooking some of the coast's most idyllic fishing villages. Palazzo Sasso reopened as a new hotel in July 1997, with a firm commitment to friendly and exceptional service.

This extraordinary hotel is under the expert and gracious leadership of general manager Stephano Gegnacorsi and associate general manager Alexandria di Palma. Few hotels are renovated so beautifully with such elegant taste. Marble tiles from three Italian cities are geometrically inlaid into the floors. Silk-covered Chippendale chairs, fountains and frescoes, grand manicured lawns of flowers, crisp white linens, and beds with 300-thread-count cotton sheets are among the elegant details. In another setting where the eye appreciates every view from every angle, we enjoyed something I had not experienced before: After a light and splendid lunch, a gleaming silver cheese trolley with more than 50 cheeses displayed was presented by the maitre d'. I selected only five. After each slice from sterling cutlery, the fork and knife were replaced by clean and polished ones, so as not to pollute the individual flavors. The ceremony was astonishingly understated. Doubles from 450 euros.

AMALFI

Autumn is the best time to drive the coast and to spend a few days in Amalfi, and the best place to stay is the Hotel Santa Caterina. The best way to get to the Almafi Coast is by Eurostar train from Rome to Naples or the Naples airport and then by car.

☆ HOTEL SANTA CATERINA
S.S. Amalfitana 9
Tel: 39-08-987-1012, www.santacaterina.it

The Santa Caterina is one of the most luxurious establishments in southern Italy below Naples and Capri. Located in lemon groves and vineyards about half a mile west of town, it is noted for its exceptional restaurant. The hotel, a seaside villa, was opened in 1904 by Giuseppe Gambardella, the town's physician; today it is owned and operated by his granddaughters, Giusy and Carmela. The 58 rooms and suites have floors of Vietri ceramics and large, soft beds. The Romeo and Juliet Chalet is an old hunting lodge in the garden, with a commanding view of the sea. From the garden, an elevator takes guests down to a small beach and swimming pool, giving perspective to the cliffs.

The cuisine of chef Domenico Cuomo focuses on the seafood brought in by the Amalfi fishermen each morning. White wines from Amalfi and Ravello are perfect in this setting. Doubles from about 350 euros, including breakfast. Dinner for two, with wine, about 130 euros.

HOTEL LUNA CONVENTO
Amalfi
Tel: 39-08-987-1002, www.lunahotel.it

A convent founded by St. Francis of Assisi in 1222, this charming place is on a cliff on the outskirts of Amalfi. The cloister has beautiful plantings, and colonnaded passageways are furnished with comfortable chairs, sofas, and appropriate artifacts. The hotel has a lovely terrace, gardens, a swimming pool, an elegant dining room, and varied bedrooms with modern furnishings, some with balconies. 50 rooms. Doubles from $150.

Amalfi's cathedral, one of the most beautiful in southern Italy, is well worth seeing. Although begun in the 9th century and remodeled in the 12th, its interior was later restored in the baroque style visible today.

If you are in the mood to shop for ceramics, head east along the coast to Vietri, a town completely devoted to colorful wares displayed on every street. The Solimena factory is the one to see first; it's in a building designed by

RAVELLO'S GARDENS

The gardens of both the Villa Rufolo and the Villa Cimbrone parade a variety of vivid flowers, plants, sweet-smelling shrubs, and herbs, all arranged in formal design.

The plan of the Cimbrone gardens was commissioned by an English nobleman, William Beckett, and is expertly manicured. From the wide green lawns, you can look as far over the coastline as your imagination can take you. The gardens are called the "Terraces of Infinity." Nearby is the Villa Maria, a small and charming 19th-century Roman villa, with its restaurant set in a vineyard shaded by grape leaves.

Villa Rufolo's magnificent gardens inspired Richard Wagner in 1880 to create the stage set for his opera *Parsifal*. Upon viewing the greenery, he allegedly stated: "Here I have found the magic garden of Klingsor." Every year, a music festival honoring Wagner takes place in the gardens. A museum in the gardens recounts the history of the families that have resided in the villa.

Next to the Rufolo gardens is the villa—now serving as a hotel—a precious gem set in a splendid mosaic.

Solari on via Madonna degli Angeli. The little tourist office on the central piazza will guide you to the latest exhibits and to demonstrations by working ceramicists.

A GOOD RESTAURANT

Cumpa 'Cosimo
Via Roma 44, Ravello
Tel: 39-08-9857-156

On a more basic and down to earth note, the Cumpa 'Cosimo restaurant is another sort of treasure. The old joke "I would like a table close to a waiter" has no credibility here; one's always nearby. Now for something wonderful, you are in the presence of somebody who instinctually knows what you want to enjoy. Proprietress Nettie Bottone, following the tradition of her grandfather and father, brings vitality to the dining experience. She supervises making the occasion easy and comes nearest to being a food psychic as anyone I have ever known. Ordering for you, she understands what your taste buds are longing for and each serving is amazingly on the culinary mark.

Seven homemade pastas with seven homemade sauces and salads from a homegrown garden are laced with tender attention. The mixed grill of fresh fish and the roasted lamb well seasoned with herbs are delicious. But the pastas and the desserts steal the show. And if that is not enough, the homemade limoncello, a liqueur made from Ravello lemons served ice cold in frosted glasses after dinner, is enough to take your breath away, a candy lemon taste that lingers on seemingly forever.

FURORE

This tiny hamlet lies in a cove at the mouth of the Vallone gorge on the way from Positano to Amalfi, between two tunnels on the most impressive section of the amazing Amalfi Highway. Over the past few years, Furore has grown dear to the hearts of a relatively small number of insiders who know it as the location of the Antica Hostaria di Bacco, a 15-room inn and restaurant owned and operated with great care by the Ferraioli family.

ANTICA HOSTARIA DI BACCO
Via G.B. Lama 9
Tel: 39-08-983-0360

Stunning views of the Mediterranean Sea and the rocky coastline are visible from the large terrace and the guest rooms, and the food keeps getting better and better. Fish is always fresh, the vegetables come from the family's kitchen garden, and the wine is from their own vineyard. Pastas and Neopolitan-style desserts are made on the premises; the thin spaghetti with mussels is a gastronomic triumph. Their season, running well into November, begins again in late winter, and it is prudent to book early. Doubles, about $70; half-board for two (room, breakfast, and dinner), about $100. If you are not staying at the inn, a meal for two, with the house wine, can run to $75. Restaurant closed Friday. Fax: 39-08-9830-352. Note: If you should be present during a storm, you will understand why the hamlet is named Furore (Fury).

SORRENTO

Above the bays of Naples and Salerno, Sorrento's setting is awe-inspiring. This famous resort city is filled with gardens, and the countryside is covered with orange and lemon groves.

AMALFI COAST

GRAND HOTEL EXCELSIOR VITTORIA
Piazza Tasso 34
Tel: 39-08-1807-1044,
www.exvitt.it

Sorrento presents a spectacular view of the Gulf and Bay of Naples from Punta di Sorrento. The best place to stay is the Grand Hotel Excelsior Vittoria. It has 107 rooms, some with balconies; a swimming pool, and shops. Doubles from $230, including breakfast; suites from $1,200.

CAPRI

⭐ GRAND HOTEL QUISISANA
Via Camerelle 2
Tel: 39-08-1837-0788
www.quisi.com

Easily reached by daily ferries from Amalfi and Sorrento, the Grand Hotel Quisisana is one of the last surviving Old World hostelries in Italy, as the international megachains have not been able to buy it from the Morgano family, who still take an active part in its management. The hotel, which opened in the 1840s, is near the central Piazza Umberto I, the social center of Capri. Any numbers of celebrities have signed the guest book. Some of the 150 rooms and suites look out on a narrow lane that is noisy until the very early morning hours from motor scooters and occasional rowdy revelers; so be sure to request a room overlooking the garden with its bougainvillea, oleander, and jasmine, a view that takes in the sea and the Certosa, an abandoned 14th-century Carthusian monastery. Most rooms are large, with elegant neo-baroque furniture and state-of-the-art facilities. Bathrooms are spacious and sparkling, but you might have to request more towels. Children are welcome, which is unusual for Capri hotels. Most of the staff are old-timers, all

TRANSFER & TOURING

Benvenuto Exclusive Chauffeur Services
www.benvenutolimos.com
Tel: 39-334-307-8342 or 39-08-987-4024

An outstanding transfer and touring service on the Amalfi Coast. Giovanni Benvenuto, with his fleet of late-model Mercedes sedans and minivans has designed excursions that exceed every standard of excellence. Each excursion on the Amalfi Coast, including transfers from train stations and airports, has been carefully arranged so that each town chosen to visit is a delight!

There is much to explore. Naples, Amalfi, Sorrento, Pompeii, Positano, Ravello, and Capri, to name a few. Each tour, half-day or full-day, is custom arranged with courteous multilingual drivers.

Their newest service includes a ten-day grand tour of Italy. You cannot find a better company. For generations, the service has been family run, and it is now led under the expert direction of Giovanni.

very obliging. If you supply an approximate time of arrival by hydrofoil from Naples (or aboard your own yacht, of course), you'll be met at the waterfront by the hotel's dock master, appearing as a naval officer. And you'll be pleased to discover a quite comprehensive spa, essential in this sun-drenched environment. The evening restaurant, Quisi, is expensive; dinner for two with a bottle from the encyclopedic wine list can cost $250. Garden doubles from about $310, including breakfast.

2 EXPLORING THE GREAT BARRIER REEF

"Then I sailed for Australia. New Holland as it was called, and I explored this magnificent land and glorious reefs on the east coast for two thousand miles, and took over the country in the king's name."

—Captain James Cook (on the *Endeavour*, 1779)

Australia's Great Barrier Reef is one of the last remaining pristine natural environments in the world and is home to breathtaking treasures. The great reef is actually more than 2,500 separate coral reefs extending from Lizard Island to the Whitsunday chain, all thriving in clear shallow coastal waters of a spectacular tropical sea. For scuba divers, the ultimate dive. There are good trips by seaplanes to water museums, for swimming, and snorkeling.

Extending nearly 2,000 kilometers (1,200 miles) along Australia's northeast coast, the Great Barrier Reef with its colorful outcroppings of coral and its incredible clarity of water is a must-visit. The islands off the mainland are wonderful places to sail, snorkel, and dive or ride in glass-bottomed boats and semisubmersible craft.

Lagoons between the reef and the coast include several thousand small reefs and more than 600 islands. Only about 20 have resorts, but you can camp most anywhere.

The easiest way to explore the reef is on day-trips from Townsville, Cairns, Port Douglas, or a few other places along the coast. Tour companies are everywhere and offer a variety of tours. Travelers should be aware, however, that after travel time, a day-trip leaves only about three or so hours for snorkeling and diving. Boats range from large, comfortable catamarans to small, intimate yachts. Experienced divers should spend several nights aboard a dive boat and see more of the reef by sailing north of Cairns to the Coral Sea, the Yongala Wreck and Cod Hole.

Another option is to stay at one of the coral resorts. One favorite is Heron Island, reached by air or a two-hour boat ride from Gladstone. We recommend that first-time visitors stay at least two nights. It's an ideal spot for divers, nature lovers, and those wanting to get away from it all. Good dining. (Heron is a bit more formal than many of the other islands.)

You can also visit Green Island on a day-trip from Cairns, or you can overnight at its small luxury resort. The closest coral island to the mainland, Green offers good snorkeling, scuba diving, and coral viewing.

Lady Elliot (reached from Bundaberg) is the southernmost coral cay on the reef, with white-sand beaches, diving, and reef walking and fairly basic accommodations in cabins and safari tents.

OTHER POPULAR ISLANDS

Dunk Island, south of Cairns, will appeal to those who love nature. It is covered by rain forest and bougainvillea and butterflies. With its nice beaches, Dunk is a good, slightly upscale family destination.

Great Keppel Island, reached by plane or boat from Rockhampton, is an informal place managed by Contiki for young party lovers. There's something going on nearly all the time. Those who enjoy this atmosphere will want to stay a few days.

Hamilton Island is part of the Whitsunday group south of Townsville and one of the most developed on the reef, with a marine village, restaurants, cafés, bars, water sports, and a large high-rise resort. In addition to underwater attractions, there's a nature park on nearby Dent Island with emus, koalas, and kangaroos. Hamilton can be reached by air or boat.

GREAT BARRIER REEF

Hayman Island is also part of the Whitsundays and is one of the most deluxe resorts on the reef. Lying near the Tropic of Cancer, it has a beautiful lagoon. The island's 214-room hotel offers its international clientele diving and snorkeling, sailing, bush walking, golfing, and tennis. Most visitors arrive by air or boat on Hamilton Island and then take a luxury launch transfer to Hayman.

Lizard Island is the most northern of the resort islands, known for its deep-sea fishing (especially marlin), snorkeling, great scuba diving, and Cod Hole. Though informal, the island is a smart luxury resort that will appeal mainly to those who love to get away from the crowds.

⭐ LIZARD ISLAND RESORT
Tel: 61-2-8269-8010 or 800-225-9849
www.poresorts.com.au

Our favorite place is Lizard Island, located 280 kilometers (175 miles) north of Cairns, on the outer Great Barrier Reef. The entire island is a nature reserve covering about 15 square kilometers (6 square miles) and encompassing 24 beautiful beaches. Year-round temperatures are between 80°F and 90°F (26°C and 32°C) during the day, dropping to about 70°F (21°C) at night. Although it's totally isolated and somewhat difficult to reach, it's worth adding to your list of ultimate getaway spots, a luxurious 40-room hideaway.

The best rooms, all air-conditioned, are the Anchor Bay Suites (rooms 27-38, with the even-numbered ones a few steps closer to the beach). Service is friendly and responsive. Meals are served outdoors, on a veranda overlooking the Coral Sea, and the food is truly excellent, which is no small achievement considering the difficulty of bringing in supplies. Fresh items are flown in daily, and a barge carrying

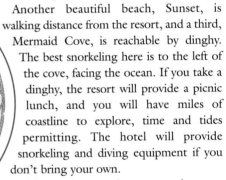

nonperishables comes every two weeks. And you'll be pleasantly surprised to find the choice of wines very satisfactory. Recreational facilities include a Zen-inspired spa with a range of treatments, all very well administered.

The snorkeling at Anchor Beach, on the resort's doorstep, is a good place to get acclimated by means of an introductory plunge. From Anchor Beach you can swim to Watsons Beach where, about 41-81 meters (100-200 yards) from shore, the underwater viewing of various species of marine life is magnificent.

Another beautiful beach, Sunset, is walking distance from the resort, and a third, Mermaid Cove, is reachable by dinghy. The best snorkeling here is to the left of the cove, facing the ocean. If you take a dinghy, the resort will provide a picnic lunch, and you will have miles of coastline to explore, time and tides permitting. The hotel will provide snorkeling and diving equipment if you don't bring your own.

Wherever you go, be sure to take water and wear good walking shoes and a hat. Insect repellent is an absolute necessity, and an itch-soothing, after-bite medication will also prove useful. Doubles from about $500 per person per day, suites from about $600, all including three meals daily as well as most activities.

BEDARRA
Tel. 61-7-4068-8233
www.bedarraisland.com

Considered by many to be the finest resort in the country, Bedarra is a private island lying off of Queensland's tropical north coast adjacent to the Great Barrier Reef. With only 15 guest villas, privacy is assured. The routine is informal;

clothing is casual at all times, including at the long lunches and relaxed dinners. Food is prepared to the highest standards. There are no locks on the doors, and you can help yourself at the bar. Most guests enjoy taking out a motorized dinghy for picnicking on nearby secluded islands. Amenities include aromatherapy burners placed in the rooms each evening. All-inclusive daily rates for double occupancy start at about $800.

HAYMAN ISLAND RESORT
Tel: 61-7-4940-1234
www.hayman.com.au

The Hayman Island Resort is an outpost of relaxed elegance. There are 214 air-conditioned rooms, including 33 suites and 11 penthouses, all beautifully furnished and fully equipped. Public spaces are filled with antiques and attractive examples of Australian art. The resort's restaurant choices include the top-of-the-line La Fontaine as well as Italian, Asian, and three casual spots. In addition to diving, Hayman Island has all water sports (saltwater and freshwater pools), racket sports, fishing, hiking, and a fitness club. Doubles start at about $325 but these are likely to be the Palm Garden rooms, some of which date back to the resort's early days. The better doubles start at about $450, suites at $850 and penthouses at $1,200, all including buffet breakfast.

THE SUNDOWNER
www.australian-trains.com

Comfort, flexibility, and a great social atmosphere have made this train one of Australia's great journeys and a favorite with travelers between Brisbane and Cairns. The journey rails its way along Queensland several times a week. The route includes the eastern coast that parallels the Great Barrier Reef.

Queenslander class is a comfortable way to travel to towns along the Reef. This premium, all-inclusive style of travel features twin sleeping accommodations, fine dining in a restaurant car, entertainment and local commentary, exceptional services, and a host of extra-special touches to make your journey a good one.

Queenslander-class compartments have a comfortable lounge that converts to upper and lower sleeping berths at night with fluffy comforters and pillows. Cabins have 240-volt power points, a private vanity, wardrobes, a full-length mirror, reading lamps, and a foldaway table.

Dining is undoubtedly the highlight of Queenslander class. Every meal aboard is prepared under the experienced hand of the onboard chef using the freshest local ingredients and served in the exclusive restaurant car by an attentive onboard staff.

❸ THE GREEN HILLS OF AFRICA

The legendary Ernest Hemingway introduced the Swahili word "safari" to the English language. He traveled in Africa two times in his life, and the experiences gave him material for short stories and novels. He created a persona, an image of the Great White Hunter, and had a true love affair with the continent's nature and wildlife

From early in his life, Hemingway traveled, like so many writers at the time. He had an enormous appetite for adventure, war, and danger. His first visit was in 1933, and, returning home, Hemingway wrote *The Green Hills Of Africa*.

Safari, anyone?

Untarnished, expansive, and exquisite, Botswana is a land greatly respected by its people and one of the few African countries to realize the importance of ecological preservation and low-impact tourism. Unique in its diversity of regions, Botswana has green wetlands, forested islands tapering into riverbanks, and rivers that eventually run dry into the parched sands of the Kalahari Desert. To see Botswana is to experience the Real Africa. Wild, unexpected, and beautiful.

Botswana was first inhabited by the seminomadic San people, Bantu-speaking tribes from the north who moved into the area before the first millennium, and before the European missionaries arrived in the mid-19th century. In 1885, to counter Boer expansion from South Africa and Ndebele incursions led by Mzilikazi from the north, Bechuanaland came under British protection. By 1895, Rhodes's British South Africa Company hoped to annex Bechuanaland, prompting three Botswana chiefs to persuade Queen Victoria to keep their land under British control.

The British administered the Bechuanaland Protectorate until 1966, when it granted the Botswana full independence under the leadership of Sir Seretse Khama.

Diamonds were discovered in 1967, which brought rapid growth to Botswana. Today, the country boasts an enviable record of democracy and human rights, has healthy foreign reserves, and is considered one of Africa's economic success stories.

While violent political action in parts of sub-Saharan Africa have discouraged many travelers from heading off on game-watching safaris, Botswana remains a very attractive destination. The country is fiscally stable and very safe, and its genuinely kind and caring citizenry supports a determined commitment to conservation and ecotourism. There are two major game reserves, the Linyati in the north and the Okavango Delta a bit farther south.

The optimum size for a safari camp is no more than 15 tented chalets. Many of the larger camps are oriented toward group tour business.

Because of the numerous details of booking a wildlife safari, the wide range of choice of camps in the area, and the significant variation in the quality of the services they offer, we recommend using the services of a qualified travel consultant to arrange your trip.

GUEST-HOUSE BUTEMBO

KIVU
CONGO BELGE

SAVUTE ELEPHANT CAMP, CHOBE NATIONAL PARK, BOTSWANA
Orient-Express Safaris
Tel: 27-11-274-1800

In the heart of the Chobe National Park, sometimes referred to as the elephant capital of the world, is Savute Elephant Camp. Found on the banks of the now-dry Savute Channel, the camp offers a spectacular bird's-eye view of elephants in their natural habitat, with an adjacent water hole just meters away from the camp's main building. The area is also known for a high concentration of predators such as the endangered wild dog, lion, leopard, cheetah, and hyena. This is a unique timeless drama with no script, played by actors who have no lines, in an environment that needs no set.

Chobe is known for its photography, exciting game viewing, and birding. It also presents the rare opportunity to view rock paintings drawn by the early Bushmen, who once inhabited the region.

Savute personifies the eternal contrast of Africa. Where other camps celebrate water and lush vegetation, Savute is an objective lesson in aridity. Rain in this dry place is rare and water is precious.

On the Savute Channel, which is an eccentric waterway that fluctuates between being bone-dry or flooding, the whole ethos of Savute Elephant Camp is to commiserate with its inhabitants and environment.

In Savute, precious little has changed on these dry plains since time began. And the realization dawns that you are privileged to be in one of the last corners of the planet governed by nature.

CHIEF'S CAMP
Maun, Botswana
Tel: 26-766-2688
www.akhotelsandresorts.com

Chief's Camp is on Chief's Island in the heart of the Okavango Delta and occupies the former hunting grounds of Botswana tribal chiefs. Intrepid travelers who feel Chobe Chilwero is too luxurious for "adventure" will find Chief's semipermanent canvas tents more in keeping with the wilderness setting, reminiscent of Hemingway. All 12 tents rest solidly on a raised wooden platform large enough to accommodate a viewing deck and a full bathroom with a shower and double sinks. Sturdy double front doors are fashioned of wood, not cloth, and hung with shutters. African masks adorn the wall above the writing desk. A ceiling fan cools the air, and although the electricity goes off during the night, storage generators keep the power flowing. The attractive public areas—a breezy dining room, casual bar, and a boutique—stretch out under a high, thatched roof. A veranda and swimming pool overlook seasonal waterways teeming with game.

Evening hors d'oeuvres, perhaps kudu skewers or chewy crocodile tail, are offered around a bonfire adjacent to the lounge. Daily rates from $270 per person (low season) to $595 per person (peak season) include meals, beverages, game drives, mokoro (dugout canoe) rides, laundry, and postage. Access by light aircraft is additional.

CHOBE CHILWERO SAFARI LODGE
Kasane, Botswana
Tel: 26-765-1362
www.akhotelsandresorts.com

Perched on a hill overlooking the Chobe River, Chobe Chilwero ("place of the high view") is now unquestionably Botswana's most lavish safari lodge. Formerly a rustic retreat an hour and a half's drive west of Victoria Falls, the property was entirely rebuilt in 2000, creating 15 elegant thatched-roof cottages with such bush luxuries as air-conditioning, hair dryers, safes, and lighted closets. Properly lit native artwork and authentic handicrafts form an integral part of the decor as do terra-cotta floors inlaid with colorful tiles. Along with a king-size bed (or twins) draped with yards of filmy mosquito netting, each cottage has a huge bathroom with a sunken soaking tub that faces a private garden enclosed by a reed fence. You can also wash off the safari dust under a rainforest showerhead either indoors or outside in the garden. The 5:30 a.m. wake-up includes coffee and cookies brought to the "sala," a thatch-covered patio. Winding pathways connect the cottages to a delightful, split-level swimming pool and grassy sunning area. A central, open-air lodge houses the dining room and a sitting room hung with an impressive African art collection. Lunches are served on an expansive terrace, which features a wood-burning pizza oven. No children under nine without prior arrangement. Daily rates of $230 per person during the wet months (December through March) and $420 per person, July through October, include all meals, beverages, twice-daily game drives in Chobe National Park, and laundry service

MOMBO CAMP
Tel: 27-11-888-4037 or 888-227-8311
www.classicafrica.com or www.africaportal.com

The Okavango Delta is the largest inland wetland in the world. Covering an area the size of Switzerland, it is packed with a dizzying array of flora and fauna. The best game viewing occurs in the Moremi Wildlife Reserve, a vast area established by the wife of Chief Moremi III in memory of her husband. Of the numerous camps in the Moremi, Mombo is one of the better choices. It offers eight deluxe permanent tented chalets featuring twin beds, an en-suite bathroom with flush toilet and shower, a sitting area, and a private viewing deck. There is also a swimming pool. Formal game viewing takes place on twice-daily Land Rover trips, but the wildlife viewing— lion, elephant, giraffe, zebra, cape buffalo, leopard,

wildebeest, and more, as well as any of more than 500 bird species—is virtually unending.

Other first-rate camps in the Okavango include Jao, Vumbura, and Chitabe. In general, daily rates run to about $450 per person, including three extraordinary meals plus an early, light breakfast and all beverages. Similar game-viewing opportunities are available in the Linyati Reserve near Chobe National Park at camps such as Savuti, Duma Tau, and King's Pool. You won't be disappointed at any of these.

KHWAI RIVER LODGE
Orient-Express Safaris
Tel: 27-11-481-6052

Nestled on the edge of a leadwood and fig tree forest, overlooking the vast Khwai River floodplains and beyond into the Moremi Wildlife Reserve, sits the luxurious Khwai River Lodge. Khwai is renowned for its large concentrations of mammals, and it is not unusual to see many different types of wildlife from the comfort of your own private deck. As a year-round destination for wildlife, predators can regularly be seen in the area, rated as one of the most prolific in Botswana for viewing wildlife. The exceptional location of Khwai makes it a regular host to elephants, buffalos, lions, leopards, cheetahs, and wild dogs. Birdlife

WHITE RHINOS

Rhinos were hunted to extinction in Botswana in the early 1900s. And after being reintroduced in the 1970s, they were decimated by severe poaching. Thus it's exciting and gratifying to report that four white rhinos—two males and two females—were reintroduced into the famed Moremi Game Reserve in the fall of 2001. Their adaptation process, which was expected to take six months or longer, has progressed so successfully that they are now seen frequently by the guests of Mombo Camp, long recognized as the best camp in Botswana. Based on this success, 20 more white rhinos are expected to be released into the Moremi Game Reserve, and plans call for at least ten black rhinos, shier and more elusive than the white rhinos, to be reintroduced as well. The conservation effort to enable these endangered species to roam freely, as once they did, is good news for all travelers who cherish the wildlife and spellbinding wilderness of Southern Africa.

can also be viewed in abundance with exceptional sightings of wildfowl and raptors near the lodge.

This is the perfect location for observing the perennial drama of the African bush and provides excellent birding.

At Khwai River Lodge, you are close to Africa's heartbeat and at the center of a world that has not altered since life began. You can sense this from the moment you arrive. Bush hats and desert boots, tall tales and long drinks, a past redolent of trophies and potent sundowners—upon entering Khwai River Lodge, you

immediately sense its big game heritage. For decades, as befits one of the most established game lodges in Botswana, it has hosted guests from all over the world on the safari trail.

EAGLE ISLAND CAMP
Orient-Express Safaris
Tel: 27-1-1481-6052

Hidden from the world, deep within Botswana's Okavango Delta, is the paradise called Eagle Island Camp. Situated on the island of Xaxaba and surrounded by Ilala Palms, the camp overlooks a lagoon fed by the tranquil waterways of the delta. The area offers exceptionally high-quality wildlife viewing with prolific birdlife and mammal sightings. It is also the site of one of the most romantic bars in the world, the Fish Eagle Bar, as voted by the *New York Times*.

The camp offers a cool retreat from the African sun and is shaded by a canopy of indigenous trees.

Xaxaba is one of the delta's most pristine natural locations, a region of myriad waterways, palm-treed islands, and vast flood plains. Bird and animal life in this region is prolific. The camp offers game viewing by mokoro (traditional dugout canoe), motorized boats, and a 14-seat Sundowner cruiser.

For intrepid explorers with an appetite for sights and sounds of the bush, it offers guided birding walks and wildlife viewing at sunset.

The magnificent twiglights can be enjoyed during times of high flood from the Fish Eagle Bar at Eagle Island or from the raised deck overlooking the lagoon. Built to blend into its environment, with private decks overlooking the surrounding lagoon, the camp affords guests a peaceful setting perfect for enjoying the sights and sounds of the Okavango Delta.

4 THE SOUTHERN CONE OF SOUTH AMERICA

Imagine a long, thin slice of California with a patch of the Sahara desert glued onto the north. Carve some of New Zealand's fjords and British Columbia's forests and lakes into the south. Press all of this against a spine of tall, rugged mountains. This is Chile, which has some of the world's most varied and dramatic landscapes.

Parts of the country, Tierra del Fuego, for example, feel like the ends of the earth. Yet Chile is one of the most modern and convenient travel destinations in South America. In many places, it has a European feel, along with European-style prices that are high in comparison with the rest of the continent.

Spanish, Irish, English, German, and Scottish immigrants, as well as Amerindians and mestizos, make up the majority of Chile's diverse population. Among their neighbors are the indigenous Mapuche, a tribe that survived colonization with its traditions intact. The complex history of Chile's settlement has made it possible to find cultural anomalies throughout the country, such as German immigrants who spoke Spanish and a revered national hero named O'Higgins.

Beginning in central Argentina and stretching from the Río Colorado to the Strait of Magellan, the vast, desolate, windswept region of Patagonia is an unspoiled haven for naturalists. You'll find all kinds of unique animals here, including guanacos, penguins, and elephant seals. With its lakes and streams, it's also a popular destination for those who like to fish, especially November through May, when trout and salmon can be hooked in the rivers and streams flowing through the Andean foothills.

The Chilean portion of Patagonia, the southernmost region of South America, is reached from Bariloche through Punta Arenas. Patagonia's rugged and varied scenery—including fjords, vast pampas, lakes, and glaciers—is filled with coastal wildlife, such as elephant seals, sea lions, and penguins. The weather is harsh, and you can expect a lot of snow and rain.

Among the area's attractions are Lago Argentino, Moreno Glacier, Glacier National Park, and the Pampas. Tierra del Fuego and a dozen national parks, including Torres del Paine National Park, are close by. Patagonia can be seen by charter plane, by four-wheel-drive vehicle, on foot, by mountain bike, or on horseback (or any combination). You can arrange to travel on horseback down to the water, followed by a raft ride past the glaciers.

Also consider a cruise through the Strait of Magellan. It's sobering to realize that, for centuries, this was Europe's main passage to the Pacific via the Americas. Thousands perished in storms there. For an idea of the rigors, you might read *Two Years Before the Mast* by Richard Dana.

BARILOCHE

Bariloche, Argentina, is South America's answer to a Swiss Alpine village. Its main street is lined with shops selling ski equipment and delicious chocolate.

GLACIER CRUISES

www.patagonia-connection.com
Tel: 56-2-225-6489

A cruise through Chile's Inside Passage, the Beagle Channel, and around the Cape Horn passage is a wondrous combination of the best of the Alaskan Inside Passage, Norwegian fjords, Antarctica, and southern New Zealand. Glaciers, flora and fauna, fishing villages, fjords, and icebergs combine to dazzle visitors, but they form only part of the experience. Passengers usually have the opportunity to disembark at various points along the way and can visit with residents to learn what it's like to live in these desolate places.

A cruise to Laguna San Rafael, set in an absolutely spectacular glacial valley dominated by beautiful mountains, is a highlight. Wide glacier icebergs are adrift in the water. It's truly an extraordinary experience to wind through these huge, floating blocks of ice and snow. Cruise through the Chilean fjords and past a thousand waterfalls until reaching the San Rafael Glacier, and then continue on to Termas de Puyuhuapi Lodge, a picture perfect spa with hot mineral springs, accessible only by boat.

☆ LLAO LLAO HOTEL AND RESORT
Av. Bustillo, Km 25, near Bariloche
Tel: 54-29-4444-8530

The Llao Llao Hotel and Resort, a few miles out of town, is a treasure offering great accommodations and facilities. Vast lakes and spectacular mountains surround the hotel, which was built in the style of a Canadian hunting and fishing lodge. There is a scenic 18-hole golf course, skiing, and windsurfing on Lake Nahuel Huapi. The dining room makes excellent German wienerschnitzel and Swiss fondues, and, of course, the grilled Argentine beef is the best in the Americas.

The most enjoyable way to reach the Chilean lakes region of Patagonia is by catamaran from the dock at Llao Llao, in Argentina, a trip of several hours that requires portaging by bus through a national forest. Puerto Montt is a common stopover site, but Puerta Varas, a scenic town on Lake Llanquihue, is a more colorful choice.

HOTEL Y CABAÑAS DEL LAGO
Klenner 195, Puerto Varas
Tel: 56-6523-2291

This hotel is an adequate choice, offering 63 rooms and 21 cabins, all nicely appointed, as well as a full range of normal hotel services, including a heated swimming pool. The best room is suite No. 500, facing the lake. Doubles from $110; cabins from $130, all including breakfast. Ibis, nearby on the lake, is an excellent restaurant featuring fresh oysters, salmon ceviche, razor clams baked with Parmesan cheese, and other specialties; dinner for two, with Chilean wine, about $40.

☆ TERMAS DE PUYUHUAPI LODGE
Tel: 56-2-225-6489, www.patagonia-connection.com
Within the lush vegetation along the banks of Dorita Bay in Patagonia is this unique lodge, Puyuhuapi Hotel & Spa.

Every day you'll start a revitalizing experience: hiking through the rain forest, excursions to the Queulat National Park, fly-fishing, bike riding on the Carretera Austral, or sailing in kayaks through the fjords of southern Chile.

At the spa, different waters converge: sea water, thermal water, and water from the waterfall, and you can enjoy thalassotherapy, relaxing massages, and beauty sessions.

A trip on the modern Patagonia Express catamaran completes the program, cruising through the fjords until reaching San Rafael Lagoon and its amazing glacier.

Some cruises dock at Puerto Natales to allow passengers some time to spend in Parque Nacional Torres del Paine. The next segment passes the most impressive fjords of Chile, a truly dramatic sight, especially when seen from the water. The area around Bahía Garibaldi (Garibaldi Bay) is known for its high concentration of ice fields and active glaciers.

From this point, the scenery becomes somewhat less dramatic, but the cruise through Beagle Channel, named for Charles Darwin's ship, HMS *Beagle,* and the passage around Cape Horn (the southernmost point of South America), provides additional opportunities for seeing glaciers, icebergs, and fjords (you'll see quite a few penguins in the area as well). Cruise ships depart from Puerto Montt. Some offer landfall on the Argentine portion of Tierra del Fuego.

TIERRA DEL FUEGO AT THE SOUTHERN TIP OF SOUTH AMERICA

Among the stories of how this southern area got its name ("Land of Fire") are the following: (1) The first explorers saw bonfires from their ships as they approached, which made the land seem to smoke; (2) Escaping underground volcanic steam makes it look like the Earth is on fire; and (3) Fog and low clouds are sometimes as thick as smoke. We can't verify any of them, but the visual effect of the latter two explanations is stunning.

This region includes all the islands of the archipelago south of the Strait of Magellan. The main island, Isla Grande de Tierra del Fuego, covers 48,000 square kilometers (18,500 square miles) and is shared by Argentina and Chile. It is a fantastic, barren region of high winds and desolate mountains with lakes and sheep farms. Those who reach the rocky, 425-meter-high (1,400-foot) area known as Cape Horn at the southern end of Chile's Horn Island should be prepared for damp, windy weather in a rugged landscape. Local sights include shoulder-high grass, beautiful flowers, birds, and the Seaman's Chapel, built of logs. We spent several hours there, and though we found it truly a fascinating experience, we're glad we did it when we were young. Most roads in the area are unpaved—at best. For hotels, tours, and maps, go to www.tierradelfuego.org.

TORRES DEL PAINE

The wildlife and scenery both inside and surrounding this park are spectacular. Glaciers creep down mountainsides, breaking off into fjords; waterfalls tumble over short cliffs; huge Patagonian hares scurry across the dry terrain; and pink flamingoes flock alongside icy blue lakes dotted with icebergs. Herds of sheep and guanacos (something like llamas), fields of wildflowers, lush green forests, fantastic birdlife (including rheas and condors), and rapidly flowing rivers round out the scene. Take a trip out to Grey Glacier, a slow-moving river of ice that feeds Grey Lake. The "torres" of the park's name are three massive granite towers of the Cordillera del Paine range that reach 3,100 meters (10,000 feet). Ambitious walkers can take a ten-day 100-kilometer/60-mile circuit around the towers and the base of the central massif called Paine Grande; there are also shorter two- or three-day walks into the high valleys. If the weather is clear, you can see some of the mountaintops as you land in Punta Arenas.

Lovers of the outdoors will enjoy rafting on the Río Serrano rapids and fishing for large brown trout (February–April). The park can also be seen as a day trip from nearby Puerto Natales or you can overnight in the park. Rainy and cold days are common even in summer, but the more time you can spend in the area, the more likely you are to have a good, sunny day.

From this part of Chile, some travelers will want to consider Balcemeda and Puerto Natales, a departure point to the penguins on Pingüineras Magdalena Island.

The Chilean lake country and the wilds of Patagonia are becoming increasingly popular destinations for travelers with a yen for mild adventure. For hotels, tours and maps, go to www.torresdelpaine.com or www.chileaustral.com.

THE HOTEL EXPLORA
Tel: 56-2-206-6060, www.explora.com

The Explora is the perfect base to explore, via guided tours, the rugged surroundings of the Torres del Paine National Park; reaching the property via a six-hour van ride from Punta Arenas. It is so remote that phone calls need a satellite hook-up. On the shore of Lake Pehoe, the hotel has 30 rooms, all but three facing the lake and the awesome twin towers of the spectacular Cordillera Paine. Some suites have Jacuzzis and king-size beds. Guides explain each day's choice of five excursion activities, which range from moderately easy to difficult walks. All are memorable, especially the trek across a wind-tossed suspension bridge over the world's third-largest ice field. There is a spa, a lap pool, and an on-site masseuse, all of which help to relax sore muscles after ambitious hiking. Food is good and plentiful; special dietary needs can be accommodated with advance notice. Weather is cool all year, and it often rains, which only adds to the challenge. Bring hiking boots, layers of clothing, and rainwear. Guests must book for a minimum of three nights, and advanced booking is absolutely necessary. Doubles from $2,700 for four nights.

PUNTA ARENAS
Punta Arenas, the main town in Chilean Patagonia, was the center of the country's shipping industry until the opening of the Panama Canal provided a cheaper and safer route than going through the Strait of Magellan. Wealthy industrialists hired European craftsmen and imported luxurious materials to build magnificent belle epoque mansions, several of which today are museums and hotels. One of the most handsome is the Hotel Jose Nogueira.

HOTEL JOSE NOGUEIRA
Tel: 56-61-24-8840
www.hotelnogueira.com

A smart 25-room property with a bar-restaurant located in a glassed-in winter garden. Best rooms are No. 311 and No. 312. Doubles from $165. There are several very good fish and seafood dishes on the menu at Sotito's Restaurant. Meat fanciers will enjoy the lamb stew. Dinner for two, with Chilean wine, about $50. There is a no-smoking section.

ATACAMA DESERT

Chile's Atacama Desert is a virtually lifeless region of volcanoes, geysers, dunes, and chalk cliffs—a sere and desolate landscape in the country's north that, nevertheless, holds great interest for adventure travelers. In the past, however, reaching the area was difficult and local accommodations barely exceeded hostel standards. But all that has changed with the inauguration of direct flights from Newark to Santiago and the opening of a luxury resort on an oasis just outside of the town of San Pedro.

EXPLORA EN ATACAMA
Tel: 56-2-206-6060 or 56-2-208-0664

This inn comes as something of a surprise in this spare environment. Its 50 rooms are situated to offer stunning desert views and utter silence. Lovely pepper and carob trees shade the grounds, and rooms connect via ramps to a central courtyard and elevated lobby and restaurant. Inside, all furniture and fabrics were produced by local artisans and walls are hung with antique Chilean textiles. Each evening, at cocktail time, English-speaking guides meet with the guests to plan the next day's excursions. Activities are the reason for coming to Explora, including leisurely horseback rides through the dunes; hiking to a natural hot spring that nestles in a grass valley where guests can bathe while sampling the Chilean national drink, Pisco sours; observing flocks of pink flamingos around a barren salt lake; or—the ultimate excursion—four days of hiking culminating in a 6,000-meter (20,000-foot) climb into a smoldering volcano. Meals, whether in the dining room or out on the trail, are excellent, an always interesting blending of continental and local ingredients and techniques.

To reach the resort, you must take a two-hour flight from Santiago to Calama, the nearest airport, where you will be met by hotel staff. Bring plenty of sunscreen, a broad-brimmed hat, and warm outerwear for the frosty nights. Minimum stay is three nights, and the rate is about $1,800 per person, including all meals, drinks, explorations, and transfers.

SANTIAGO

Santiago, Chile's lovely capital, is a very European-style city. It's an energized metropolis of majestic neoclassic buildings that could just as well be in Brussels or Paris. There are quiet, well-kept parks, beautiful stucco mansions, and flowers everywhere. On a clear day, the beauty of the Andes,

serving as a backdrop, will take your breath away. Santiago is one of the few capital cities where ski slopes and beaches are easily accessible. And don't forget the vineyards in the surrounding countryside!

HYATT REGENCY
Kennedy Avenue #4601
Tel: 56-2-950-1234, www.santiago.regency.hyatt.com

The Hyatt Regency in Santiago is a full-service luxury hotel that provides so many amenities that it can function with equal satisfaction as a resort in the middle of a city or as a business destination. The 310-room haven is located in an elegant neighborhood of diplomatic residences and expensive homes, minutes from midtown. Locals find it a convenient and posh place for social or business meetings. The marble and wood lobby is part of a dramatic, soaring atrium tower that is the major public space of the hotel. Guest rooms are located in two 24-story adjacent wings and have views of downtown Santiago and the Andes Mountains. The deluxe rooms, quite large by most hotel standards, have comfortable seating areas with couches and executive desks. Many of the top suites are cantilevered and overlook a 900-meter (3,000-foot), lagoon-style swimming pool with a waterfall and landscaped gardens. Every room has modern equipment, including minibars, satellite TV, and international direct-dial telephones. Four floors are dedicated to the Regency Club, with continental breakfast, early evening cocktails, tea and coffee service, the aid of a concierge, and a billiard room. Well-lit, marbled bathrooms are conveniently divided into three areas for separate shower, toilet, and sink compartments.

The hotel has two restaurants: Crostini's, with a variety of Northern Italian specialties, and Anakena, a good spot for Chilean seafood. Dinner for two at either restaurant, with wine, about $75.

★ THE RITZ-CARLTON, SANTIAGO
Calle El Alcalde 15
Las Condes
Telephone: 56-2-470-8500, www.ritzcarlton.com

An outstanding hotel strategically located in the capital's most prestigious and refined neighborhood, El Golf. The 205-room hotel is just 30 minutes from Santiago International Airport and within walking distance of exclusive boutiques and restaurants. The rooms have every Ritz-Carlton advantage, stylish and comfortable.

★ HOTEL ORLY
Av. Pedro de Valdivia 027s
Tel: 56-2-231-8947
www.orlyhotel.com

A rare find and a moderately priced hotel with many of the comforts of those costing twice as much. That you can find a treasure like this in the middle of Providencia is nothing short of a miracle. The shiny wood floors, country-manor furnishings, and glass-domed breakfast room make this hotel as sweet as it is economical. Rooms come in all shapes and sizes, so ask to see a few before you decide. Cafetto, the downstairs café, serves some of the finest coffee drinks in town. There are 25 rooms and 3 suites, plus restaurant, café, room service, in-room safes, minibars, cable TV, in-room data ports, bicycles, laundry service, Internet, free parking, and full breakfast.

THE SOUTHERN CONE

On a day trip south to Rancagua, another of Chile's several Swiss chefs blends European training with Chilean provender at Termas de Cauquenes, originally a 15th-century thermal spa. Razor clams, a national dish, come coated in Parmesan à la Rockefeller or steeped in red wine. A creamy conger-eel soup is good enough to convert the squeamish. But if not, move right on to the bacon-wrapped snapper or lamb chops served with fried quail eggs and frites. Dinner for two, without wine, about $65.

SHOPPING IN SANTIAGO

The cobblestoned Paseo Ahumada is a heavily commercial pedestrian street full of shops, fast-food restaurants, department stores, clowns, musicians, and pickpockets. There more ice-cream shops and outdoor candy stands than probably anywhere else on Earth. On this street is the Pasaje Crillon, which has several nice shops, including Murillo, a good source for silver.

For a concentration of exclusive shops, make your way to the little shopping neighborhood where Avenida Providencia meets Suecia. Walk one block toward the river to General Holley Street, where among other smart stores you'll find both the Galeria Fundacion, which showcases contemporary Chilean artists, and a sort of Swiss-English "village" with clothing stores, jewelers, and design shops.

For a pleasant afternoon, go to the very end of Apoquindo to the little village next to the church at Los Dominicos. Here, at the artisan's fair, you'll find some really beautiful handicrafts—lapis lazuli and sweaters from the south, traditional ceramics. A chattering brook runs

through the little village, adding its noise to the cheerful hammering of silversmiths. Somewhat stagey, but fun.

The Mercado Central (Central Market), in a wrought-iron exposition building constructed in England to Chilean specifications in the late 19th century, is a popular spot at lunchtime and on holidays.

SKIING IN CHILE: PORTILLO

This world-famous winter resort offers excellent skiing, both downhill and cross-country, ice skating on Laguna del Inca, and splendid mountain views. Many European, Canadian, and U.S. ski teams keep in shape on the slopes of Portillo during the Northern Hemisphere's summer. The ski season is June–September, with August being best.

While there, you'll also want to see the Christ of the Andes statue atop a nearby 3,650-meter (12,000-foot) mountain. The bronze statue, cast from melted-down cannon, commemorates a Chilean-Argentine peace treaty. The drive to Portillo from can be exhilarating—there are no guardrails along the road—passing through the Aconcagua Valley along the Río Blanco. Other ski areas in the region include Farellones-El Colorado (55 kilometers/35 miles east of Santiago) and La Parva. All offer lifts and skiing at elevations of 2,200–2,700 meters (7,500–9,000 feet). A fairly new ski resort, Valle Nevado, caters to a young, international crowd. For more information, see www.skiportillo.com.

VALPARAISO

Founded in 1536, Valparaiso is Chile's oldest and largest port city (pop. 279,000). We think a day trip allows enough time to see the main sites in the interesting old section of town, including colonial buildings, the church of La Matriz, Victoria Square, and the Naval and Maritime Museum. The old-seaport atmosphere of Valparaiso is best appreciated by spending a few hours wandering the steep and winding cobblestone alleyways through the town's colorful working-class neighborhoods. We enjoyed our visit to La Sebastiana, one of Chilean poet Pablo Neruda's eclectically decorated homes, located high above the harbor. You should also plan to visit Neruda's home at Isla Negra, a beautiful stretch of shoreline south of Valparaiso. (It's called Isla Negra—Spanish for "Black Island"—but it's not an island at all.) The house contains a museum with items belonging to the great poet.

What makes Valparaiso distinctive is its rickety-but-reliable network of *ascensores* (funicular cable cars), which were built at the turn of the 20th century. Though they might not look like much, they are true feats of engineering that your feet will be thankful for. Valparaiso also has a number of good waterfront restaurants and a lively, if rather seedy, nightlife.

★ BRIGHTON B&B
Paseo Atkinson 151
Tel: 56-32-223-513

A bright yellow Victorian house on Cerro Concepcíon has a great neighborhood and spectacular view. Owner Nelson Morgado, a professor of architecture at the University of Barcelona, furnished the house with his own antiques. Six rooms overlook the ocean and bay with private balconies. Prices include continental breakfast in a lovely café.

VINA DEL MAR

Just up the coast from Valparaiso, Vina del Mar is Chile's chief seaside resort (pop. 302,000), and it is the polar opposite of its somewhat gritty southern neighbor: It's shiny, slick, and chic, offering golf, tennis, very nice hotels, casinos, parks, shopping, good nightlife, a summer palace, and beaches (though the water is often murky or even muddy). Most people go there to lie on the beach (the main season is January–March), but before you swim you ought to know that the ocean is cold at these latitudes. From Santiago, consider taking the train (about a three-hour trip one way)—the scenery is impressive. To get around Vina del Mar, use the fairly inexpensive horse-drawn fiacres. The town's derby (horse races), held the first Sunday in February, attracts thousands, so reserve hotel space early if you plan to stay for it.

If Vina del Mar is too crowded for your taste, you can always go north to Zapallar or Cachagua, which have the area's most exclusive resorts. There you can find a quiet stay among Chilean aristocracy. Another good destination within easy reach of Vina del Mar is La Campana National Park, a park full of huge native palms; several trails lead to overlooks that reveal the Andes on one side and the Pacific Ocean on the other.

5 THE PAMPAS, POLO, & TANGO

The seduction begins in Buenos Aires. While the world sways to the rhythm of the tango, Buenos Aires pulses with a more frenetic beat. Traffic is the first thing to notice. It is uproariously bad, and discourteous driving is the norm. The accident rate is high. But BA is an amazing place. The city was designed by the French, and in Recolta, upscale and residential with restaurants of every description, are smart shops, swank boutiques, and fashionable Argentines.

Behind this urban landscape of memorable architecture, wide boulevards, and magnificent gardens are the great tango palaces. It is a place where people dance easily to a different tempo in another time.

This is a land with no better polo or gaucho, and I found restaurants and hotels ranking with the best in the world. We've listed selections, places on the pampas, excursions to estancias, and colonial Salta where we took the "Train to the Clouds."

This beautiful country has always attracted visitors. Argentina has arguably the tastiest beef, the sexiest dance, the best-looking people, some of the cutest penguins, the highest peak, and the most cosmopolitan city in South America. Add to that its vast plains and deserts, glistening lakes, thundering glaciers, and some of the greatest waterfalls on Earth, and you have a destination you won't forget.

☆ ALVEAR PALACE
Avenida Alvear 1891
Tel: 54-11- 4808-7777
www.alvearpalace.com

The Alvear Palace is still the most elegant Old World hotel in Buenos Aires. Since 1932 it has been the place where heads of state usually stay and where high government officials still lunch. It is located in Recoleta, the city's best residential neighborhood, amid an atmosphere much calmer than the city center. A butler on each floor is available to help you with any requests. Despite its age, the hotel is maintained to a high order, and the in-room electronics and entertainment equipment is up-to-date. Public rooms and many of the 210 guest rooms (including 125 suites) are decorated in a quiet Louis XVI or Empire style. Almost all of the

BEST RANCH

ESTANCIA LA JOSEFINA
Chascomus
Tel: 54-11-4811-9434

One of the prettiest ranches not too far from Buenos Aires is Estancia la Josefina, a 2,500-hectare (6,250-acre) spread in the pampas with a lovely great house tastefully decorated with antiques and memorabilia. The drive will take you about two hours, but it's worth it. You can come for a day visit or stay one or more nights—there are five comfortable guest bedrooms. The owner, Angela Behrendt, raises cattle organically and has a large organic vegetable garden; much of the produce ends up in the terrific food that's included in your visit. Basque gauchos will take you on horseback or carriage rides and entertain you at picnics of meats and fish grilled over wood fires. There's a swimming pool and the area is a great one for birders. A day visit, which includes a sumptuous barbeque, is about $85 per person. Overnight rates start at about $200 per person and include breakfast, lunch, tea, and dinner.

Buenos Aires: Tango Town

Buenos Aires is a bright city of melancholia set to a dance step. A tango town of once-fabulous wealth and now of nostalgic mansions has gone to delicious decrepitude. City of jackbooted generals and the Mothers of the Disappeared, of Maradona, and even, briefly, of Madonna.

In Recoleta they often die as they have lived, beyond their means. Buenos Aires' most prestigious suburb, Recoleta, has its own exclusive necropolis where row upon row of marble vaults accommodate the dusty repose of the city's once-gilded elite.

Imagine a cemetery populated exclusively by pedigree surnames, and right in the middle, lowering the tone, rests a scrap metal dealer or Lotto winner. That's Recoleta Cemetery. In this case, the post-mortem gatecrasher is Eva Perón. Loved in life by the poor, she is surrounded in death by the rich who despised her then and still do.

Eva Duarte Perón, the second wife of Argentinean President General Juan Perón, died of cancer at age 33 in 1952. She divides Argentineans in death as she did in life: Some think of the ex-actress as an almost saintly friend to the poor, while others consider her little more than a social-climbing tart.

There's more to "BA" than memories of tarts, tango, and generalissimos. This city of Belle Époque elegance and endless wide avenues is like no other Latin American capital. From the red, pink, and blue houses of Caminita to the center's grandiose edifices, BA is a city of fascination. The coffee's great, as are the coffee shops, like the famous Café Tortoni, founded in 1858 and once patronized by writers such as Lorca and Pirandello. And Argentinean steaks are as large as your placemat. The wealth, mostly generated by the export of pampas beef, mutton, and wheat, that once created this New World melding of Paris, Rome, and New York must have been astounding.

The taxis are metered. The public buses are good. But the walking is even better. And this is what I did, letting the city's vast, flat blocks crowd me with their impressions. A sunlit city with the grumps, I thought at first. (In fact, Porteños, the inhabitants of Buenos Aires, are famously unhappy and are said to have two addictions, coffee and psychoanalysis.) BA's endowment of riches may have been squandered by generals and later choked off by changes in world commodity prices, often leaving the city's sumptuous old buildings in need of renovation, but, walking its streets, the patina of history rubs off on one's elbows, almost literally.

The first Spanish settlement here, on the banks of the Río de La Plata, was founded in 1536. Much later, in 1807, the British invaded and were booted straight back out. The Spanish colonial masters received their own marching orders just a few years later. By the turn of the 20th century, Buenos Aires was the largest city in Latin America, with a population of more than a million. Massive immigration added German, Welsh, Basque, Irish, Italian, and English blood to that of the earlier Spaniards and Amerindians.

In the harbor suburb of Boca, where Diego Maradona started his soccer career at Boca Juniors club, one old street has been reborn as a walk-through art galley. Closer to an alley than an avenue, Caminita is more notable for its buildings, multistoried structures made entirely of corrugated iron and painted like grand, primary-colored cubes, than for its art, which is mostly nostalgic images of zoot-suited blokes with Brylcreem hair and bedroom eyes, tango dancing with slinky dames.

Nearby in the San Telmo district, the plazas, cobbled streets, and outdoor cafés seem so European that this could be Italy in the 1950s, or even General Franco's Spain. One guidebook notes, "BA doesn't look like Europe; it looks like a postcard of Europe."

Yet this is always Argentina, with tango tunes trotting in the background.

Theatre Colon, the grand 1908 opera house, seems like it just drifted down a canal from Venice. There's no such whimsy attached to the imposing La Casa Rosada, the President's Palace, from whose balcony Juan and Eva Perón stirred the crowds with jingoism—as later did President Leopoldo Galtieri when, in 1982, he quixotically led Argentina to war against England over the

Malvinas (Falkland Islands). There's Avenue Ninth of July; at 16 lanes across, it's the world's widest city street. And, of course, the Porteños.

Almost 40 percent of Argentina's 34 million people live in greater Buenos Aires. Beyond the elegant architecture and touristy tango clubs, it is the Porteños who make the place. In BA, "personality" still means the triumph of substance over style. Everywhere, you see people with a resilience.

Individualism is still intact, along with a touch of their own class and a slightly fierce glint in their eyes. People here are more than just the sum of their clothes. It's the spirit that regained Argentineans a civilian democracy in 1983 after too many generations of generals.

At a fashionable outdoor café in Recoleta on a crowded, sunny Sunday afternoon, I saw a display of "who-gives-a-hoot" pleasure, at once both intensely private and public, that one might wait a month of Sundays and still not see in other, more self-conscious, cities:

A well-heeled woman of about 60 sat at a table with her bicycle parked beside her. A bottle of mineral water and a coffee waited, only half-consumed on the table. Her tanned, smooth midriff was bare, her sneakered feet were propped on a chair. She leaned back with eyes closed in bliss as the Buenos Aires summer sun poured down in benediction.

—JOHN BORTHWICK

John Borthwick is one of Australia's leading travel writers. When he's not traveling, writer/photographer Borthwick calls Sydney home. He is the author of numerous travel articles (most illustrated by his own photographs) and books, including a collection of his travel essays.

rooms have a Jacuzzi tub. The fitness facilities include a beautiful indoor pool. Everyone on the staff, from the managers to the housekeepers, is determined to measure up to the Alvear's fine reputation. Doubles from about $300, including breakfast.

⭐ CAESAR PARK
Posadas 1232
Tel: 54-11-4819-1100
www.lhw.com

A good choice hotel located in the Recoleta district, across from the elegant Patio Bullrich shopping plaza, is the Caesar Park. It is a stylish facility with 170 spacious rooms tastefully dressed in Empire furnishings and with huge marble baths and windows that open. Some floors are are designated "non-smoking," an unusual practice in this country. Cell phones are provided for guests' use. Several restaurants, fitness center with indoor pool. Doubles from $460.

⭐ THE FOUR SEASONS
Posadas 1086
Tel. 54-11-4321-1200 or 800-819-5053

Also in the Recoleta district is the beautiful Four Seasons hotel, with accommodations that exceed luxury in its Mansion, an elegant turn-of-the-century French townhouse that was, until 1976, a private home and then was carefully incorporated into the hotel's construction in 1992. The living, dining, and billiard rooms of the Mansion retain much of their original character.

There are seven guest suites, each individually decorated with antique furnishings, marble baths, Oriental carpets, and potted palms. The house has its own private garden with a heated swimming pool. Comprehensive valet service is included. Mansion suites start at about $550.

The rest of the hotel offers all of the quality and attention to service that have earned the Four Seasons group its enviable reputation. The 165 well-proportioned guest rooms are nicely furnished and have well-designed, marble bathrooms, all featuring oversized tubs. Club floors offer a private concierge service, a lounge, and complimentary breakfast, tea, cocktails, and hors d'oeuvres.

The fitness center is well equipped, and there is a striking heated outdoor pool in the Mansion garden. Doubles from about $350.

HOTEL SOFITEL BUENOS AIRES
Arroyo 841–849
Tel: 54-11-4131-0000, www.sofitel.com

A charming hotel, totally renovated, the Sofitel is located in a historic art deco building of the 1920s. It is situated in Retiro, one of the most elegant areas in the heart of the city, close to the financial district. Café Arroyo is reminiscent of the traditional Buenos Aires cafés.

OF INTEREST

Throughout the center of the city, you'll find any number of *confiterias,* coffeehouses that serve a changing selection of food items throughout the day and late into the evening. In the morning, locals stop for coffee and toast or *medialunas,* small croissant-like pastries. By noon, patrons are having an early aperitif to tide them over until lunch. At teatime, the confiterias serve tea, coffee, drinks, and sandwiches, and then

FINE STEAK HOUSE

⭐ LA CABANA
Rodriguez Peña 1967, Buenos Aires
Tel: 54-11-4814-0001

La Cabana is located in La Recoleta and within easy walking distance to the Four Seasons, Alvear Palace, Caesar Park, and the Jockey Club. Mirco Zampieri is the talented and charming General Manager of La Cabana. He was brought in to oversee the creation of the restaurant from the Cipriani Group.

La Cabana is a faithful re-creation of the famous Buenos Aires Steak House. From the early 1930s, the restaurant has welcomed VIPs, celebrities, the famous and infamous from all over the world, serving what many considered to be the best steak on Earth. La Cabana's dining areas is inspired by different regions and provinces of Argentina such as Pampa, Patagonia, and Salta, combined with classic gaucho style, featuring large open fireplaces and walls lined with wine bottles. There is no better steak house in the world.

throughout the evening, cordials and still more coffee. There are several that are exceptional. La Biela is the most fashionable. Clasica y Moderna is stylish and upscale, with a bookshop, interesting menu, and tango and flamenco evenings. Richmond is a leathery spot with chess and billiards.

I very much enjoyed Dora, a casual place with wonderful food and gracious waiters. The menu and the portions are huge. As in many Buenos Aires restaurants, if you arrive before 9 p.m., you probably won't need a reservation. Try the chicken with garlic and sherry, the creamed spinach, the ensalata Dora, and the flan with dulce de leche. Many people consider La Bourgogne, in the Alvear Palace Hotel, Argentina's best restaurant. Chef Jean-Paul Bondoux serves classic French and international cuisine in elegant surroundings. It is the only Buenos Aires restaurant to carry the Relais Gourmand designation.

⭐ CONFITERIA IDEAL
Suipacha 384, 1° piso (first floor)

Tango has enjoyed a huge revival during Argentina's current political and economic crisis. La Confiteria Ideal, a Buenos Aires dance hall, is where fervent devotees of tango flock to escape everyday life.

The Confiteria Ideal is a century-old, two-story building with 6-meter (20-foot) ceilings on each floor. The European coffeehouse is on the first level with walls in dark wood paneling. The floors and round columns around the room are marble with art deco chandeliers. It's similar to Café Tortoni, located nearby on Avenida de Mayo. It is also very reminiscent of the Gran Vía in Madrid. The Confiteria Ideal is authentic with style and dusty elegance.

At Confiteria Ideal, the walls, floors, and ceilings look not to have been touched for a hundred years. The tables are well spaced throughout this giant room, which must be 30 meters (100 feet) wide by 45 meters (150 feet) deep. Ceiling fans whir and turn. To the left is a metal elevator cage. The wrought iron is brass with the patina of a century. A beautiful marble staircase leads to the dance floor upstairs and a continuous tango experience. The dance floor is large and the marble floor quite uncertain. With the music, the twentieth century has not yet arrived, falling into a reverie recalling a long ago past.

Classes begin at noon and the *milongas* follow into the afternoon and late evening.

TANGO PARTNERS IN BUENOS AIRES

⭐ JULIO EDUARDO CORAZZA
tango_partner_ba@yahoo.com.ar
Tel: 54-11-4752-0213

Our friend Julio Eduardo Corazza has created a one-stop service for tango lessons, including arrangements for hotels and guides.

He arranges airport pickup and tours in Argentina, and if you advise him of your goals, skills, needs, and budget, he will make effort to provide you with a custom itinerary and personalized service.

There are over 180 *milongas* (dances) a week and hundreds of events, teachers, and classes in BA. Julio is a delightful insider and knows the best Buenos Aires has to offer, including cultural events, shows, and tango concerts with the best orchestras.

With his experience and knowledge, you can make the most of your visit, saving a lot of time, and his services are reasonably affordable. Services include:

- Transfer to and from airport
- Lodging recommendation and reservations: Hotels, apartments, or guest houses
- Interpreters
- Transfers to/from milongas every day
- Tango protocol
- A staff of outstanding dancers to accompany you
- Table and class reservations at milongas
- Tango teachers and classes
- Sightseeing
- Boat trips to the islands
- Tours in Argentina

SHOPPING & SIGHTSEEING

Buenos Aires offers great leather goods, including shoes and boots, gems, and brand-name products such as Gucci and Dior. Other items to look for include rugs, gaucho souvenirs, sheepskin products, wines, guitars, art, handicrafts, yerba-mate paraphernalia such as gourds and bombilla, metal straws with a filter at the bottom, and vicuña products. You may also want to get a pair of gaucho trousers, *bombachas,* or perhaps a poncho. In Buenos Aires, stroll down Calle Florida and Avenida Santa Fe for upscale stores, where leather goods and custom-made suits are a good buy. There are also many markets and department stores for bargain shoppers. Low-key bargaining may get you a better price outside of department stores or on any big-ticket item. Palermo Viejo is often noted for its lovely boutiques, designer outlets, lingerie craft couture and dozens of quirky shops.

BA's best shops are on Avenida Santa Fe and in the Galerías Pacífico and Patio Bullrich malls. The Buenos Aires Design Center has about 100 shops specializing in interior decoration, arts, and crafts. La Martina specializes in polo gear but also carries fine handbags, jackets, and accessories. Valmont is a distinguished dealer in fine art. Zurbura sells the best of Argentine art. Among the best antique shops are Los Siglos Pasados and Corinto for European selections. America Antiguedades is another good antiques dealer with unusual items and good prices

Some of the most enjoyable shopping is to be had at the weekend outdoor markets. The best of this lot takes place on Sundays in the San Telmo area main square and spilling over onto surrounding streets. It is very lively, like a Fellini parade with music and original costumes.

The Plaza de Mayo is Buenos Aires' main square, named to commemorate independence from the Spanish viceroy on May 25, 1810. Two blocks long, it is an area of wide geometric pathways, flowerbeds, fountains, ponds, and trees. It's also the scene of political rallies. Several important buildings surround it.

Casa Rosada is the Argentine president's headquarters. It's not generally open to visitors, but for special permission to tour it, which may or may not be granted, contact the National Tourism Office. El Cabildo (The Council House) was originally built in 1711 to house the Spanish viceroy's counselors. It's now a museum with mementos of the 1810 uprising. Guards wear 19th-century ceremonial uniforms.

The cathedral, Rivadavia 450, is on the site of the first Buenos Aires church. It has a Greek facade with a frieze depicting Joseph and his brethren. The 1878 tomb of General San Martin is inside. Just two blocks away, at Calles Alsina and Bolivar 225, is the Church of San Ignacio de Loyola, the oldest colonial building in BA. It was founded in 1710. And one block from it, at Alsina and Defensa, is the Church of San Francisco, inaugurated in 1754. Its facade dates back to 1808.

The Palacio del Congreso is about 13 blocks up the Avenida de Mayo at Entre Rios 53. It's an impressive white Greco-Roman building in which the Senate and Chamber of Deputies meet. You can sit in on legislative sessions, but you must present your passport at the entrance desk.

Palermo Park is a magical spot, full of beautiful avenues and statues. It has a famous rose garden, an Andalusian patio, a Japanese garden where you can feed the fish, and the Hipodromo Argentino, BA.s world-famous racetrack. The track has an old wooden clubhouse, seats 45,000 spectators, and is the site of many big races throughout the year. El Premio Nacional, Argentina's equivalent of the Kentucky Derby, takes place in October.

Across are the Palermo Polo Fields and stadium, home to the greatest polo in the world, especially during the championship tournaments in December.

The Cemetery of Recoleta has a great deal of interesting statuary, some of it surprisingly cheerful and lighthearted, as well as a variety of architectural styles, all adapted to suit these "mini-mansions" of the dead. The crypt of Eva Perón is tastefully tucked away, but any of the caretakers will gladly lead you to it. Just ask to see "Evita."

San Telmo is an old barrio that still has late-colonial buildings where cattle barons used to live, cobblestone streets, and narrow alleyways. It is an artistic center with many cafés and first-class antique shops. On Sundays, a large antiques market occupies Plaza Dorrego, where a

TANGO FACTS

"There are shortcuts to happiness, and dancing is one of them."

— Vicki Baum

- Tango developed in the 19th century among the immigrants who reached Argentina from Africa and Europe.
- The music and dance steps combine African influence with rural Argentine traditions—which in turn reflect both Spanish and native South American origins.
- Tango was first danced in Europe during the first decade of the 20th century.
- It probably reached France first through the port of Marseille, where Argentine sailors would dance with the local girls.
- The fall of the military junta in Argentina in 1983 began a tango renaissance in Buenos Aires.

colorful and original costumed parade led by an orchestra, is in full force and is worth the trip alone. At night, San Telmo comes to life with the tango on an entire street of tango bars and cabarets.

The Teatro Colón, almost a whole city block, is unquestionably one of the world's great opera houses. Its interior is red plush and gilded, its stage almost a block long, and its highest balcony, for obvious reasons, is called El Paraiso. Guided tours of the building are available. The season runs from March to November, and tickets go on sale three days before a performance. Men customarily wear a jacket and tie.

Another theater, the Cervantes, is also old and venerable and is the home of classical drama. Occasionally a touring English-language company makes its appearance there.

The Museo de Bellas Artes is Argentina's best art gallery. It has modern Argentine works, wooden carvings from the interior, 16th- and 17th-century paintings representing the conquest of Mexico, and American and European works.

The National Historical Museum contains General José de San Martín's uniforms and furniture, a copy of his famous curved saber, and trophies and memorabilia of historic events. Visits are available in the afternoon.

Museo de Arte Hispanoamericano Isaac Fernandez Blanco is in a beautiful colonial mansion containing an interesting and valuable collection of colonial art, especially silver.

Ski resorts in the Argentine Andes include Mendoza, Villavicencio, and Valle de las Lenas. Villavicencio has very good facilities, is in a beautiful setting, and is near some interesting ruins; and Valle de las Lenas is a world class ski resort with excellent powder skiing.

SALTA

✮ THE TRAIN TO THE CLOUDS

www.turismosalta.gov or www.ripioturismo.com.ar/esla.htm

Salta, founded in 1582, still has a very Spanish feel. From here, an excursion can be made to Cafayate, passing over mountain ranges, deep gorges, and beautiful scenery, the landscapes changing colors, as time passes through the day. This is a startling feat of engineering and one of the great train ride adventures of the world.

To touch the clouds is the ultimate experience, a trip full of sensations and surprises and railing straight to heaven, embracing along the way small Andean villages and ruins of thousand-year-old civilizations.

One of the three highest railroads in the world, the carriages seem to be hanging from peaks and mountains, and travelers feel as if they were hanging from the clouds. The train treks across some of the region's most spectacular scenery.

SHOPPING EXTRA

✮ CASA WALTON
Montanesses 2705v
Alt. Av. Libertador 6
Tel: 54-11-4787-1739

For the best custom-made boots and saddles, there is none better than Casa Walton. Expect to pay $250 for English riding or polo boots, with a choice of styles and two fittings, constructed from the finest Argentine leather. Custom wooden boot trees, too, at only $60. Comparable merchandise in England and France costs $1,800. Their bench-made saddles are superb and as good in craftsmanship as a $4,000 Hermès.

North & South

Two of the must-see, must-stay places and side excursions in Argentina are Salta in the north (see pp. 270–273) and the resort of Bariloche in the south.

Bariloche (www.bariloche.com/english) is an Andean village that looks like it belongs in Switzerland. It's easy to see why so many people go—it's in a magnificent area. Located on the shores of Lake Nahuel Huapi, in the midst of Nahuel Huapi National Park, Bariloche is surrounded by dense forests, alpine lakes, and 3,600-meter (12,000-foot) mountains.

The village itself has Swiss chalet hotels and a number of sights worth seeing, including a small museum with displays about the area's founder, Francisco Moreno. But our favorite activities and everyone else's can be found on the main street and the slopes: shopping and skiing. Sample some of the many varieties of jellies and jams made from native fruits found nowhere else in the world, and each day you are there, stop in a different chocolate shop to try to determine whose version of the local specialty, papas de Bariloche, you like best. Skiing sometimes starts in May at Cerro Cathedral, 20 kilometers (12 miles) from town, but the best time to hit the slopes is July through October. During the warm

months, you can fish for salmon in clear mountain streams, take a boat ride to pretty Isla Victoria, or take in a great view from atop Otto Hill reached by aerial gondolas. Other impressive sights are towering Mt. Tronador, a great climb in summer, and the nearby glacier field.

Located on a small hill between Lakes Nahuel Huapi and Moreno is the magnificent Hotel Llao Llao, surrounded with old cypress, coigue, and arrayan woods and framed by Lopez, Capilla, and the majestic Tronador mountain peaks.

Canadian-style with Norman roof tiles and visible cypress logs blending with the region's green stone, the setting and landscapes are amazing. Since its early years, the hotel has attracted the cream of the Argentine society.

A trip to Bariloche can be combined with an excursion to Chile. If possible, take a tour that overnights along the way; a nonstop trip to Puerto Montt, Chile, is complicated and tiring, although feasible. Trips go from Bariloche to Puerto Blest by boat (past waterfalls), by bus, by boat again, then by bus through some of the most beautiful, peaceful scenery in South America, including dormant volcanoes and milky green water.

At the End of the World

Ushuaia is the capital of the province of Tierra del Fuego. Located at the Beagle Channel side and surrounded by the Martial chain, this town offers a unique landscape in Argentina. Ushuaia is a beautiful combination of mountains, sea, glaciers, and forest. It is possible to go through the old part of the city, watching the typical fuegian architecture, as well as the End of the World Museum and the maritime museum with local painters, photographers, and artisans, around the Culture House. As if that is not enough, it is a great place for shopping: The whole island is a tax-free zone, so you can find a myriad of imported goods along with regional products.

Ushuaia is called the "Land of the End of the World" because of its infinite landscapes and it is the departure point of the most diverse excursions. There is a footpath to the base of the Martial Glacier for nature lovers, from whence there is a wonderful view of the city, Beagle Channel, and the glacier itself—a fascinating experience that is unique to this world.

In September 1884, an Argentine expedition arrived with the purpose of establishing a subprefecture. October 12 that same year the Argentine flag was hoisted in front of Ushuaia Bay, constituting that date as the official day of the city's foundation.

All year long you can entirely enjoy this wonderful city. In summer there is the adventure tourism: trekking, horseback riding, mountain biking, fishing, and the most incredible rides along Beagle Channel, Cape Horn, and Argentine Antarctica.

Tierra del Fuego National Park belongs to the protected Andean Patagonian natural areas system and borders the republic of Chile. Visiting the park enables the discovery of Escondido and Fagnano Lakes and Martial Glacier. Not very far from this site you can find the small village of Tolhuin, as picturesque as nearby Chepelmut and Yehuin Lakes.

In winter the snowy scenery changes Ushuaia's appearance completely. Only 15 kilometers (9 miles) away from the city you have the Mount Castor ski center on Krund Hill.

Ushuaia International Airport's runway, operating since December 1995, allows the landing of all kinds of planes. The Concorde landed at the airport in its farewell flight around the world in January and November 1999. Ushuaia is thus daily connected with 3-hour flights non-stop from Buenos Aires, 3,000 kilometers (1,800 miles) away, and other regular flights.

Ushuaia is a paradisiacal place. It's the end of the world, and that is barely enough to say.

During the 15-hour journey, the train provides meals in the buffet car, and there is a medical cabin. Over the years, the "Train to the Clouds," built in the first half of 20th century, has become one of the most beautiful attractions in Argentina.

PLAY POLO

EL METEJÓN POLO RANCH
Vicente Casares, on Ruta 205
55 kilometers (33 miles) from Buenos Aires
Tel: 54-222-643-226,
www.elmetejon.com.ar

El Metejón Polo Ranch has become a by-word in international polo ever since 1998. Every year, players from all over the world gather here to enjoy the game and the lifestyle that is such an intrinsic part of polo.

The owners of El Metejón are the best assurance of guaranteed quality. Diego, Alicia, and Catalina Richini and Maria and Santiago Chavanne, as polo fans and lovers, decided to create the ideal resort in which to share their passion for this handicap sport. They have all left their mark within the Argentine polo world, each from a different perspective, and it is a pleasure to meet them.

Maria Chavanne is a world-class player. If you want to learn polo or improve your game, this is the best polo experience in the world. You will play with great players, and there are more than 300 polo ponies to ride.

⑥ PRAGUE SPRING: THE MOST EXTRAORDINARY MUSIC FESTIVAL IN THE WORLD

Prague is a looking glass image of Paris a hundred years ago and one of the most romantic cities in Europe. There is a saying in Prague that every other Czech must be a musician.

May is a good time to visit the Republic, in time for Prague Spring. The town becomes symphonic with more than 20 concerts everyday. Performances take place in landmarks of 900 years of architecture, Romanesque, Gothic, Renaissance, baroque, 19th-century revival, and art nouveau. String quartets play in a dozen medieval châteaus and castles. Musical interludes include classical, modern jazz and rock, opera and ballet, and avant-garde musicals in theaters, museums, and galleries.

⭐ THE ARIA HOTEL
Trziste No. 9, Mala Strana
Tel: 420-225-334-111
www.ariahotel.net

The luxurious new Aria Hotel is superbly located in Mala Strana, the most architecturally beautiful area of Prague, just a stone's throw away from the Charles Bridge and walking distance to all of the great historical sites, such as St. Nicholas Cathedral, Prague Castle, and Old Town Square. A view of Prague from the Roof Garden Terrace will leave no doubt you are in the most prestigious quarter of the Old City.

The ultimate haven for lovers of music, the design and decor of the Aria Hotel celebrates the work of some of the greatest composers of all time. Each floor is dedicated to an

VISITING PRAGUE

www.festival.cz
Tel: 420-257-312-547

Spring is a perfect time to visit Prague if you want to avoid the crowds, but summer is better if you want to avoid the rain. October is chilly and wet but appealing for visiting museums, while during winter Prague is cold and foggy.

The Prague Spring International Music Festival is a permanent showcase for outstanding performing artists, symphony orchestras, and chamber music ensembles of the world. The festival, first held in 1946, commemorates important musical anniversaries by including works by the composers honored on its programs. It presents Czech as well as world premieres of compositions by contemporary artists.

Great artists and orchestras are invited to perform. A few of the inexhaustible galaxy of stars who have appeared at Prague Spring are Sviatoslav Richter, Lorin Maazel, Herbert von Karajan, Mstislav Rostropovich, Lucia Popp, Boris Pergamenschikow, Kim Borg, Sir Colin Davis, Maurice André, Paul Klecki, Dmitri Sitkovecki, Leonid Kogan, Gustav Leonhardt, Heinrich Schiff, Anne-Sophie Mutter, Alfred Brendel, Leopold Stokowski, Arthur Honegger, and Arthur Rubinstein.

important genre of music, such as opera, jazz, contemporary, and classical. Each room then honors of one great artist or composer of that genre, with music, art, and books highlighting his or her work. Some of the featured artists include Puccini, Dizzy Gillespie, Dvorak, Louis Armstrong, and, of course, Mozart.

Respecting the magnificent Italian Renaissance architecture for which Mala Strana is known, Italian designer Rocco Magnoli was commissioned to make the Aria Hotel the most architecturally distinctive and beautiful hotel in the city. One of the most original features is the Italian mosaic tile with magnificent musical note patterns that recall an ancient Gregorian chant, leading guests from the wrought-iron gated entrance, through reception, and into the Winter Garden where it builds to a crescendo.

THE CAFE EUROPA
Václavské námestí 826/25
Tel: 420-224-215-387 or 420-224-213-914

In the Hotel Europa, a spectacular art nouveau building on Wenceslas Square. Over a good, simple breakfast of scrambled eggs, ham, toast, and frothy cinnamon-sprinkled coffee, served in a heavy glass, you can relax amid the art nouveau furnishings in perfect early morning calm.

OF INTEREST

The best place to start a tour is at Hradcany Castle, founded in the ninth century and the former residence of Bohemian kings. Although it is the official residence of the country's president, the castle is open to the public every day except Monday.

Inside the castle gates are a series of four courtyards. The main building is the Royal Palace, which can be toured in about 45 minutes. The grand hall once was the stage for jousting tournaments, and the wide entrance stairway was designed to allow horses to gallop in and out. The "real estate records rooms" are particularly beautiful, with painted land titles on the walls and ceilings.

St. Vitus Cathedral is in the center of the castle complex and is the mausoleum of many Bohemian kings. Be sure to take note of the elaborate tombs on the right aisle and the stained-glass window by Mucha on the left near the back of the church.

St. George's Convent, also part of the castle complex, is now the National Gallery of Czech Art. It contains examples of works dating from the Middle Ages to the 18th century.

An elaborate changing of the guard ceremony takes place at noon each day in the first courtyard. Drummers and trombone players accompany the pageantry, which lasts about a half-hour.

Near Hradcany Castle, up around the next bend of the Vltava River, is the Strahov Monastery, founded in the 12th century. It houses one of the best-preserved medieval libraries in Europe in a gorgeous setting of frescoed, vaulted halls and rooms. Some of the original Baroque furniture survives, as well as a group of 17th- and 18th-century globes. The library is open for visits, and manuscripts are available to scholars for study. From behind the monastery, the panoramic view of the city, including the castle, is spectacular.

The most famous bridge in Prague is Charles Bridge, dating from the 14th century. It is a long pedestrian crossing that is lined with 30 18th-century statues of saints.

Locals and tourists alike use it as a rendezvous point and gathering place, especially on weekends in summer.

The Josefov section of town is the Jewish quarter. During World War II, the Germans deported most of Prague's Jews, but decided to leave the ghetto intact, planning to turn it into a "museum of a vanished race" after the war. Confiscated possessions of deported Jews from all over Europe were amassed here for that purpose. The oldest functioning synagogue in Europe is also located here—the Altneushul, a 13th-century Gothic building, very small and very precious.

Of great interest is the Jewish cemetery where as many as 100,000 people are buried up to 12 deep in a small area. It was used from 1439 to 1787, and as more tombs were added, the headstones became all jumbled together. It's as though an earth tremor upset the stones, leaving them leaning in all directions. Buried here is Jehuda Loew ben Bezalel, the rabbi who, according to legend, created an artificial human being, the Golem.

In the Old Town Square, the celebrated astronomical clock marks not only the minutes and hours but also the days of the week, the dates of the month, the phases of the moon, and the signs of the zodiac. Each hour, on the hour, figures of the apostles twirl to the chimes, and other figures move about until a cock crows, signaling the end of the performance for another hour.

Lesser Town Square, or Malostranske Namesti, is a busy area containing many lovely 16th-century houses, including

the beautiful Waldstein Palace, and the fabulous Baroque Church of St. Nicholas, which was built in 1735 by a Czech architect, Dientzenhofer. This is one of the most elaborate churches in Europe. Of special interest are the massive organ and choir loft and the lavishly decorated gold-leaf pulpit.

Wenceslas Square (also called New Town Square) is now the "Champs Elysees" of Prague. It is actually a long, wide shopping boulevard with a large equestrian statue of St. Wenceslas at the upper end. Behind it, the National Museum has an interesting ethnographical collection, but if you plan to visit, be aware that every imaginable kind of sidewalk hustler makes a living working the tourists in this area.

Prague has many other museums as well. The National Gallery, in Sternberg Palace, has a collection of Western European art, mainly Italian, Dutch, Flemish, French, and German. (Don't miss Breughel's large, peopled landscape representing spring.) The Museum of Applied Arts, in a beautiful neoclassical building, is really a display of decorative arts, much of it quite impressive. The Museum of 19th-Century Czech Art is the continuation of the collection found in St. George's Convent.

The Tyl (Estates) Theater is where Mozart's *Don Giovanni* was first performed on October 29, 1787, with the composer conducting. The Lanterna Magica Theater is very popular for its outstanding multi-media performances.

A small Dvorak Museum, with memorabilia of the composer, is located at 20 Ke Karlovu Street.

A FEW DAYS IN THE COUNTRY

KARLOVY VARY

Karlovy Vary is probably the Czech Republic's second most popular city after Prague. World-famous for its regenerative waters, it is the oldest of the Bohemian spas.

Two hours away by train, the mineral waters from the town's 12 hot springs range between 43°C and 72°C (110°F and 162°F). Locals say the 13th spring is Becherovka, a popular herb and liqueur that originated here. King Charles IV discovered the springs in the 14th century. A short time later, Karlovy became a favorite watering hole for the Hapsburgs.

There is even a royal bath in the same tub room as Edward VII, and the most difficult task is selecting from a menu of 20 different aquatic therapies. The peppermint aromatic hydra massage is refreshing.

Many visitors purchase a silver cup at the Vridelni Kolonada, a glass-enclosed structure housing several springs, and stroll the tree-lined promenade following the river, greeting fellow pilgrims. Passing art nouveau buildings, they sip the hot mineral water, replenished from stations every few hundred meters.

✫ GRANDHOTEL PUPP
Mirove Namesti 2
Tel: 420-35-310-9111
www.pupp.cz

The five-star Grandhotel Pupp is an elegant baroque building constructed in 1701. All of its rooms and suites have been remodeled since the hotel's privatization. Attractive pastel decor has replaced the formerly heavy, Communist-era furnishings. Ask for a room with a view of the river. The hotel's Grand Restaurant is belle epoque, with crystal chandeliers, high ceilings, and quiet, efficient service.

⑦ SAILING THE RIVIERA & SEEING FLORENCE

PORTS ALONG THE WAY

Before boarding your vessel in Nice, explore the town's casual affluence, flower-lined streets, flourishing markets, and interesting museums. The Musée Chagall and Musée Matisse are highlights. Nice is a charming introduction to the spirit of the Côte d'Azur with wide sunny boulevards, broken here and there by shady gardens and parks.

Monte-Carlo glitters with opulence and jet-set glamour, and the action centers around its famed casino. Inside, under gilt-edged ceilings and ornate frescoes, fortunes are made or lost. Elsewhere in Monaco are the Prince's Palace, from which the Grimaldi dynasty has ruled since 1297; the cathedral where Grace Kelly married Prince Rainier; and the Rock of Monaco, where gardens cascade to the sea.

Portofino, east across the Italy border, is considered by many yachtsmen to be the "world's most beautiful small port." From the sea, the entrance to town is a narrow waterway, usually crowded with yachts and sailboats. Tall cliffs rise steeply above the port, dotted with expensive villas and an imposing castle. Along the water, restaurants with outdoor tables and colorful umbrellas offer refuge to some of Europe's wealthiest and most discerning pleasure-seekers.

GETTING THERE

TWO GREAT SAILING SHIPS, ONE GREAT ITINERARY

Sailing on the Windstar or the Star Clipper provides a perfect way to tour this part of the Italian Riviera, from Nice to Monte-Carlo, with Portofino, Portovenere, Sicily, Corsica, and Florence in between.

The Windstar, part of a fleet of sailing vessels, sails these ports and many parts of the world. The Windstar service was created to offer an alternative to the typical cruise or resort vacation. For an elegant ship with a delightful crew and service, it is one of our favorites. The Star Clipper is smart true sailing experience.

WINDSTAR
www.windstar.com

STAR CLIPPERS
www.starclippers.com

Stop in for lunch at the Hotel Splendido for a lovely lunch under a canopy of grape trees, next to its own olive press, with its fabulous view of the harbor.

★ HOTEL SPLENDIDO
Salita Baratta, 16, Portofino
Tel: 39-018-526-7801, www.hotelsplendido.com

Gliding into the town of Portoferraio on Elba, you can see why Napoléon chose this island of pink granite, pine forests, and pristine beaches for his exile. The contrasts of the Elba countryside—from its typical fishing villages and high

TROMPE L'OEIL

Not far from Portofino, in Nervi, south of Genoa, are Ligurian towns that specialized in trompe l'oeil.

In this part of the world, all house painters are artists. Genoa, Camogli, and Bogliasco have house painters who surely bear very little relation to the trade anywhere else in the world.

According to Richard Spear, a professor of art history at the University of Maryland and a scholar with at the Liguria Study Center, "The painted facades of modern Liguria remind me of the Renaissance.

Some benchmark examples are Mantegna's illusionist frescoes in the Camera degli Sposi in Mantua, Correggio's proto-Baroque domes in Parma, and Veronese's optical tricks in the Villa Barbaro, Maser, in the Veneto. As in the Ligurian facades, the key to their trompe l'oeil success is mastery of perspective.

For general information about Liguria, consult the website of the Regional Tourism Promotion Board in Genoa, at www.turismoin liguria.it

Or contact APT Genova, a tourism organization with offices at the main (Principe) train station. Tel: 39-01-057-6791, www.aptgenova.it.

mountain passes to its stylish summer resorts on the coast—are enchanting. Elba's restaurants feature excellent seafood, and small private vineyards produce local Moscato and Aleatico wines.

Portovenere's small colorful houses—some only 3 meters (9 feet) wide and as much as 7 stories tall—climb steeply up the hillside. Wander its maze of tiny alleyways; this is a fascinating small town to explore. From the harabor, the steeple of the 12th-century church of San Lorenzo can be seen, along with the simple Gothic church of San Pietro built on a promontory above the harbor. Also available from Portovenere is a motorcoach transfer to nearby Florence, where you'll have the day to explore that city's fabulous art, architecture, and museums.

FLORENCE

Florence casts its spell the way few other cities can. Sublime art, architecture, and views at sunset with colors all their own are just as enjoyable here as are a plate of food and a glass of wine—all are a delight to the senses.

Florence has not changed much since the 16th century. Part of the Grand Tour since the 18th century, it is still a favorite for travelers and romantics, who, on the banks of the Arno, drift and reflect upon its wondrous past.

RESTAURANTS

BECCOFINO
Piazza Scarlatti 1
Tel: 39-055-290-076, www.beccofino.com

A wine bar and evening restaurant on the left side of the Arno, Beccofino has lately become a hangout for a flashy international crowd. Nevertheless, it has managed to maintain its roots in Tuscan tradition. The restaurant looks out on the river, near the Ponte Santa Trinità, and is within walking distance of the Pitti Palace. The wine bar offers not only various Chiantis by the glass, but also soups, salads, and pasta for a quick meal. The restaurant serves excellent pastas, scampi, tender steaks cooked in wine, and a chocolate cake with a lemony cream that seems to be everyone's favorite. Dinner for two, with a bottle of Chianti, about $80. Closed Sunday.

AL LUME DI CANDELA
Via delle Terme 23r
Tel: 39-055-294-566

Dark old beams, fresh flowers, candlelight, and good food. Dinner for two, without wine, about $120.

THE ENOTECA PINCHIORRI
Via Ghibellina 87
Tel: 39-055-242-777, www.enotecapinchiorri.com

On two levels of a Renaissance palazzo east of the Piazza della Signoria is a refined establishment with a beige-and-pink color scheme and wood paneling. Giorgio Pinchiorri, with Annie Feolde in the kitchen, has transformed what was an ordinary wine-and-food place into a Michelin two-star restaurant that attracts a super-solvent international clientele. Closed Sunday and at lunchtime on Monday.

HARRY'S BAR
Lungarno Vespucci 22r
Tel: 39-055-239-6700

Near the Excelsior Hotel is an intimate, appealing place that offers good food and service. Dinner for two, without wine, about $120.

IL CIBREO
Via dei Macci 118r
Tel: 39-055-234-1100

Il Cibreo, on the corner of Piazza Ghiberti, is probably the best authentically Florentine restaurant next to the superb (and very pricey) Enoteca Pinchiorri. More than 20 years ago, Fabio Picchi opened a simple trattoria off a food market in an unfashionable eastern neighborhood of the historic center. It has since expanded at the same location and, today, Fabio presides over a complex that includes a restaurant, a wine bar, a food store, and a coffee bar. The wine list focuses on Chiantis and other Tuscan vintages. Dinner for two, with a bottle of medium-priced Chianti, about $110. Prices are about 20 percent lower in the wine bar, Vineria Cibreino, where seating is on a first-come, first-served basis, without reservations. Closed Sunday and Monday.

LA SACRESTIA
Via Guicciardini 27
Tel: 39-055-210-003

This handy restaurant, especially for lunch, is located between the Ponte Vecchio and the Pitti Palace. A three-course meal for two, with a little wine, costs about $75.

LE QUATTRO STAGIONI
Via Maggio 61r
Tel: 39-055-218-906

A pleasant trattoria near the Pitti Palace, Le Quattro Stagioni is on a street lined with antique shops. It serves traditional cuisine and honest wines. Dinner for two, without wine, about $100.

and keeps its prices comparatively moderate. Florentine steak is king and there isn't much in the way of seafood. Excellent pasta dishes, polenta, vegetables, desserts, and a good wine list. Dinner for two about $100. Closed Sunday.

SABATINI
Via dei Panzani 9A
Tel: 39-055-211-559

Where the locals go when they want to splurge. The cuisine at this discreet restaurant is classic Tuscan, with splendid pasta dishes, fresh fish, tender steaks, game, and fine desserts. Connoisseurs are especially pleased with the wine list. Excellent service. Dinner for two, without wine, about $150. Closed Monday.

SOSTANZA
Via della Porcellana 25r
Tel: 39-055-212-691

Very popular in Florence are the "kitchen" restaurants like the well-known Sostanza. There are white-tiled walls, communal tables, the clanging of saucepans, and a steamy kitchen in the background. No booking, no credit cards. The atmosphere and food are genuinely Florentine.

ALLA VECCHIA BATTOLA
Viale Ludovico Ariosto 32r
Tel: 39-055-224-158

A recommended restaurant. Dinner for two, without wine, about $50.

SHOPPING IN FLORENCE
Stores are generally open from 9 a.m. to 1 p.m. and again from 3:30 or 4 p.m. to 7:30 or 8 p.m. Closed on Monday mornings in winter and on Saturday afternoons in summer.

LE RAMPE
Viale G. Poggi 1
Piazzale Michelangelo
Tel: 39-055-681-1891

The most scenic pizza place in town is Le Rampe. Here, at sunset, both Florentines and tourists lean over the parapet looking down at the city—a rather striking view. Dinner for two, without wine, about $50.

OLIVIERO
Via delle Terme 51
Tel: 39-055-287-643

Near the right bank of the Arno, west of the Uffizi Gallery and the Ponte Vecchio, is an old and glorious restaurant that for a few years was converted into a not-very-successful branch of the El Toula chain. It has reopened under its original name with new management. Clearly aiming at a knowledgeable local clientele rather than at one-shot tourists, the new-old Oliviero changes its menu frequently

On the Via de' Tornabuoni, the city's most elegant shopping street, Gucci, Yves Saint-Laurent, Trussardi, Louis Vuitton, Hermes, etc., have replaced long-familiar businesses such as Alinari Brothers, with their wonderful period photos (now moved to Via Nazionale 6), the hairdresser Valentino, and even the Cafe Doney where the beautiful people used to meet for cappuccino, Campari, and gossip. Doney's premises have been taken over by the Beltrami fashion house, and a new, smaller Doney has opened at Piazza Strozzi 5, next to an Armani store with which it is allied.

If you don't need designer labels to show your style, the Borgo San Jacopo, in the Oltrarno, can be a fascinating shopping experience.

CELLERINI
Via del Sole 37r
Tel: 39-055-252-533

The Florentine tradition of leather-making has been preserved at Cellerini, probably the bst place in Florence to find leather. It's not cheap, but the quality is superior. Orders can be made to order.

JOHN F.
Lungarno Corsini 2
For leather handbags, briefcases, wallets, and clothes.

FARAONE-SETTEPASSI
Via Tornabuoni 24r
Tel: 39-055-215-506

Renowned for jewelry.

BIJOUX CASCIO
Via Tornabuoni 32r
For costume jewelry that looks genuine.

FLORENTINE PAPER

Florentine papier à la cuve is known and valued throughout the world. Based on techniques developed in the 17th century, it is handmade and looks like marbled paper. And no two designs are exactly the same.

It's sold by the sheet and can be used to cover boxes, frames, pencils, diaries, and albums. Try these boutiques for some of the loviest papers.

GIULIO GIANNINI E FIGLIO
Piazza Pitti 37r
Tel: 39-055-212-621

IL PAPIRO
Via Cavour 55r

BOTTEGA ARTIGIANA DEL LIBRO
Lungarno Corsini 38-40r

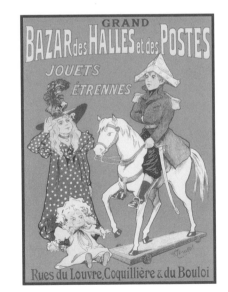

OUTSIDE FLORENCE

Fiesole, about 8 kilometers (5 miles) outside of Florence, is an ancient Etruscan and Roman city set in the Tuscan hills. Among the villas that cover these hills is the Villa Palmieri, where Boccaccio wrote and which was the setting for the *Decameron.*

In Fiesole, the Monastery of San Francesco offers a wonderful view of Florence. St. Bernardino of Siena once occupied a tiny spartan cell here. The Roman theater and archaeological zone here, dating from 80 B.C., include the temple ruins, baths, and an Etruscan gate and wall. The Bandini Museum contains della Robbia terra-cottas and 15th-century masterworks, and the 11th-century cathedral has important works of Mino da Fiesole. Near Fiesole, in the Convent of San Domenico, Fra Angelico took his vows and painted the *Madonna and Saints,* as well as a fresco of the Crucifixion.

The road to Settignano, a picturesque town, winds through pines and cypresses. One of the noteworthy sites along the way is the Villa Gamberaia, where the famous garden inspired Longwood Gardens in Pennsylvania.

I Tatti, the former villa of Bernard Berenson, the well-known art historian who bequeathed it to Harvard University, can be visited. To do so, write several weeks in advance to I Tatti, Via di Vincigliata 26, Settignano, Florence, Italy 50135. There is a tour one day a week for a maximum of five people, although they prefer only two.

Vallombrosa, 33 kilometers (21 miles) east of Florence, presents a glorious setting and interesting views. The Monastery of Vallombrosa was founded in the 11th century.

The five ancient fishing villages of Monterosso, Vernazza, Corniglia, Manarola, and Riomaggiore—known as Cinque Terre—are located on a particularly rugged 10-kilometer (6-mile) stretch of the Italian Riviera between La Spezia and Genoa. Each village is secluded in a little cove, some have tiny beaches, and all are linked by an easy footpath, the Via dell'Amore.

⭐ THE VILLA SAN MICHELE
Via di Doccia 4, Fiesole
Tel: 39-055-567-8200
www.villasanmichele.com

A prestigious, quiet, top hotel on the Fiesole hillside 8 kilometers (5 miles) northeast of Florence. The 15th-century building, which was a convent until 1808 and then a private mansion, has been magically transformed into an exclusive hotel by Orient-Express. It offers a portico inspired by Michelangelo, a lush park with its own swimming pool, and a panoramic view looking to the city of Florence below.

VILLA VILLORESI
Via delle Torri 63
Tel: 39-055-448-9032, www.ila-chateau.com/villores

The 12th-century Tuscan Villa Villoresi, about 10 kilometers (6 miles) from Florence, is adorned with frescoed walls and antique furnishings. In winter, classes are offered in painting, sculpture, lithography, art history, and cooking.

VISIT TO A HISTORIC LIST

From a historical point of view, more has been written about Renaissance Florence than perhaps any city in the world. One can profitably devote a lifetime to studying the buildings, the sculpture, and the paintings to be seen here and to understanding their place in the development of Western culture. Here are only a relative few of the city's treasures, recommendations for what you should not miss.

The Galleria dell'Accademia's principal attraction is Michelangelo's magnificent sculpture "David." It stands in splendid isolation in a rotunda, protected by a shield erected after it had been damaged by a lunatic. The statue is preceded by two rows of "captives," uncompleted statues by Michelangelo, whose figures appear to be struggling to free themselves from the granite blocks out of which they were partially carved.

In the Piazza del Duomo stand three of the supreme architectural achievements of history, the cathedral of Santa Maria del Fiore, the Campanile, and the Baptistery of St. John.

The cathedral of Santa Maria del Fiore (Il Duomo) is capped by Brunelleschi's great dome, a stupendous feat. The 15th-century artist succeeded in erecting the dome using techniques that had never before been tried and that are still not fully understood. If you have the physical stamina, you may climb to the base of the lantern that tops the dome. The ornamental exterior of the Duomo was completed in the late 19th century, while the somewhat severe interior belongs to much earlier periods and displays the works of many of Renaissance masters.

The 14th-century Campanile is one of Italy's finest bell towers. From its top (414 steps), there is an unparalleled view of the city.

The East Door of the Baptistery of San Giovanni, across from the Duomo, is the site of a constant mob scene as tourists fight to view and photograph Ghiberti's exquisitely wrought panels— justifiably so. The North and South Doors are also worth a great deal of attention. Inside the Baptistery, the dome-mosaics and works by Donatello are of special interest.

The Galleria degli Uffizi, one of the world's great art museums, was built as public offices in the 16th century by Vasari for Cosimo I de'Medici, the Duke of Florence. The building overflows with masterpieces, particularly the 15th-century Florentines including Michelangelo, Botticelli, and Leonardo as well as works by Raphael, Titian, and Rubens.

The gallery is slowly recovering from the terrorist bombing of May 1993. The damage done to both of Vasari's 400-year-old buildings housing the gallery was more extensive than had originally been estimated. Among the changes introduced in the reconstruction, a new snack bar has been constructed on the top floor of the east wing, and there's now a bookstore near the exit on the ground floor.

The Uffizi is always inundated with people, including tour leaders loudly declaiming in a babble of English, French, Spanish, Italian, and Greek. Overcrowding is a serious problem at all the popular sites in Florence, which is why early morning is the best time to see just about anything in the city.

The Piazza della Signoria is one of the great historic sites of Florence—a place where Florentines gathered when momentous events were in the making. Here unfortunates were hurled to their deaths from the Palazzo Vecchio, Savonarola was burned at the stake (a plaque marks the spot), and titans such as Dante, Machiavelli, the Medici, and various emperors and popes acted out the great drama of the Renaissance.

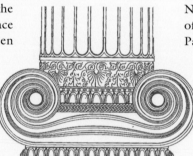

Here also are the Fountain of Neptune, equestrian statues, and, in the Loggia dei Lanzi (an outdoor museum), Giambologna's "Rape of the Sabines," and much more. After Michelangelo's "David" was removed to the Accademia to preserve it from pollution, a poor copy was erected in the Piazza. As a matter of fact, even art-minded Florentines are now at a loss to determine which of several of the sculptures are authentic, here and elsewhere in public spaces. Over the last few years, much of the outdoor statuary was quietly removed to indoor sites for protection from vandalism and pollution, and copies have replaced them. In the Piazza della Signoria, the latest statue to be removed from the Loggia is Cellini's "Perseus," which was badly corroded.

The Piazzale degli Uffizi contains more statuary, particularly Bandinelli's "Hercules and Cacus."

Nearby, on the Lungarno (the road along the Arno), in the Piazza dei Giudici, is the Museum of the History of Science, missed by many visitors but offering an interesting collection of scientific instruments, including several of Galileo's telescopes. One of Galileo's index fingers is also on view, removed from his corpse when the body was disinterred for reburial.

The Bargello Palace houses the National Museum, with its large collection of Italian art dating from the Middle Ages. Particularly noteworthy is its display of Tuscan sculpture, the best anywhere.

The church of Santa Croce is a beautiful 13th-century Franciscan church that contains the tombs of Machiavelli, Michelangelo, Galileo, and other notables. Frescoes (some by Giotto), sculpture (Donatello and others), and terra-cotta works by della Robbia adorn the chapels. The Pazzi Chapel was designed by Brunelleschi in his characteristic manner, a circle within a square, which became a hallmark of quattrocento architecture. An adjoining museum displays the famous Cimabue crucifix.

The Ponte Vecchio is likely to disappoint. Jewelry shops extend along both sides for its whole length, and souvenir hawkers are everywhere. The areas around each end of the bridge are densely packed with shops catering to tourists. So after you've fought your way across once (it's the most direct route to the Pitti Palace), you may prefer to cross the Arno over one of the other bridges that are less crowded and offer an unobstructed view of the river.

The imposing Pitti Place has a wonderful collection of paintings (11 by Raphael), richly ornamented apartments, a silver museum, and the Gallery of Modern Art. Just behind the Pitti Palace are the Boboli Gardens, which ascend in terraces to an elevation that offers a lovely view of Florence. The adjacent Pallazina della Meridiana houses the Costume Gallery. Across the street from the palace is the apartment in which the poet Robert Browning lived. It's open to the public.

The church of San Marco, in the pleasant piazza of the same name, has an attractive cloister as well as a lovely collection of frescoes by Fra Angelico. Upstairs are the monks' cells, one of which is reputed to have been occupied by the 15th-century religious reformer, Savonarola.

The church of San Lorenzo was the parish church of the Medicis. Here and in the adjacent Medici Chapels and Laurentian Library, the family lavished its patronage on Michelangelo, Brunelleschi, Donatello, and others, creating edifices that stand at the height of Florentine architectural achievement.

In the Medici Chapels are Michelangelo's superb tombs of two of the Medici dukes—Lorenzo, Duke of Urbino, and Giuliano, Duke of Nemours. The Laurentian Library contains many priceless manuscripts and codices. Outside the church is an interesting, rambling open market that sells clothes, leather, souvenirs, and you name it.

The Brancacci Chapel, in Santa Maria del Carmine, has beautifully restored frescoes of Masaccio and

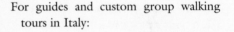

Masolino da Panicale. Michelangelo frequently visited the chapel to copy the Masaccio frescoes.

Santa Maria Novella is a large Dominican church with lovely frescoes and an attractive cloister. There's a story, probably apocryphal but amusing, about Donatello and Brunelleschi agreeing to a friendly contest to carve the most beautiful crucifix. As the story goes, when Donatello visited Brunelleschi's studio for lunch one day, he was so taken by the beauty of Brunelleschi's crucifix that he dropped the eggs he was carrying in his artisan's apron. Brunelleschi's crucifix now hangs by itself in a chapel here.

Here are several excellent sources for guides who can efficiently organize a tour of the sites you may want to select and point you in the right direction.

For guides and custom group walking tours in Italy:

AVVENTURE BELLISSIME TOURS
2442/A San Marco, Venice 30124
Tel: 39-0-41-520-8616
www.tours-italy.com
or Via Villanova n.27, 33170 Pordenone
Paola Barubiani

WALKS INSIDE FLORENCE
guide@walksinsideflorence.it
www.walksinsideflorence.it

THE ORIGINAL & BEST WALKING TOURS OF FLORENCE
Piazza Santo Stefano 2, Florence
Tel: 39-0-55-264-5033 or 329-6132730

8 THE OLD WORLD CITIES OF RAJASTHAN

Even before Indira Gandhi reneged on an earlier arrangement and stopped supporting India's princes in 1972, economic reality had pushed many of Rajasthan's maharajas into converting their palaces to "heritage hotels." It enabled the royals to make a living and their guests to enjoy some of the world's most gorgeous properties.

Rajasthan's martial history has produced massive forts such as Jodhpur's Meherengarh. Its merchants, enriched by their strategic location on the east-west silk routes, developed a splendidly distinctive architectural style that adorns palaces in Jaisalmer, Bikaner, and other cities. The culture is vibrant and exotic. At society functions, ladies parade spectacular saris and embroidered silks, and men flaunt turbans and ceremonial swords.

JAIPUR

RAJVILAS
Gioner Road
Tel: 91-141-64-0101

Near Jaipur, the "Pink City" of Rajasthan, the Oberoi hotel group has created a 71-room princely fantasy, a breathtaking work that exudes the sophistication commonly associated with Southeast Asia's Aman resorts. The resort occupies a 13-hectare (32-acre) site on which stand smooth-surfaced buildings made of the indigenous pastel-pink sandstone and stylized with Hindu motifs and objets d'art. The main building echoes a Rajasthani fortress, complete with towers and a moat. The most striking guest quarters are the huge and luxuriously furnished hunting tents, each of which has two terraces, one for dining and one for lounging.

Encircling the tents are mud walls, unfortunately not high enough to provide real privacy, but newly planted trees will ultimately enhance the seclusion. For a somewhat less pampered ambiance, you can book a room in the tent village on the resort's northerly flank. The tents may strike you as a bit gimmicky, but Vikram Oberoi, the general manager, explains their use as reflective of the traditional lifestyle of the maharajas while out on hunting trips.

Somewhat more practical in their layouts, yet just as appealing, are the deluxe rooms. Bathrooms of marble and glass have sunken tubs that look out on bougainvillea-draped gardens. If the maharaja style really overwhelms you, consider one of the villas, the topmost of which includes a palatial pool and a dining gazebo.

Much of the pleasure of a Rajvilas stay can be credited to a staff of friendly, efficient, and well-educated service personnel. The property is easily reached from New Delhi via the Pink City Express train in about five hours. Deluxe doubles from $300; hunting tents from $400; villas from $1,000.

RAJASTHAN

The Rambagh Palace
Bhawani Singh Road
Tel: 91-141-238-1919
www.tajhotels.com.

A popular destination with European visitors since 1972 when the Taj management took over, this is an imposing structure, once the residence of the Rajasthani royal family, and is the best base from which to tour Jaipur and surrounding areas. Elaborately costumed and turbaned doorkeepers hark back to the days of the Raj. Rooms and suites are large and lavishly furnished in a local manner; we like the superior rooms best for their spaciousness. Public areas are imposing. The dining room is a luxurious space but, alas, the food is only ordinary. Tea on the lawn, in wicker chairs and amid browsing peacocks, is a memorable affair.

ELEPHANT RIDES

I took a two-hour elephant ride across Rajasthan's eerie landscape and through farm villages and did not mind reliving the traditional lifestyle of the maharajas on a hunting trip, ending with a high-style picnic under an umbrella. Dining is delightful, either on your terrace or in the colonnade overlooking lily ponds, lawns, and a 250-year-old Shiva temple. Afterward the real hunting was targeting the bazaars—shopping for uncut gems, antique jewelry, tie-dyed fabrics, carpets and dhurries, blue pottery, and camel-leather goods—and visiting the historic sites in Jaipur.

BAZAARS
Jaipur's markets are legendary. You'll find all kinds of costume jewelry, handicrafts, rugs, pottery, brassware, and traditional Jaipur minakari work. When you're all shopped out, treat yourself to a traditional henna design on your palms.

The Marketplace
Tambaku Bazaar

Maharani Art Exporters, in the Tambaku Bazaar, is a long-established marketplace with eight floors of textiles, including everything from bedspreads to cushion covers. Pashmina shawls at an average price of $40 are a great bargain.

Mohanlal Verhomal
209B Vegetable Market, near the Clock Tower
www.mvspices.com

Walls are covered with testimonials from an international A-list of direct mail buyers. Expect Mohanlal to take your photo with his digital camera and send a copy to you via e-mail. His rather eccentric website is worth browsing

UDAIPUR

Shiv Niwas Palace Hotel
Tel: 91-294-252-8016
www.hrhindia.com

This incomparable hotel, more than any other hotel we visited in Rajasthan, captures the essence of the palace lifestyle with spacious suites, sumptuous decor, and original furnishings, including chandeliers and carpets. Its bathrooms, however, although large, are rather plain. The hotel is part of the sprawling City Palace complex overlooking

Lake Pichola. It has 18 deluxe rooms and 17 suites, with each accommodation a different size and layout. We prefer the terrace suites, where lattice-worked stone balconies (*jharokhas*) and turrets overlook courtyards with gilded colonnades. Cocktails in the Paneera Bar, with its coffered ceiling and huge armchairs, is an elegant preamble to dining either outdoors at candlelit tables in the garden or in the formal dining room.

FATEH PRAKASH PALACE HOTEL
Tel: 91-294-252-8016, www.hrhindia.com

An annex to the Shiv Niwas, the Fateh Prakash is slightly smaller, with 28 rooms and suites, and it does not have quite the same ambiance. However, the suites are spacious and opulently furnished, and they provide much of the palace experience at excellent values. The gallery in the durbar hall displays what is probably the largest private collection of crystal in the world.

UDAIVILAS
Haridasji Ki Magri
Tel: 91-994-243-3300

This Oberoi resort property on the banks of Lake Pichola opened in September 2002. It is almost overpowering in its visual impact and no-expense-spared attention to detail. Designed as a traditional palace, there are 85 rooms and five suites. Guests are met at the airport by a private limousine and transferred to a private jetty for a boat trip across the lake. The lobby's reception area, with its enormous dome, glittering chandelier, and fountain, establish the hotel's ambiance. Standard rooms are 56 square meters (600 square feet), with a sitting area and private balcony; suites are 107 square meters (1,150 square feet). All have top-quality, Indian antique-reproduction furnishings; bathrooms are white marble.

Doubles from about $370; superior deluxe rooms $450; suites $1,250. The 250-square-meter (2,650-square-foot) Kohinoor suite is luxurious beyond all expectations. With two bedrooms, its rate is about $2,000 per night.

BIKANER

In the middle of the desert, in the heart of camel country, you'll discover this royal fortified city, established in 1488. Its red-pink forts and palaces bespeak its rich history, its modern-day bazaars full of life.

THE LALGARH PALACE HOTEL
Tel: 91-11-686-8992, www.welcomheritage.com

The former Lalgarh Palace in Bikaner was so large that two branches of the royal family were able to turn it into separate hotels. The first to be converted was the Lalgarh Palace Hotel. Its 38 rooms are enormous and comfortably furnished, and many have cavernous bathrooms with stretch-limo-size tubs. Doubles, about $60.

LAXMI NIWAS PALACE HOTEL
Tel: 91-151-202-777, www.laxminiwaspalace.com

The other half of the original Lalgarh Palace is called the Laxmi Niwas Palace. Under the same ownership as the Fort Rajwada in Jaisalmer, the Niwas is where Bikaner's former maharaja lived and put up his guests. The opulence of his reign is reflected in the impressive portico entrance, the sandstone-arched lobby (once the state drawing room), superior furnishings (gold-painted walls, carved-wood ceilings, king-size beds), and spacious public areas, including a billiard room, card room, and trophy bar. The restaurant's tandoori dishes, biryani, and lamb curry are exceptional. Deluxe doubles from about $90, and the magnificent royal suite is only about $135.

TWO SMALL SHOPS

KALAKAR ARTS
Sardar Hall, Lalgarh Palace Road

SWAMI ART KRISHNA BLOCK
These are two of the best crafts shops in and near the bazaar. Raju Swami, who operates them, is a fascinating miniaturist. If he hasn't sold it yet, ask to see his "Banyan Tree," which includes 17,480 leaves (his count, not ours), each clearly visible under a magnifying glass.

RAJASTHAN TOURS
www.indianholiday.com
This group in Bikaner is able to provide excellent guides for Udaipur and Jaisalmer as well as Bikaner.

9 RETURN TO SHANGHAI

Even three weeks is not enough time to get more than taste for today's China. The country is so vast and varied that the only sensible plan is to select a few major destinations, cities, natural wonders, historic sites, and cultural icons and to experience the uniqueness of each one. China is better known to the West today than it has been for more than half a century, and yet you will be surprised again and again by what you see and experience. "Did you ever think China was like this?" became the mantra for our journey.

Unlike Beijing, a royal city for centuries, Shanghai's history is not dramatic. Until the mid-19th century it was just a fishing village. Then it expanded into a trade center, colonized by the British. A stunning residential neighborhood remains today. The old city is rapidly disappearing, although preservationists are attempting to save as much as they can.

Shanghai is the gateway to the mighty Yangtze River. But when the British opened their first concession here in 1842, after the after the Treaty of Nanking that ended the first Opium War, it was little more than a small town supported by fishing and weaving. Change was rapid. The French came in 1847 and it wasn't long before an international settlement was established. Before 1895 the city was being parceled up into settlements, all autonomous and immune from Chinese law. Enter China's first fully fledged Special Economic Zone.

The world's greatest houses of finance and commerce descended on Shanghai in the 1930s. The place had the tallest buildings in Asia, and more motor vehicles on its streets than the rest of China put together. Shanghai became a byword for exploitation and vice, in countless opium dens and gambling joints, in myriad brothels. Guarding it all were the American, French, and Italian marines, British Tommies, and Japanese bluejackets.

By the time the Communists said enough was enough in 1947, they had the job of eradicating slums, rehabilitating hundreds of thousands of opium addicts, and stamping out child and slave labor. For the West, the party was over in Shanghai. But the 1990s have seen invitations go out again to capitalist business interests as the central government hunts foreign capital to help reinvent this whirlwind metropolis.

The city continues to grow with new underground stations, highways crisscrossing the city, the most modern stock exchange in Asia and perhaps the world, and two new cultural institutions. However, despite the growth and international investment, Shanghai is still a city of contradictions as poverty is still prevalent.

It is the most populous city in China. New high-rise buildings, especially in Pudong on the east side of the Huangpu River, have been developed at such a dizzying rate that there is now talk of legislation to limit further construction of this type. By contrast, the Bund, on the west bank of the river, is a 1.5-kilometer-long (mile-long) promenade lined with 1930s buildings constructed in styles reflecting the architecture of the various countries with commercial interests in Shanghai at that time. In the city's modern sectors, women are dressed for London's West End or New York's Park Avenue, obviously having very much bought into Western fashion trends. At the same time, however, you still see the occasional Mao jacket, and you can leave your high-rise hotel and turn a corner into a 1920s street scene straight

out of a Hollywood movie, pajama-clad people and all. Within an hour's drive of the city, you can enter towns whose 1,000-year-old shopping alleys have stalls selling things you can't even identify. The yin and yang of Shanghai's culture are overwhelming.

Overall, the city is very clean, with ample public facilities, most of them very acceptable. The air quality is considerably better than in Beijing and little different than that of Los Angeles on a normal day. Traffic is often so heavy that you should allot extra time to go anywhere.

Although many Shanghainese understand and speak English, with more than 16 million people in the city, the vast majority do not. So unless you want to limit your experience to the city's westernized and tourist-oriented attractions, it is imperative that you arrange for the services of a guide. Our visit was made immeasurably more enjoyable by East Travel (www.east-tours.com). They are professional, knowlegeable, and attentive to every detail.

One of the most exciting and enjoyable aspects of time spent in Shanghai is the opportunity to eat multitudes of unfamiliar food. Street food in the Old Town is very tempting. The area around Yu Garden is a little maze of colorful Ming- and Manchu-style pedestrian streets chockfull of food stands where everything is prepared as you watch. If the ingredients look fresh and are served hot off the wok, you should experience no ill effects, and you'll sample some wonderful food that somehow tastes better than it does indoors.

Shanghai's famous Bund—an Anglo-Indian term for muddy enbankment—with its row of Western institutional banks and business buildings, was once the most important financial street in Asia. Although all the buildings that formerly bore major international names have been taken over, mostly by government offices, the Bund (the Waitan in Chinese) still retains its proud atmosphere. The broad boulevard is a museum of turn-of-the-20th-century Western architecture, with stately columns and porticoes.

The promenade along the Huangpu River, across from the Bund, is a popular place for locals to meet. They go there to stroll, practice ballroom dancing or tai chi, buy souvenirs or snacks, and chat with foreign visitors—a popular pastime.

South of the Bund, the ancient city (Nanshi), once surrounded by walls, is a lively, earthy place whose crowded, narrow streets bring old Shanghai instantly to mind. In this traditional neighborhood, people seem to live in the streets—shopping for vegetables, smoking, eating, gossiping, or reading.

Nearby, the walled Yuyuan Garden is an ancient park of rock formations, pavilions, towers, and man-made lotus ponds designed by a Ming dynasty family. And although the crowds of sightseers have destroyed the garden's tranquility, it still retains the feel of traditional China. The zigzag Bridge of Nine Turnings, one of the best-known sights in Shanghai, crosses an artificial lake to Huxingtang, a beautiful little pavilion that holds a classic Chinese-style teahouse. It is a perfect image of traditional China.

Nanking Road, from the Bund to the Portman Ritz-Carlton Hotel, takes you through several blocks of wide pedestrian streets lined with shops of every kind. What's more, it's one of the city's best people watching locales.

In Old Town, the basement of the Huabaolou Department Store includes an area of rather elegant antique stalls. Bargaining is expected.

The Dongtai Lu and Liuhe Lu antiques markets are fun, but don't expect to find anything spectacular, and be wary of "altered" merchandise. Bargaining is the norm, so don't be shy.

Tai Ping Yang Department Store and Digital Square are two huge stores opposite each other at the corner of Huai Hai Lu and Hang Pi Lu. The former is China's answer to Macy's; anything you might need, from luggage to designer cosmetics, is available. The latter is a huge store selling everything imaginable in electronics, including some things you never knew existed.

If your schedule permits, there are two very interesting and easily reached destinations outside of the city that are worth visiting.

Zhujiajiao is a village crisscrossed by picturesque bridges and waterways, in some respects a Chinese Venice, about an hour by car west of Shanghai. It has many original buildings and quaint streets and canals dating from the Ming dynasty (14th to 17th centuries) and its successor, the Ch'ing or Manchu dynasty, China's last monarchy. You can take a boat ride on the canals and walk through the warren of ancient, cobbled streets, where you'll find lively shopping as well as dozens of food vendors and little restaurants. It's worthwhile for a half-day, but avoid weekends.

A two-hour drive from Shanghai takes you to Suzhou, a renowned garden city that's a popular day-trip destination for the Shanghainese. The drive, past farmlands and surprisingly extravagant, single-family farm homes, is very pleasant. You'll also go through a vast new industrial complex that has to be seen to be believed.

Don't be disappointed to find that Suzhou is another big city with lots of air pollution; it's also home to quite beautiful gardens. The largest and most famous one is called the "Garden of the Humble Administrator," another is called the "Garden of the Master of the Nets." A portion of this latter garden has been exactly re-created in the Metropolitan Museum of Art in New York City. Still another garden, Tiger Hill, is the former home of architect I. M. Pei, who was born in Suzhou.

Another worthwhile attraction is the Silk Embroidery Institute, which might sound like a hangover from collectivist days but is a lively enterprise producing highly desirable work. You'll see crafts workers turning out gorgeous embroidered artifacts. There's a large gift shop on the premises with a huge selection of embroidered

work. Prices are higher here than at street stalls with similar but inferior pieces, and the institute salespeople are readily willing to bargain.

A good place for lunch in Suzhou is the Emerald Palace on the second floor of the large and modern Bamboo Grove Hotel. The menu offers local Suzhou dishes, including a sweet fried pork dish made with cherries, biluo-tea-flavored shrimp, and a chicken-and-

watermelon preparation. The appropriate drink is one of the locally grown teas.

THE PEACE HOTEL
20 Nanjing Road East
Tel: 86-21-6321-6888
www.shanghaipeacehotel.com

As far as accommodations back in Shanghai, worth considering is the Peace Hotel, the best of Shanghai's few old hotels that still provide pleasant accommodations. When it opened, as the Cathay in the late 1920s, it was the grandest hotel in the country. Today, it offers 380 air-conditioned and well-equipped rooms, the best of which are the superior doubles with harbor view. Its interesting art deco suites of Nine Nations (China, Britain, America, France, Japan, Italy, Germany, India, and Spain), which date back to the founding of the hotel, are decorated and furnished in the Shanghai version of each country's style. All these suites face the Bund and the Huangpu River and are quite appealing in their nostalgic ambiance. And even if you don't stay here, you should see the hotel's Old Jazz Band, six men in their 70s who play jazz and swing nightly in the hotel bar. Superior doubles from about $200.

THE PORTMAN RITZ-CARLTON
1376 Nanjing Xi Lu
Tel: 86-21-627-9888 or 800-241-3333

A top property, with a location on Nanjing Road, the most interesting street for shopping and restaurants.

THE FOUR SEASONS
500 Weihai Road
Tel: 86-21-6256-8888

A stunning and first-rate hotel, matchless in service, as you would expect of Four Seasons.

Report from Beijing

Coordinating a trip to China can be an overwhelming experience but the personalized, professional, and educated tour design by East Travel alleviates any concern or confusion. Michelle Lin at East Travel created a unique itinerary for Shanghai and Beijing that was seamless from preparation through departure. Here is my report from Beijng.

Our young and knowledgeable guide, Grant, met us with his driver at Xinggang Pier as we disembarked the *Crystal Harmony* outside of Beijing. Our 3.5-hour drive to the Great Wall, Mutianyu Section, seemed short, with the informative conversations on Chinese culture that we shared with Grant along the way. Before arriving at the Great Wall, we stopped for lunch at Red Capital Ranch, a fascinating countryside resort designed in a traditional Chinese Feng Shui manner. This special retreat is truly one of a kind, much like its brother property, the Red Capital Residence and the Red Capital Club restaurant. We worked off our lunch during a private escorted excursion to the Great Wall. The Mutianyu Section is approximately 25 kilometers (42 miles) northeast of the city center. It is quite well preserved and winds over 2.5 kilometers (1.6 miles) with 23 watchtowers. The construction of this section started during China's Northern Dynasties (during Qi, in the 6th century after Tang) but was restored to the current status in the Ming dynasty. Many consider this section to be the most scenic, quiet, and untouristy part to visit. We rode a cable car up to the mountain followed by some brisk hiking and spectacular views.

In the early evening we arrived at the Shangri-La China World Hotel in downtown Beijing. This bustling city has been the proud capital of China for hundreds of years. Beijing's importance is not just in its politics but also in the fact that it is the soul of Chinese culture and history. After a short rest, we traveled to the Red Capital Residence, a boutique hotel restored and transformed from a Courtyard House. Red Capital Residence has an impressive history and an intriguing setting. We ended the day with a very good Chinese dinner at the popular Red Capital Club, to which we were transported to in style by rickshaw.

We began our morning with Grant on a private excursion to Tiananmen Square. This is the world's largest public square and represents the heart of "Imperial" and "Tourist" Beijing. It is probably the gray tone of the setting and the historical tragedies that make many Western travelers distance Tiananmen from "Gate of Heavenly Peace." However, after actually being there and getting a feel of the historical and political importance, as well as its power and authority, people change their impression about this "infamous" place. We continued our walk across the street to the Forbidden City. This architectural marvel was completed in 1420 after 14 years of hard work by 200,000 laborers and, fortunately, is still the best-preserved collection of ancient buildings in China. It was the symbol of imperial power for more than 500 years and was the home of 24 emperors from the Ming and Qing dynasties. Seeing the beauty of the palace is not enough; in order to appreciate it at a deeper level, you must learn about the ideas of design, the feng shui, as well as the legends of the imperial families.

Next we ventured to the Houhai District near the Forbidden City, an old neighborhood with well-preserved Chinese courtyard housing and ancient back alleys and passageways known as *hutongs*. We explored these small winding alleys both on foot and by rickshaw, which was a fascinating and delightful experience. It really gives you the best opportunity to see a traditional Chinese communal lifestyle that has existed for hundreds of years. These neighborhoods have their origins in the Yuan (Mongol) dynasty and are the birthplace of Beijing's folk art. The majority of those banned from the Forbidden City created their own enriching lifestyle right inside hutongs. There are more than 7,000 hutongs in Beijing and none of them are the same. Each has its own unique story and history and you can tell a little by their names. Some are called after historical figures, some after the nearby markets, and others just by local expressions. Hutongs and *dazayuan* (Chinese courtyard "condo" homes shared by several families) are unique Chinese structures and can be found nowhere else outside China. By taking an excursion here, you'll experience the more authentic parts of the city and really get acquainted with the old Beijing.

We enjoyed a late lunch at the famous Fangshan Imperial Restaurant inside Beihai Park (formerly the back

garden of royalty), where the Empress Cixi often held 120-course banquets. Though we were hungry we didn't do 120 courses. We were quite fulfilled sampling several of the famous dishes and snacks.

After lunch, Grant took us on an escorted tour to Yihe Yuan. In 1888, Qing's most powerful Empress Cixi diverted 30 million silver dollars from the Chinese North Ocean Navy to construct the Summer Palace as a gift for herself for her 60th birthday. She placed an order to imitate the West Lake of Hangzhou and the gardens in Suzhou and absorb the beauty into the creation of Yihe Yuan—the Garden of Spirit and Harmony or the Summer Palace, as most people know it. The garden was almost completely destroyed during the Eight-Power Allied troops' invasion of Beijing in 1900. When Cixi returned to Beijing from Xi'an, she ordered the garden rebuilt. History records show that Cixi rebuilt the Summer Palace with unbounded extravagance, spending some 40,000 silver taels per day. You can still see how luxurious it is even now. Since this palace was for summer holiday use, the emphasis was on the cooling features, such as a natural underground stone cooler.

For our last night, Grant took us to a dinner performance of the Beijing Night Show. This lavishly costumed and choreographed stage show was highly entertaining as it took us through many of China's cultural and historical accomplishments. It was the perfect ending to our very short but highly informative tour of Beijing. Without Michelle Lin's thoughtful itinerary, it would have been impossible to experience such a significant overview of Beijing in only two days.

MICHELE LIN, EAST TRAVEL CONSULTING
SERVICES INC.
Tel: 866-402-4462, www.east-tours.com

⑩ LIVING ICE: GHOSTS OF ANTARCTICA

For guests of our planet, Antarctica is the last stop on the train, a continent where passports are unnecessary and where the fringing ocean still stirs with life in a way great stretches of the Atlantic and Pacific no longer do. It's no exaggeration to call Antarctica the coldest, windiest, and driest place on Earth. Unexplored valleys and unscaled mountains are everywhere in this white brocade desert, with its ferocious winds and curve-of-the-Earth vistas. What, really, will you find here? A very different experience.

Travel in Antarctica has been confined largely to the Antarctic Peninsula, 965 kilometers (600 miles) south of Cape Horn. But with more ice-capable cruise ships, ski planes, and dogsleds, explorers can press farther and wider to South Pole destinations such as the McMurdo Dry Valleys, the Vinson Massif in the Ellsworth Mountains, and historic Beardmore Glacier, where early polar expeditions crossed.

In Antarctica, the landscape is reduced to its barest elements: ice, rock, water, and sky. But within this natural environment are surprising discoveries. Ice freezes in endless shapes and colors, from sheets to shelves. There is old ice and fast ice, grease ice and pancake ice, striated ice and fractured ice. And, of course, there is thin ice—the element of the unknown that sometimes makes travelers realize their vulnerability on the coldest, driest, windiest, highest, and remotest of continents.

But then that's why we go there. Nearly 100 years ago, the explorer Sir Ernest Shackleton wrote of Antarctica's lure: "Some are actuated simply by a love of adventure, some have the keen thirst for scientific knowledge, and others again are drawn away from the trodden paths by the 'lure of little voices,' the mysterious fascination of the unknown." Whatever the exact purpose, a visit to Antarctica is not just a trip: It's an unpredictable journey. But once you arrive, you'll be rewarded with an incredible view of a world few people have seen: thousands of penguins, elephant seals, and icebergs—even volcanoes and thermal springs.

In the past few years, Antarctica has gotten so popular, especially with travelers interested in nature-based tourism, that concerns have been raised about the continent's delicate ecosystem. Proposals have been made to protect it by restricting the number of visitors, but none has yet been adopted. For now, tour operators are supposed to ensure that travelers have as little impact as possible on the wildlife and the environment.

Antarctica is about 50 percent larger than the United States and occupies nearly one-tenth of the world's landmass. With its mountains reaching heights of 5,139 meters (16,860 feet), it's the highest continent in the world in average altitude, and the least visited.

For information and a list of tour operators, contact the International Association of Antarctica Tour Operators at 970-704-1047 or iaato@iaato.org.

MACQUARIE ISLAND

Roughly halfway between Tasmania and the Antarctic continent, Macquarie Island has one of the highest concentrations of wildlife in the sub-Antarctic region. Australia's Sir Douglas Mawson built a wireless radio relay base on the island when he first brought modern communications to the Antarctic region in 1911. (Until then, the island was frequented only by sealers who boiled down penguin and seal blubber for oil.) Mawson's subsequent conservation efforts saved the penguin colonies on Macquarie, and the Australian government now staffs an important wildlife research station there. The island is home to tens of thousands of seals and some four million penguins. It has the world's only royal penguin rookery (to which the number of visitors is restricted) and a massive king penguin colony, which visitors may visit by Zodiac only.

McMURDO STATION

Located on Ross Island, McMurdo is the largest settlement in Antarctica. It's home to about 1,000 residents during the summer season. The station is operated by the United States, but it's supplied by air from New Zealand (New Zealand's Scott Station is a near neighbor). Residents put on the McMurdo Golf Tournament each year, perhaps the only golf match in which there is no difference between the fairway and the rough—it's all rough. A hut built by Robert Scott's expedition in 1902 is also there, set off from the base by a rope railing but open to careful travelers.

MOUNT EREBUS

Named for one of the ships of explorer James Clark Ross and located on Ross Island, Mount Erebus is Antarctica's only active volcano. How active is it? Scientists estimate that the volcano erupts at least once or twice a day. One of only three volcanos in the world that has a permanent lava lake, Erebus vents significantmounts of chlorine, sulfur dioxide, and fluorine, contributing to the growing diameter of the area's infamous ozone hole. The completely snowcapped peak is 3,800 meters (12,450 feet) high and is visible from McMurdo Station. The volcano was first climbed and measured in 1908 by a party that included Australian Sir Douglas Mawson.

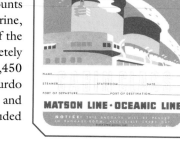

ROSS ICE SHELF

Like thick syrup pouring over the top of a bowling ball, ice slowly and relentlessly moves down from the South Pole plateau to the edges of the Antarctic continent. One such edge culminates in the Ross Ice Shelf, a thick layer of ice that covers much of McMurdo Sound, the side of Antarctica directly below Australia and New Zealand. Cruises to this area allow you to see this immense wall of ice, in some places hundreds of feet high, resembling the walls of a glittering white fortress. Periodically, parts of the wall shear off—a process known as calving—and a new iceberg is born. The coastal area produces many icebergs, some as large as the state of Rhode Island! McMurdo Bay, which is covered in ice up to 700 meters (2,300 feet) thick, is home to the major research stations of McMurdo and Scott, as well as Mount Erebus.

SOUTH ORKNEY ISLANDS

Claimed by both Argentina and the United Kingdom, the South Orkneys were used as a base for whalers in the 19th century. Today, the main island, Coronation, is the site of a British research station where scientists are studying the nesting habits of the snow and cape petrels. Note the beached icebergs in the harbor.

SOUTH POLE

Undiscovered by human eyes until the Norwegian explorer Roald Amundsen arrived in 1911, the South Pole now has permanent residents. The U.S. Amundsen-Scott South Pole Station is currently housed in a geodesic dome, but a new station is under construction. Only a small number of tourists a year actually get to the Pole and see the mirror ball on the

WHITE CONTINENT

Though writings of the ancient Greeks cryptically refer to a massive southern region of the world, the discovery of the "White Continent" is generally attributed to Edward Bransfield, a British naval officer. Bransfield discovered the northwestern coast of the Antarctic Peninsula on January 30, 1820, and called it Trinity Land. However, the land mass was first touched in the 1840s by a party of Norwegians, and it was the Norwegian Roald Amundsen who, on December 14, 1911, first reached the South Pole. (Robert Scott, an Englishman, reached the Pole just weeks after Amundsen. He never returned.) Not until 1956 did the first tourists—a group of Chileans—make trips to Antarctica.

Since Antarctica's discovery, some 26 nations, including Russia, the United States, Norway, China, Great Britain, Chile, Argentina, Poland, Australia, South Africa, Belgium, France, Japan, and New Zealand, have laid claim to various sections of it. Today the continent is effectively a shared territory, and the occupying countries have agreed to cooperate in protecting Antarctica's many environmental treasures and its pristine beauty.

pole's actual location or the sign with the quotes from Scott and Amundsen on them. Those who do generally come via Adventure Network International, which flies a small plane from its base camp at Patriot Hills onto the ice airstrip at the pole during the summer season. The groups tend to be quite small (2–4 people), and the stay is only a few hours. The station will provide a hot drink to visitors in the cafeteria, but is not set up for tours or other amenities. The station does operate a small gift shop (U.S. dollars accepted only).

SOUTH SHETLAND ISLANDS

The Shetlands, unlike the ponies of the same name, are not cute and cuddly. They're cold and wet and covered with lichens, peat, and moss. Casual tourists are unlikely to find their way there—and they would find little to see and less to do. These 11 islands, first explored in 1819 and claimed by Great Britain, Chile, and Argentina, lie just off the Antarctic Peninsula. Primarily used as research stations, the islands have a rather international community. Brazilians, Chileans, Uruguayans, Argentines, Poles, Russians, and Chinese all share the South Shetlands.

CRUISES

THE INTERNATIONAL ASSOCIATION OF ANTARCTICA TOUR OPERATORS (IAATO)
www.iaato.org

For travelers, the most popular—and practically the only—way of seeing Antarctica is by ship. Antarctic cruises visit ice-free coastal areas and sub-Antarctic islands from November to March. The harsh weather, daunting logistics, and lack of on-site support facilities discourage most other types of travel. The only people who don't see Antarctica on an escorted tour/cruise are research scientists living and studying there. It's simply not practical to try to see it on your own (only the very rich could even consider it). Most trips depart from Ushuaia, Argentina, or Punta Arenas, Chile. For longer voyages, you may board in Australia, New Zealand, or the Falkland Islands.

There are about a dozen cruise lines worldwide that

Eden in Ice

One of our favorite correspondents and contributors to this volume is John Borthwick. He is the author of hundreds of travel articles (most illustrated by his own photographs) and numerous books, including a collection of his travel essays, *The Circumference of the Knowable World;* an anthology of train stories, *Off the Rails;* and an edited collection of the late Peter Pinney's travel writings, *The Road to Anywhere.*

Among his principal outlets are newspapers *The Australian, The Age* (Melbourne), and the *Sunday Telegraph* (Sydney) and color magazines such as the *South China Morning Posts Sunday Magazine* and *Australian Gourmet Traveller.* Here are his thoughts on Antarctica.

Welcome to the Lemaire Channel. Welcome to Antarctica. With walls of black basalt and ice rising 300 meters (1,000 feet) on each side of the narrow channel, this impression—of cruising through a high mountain valley—is not far from the truth. Since the Antarctic Peninsula is the ancient coccyx of the Andes' spine, we are sailing between what were, long ago, Andean peaks.

It's like sailing through the middle of the Andes. As if that weren't enough, we're slaloming down a field of

ice floes, dodging bergs as big as apartment blocks.

Our captain is a nuggety, crew-cut Russian named Kalashnikov—not the sort of man you'd jokingly call "AK-47"—who, with a marksman's accuracy, maneuvers our 117-meter- (384-foot) ice-strengthened vessel through the bergs. The vessel moves with the shipshape grace that travel writer Jonathan Raban once aptly described (in reference to another ship) as "the ponderous delicacy of an elephant sidestepping the tea things in a drawing room."

Some of the bergs are an improbable powder blue; others have downy-white shelves on which languid Weddell seals sun themselves. From their floating sun lounges (yes, this is summer in Antarctica—a balmy 0°C/32°F) the seals consider our passing; a few shuffle and plop into the sea, but most are too lazy to even feign interest.

Such is a day in the Antarctic, with more "once in a lifetime" encounters—with calving glaciers, humpback whales, insouciant seals, and teeming penguin rookeries—than I could have thought possible.

I have joined an 11-night cruise aboard a Canadian-chartered, Russian-flagged vessel with the slightly pedantic name of *Akademik Sergey Vavilov*. The *Vavilov*'s operators, Canadian company Marine Expeditions, have also badged the ship as the plain *Marine Discoverer*—perhaps for those die-hard capitalists who are still "Red sensitive" or just syllabically challenged. Belonging to the Soviet Academy of Sciences, this former "research ship" (for which, read "submarine listening ship") is only ten years old and, being Finnish-built, is equipped with plenty of creature comforts, including en suite bathrooms in each cabin, a sauna, library, and (indispensable in the Antarctic) a fleet of inflatable Zodiac boats that will ferry us ashore twice daily.

When market forces caught up with the Soviet Union in the early 1990s, many of its big-ticket research-cum-defense projects were moth-balled. Expensive hardware like the *Vavilov* had to earn its keep, and soon this and similar vessels were chartered for Arctic and Antarctic cruises.

With 74 passengers and 50 crew on board, our journey starts from Ushuaia, southern Argentina. South America's last resort (so to speak), Ushuaia is an outpost of rutted roads and nervous-wreck pop music, surrounded by the forested peaks of Tierra del Fuego and the vast waters of the Beagle Passage.

A 40-hour crossing of the infamously rough Drake Passage, between South America and Antarctica, lies before us. "'Drake-proof' your cabin," advises Brad Rhees, our expedition leader. Although we batten down all bottles and loose items, this time, mercifully, there is only a moderate swell. We arrive at the doorstep of Antarctica, Deception Island in the South Shetland Islands, and moor in a massive bay formed by the rim of a volcanic crater. After donning kilos of thermal underwear, Goretex, and gumboots, all topped off by mandatory red life jackets, we pile into the Zodiacs for our first landfall. The cruise crew (mostly North American and British) makes sure no one takes a frigid dunking between the ladder and the boats or between the surf and the shore.

On the pebbly beach we immediately encounter the first of the thousands of penguins we will meet over the next week and a half. The aroma of their rookeries is pervasive, although after a while, "penguano" pong is no worse than the aroma from one's local fishmarket. Gentoo penguins are by far the most prevalent species, followed by the aptly named chinstraps (who have a small, dark "chinstrap" marking), plus a few adelie and so-called macaroni penguins.

The ruins of Deception Island's huge whaling station stand rusting in the polar wind. Abandoned around 1918, this corroding mountain of industrial archaeology, with its vats and tanks and huts, plus the bones of old lighters buried in the volcanic sands, is an eerie, Apocalyptic introduction to the sub-Antarctic.

Back on board, we passengers get to know each other, as well as our cruise staff and the ship's Russian sailing crew. The passengers are predominantly well-traveled North Americans and Europeans, plus a few from Hong Kong and Japan. While mostly "over-40s," these are no blue-rinse superannuants who might be content to scan the shoreline penguin parades via their deck-chair binoculars. Every one of our excursions ashore is packed by alarmingly keen people, all bristling with cameras and Antarctic knowledge, hoofing up snow slopes for a better photo angle, glissading down again on their backsides, and generally being up to the hilt in whatever's going.

PENGUIN CRAZY

The most eccentric passengers are a flock of earnest British birdwatchers ("twitchers," according to their own slang) who tick off on their lists every albatross, giant petrel, tern, skua, and blue-eyed shag that moves across land, sea, or berg. ("Goodness. I've already spotted three new species of goose," announced one twitcher woman before we were even out of Ushuaia Airport.) The men tend to look like the late British actor Denholm Elliott and are often called Nigel, their leading Nigel being distinguished by the Hubble Junior–size telescope that he hoists before his flock like a bishop's crook.

"That's it—the big seven!" announces a woman from New York on the morning that we step for the first time onto the Antarctic Peninsula proper, at Paradise Bay. Antarctica is the seventh continent and for many of these travelers, setting foot here completes their global "score."

Along the indented shores of the Antarctic Peninsula we venture out twice daily in our Zodiacs to blitz the penguin rookeries and fur seal colonies with camera action, or just contemplation. Or to meander in the boats through stupendous fields of "bergy bits"—white galleries of Daliesque ice sculpted by the sun to surreal extremes. Gothic bergs that bristle like a Chartres Cathedral in ice. Translucent arks, scrimshaw swans, and ivory aircraft carriers. One pioneer explorer described his vision in ice floes as "a gondola steered by a giraffe ran afoul of us, which much amused a duck sitting on a crocodile's head."

On these excursions, humpback whales sometimes surface near our Zodiacs. Around the bays, the continent's ancient ice cap creeps inexorably down to the sea in shelves that crack and avalanche with the sound of howitzer blasts. Here the extraordinary is recurrent.

We've been well instructed to remain at least 5 meters (16 feet) clear of the penguins (and much farther from the cantankerous fur seals); however, the penguins haven't been similarly educated, and soon they are zigzagging around us, indeed almost between our legs. This is late summer, penguin fledgling season, when the mothers are trying to teach their goofy, fluffball offspring a little common sense. Such as: "No, I won't feed you fish (via beak-to-beak regurgitation) every time you wail; no, don't follow me everywhere; and yes, there's the sea—now go and learn to swim and fish for yourself."

At such times a penguin rookery resembles a pratfall training camp for a Three Stooges movie. As a mother gentoo penguin flees downhill from her frantically pestering offspring (plus another hanger-on or two), the whole train trips over itself, squawking and skidding uncontrollably—like David Attenborough gone slapstick.

RESEARCH ON ICE

Antarctica is like God's hand let loose, an Eden in ice. On the shores of aptly-named Paradise Bay sits little Almirante Brown base, one of several research stations—British, Polish, and Argentinian—that we visit. It's not much more than an outpost of tin and wind: two orange huts and an Argentine flag shredding itself in the gale. Such "scientific bases" are maintained by a number of South American nations in order to literally "wave the flag" in hope of reinforcing their claim to some slice of rock and ice. In Paradise Bay's case, Argentina claims it along with both Chile and the United Kingdom.

Almirante Brown base used to be much larger than its current pair of curiously singed-looking huts. The Antarctic urban legend goes that in the mid-1980s the base doctor, perhaps stuck down here too long, became unhinged. When he heard that a ship was coming to relieve him of his duties—and possibly in a straitjacket—he took the line of, "If I'm going, so is everyone else," and he torched the base. Personally, I suspect that his fellow workers passed the hat around and encouraged him with several thousand pesos (and a box of matches) to hasten their repatriation en masse back to Argentina.

ZODIAC LIFE

Life on board our ship seems to be much about digestion— of scenery, Antarctic in- formation, and, of course, meals. On most days we enjoy specialist lectures in Antarctic ecology, the complex local birdlife, whales, and, of course, the heroic/tragic history of polar exploration. The meals, too, are excellent, and on several afternoons we enjoy that polar improbability, of a barbecue on the Vavilov's sunny aft deck.

But it is from the close quarters of the Zodiac, or in delicately creeping through a rookery, that our greatest impressions come. A school of crabeater seals surfs the turquoise surge around the base of a grounded iceberg. Elephant seals snooze side by side on the beach like obese, comatose cigars or waddle into the water to swim like rocks. Giant whale vertebrae lie beached and bleached on the shore like prehistoric bone propellers. And summer's growling avalanches of blue ice—the gods of "The Freezer" (as Attenborough called this place) at their annual defrosting.

"So much ice for gin and tonics!" I overhear one tippler sighing at the sight of fields of pure ice. It's easy to forget that Antarctica is in fact a desert, one of the world's driest places; a desert covered with an ice sheet more than 2,100 meters (6,900 feet) thick that contains 70 percent of our planet's fresh water.

The world's lowest temperature, -89.2°C (-128.6°F), was recorded in Antarctica, although summer along the Peninsula—the area most commonly visited by cruise ships—can be as warm as 15°C (59°F). This is mid-February and it's 0°C (32°F) on deck; even so, the couple opposite me at breakfast is celebrating: "This is our summer vacation. It was -21F (-29°C) when we left Chicago."

Some 15 ships—departing from Ushuaia, Christchurch, and Hobart—now bring around 10,000 visitors to the Antarctic waters, from South Georgia Island to the Ross Sea, during the November– March cruising season. It's a figure that many fear may be already nearing the impact limit. The frequently voiced opinion of "Don't open the door any wider," after one's own visit, is paradoxically both selfish and protectionist.

I climb a steep snow ridge above a beautiful inlet named Neko Harbour and look down into its glacier-framed bay where, amid a litter of ivory bergs, the *Akademik Vavilov* rides on a mirror sea. This could be a J. M. W. Turner image, painted not in fire but ice. As they say, the last virgin continent. May it stay that way. No more travel writers, at least, should be allowed.

—JOHN BORTHWICK

DINING

The food eaten at the Antarctic bases is very hearty home-style cooking and reflects the national cuisine of the host nation. Absolutely everything except water must be flown or shipped in, so take only as much as you will eat when dining at a base cafeteria. The cruise ships offer more variety, but not like the feasts-of-plenty available on standard cruises.

belong to IAATO. These companies offer a variety of voyages, generally on icebreakers or research vessels that have been transformed into passenger ships. This isn't Caribbean-style cruising, with floor shows and shuffleboard—it's more an expedition than a cruise. You will, however, almost always receive many informative lectures en route on the region's geology, history, and climate.

Itineraries vary, depending in part on the kind of vessel you choose. If you want to venture beyond the Antarctic Peninsula, for example, you'll probably wind up on an icebreaker. Cruises can be one to three weeks in length, stopping at various points of interest or bases on the peninsula, coast, or islands. Activities on the tours include viewing penguins, elephant seals, and other polar animals, as well as ice walks and opportunities to visit research bases and meet the scientists who work there. Every cruise offers the chance for spectacular views of icebergs, and you may get to see an ice shelf or glacier calve into an iceberg. Many icebergs are beautifully colored, showing green, blue, or purple ice and crevasses where the sea water has hollowed

them out or melted them into fantastic shapes.

Much of the sightseeing is done in Zodiacs—the small inflatable boats powered by outboard engines. One of the larger icebreakers has helicopters for transporting passengers ashore to visit research stations. Some tours visit sites made famous by such explorers as Robert Scott and Sir Ernest Shackleton (you can still see remnants of their doomed expedition). Shore visits are supervised and conducted by shipboard staff, which typically includes one staff member for each 10–20 passengers. Such staff generally includes ornithologists, marine biologists, general biologists, geologists, glaciologists, historians, and naturalists. It is very important to be realistic about the sort of rigors your particular trip will entail and to be honest with the tour operator about your ability or desire to partake in the more difficult parts of the trip. For example, if you don't like the thought of being in rough seas for three hours in an open rubber boat, then opt out of that particular excursion. If you choose a ski jaunt but don't want to do the mountaineering portion, discuss this with your tour operator prior to the activity.

Most travelers opt for the shorter, less strenuous cruises that depart from South America and make a two-day passage to the Antarctic Peninsula. On these cruises, you cross the Weddell Sea and visit the islands and coastal areas. A cruise through LeMaire Channel is a great option, passing spectacular mountains and huge blocks of floating ice. For longer voyages, the best bet is to board in Australia or New Zealand. These routes present the best opportunity to see the historic sites of the Ross Sea area, including Shackleton's hut and the penguin rookery at Cape Royds. You can also take in the sprawling American research base and Scott's century-old huts, now ghostly and evocative.

Given the small number of Antarctic tour operators, the short tourist season, and the limited number of tourists that can be accommodated, many cruises fill up fast. You should plan at least six months ahead when making arrangements to take an Antarctic cruise and research your options carefully.

OVERFLIGHTS

QANTAS AIRLINES
www.qantas.com

For exploring travelers who want to see Antarctica without the hassle of the cold or of cramped ship's quarters, Australia's Qantas Airlines offers sightseeing flights over Antarctica November–February. The flights are conducted on Boeing 747s and last approximately 12 hours. All of the excursions spend 3 to 4 hours over the continent, flying high enough (about 3,100 meters/10,000 feet above sea level) to avoid the mountain peaks but still affording great opportunities for unforgettable photographs. Among the attractions are the historic huts of Sir Douglas Mawson at Cape Adare and the Mertz Glacier. (The aircraft flies figure-eights over some areas so that passengers on both sides of the aircraft get to see the stunning views.) Although you do not get to touch down on the continent or see its wildlife, the flights offer many of the same educational experiences as cruises, including experts giving talks on polar sciences and history. A camera on the flight deck gives you the pilot's view of the scenery. Two full meals are served, plus a snack and bar service.

Flights depart from Sydney, Melbourne, and Adelaide. The journey is regarded as a domestic route and thus leaves from the domestic area of the departure airport.

FLUGFÉLAG ÍSLANDS

PRIVATE EXPEDITIONS

The most authentic way to experience the White Continent is to undertake a trek to the interior. While a cruise will confine you to explorations of the coast and overflights don't get you on the ground, a private expedition allows you to set your own itinerary and to envelop yourself for days or weeks in the intensity, mystery, and wonderful strangeness of the Antarctic continent. Such a journey requires a traveler to be in good physical shape, to be willing to camp in tents for extended periods, to be a reasonably good cross-country skier, and even to possess some mountaineering skills. It also comes with a hefty price tag—anywhere from $10,000 to $25,000 is typical.

Above all, you must understand that even a pricey private expedition will be subject to the vagaries of the weather and that you are dependent on the quality of your guide and equipment. But if you're in shape and your wallet doesn't flinch, a ground voyage can give you the experience of a lifetime.

At press time, Adventure Network International (ANI) was the only company staging private expeditions in Antarctica. The packages include "ski safaris" and mountaineering experiences lasting from a few days to more than a month. Though ANI operates out of Punta Arenas, Chile, the company's Antarctic base camp is six hours from Chile at Patriot Hills, at the base of the Ellsworth Mountains, 1,080 kilometers (670 miles) from the nearest inhabited area. This outpost is the departure point for the guided expeditions. Up to 60 travelers stay there at a time, living in insulated tents, eating in the dining tent, and reading in the library tent.

Needless to say, hygiene arrangements are minimal—there are central toilet facilities but no showers or laundry services. ANI is fastidious about protecting the environment, and all waste is carried out after an expedition. A medical doctor is on site.

ADVENTURE NETWORK INTERNATIONAL (ANI)
www.adventure-network.com

⑪ THE BLUE TRAIN

The Blue Train (27-12-334-8459, www.bluetrain.co.za) is not merely a train; it combines the luxury of a leading hotel with the adventure of train travel. It as an all-inclusive luxury rail cruise with an opportunity to view South Africa's spectacular landscapes and attractions along the way. Take a journey into a timeless world of grace, elegance, and romance, with spectacular scenery and luxurious comfort.

It's the journey of a lifetime.

Southern Africa has always attracted adventurous, romantic, discerning travelers who crossed the land in as much comfort as possible. Then, when the first luxury train was introduced between Johannesburg and Cape Town, truly comfortable travel became a reality.

With interiors created by a leading interior architectural design company, the New Blue rivals many a five-star hotel in terms of grace and style. The suites have been superbly redesigned to offer guests the best that modern technology and superior craftsmanship can offer.

In the beginning, the train with distinctive sapphire-blue carriages was known southbound as the *Union Limited,* and on its return journey, the *Union Express.* Everyone soon began referring to them as "those blue trains," and so a legend was born.

Before the turn of the 20th century, advertisements offered direct-route journeys to the gold and diamond fields of South Africa. "It is not difficult to imagine what conditions must have been like on these early trains. The extremes of heat and cold, the dust, the multiplicity of insects and the smoke and coal dust from the locomotive would all have added up to an experience of tedious discomfort," writes author David Robbins in *The Blue Train.*

At the same time, Cecil John Rhodes, who built his influence and wealth on the Kimberley diamond fields and who founded the De Beers Mining Company, was forging ahead with his dream of "painting the map red," a euphemism for extending the British Empire. His dream included a Trans-African railway between Cape Town and Cairo. Although this never materialized, he achieved the construction of a line between South Africa and the then Congo Free State, later known as Zaire, now the Democratic Republic of the Congo.

The accommodation and level of passenger comfort on the trains soon improved as the first years of the 20th century brought a new breed of trains that were considered to be the most luxurious anywhere in the world at the time. World War II caused a suspension of service, which resumed in 1946. Steam reluctantly gave way to electrification and diesel as the grand all-steel blue icon adapted to progress, tirelessly journeying backward and forward. More and more people booked on the Blue Train for the sheer pleasure of the experience. The train's reputation for comfort, excellent service, food, punctuality, Irish linen, crystal, and silverware in the heart of some of the world's most rugged and spectacular scenery soon spread around the world.

Now each Blue Train suite has a fully appointed bathroom en suite, featuring either a bath or shower; a telephone; and a TV monitor. A Club Car, designed like a gentleman's club, is an ideal place to enjoy an after-dinner cigar and relax over a cup of coffee. Finally, to ensure the ultimate in hospitality, professionally trained personnel are on call for guests in each suite 24 hours a day.

The Blue Train operates a total of four routes. Offering the biggest attractions the Pretoria to Cape Town route gives a discerning traveler a glimpse of some of Southern Africa's natural beauties such as the great plains of the Southwest and Victoria Falls. During this trip, guests spend two nights on board the train.

The journey begins in Pretoria, home of The Blue Train and site of the historic presidential inauguration in 1994 of South Africa's best-loved national hero, Nelson Mandela.

This is an opportunity to follow in the footsteps of missionary-explorer Dr. David Livingstone, who traveled deep into the African continent in search of the greatest curtain of falling water on Earth, Victoria Falls.

Travel west to Mafikeng and across the border into Botswana before turning north through the capital,

Gaborone, and onward over the undulating expanses of the savanna, the enduring African plains of thorn bush and grass, unchanged for millions of years.

The train stops in Kwa Bulawayo for an off-board excursion in the unique landscape of the Matobo Hills National Park. These hills were given their name by a Zulu warlord and founder of the Ndebele nation.

The most spectacular sights of the Matobo Hills are landscapes, dams, and wildlife and the site where Cecil Rhodes is buried. Not far from his grave is the large and imposing memorial to the Shangaan Patrol, a tribute to the 20 men who engaged in the battle with 30,000 Zulu warriors during the Matebele Wars of 1893. In essence, the Matobo Hills are packed with history and myth of Shona dynasties and the countless battles fought between Ndebele armies and British colonists.

The train then journeys toward the thundering Victoria Falls, named after Queen Victoria by British explorer Livingstone in 1855. "Scenes so lovely must have been gazed upon by angels in their flight," exclaimed Dr. Livingstone when he first saw them.

Known in Zimbabwe as Mosi-oa-Thunya, the "smoke that thunders," the falls are one-and-a-half times as wide and twice as high as Niagara Falls. The water plunges almost 450 meters (1,476 feet) in a sheer drop. This magnificent seasonal waterfall carries 500 million liters (130 million gallons) of water a minute, when in full flood, creating a permanent rain forest and a cloud of spray that rises high into the sky and that I could see 80 kilometers (50 miles) away.

A tour of the valley, including a visit to the Kwa Bulawayo museum, an original home of royal citadel of

Lobengula, mighty king of the Matebele, makes this journey memorable.

On the return trip from Victoria Falls, a stopover is made at Hwange National Park, home to Africa's last great elephant sanctuaries. An open 4X4 vehicle drives to a spectacular game-viewing area in one of Africa's most abundant wildlife regions.

⑫ IN THE WAKE OF JOSEPH CONRAD: SAILING FROM SINGAPORE TO PHUKET ABOARD THE *STAR CLIPPER*

It was natural that Joseph Conrad, a young man from Poland setting his heart on travel, should turn his eye first to the sea. The novelist navigated the Spice Islands of the Malay Archipelago. His close acquaintance with those shores is measured in his writing and were the most enriching of his life. We followed in his wake.

The journey began and ended in Singapore, a fascinating, startling combination of contemporary glass-and-steel architecture relieved by pockets of tropical greenery. Its proximity to the equator means that Singapore is almost always hot and humid, but for a chance to enjoy one of the world's most extensive banquet of cuisines and to stay in one of the world's most evocative hotels, it's worth accommodating to the local conditions. Singapore's location at the tip of the Malay Peninsula makes it a major trade center, and its harbor is the second busiest in the world, combining to produce one of the truly great international cities.

Singapore is a city of spires. Its skyscrapers look like a big bar graph along the skyline. It is incredibly clean, and crime is virtually unknown. But amid this obsessive neatness is a mad mix of peoples and cultures, drawn to Singapore. Emerald Hill has charming pavilioned prewar homes, the Victorian botanic garden, and the green lawns of the Padang Cricket Club.

SINGAPORE

★ RAFFLES HOTEL
1 Beach Road
Tel: 65-6-337-1886, www.raffleshotel.com

Established in 1886, the Raffles is one of the last great 19th-century hotels. Famous writers Somerset Maugham, Rudyard Kipling, and Joseph Conrad stayed here during their travels. Though it lacks the superb harbor views of some of its competitors, the millions of dollars that were invested in a complete rebuilding in the early 1990s have added luxury and service without sacrificing the house's legendary heritage. Maugham would still love the place.

Its 104 suites are spacious and luxuriously furnished, with much of the original furniture saved and blended with newer pieces that have the old look. Our favorite rooms face the Palm Courtyard and include sitting rooms, dark polished wooden floors, large bathrooms, and high ceilings. All are air-conditioned and each is attended by a personal valet. Second-floor rooms are quietest. The entrance is imposing, surrounding gardens are luxurious, and the famous Writers Bar in the lobby, where the Singapore Sling was reputedly first concocted, remains intact. Despite its being surrounded by multistoried skyscrapers, you can still

STAR CLIPPER

"One ship, the Vidar *owned by an Arab sailed under the Dutch flag, with an English master. He pleased me at once by his manners, which were distinguished and reserved; one of the first things he told me was that he was a foreigner by birth, which I had already guessed from his accent.*

The ship included two European engineers, and one Chinese; With one other mate, Mahamat; eleven Malays, and eighty-two Chinamen who were used for loading and unloading gum and resin, we took the regular run on the Vidar *through the Malaician straights to the islet of Laut, and that held great beauty and fascination."*

— Joseph Conrad (aboard the *Vidar*)

go for a late-night swim in the splendid pool around palms and lush greenery.

THE RITZ-CARLTON MILLENIA
7 Raffles Avenue
Tel: 65-6-337-8888, www.ritzcarlton.com

A striking high-rise on the city's bayfront. The best of the 32-story hotel's accommodations are on the top floors, especially at the corners where you get superb views either of the harbor or Marina Bay or back into the city itself. All rooms are spacious, with especially large and nicely designed bathrooms. With Frank Stella sculptures and huge art-glass pieces in the lobby, the overall look blends classic Asian and starkly modern design. Service throughout is usually well up to the high Southeast Asia standard.

⭑ THE FOUR SEASONS HOTEL SINGAPORE
190 Orchard Boulevard
Tel: 65-6-734-1110
www.fourseasons.com/singapore

Providing a touch of understated elegance and set in a parklike enclave of calm and civility, conveniently located around the corner from Orchard Road, this intimate retreat is run more like a residential club than a commercial hotel. The ground level of the hotel is linked to one of the city's most attractive and easily navigated promenades and is filled with some of the finest and most tasteful international designer boutiques and art galleries. The small lobby has an extravagant gold-leaf vaulted ceiling that leads the eye to the second floor, where you'll find the reception and concierge areas as well as a bar and two restaurants. The One Ninety specializes in innovative Italian/California-style cuisine with an Asian touch and also features fresh seafood and grills. The smaller, informal bar offers light snacks, afternoon tea, and cocktails.

The hotel's outstanding Chinese restaurant, Jiang-Nan Chun, is reached by way of a grand, sweeping black marble staircase. The room is decidedly not Chinese in design, with an undercurrent of art deco evident in its stylized furniture and chic black-and-white tableware. Tubular lighting that rings the ceiling softens the starkly dramatic black and charcoal decor, with a contemporary sculpture and stunning chairs that are upholstered in unusual bronze leather. The wall coverings have gold threads woven into them, and the overall effect is warmly masculine. The Cantonese cuisine is the finest in Singapore, rivaled only by the Lai Ching Heen restaurant in Hong Kong's Regent Hotel. Menu favorites include bird's nest soup, duck, abalone, seafood, and hot oshibori; and the wine list is wide-ranging in choice and diverse in label and price. Service is smooth and savvy.

GOODWOOD PARK
22 Scotts Road
Tel: 65-6-737-7411
www.goodwoodparkhotel.com.sg

A vintage structure dating back to 1900 in the center of town, Goodwood Park is surrounded by tropical gardens. Its 235 rooms are comfortable and have contemporary touches. There are eight restaurants, a business center, two outdoor pools, and a gym.

SHOPPING

The main shopping area is Orchard Road, which is lined with shopping malls, many of them several stories high. Start at the Dynasty Hotel and turn left as you come out. You will then find a dozen or so malls within a few short blocks on either side of Orchard Road. Some malls specialize in certain kinds of goods. The Tanglin Shopping Centre features antiques. The Forum Galleria is a heaven on Earth for children or the young at heart. Palais Renaissance is noted for fashion and high luxury. And the Far East Shopping Centre specializes in Asian antiques. There, on level three, the Kwok Gallery is an excellent source of rare porcelains, jade, and fine ivory pieces.

While Singapore shopping malls are interesting, they are really just enlarged versions of what you can find at home, with better prices. If you decide to buy jewelry, stick to gold or silver that is marked properly, and buy gemstones only from established dealers.

Arab Street consists of all kinds of tiny shops where you

can bargain. Those along Arab, Baghdad, Muscat, and Bussorah Streets offer rugs, beautifully made baskets, and fine rattan furniture. Especially good are the shops at 40 and 42 Arab Street. At No. 18 you'll find lovely cloisonné boxes. If it gets too hot, you can cool off in the Golden Landmark shopping complex at the corner of North Bridge Road and Arab Street.

Allow time for shopping in Chinatown. Smith, Temple, and Pagoda Streets deserve the attention. You'll find significant items jumbled together with the insignificant, jade figurines sitting next to plastic chopsticks, silk robes adjacent to paper kites.

MING VILLAGE
32 Pandan Road

Chinese porcelain is made here exactly as it was centuries ago. Singapore Gems and Metals Company offers another instructive experience. There, precious gems are cut and fashioned into jewelry. The perfume bottles inlaid with precious stones are particularly attractive.

AFTER SINGAPORE

We set sail in the *Star Clipper,* cruising the Malacca Straits following in the wake of Conrad. *Star Clipper* and her sister ship *Star Flyer* are as fleet as the wind and as graceful as swans. These are true clippers, reflecting their proud heritage in every inch of polished brass and gleaming brightwork.

Stepping aboard enters a new age of sail, where traditions of the past are happily married to the comforts of the present. The *Clipper* is modern ship in every way, created for sail and adventure, for those who love the traditions and romance of the legendary era of sailing ships.

She is 110 meters (360 feet) long and carries just 170 guests. Life aboard is relaxed, much like traveling on a private yacht. The ship offers pleasing accommodations and expansive teak decks with ample space for relaxing and play.

Recalling the grand age of sail, antique prints and paintings of famous sailing ships and teak with gleaming mahogany rails establish a rich nautical ambiance.

VISITING SINGAPORE

LITTLE INDIA
The spice-scented streets call shoppers to a treasure trove of ethnic jewelry, jasmine garlands, brassware, and Kashmiri silk.

BUGIS STREET
Its old-style shop houses provide the venue for outdoor cabaret, a beer garden, and a hawker center. Up to 850 people during the day and 1,600 people during the night can party and dine on some of the best "hawker" food while being entertained by wandering musicians.

MOUNT FABER
The second highest point in Singapore after Bukit Timah Hill, Mount Faber offers a view of the harbor and surrounding districts and a tranquil place to take a break in the city. A cable car leaves here for Sentosa.

CAMERON HIGHLANDS

Shortly after setting sail, the *Clipper* comes to place where in 1885 a surveyor, William Cameron, went for a long walk in the Malayan jungle. After weeks hacking at steep, dense rain forest, he happened across a landscape with "gentle slopes and rounded hills" at around 1,500 meters (5,000 feet), but without the help of satellite positioning, it was ages before anyone found it again. Once on the map, Cameron's garden of Eden developed into a hill-station for colonials looking to cool their heels, grow wisteria, walk, and come home to their Tudor bungalows for slap-up cream teas by a roaring log fire.

In newly rediscovered Cameron Highlands, jungle walks, waterfalls, tea and rubber plantations, and gardens intermingle with wild flowers.

ISLANDS IN THE STRAIT

Under full sail, we reach Tioman Island, off the eastern coast of Malaysia in the South China Sea. Here are beautiful beaches, clear coral-filled water, Technicolor marine life, virtually unpopulated jungle highlands, crystal clear streams, and the peaks of Batu Sirau and Nenek Semukut. Tioman is gifted with exotic place names like "Pond-Frond Hill" and "Village of Doubt," and was the setting for the mythical Bali Hai in the film "South Pacific." It's located midway between Singapore and the island of Pankor Laut.

"It is not down in any map; true places never are."
—Herman Melville

⭐ PANGKOR LAUT
www.pangkorlautresort.com
The resort is like a British Raj dream. Following Conrad's route, tacking through the Strait of Malacca to the island of

A Guide to Good Shopping in Southeast Asia

Sir David Landale's family founded the noted firm of Jardine Mathison in Hong Kong more than 200 years ago. As a top aide to Prince Charles, David was keeper of the records of the Duchy of Cornwall. A classmate of mine at Oxford and a dear friend, he has offered keen insights over the years as our consulting guide to Southeast Asia, including the following on shopping and bargaining for all things in Asia.

Shopping in Southeast Asia is fun, and with a little care, rewarding. Each locale is renowned for certain items: Bangkok for gems, Hong Kong and Bangkok for jewelry and tailoring, Jakarta for batik.

Compare prices and bargain, except where a fixed price is displayed. Enjoy your shopping excursions and buy what you find attractive rather than what you consider a bargain. Remember, what appears to be genuine may not always be; if it is an antique or art, ask for a certificate of authenticity.

HONG KONG

From bird cages to bone china, brand names, and nighttime bazaars, Hong Kong is a veritable supermarket of the Orient, offering everything from high fashion to low-cost knick-knacks. You visit malls like Pacific Place, the Landmark, Ocean Centre, and Ocean Terminal for designer brands or browse through Stanley Market for everything from gift ideas to clothing, linen, and silk goods. Stroll along Hollywood Road for antiques and fascinating bits of history such as Mao badges. Not far from the Regent Hotel are the Jade Market in Yau Mau Tei and Bird Alley in Mongkok, both rich in local color. In the evening visit Temple Street Market for souvenirs, T-shirts sportswear, and gadgets or stop to have your fortune read.

Hong Kong is one of the world's largest diamond-trading centers and a major exporter known for its sophisticated design. Cultured and freshwater pearls, jade, and other semiprecious stones are abundant. Exclusive brands of watches are attractively priced. Custom tailoring is good value, but allow time for three fittings.

Typically, the prices of electronics, computer equipment, and cameras are no lower than discount prices in the West. Depending on where you live, though, the savings are probable thanks to Hong Kong's "no tax" status. If you do want something in these categories, compare prices, make sure there is a valid international guarantee and that accessories are included, and check that the package you receive includes the exact goods you selected.

MACAO

One hour away from Hong Kong by high-speed jetfoil is the former Portuguese enclave of Macao off the Chinese mainland. With its plethora of casinos, it's quickly becoming known as the Las Vegas of the East. Its many winding streets have antique shops with colonial curios and bits and pieces from a China of long ago. There are also shops selling good reproduction Chinese furniture and household items at truly bargain prices. A visit makes for an interesting day of shopping with delicious country-style Portuguese cuisine and wines to top it off.

SINGAPORE

Singapore is a shopper's paradise, an emporium of the South Seas. There's no duty on most items, and just about everything you could wish for is here, from the latest fashions (look for the creations of respected locals Benny Ong, Celia Lo, and Tan Yoong) to gold, silver, jade, pewter, pearls, leather shoes, silk, batik, antiques, and handicrafts from all over Asia. And that's just a start.

Orchard Road is Singapore's Fifth Avenue, with huge department stores like Takashimaya and Tang's along with shopping centers like the Promenade, Centerpoint, and Lucky Plaza for cameras and electronic items.

Take a break from the glitter and glass and discover interesting buys on a ramble through Chinatown, Little India, and Arab Street, where tiny lanes harbor shops full of unknown treasures. On Northbridge Road and in People's Park, reputable goldsmiths sell items by weight, set at the day's prices. Precious stones are also a good buy. For antiques, browse in the shop houses of Cuppage Road. The night market at the Singapore Handicraft Centre sells work from 16 Asian countries. The Consumer's Association and Singapore Tourist Promotion Board–approved shops display the Merlion sign, a lion-headed mermaid. The STPB has excellent shopping guides. The one problem with Singapore is knowing when to stop!

BANGKOK

How would you like your sapphire? Black or blue, star or plain? Bangkok is famous for precious gems and jewelry at very fair prices. Jewelry is best at shops displaying the trade's official emblem: a gold ring mounted with a ruby. Be sure to obtain a detailed receipt and certificate of authenticity. Check the workmanship carefully, as this varies from shop to shop. Thai silk is also sought after, including the famous tie-dyed mat mee silks of the Northeast, and the tailors are phenomenal. Much celadon pottery matches the finest from China, and there are plenty of beguiling handicrafts like dolls and spirit houses. Remember that you can't take Buddha images out of Thailand, and antiques and works of art require a license. For a wide range of folk arts and handicrafts, visit one of the Chitra-Ladda support foundation shops that are under the patronage of Her Majesty the Queen. A special buy here are the decorative rattan baskets made in the traditional way, a craft the queen herself revived as a way to give rural farmers an alternative source of income.

CHIANG MAI

Shinawatra Trading is one of the oldest and largest silk factories here, with top-quality bolts of silk, bedroom slippers, ties, and men's and women's silk suits. Jolie Femme sells silk in many forms, with an emphasis on women's clothing.

Napa Lacquer is one of many interesting lacquerware factory show-rooms. It has especially handsome boxes, as well as many nice gift items.

Iyara Art Company has wonderful terra-cotta pieces and antique furniture. Chiang Mai Silverware engraves intricate designs on soft silver: bowls, furniture, and jewelry. You can watch the entire work process.

Prempracha's Collection has an enormous complex of showrooms with a variety of goods: silks, textiles, antiques, furniture, and wood carvings, as well as whimsical blue-and-white porcelain. The Umbrella-Making Center sells charming hand-painted umbrellas and parasols. Lanna Thai has some of the best prices for high-quality Thai silver at 79 Chiang Mai-Sankampaeng Road.

If you're adventurous, try the Night Bazaar after dinner. It's located on Changklang Road near the junction of Suriwong Road and operates from 7–10 p.m. It's a crowded, crazy, carnival atmosphere. Watch your wallet.

JAKARTA

Look for Javanese carvings, Wayang puppets, hand-painted silk batiks, Sumatra songkets, Sulawesi silks, haute couture, Palembang jumputan, and contemporary jewelry. Striking jewelry, sensational fashions, and stunning paintings show that Indonesia offers more than puppets and batik. But don't pass those up—you'll find them splendid buys, too.

Jalan Surabaya is Jakarta's main open-air curio market with crafts from all the major islands. It's advisable to bargain for at least 50 percent off the starting price. The market on Jln Ciputat Raya is great for antique furniture. Serious art collectors should visit Edwin's Gallery for paintings, old maps, original lithographs, and prints, and Duta Fine Arts for its well-priced works by Indonesian artists. Obin House in Menteng is another great secret. It sells not only art but also gold, gemstones, handmade batiks, Java tea, and tobacco. For Chinese porcelain left by traders of centuries ago, head for Jln Kebon Sirih Timur Dalam or Cony Art and Curio in Melawai for Sung, Yuan, Ming, and Ching porcelain.

Tradition and the modern world inspire local jewelers. They work in gold (prices are good), silver, and other metals using cultured and baroque pearls, precious and semi-precious gems, and opals, including the bewitching black opal. Blok M is a good area to look around, with its department stores, plazas, and shops of well-known local jewelers. For excellent pearl and gemstone bargains, make a trip to Fandiasta in West Jakarta.

Crafts to look for include Sumba blankets, Sumatra songkets, South Sulawesi silks, Balinese wood carvings, masks and puppets from Java, rattan baskets from Lombok, jumputan or tie-dye from Palembang (also haute-couture palembang by renowned Indonesian designer Ghea Sukarya), and primitive arts from Irian Jaya. Or go to Jaya Ancol Dreamland with its arts and craft center, where you can see craftsmen making such items as exquisitely carved teak furniture. For something unique, take a day out to Bogor and visit Bengkel Gamelan, one of Indonesia's few remaining gong factories. Bargain at least 10 percent off the price.

You can't leave without at least one batik. For magnificent examples, visit Danar Hadi and Iwan Tirta. Indeed wherever you go in Indonesia, you'll find an abundance of creativity!

Pulau Pangkor, a 20-kilometer-long (12-mile) brush with rural Malaysian reality, the ship cuts past landscaped ports to craggy volcano peaks rising out of the water in a crystal sea, under hanging white clouds, as if to pay tribute to the gods. The Batong Islands are close to the Malaysian island of Langkawi and are characterized by towering rock formations and beautiful beaches. Crystal clear seas team with marine life, ideal for snorkeling and diving or simply enjoying a relaxing swim. The coves are all yours.

The breathtaking Malaysian island of Langkawi is one of a group of 104 islands scattered in the calm seas off the northernmost tip of Peninsular Malaysia. The clear tropical  waters here provide some of the most spectacular swimming and diving in the world, while scenes of paddy fields contoured into limestone hillsides, lush tropical forests, and high tumbling waterfalls entrance nature lovers on land.

Malacca and the Spice Trade are inseparably associated. From the time of the early Renaissance explorers onward, it was the control of the Malaccan Straits that dictated who would own the most precious treasures of the Orient, its spices. The Portuguese, the Dutch, and the British each ruled Malacca at one time or another. Explore opulent private mansions built in the distinctive Peranakan colonial style and filled with priceless Chinese antiques.

Reaching Thailand, the sheer-sided sea mountains rising vertically out of Phang Nga Bay are some of Thailand's most spectacular scenery. The islands have crisp white sandy beaches and superb coral reefs. Ko Hong, part of the Ko Hong archipelago, has a spacious lagoon. One of the prettiest bays in the area, huge monolithic rocks provide shade all day long on a beautiful white silica sand beach.

"It is part of my sea life to which my memory returns most often, since there is nothing to remember but what is good and I assure you, I have preserved that voyage with warm regard and happy memory."

— Joseph Conrad

PHUKET ISLAND

Phuket, Thailand's largest island, lies in the Andaman Sea and is joined to the mainland by a causeway. The landscape is one of lush green hills, coconut groves, and rubber plantations, with a coastline dotted with a dozen spectacular beaches. Phuket is a paradise with the lively area of Patong providing the up-beat resort life with its many shops, leaving the rest of the island to show off her natural beauty and unspoiled culture. Making a tsunami comeback, Phuket has restored many fine beaches and accommodations.

AMANPURI
Pansea Beach
Tel: 66-76-324-333
www.amanresorts.com

A super place to stay in Phuket is Amanpuri, a glamorous hotel that occupies a splendid location on Pansea Beach. With a number of oceanfront pavilions on stilts, each with a large bedroom, bath-and-dressing room combination, and an open-air terrace with a temple like gazebo, the decor is tastefully understated.

THE BANYAN TREE PHUKET
Tel: 66-76-324-374
www.banyantree.com

A favored resort that offers the ultimate in privacy. You'll find the main pool by the lodge virtually deserted because most guests prefer the comfort and intimacy of their own villas, especially the accommodations that include a private pool or a spa pool.

It's refreshing to wake up in a spa pool villa, press a button that opens the curtains and find that your bed sits in a glass cube surrounded by lily ponds. High walls surround the villa, ensuring privacy. A superbly trained staff that attends to villa guests alone will arrange for all of your meals to be served on your patio, or in your living room if you prefer. The private pool villas are also luxurious but are smaller, with a small anteroom and a bedroom. They have splendid bathrooms with outdoor sunken rock bathtubs.

LE ROYAL MERIDIEN PHUKET YACHT CLUB HOTEL
Nai Harn Beach
Tel: 66-76-381-156
www.phuket-yachtclub.com

The hotel stands at one end of pretty crescent-shaped Nai Harn Beach and is built up a hillside in nine steps, each step being a floor. The elevator goes only to the sixth floor, but the best rooms are on floors seven through nine (No. 01 to No. 08 on each floor). In all, there are 109 rooms.

BANGKOK

Called the "city of angels," Bangkok's real name in Thai is Krungthep Mahanakorn Amorn Ratanakosindra Ayuthaya Mahadirok-phop Nopharatana Rachathanee Burirom Udomrachanivet Mahasthan amorn Pimarn Avatarn Sathit Sakkatuttiya Vishnukarm Prasit. It is listed in the Guinness Book of World Records as the longest name of any place in the world. For short, this

metropolis is called Krungthep Mahanakorn—translation: "city of angels."

While watching the sunrise at a temple and monks collecting alms, I marveled at what peace can be found in the midst of such a chaotic metropolis. If you're stuck in a typically nasty traffic jam, you'll wonder if any magnificent sight or the warmth of the Thai people could possibly be worth the frustration of trying to get from one place to the next. But this cultural hub in Southeast Asia has much to catch your interest. Most certainly, Bangkok will assault your senses. It's fascinating and indulgent, but it requires time and patience.

You might want to lose your way intentionally to discover the hidden parts of the city that you might otherwise miss. You can always find a taxi to take you back to your hotel.

All through Thailand, you'll find fabulous architecture, beautiful beaches and islands, inexpensive shopping, fantastic food, exotic hill-tribe villages, ancient ruins, and all the amenities as well. Thailand is a place that can excite the mind, tantalize the senses, and take care of most everyday needs. The balance between comfort and excitement is near perfect.

★ THE ORIENTAL BANGKOK
48 Oriental Avenue
Tel: 66-2-236-0400

Truly one of the world's outstanding hotels. The entrance lounge with handsome teakwood-bell chandeliers establishes an elegant atmosphere. Appointments and colors are exceptionally pleasing and restful. Hostesses wear Thai *chitrlada* costumes in harmonizing colors. Each of its 396 rooms has a slightly different decor. You will have superb service and luxurious living.

The hotel is on the Chao Phraya River, where there is constant activity. Outdoor breakfasts overlooking the river are memorable, and the sumptuous nightly barbecue feasts on the terrace with countless Thai dishes are an experience you will remember. Try Lord Jim's for seafood, Sola Rim Naam for Thai food, or the Normandie for French cuisine.

The Oriental is home to its famous cooking school where guests learn to prepared exquisite Thai dishes.

SHANGRI-LA HOTEL
89 Soi Wat Suan Plu, New Road, Bangrak
Tel: 66-2-236-7777

The 868-room Shangri-La Hotel provides deluxe amenities, and the housekeeping is impeccable. Its most desirable section is the 174-room Krungthep Wing, which has its own entrance. Every room in this part of the hotel enjoys an uninterrupted view of the Chao Phraya River from individual terraces. The four-story atrium lobby, with arched bridges over running streams surrounded by tropical greenery, is a welcome refuge. Room amenities are similar to those in the main hotel, except for bidets, walk-in closets, and a separate bath, shower, toilet, and vanity. Appointments are more elegant. The wing also has its own restaurant, the Veranda, on the second floor, and a riverside swimming pool.

☆ THE PENINSULA BANGKOK
333 Charoennakorn Road, Klongsan
Tel: 66-2-861 2888
www.peninsula.com

The Peninsula Bangkok is an outpost retaining all the high service standards international travelers have come to expect from the Peninsula Group. The hotel takes full advantage of its location on the Chao Phraya River, with each of its 370

SHOPPING IN THAILAND

Thailand's capital is a shopper's paradise. It is a leader in gemstones, so you can expect settings and designs in the better jewelry shops to be comparable to those available in Western capitals. Precious and semiprecious stones are among the best buys, especially sapphires and rubies. Prices of Burmese jade and Phuket pearls are about half of what you would expect to pay for comparable quality and settings in New York. But if you aren't gemstone savvy, be careful, as fakes abound. Shop only at stores that display the emblem of the Thai Gem & Jewelry Traders Association, and with pricier purchases always request a certification of authenticity.

Bangkok's other special values include Thai silks, which are thicker than most other silks and very durable. Thai cotton has durable quality and varied designs. Many strikingly original batik patterns are available.

Lacquerware, pewter, enamel, and ceramics are all produced in Thailand and are good buys. Look also for Burmese crafts such as gold-and-black lacquerware, kalaga bas-relief wall hangings, and wooden puppets and marionettes, all moderately priced.

Most of the best stores are in giant vertical shopping malls. Usually three or four stories high, they are bursting with individual shops. The malls are reached by shuttle boats from hotels such at the Oriental and the Shangri-La. Taxis are inexpensive; it's best to travel mid-morning or mid-afternoon. Use only metered taxis.

The best values are clothes, especially custom-made clothes. The many tailors compete with those in Hong Kong for quality and price.

THE SIAM SOCIETY

RAMA I ROAD

Founded in 1904 under royal patronage, the Siam Society sponsors lectures and artistic performances. It also regularly conducts one- to seven-day tours of cultural interest in Thailand and neighboring countries. All are done in English, and we feel they are superior to those offered by the Oriental Hotel's Thai Cultural Program.

The Kamthieng House, on the society's grounds, is a quiet oasis at the center of this very animated city. It is itself a historical treasure of 19th-century northern Thai architecture and artifacts.

The society's excellent library houses approximately 20,000 books on Southeast Asia.

large rooms offering fine river views. Decor is tasteful, making extensive use of Asian contemporary art, especially work from Thailand and Vietnam.

BANGKOK'S REGENT FOUR SEASONS HOTEL
155 Rajdamri Road
Tel: 66-2-251-6127

Not on the river but located nearer the city's center and opposite the Royal Bangkok Racetrack, this hotel's rooms are attractive and done in excellent taste. An outdoor pool, squash court, and luxury spa are across the river. It has several restaurants, including the excellent Spice Market.

THE GRAND HYATT ERAWAN
494 Rajdamri Road
Tel: 66-2-254-1234

The Grand Hyatt has risen, phoenix-like, on the site of the old Erawan Hotel. Its design captures the essence of a palatial Thai residence. The striking atrium lobby of landscaped silk-foliage trees is complete with cascading streams, and the $1 million art collection even spills over into the restrooms. Hardwood floors with accent rugs are standard in all 400 rooms, and amenities include executive desks, walk-in closets, and bay-window views of the city. There are two good restaurants, a jogging track, a terraced swimming pool, and tennis and squash courts.

SHOPPING

JIM THOMPSON STORES
Oriental Place Shopping Arcade, 9 Surawong Road
Tel: 66-2-234-4900

The inventory includes dresses, evening gowns, blouses, and other clothing, all either ready-made or to-measure. Also there is an abundance of handbags, neckties, accessories, and yard goods. (Also at 30/1 Soi Charoen Krung and 38 Charoen Krung Road.)

COTTON HOUSE
Phayathai Road near Siam Square
Tel: 66-2-251-7549

A shop packed with unusual new and antique clothing items of Thai, Cambodian, and Laotian fabrics. The materials are also available in narrow rectangular lengths just as they came off the hand looms intended to be made up into traditional sarongs.

THE RIVER CITY SHOPPING COMPLEX
Next to the Royal Orchid Sheraton Hotel
23 Trok Rongnamkhaeng, Yota Road

This complex holds the greatest concentration of Asian antique shops in Bangkok, with beautiful paintings, scrolls, brass sculpture, wood temple reliefs, jewelry, and furniture from Thailand, Burma, Cambodia, and China. It's relatively expensive, and bargaining is expected. Buddhas of any size or shape cannot be exported. An antiques auction is held here on the first Saturday of every month.

CHAROEN KRUNG
AND SI PHRAYA ROADS
Ne Old, 149/2-3 Suriwongse Road

A noted antiques dealership, this establishment is known for its many bona fide treasures, which, though expensive, can be negotiated. It is located a few blocks from Jim Thompson's.

⭑ WORLD GROUP TAILORS
Near the Oriental Hotel
Tel: 66-2-234-4799 or 66-2-237-5274

Modestly without mention, this group is the custom tailor for the king. These tailors are among the best and are reasonably priced. They are my tailors.

World Group offers wide range of quality fabrics imported from England, Scotland, France, India, and China, along with fabrics made in Thailand. Silks, cottons, wools, wool blends, linen, super 100 wool, super 110, 120, 150, and super 180 wools are always in stock, including classic worsteds in wool to twills in cottons and wools and gabardine, alpaca and super merino wool, cashmeres and cashmere blends. A suit with two fittings can be constructed in less than a week.

For shirts, there are cotton twills, oxford, and Egyptian cottons. Chinese silk and Thai silks, along with silk blends,

are available for blouses and dresses. Patterns and plain materials are used for their custom-tailored clothing: classic stripe, windowpane check, twill, end-on-end weave, and white-on-white patterns.

Materials for suits are offered in flannels, wools, cashmere blends, pinstripes, chalk stripe, Prince of Wales check, and windowpane check all in the classic colors. Sports jackets and blazers can be made in blue flannel, linen, hounds tooth, dogtooth, tweed, or Harris Tweed.

Should a particular fabric, color, or pattern not be found, they will locate it and provide the best for you.

⭑ JAMES FASHION
344/2-6 Sukhothai Road
Suanchitlada, Dusit
Tel: 66-6-686-9903

James Fashion is arguably one of Bangkok's most popular and best tailors. The staff is very friendly and knowledgeable, and you can't help but feel special for the way you are treated from the moment you step inside the store. They offer and have on display an enormous range of fabrics and styles. Bolts of beautiful Thai silks, English and Italian wools and blends, and Egyptian cottons fill both floors of the bustling establishment. They provide hotel drop-offs free of charge and their prices are startlingly inexpensive, given the attention to detail and quality of the materials they provide. This company will even accommodate the oversees clients by sending swatches in return for measurements or a perfectly tailored garment in return for one of their handmade duplicates or original pieces. London shirtmakers are charging upward of $240 a shirt these days. James has the same quality for $40.

They have a wide range of fabrics and styles to choose from. Suits, shirts, pants, coats, jackets, tuxedos, and dresses can be made to measure and custom tailored to fit before being shipped to the client's doorstep via international couriers for safe and fast door-to-door delivery. Quality and fit are guaranteed; turnaround and delivery are amazing.

SEEING BANGKOK

The Grand Palace is Bangkok's leading attraction. It was completely restored in 1982. Adjoining it is Wat Phra Keo, the royal chapel, in which the king carries out his religious duties, and where the famous Emerald Buddha resides.

Bang Pa-In, the summer palace of Thai kings, is about 70 kilometers (45 miles) north of Bangkok. The small pavilion in the middle of the lake, Aisawan Thi Paya, is one of the finest extant examples of Thai architecture. A pleasant way to get to Bang Pa is by boat on either the *Oriental Queen* or *Orchid Queen*.

Farther north and also reachable by the two *Queen* boats is Ayuthaya, the ancient capital of Siam. Nearby are Wat Mahathat and Wat Phra Sri Samphet, 14th-century Khmer monasteries. They were built with flat bricks, covered with stucco, and then gold. However, the buildings were sacked by the Burmese in 1767, and the gold was removed.

Within the city there are more than 300 wats, Thai monastery-temple compounds.

CHIANG MAI

From the frenetic capital, the hill-country gateway of Chiang Mai is accessible by train or an easy one-hour flight. The "Rose of the North" is the nation's second largest city and has excellent food and accommodations. It's also increasingly making a name for itself in the arts, especially accessories of modern design. It's refreshingly cooler than Bangkok, and it doesn't have the fast pace, traffic, or pollution.

Chiang Mai is in the hilly Golden Triangle, the region where much of the world's opium is grown. It is an ancient city and was once the capital of an independent kingdom. The moat around the original town is still intact.

There are several old and interesting temples, among them Wat Suan Dawk and Wat Chiang Man, historically the most important temple in the city and the oldest, dating from 1300. It is notable for its small, ancient Buddha-image made of precious stones.

Wat Chedi Luang is the largest relic in northern Thailand and an impressive leftover from Chiang Mai's golden age. It contains a huge reclining Buddha.

Phra Tat Doi Suthep, at a height of 1,100 meters (3,600 feet), is the temple most people want to see. According to legend, the site was chosen by a royal elephant. The view is splendid.

THE REGENT RESORT CHIANG MAI
502 Mae Rim, Samoeng Road
Tel: 66-5-329-8181

Offering luxurious accommodations in two-story Lanna-style villas with polished teakwood floors, a spa bath, living and dining areas, and your own personal housekeeper, this is a perfect place to stay as a base for side excursions.

The best shopping is located east of the city on Sankampaeng Road. It has a multitude of factory

Traveling Past a Thousand Shades of Khaki

The best way to return back to Singapore is by the *Eastern & Oriental Express* (www.orient-express.com). Following the success of the famous *Venice-Simplon-Orient-Express,* the *Eastern & Oriental Express* made history as the first-ever train to transport passengers directly from Singapore and Kuala Lumpur to Bangkok and return.

This luxury train was first built in Japan in 1972 and operated as the Silver Star train in New Zealand. Its carriages were then remodeled and designed by Gérard Gallet, who with James Sherwood, supervised refurbishment of both the British Pullman and the *Venice-Simplon–Orient-Express.*

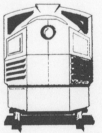

An enormous amount of work went on behind the scenes to put the *E&O* on the rails. The same team of people who had worked on the *Orient-Express* created the interiors. They added the required air-conditioning system, made the carriages compatible with the Malaysian and Thai railway systems, and extended the windows in the dining cars for panoramic views.

The inspiration for the interiors is derived from the East.

The carriage walls are decorated with veneers of wooden marquetry with Eastern designs, while the bar and restaurant cars are decorated in Chinese and Thai lacquer using Malaysian motifs with Thai wall carvings and engraved mirrors. The open deck of the Observation Car also has an Asian theme, and for much of the train local materials have been used.

On board the *E&O,* the atmosphere returns to the colonial age of rattan chairs on the veranda, linen suits, and tea dances. The onboard cuisine continues the same very high standards already established by the *Orient-Express* in Europe.

The inaugural journey departed in September 1993, and the *E&O* quickly built for itself a high reputation for providing one of the most adventurous and exciting rail journeys in the world. In addition to the two-night journey between Singapore and Bangkok, and return, the *E&O* also travels overnight to Chiang Mai from Bangkok.

Whichever journey you take, you are assured of the highest quality food and service while enjoying dramatic views across the Southeast Asian landscape.

Eastern & Oriental Express
Singapore • Kuala Lumpur • Butterworth • Kwai • Bangkok

showrooms and workshops bursting with crafts: parasols, silks, cottons, jewelry, silver, leather, ceramics, lacquerware, and more. If you see something you like, buy it right away, because it may be gone by the time you make up your mind. This doesn't preclude bargaining over the price, however. The night market showcases all kinds of wares, and you can watch local hill-tribe members buying and selling.

BEYOND CHIANG MAI

The city's sights can be seen in a day, but most people use the town as a jumping-off point for exploring the region. Several hill tribes live in the area, and trekkers can visit tribal villages.

If you're looking for a day trip, go see the elephants being trained at the Elephant Conservation Center near Lampang, a two-hour drive to the southeast (buses leave every 20 minutes). This village also has interesting blue-and-white pottery and an old fortress temple, Wat Lampang Luang.

Other day-trip possibilities include Lamphun, just south of Chiang Mai, which has 60 Buddhas standing in niches on the outside its famous temple, and Baw Sang for its lacquerware, textile, bronze, umbrella, and jade factories. For another driving excursion, a half-hour away, is Phuping Palace, the royal family's winter residence

Mae Sai, the northernmost point in Thailand, is a four-hour bus journey from Chiang Mai. There are wonderful markets, including a puppet market and the import point for Myanmar's rubies and sapphires. The gem market, where you can watch the bidding on imported stones, is downtown, across the street from the police station.

Chiang Rai, northeast of Chiang Mai, is a small town in the Himalayan foothills, close to the border of Laos, in the Golden Triangle.

⑬ HISTORY ON HORSEBACK: TEN DAYS THROUGH THE LOIRE VALLEY

What better way to discover the Loire than on horseback and, at the end of the day, to be met by your groom and greeted by your host, a count at his castle.

There are breathtaking sights along the ride. Beautiful Chenonceau, built over a bridge and the River Cher, with one wing on the right bank, the other on the left, and the intimate Azay-le-Rideau, built at the same time in 1515, are highlights. Each day, take a picnic break at a landmark setting. Each evening, accommodations can be at country inns and châteaus.

Patrick Germaine, an Olympic equestrian, was our guide; the horses were good and well groomed. The ride averaged five hours a day for medium to professional riders.

France is ideally suited for a horseback-riding vacation. Here the idea of equestrian travel was reborn and is most highly developed. Ride leaders in France are required to take long courses and pass exams on leading riding tours and horsemanship.

The countryside in many parts of France is unspoiled and beautiful with many rights-of-way kept open, which makes riding through it on horseback a real pleasure. Riding trails in France usually avoid paved roads. Spectacular castles, walled towns, and ancient monasteries are everywhere. It is a thrill to ride into a castle courtyard on horseback like a traveler of old.

Each region has a unique character with its own history, cuisine, wine, architecture, and topography. French food and wine are justly famous, and you will have every opportunity to savor them, with an appetite made keener by an active day of horseback riding. Accommodations vary from small village hotels to châteaus, but are generally picturesque and comfortable.

Equitours is a company offering rides on horseback in 70 countries around the world. For more information go to www.equitours.com.

JEWELS OF THE LOIRE

This riding tour visits many of the most famous castles in France—indeed, in the world— including Chenonceau and Cheverny. In the centuries before the French Revolution, this valley was the scene of an unprecedented flowering of culture when French kings and nobles vied with one another to build the most magnificent structures and to decorate them exquisitely. There are wonderful opportunities for gallops through some of the old hunting preserves of the French nobility. Staying in smaller private châteaus contributes to the spirit of this grand adventure.

DAY 1
We were met at the railway station in Blois at 7 p.m. and transferred to the hotel for dinner and overnight. There was a briefing on handling the horses.

DAY 2
We departed the hotel at 8:00 a.m. and transferred to the stable. I was introduced to my horse, a fine thoroughbred called Jean-Philippe. There were ten of us from all over the world, and all spoke English. We mounted and headed toward the south across the wild region of forests and vineyards (famous for its wild game) known as the Sologne and the valley of the kings. A picnic lunch was served in the forest. In the afternoon we rode toward the banks of the River Cher and the Gallo-Roman ruins of Thésée. We overnighted in Montrichard.

DAY 3
After breakfast we transferred to the horses and rode out across the Sologne into the

ILE DE FRANCE

PASSENGER'S NAME

CABIN NO. _____ SAILING

FINAL DESTINATION

French Line

EQUITOURS

Equitours offers tested and proven horseback riding vacations on six continents. Here's why.

Careful Selection. Over the last 30 years they have developed a broad range of riding vacations for your enjoyment and fulfillment as a traveler. Only a few of the best horseback riding opportunities in each category have been included after careful research. Equitours constantly monitors the quality of the tours they sponsor. Your safety is always a priority with them and you will find these vacations give terrific value for the price. There is a wide choice in price, geographical location and riding ability required.

Expert Advice. Knowledgeable ride consultants are a wonderful resource entirely at your disposal. They have many years of collective experience with horseback-riding vacations and can answer all your specific questions about a given holiday. The consultants are thoroughly acquainted with the trips they handle and have taken most of them personally. They can advise you wisely in choosing the best options to meet your personal vacation goals.

Equitours has a unique advantage in organizing and understanding these tours because the owners, Bayard, Mel, and Richard, have their own Wyoming dude ranch where they have offered horseback riding vacations since 1971. The ranch raises and trains horses and provides insight to all aspects of a riding vacation. They ride personally with their guests every day during the season and stay in close touch with preferences and equestrian goals.

Equitours believes in equestrian travel as a way to practice a fascinating sport and at the same time to interact with a different culture and other peoples. You will find that a common love of the horse is very effective in forming bonds of friendship quickly with people all over the world. They travel in small groups to visit places which are often well off the beaten track and sometimes so far off that tourists are a curiosity. You can sip tea with a prince in remote in Rajasthan or drink ouzo with a Greek fisherman in an isolated Aegean village.

The company makes every effort to ensure that all riders are well matched to the ride and the difficulties are explained as clearly as possible. Equitours encourages those who want to test and hone their skills to come first to the ranch, where you can always ride at your own level or choose a lesson program or an easy European ride.

WORLDWIDE HORSEBACK RIDING ADVENTURES
10 Stalnaker Street, Dubois, Wyoming
Tel: 307-455-3363

beginnings of the vineyards of Touraine, stopping to have lunch at the Château de Chemery (13th, 15th, and 16th centuries). In the afternoon we visited that beautiful part of the Sologne where grapes for the excellent local wine are grown. We enjoyed some long canters, then stopped at the winery of Mr. August Bodin in Touraine and tasted his wines. We continued on to reach the magical Château of Gué Péan with stables. We spent the night at Château Razay after dinner at the inn of Château Montpoupon. After an exhilarating last few days, I soaked for hours in a hot tub, then borrowed an inn pillow to cushion my sore derrière.

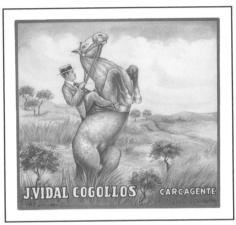

DAY 4

At Gué Péan, we trotted through the valley of the Cher by way of Thésée. We crossed the Cher over the bridge at Anges and walked along the river where the hillsides were covered with grapevines, until we reach the Abbaye d'Aiguevives, where we had lunch with an impressive view of the surrounding countryside. The delightful Château de Montpoupon is a fascinating hunting museum. We left the horses at les Bourdinières for the night.

DAY 5

In the Vallières les Grandes, we left the farm of Lereau to gallop northwest through forests and countryside to the Château of Amboise, where we had a tasteful and well deserved lunch. Afterward, a visit the château was followed by a return to the farm in Lereau.

DAY 6

After breakfast, we rejoined our horses and made our way again across the countryside and through the forests to the Château of Chaumont on the Loire, which we approached on horseback. Lunch was at the Club Hippique les Frileuses. Afterward, we visited the château, then continued along the Loire to Candé, where we spent the night.

DAY 7

After mounting up at Candé, we rode southwest through vineyards, forests, and countryside to reach Château Fougerès for lunch. In the afternoon we cantered to Cheverny, one of the finest jewels of the Loire.

DAY 8

After a fine breakfast we transferred to the Château of Chambord and to the Blois railway station.

⑭ THE SILK ROAD

As far back in history as the first century, silk and other precious commodities have been transported by caravan between China and the Middle East along several alternative routes for mountains and deserts. Even Rome was formidably influenced by the rigorous path the exotic fabric had to travel over the Silk Road.

Following the route of Marco Polo along the fabled road through Imperial China, from oasis to oasis, exotic city

to remote outpost, exploring ancient treasures and artifacts, is a rigorous undertaking made easier by a modern caravan of private trains, carrying you comfortably on an epic overland journey along a great highway of trade. Or you may fly.

The journey really begins in Kashgar, or Kashi, some 3,200 kilometers (2,000 miles) by air from Beijing. Two thousand years ago it was a great trading center, where long camel caravans that crossed the forbidding Taklamakan Desert brought goods from Xi'an. Other caravans continued north to Mongolia and Russia, west to Persia and the Mediterranean, or south to India.

Even after the Silk Road collapsed in the 12th century, Kashgar maintained its trading prominence because of its favored location surrounded on three sides by the huge mountain ranges of the Pamirs, Karakoram, and Tsien Shan. On the other side of these mountains lived the Mongols, Uzbecks, Tajicks, and Indians, all of whom congregated in Kashgar to trade. Still today, the Sunday market is one of the world's great sights.

Soon after the emergence of Buddhism in what today is northern India and Pakistan, followers traveled the Silk Road into China, where great monuments, tombs, caves, and other relics remain and make Turkistan a treasure trove. In the 12th century, Islam, following the same route, pushed Buddhism farther east and is now the predominant religion in Chinese Turkistan.

In the late 19th and early 20th centuries, Kashgar was the nerve center of the Great Game, the contest between Imperial Russia and Great Britain for the area. The great British and Russian consulates still stand.

From Xi'an in China, a westward-wandering caravan trail traveled over the mountain passes of Central Asia and across the deserts of Persia to the plains of India. Later, shipping routes took to the sea, and the Silk Road became a dusty trail.

Travelers today can trace the major stops of the Silk Route crossing Central Asia, from Beijing or Xi'an, the starting or ending points for the great trade caravans to Kashgar in Xinjiang region, and even to the fabled Samarkand and Tashkent.

A major garrison on the Silk Road is Lanzhou on the Yellow River. Through this corridor, Buddhism traveled east, with caravans passing Jiayuguan, the farthest point of the Great Wall, of which there still remains a remote section. Equally notable is the 1372 Jiayuguan Fort, the "impregnable pass under heaven," that dominates the city. Mountains soon level to arid lands and travelers on the Silk Route marvel at the stunning Buddhist art and the Singing Sands Mountains and Crescent Moon Lake.

The Taklamakan Desert oasis of Turpan eventually leads to the Tienshan and the celestial scenery at Tianche called Heaven Lake.

Many travelers fly to Beijing before flying to Kashgar to embark on the Silk Road.

CITS (www.cits.net) offers a variety of Silk Road tours.

SILK ROAD

BEIJING

At first sight, clusters of office skyscrapers and 40-story apartment buildings, intersected by huge boulevards with as many as 16 lanes, are all clogged with traffic. The airport is beautiful and efficiently designed. All taxis are metered and inexpensive; expect to pay about $3–$4 for the ride into the city. Have your hotel name and address written in Chinese to show to the driver, and, if possible, one person should sit next to driver as there is no leg room in the back seat.

Traffic completely disregards pedestrians; it can be virtually impossible to cross a boulevard. This is a good reason to stay at the Kempinski Hotel rather than the more conveniently located Palace: Although the Palace is within walking distance to the Forbidden City, the traffic makes walking dangerous.

KASHGAR

A landmark on the Silk Road is Kashgar. As early as 2,000 years ago, the city was a great trading center, and even today on a Sunday, Kashgar's market, the largest market in China, explodes with thousands of people trading in colonnaded bazaars, buying or selling, carpets to camels.

The walls of the Pamir Mountains rise to the south; its gaps are the old trading passes leading to Afghanistan, India, and Russia. The Silk Road goes on to the borders of China, to Uzbekistan's capital, Tashkent, and to the three pearls of the road: Samarkand, Bukhara, and the walled city of Khiva.

Kashgar is a dusty collection of mud houses and only the most hardened traveler would want to stay overnight in the town as the only lodging, the Seman Hotel, and is falling apart. But if you want to experience the Sunday market, you should do so either early in the morning or later in the afternoon, with one night in the city. The town does have a spotlessly clean haven of sorts, a coffee shop called the Caravan, run by an expat American. If you're game enough to survive a second night at the Seman Hotel, hire a car and driver for an excursion into the high Pamirs up to 3,600 meters (12,000 feet) to Karakuli Lake, which is surrounded by 24,000 peaks and is breathtaking. It's about 200 kilometers (125 miles) each way over a badly paved road that may be impassable in parts because of landslides. Hotels in the more remote Silk Road towns are inexpensive.

DUNHUANG

The next stop in retracing the Silk Route is Dunhuang, a gateway to several important sites. You can fly or take the train.

Mainline trains are comfortable, comparable to Russia's Trans-Siberian railroad, only much cleaner and efficient. The track is well maintained and smooth. All "Soft Class" compartments are for four, so if you wish privacy, insist on a double compartment, paying additionally for the other two seats. There is no sink or running water in the compartment, but washing and toilet facilities at the end of the car are clean. You may have the national travel service reserve and prepay for your meal in the dining car. Turpan station is about a two-hour drive from the city, and there is another four-hour drive across the desert from the Dunhuang station to the town. The Dunhuang Hotel is the nicest in town, offering accommodations that can be described as basic.

About 32 kilometers (20 miles) away are the ancient Buddhist murals and sculpture within the Mogao Caves, one of China's cultural highlights and one of the great artistic treasures of the world. Hire a local guide to escort you through a dozen of the more than 500 caves, and be sure to see the Library Cave. A few miles out of town are the world's highest sand dunes. From Dunhuang, it is about a five-hour drive across the Gobi Desert to Jiayaguan.

For hundreds of years, Jiayaguan was China's western boundary, and it's worth the effort to reach the city just to see the great Ming fortress at the far western end of the Great Wall. The Great Wall Hotel in Jiayaguan is new and very comfortable and has Internet access in the lobby. Ask for one of the remodeled rooms. When leaving in the morning, have your driver stop about half a kilometer (a quarter mile) from the edge of town. Climb the low hill on the left of the road for a magnificent view of the fortress. About 35 kilometers (20 miles) from town there is a small village with a enchanting mosque. From Jiayaguan, it is a short flight to the next stop on the itinerary.

LANZHOU

The sun is hardly ever seen in Lanzhou, the town with the country's worst air pollution. It has a great history dating back to the Bronze Age due to its strategic location on the Yellow River at the gateway to the Hexi corridor, the main communications link between China and Central Asia.

Lanzhou was a major station on the Silk Road. The Feitian Hotel is a newish high-rise with a Western restaurant. Ask for a room overlooking the main square and make time to visit the Gansu Provincial Museum, a Silk Road treasure house.

Labrang Lamasery is an exciting six-hour drive through rugged mountains, climbing to 2,700 meters (9,000 feet). At about the halfway point you come to Linxia, with its Great Mosque and its Great North Street, where there are a good many antiques shops. The merchandise is good, but much of it is likely to be recent reproductions. There is also a large selection of Tibetan and other carpets as well as many fox and wildcat pelts. After Linxia the drive winds through forbidding mountains and across flat alluvial plains that are farmed by Tibetans using wooden plows.

The Labrang Lamasery is home to some 3,000 monks. It dominates the small town of Xiahe. Here the streets are loaded with antique shops and are mixed with Tibetan country folk and red-robed monks. If you decide to overnight here, be up at sunrise and observe hundreds of chanting monks and parades of pilgrims journeying to the monastery.

XI'AN

The last stop is the ancient city of Xi'an. After the Great Wall, China's most interesting attraction is this city, originally known as Chang'an, with its army of some 8,000 life-size terra-cotta soldiers in battle formation, marching to the beat of the third-century B.C. The Emperor Qin Shihuang, who was enthroned at age 13, spent his life attempting to ensure his immortality. Fearing enemies in the afterlife, he had this column of warriors face east, the only direction from which Xi'an is unprotected by mountains.

Emperor Qin's terra-cotta army was discovered by a farmer in 1924, partially excavated and restored by archaeologists, and maintained with care during succeeding decades. The figures are strikingly realistic, each one with a face and stance that suggests an individual personality. Altogether, it is really a tour de force you won't regret.

Just as impressive is the size of the memorial, which occupies a roofed-in space as large as an old airplane hangar. From a pedestrian walkway there are views from every angle. Two of the royal bronze carriages in an adjoining building have clever details such as a tinted one-way window.

The city has several first-rate hotels, and it is a popular destination for visitors to China. Some travelers fly in and out in a day, just to see the terra-cotta figures, but an overnight stay is more rewarding.

Taking year-round rain and varying temperatures into account, May, September, and October are the best months to visit Xi'an. The city is about two hours from Beijing by air and more than three hours from Hong Kong. The 37-kilometer (23-mile) ride into the city from the airport is past wheat and cotton fields. The city itself is a major manufacturing center with a population of 6 million. Its factories and housing for workers sprawl at every approach, but once inside the old walled city you escape and can begin to enjoy its exotic atmosphere.

The promenade leading to Emperor Qin's museum is packed with stores and clamoring vendors, and your instinct may be to dismiss the lot of them. But the reproduction soldiers, chariots, and swords are near works of art. Your concierge can direct you to the many specialized markets selling clothing, porcelain, antiques, and beautifully crafted needlepoint rugs. Near the Xi'an Garden Hotel, there are a large number of upscale shops offering jade, watches, silks, and ancestral portraits.

This marks the end of the famed Silk Road that stretches 6,700 kilometers (4,200 miles) through the Mediterranean and over the centuries was the route of adventurers and traders seeking Asian treasure.

HONG KONG

Many adventure travelers journey on to Hong Kong, a city not to be missed. To travel from the Silk Road to Salisbury

THE SPA

PLATEAU AT THE GRAND HYATT
www.plateau.com/hk

A Hong Kong spa with a difference, Plateau at the Grand Hyatt provides a true resort spa experience in the heart of the city. With 7,500 square meters (80,000 square feet) dedicated to aesthetics, relaxation, fitness, and culinary excellence, Plateau provides a self-sufficient spa environment with a range of treatments as well as residential accommodation. The 23 guest rooms and suites are designed for guests who want the special convenience of the adjacent athletic, garden, and recreation facilities together with a unique guest room experience. Accessible via the 11th floor of the Grand Hyatt Hong Kong, Plateau is also available to outside visitors by appointment.

With fountains, pools, a waterfall, and extensive landscaping combining to form a peaceful oasis in the middle of Hong Kong, the special spa environment at Plateau assures privacy, seclusion, and a quiet escape, whether for a few hours, an entire day, or longer.

Specialists are available by appointment for a variety of spa services aimed at total relaxation, including massage, reflexology, and hydrotherapeutic massage. Private pools, sauna steam rooms, and peaceful surroundings are all part of the total spa experience.

Road is a transition into luxury. Hong Kong's Peninsula is the peak hotel experience in this exciting city. The new Grand Hyatt is also very special and with the new Plateau Spa, a perfect way to rejuvenate after after following Marco Polo's footsteps.

★ THE PENINSULA HONG KONG
Salisbury Road, Kowloon
Tel: 852-2920-2888

The Peninsula Hong Kong is one of the finest hotels in the world, if not the finest. Created in the glamorous 1920s, the legendary "Grande Dame of the Far East" continues to set hotel standards worldwide, offering a blend of the best of Eastern and Western hospitality in an atmosphere of unmatched grandeur and elegance.

It offers the ultimate in luxury accommodations with the most spacious hotel rooms and suites in Hong Kong. Each one of the hotel's opulent guest rooms is comfortable and stylish and equipped with advanced technology for the convenience of hotel guests, underlined, of course, by the world-famous Peninsula service.

The hotel's celebrated fleet of Rolls-Royce limousines, together with the Peninsula's helicopter shuttle service from the hotel's rooftop helipad, offer hotel guests luxurious transportation to and from Hong Kong International Airport and around Hong Kong.

The restaurants and bars at the Peninsula Hong Kong are among the most exclusive and most elegant in Hong Kong. Renowned as one of the best French restaurants in Asia, Gaddi's is Hong Kong's most elegant dining experience, while Felix offers a sleek and stylish city rendezvous with stunning views across the harbor. High tea at the Peninsula's Lobby is a Hong Kong institution, and the best authentic Cantonese food in town is served at Spring Moon.

STAY THE NIGHT IN XI'AN

SHANGRI-LA GOLDEN FLOWER HOTEL
8 Chang Le Road West
Tel: 86-29-323-2981
Outside the east wall and about 45 minutes from the archaeological site.

———•———

HYATT REGENCY XI'AN
158 Dong Da Jie
Tel: 86-29-723-1234
A reliable choice within the Old City walls.

———•———

XI'AN GARDEN
4 Dong Yan Yin Lu, Da Yan Ta
Tel: 86-29-526-1111
A more traditional hotel is this quiet inn with pagoda roofs, courtyard garden ponds, and walking bridges.

The Peninsula Spa is one of Hong Kong's most luxurious hotel spa facilities, complete with a state-of-the-art health club, huge Roman-style swimming pool, and beauty and hairdressing salon. The pool opens onto the hotel's sun terrace, providing an incredible view of Victoria Harbor and Hong Kong Island.

GRAND HYATT HONG KONG
1 Harbour Road
Tel: 852-2588-1234

The Grand Hyatt Hong Kong is Hyatt International's flagship property. Positioned among the finest hotels in the world and with magnificent views of Hong Kong's renowned Victoria Harbor, it lies in the very heart of this vibrant and exciting city. Of the Grand Hyatt Hong Kong's 556 guest rooms and suites, more than 70 percent of the accommodations command spectacular views of the harbor. Each one of the hotel guest rooms combines the subtle ambience of a contemporary residence with the latest business and entertainment technology.

The eight restaurants and bars at the Grand Hyatt offer a diverse array of dining and entertainment options. Gourmet cuisine created by some of Asia's most innovative chefs is complemented by five-star service and elegant surroundings. Grand Hyatt Hong Kong also offers 24-hour room service.

Guests can enjoy Cantonese delicacies in One Harbour Road, the hotel's 196-seat dual-level restaurant, while the chic Japanese restaurant Kaetsu features classic Japanese cuisine and an extensive sake menu. For those seeking more international dining options, why not try the authentic Italian cuisine in Grissini, all-day dining in the Grand Café, or afternoon tea and desserts in Tiffin.

15 CUBA REVISITED: ROMANCE, REVOLUTION, AND RENEWAL

Havana. The first time I saw this romantic colonial city was with my father in the 1950s. He was a distinguished doctor, a visiting professor at the University of Havana, and a close friend of Ernest Hemingway's. He took me along to be a guest at Finca Vigía, Hemingway's home, sitting above a pastel-painted, hilltop town called San

Francisco de Paula on the outskirts of Havana. I loved the adventure of it all.

Ernest Hemingway, with his wife, Mary, and 15 cats, lived in this simple, Spanish-style house for 20 years between assignments, starting in 1940. Among my most valued books are the ones he inscribed in his own hand to me. In his rough, raspy voice, he asked that I call him Papa, which I did.

When Papa wasn't standing at his mantle writing narrative or sitting at his Remington tapping dialogue, he took me fishing in the Gulf Stream—the "great blue river" he called it—for marlin, on his fabled *Pilar,* and then shooting at sugar plantations in Camagüey.

He downed daiquiris at the Floridida bar, shot clay pigeons at the Club de Cazadores, and trolled the Caribbean for German submarines, his inspiration for *Islands in the Stream.* When he left Cuba after Castro came to power, he offered his home to the country.

I remember Havana, the images framed with music and words, like a Walker Evans photograph: a dapper man in a white suit by a shoeshine stand; the grand wedding cake called the Hotel National; a cool mojito at Bodequita del Medio; the spectacular moving mambo bands outdoors at the Tropicana night club; the pretty girls strolling past the colonnades in their summer dresses; and music, always the music. Yes, I remember.

Forty years later, I returned with Andrew to this magnificent island as a fellow of the Center for Cuban Studies. Father and son enjoyed the same colorful painting, the same timeless landscape found only in Havana. In the evening, cigars are smoked and rum is tasted, in this interlude of memory.

The music and themes of Cuba are notes transcending time. The fragrance of verbena blooms, like the music, takes me back. Memory floats though open shutters and Palladian windows, to the sea, following the beautiful serpentine drive, the Malecon.

With that memory, I realize that whatever Havana may have lost, she has not lost her spirit.

HAVANA

The Old City resounds with a salsa beat. In room 511 at the Hotel Ambos Mundos is where Hemingway began writing *For Whom the Bell Tolls.* Outside the hotel, bands play in virtually every square, and many restaurants have live music at lunch and dinner.

Most of Havana is now charmingly decrepit, as few buildings beyond the Old City have been restored in the past 50 years. It appears that time has stood still since 1959.

But recognizing the tourist potential of the Old City, the government and private entrepreneurs have been investing, restoring, rebuilding, and upgrading there for some time. Old palaces are being converted into attractive hotels that retain their colonial atmosphere.

Old Havana has far more to offer in historic and colonial atmosphere than similar cities such as San Juan and Cartagena, and most people are invariably friendly and speak at least some English. Taxis are plentiful, and you'll see many ancient American cars that appear to be in a state of imminent collapse. Recently, Castro mandated that the dollar is no longer accepted currency and must be converted to pesos.

There is much to enjoy and see in Cuba, from the Hotel Nacional, and many fine restaurants like the open-air El Aljibe in Miramar, to the *paladares,* tables in private houses licensed by the government.

Not far from Havana are the lush green rolling hills of the Vuelta Abajo, a landscape of royal palms and tobacco plants topping rich red clay. Farther afield are the cities of Santiago de Cuba, Varadaro, Trinidad, Pinar del Rio, and the town of Viñales. Cuba is history in the making.

AMBOS MUNDOS
Obispo & Mercaderes
Tel: 53-7-33-9529

The Ambos Mundos was Hemingway's favorite; his room is kept as a shrine and is not available for guests. The hotel is probably best reserved for diehard Hemingway fans. There are 53 rooms, starting at about $100.

GOLDEN TULIP PARQUE CENTRAL
Neptuno e/ Prado y Zulueta
Tel: 53-7-66-6627

Located in the heart of the city, this is a contemporary hotel run by a Dutch group. It has a good feel about it, neither teeming with tourists nor, with 278 rooms, too small to offer extensive services. Its second-floor outdoor pool has a spa area offering wonderful views of the nearby Central Park and the Capitolio, the former Cuban Congress building that is a copy of the U.S. Capitol. The hotel is within walking distance of the Old Havana attractions. Doubles from $180.

★ THE HOTEL NACIONAL
Calles 21 & O
Tel: 53-7-33-3564, www.hotelnacionaldecuba.com

In the Vedado section, she has reigned over Havana's nightlife since being built in 1930 and still offers a Las Vegas–type revue, complete with "feather ladies." Situated on a bluff overlooking the sea, the hotel was designed to resemble the Breakers in Palm Beach, and it still has a palmy, art deco atmosphere. Its 450 rooms are large and still reasonably attractive, helping you to recall the Havana of old. Most rooms have sea views. There is a pool and an interior terrace that's a tranquil spot for relaxing with a mojito, the delicious cocktail of rum, lime juice, and fresh mint. Doubles from about $170.

CUBA'S BEST GUIDE

JULIO CÉSAR MOLINET
Tel: 53-7-30-8915
or at Havanatour: 53-7-33-0209

Unquestionably the best guide in Cuba, a gracious friend, a knowledgeable and gentle man.

CUBA REVISITED

HOTEL SANTA ISABEL
Calle Baratillo 9
Tel: 53-7-33-8201

The Hotel Santa Isabel is one of the most satisfying lodgings in Havana. It occupies a stunningly renovated 17th-century palace just off the Plaza de Armas, the square at the heart of the Old City. Its 27 air-conditioned rooms are large high-ceiling spaces attractively furnished in colonial style; bathrooms (marble) are huge. The staff is very helpful. Room 308, and others like it, has a terrace overlooking the square. The view from the roof, with the plaza on one side and the harbor and Morro Castle on the other, is memorable. There is no pool and the bustle on the square may be a bit taxing, but for interior atmosphere, this place can't be beat. Small, elegant dining room. Doubles from about $190, including a full breakfast.

MELIA COHIBA
Calle Paseo
Tel: 53-7-33-3636

In Vedado is the Melia Cohiba, located next to the Malecon, Havana's seaside promenade. It's a 22-story glass monolith with 460 rooms, shops, restaurants, bars, a fitness center with sauna, and two swimming pools—all in all, the type of contemporary hotel seen around the world and favored by business travelers. Doubles from about $190.

SOFITEL SEVILLA LA HABANA
Trocadero 55
Tel: 53-7-860-8560, www.sofitel.com

Completed in 1908, it has an exotic faux Moorish decor complete with a handsomely tiled lobby and bar. Graham Greene used the hotel as one of the settings in his novel *Our Man in Havana*. It is well located for visiting Old Havana, where most of the interesting attractions are to be found. Run by the French Accor group, all 178 rooms are air-conditioned and decorated a bit frowzily, but comfortably nevertheless. There is a lovely, open-air swimming pool and, in a city where good restaurants are scarce, a rooftop dining room that not only has splendid views but serves reasonably good food at acceptable prices. Have the grilled rock lobster and a bottle of the white Torres Viña Sol. Doubles from $100.

★ HOTEL COPACABANA
Calle 1ra. e/ 44 & 46, Playa
Telephone: 53-7-24-1037

The Copacabana is a unique hotel open to the sea, right on the Atlantic with a nautical flavor. Since 1957, the Copacabana has been part of the exclusive Miramar district in the western area of Havana. In 1992, it was remodeled and expanded. Its architecture is attractive and functional, and it has one of the great natural swimming pools in the world, built into the sea. The rooms are simple and very

nice. The Copacabana also has a freshwater pool. It is fully equipped for all sports.

The Copacabana's accommodations and restaurants all have Brazilian names. Some of the most characteristic are the typical and nice Itapoa and Tucán restaurants, the Caipirinha snack bar, and the widely known Ipanema discotheque. Its location near Quinta Avenida makes it easy to reach in just a few minutes. Doubles from $85.

RESTAURANTS

☆ EL ALJIBE
7ma avenida e/ calle 24-26, Miramar
Tel: 53-7-22-1584

One of our favorite restaurants in the world, the open-air El Aljibe grills fantastic chicken dishes in a tamarind-vinegar herb marinated sauce like no other, particularly the *pollo criollo*. It is served with rice, salad, fried plantains, and potatoes. The caramel-flavored ice cream for dessert is a joy. Dinner for two, without beverage, about $50.

EL PATIO
Calle San Ignacio & Emperado
Tel: 53-7-63-0862

A very pleasant place for lunch. Dishes of roast pork and grilled fish are tasty, and a singing guitar troupe animates the pretty colonial courtyard setting. Lunch for two, about $50.

EL TOCORORO
Calle 18 & 3ra avenida
Tel: 53-7-33-2209

El Tocororo is a favorite with the diplomatic community for its lobster and shellfish. Dinner for two, without wine, about $80.

THE DOCTORS OF MUSIC

One evening, just returning from the day's assignment with my colleague, Julio Molinet, a melody floated up to my bedroom terrace at the Hotel Nacional. It was curiously coming from a two-story open hacienda outside on the grounds of the hotel, a song by Isolina Carillo.

I went down to the hacienda to listen to the small Cuban band, and Julio introduced me to the musicians. They played with great spirit.

Performing at the Nacional was their night-time profession. I was amazed to discover they were all doctors.

As doctors during the day, each worked at a different clinic in the city. Because of Cuba's economic woes, there was never enough money to be had, or medicine to prescribe, but somehow they made it through the day.

Each afternoon, they examined patients, made rounds, and comforted the poor. In the evening, they were musicians, playing with all their heart.

They had met in medical school at the University of Havana and had all wanted to be musicians. In the end, they chose medicine. Music gave them their humanity, their vitality. As I listened into the night, they played songs that spoke eloquently of it all.

The Floridita
Calle Obispo & Avenida de Belgica
Tel: 53-7-63-1060

Happily, the Floridita, where Hemingway drained his daiquiris, is still a delightful place not only for a drink but also for dinner. The mood is still '50s New York sophisticate, and the drinks, served with house-made potato chips, are excellent. The dining room, air-conditioned and with fine service, is almost worth its stiff prices. Start with the fresh oyster cocktail and follow with roasted rock lobster. Dinner for two, with wine, about $125.

La Bodeguita del Medio
Calle Emperado 207
Tel: 53-7-61-8442

Unfortunately, another of Hemingway's hangouts, La Bodeguita del Medio, has become nothing more than an tourist trap. The food is just minimally acceptable, the whole place could use a good scrubbing, and the service is indifferent. Still, as an attraction, it's worth dropping in for one of Papa's adored mojitos.

La Ferminia
5ta avenida e/ calle 182-184
Tel: 53-7-24-6555

Many Cubans name La Ferminia as the city's best international restaurant. Its mahogany-furnished dining room, with embroidered tablecloths and potted plants is certainly elegant. The grilled meats and fish are satisfactory. Dinner for two, without wine, about $100.

La Guarida
Concordia 418
Tel: 53-7-62-4940

A fine privately owned restaurant featured in the Cuban film *Strawberries and Chocolate*. Located in a crumbling old palace, you climb a rickety staircase past laundry-hung balconies to a top-floor apartment that comes as a pleasant surprise—paneled walls, nice old furniture, and decent art. The menu, which changes nightly, might feature rabbit or grilled swordfish, preceded by a tangy cold spinach soup and followed by a feather-light lemon tart. Dinner for two, without wine, about $50

SHOPPING

Even non-smokers seem to fall under the spell of the famed Cuban cigar when at the source. You can visit the Fabrica de Tabacos Partagas in Old Havana, watch them being made, and buy some. A box of top cigars at hotel shops can cost more than $350. It's best to ignore anyone trying to sell cigars on the street. Dark Havana Club Añejo Reserve, one of the best rums, costs less than $10. Locally produced art requires a special permit or an official store receipt to take out of the country. The Carlos III shopping center on

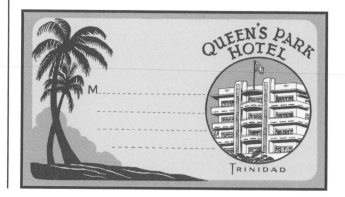

avenida Simon Bolivar is incongruously chic for Havana. One of the best buys there is an ice cream cone from the stand on the ground floor.

TRINIDAD

Trinidad, a quiet town on the island's southern coast, offers an enchanting vision of Spanish colonial life preserved almost intact. It was founded in 1514 and prospered as a sugar- and shipping town until the introduction of the sugar beet in Europe caused exports to collapse at the beginning of the 19th century. There are several charming museums, the best of which are the Museo Romantico, with its impressive collection of 18th- and 19th-century art and furniture, and the Museo de Arquitectura Colonial, showcasing the town's remarkable architectural treasures.

The great pleasure to be experienced here, however, is simply strolling the old cobbled streets and catching glimpses of superb colonial interiors through open windows. Although several guidebooks suggest spending a few days here, local accommodations are unsatisfactory. A day trip from Havana or Varadero will suffice to bring Trinidad and its heritage to life in sounds and images you will long remember. Cubana Airlines has daily trips connecting Havana, Varadero, and Trinidad; and it is possible to arrive by 9 a.m., have a leisurely day to explore the town, and catch the 6 p.m. flight back to Varadero. For lunch, try the Trinidad Colonial, with its handsome colonial decor and reasonably appetizing creole cooking.

VARADERO

This palm-fringed finger of sand sticking out into the intersection of the Gulf Stream and the Gulf of Mexico is

WHERE TO STAY IN VARADERO

HOTEL INTERNATIONAL
Avenida de las Americas
Tel: 53-5-66-7038

Opened in 1950 as a sister property to Miami's Fontainebleau Hotel. Although not as up-to-date as some of the newer properties, it's right on the beach and has a certain faded charm. Doubles from $80.

—·—

MELIA LAS AMERICAS
Avenida de las Americas
Tel: 53-45-66-7600

MELIA VARADERO
Avenida de las Americas
Tel: 53-45-66-7013

MELIA SOL PALMERAS
Avenida de las Americas
Tel: 53-45-66-7009

Three Melia hotels stand at the eastern end of the peninsula. Guests staying at any one of these can use all of the facilities of the other two—restaurants, recreational facilities, and pools. The appeal of these places rests on their beachfront location. Rooms are air-conditioned and comfortably furnished. Insist on a seaview room when booking and go for the half-board plan as the only other restaurants worth seeking out are a tiny Chinese one in the Melia complex and the dining room of the DuPont mansion, where quite good food is served in a former library.

the queen of Cuban beach resorts. Its appeal was recognized by Alfred Irenée DuPont de Nemours, who built a stunning villa here in 1930 and sold building lots to wealthy friends. Until Castro's revolution, Varadero was a North American St. Tropez, with casinos and a Palm Beach–style social circuit. Today it is being developed by Canadian and European hotel groups.

Because of the occasionally noxious fumes from an oil refinery across the bay, we recommend staying on the eastern end of the peninsula rather than in town. Also, when booking a room, insist on one that faces the sea, not only for the view, but because the main highway, running the length of the peninsula, is noisy well into the night. Fans of 1950s vintage architecture and anyone looking for moderately priced accommodations might consider Hotel Internacional.

The elegant Varadero Golf Club offers accommodations and gorgeous greens in a luxurious atmosphere. Headquartered in the Villa Dupont, a most extravagant mansion in Cuba when it was built in 1928, it has become one of the nicest hotels Cuba has to offer. Seven guest rooms are available, and they throw in the greens fee when you are in residence. Play the links, have a mojito in the Bar Mirador, and dine on lobster in Las Americas, the French restaurant on site. For those who can manage it, life doesn't get any better in Cuba.

Or, if you want a bit of local flavor, stay at one of the quite affordable downtown hotels. And for a view into the real Cuba, the sleepy little town of Cardenas is only a few miles away.

GUARDALAVACA

This small area, with several resort enclaves, lies 55 kilometers (35 miles) north of Holguin. It has great scuba

diving and is gorgeous. Like many beach areas, Guardalavaca is undergoing development aimed at attracting foreign travelers, especially Canadians and Europeans.

Another beautiful site being groomed for development is Cayo Coco, an island off the northern coast. The Hotel Jardines de Los Cocos on Cayo Coco is a Caribbean village-style complex. The area guards a significant concentration of fauna, including huge flocks of flamingoes. (There is some question of whether the wildlife can survive further development, despite the Cuban Academy of Sciences' claim that 16,000 rooms can be built without harming the environment.) We find the more low-key Cayo Guillermo, a short distance along the causeway to the northwest, more attractive than Cayo Coco, with its beautiful beach, a very pleasant setting, and lots of water activities, especially deep-sea and fresh-water fishing.

We were less impressed with the accommodations at Playa Giron on the Bay of Pigs. The diving and snorkeling opportunities offshore are excellent, however. A Bay of Pigs Museum details the story of the ill-fated CIA-sponsored operation to overthrow Castro in 1961. Though there are a few captured airplanes and tanks on display outside, it's a rather low-energy museum.

Don't expect to find much in the way of Cuban culture at the beach resorts. Cubans aren't allowed to go to most of them, except as employees. In fact, guards often keep the locals at a distance. One exception to this rule we discovered, is Playas del Este, a nice beach area about 16 kilometers (10 miles) east of Havana. Cuban vacationers can be found there in abundance, and activities range from diving to boat trips. Though the hotels in that area are far more humble than at the newer tourist resorts, a visit there does give you a better sense that you're truly in Cuba.

CAMAGÜEY

A charming Spanish colonial city, the third largest in Cuba, is in the middle of a cattle-ranching region. Camagüey is

associated with early revolutionary Ignacio Agramonte, who led unsuccessful revolts against the Spanish in the mid-1800s. Sights include La Soledad and other historic churches, plus one of Cuba's largest museums, the Museo Provincial Ignacio Agramonte, which has exhibits on the history and fine art of the region.

As elsewhere, local authorities actively discourage contact between locals and foreigners, but you can hear a form of music indigenous to Cuba, *la trova* (performers singing ballads with guitar accompaniment), nightly at the Casa de la Trova in Agramonte Park. Also, try to see a Cuban rodeo while you're in the area. Cuban cowboys *(vaqueros)* have their own unique style. Outside of town is the Sierra de Cubitas, river gorges with dramatic cliffs.

Within the province of Camagüey, there are some beach areas worth checking out, too. Lesser-known than Varadero and Cayo Largo is the Santa Lucia area on the north coast, which is especially popular for its diving and snorkeling. Resorts like the Cuatro Vientos and Vita Club Caracol already show that Santa Lucia has the potential to become another Varadero. You'll also want to spend some time on the sand at Playa Los Cocos, which is 6 kilometers (4 miles) northwest of Santa Lucia. In the morning you'll be alone; later you'll share it with locals, a rather rare treat in Cuba.

CAYO LARGO

Located south of the main island of Cuba, Cayo Largo has one of the best stretches of sand and water in the Caribbean, and the feel of the place is definitely paradise found. (Alas, millions of mosquitoes feel the same way, so strong repellent is essential, especially at dusk.) Snorkeling, diving, windsurfing, and fishing are all available. Boat excursions to Playa Sirena, the most

THE CENTER FOR CUBAN STUDIES

124 West 23rd Street, New York, NY
Tel: 212- 242-0559, www.cubaupdate.org

One way Americans can visit Cuba legally is by participating in programs organized by the center, which arranges history and art tours on a regular basis, packaging travel arrangements, providing expert guides and good accommodations. The Center for Cuban Studies opened in New York City in 1972, organized by a group of scholars, writers, artists, and other professionals who hoped to counter the effects of U.S. policy toward Cuba. The 1961 U.S. ban on trade with and travel to Cuba, followed by the break in diplomatic relations, had created a de facto embargo on information about Cuba. The center has served as a vital communication link between the United States and Cuba through its publications, organized tours, library services, exchange programs, and art projects.

MEMBERSHIP

The center relies on membership to continue its work. All members receive the CUBA Update and regular mailings about Center-sponsored events, trips, and developments in U.S.-Cuba relations. Supporting and sustaining members, in addition, receive notices about visiting Cuban artists and experts, are invited to special events, and can call upon staff for special requests.

Annual memberships are $60 (regular), $100 (supporting), and $150–$250 (sustaining). Institutional and foreign membership is $70. Students and senior citizens from the U.S. can join at the special rate of $40.

beautiful beach, take place in the glaring midday hours and, unfortunately, depart before the early evening magic sets in.

The new Sol Club is one of the best resorts on the island. The Hotel Pelicano is recommended as well, and the Isla del Sur Resort is a favorite with Germans. Nightlife is confined to what's available at the resorts or the Discoteca Blue Lake in the airport terminal. One thing to know, though: The government forbids Cubans from setting foot on Cayo Largo unless they work on the island.

SAN FRANCISCO DE PAULA, LA VIGIA

In the hills beyond Havana, Ernest Hemingway's home of 21 years has been preserved. The rooms, empty rum bottles and all, remain as they were when he died in 1961. While you can't actually enter the house, you can view the rooms through the windows. Jars of formaldehyde containing snakes and iguanas decorate the bathroom. Many of the other rooms contain his stuffed hunting trophies and weapons from Africa. His yacht, the *Pilar,* is oddly on display in the backyard next to the empty swimming pool, and there's a small graveyard nearby for his four beloved dogs: Black, Negrita, Linda, and Neron. Be aware that you will be charged $3–$5 for each photograph you take at La Vigia. U.S. scholars have finally been given permission to conserve Hemingway's written legacy, the thousands of documents stored at La Vigia.

ISLA DE LA JUVENTUD

Sitting some distance from the main island of Cuba, Isla de la Juventud has great beaches around Punta del Este in the south (in a military zone), but it's not primarily a beach destination—similar beaches can be found all over the mainland. It's special because of its reefs. Offshore diving expeditions, among the most professionally organized outings in Cuba, leave the island's west side.

Though lacking the impressive colonial architecture found on the Cuban mainland, the island has several landmarks that revolve around (and glorify) the Cuban Revolution. Among them is the desolate and surreal Modelo Prison, where Fidel Castro and his followers were once imprisoned. Other sights include the Museo de la Lucha Clandestina, which details the underground movement against Batista, and El Abra House, where Cuban independence hero José Martí once was held. Prior to the early 1990s, the island was the home of thousands of students from Cuba-friendly countries; when we visited, we saw only deserted, run-down buildings and dormitories containing a few students from North Korea and the Western Sahara.

PINAR DEL RIO

This province (with a capital city of the same name, pop. 112,000) in western Cuba is one of the most beautiful in the country: Stunning *mogotes* (limestone mountains) tower over lush fields of the tobacco used in the legendary Cuban cigars. The highest-quality tobaccos are grown in Vuelta Abajo and in Hoyo de Monterrey, both southwest of the city of Pinar del Rio. (The growing season is December–April.) Tour buses leave for daylong trips from Havana and stop at a cigar factory in the city of Pinar del Rio

HOTEL DES ETRANGERS

along the way. We recommend renting a car to make the trip. That will allow you to stop when you want to take photos. Good country-style restaurants are found at the Valley of Prehistory (where restaurant patrons have an excellent view of a 180-meter/590-foot mural that adorns the cliff face of Mogote Dos Hermanos) and at the Cueva del Indio (site of an eerie subterranean river that can be toured by boat).

For the best views of the countryside, take the main highway toward Pinar del Rio city to the exit for Viñales. Though the road is potholed in some parts, the scenery becomes quite nice as you approach Viñales. The stretch of road between Viñales and the coast is the most dramatic, with limestone outcroppings etched with almost lacy patterns and interspersed with green mountains. You can stop along the way for refreshments (or a dance) at a cave that has been converted into a disco bar. Stay with the northern coastal road on the way back to Havana (the water is on your left, beautiful hills and valleys to your right). Although the entire drive can be made as a day trip from Havana, we recommend taking things at a slower pace, with an overnight along the way.

Southwest of Pinar del Rio, lying on the southwestern tip of Cuba itself, is Maria La Gorda. It's definitely off the beaten track, but divers rave about the untouched reefs teeming with marine life close to shore. At least 8 kilometers (5 miles) of splendid white-sand beach front the warm, crystal-clear water. The only hotel is very small and basic, but diving enthusiasts won't really mind.

BARACOA

On the eastern tip of Cuba, Baracoa may be the place that Columbus first landed in Cuba, and it was definitely the first Spanish settlement on the island. Set among palm trees and lush vegetation, Baracoa was cut off from the rest of the island by a range of mountains until the early 1960s. It's a great place to escape for days or weeks. A fort from the 1700s that overlooks the town has been turned into the Hotel Castillo.

Spend your time rambling through town and meeting the great local characters. We recommend you take some time to tour the beautiful—and largely untouched—rain forests and rivers in the surrounding countryside. A good place to sample Baracoa's cuisine, one of the best outside of Havana, is in the restaurant located in La Punta fortress. And if you're there on a Saturday, don't miss Noche Cubana, when food stalls spring up along Calle Antonio Maceo and street musicians entertain the dancing crowd.

SANTIAGO DE CUBA

A bumpy, one-stop flight from Havana on an Aero Caribbean, Russian-built Ilyushin 18 is Santiago de Cuba, the city that Cubans consider the birthplace of their vibrant, African-inspired art and music as well as the point of origin of the Castro-led revolution. Seemingly on every downtown street corner around Parque Cespedes, the main square, there are musicians pouring out their infectious rhythms and craftspeople selling papier-mâché masks or carvings. Dance performances that reflect African and Haitian influences can be seen at the Museo del Carnaval at Calle Heredia 30, and there are nightly music performances at the Casa Trova, a cultural center at Calle Heredia 208. Be forewarned, however: It's smoky and steaming.

Here on the eastern end of the island and some

A NICE PLACE TO STAY

THE CASA GRANDA
Calle Heredia 201, Santiago de Cuba
Tel: 53-226-54384

A smart colonial hotel overlooking the main square. This ornately refurbished and air-conditioned 52-room property is now managed by the Sofitel chain. Its rooftop restaurant serves a limited but well-prepared menu, with dinner for two running to about $50. Doubles from about $80.

---

distance from Havana is one of Cuba's oldest cities, but it doesn't really look like it. Earthquakes have damaged it repeatedly. Most of the buildings are from the 1800s and early 1900s. But the city itself has a beautiful setting at the foot of the Sierra Maestra Mountains and overlooks a magnificent bay.

The Parque Cespedes area holds most of the city's attractions, which include the cathedral and the Colonial Museum (located in the house that supposedly belonged to conquistador Diego Velazquez). The restored Hotel Casa Granda is adjacent to the square and was a favorite hangout of author Graham Greene. Even if you don't stay there, visit the hotel veranda or rooftop bar to hear live music and soak up the atmosphere that attracted Greene.

We also recommend the piracy museum in the Morro Castle and the Moncada Barracks. Castro and his men quixotically attacked Moncada on July 26, 1953, the first armed uprising of the Cuban Revolution. (The bullet holes on the facade are re-creations.) Take the time to visit the city cemetery—you'll find the graves of such diverse Cuban heroes as José Marti and the Bacardi brothers.

Only true history buffs will want to visit San Juan Hill to see where Teddy Roosevelt and his Rough Riders defeated the Spanish in 1898. Today, only a small monument commemorates the event, and a rusting Ferris wheel nearby does nothing to add to the site's allure.

Santiago's African heritage has led to the creation of a vibrant local culture. Many Cuban musical styles, such as *son*, originated in the region, and Santiago's Carnival (in July) is the most famous in Cuba.

Santiago offers many excursions. A trip to the Gran Piedra mountain (1,234 meters/4,047 feet) in the Parque Baconao makes a cool and refreshing break from the usually steaming hot city. Farther east you will find beaches and two hotels, LTI Los Corales and Club Bucanero (many of their clients arrive from Canada and Germany).

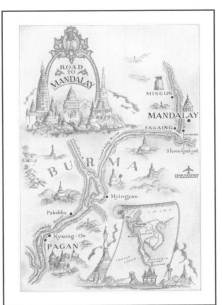

You can take a day trip to Guantánamo (70 kilometers/45 miles east of Santiago de Cuba) to see its Spanish buildings from the 1800s, but the city has very few attractions: It's one of the poorest in Cuba. Nearby is the U.S. naval base at Guantánamo (held by the U.S. since 1903), but you won't be allowed to visit this installation. You can, however, arrange a fascinating trip to an observation point in Cuban territory near the naval base. A short distance east of town, after crossing through a military checkpoint, you travel about 15 kilometers (9 miles) through cactus-covered hills to a former military lookout post called Mirador Malone (now a restaurant). Old Soviet-made binoculars are provided so that you can get a better look at the U.S. base. In dramatic contrast with the Cuban territory around it, the base looks like an idealized U.S. town: Late-model cars cruise past split-level suburban homes surrounding a golf course, and there's even a McDonald's. It's quite surreal. You might be able to spot a flash of orange overalls (perhaps belonging to one of the unnamed detainees alleged to have ties to al Queda or the Taliban) in the distance while you're having lunch under camouflage netting at the observation point/restaurant—where there are no Big Macs for sale, but Cuban army souvenirs can be purchased. Cuban authorities are less inclined these days to let tourists have a peek. Only strictly supervised groups are allowed access.

16 KIPLING'S ROAD TO MANDALAY: CRUISING OLD BURMA AND NEW MYANMAR

In Rangoon, the 2,500-year-old Shwedagon Pagoda is plated with 60 tons of gold, its summit ornamented with 8,000 diamonds, rubies, and sapphires. A stone's throw away is the famed Scott's Market, teeming with gems and silks. At Bagan, in the center of the country, where 13,000 temples and monuments were built eight centuries ago, I marveled at the

THE ROAD TO MANDALAY

Rudyard Kipling summed it up a century ago, "*This is Burma*," he wrote, "*and it will be quite unlike any land you know about.*"

> *By the old Moulmein Pagoda,*
> *lookin' eastward to the sea,*
> *There's a Burma girl a-settin',*
> *and I know she thinks o' me;*
> *For the wind is in the palm-trees,*
> *and the temple-bells they say:*
> *Come you back, you British soldier;*
> *come you back to Mandalay!*
> *Come you back to Mandalay,*
> *Where the old Flotilla lay:*
> *Can't you 'ear their paddles chunkin'*
> *from Rangoon to Mandalay?*
> *On the road to Mandalay,*
> *Where the flyin'-fishes play,*
> *An' the dawn comes up like thunder*
> *outer China 'crost the Bay!*

2,000 that still stand. In Mandalay's Mahamuni Pagoda, devotees plaster gold leaf every day on a 13-foot-high Buddha already so overlaid with leaf that its profile is unrecognizable.

★ THE ROAD TO MANDALAY
www.orient-express.com

Life along the Irrawaddy is a movie screen of exotic activity: farmers plowing behind oxen, women in fishing villages beating their laundry against rocky banks, saffron-robed monks marching in single file toward gold-domed pagodas.

Myanmar (Burma) is still relatively unknown to Western travelers. I was taken by sights and monuments that rival Angkor Wat and the Taj Mahal, by the country's distinctive handicrafts and artifacts, its smiling people, and, above all, by a culture that engages the hearts and minds of almost everyone.

Formerly called Burma, Myanmar has always been a fascinating destination for the venturesome traveler, and it remains so today, despite its regrettable political situation. The country's military government, once known as SLORC (State Law and Order Restoration Council), has adopted the gentler name of State Peace and Development Council, and it is aggressively courting foreign investors and foreign visitors. Nevertheless, a land excursion can be challenging. The country's infrastructure is largely undeveloped. Roads are poor, restaurants are limited, and red tape complicates each move. Internal airlines, laden with foreign entrepreneurs, are frequently overbooked. Fortunately, a very attractive alternative is available: a cruise along the Irrawaddy River, Myanmar's lifeline, aboard the Orient-Express's elegant vessel *Road to Mandalay*.

The 180-kilometer (114-mile) voyage presents some of the best of Myanmar from the vantage point of an elegant floating hotel. The ship, built in Germany in 1964 and equipped with state-of-the-art navigational aids, offers 64 air-conditioned cabins, compact but comfortable. Each is decorated in soft colors, with old Burmese prints and handsome chests and cupboards of polished teak. However, there is no storage space for luggage in most of the cabins. Some of the single cabins have their beds perched above a tricky set of steps. The 14 double-width State Cabins, with big beds, double granite sinks, and relatively generous storage and sitting space, are worth the considerable premium they command.

Recreational facilities include a swimming pool on the shaded top deck and a large observation lounge used for Burmese puppet shows, crafts demonstrations, and talks by the guide staff. The 76-person crew includes 15 who work in the immaculately clean galley and 28 "hotel" staffers. Much of the food and all of the wine and liquor are shipped in from Singapore. We had no concern for the safety of the food served aboard. The chef at the time, Welsh-born Jeramie Garlick, a veteran of the *QE2* and the *Vistafjord,* is expert at preparing gentle versions of Asian dishes.

From October to May, after the rainy season, the ship sails on three-, four-, or seven-day itineraries between the ancient royal capitals of Mandalay and Bagan. Bring a sufficient wardrobe for the entire length of your cruise; laundry service is not available.

If you're traveling in Myanmar independently, you can traverse the Irrawaddy between Mandalay and Bagan on one of the scheduled ferries that leave at around 6 a.m. every day in each direction. The trip takes about nine hours and calls at a half-dozen villages en route, delivering and taking on passengers and freight.

Traveling in Myanmar presents an opportunity to experience colonial living and to try exotic and sometimes exceptional Asian cuisine.

PANDAW 3
www.pandaw.com

Another alternative is to cruise on a purpose-built boat such as the *Pandaw 3,* which has 40 spacious cabins, polished teak interiors, elegant furnishings and a huge observation deck from which to watch the endlessly fascinating river traffic. As a bonus, the food aboard is excellent. The ship anchors overnight and calls by day at interesting stops such as Ava and Sagaing. Other Pandaw

YANGON RESTAURANTS

LE PLANTEUR
16 Sawmaha Street
Tel: 95-1-549-389

The most exceptional restaurant in Yangon is Le Planteur, where Swiss chef Boris Granges prepares creative versions of Indo-French food using local spices to enhance seafood, suckling pig, Australian venison, and more. It's located in a colonial bungalow-style house by the side of Kandawgyi Lake. The wine list is remarkably broad and well chosen. Dinner for two, without wine, about $70.

———•———

MANDALAY RESTAURANT
Governor's Residence, 35 Taw Win Road
Tel: 95-1-221-462

Chef Lionel Auvray combines French and Burmese cuisine to produce dishes such as pan-fried tiger prawns with tamarind sauce and crispy fried garlic. His warm mango tarte tatin dessert is quite special. Dinner for two, without wine, about $65.

———•———

THE GREEN ELEPHANT
U Wisara Road
Tel: 95-1-535-231

The best place to sample authentic Burmese food (and buy antiques) is the Green Elephant in Kamayut Township. Rice and copious quantities of palm oil are the basic ingredients, and so the curries and tempura-fried fish tend to be a bit oily. But if you can handle this cooking, the butterfish curry is exceptional. Otherwise, stick to appetizers, lentil soup, and vegetable dishes. Locals dine early; if you arrive after 6:30 p.m., you're likely to be eating alone. Dinner for two, with local beer, about $20.

cruises last for from five to ten nights, exploring the north and south of the country.

YANGON

TRADERS
233 Sule Pagoda Road
Tel: 95-1-242-828 or 800-942-5050
www.shangri-la.com/yangon/traders

Having anticipated a more rapidly developing tourism industry, Yangon has an oversupply of hotel rooms, and you can expect discount rates. In the city center, the most popular choice is Traders, a property of the Shangri-La group. At 22 stories, it's the city's tallest building, and hence it offers panoramic views, particularly from rooms facing the Shwedagon Pagoda. The 407 guest rooms provide all the expected amenities, including TV in eight languages. There are four restaurants, a fitness center with pool, saunas, and Jacuzzis. The Summer Palace serves excellent Cantonese food, with dinner for two running to about $50, unless you order shark's fin soup at about $50 per person. Doubles from about $150, including breakfast, airport transfers, and dry cleaning. Wheelchair accessible.

★ THE STRAND
92 Strand Road
Tel: 95-1-243-377

When the Strand first opened in 1901, it was touted as "the finest hostelry east of Suez." It suffered severe damage in World War II and deteriorated thereafter to the point where by the 1980s it was a sad shell with despondent waiters padding silently around ghostly halls. Fortunately it has been restored to something approaching its old splendor. Its 32 suites are graced by such modern amenities

as functioning plumbing, a treat in Myanmar, and huge closets and bathrooms. Decor is a successful blending of Asian and Western influences. Ask for a room at the front, overlooking the Yangon River that, although grubby, is lively and interesting. The bar makes a wicked Mandalay rum sour, and the principal dining room has good but rather expensive food. Doubles from about $350.

★ THE GOVERNOR'S RESIDENCE
Pansea Orient-Express Hotels
35 Taw Win Roa
Tel: 95-1-229860

For a smaller boutique hotel, the Governor's Residence, now part of Orient-Express, is located in a quiet, residential area. It is a spectacular 49-room hotel, an imposing Burmese teak mansion restored to its pristine glory, standing majestically amid a lotus garden. Its spacious teak rooms are luxuriously decorated in tropical cottons and silks, looking over the garden and free-form pool, and each has a large handmade, free-form bath. Nearby is the Shwedagon Pagoda, one of the world's great treasures, and not to be missed.

BAGAN

Bagan produces most of Myanmar's fine lacquerware. One of the best places to see it manufactured and to buy it is the Golden Cuckoo. You can visit the shop, which has been in business for four generations, or the workshops located in Myin Ka Par Village on the outskirts of the city. Look for boxes, vases, finger bowls, nut bowls, and trays, all made of woven bamboo and horsehair overlaid with up to 14 successive layers of lacquer.

THIRIPYITSAYA SAKURA HOTEL
Tel: 95-62-702-8790, www.thiripyitsaya.com
The villas at the Thiripyitsaya Sakura Hotel are attractively decorated and furnished in traditional Myanmar style. The property is a former government guest house located in a garden setting along the Irrawaddy River—a tranquil spot for relaxing and not doing much else. The food is good, with some welcome international choices, and the service is discreet and caring, in typical Myanmar fashion. Doubles from about $65.

BAGAN THANDE HOTEL
Tel: 95-62-70-144, www.baganthandehotel.com
A bit farther along the river bank, the Bagan Thande Hotel offers similar accommodations in a similarly tranquil setting. The teak walls and furniture in your room will put you in mind of a chalet in the Alps, until you look out of the window. Deluxe riverside rooms are the best, by far. Doubles from about $50, including breakfast.

THE BAGAN GOLF RESORT HOTEL
Tel: 95-62-70-187
Close to the old city in a country-like setting. Rooms and bungalows are spacious and attractive and offer the opportunity to play a round of golf on what is perhaps the only 18-hole course overlooked by pagodas. Doubles from about $65, including breakfast.

YANGON TIPS

– Watch for the teams of artists who roam the city, painting movie billboards by hand.

– For camera repairs, go to U Hla Myint, 3rd Floor, 141, 34th Street.

– From Central Station—which, as with many such British colonial structures, resembles a Gothic cathedral—the Circle Train works its way around Yangon, providing three hours of local color and entertainment.

– Visit Natmimae Thanaka Industry at 12th Street to see the making of the distinctive thanaka cosmetic that most Burmese women and children use as facial makeup and sun barrier.

INLE LAKE

Inle Lake, an hour by plane from Mandalay and another hour by taxi from Heho airport, is home to 150,000 people who cluster around the shore or live in floating villages perched on stilts over the water.

Try to make it to the daily, early-morning market with its tribal people in colorful costumes. Textiles are a good buy; shirts and shawls made here find their way to upmarket stores all over the world. You will also find excellent work done by silversmiths, wood carvers, and shoulder-bag makers. Inle produces most of the cheroots that Burmese men and women smoke incessantly. They are made of tobacco stalks and additives such as tamarind, all wrapped in a leaf and finished with a filter of shredded newspapers and pieces of sugar cane fiber. The occasional showers of sparks they throw off redefine the term "smoking jacket."

GOLDEN ISLAND COTTAGES
Near Nampan Village
Tel: 95-81-23-136
www.gicmyanmar.com

Take one of the basic cottages with little more than a hot-water shower stall and a mosquito-netted bed, and consider yourself to have experienced something few Western travelers have done. The most appealing aspect of inn is the helpful and smiling service of the staff. Food at the restaurant is limited to local dishes. Cottages from about $50, including breakfast.

LAKE VIEW RESORT
Tel: 95-81-29-332

A boutique hotel located on a 5-hectare (12-acre) site overlooking the lake. Accommodations consist of 20 rooms and 12 villa-type junior suites that are by far the more comfortable; all are furnished in colonial style. The dining room offers the best choice and quality of food in the area. No air-conditioning. Villas, about $100, including breakfast.

INLE PRINCESS RESORT
Tel: 95-81-21-347

One of the best looking of the lake properties, this resort has 25 well-furnished, spacious wood-and-bamboo cottages. Other than that, facilities are few; no phones, no air-conditioning, and only mediocre food. Cottages from about $100, including breakfast.

MANDALAY
There are two recommendable accommodations in Myanmar's second city.

SEDONA HOTEL MANDALAY
Tel: 95-2-36-488, www.sedonamyanmar.com

A contemporary resort-style hotel with 247 attractively furnished rooms, a swimming pool, and a fitness center. The restaurants serve reliable but unexceptional food. Doubles from about $200, including breakfast, but expect a big discount from the rack rate or an upgrade to a suite.

MANDALAY HILL RESORT HOTEL
Tel: 95-2-35-638, www.mandalayhillresorthotel.com

A incongruous-looking 206-room high-rise located at the foot of the Mandalay Hill. Rooms are well-equipped and comfortable, although a bit institutional; ask for a deluxe with a Mandalay Hill view. Doubles from about $100 before discount.

Mandalay, too, has a Green Elephant restaurant with the same ownership as the one in Yangon and the same culinary qualifications. Ask for directions at the Sedona Hotel. Another interesting dining spot is the Hot Pot Suki restaurant at the Swan Hotel, 26th and 68th Streets. Its Asian fondue is excellent.

The town has countless workshops producing crafts and so-called Nirvana (Buddhism-related) articles. Thein Hteik Shin, just inside the east entrance of the Mahamuni Pagoda, is a reliable shop for these items. The pagoda is the sanctuary of the country's most famous Buddha. If you go there at 4:30 in the morning, you will see guardians washing its face and occasionally coating it with a sticky lacquer to ensure that it retains the thousands of gold leaf squares that the faithful plaster on it every day.

By all means, visit a nearby gold leaf workshop. Men stripped to the waist, glistening with sweat, wield long-handled sledgehammers to pound pieces of gold wrapped in deer skin. The battering continues until the metal is so thin that the leaf from a one-ounce nugget will cover 10 square meters (100 square feet). Next door, in stifling heat (no fans are allowed), young girls manipulate the fragile leaf with tweezers, cutting it into five-centimeter (two-inch) squares and packing it between sheets of oiled bamboo paper for delivery to the Mahamuni and other shrines throughout the country.

Despite continued political problems, visitors' security has never been a problem in Myanmar. Providing you don't engage in political demonstrations or otherwise act suspiciously, you'll run no risk of arbitrary arrest. And there is virtually no petty crime, at least one benefit of a military administration!

MYANMAR AIRWAYS INTERNATIONAL

www.maiair.com

Since January 2001, MAI has been working hard to reinvent itself. Today, while it continues to strive for improvement, it should be pleased with its achievements and proud of the high level of service it provides to its increasing number of passengers. The service concept is captured in the tag line "modern comforts, gentle traditions." Operationally, it continues to grow with an all-Boeing fleet flying from Yangon to Bangkok, Kuala Lumpur, Singapore, and New Delhi. The flights to and from Bangkok are operated on a code-share basis with Thai Airways International, and together, provide visitors traveling between Myanmar and Thailand with a wide selection of 23 flights per week. More flights are being planned to new destinations within Asia. Everything is geared toward one main objective: to bring you the character and unspoiled sights of Myanmar, in a safe and efficient manner.

17 A GARDEN & WALKING TOUR THROUGH LITERARY ENGLAND

Contributor and distinguished author Frank Delaney was born in Tipperary, Ireland, host of the award-winning *Bookshelf,* for BBC Radio Four, and author of many books including *Ireland, A Novel.*

"Place is memory. All our lives tell us so. Why is it we remember forever not what we were wearing or doing or feeling, but where we were at the most crucial moments? There is a wider sense of place, planted in our memories by people we have never known or met. The Lake District of northwest England is immortalized by mighty poets. Their verses fill the universe's memory bank with crags and gray satin waters, and hills of trees down to the lakeshores. Ullswater, Buttermere, Derwentwater—these places with their sweet-sounding names stretched my heart even before I saw them. Wordsworth's sister, Dorothy, believed that

Grasmere "calls home the heart to quietness." Keats, that doomed diamond, said that Windermere "makes one forget the divisions of life: age, youth, poverty, and riches."

There are opportunities to be alone in the Lake District and in the company of the poets. In my own deck of recollection, a man in tweeds walks across a stone bridge outside Applethwaite, and a stream pours its black-silver ribbon straight down the heights of High Stile. And I'll always remember a visit to the farmhouse of Beatrix Potter. Her stories were world-famous when she went to live there. At the Lakes she met a local lawyer, a tall and decent man called William Heelis, and he cared for her and married her and gave her the freedom to be as she wished.

She wished to live unnoticed and to be of the countryside. Here she knew her greatest pride. It came not from Peter Rabbit or Jemima Puddleduck (whose descendants still waddle round Hill Top Farm) but from the prizes she won for the sheep she bred.

That, too, defines the Lake District, a natural award for nature's sober excellence, which never leaves your spirit. And which your spirit never leaves."

If anywhere is the heart and soul of walking in England,

it's the Lake District in the northwest of the country, a wonderful land of high mountains, deep valleys and of course, deep blue, glacially formed lakes.

The reason for its popularity may be historical, with a strong connection to the literature of England; this is where Potter, William Wordsworth, and the Romantic writers first engaged in walking and enjoying the outdoors for aesthetic or spiritual reasons only, rather than just as a means of transportation. Many famous walkers, from Sir Walter Scott to Queen Victoria, became frequent visitors of this "earthly paradise that only England knows."

In the very heart of the Lake District is the charming village of Hawkshead, the "Vale of Grasmere," with is lovely town and lake, Rydal Mount, the Wordsworth home, and beautiful Borrowdale. Each day walkers are surrounded by ever watchful mountains and fells, wild and rugged, with the quiet lapping waters of the Lakes Grasmere, Windermere, Rydal Water, and Derwentwater—created by glaciers 10,000 years ago, now reflecting each day's moods—dazzling blue, deep green, slate gray. A walk you can experience offers valleys, stretches of water, hills, and villages of the great writers.

England's Lake District covers an area of about 90 square kilometers (35 square miles) north of Manchester, mainly in Cumbria, plus a very small segment of Lancashire. Despite its small size, the Lake District encompasses an astonishing variety of natural forms that give it an air of wildness and scenic beauty unmatched anywhere else in England. It formed the geographical nexus of the "Lake School," a group of literary figures led by Wordsworth, Coleridge, and Southey. Most of the area has been designated a national park, and to Wordsworth it was "the loveliest spot that man hath ever found."

If you're reasonably fit and are up to walking in the

WALKING TOURS

⭐ COUNTRY WALKERS
P.O. Box 180
Waterbury, Vermont
Tel: 802-244-1387 or 800-464-9255

———•———

THE WAYFARERS
Tel: 44-(0)-1242-620-871 or 800-249-4620
www.thewayfarers.com

———•———

CROSS COUNTRY INTERNATIONAL
P.O. Box 1170, Milbrook, New York
Tel.: 800-828-8768
www.walkingvacations.com

———•———

ENGLISH LAKELAND RAMBLERS
Tel: 212-505-1020 or 800-724-8801
E-mail: Britwalks@aol.com

footsteps of some great poets, and for a literary touring experience, consider this walking vacation. There are a number of first-rate operators offering deluxe walking experiences in almost any part of the world that might interest you. One such ramble across England under the guidance of Country Walkers or The Wayfarers could not be better planned.

My coast-to-coast walk took six days, averaging 22 kilometers (14 miles) a day and following a route from the Irish Sea to the North Sea through the Lake Country, the Yorkshire Dales, and the North York Moors, walking where sheep and cows graze and where few people live in one of the most poetic landscapes imaginable.

Hiking days were long, starting at 9 a.m. after a proper English breakfast of bangers, eggs, stewed tomatoes, porridge, toast, preserves, and coffee, and ending around 7 p.m. with a hot bath, cocktails, and a long leisurely dinner with good French wines. All meals were of very fine quality, with several menu choices and rich and satisfying desserts. I found my experience to be so stimulating that the day's end found me more exhilarated than tired.

My group of 15 was directed by an experienced leader. Unlike bicycle touring, where you follow your own map and join up with your fellow travelers at meals, on my trip we followed the leader as a group, and there was no worry about misreading directions and getting lost. A van, driven by the trip manager, met us at mid-morning and afternoon for snacks and to pick up any stragglers who were ready to stop walking for the day. Lunches were taken at local pubs, and lodging was arranged at country house estates or historic hotels and inns.

A few rituals served to make my trip even more memorable: On our first day, we dipped our toes into the Irish Sea, and on our last, we did the same at Whitby, a fishing village bordering the North Sea, and then raised a champagne toast to our accomplishment.

The best times to visit are in spring, early summer, and fall. In July and August, hordes of tourists swarm all over the area, jamming facilities and crowding scenic spots.

If driving, most travelers start at Windermere, England's largest but very narrow lake, and find their way into the wilder and more impressive scenic areas. Driving is difficult, particularly in summer. Parking is always very tight. The roads wind a great deal, but are in good condition. Hikers are in their element and walking is really the best way to explore the district.

ENGLAND'S CHEESES

"The poets have been mysteriously silent on the subject of cheese."

— G. K. Chesterton (1874–1936)

English cheeses have long lived in the shadow of those made in France. During World War II, cheesemaking in England fell to almost zero because of a shortage of farm workers and because there were more important uses for milk. By 1954, when rationing finally ended, many cheese-making skills had been lost. Fewer than 150 cheesemakers were left of the more than 15,000 who were in business before the war. As a result, until about 10 or 15 years ago, most English cheese was made in bulk. But then several cheesemakers started making craft cheese once again.

Ideally the best milk comes from cows, sheep, and goats allowed to graze in pastures filled with wildflowers. Plant oils derived from grasses and flowers are found in the grazing animals' fat and milk, giving naturally produced cheese an aroma and flavor not found in bulk cheese.

Today, England has some 300 cheesemakers, producing more than 500 varieties in an artisanal manner. Here is a selection of some to look for, most of them available at many of London's best cheese shops and department stores such as Fortnum & Mason, Harvey Nichols, and Harrod's.

◻ BEENLEIGH BLUE is a blue sheep's milk cheese, moist but crumbly, piquant with a burnt caramel sweetness typical of quality sheep's milk cheese. Available from August to January. Ideal with beer.

◻ BUTTON/INNES is a fragile goat's milk cheese that literally melts in your mouth. It is made in Staffordshire.

◻ CAERPHILLY is a cheese made in Wales. It is quite mild in taste and goes well with salads.

◻ CERNEY is a connoisseur's cheese, created by Lady Angus using unpasteurized milk. Each of several varieties has a slightly sharp zing to it with a hint of lemon and a nice goaty texture. It is high in fat and is best when about ten days old.

◻ CHEDDAR—the authentic variety—is made from the milk of cows that have been fed on a diet of green grass, buttercups, and daisies. Unfortunately Cheddar's name, unlike cheeses of Europe, is not protected and, therefore, there are hundreds of bad imitations. England now has only six traditional Cheddar cheesemakers: Chewton in Somerset; Denhay and Quickies in Devon; Green's in Somerset; and Keen's and Montgomery's in Somerset.

◻ CHESHIRE CHEESE, mentioned in the Domesday Book, is one of Britain's oldest cheeses. Its distinct character comes from the salt marshes upon which the cows graze.

COQUETDALE is made from the milk of Friesland sheep and is ripened in old Northumberland caves. Sweet, nutty.

CORNISH YARG is made according to a 17th-century recipe. It comes in a nettle wrapping, which gives a very slight flavor to the cheese.

COTHERSTONE comes from Durham. It has the acidic flavor of white wine and is one of the few traditional cheeses being made in the Pennines.

CURWORTHY comes from the Stockbearne Farm in Devon and has a delicate, buttery flavor. A variety of Curworthy known as Meldon is flavored with Chiltern ale and whole grain mustard.

DERBY has been called England's worst cheese; it was the first of Britain's cheeses to be mass produced during the Industrial Revolution. Handmade Derby, quite similar to Cheddar, is usually sold too young.

DORSET BLUE VINNEY is a hard blue cheese with a pronounced taste of wet leather. Don't confuse this with imitations made elsewhere.

EMLETT is a cream cheese that softens when mature to the consistency of ice cream. It has a sweet acidic and nutty taste.

FINN is the only triple-cream cheese produced in England. It is firm, very rich (fat content is 75 percent), and has a hint of mushrooms in the flavor.

GLOUCESTER (both single and double) dates back to the 16th century. Double Gloucester, with a nutty flavor, is made from full-cream milk. Single Gloucester is made from skimmed milk; it is popular for its low fat content.

HEREFORD HOP has a rind made from crunchy hops, which gives it a yeasty taste. An old recipe for it was revived in 1988 by Charles Martell.

LANCASHIRE was one of the first cheeses to be factory made, and it has declined ever since. When young, real Lancashire is quite creamy.

LINCOLNSHIRE POACHER comes from Holstein cows. An unpasteurized hard cheese, it is simple and unsophisticated but, when handmade, quite delicious.

LODDISWELL AVONDALE is a new English cheese, semisoft with an aroma of almonds.

MALVERN is a sheep's milk cheese that has a slight butterscotch taste with a hint of thyme. It's a solid cheese that can be eaten daily.

RED LEICESTER has a firm body with a slightly sweet taste. As it gets older, it develops a complex mixture of butterscotch and nut flavors.

SAGE DERBY is a popular Cheddar cheese flavored with sage. It has subtle differences from other Cheddars.

SHROPSHIRE BLUE, similar to Stilton, has an orange color from added annatto.

STILTON, rich, creamy, and slightly crumbly, comes in two varieties, blue and white. Genuine only if it comes from Nottinghamshire, Derbyshire, or Leicestershire, it is made from cow's milk and aged for four to six months, during which time it's skewered to encourage the growth of *Pencillium roqueforti* mold.

STINKING BISHOP, aptly named, is creamy and delicious. It tastes better as it gets smellier with age.

WENSLEYDALE is best made with sheep's milk from a recipe that came to England along with William the Conqueror in 1066. It has a supple, crumbly texture and lends itself to being flavored.

WIGMORE, produced by Village Maid Cheese, is a new variety that's made by washing the curd to remove excessive whey then packing it in molds to drain. The result is a low-acid cheese with the sweetness of milk and a somewhat yeasty aroma acquired from the rind.

YORKSHIRE BLUE has a subtle, typically blue cheese flavor that develops more pungency as it matures. This cheese is best when about ten weeks old.

If you're walking on your own, keep the following villages and accommodations in mind.

THE WALKS

The village of Carlisle lies 11 kilometers (7 miles) south of the Scottish border. Originally an important military outpost in Roman times, it remained a center of conflict between the English and the Scots for many years. Although now principally an industrial and farming town, it has innumerable Queen Anne houses and small shops lining its winding streets.

Carlisle has a small but quite interesting cathedral. Worth visiting, too, is the Tullie House Museum, in a small Jacobean mansion, where there is a good collection of local antiquities, many from the Roman period. Carlisle Castle dates from 1092; it stands on a bluff above the Eden River and contains a regimental museum.

THE CROWN AND MITRE HOTEL
Tel: 44-(0)-1228-525491
www.crownandmitre-hotel-carlisle.com

An acceptable place to stay, the Crown and Mitre occupies a gabled Edwardian house of 98 rooms, each with a private bath. There are two bars and an indoor swimming pool. Doubles from $185.

About 5 kilometers (3 miles) south of Carlisle is Keswick. It's an old market town near Derwentwater, considered by many to be England's most beautiful lake. The town is sheltered by the impressive Skiddaw Mountain. Derwentwater's shoreline is a mixture of crags, wooded slopes, and mountainside, and the lake is dotted with islets and swarming with trout and salmon. Good spots for views of the lake are Castle Head and Friar's Crag, where there is a memorial to John Ruskin.

The Fitz Park Museum exhibits manuscripts and memorabilia of the Lake School poets. Southey's home, Greta Hall, is now a school. (He's buried in the Crosthwaite churchyard.)

HILTON KESWICK LADORE
Tel: 44-(0)-17687-77285

Keswick's best accommodations are to be had in this 68-room hotel that offers fine views and a good restaurant. Doubles from $280.

From Keswick, continue into Borrowdale, a lovely valley. If you circle the lake you'll see the Falls of Lodore, subject of a well-known poem by Southey.

Cruises on Windermere, Ullswater, and Derwentwater are a popular pastime. Water sports, fishing, and swimming are common on most of the lakes. Many travelers like to skirt the lakes, visiting towns and villages along the way. Heartier souls take on the rugged terrain for some rewarding walks.

Ambleside, a short distance north of Lake Windermere, overlooks the lake from its hilltop position. This is where many travelers begin their tour of the district. The area offers tennis, golf, fishing, water sports, and good nature trails. Ducks sometimes strut across the golf course, and, according to the local citizenry, they have the right of way. There are even traffic signs that read: "Beware—Ducks Crossing."

ROTHAY MANOR
Ambleside
Tel: 44-(0)-15394-33605, www.rothaymanor.co.uk

A very pleasant place to stay, the Rothay Manor offers lots of fresh flowers and friendly service. There are two lounges, both with working fireplaces, and its 15 rooms are inviting. The restaurant, decorated with antique furnishings, has a good menu. Set on attractive grounds. Doubles from $200.

THE SAMLING
Ambleside Road, Windermere
Tel: 44-(0)-15394-31922

Here's an out-of-the-ordinary retreat, a small country house hotel with stunning views over Lake Windermere. It has ten delightful rooms and suites and beautiful grounds and gardens. All kinds of internationally known luminaries have entertained friends and family here. It may be booked only in its entirety, and the minimum charge is $5,000 per night, which includes early morning tea, breakfast, lunch, afternoon tea, and dinner for six couples or ten singles. The maximum number accommodated is ten couples, and for that number, the cost is about $8,000 per night.

Just past the Salutation Hotel in Ambleside is Stock Gill Force, a charming waterfall. St. Mary's Church (1854) has a memorial to Wordsworth.

Near Ambleside is Rydal, a village at one end of Rydal Water, another pleasant little lake. Wordsworth lived here at Rydal Mount from 1813 until he died in 1850. The house contains memorabilia as well as his library. A bit farther along

BEERS IN ENGLAND

Bass is one of England's biggest breweries and its "red triangle" beer is a good everyday choice. Less well known, however, is "Bass No. 1" ("red diamond"), a little hard to find but worth looking for. It is matured in the cask for 12 months and has a bitter oaky flavor, quite strange at first, but the more you try it, the more you will like it.

Freedom Premium Pilsener is brewed by a relatively new company in London and is rated by many as being the best bottled lager produced in the United Kingdom. Its formula uses Bavarian yeast, Czech and aromatic American hops, and English malted barley from East Anglia.

Marston's Pedigree Bitter is made in Burton-on-Trent, a town that has been famous for its beers since the Middle Ages. The waters found in the Trent Valley are rich in gypsum and magnesium salts, which give a crisp sparkle to pale ales. Marston's is the only brewery in the world using the "union room" method of fermentation in a linked series of oak casks. This process gives Pedigree its wonderfully complex and subtle flavors. Marston's also produces Owd Rodger, a heavy old ale with a slight licorice flavor and a creamy body, and Oyster Stout, which has a fruity flavor with a suggestion of onion and cedar. It is, in fact, ideal to drink with oysters.

Samuel Smith's Taddy Porter, a deep red-black beer with the aroma of well-done buttered toast, is one of the finest porters brewed. The brewery was founded in 1758, making it the oldest in Yorkshire. Charles Dickens mentioned it in *A Tale of Two Cities*.

Wychwood Hobgoblin, created as recently as 1995, is a full-bodied, copper-colored, well-balanced brew. Wychwood produces a number of other brews including Dog's Bollocks and Old Devil.

ENGLAND, SCOTLAND, & WALES

Martin O'Brien lives in Gloucester and works as a freelance journalist and photographer. Formerly travel editor at *Vogue* (UK) and editorial director for UPL Films in London and Los Angeles, he has contributed travel features to a variety of newspapers and magazines worldwide. He has published two books: *60 Years of Travel in Vogue* (1980) and *All The Girls* (1982), described by Auberon Waugh as "a classic among travel books." Here are his reminiscences on Great Britain.

There was never a country so built for the senses as Britain. The skirl and wheeze of a lonely bagpipe drifting down a Scottish glen; the tug of a Hampshire trout stream pummeling at your waders; the college spires of Oxford floating above dawn mists; the flavors of tender Welsh lamb laced with mint, Cromer crab, and Dover sole. And most memorable, for this is an island after all, the salty tang of the sea as it hisses over broad Northumberland sands, thunders against rugged Pembrokeshire cliffs, or shuffles like a cardsharp through the shingle of a Sussex beach. And for each of these sensory treats there's a thousand more.

As islands go, Britain is a sizable proposition, sitting on the edge of northern Europe like an old maid dipping her foot in the wide Atlantic, a little more than 1,400 kilometers (870

miles) from her head to her toe. Between Land's End and Dunnet Head, 3 kilometers (2 miles) closer to the Arctic Circle than the better-known John O'Groats, lie 230,000 square kilometers (9,000 square miles) of unforgettable country, with nowhere farther than 46 kilometers (74 miles) from the sea.

More than anything else, it is the sea that has defined Britain's character. As well as carving out the country's peculiarly craggy profile with its scouring surf and shifting tides, it has provided Britain with the means to prosper, the country's trading wealth and far-flung empire founded on its maritime skills, its great admirals and seaports like Plymouth and Portsmouth, Southampton and London, Liverpool and Glasgow. And if fortunes have flagged with the fading of Empire, the seafaring spirit along Britain's coastline is as strong as ever— its fishing ports, marinas, and quays crowded with every kind of craft.

And what a coastline, ranging from gull-dotted cliffs and palm-fringed coves in Devon and Cornwall to the reedy shallows of the Norfolk Broads, from wide strands and scalloped bays in the wild northeast to the deeply gouged, fjord-like firths that riddle Scotland's rocky coast. Here, along the shore, are Roman forts, Norman castles, Tudor blockhouses, and 19th-century Martello Towers put up to defend the realm; ancient abbeys built wherever the first Christians stepped ashore; and scores of wind-lashed lighthouses, flashing out their warning to centuries of shipping. And strung between them, like a necklace of lights, wherever the climate is mild, the sea safe and the sands golden, traditional seaside resorts like Brighton and Blackpool, Scarborough and Skegness, with their piers and promenades, their "Kiss-Me-Quick" hats, roller-coaster rides, and cotton candy stalls.

But Britain's coast is only half the story, a ribbon of sea and sand tied around an interior that lures and seduces with equal intent. Far to the north, Scotland accounts for some of the wildest, remotest, and most romantic country in Britain. In its highlands and lowlands are haunting, mirror-flat lochs like Rannoch and Tay, Trool and Lomond, eagle-soaring crags like Ben Nevis and Merrick, fairy-tale turreted castles like Blair and Craigievar, and celebrated salmon rivers like the Tweed, the Spey, and the Dee. Here are fine northern cities like Glasgow, set firmly on the Clyde yet within easy reach of the Trossachs; Edinburgh, one of Europe's finest capitals, with its elegant Georgian terraces and annual festival of music and drama; Aberdeen, prosperous port of departure for the North Sea oilfields; and smaller settlements, too, like Kelso with its cobbled market square; Port Logan where the cod can be fed by hand; and Arisaig with its grand views of the western isles.

Wales, too, has a wild, inspiring beauty, its narrow coastal pasturelands rising dramatically into the high peaks of the Brecon Beacons, the Black Mountains, and lofty Snowdonia. Like Scotland, too, it has its own tongue-twisting language, remains fervently nationalist, and boasts a long line of homegrown heroes who fought for their independence against Roman, Saxon, and Norman invaders. This is good country for fishing, trekking, and climbing—

the first men to reach the summit of Everest trained in Snowdonia—with unexpected delights like the Lleyn Peninsular and the waterfall country of Rheidol, the Plynlimon Hills, Dovey Valley, and the Vale of Llangollen.

Not surprisingly, England has a little bit of both its neighbors, most evident in the uplands of Dartmoor and Exmoor, the rolling Yorkshire Dales, the Peak District, and Wordsworth's timeless Lakeland, similar in all but scale to the wild reaches of Wales and Scotland. Where England differs is in its compactness.

Despite its size, nothing seems too far away. Only a few hours from London are the orchards of Kent and the lavender fields of Norfolk, the rolling Downs of Sussex and  ancient forests like Sherwood, Dean, and the oddly named New Forest, declared a royal hunting preserve by William the Conqueror nearly a thousand years ago.

Along the way are elegant spa towns like Bath, Cheltenham, and Royal Leamington Spa; the hallowed univversity grounds of Oxford and Cambridge; and bustling midland cities like Birmingham and Nottingham, Manchester and Sheffield, heartland of the Industrial Revolution. Also within easy reach are grand stately houses like Chatsworth and Longleat, Petworth, and Blenheim Palace; medieval castles like Arundel, Warwick, and Windsor; and the soaring cathedral cities of Salisbury, Winchester, Lincoln, and Durham.

In a single day you could watch the sun rise over Stonehenge, search for King Arthur in the depths of Somerset, fish for trout in the River Itchen, and return to London for a West End play, reach Glyndebourne in time for an evening's opera, or make Stratford-upon-Avon for a date with the Bard.

The only problem you'll encounter is deciding what to do first.

LITERARY ENGLAND

is Nab Cottage, Thomas de Quincey's home, briefly, in 1806.

Bowness-on-Windermere is the major destination on the lake and gets very crowded in summer. It's the gateway to many villages along narrow, winding roads. The town's 15th-century church has a beautiful stained-glass window.

THE BELSFIELD HOTEL
Kendall Road, Bowness
1.6 kilometers (1 mile) south of Windermere
Tel: 44-(0)-87060-96109

This hotel commands a striking view of the lake and has nice public rooms. Some bedrooms contain period furniture. Garden, indoor swimming pool, tennis, and sauna. 62 rooms. Doubles from $140.

MILLER HOWE HOTEL
Rayrigg Road, Windermere
Tel: 44-(0)-15394-42536, www.millerhowe.com

This Windermere establishment is well-known for its food, served in very pleasant surroundings. It has 13 rooms, each individually decorated, with many antiques. Excellent views of the lake and mountains, and there's a garden. Doubles from $160.

OLD ENGLAND HOTEL
Church Street, Bowness, 1.6 kilometers
(1 mile) south of Windermere
Tel: 44-(0)-15394-42444

This hotel, too, has fine views of the lake. Good-size bedrooms and tasteful decor. Also, an outdoor swimming pool and a garden. 78 rooms. Doubles from $200.

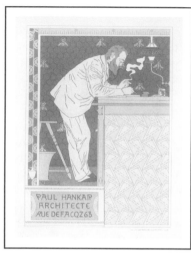

PAUL HANKAR
ARCHITECTE
RUE DEFACQZ63

LINTHWAITE HOUSE
Crook Road, Windermere
Tel: 44-(0)-15394-88600
www.linthwaite.com

Set on a grassy knoll overlooking Lake Windermere, Linthwaite House takes an "unstuffy" approach to country living. Built in 1900, the hotel offers 26 rooms, the best having lake views, and all with large, well-appointed baths. Owner/manager Mike Bevans promises "no chinz." He favors a tailored Ralph Lauren look, complete with teddy bears. Homey touches such as stacks of well-used leather suitcases and duck decoys decorate the lounge and conservatory bar. The 6-hectare (14-acre) grounds include a view terrace and a tarn for fly-fishing. The restaurant's dinner menu changes daily. Cheese lovers shouldn't miss the creamy Yorkshire Blue. Dinner for two, without wine, about $150. Doubles from about $220.

The village of Hawkshead is a few miles west of Lake Windermere. It has charming old stone houses and a 16th-century church. Wordsworth attended its grammar school.

Coniston rests in a splendid setting beneath Old Man and Yewdale crags, a kilometer (half-mile) from Coniston Water. John Ruskin is buried in the churchyard, and the town is the site of the Ruskin Museum with drawings, manuscripts, books and memorabilia. Ruskin lived in Brantwood, on the east side of the lake. Nearby is Tarn Hows, with an outstanding view, and Duddon Valley, both described in Wordsworth sonnets.

Grasmere Village is a bit north of Lake Grasmere, at the center of the Lake District. Wordsworth lived here in Dove

Cottage from 1799 to 1808, followed by Thomas de Quincey. The area received loving attention in Wordsworth's poems, and he is buried in the churchyard of St. Oswald, as are his wife and sister.

BRIDGE HOUSE HOTEL
Church Bridge, Grasmere
Tel: 44-(0)-15394-35425, www.bridgehousegrasmere.co.uk

Perched on two acres of woodlands in Grasmere village, this charming, family-run hotel makes you feel right at home. Eighteen guest rooms include modern amenities. Two lounges with working fireplaces. The restaurant's menu changes daily. Doubles from $70.

A Wordsworth favorite, Scafell Pike, at 978 meters high (3,210 feet), offers the most interesting climb in the Lake District. It takes two or three hours.

Grange is a charming town overlooking Morecambe Bay at the southern end of the Lake District. It contains an interesting mélange of Victorian houses.

Penrith is the gateway to Ullswater, England's second largest lake, and one of the most scenic, especially as you near its head. Patterdale, a tiny village, has a lovely setting at the head of the lake and is a good base for excursions around it. Glenridding is also nicely situated and a good center for hiking in the area. Aira Force, a beautiful, 20-meter (65-foot) waterfall in romantic surroundings, is located off the road between Penrith and Patterdale, a short distance from the entrance to Gobarrow Park.

THE SHARROW BAY COUNTRY HOUSE HOTEL
Lake Ullswater, near Penrith
Tel: 44-(0)-17684-86301
www.sharrow-bay.com

This has the finest view of any hotel that looks westward along the length of Lake Ullswater. Its two lounges are crowded with overstuffed furniture, and fluffy pillows predominate. There are tall Victorian lamps with fringed silk shades and the mantels and tables are jammed with knick-knacks. There are 28 attractive rooms, some in a beautifully situated annex. Excellent restaurant. Fishing available. Doubles from $325.

LEEMING HOUSE
Watermillock, Ullswater
Tel: 44-(0)-17684-86622

Enjoying a lovely location overlooking Lake Ullswater, its 39 spacious rooms are well appointed, and the food in its restaurant won't disappoint—nor will the service. Nice garden. Doubles from $200.

⑱ ON THE WAY TO NEW ZEALAND'S MILFORD SOUND: THE LORD OF THE RINGS COUNTRY

Queenstown may very well be New Zealand's premier tourist destination. From here, helicopters lift off to show visitors the awesome scope in this Lord of the Rings country, most of which cannot be accessed by road. Passing over expansive lakes and mountains, stopping only for a picnic and photo or two on top of the world's tallest glacier, I discovered that this is perhaps the most breathtaking scenery in the world.

Once at Milford Sound, there are cruises that pass by falling waterfalls, glaciers, sheer cliffs, and rain forests. I saw fur seals, dolphins, and penguins from boats with names like the *Milford Wanderer* and *Milford Mariner,* the latter built along the lines of a traditional trading scow with all the romance of sails. They are much the same as when they were launched in 1912, the same year as the *Titanic,* but there definitely are no icebergs in sight.

There are overnight options on these vessels, which go out to the open sea before settling in Harrison Cove for a good night's sleep.

And that is just a tiny taste of what this great land has to offer.

MOST ROMANTIC INN

MATAKAURI LODGE
Closeburn, Glenorchy Road
Queenstown on the road to Glenorchy
Tel: 64-3-441-1008
www.matakauri.co.nz

In 1999 Matakauri Lodge opened and quickly became home to one of the best and most romantic of New Zealand's lodges. With cedar walls and beech floors, each mini-villa has a natural design of warmth and comfort. The views from the duplex chalets are breathtaking. This is a terrific accommodation with the huge double spa bath in each bathroom. An exceedingly friendly staff attends to every detail. Looking out over Lake Wakatipu in the evening, with a warm fire in your living room, you'll be delighted.

If you love the outdoors, and scenery jumping out of postcards, glaciers and lakes, mountains, plenty of rolling green hills, scenery topping scenery, you will love New Zealand. With spectacular natural landscapes, and the sight of thousands and thousands of sheep, there is much to do before you sleep. New Zealand is approximately the size of Great Britain and has similar weather. During New Zealand's summer season, it never gets too hot no matter where you go.

A fisherman's paradise, with some of the best sport fishing in the world, New Zealand has many fishing clubs and local guides to direct and help. The country has no snakes, poisonous spiders, or animals to fear—good news for hikers and campers.

New Zealand comprises two main islands, the North and the South, plus the small, minor Stewart Island at the southernmost point. The North Island has a subtropical climate. The South Island is in the temperate zone. There are no extreme variations in weather, but it is most consistently pleasant from December through April. New Zealanders take their vacations en masse between mid-December and mid-January, however, and service deteriorates for lack of help.

The country's most enjoyable accommodations are its lodges and boutique inns. By and large, each has fewer than 20 rooms and is presided over by caring owner-managers who will go out of their way to make you feel welcome. Most lodges are expensive, although it is not unusual for the rate to include breakfast, dinner with wine, cocktails, and other amenities.

Of note: Grilled lamb is a specialty of New Zealand. Many restaurants pride themselves on their sauces. One particular favorite of ours is a mint sauce, combined with honey, brown sugar and vinegar settled together and a delicious complement.

THE SOUTH ISLAND

QUEENSTOWN

Queenstown, New Zealand's "adventure capital," is the South Island's most important year-round resort. It is located in a spectacular setting on lovely Lake Wakatipu and surrounded by hills and jagged summits. There are outstanding views from Bob's Peak and Coronet Peak.

Skiing in winter is very popular with New Zealanders as well as visitors. In summer, there are many water excursions via ferries, jet boats on the Dart River, hydrofoils, white-water rafts, and boats that sail to high-country sheep and cattle stations. Half-day and all-day horseback rides are popular, as are fishing and hiking. For an easy, pleasant walk, try the "fitness track" that starts in the park at the end of the lake, opposite the Parkroyal Hotel. Despite the huge snowfall that hits the mountains, the valley below remains relatively snow-free most of the time. So you can ski and play golf or go boating on the same day.

PARKROYAL QUEENSTOWN
Beach Street, Queenstown
Tel: 64-3-442-7800

A good hotel, with 139 pleasant rooms. Most face the lake and mountains. Doubles from $150.

⭐ EICHARDT'S BOUTIQUE HOTEL
Marine Parade, Queenstown
Tel: 64-3-441-0450, www.eichardtshotel.co.nz

The Shaw family, under the leadership of Victoria Shaw, has created one of the most beautiful boutique hotels in the world. It is a combination of contemporary provincial elegance, with distinctive antiques and luxurious furnishings.

The rooms all feature a super-king bed, fireplace, minibar, dressing room, a bathroom with generous bath, double vanity, separate shower, and heated mirror and floor. Each is fully entertainment and business integrated, with personal audiovisual systems, along with e-mail and Internet access.

All rooms are generously proportioned, and the hotel has ample spaces for privacy and quiet, whether reading by an open log fire in the parlor or enjoying a late morning espresso in the house bar.

Overlooking a mirror of crystal water with splendid views of snowcapped peaks in the background, this hotel sets its own standard for gracious, luxury accommodations with the confident strokes and flawless symmetry by New Zealand's leading interior designer, Virginia Fisher.

You will appreciate the details: fresh flowers, stunning bathrooms, custom amenities of soap and cologne, and the plates of fruit, port wine, and cheese fireside in your suite each evening.

All this beauty and alpine splendor is a world apart, yet right outside is the bright buzz of Queenstown's vibrant cafés, dining, shopping, and nightlife. It has all the facilities and amenities you would expect in a world-class resort. Victoria serves up a delicious breakfast in the library.

SOUTH ISLAND FROM ABOVE

OVER THE TOP HELICOPTER TOURS
Tel: 64-3-442-2233
www.flynz.co.nz

For a truly thrilling way to experience the Queenstown area, take a helicopter tour over spectacular mountain tops, dropping into beautiful valleys and lingering at some of the area's many waterfalls. Over the Top Helicopter Company offers a selection of different tours, all of which can be altered to suit your needs.

One of the most popular tours is the Glacier Experience, where you land on top of a glacier and truly feel on top of the world. Another option is Picnic on a Peak, in which you'll be flown to a secluded area for a leisurely champagne lunch. High Country Explorer showcases the best of the South Island's high country, including a hospitality stop at a historic goldminer's cottage. And, for the daredevils, there's the Heli Bungy tour, in which you'll be delivered to the bungy platform, take a terrifying leap, and step back into the helicopter for your trip home. For information, tel: 64-3-442-2233, E-mail: bookings@flynz.co.nz. Prices begin at $150.

BLANKET BAY
Glenorchy Road, Glenorchy
Tel: 64-3-442-9442

A fine inn near Queenstown, Blanket Bay is a massive stone-and-wood lodge that sits right on the shore of Lake Wakatipu near the mouths of the Rees and Dart Rivers. The views of the surrounding 3,000-meter (10,000-foot) Humboldt Mountains are spectacular, and the scale of the rooms seems almost as massive as the natural surroundings. A good choice among the rooms is the Mt. Earnslaw suite, an attractive and comfortable accommodation with a superior bathroom. The dining room is exceptional. Lodge suites from about $685, including breakfast and dinner.

NELSON

THE LODGE AT PARATIHO FARMS
545 Waiwhero Rd., RD 2, Upper Moutere, Nelson
New ZealandTel: 64-3-528-2100
www.paratiho.co.nz

Not far from Nelson on the South Island is this lodge in an area of farms, vineyards, beaches, and mountainous national parks. *Paratiho* is a Maori word meaning "paradise," and once you've settled into your beautifully decorated guest quarters, you'll understand the relevance of the name. Furnishings throughout the lodge, the common rooms, and the guest suites are quite beautiful; and the owners' fine personal art collection is displayed everywhere. There are only six suites, all separate from the lodge, with fireplaces, splendid bathrooms, and many thoughtful amenities, including a bedside jar of cookies baked fresh and restocked daily. The property was developed by Sally and Bob Hunt, who seem to have taken exquisite pains to assure the comfort and satisfaction of their guests. A talented chef produces excellent cuisine, which is served either in the breakfast room off the kitchen or in the dining room. Table settings are lavish. Facilities include fitness center with spa rooms and swimming pool, a petanque court, tennis, croquet, and a putting green. The staff will arrange excursions, perhaps to the artists' colony of growing renown. Doubles from about $1,000 for two persons, including all meals.

BLENHEIM

TIMARA LODGE
Dog Point Road-RD-2, Blenheim
Tel: 64-3-572-8276

Timara Lodge, in the heart of the Marlborough wine country, is a very appealing luxury escape. This 100-year-old house on a magnificent estate has extensive lawns, a swimming pool, tennis court, lake, flower gardens, and many big old trees. There are only four guest rooms, each decorated differently and elegantly. Beds have sheepskin mattress pads for extra comfort. Good food. Lots of tropical fruits, local fish, and lamb. Doubles from $500, including two meals.

FINE DINING

C'EST LA VIE
33 Rue Lavaud, Akaroa
Tel: 64-3-304-7314

French cuisine in a candlelit setting, in a French-settled town.

CHRISTCHURCH

Christchurch, the most English town outside England, was founded by the Anglican Church in 1850. It is called the "Garden City" because of its unusual number of parks and gardens, and its Botanical Gardens are world-renowned. There is an annual competition to determine the best home gardens. Most gardens are open to the public at specified hours. The Avon River meanders throughout the city, with trees and gardens on both banks. All told, it is really a lovely town, with much Edwardian and Victorian architecture.

Be sure to visit the Canterbury Museum, with its charming 19th-century street replica and displays of Polynesian artifacts.

RYDGES CHRISTCHURCH (FORMERLY NOAH'S HOTEL)
Worcester Street and Oxford Terrace, Christchurch
Tel: 64-3-379-4700

In a central location, Rydges provides good accommodations and a pleasant ambience. 208 rooms. Doubles from about $100.

PARK ROYAL HOTEL
Kilmare and Durham Streets, Christchurch
Tel: 64-3-365-7799

With a pyramidal shape and an attractive atrium lobby, the Park Royal is in a good location. Facilities include a business center and gym. 300 rooms. Doubles from about $200.

For an enjoyable excursion from Christchurch, go to the village of Akaroa, originally settled by the French.

MILFORD SOUND

Milford Sound, in the South Island's southwest and part

of Fiordland National Park, is one of the most beautiful and out-of-the-way places in the country. It receives more than 500 centimeters (200 inches) of rain annually. You can drive or bus here from Te Anau in about three hours. En route you might want to stop to look into chasms, observe Mirror Lake, and try a portion of the nature walk to Gunn Lake.

A more adventurous way to visit Milford Sound is by helicopter, stopping on top of a glacier on the way. Southern Scenic Air Service has scheduled one-hour flights from Queenstown in eight-seat planes, weather permitting. The plane flies the entire length of the sound only a hundred meters or so (a few hundred feet) above the water, and your wings seem to be scraping the walls of fjords compared to those of Norway.

Energetic and fit hikers with sufficient time can make the 53-kilometer (33-mile) trek between Te Anau and Milford Sound on the famed Milford Track in three days. Many people consider this to be the most beautiful walk in the world. It is physically challenging, with lots of hills: Outfitters will not take anyone incapable of going the entire distance.

There are two ways to make the trip: deluxe and basic. Deluxe provides comfortable bungalows, where guests sleep in dormitory style—men in one room, women in another—and good meals. The basic-level trip is essentially for backpackers. Nighttime shelter is provided, but you carry your own sleeping bag and provisions. Reservations must be made at least six months ahead of time through a travel agent or with the Milford Track Office.

Another option to visit the sound is to take one of the highly recommended launch cruises, but not one that serves lunch. While you're dining inside, the spectacular scenery will be passing by unseen. You'll see Mitre Peak, 1.6 kilometers (1-mile) high, and many other steep

mountains, inlets, islands, and "hanging valleys"—truly the "eighth wonder of the world," just as Rudyard Kipling described them when he visited in the 19th century. There is also a "Doubtful Sound" trip, involving two launches and a bus ride—worth taking if you have the time.

MOUNT COOK NATIONAL PARK

Mount Cook National Park is a scenic wonder offering views of 27 peaks that ring the area. If you are traveling between Christchurch and Queenstown, and if the weather is good, an unforgettable experience is to take a ski-plane flight from Mount Cook to the Tasman Glacier, at the side of the 3,764-meter (12,349-foot) mountain.

The tiny Mount Cook "village" is in an unspoiled valley surrounded by mountains. You'll discover beautiful trails at all levels of effort. For example, the Governor's Track is easy. It hugs the bottom of a mountain. The thick bushy area supports many different kinds of trees and ferns interspersed with open meadows that are filled with lupines of every color.

Arrowtown, a nearby deserted gold-rush relic, makes a pleasant excursion. The scenery en route is beautiful.

THE HERMITAGE HOTEL
Mt. Cook National Park
Tel: 64-3-435-1809

This sprawling mountain resort overlooks the Hooker Valley and Mount Cook. Ask for a room with a balcony and view of the mountains. Rooms are not deluxe but comfortable, and there are two restaurants, including the award-winning Panorama Restaurant. 104 rooms. Doubles from $150, includes continental breakfast.

LAKE MOERAKI WILDERNESS LODGE
South Westland
Tel: 64-3-288-750-0881

New Zealand's largest lowland rain forest and wilderness lies midway between Queenstown and Greymouth. Of the few accommodations in this area, the best choice is this lodge, a basic 18-unit outpost, with small, neat rooms that are reminiscent of a 1950s motel. The restaurant overlooks the Moeraki rapids. Nature study activities excellent—your guide will introduce you to crested penguins, fur seals, and giant tame eels. Doubles from $225.

From Queenstown, it's a three-hour drive through mountains and past sheep, cattle, and deer stations to the small town of Te Anau on Lake Te Anau. It also borders

Fjordland National Park, one of the world's most beautiful parks, with superb mountain and woodland scenery. If you are not a hardy hiker or camper, you can stay in Te Anau and take day trips into the park.

The boat trip across the lake to the impressive Te Anau Caves is recommended. Here you will see waterfalls, limestone formations, and a glowworm grotto similar to Waitomo's, and hear an excellent talk by a park ranger about the ancient caves' history and about glowworms.

TE ANAU TRAVEL LODGE
64 THE TERRACE, TE ANAU
Tel: 64-3-249-7411

The best hotel in town is the Te Anau Travelodge, with 112 acceptable units, a business center, a heated pool, spa, fishing, and boating. Doubles from $125.

THE NORTH ISLAND

COROMANDEL PENINSULA

The Coromandel Peninsula, west of Auckland, is an unspoiled area, forested and wild, with good beaches, hunting, and fishing. It was once a gold-mining center.

PUKA PARK RESORT
Mount Avenue, Pauanui Beach
Tel: 64-7-864-8088
www.pukapark.co.nz

The best base from which to enjoy the natural surroundings. It is restful, with 48 chalets and a pool.

They will arrange hiking, boating, fishing, shooting, and so on. Doubles from $250, including breakfast.

CASSIMIR
Williams Road, Tauranga
Tel: 64-7-543-2000

A grand 1890 colonial villa that overlooks the Coromandel coast to the Pacific Ocean. Owner Reg Turner has created a first-class lodge on 20 hectares (50 acres) of pasture and native forest with an abundance of wildlife as well as small herds of sheep and cattle. The six rooms are comfortable, and there are a spa, solarium, and library. Activities include clay-pigeon shooting and hot-air ballooning. Doubles from $250, including breakfast, dinner, and cocktails.

LAKE TAUPO

Taupo, the largest lake in New Zealand, offers a variety of sports activities including a bungee-jump site over a beautiful gorge. Fishing is excellent, and you can charter a boat and crew for a day's excursion on the lake.

HUKA LODGE
Taupo
Tel: 64-7-378-5791, www.hukalodge.com

Huka Lodge is about an hour's drive from Rotorua or a four-hour drive from Auckland through beautiful countryside. You can also fly directly to Lake Taupo. The lodge began as a fishermen's tent camp in the 1920s, located on 7 hectares (17 acres) along the Waikato River leading to Huka Falls.

Twenty bungalow rooms are arranged in pairs and situated along a wooded trail. All rooms face the river and are the essence of secluded comfort. Your serenity will not be disturbed by telephone, e-mail, or TV, unless you ask to have them. Dining is at large tables for eight or, if you make advance arrangements, at any of several charming private areas. The food is outstanding and the service impeccable. Doubles from about $500 per person, including breakfast and dinner.

NAPIER

Napier, in the North Island's southeast, features stunning art deco architecture from the 1930s and a buzzing café culture—more than 30 cafés do business here. Marine Parade, a lush walkway along the sea bedecked with gardens and fountains, has a fabulous aquarium that families shouldn't miss. Nearby await a gannet colony at Cape Kidnappers and plenty of Hawke's Bay wineries in the heart of New Zealand's oldest wine-growing region.

MANGAPAPA LODGE
466 Napier Road (15 minutes from Napier)
Tel: 64-6-878-3234

The former country homestead of Sir James Watte, a wealthy New Zealander who sold his canning business to the H. J. Heinz Company, was restored in 1994 by a German couple, Shirley and Guenter Engels. Each of its nine spacious suites reflects a different European ambience; the Macon (French) and Seefeld (Austrian) are particularly attractive. There is an outdoor swimming pool, tennis courts, Jacuzzi, and an orchard. Deluxe and cottage suites from $450, including breakfast, dinner, and cocktails. The dining room is open to nonguests.

MASTER'S LODGE
10 Elizabeth Road, Bluff Hill, Napier
Tel: 64-6-834-1946

Overlooking the coast, the lodge was built by a local cigarette baron and is now owned and managed by a Swiss couple, Doris and Urs Blum. There are only two rooms, both of them huge and nicely furnished, and one with a sun porch. For any service in your room, you just pull the old-fashioned bell cord. Doubles from $260, including breakfast. Swiss dinner for two, including wine, about $60.

EATING OUT

MISSION ESTATE WINERY
Church Road, Taradale
Tel: 64-6-844-2259

An interesting attraction, rather than a fine dining experience. The winery is the oldest in New Zealand, having been founded in 1851 by the brothers of the Society of Mary. Their vintages have won numerous awards. Lunch or dinner for two, with wine, about $50.

——— · ———

BAYSWATER
Hardaige Road, Napier
Tel: 64-6-835-8517

A small restaurant noted for its unusual selections, including apple soup and starters made of kangaroo and crocodile. Dinner for two, without wine, about $60.

THE LODGE AT KAURI CLIFFS

Near Matauri Bay, Northland
Tel: 64-9-405-1900
www.kauricliffs.com

On the Bay of Islands, about 300 kilometers (185 miles) north of Auckland and about as far north as you can go in New Zealand, set on 2,500 hectares (6,000 acres) of rolling country and cliffsides dropping down to the Pacific Ocean, this lodge's biggest draw is its championship golf course. The main lodge is a plantation-style building that houses the lounge, dining room, and other guest facilities; accommodations are in eight cottages, each with two guest rooms that are tastefully designed and furnished. We prefer the cottage farthest from the lodge for its greater privacy. Food service is excellent and is particularly enjoyable at the outdoor tables on the verandas. High season (October to March) doubles from about $800 per person, including breakfast and dinner. Golf fees are extra.

Although there are convenient flights from Auckland to Kerikeri, the closest airport, there is a great deal to see in the area, so you should consider driving from Auckland, a trip of about four hours on a good road with spectacular scenery. Be sure to visit the Waitangi National Reserve, the most important Maori site in New Zealand. Take a walk through one of the kauri forests that abound in the area. There is one very near the hotel with marked paths of varying lengths. Several of the seaside villages in the area are also worth a visit. If you are out and about and want a lunch spot, try the Marsden Winery, on the road to the Kerikeri airport. Another decent spot is Marx (310 Kerikeri Road). And if you visit the town of Russell (via ferry from Opua), try the Duke of Marlborough Pub.

ROTORUA

Perched on the southern shore of Lake Rotorua in the Bay of Plenty, Rotorua has been a spa resort for more than a century. It has some lovely botanical gardens, charming architecture, and, at Kuirau Park, some remarkable hot bubbling mud pools.

Rotorua is also a good place to learn about the Maori culture. The Arawa tribe has lived here for about 600 years. Start your visit with a tour of the Whakarewarewa Thermal Reserve ("Whaka" for short). You'll see a profusion of thermal phenomena right in the middle of a functioning Maori village. Also worth visiting is the Maori Arts and Crafts Institute on Hemo Road. It's a government supported woodcarving school designed to maintain the state of the art, which came close to being lost before the program was launched.

Of special interest in Rotorua is the *hangi,* a traditional Maori feast, supplemented by music and dancing. The best place to enjoy a hangi with music is the Centra Rotorua Hotel. Music and dancing alone are offered at the Maori Cultural Theater on Eureka Street, and at the Tamatekapua Meeting House in nearby Ohinemutu Village.

In town, you'll see some really excellent examples of Maori woodcarving. The meeting house is carved with scenes from Arawa tribal history. Near it is a church with a hall decorated by Maoris, combining native and European themes.

A worthwhile non-Maori event takes place in Rotorua's Agrodome: an exhibition of New Zealand's best breeds of sheep. There is also a working sheepdog exhibition, and don't miss the good sheepskin store at the Agrodome.

On the other hand, you can skip the Rainbow and Fairy Springs. Despite the stocked trout pools, the kiwis, and the wild pigs, it's pretty dull.

A noted landmark just a short distance from Rotorua is the Te Wairoa Buried Village, a victim of the volcanic eruption of 1886. The museum here exhibits objects unearthed from the site, along with before-and-after photographs. You can also visit a number of ongoing excavations.

MAORI TRADITION

The Maori, who came from Polynesia, reached New Zealand almost 500 years before the Europeans. Today, about a third of the people identified as Maori are actually of a pure Maori strain. Most are of mixed ancestry and most still live on the North Island. Since the 1940s there has been a mass exodus of Maori from rural areas to cities in search of employment. Thus, most Maori now are urban dwellers. All these changes, however, as profound as they've been, have not entirely destroyed the cultural heritage of the Maori. And efforts are being made to keep it alive as a national treasure.

MILLENNIUM ROTORUA
Eruera and Hinemaru Streets, Rotorua
Tel: 64-7-347-1234

The best choice in town is a 227-room establishment in the town center. Rooms on higher floors have views of the lake. Doubles from $120.

MOOSE LODGE
State Highway 30
Tel: 64-7-362-7823

Naturally beautiful and less than ten minutes from the Rotorua Airport is a 7-hectare (18-acre) retreat overlooking Lake Rotoiti. The lodge includes 20 individually decorated rooms, all with lakefront views and three with spa baths.

Guests have use of an all-weather tennis court, a billiard room, sailboats, the lodge's 8.5-meter (28-foot) launch, windsurfers, kayaks, a volleyball court, bicycles, and a gym. The inviting public rooms are filled with antiques, and an elegant five-course dinner is served each evening in one of three intimate dining rooms. Doubles from $570, including breakfast, pre-dinner cocktails, and dinner.

SOLITAIRE LODGE
19 Ronald Road, Lake Tarawera
Tel: 64-7-362-8208

This lodge is thought by many to be the most elegant lodge in the Pacific, and it surely is the finest in the Rotorua area. Solitaire overlooks Lake Tarawera with its record-size rainbow trout. Each of the ten rooms and suites offers a marvelous view of the lake, with the best, perhaps, being the Solitaire and Tarawera suites. Only slightly less grand are the Spencer and Arawa suites. Guests may dine in their rooms or join others for cocktails and dinner in the dining room. Activities include tennis, sailing, fishing, and water skiing. The property, a member of the Small Luxury Hotels of the World, is under the careful and considerate management of Jennifer Klein. Doubles and suites from $630, including three meals, use of fishing gear and sailing yachts, and Rotorua airport transfers.

WELLINGTON

Wellington, the capital of New Zealand, is at the southern tip of the North Island on a very hilly, beautiful site overlooking the harbor. It is a rather conventional, conservative city. There are no truly deluxe hotels. Te Papa, the National Museum, has an outstanding Maori collection of South Island tribal artifacts, including the carved Te Hauki-Turanga meeting house.

WELLINGTON'S BEST SITES

- Parliament and Government buildings, an attractive mix of old and new buildings
- Botanical Gardens (go via cable car)
- Te Papa, the National Museum, with its fascinating exhibits on New Zealand history and culture
- Alexander Turnbull Library, specializing in Pacific geography and history
- Willis Street for New Zealand's best shopping

PARK ROYAL WELLINGTON
147 The Terrace, Wellington
Tel: 64-4-499-9500

The Park Royal has 233 rooms, a health and fitness club, an indoor pool, and a spa. Doubles from $200. It is near the harbor, the commercial district, and the James Cook Centre.

★ WHAREKAUHAU COUNTRY ESTATE
Western Lake Road, Palliser Bay
Tel: 64-6-307-7581

A spectacular accommodation in the Wellington area. We strongly recommend staying here. Located 10 minutes from Wellington by helicopter, or two hours by car, it is situated on a 2,000-hectare (5,000-acre) sheep station at the foot of the Rimutaka Mountains. The beautifully appointed property has accommodations for up to 20 guests in several Celtic cottages and villa-style buildings. All are very comfortable and equipped with every modern convenience on expansive landscapes of endless rolling hills to the sea.

The food is on a par with that of the best restaurants. The managers can arrange fishing, hiking, hunting, golfing, and touring the station. Per person, double occupancy rates, from $350 including breakfast and dinner.

AUCKLAND

Auckland, the international gateway to New Zealand, is laid out with stylish informality around one of the most beautiful harbors in the world. The "City of Sails" is surrounded by water, so the maritime environment is predominant and sailing is a major pastime. A trip to the top of Mount Eden, an extinct volcano, provides a superb panoramic vista of the city. The beaches, miles of them, are very nice, and you might want to see the races at Ellerslie Racecourse. Parnell Village is an attractive area filled with boutiques and restaurants.

The Auckland City Art Gallery exhibits Western art, the country's best such collection. The Museum of Transport and Technology features airplanes, photography, printing, and colonial furnishings. At Auckland's zoo, you can see the kiwi, New Zealand's national bird, and the tuatara lizard. Don't miss the War Memorial Museum, with one of the finest Maori collections in the world, mostly oriented toward North Island tribes. It includes a carved 25-meter (82-foot) war canoe; the carved Hotunui meeting house, depicting the ancestral legacy of the Ngati Maru tribe; and the really splendid Rangitakaroro carved gateway.

★ HYATT REGENCY AUCKLAND
Corner of Princes St. and Waterloo Quadrant, Auckland
Tel: 64-9-355-1234

Right in the middle of this incredible city is a very special hotel, the Hyatt Regency. With its stunning views of the Auckland harbor and parks, it is located just a few minutes' walk from the city center. We prefer this hotel over any in the city.

In 2003, the hotel added 120 new rooms, studio suites, one- and two-bedroom all-suite apartments, and penthouses, each with balconies. The suites have spacious bathrooms with separate bath and shower and large double vanities, along with a lounge, dining area and kitchen facilities. The new suites complement the hotel's other 274 European-style rooms.

Guests have access to Spa at the Hyatt—a health club, lifestyle, and fitness center with a fully equipped gym, heated pool, Jacuzzi, steam room, and sauna. Facial, massage and spa therapy treatments with New Zealand and international products are also available.

The hotel has a full range of business facilities, a business club lounge (Regency Club), Lobby Bar, outdoor dining area, and a delicious range of local and international cuisine in its restaurant, the Café.

⭐ HILTON AUCKLAND
Princes Wharf, 147 Quay Street
Tel: 64-9-978-2000

The Hilton is in the unique position of being located on the end of Prince's Wharf, offering guests beautiful views across Auckland's inner harbor. A contemporary, luxury boutique-style hotel featuring 138 king-bed and 20 twin-bed stylish guest rooms, plus 8 suites. It has the most unique swimming pool in New Zealand, and Whytes Restaurant is one of the best.

⭐ MCMAHON'S VILLA HOTEL
42 St. Stephens Avenue, Parnell
Tel: 64-9-309-7788

Six delightful rooms with equally delightful hosts who could not be more accommodating. As an alternate to hotels, not far from the town's center but residential, McMahon's is truly outstanding in every respect. Each room is furnished with fresh linens, flowers, and tasteful antiques.

WAIHEKE ISLAND

The short ferry ride from Auckland to Waiheke is recommended. It is a very attractive part of the world and a hidden treasure with outstanding scenery and great wines. The mere mention of Waiheke is enough to put a smile on any North Islander's face. It's the place they go to loosen up, kick back, and have fun. Some people are even lucky enough to live there.

Waiheke is one of the larger Hauraki Gulf islands, and its landscape is a picturesque blend of farmland, forest, beaches, vineyards, and olive groves. The unique climate and soil conditions produce consistently excellent wines, particularly Cabernet and Merlot blends. The island seems to have a similar effect on the local art scene. Waiheke artists and craftspeople are credited with producing some of the country's most respected work in recent years.

A day trip could include visits to vineyards and art studios, swimming at Onetangi or Palm Beach, and lunch at an Oneroa café. Ask the locals to point you toward Stony Batter, a massive underground tunnel network built during World War II. You'll need a comfortable pair of walking shoes and a flashlight.

If you want to stay for a few days, there's a nice choice of accommodations. For a real getaway, why not rent a beach house and live the dream? Waiheke is considered by many to be the ultimate lifestyle choice, so the traditional New Zealand beach houses (known to Kiwis as a "bach") are scattered all around the Waiheke coastline. Activities such as horseback riding, golf, and sea kayaking will keep you busy— or simply find a perfect beach and let the days wash over you.

A TASTING LUNCH

TE WHAU VINEYARD RESTAURANT
218 Te Whau Dr., Waiheke Island
Tel: 64-9-372-7191

Surrounded by breathtaking views of Waiheke Island, this spectacular restaurant, located on the top level of Te Whau winery, features fresh New Zealand/Pacific Rim cuisine, a wine bar, and the finest wine list in New Zealand. Each year since 2002, Wine Spectator has designated it "One of the Best Restaurants in the World for Wine Lovers." This Award of Excellence is made based on the strength and depth of their wine list, which features the very best of New Zealand wines, Te Whau vintages, and many unobtainable Waiheke Island wines.

Two Great Vineyards

STONYRIDGE VINEYARD

Stephan White's Stonyridge Vineyard was conceived and operated with the sole intention of making the greatest Bordeaux-style red wine in the world. This is a blend of Cabernet Sauvignon, Merlot, Cabernet Franc, Malbec, and Petit Verdot and is named Larose as a tribute to the rose, the most aromatic, colorful, intense, and beautiful of all flowers.

The vineyard site was chosen specifically to produce this style of wine. Its gentle north-facing slopes are sheltered from the cold south westerly winds by the ridge that bears the vineyard's name. Summer temperatures regularly reach more than 30°C (85°F) with the highest temperature being 36°C (97°F) degrees. Combined with north-facing rows and excellent viticulture, the grapes achieve perfect ripeness in normal years.

The grapes are handpicked and immediately transported to the winery, where they are crushed, de-stemmed, and pumped into stainless steel fermentation tanks. A warm fermentation is followed by a two-week maceration before being basket pressed. Malolactic fermentation is completed in  barrel in the warmed chai or barrel cellar. The wine is 100 percent oak aged in French and some American barriques.

Larose is aged for more than a year in oak, racked regularly, rarely fined, and never filtered. It's available either "En Primeur" on the mailing list, in the vineyard café, or from selected retail outlets and prestige restaurants. The vineyard is located at 80 Onetangi Road, Waiheke Island, Tel: 64-9-372-8822.

TE WHAU VINEYARD

Terry Forsyth's vineyard has one aim: to produce grapes of the highest possible quality that fully reflect the characteristics of the site.

Their red grapes, two hectares (five acres) of Cabernet Sauvignon, Merlot, Cabernet Franc, and Malbec, are grown on a steep (20°) north-facing slope just back from the point of the peninsula. The vineyard's topography ensures shelter from the prevailing cool south winds as well as extra ripening potential from the steepness of the slope and its orientation toward the sun. The vineyard is located at 218 Te Whau Dr., Waiheke Island, Tel: 64-9-372-7191, www.tewhau.co.nz. Its restaurant offers the perfect chance to taste some fine wines with exquisite cuisine (see sidebar).

WAIHEKE ISLAND VISITOR INFORMATION CENTRE
2 Korora Road
Phone: 64-9-372-1234

⭐ GIVERNY INN
44 Queens Drive, Oneroa
Tel: 64-9-372-2200, www.giverny.co.nz

Set in Mediterranean-style gardens and nestled on a bush-clad hill on Waiheke Island is Giverny Inn, a Tuscan-inspired lodge providing luxury accommodation, with three suites, a superb range of facilities, Jacuzzi, gourmet breakfasts, in-house massage, and beauty therapy. Its dramatic 200-degree views of the mighty Coromandel Peninsula, the enchanting Hauraki Gulf islands, and stunning Oneroa Bay offer guests an unforgettable taste of paradise.

Style, elegance and privacy, the enchantment of island life, the delights of fresh local and indigenous produce, pampering spa and beauty treatments—all are features that make a stay at Giverny Inn an extraordinary experience. Just a 35-minute ferry ride from the bustle of downtown Auckland or a 30-minute flight from Auckland International airport, Giverny's guests feel they are a world away from city life.

LONGHOUSE
155 Nick Johnstone Drive, Church Bay
Tel: 64-9-372-9619

As the Waiheke Ferry glides into Matiatia Bay, 35 minutes from Auckland City, cast your eyes to the headland on your right, and there rests Longhouse, the perfect island retreat with rolling countryside, ancient Pohutukawa trees, vineyards, olive groves, and a tiny cove with coastal walkways. Recently completed, Longhouse is an elegant structure of high ceilings and soft plastered surfaces, with an enclosed courtyard, three guest rooms with en-suite facilities, and views across the ocean to die for.

⑲ THE GREECE OF ARISTOPHANES, EURIPIDES, & HOMER

The impact of ancient Greece on the Western world can't be overstated. The rediscovery of Greek classics of philosophy, science, and literature in the 14th and 15th centuries had a profound influence on the development of Western thought, leading Europe into the Renaissance.

The notion of democracy, the concept of the atom, the image of the Earth as round, the scientific method itself, all these and more had their birth in the thinking and writing of ancient Greece.

Though its recorded history goes back thousands of years, modern-day Greece was largely shaped by the past several centuries. The Ottoman Empire took control of Greece in the 15th century and governed until 1821, when the War of Independence began. A monarchy, installed in 1832 under Prince Otto of Bavaria, was abolished and reinstated twice during the 20th century. A military junta took power in 1967, but was booted out in 1974. That year, the nation finally returned to democracy.

The following years brought a period of political stability and economic development. Greece obtained full membership in the European Community in 1981, and replaced the drachma with the euro in 2002.

The best time to visit Greece is from mid-May to mid-June and from mid-September to the end of October, when temperatures are mild. The end of June to the beginning of September is crowded with tourists and hot. During winter, temperatures are often below 10°C (50°F), which is okay for touring but too cold to swim or lie on the beach.

Greece has little rain year-round, while during the summer the breezes (*meltemi*) keep the temperatures bearable. Though Athens, like Rome and Jerusalem, is known for its glorious past, few become impressed with the modern city.

ATHENS

The Acropolis stands sentinel over the smoggy urban sprawl of Athens and can be seen from almost everywhere in the city. In this complex of ancient buildings, the Parthenon stands out for its unsurpassed grace and beauty. The

nearby Erechtheion is recognized immediately for the much-photographed Caryatids, the six stone maidens who take the place of columns. The ancient theater of Dionysus, where every citizen of Athens took a turn in the chorus of Greek tragedies, is on the Acropolis's southern slope and still hosts dramatic events.

ANDROMEDA ATHENS HOTEL
22 Timoleontos Vassou (next to the U.S. Embassy, 1.5 kilometers [1 mile] from the center of town)
Tel: 30-281-030-0330
www.ellada.net/andromeda

The Andromeda Athens Hotel is a small, stylish establishment à la Philippe Starck. It has 17 double rooms, four studios with kitchenettes, nine suites, and a penthouse. All have satellite TV, minibars, and computer outlets. Bathrooms include hair dryers and phones. There are two restaurants, one a café bar specializing in Polynesian and Asian food; the other, Michelangelo, is one of the city's better restaurants. Twenty-four-hour room service and free parking. Doubles from $300.

ASTIR PALACE RESORT
Vouliagmeni Beach
Tel: 30-210-890-2000

A very nice resort only a few miles out of the city, the Astir Palace Resort comprises three hotels with air-conditioned rooms, suites with balconies, and a number of bungalows, all with marble bathrooms. Wonderful views of the sea, plus a private beach, swimming pool, roof garden, and tennis courts.

GREECE

ATHENS HILTON
46 Vasilissis Sofias Avenue
Tel: 30-210-728-1000, www.athenshilton.com

This 453-room Hilton is one of the better representatives of the international chain. It is located across the street from the National Gallery, somewhat away from the city center. The hotel has spacious rooms, good restaurants, huge outdoor swimming pool, sauna, and outstanding views from rooms facing the Acropolis.

HOTEL GRANDE BRETAGNE
Constitution Square
Tel: 30-210-333-0000, www.grandebretagne.gr

Competing with the Ledra Marriott for recognition as the city's best hotel is the old lady of Athens, the Grande Bretagne. This 364-room accommodation dates back to 1842 and has become a landmark presiding over the central Constitution Square, opposite the House of Parliament. The Grande Bretagne is draped in history: During World War II, it became a strategic headquarters, first for the Germans and then for the British. In 1944, the staff foiled a bomb plot to kill Churchill when he stayed at the hotel. The rooms are palatial, with antique furnishings and a turn-of-the-20thcentury ambiance. Notably absent are leisure facilities—no gym and no pool. Doubles from $350.

HOTEL PLAKA
7 Kapnikareas
Tel: 30-210-322-2096, www.plakahotel.gr

It may only be a three-star hotel, but no accommodation in Athens has a better location than the Hotel Plaka. Situated at the heart of the historic Plaka district, there are 67 rooms that offer fantastic views of the Acropolis. All were renovated in 1995, and though they are basic they

TRAVELERS BEWARE

Beware of taxi drivers in Athens. It is not uncommon for them to claim that their meters are broken in order to jack up the price. And don't ask for a restaurant recommendation. They'll take you to a place that pays drivers for depositing innocent tourists at its doorstep. Inside, you'll pay sky-high prices for second-rate food.

are comfortable. The hotel also has a rooftop café that is very popular in summer. If you are looking for a value-conscious option without having to sacrifice location or view, the Plaka is a good choice. Doubles from $60.

LEDRA MARRIOTT
113–115 Syngrou Avenue
Tel: 30-210-930-0000, www.marriott.com

A five-star hotel with 259 guest rooms and seven suites. It's ideally located on busy Syngrou Avenue, which runs from the city center to the airport. Many rooms have balconies that offer views of the Acropolis, although the incessant traffic can be off-putting. The rooftop pool is a highlight, and the recently opened health club and business center have improved a hotel that was starting to look slightly outdated.

MUSEUMS

THE NATIONAL ARCHAEOLOGICAL MUSEUM
Patission 44 Street
Tel: 30-210-821-7717

A treasure-house of ancient Greek artifacts. Be sure to see the Minoan wall paintings from Thera.

GREECE

THE JEWISH MUSEUM
36 Amalias Avenue
Tel: 30-210-323-1577, www.jewishmuseum.gr

The Jewish Museum is small and beautiful. The Jewish community in Greece dates from at least the third and perhaps the fifth century B.C.

THE MUSEUM OF CYCLADIC AND ANCIENT ART
4 Neof Douka Street
Tel: 30-210-722-8321, www.cycladic-m.gr

A small, private collection. Of the items displayed on its three floors, the cycladic figurines are the most striking. They date from the second millennium B.C. to the fifth century A.D.

BENAKI MUSEUM
22 Vassilissis Sofias Avenue
Tel: 30-210-367-1000, www.benaki.gr

The former house of the Benaki family contains Greek art from ancient to modern times (jewelry in particular), Byzantine art, and Greek folk art. Also Chinese porcelain.

BYZANTINE MUSEUM
22 Vassilissis Sofias Avenue
Tel: 30-210-721-1027

Occupying the Duchess of Plaisance's mansion, this lovely museum features sculpture, frescoes, icons, woodcarvings, jewelry, and more.

AGORA MUSEUM
Stoa Attalou
Tel: 30-210-321-0185

The finds from excavations of the southern slope of the Acropolis and Pnyx hill are exhibited herre, including pottery, jewelry, ivory, and sculpture.

NATIONAL HISTORIC MUSEUM
13 Stadiou Street
Tel: 30-210-323-7617

The crown jewels of Greece and art and mementoes of Greece's struggle for independence in the 19th century are on display.

NATIONAL PICTURE GALLERY
50 Vassilissis Konstantinou
Tel: 30-210-723-5857

This wonderful museum showcases paintings by Greek artists, the Italian and Flemish schools, and El Greco—keep an eye out especially for drawings by Rembrandt, Van Dyck, and Watteau, as well as engravings by Dürer, Brueghel, Braque, and Picasso.

RESTAURANTS

O DAMIGOS
41 Kidathineon Street
Tel: 30-210-322-5084

Open only between October and May, this traditional gem right in the heart of Plaka is unknown to most travelers. The basement taverna serves up homey cuisine in sparse surroundings. Most of the diners are neighborhood folk who come to enjoy the local retsina and olive-oil-laden food. Highlights on the short two-page menu are the large salads, including a very delicious one with shrimp in oil sparked by a touch of lemon. The baklava desserts are outstanding. Dinner for two, without wine, about $35.

THE OLIVE GARDEN
In the Titania Hotel, 52 Panepistimou Street
Tel: 30-210-383-8511

Many hotels in Athens offer restaurants with great views. The centrally located Olive Garden, with its fabulous view, serves up tasty Mediterranean cuisine. The service is attentive and the menu offers good value. The "three different tarts" starter offers some tasty concoctions, including Gruyère and fresh thyme as well as wild mushrooms with grilled red pepper and walnuts. Salads are excellent, as are the seafood main courses, which feature grouper, monkfish, salmon, and the exotic scorpion fish steamed in a crabmeat sauce. The wine list consists primarily of the varieties found in most Athens restaurants, but you'll also find some excellent vintages from the Peloponnese. Dinner for two, without wine, about $60.

RESTAURANT DIONYSOS
Lykavittos Hill
Tel: 30-210-722-6374.

No restaurant offers a finer view than Restaurant Dionysos, which enjoys sweeping vistas from its location atop Lykavittos Hill. Part of the fun here is taking the funicular up and enjoying the city skyline, which is especially stunning at night. Most locals automatically recommend Dionysos to visitors, which has brought success to its operators and indifferent food to its diners. By all means go to the restaurant, but maybe skip dinner—just opt for a snack and coffee. Dinner for two, without wine, about $75.

EXCURSIONS FROM ATHENS

Most visitors to Athens see only the downtown area before moving on. Yet it is easy to get a fuller Greek experience simply by traveling a few miles to explore the areas immediately around the city. You will have to pass through the apparently endless, sometimes industrial, suburbs first, but the reward is the chance to have some classical sites all to yourself, particularly if traveling out of high season.

DAPHNI MONASTERY
Daphni, a bit more than 3 kilometers (2 miles) west of Athens, has the most important Byzantine church in Attica. It was built in the 11th century and dedicated to the Dormition of the Virgin. Architecturally its most remarkable feature is the majestic dome, some 8 meters (27 feet) in diameter and 15 meters (50 feet) high. Resting on an eight-sided base, the dome virtually caps the entire church. A hypnotic Pantokrator stares down

Postcard from Greece

It's a heady feeling to walk on stones that may have been trod by Plato, Homer, or Agamemnon. But at many places in Greece, where ancient ruins are surrounded by the noise and smells of traffic, or where pristine island beaches are packed by topless sunbathers, it's apparent that the influence works the other way as well: Greece, it sometimes seems, has been overtaken by the modern world it spawned.

The trick for travelers to Greece is to find the golden mean, in this case, the balance between environment and history, between crowds and quiet, between ancient and modern. With a bit of planning (and maybe a query to Delphi's oracle), you can find beautiful settings that can soothe your soul, while centuries of art and history invigorate your mind. And, very likely, you'll be as charmed by the Greek people as you are by their landscape.

SIGHTS

Mention Athens, and most people will think of the Acropolis. In spite of the ravages of weather and pollution, one cannot help but be moved by the grandeur of its setting and the beauty of its architecture. Be sure to visit the Acropolis Museum; it contains almost all the movable objects unearthed since the early 19th century.

The Plaka is Athens's old quarter. There you can see Hadrian's Library, the Lysicrates Monument, the Tower of the Winds, and many interesting old houses. Here too are Hadrian's Arch and the columns left standing from the Temple of Olympian Zeus.

At the ancient site of Delphi, northwest of Athens, where the Greeks once consulted the Oracle about the future, there's a small round sculpture. It's known as the *omphalos*—the cosmic belly button. The Greeks believed that Delphi was the very center of the world, the place where it all came into being. Indeed, many aspects of Western culture came into being in Greece: drama, art, philosophy, and science.

And then there are the islands.

Off the western coast, in the Ionian Sea, are the Ionian Islands (Cephalonia, Corfu, Ithaca, Lefkada, Paxi, and Zakinthos), the only island group not in the Aegean Sea. In many ways they remind visitors of Italy. Anyone who wanders into the backcountry will be rewarded with unspoiled villages. Corfu is the most beautiful. Close to Italy and Albania, it has been touched over the years by several foreign cultures. As a result it has acquired a certain sophistication and an offbeat charm.

Islands off the eastern coast, in the Aegean, include the Dodecanese Islands (Kalimnos, Kos, Patmos, and Rhodes); the Cyclades (220 islands, including Paros, Delos, Ios,

Mykonos, Naxos, Santorini, Siros, and Tinos), the Sporades (Skiathos, Skopelos, and Skyros), and the large islands of Samos, Ikaria, Chios, Lesbos, Limnos, and Samothrace.

The Dodecanese islands of Lipsi and Tilos have fantastic beaches without the large crowds, while the far-flung Agathonisi, Kastellorizo and Kassos, in the same island group, are good places to experience traditional island life. Santorini (also known as Thira) in the Cyclades is regarded by many as the most spectacular of the Greek islands, with its whitewashed buildings perched high above a dazzling turquoise sea. Some come each year for a look at its sea-filled caldera, evidence of what was probably the modern world's largest volcanic eruption. Santorini's unique appearance—black-sand beaches and mighty cliffs—holds a distinct allure, despite the crowds that come in the summer.

Just off the southern coast are the Saronic Islands (Aegina, Poros, Spetses, Hydra, and Kythira), easily accessible to Athens. Hydra was discovered in the 1950s by bohemian artists and became a very fashionable hangout, which it remains to this day. The island is too rugged to be spoiled, and it retains a chic charm around the harbor area.

And, finally, there's Crete, Greece's largest and southernmost island. With its long history of fierce independence and patriotic citizens, Crete is more a country than an island. First impressions of its capital, Iraklio—a big and noisy city by Greek island standards—are seldom favorable, but even here the Cretan charm can work its magic as you get beneath the skin of the city.

CUISINE

There is amazing food in Greece, and its preparation is usually quite simple, with olive oil as a staple ingredient.

After all, the Greeks have an olive-growing tradition that dates back 5,000 years. The Greeks also love to make dishes from fresh vegetables, such as eggplants, beans, and tomatoes, and they commonly use lamb and fish. This means that there's more to Greek food than gyros: If you've experienced Greek cuisine only as fast food in another country, you're in for a treat. Athens has a wide variety of restaurants, ranging from traditional eateries to world-class gourmet restaurants. You are well-advised to avoid the tourist traps of Plaka and to eat in tavernas frequented by Greeks, such as the ones found in Psiri. Estiatorion are the more expensive conventional restaurants; tavernas are informal, family-run establishments; psistarias offer mostly grilled meats; and psarotavernas specialize in seafood dishes.

Common everywhere are *tsatsiki* (garlic-yogurt spread), *souvlakia* (lamb kebabs marinated in garlic), *spanakopita* (spinach pie), and *tiropita* (cheese pie). There is also a huge variety of regional specialties ranging, for example, from numerous pita pies (with several fillings such as meat or vegetables) in the northern regions of Macedonia and Epirus to traditional goat and snail dishes on the island of Crete. Seafood, including fish, squid, and octopus, is also very popular in Greece and especially on the islands, usually grilled and marinated with lemon and olive oil. Pastries made from filo dough, nuts, and honey, such as baklava, shouldn't be missed.

Greek wines and liqueurs are distinctive and potent. The anise liqueur ouzo is often drunk with water. Metaxa is a common brandy. Wines vary widely in taste and quality. The last two decades have seen a renaissance in the age-old Greek winemaking tradition. The introduction of new vines and the use of better techniques have resulted in some excellent reds and whites on par with the world's best wines.

from its center. Within the church are some of the most beautiful Byzantine mosaics in Greece. Although not all have survived the centuries, the ceilings and upper walls are still blazing with archangels, saints, prophets, martyrs, bishops, and monks. Much has been restored, but in a discreet, old-fashioned way. The surviving mosaics were delicately reaffixed, while the rest has been left cleaned and protected.

CAPE SOUNION

Cape Sounion, about 30 kilometers (18 miles) southeast of Athens, was once a distant part of the city-state. It is the site of the lovely fifth-century B.C. Temple of Poseidon, where Athenians sought to propitiate the sometimes vengeful sea god. Over the years, its shining columns have stood as beacons for passing ships. The promontory is dangerous in stormy weather, but the temple signals safety in its little harbor. The graceful temple architecture and the commanding position on which it stands combine to make a stunning sight.

DELPHI AND METEORA

The ancient Greeks considered Delphi the center of the world. When you visit Delphi, you are part of a tradition that goes back over 3,000 years. In the 12th century B.C., the first pilgrims began to come here to seek advice from the Pythia, the most famous oracle of the ancient world. You'll see the Rock of the Sibyl, which stands on the spot where the oracle—a woman usually over the age of 50 deemed to

have been given the powers of the prophecy by the god Apollo—was consulted; along with the Sacred Way, the remains of the Temple of Apollo, and the theater.

The monastery at Meteora are on every visitor's list of essential sights in Greece. Meteora means "rocks in air," very descriptive of what you'll see. Hermits and ascetics lived among the rocks in the 11th century. The Great Meteoron Monastery was the first to be built here on a high rock peak, and, by the end of the 16th century, there were 24 monasteries here in all.

The first inhabitants ascended via ladders fitted in rock crevices or were hauled up in baskets with rope pulleys. You will be awed by the obvious hardships involved in building these structures, including the frightening ascents and descents. Centuries later, the ladders were removed and small stone steps were carved into the rocks.

Today there are only five monasteries in use that can be visited (one is now a convent). They are the Great Meteoron (Monastery of the Transfiguration); Barlaam (All Saints Monastery); Monastery of the Holy Trinity; Holy Monastery of St. Nicholas Anapafsas; and Saints Stephen and Charalambos Convent. The Rousanou Monastery can be viewed from afar, but not visited.

The Great Meteoron and Barlaam Monasteries are the largest and most impressive. Each is reached by ascending a great many steps, a challenging but relatively safe undertaking. They have lovely frescoes in the chapels and interesting artifacts.

St. Stephen's is interesting, but most tour groups visit it because there is an easy and quick access via a bridge, so it gets a bit crowded.

To reach Delphi and Meteora, you can go by hired car with or without a driver, or you can take one of the CHAT bus tours. No matter how you visit, a day trip to Delphi means an early start and a late arrival back in Athens. If you go on to Meteora, it's a three-day trip, and you might want to stay in one of Delphi's little hotels the first night.

You'll probably arrive in Delphi about mid- to late morning and have a guided tour of the magnificent site of the ancient oracle and the museum. After lunch, we suggest you return to the ruins on your own and enjoy them without crowds. You'll also want to explore the small town of Delphi, built on the side of a steep hill.

The next day you could go to Kalambaka, site of the Meteora monastery. If you don't care to drive or bus from Athens, you can take the morning Olympic Airlines flight from Athens to Larissa (about an hour) and rent a car at the airport. Kalambaka is about 40 kilometers (25 miles) away.

AMALIA HOTEL
Delphi
Tel: 30-226-508-2101

This reasonably comfortable, modern, and attractive hotel is located within walking distance to Delphi's main sites. 185 rooms. Swimming pool. Doubles from $120, including breakfast.

DIVANI MOTEL
National Rd, Trikala, Meteora
Tel: 30-243-202-3330

If your plans allow an overnight stay in Meteora, the 165-room Divani Motel, although not deluxe, is pleasant and

AEGEAN HIKING & BIKING CRUISE

One of the most enjoyable features of Butterfield & Robinson's hiking and biking cruise in the Aegean is the fact that—with the exception of Santorini—each island on the itinerary is likely to be a new experience even for weathered Greece travelers. The trip begins in Athens, where you connect to a flight to Rhodes to board the *Callisto*, a very comfortable 15-stateroom yacht. For the next nine days, you cruise to five or six islands in the Dodecanese and the Cyclades before returning to Athens. Each island is a revelation, marked by its own distinct history and culture— Symi, a travel-poster stunner with pastel-painted neoclassic mansions terraced in tiers above a horseshoe-shaped harbor; Amorgos, with its medieval village, Byzantine monastery, and 13th-century fortress; Sifnos, dotted with typical Cycladic white cubic houses; and Paros famed for its prized translucent marble.

The tour is led by three charmers: an Oxford classicist, a field archaeologist, and a Greek painter who is the real Zorba. The itinerary includes active days filled with hiking, biking, and beaches as well as relaxing hours both aboard the *Callisto* and in friendly tavernas.

With irregular ferry and plane connections among the islands, this is a tour that would be difficult to duplicate on your own. And where else will you have the opportunity for such frequent contacts with locals that weave you directly into the warp of local culture?

Classical Greek Islands by Sea tour by Butterfield & Robinson, Tel: 800-678-1147, www.butterfield.com. Rates from $8,950.

ELOUNDA BEACH HOTEL

180 ELOUNDA BEACH, ELOUNDA
Tel: 30-841-4-1412
www.eloundabeach.gr

The Elounda Beach Hotel is beautiful, with every last detail for comfort, enjoyment, and scenic beauty. All rooms and bungalows have balconies or patios. There are two main buildings. Bungalows are either near the sea or in the beautifully maintained gardens.

The saltwater pool is extremely large, and there is also swimming from the beach or off the rocks near the bungalows. The water is a clear, transparent blue-green. Tennis courts, an amphitheater for movies, water sports, boutiques, and a model village are among the many attractions.

The dining room serves lavish buffet breakfasts, as well as lunch and dinner. There is also a taverna offering Greek food and entertainment, as well as an outdoor snack bar open for breakfast and lunch. 260 rooms. Doubles from $180.

quite convenient to the town. Try to get a room at the back for the better views of the mountains. Doubles from $120, including breakfast.

CORINTH

Corinth, about 30 kilometers (20 miles) west of Athens on the Peloponnese Peninsula, is the site of many significant Greek and Roman ruins within the confines of its ancient city limits. Particularly notable is the Acrocorinth, the highest citadel in Greece. The Excavation Museum documents the wealth of Roman Corinth with extensive collections of statues of imperial figures and of mosaics, including one depicting a sunburned Pan piping to several besotted heifers.

CRETE

Crete, the largest island in Greece, is a separate Greek world, with an incomparable history and spectacular scenery. It also has some luxurious resort hotels and a few fine restaurants.

Very briefly, early Cretan culture is seen in the remains of the fascinating Minoan civilization (about 3000–1000 B.C.)—most notably, the fabulous Knossos palace. Subsequently, the island was ruled by the Romans, Arabs, and Byzantines. In 1210, Venice began an occupation that lasted more than 400 years. The Venetians were followed in 1669 by the Ottomans, who ruled for more than 200 years. It was only in 1913 that Crete joined the modern Greek state.

Some visitors rent cars and travel on their own. If you are game, and careful, this is a good idea. Keep in mind, however, that cars coming around blind curves from the other direction may well enter your lane; there are no railings on many high, precipitous mountain roads; and gas stations are few and far between. As an alternative, there are good bus excursions from the major cities.

Crete's best weather occurs in spring and fall. Summer is very hot.

CHANIA AND WESTERN CRETE

The Old Town of Chania, in western Crete, is enclosed by 16th-century Venetian walls. The archaeological museum, located on Halidon Street, the main thoroughfare, has a fine display of Minoan, Greek, and Roman antiquities. On Angelou Street near the Naval Museum are a number of worthwhile stores: Look for locally produced ceramics and high-quality textiles, as well asgold and silver jewelry as well as silver and gold objects and semiprecious stones. Eat dinner at the Oleander in the Old Town in what used to be a Venetian warehouse.

CASA DELFINO
9 Theofanous Street
Tel: 30-282-109-3098, www.casadelfino.com

The 12-suite Casa Delfino, near the Venetian harbor, is a pleasant place to stay. Breakfast, included in rates, is served in your suite or in a courtyard. Doubles from $100.

THE KYDON HOTEL
Platia Agoras
Tel: 30-282-105-2280, www.kydon-hotel.com

With 112 rooms, this is the only other acceptable choice in town. It is well situated. Doubles from $60, including two meals.

Near Chania, if you are up to a five- to seven-hour walk, you can either go on your own or take a guided tour down the Samaria Gorge, the steep, beautiful ravine running 17 kilometers (11 miles) from Xylokastro, in the White Mountains, down to Aghia Roumeli, on the Libyan Sea. It's the longest gorge in Europe, and the scenery is outstanding. To return you must take a ferry.

To see the gorge without taking such a long hike, drive through Souda and Vrises, past the green Askyfou Plateau, and wind down the Imvrou Ravine to Chora Sfakion. The views are startling. Take the one-hour ferry ride to Aghia Roumeli, and walk up the gorge as far as you like. There are a few good restaurants where you can have lunch, and then take the ferry back to Chora Sfakion.

The Akrotiri Peninsula, just east of Chania, is known in Greek history for its association with the statesman Eleftherios Venizelos. The Monastery of Aghia Triada, a fine 17th-century Venetian building, was founded by a Venetian convert to Greek orthodoxy. To the north is the Monastery of Gouverneto.

EASTERN CRETE

MINOS BEACH ART HOTEL
Akti Ilia Sotirhou, Amoudi, Agios Nikolaos
Tel: 30-284-102-2345

In the attractive resort town of Agios Nikolaos, the Minos Beach Hotel is a good place to stay. You have a choice of room or bungalow, some with a view of the sea. There's also a pool, beach, and tennis courts. It's a smaller, lower-key kind of operation than the hotels in Elounda, and some people prefer it for that reason. Doubles from $100, including breakfast.

ST. NICOLAS BAY HOTEL
Agios Nikolaos
Tel: 30-281-030-0330

Comfortable bungalows in traditional Crete style in a garden setting overlooking Mirabello Bay. Poseidon Spa offers a wide range of treatments. Doubles from $150, including breakfast.

20 NORWAY: FROM BERGEN TO THE FJORDS

Summer in Norway is a season of enchantment, a time to move through hours of almost endless light or to sit in a garden or on a sea rock, reading or watching a lone fisherman calmly casting his line into the still waters of a fjord. I cruised the coastal waters under ghostly wisps of clouds suspended in the distance, falling over mountains into meadows.

A midsummer night solstice, the longest day, is celebrated on June 23, after much anticipation. As my "post office boat" comes to a drift in the twilight waters, I see people singing around campfires on shore, and the fjord comes alive with celebration.

NORTH CAPE CRUISES
Tel: 212-480-4521
www.cruisenorway.com or www.norwegiancoastalcruises.com

There are two ways to take a North Cape cruise. You can sail on a big and luxurious ocean liner, such as a Royal Viking Lines ship, or you can take a simpler, more Spartan post office boat, which leaves Bergen daily and stops at as many as 30 ports along the coast, picking up freight, mail, and passengers. There are a lot of fjords and interesting coastline to look at on these trips, but some people will object that the accommodations are a bit too basic and the food monotonous. However, to vary the experience, several shore excursions are available, including a visit to Trondheim and its Ringve Museum; a trip up the North Cape (after June 1, when mountain roads reopen); and an overland trip from Harstad, crossing two fjords, and then rejoining the ship at Sortland.

Norwegian Coastal Voyages

The Norwegian Coastal Voyage cruise is known as the world's most beautiful voyage. This unique nature cruise is unlike any other cruise around the world, as the 11 ships of the Norwegian Coastal Voyage fleet are still combined working ships, public transport for the locals living along the coast, and cruise ships carrying cruise passengers from around the world. Being domestic public transportation, the ships' crews consist of Norwegians only.

The extensive number of stops at tiny ports and main cities along the coast offers you a unique opportunity to experience the authentic coastal Norway. The sea journey is comfortable and relaxing, with the nature and beauty of the coast and fjords as the main focus of the cruise. You can, however, take part in a wide selection of interesting and adventurous optional shore excursions en route. Enjoy the Midnight Sun and the bright nights on a summer cruise, the spectacular Northern Lights during an exotic winter cruise, or a traditional Norwegian Christmas onboard during that holiday season.

No words do justice to the Norwegian coast, and no trip you may have taken before can prepare you for the visual beauty you will encounter along the way. Physically, the Alaskan coastline comes close, but the architecture and style of Norway is so different that comparisons between the two don't really stand. Both of them are terrific, but I give Norway the edge. And this voyage is the only way to really see it.

Every day of the year, one of these coastal ships departs Bergen for the north, and if you have the time to take the full 12-day round trip, you will sail about 4,000 kilometers (2,500 miles) through some of the world's most scenic waters.

This voyage passes among 600 islands between Bergen and Kirkenes, a few miles from the Russian border. Along the way, it makes 30 or so stops, taking on and discharging local passengers and cargo. The northbound voyage takes seven days; the southbound, six.

Ports visited at night in one direction are daytime stops in the other direction. Cabins have two lower berths, bathrooms with showers, and nice furnishings. Breakfast and luncheon buffets are plentiful, featuring delicious Norwegian specialties.

NORWEGIAN COASTAL VOYAGE cruise program
See web addresses opposite or telephone:
Fjord Travel Norway
Tel: 47-5513-1310

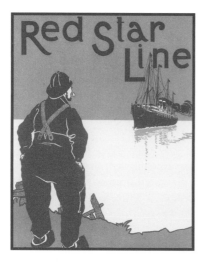

The Norwegian Coastal Voyages (see previous page) is one of the world's last remaining long-haul transportation systems for passengers and cargo. Nature and geology have provided Norway with a spectacular beauty, but its craggy, rocky, and often isolated nature really never facilitated land links. So the coastal route has been Norway's lifeline since 1893, when seafarer Richard With demonstrated the benefits of regular steamship services to Norway's coastal communities, organizing a north–south link along Norway's coastline.

The service has run almost without interruption since its beginning, hardly stopping for German occupation during World War II; in those difficult times it slowed, but the service never totally shut down.

Because of the need for daily transport of people, goods, and mail, vessels generally appeared in multiples, as six sisters, the *Kong Harald, Nordkapp, Nordlys, Nordnorge, Polarlys,* and *Richard With*. So vital are these vessels that Norway's parliament years ago chartered them

as Highway 1, and if you look closely at the superstructure of any of them, right near the bridge wing, you will see a little painted rectangle with the number one in it—the equivalent of a highway signpost.

The Norwegian Coastal Voyage line recently introduced three new ships to the market. These ships are modern, with the latest technology and comfort you would expect to find on new cruise ships. The 2003-built, 15,000-ton, 674-passenger ship M.S. *Midnatsol* has a modern design. The ship's interior is dedicated to the Norwegian summer. *Midnatsol* means "Midnight Sun," and large glass surfaces allow the outside light to enter, creating a proximity to nature throughout the ship. It has a large two-story panoramic lounge on the two upper decks and a top deck with saunas, a gym, a bar, and a large sundeck. Deck 5 houses the main restaurant, cafés, an arcade with playroom, shops, and lounges. Deck 8 also has several lounges, including an Internet café, TV lounge, and a library. There are 19 suites, some with balconies. All cabins have telephones and heated bathroom floors. The suites and inside cabins all have TVs.

The 2002-built, 643-passenger M.S. *Finnmarken* is decorated in art nouveau style, reminiscent of the first Coastal Voyage ships' Old World elegance. Norwegian artists have decorated Finnmarken with drawings, watercolors, oil paintings, charcoal drawings, lithographs, and sculptures. There are 32 suites, some with a balcony and Jacuzzi. All cabins have telephones and TVs. The bathrooms have heated floors. The fitness center, on deck 8, has saunas and a massage parlor. You will also find a hair salon and an Internet café on deck 8, while the outdoor swimming pool is on deck 7. Several restaurants, bars, panoramic lounges, observation areas, and indoor and outdoor cafés are located throughout the ship.

The 2002-built M.S. *Trollfjord* is *Midnatsol*'s sister-ship. M.S. *Trollfjord* has Norwegian wood and stone throughout the interior. Large windows let the light and scenery into the public areas—even the elevators are made out of glass. Norwegian artists have also decorated this ship. The sauna and fitness area are located on the top deck. Here passengers can enjoy the spectacular views from the large outdoor area or from the panoramic balcony. On deck 8, there are numerous bars, panoramic areas, a library, and an Internet café. Deck 5 houses two restaurants and several cafés. There are 19 suites, some with a balcony. Suites and inside cabins have TVs. All cabins have heated bathroom floors.

BY RAIL

www.eurorailways.com

If you do not wish to cruise, another way to see more of Norway is to take the train from Oslo to Bergen, stay a day, and return either by train or by fjord cruise to Flam. You can then pick up the Oslo train at nearby Myrdal. The Bergen train run is considered one of Europe's finest trips. It departs from Oslo's Ost Station, reaching Bergen in about eight hours. All seats must be reserved.

Without the railroad, Bergen would have been pretty much isolated from the rest of Norway. As the train climbs and winds through the mountains and over the Hardanger Plateau and Ice Cap, you reach the highest point on the trip, more than 1,280 meters (4,200 feet). The plateau

is a desolate area of glacier-decimated mountains. Along the way you stop at pleasant villages and lakes and go on beyond the enormous Folgefonn Glacier overlooking Hardanger Fjord. Over part of the route, you will notice wooden sheds that shelter the tracks from periodic avalanches.

At Myrdal, you suddenly get a striking view of the Flam Valley as the train drives down through gorges and waterfalls into the flower-bedecked area of Bergen, reached in early afternoon.

BERGEN

Gateway to the fjords, Bergen presents about a day's worth of sightseeing. Norway's second city was the home of the composer Edvard Grieg (1843-1907), in Troldhaugen, 13 kilometers (8 miles) to the south. Bergen is an old city, hilly and with picturesque harbor views. It would be worth devoting more time to the area if you are interested in visiting any of the outlying fjord resorts.

CLASSIC HOTEL NORGE
Ole Bulls Plass 4, near the main square
Tel: 47-55-21-0100.

Bergen's best hotel is the 347-room Hotel Norge, one of the few world-class hotels in all of Norway. Very well run and very busy. It has several excellent restaurants. Doubles, $210 to $245.

GODOYSUND FJORD HOTEL
5682 Godoysund
Tel: 47-53-43-1404

Not many people know about this nice

outlying resort on a private, scenic island right on the water. There are 47 rooms, about half with private balconies. You get there by ferry from Bergen, or via a bus and boat. Especially pleasant for fishing and walking. Doubles, $100.

GRAND TERMINUS HOTEL
Zander Kaaesgate 6
Tel: 47-55-31-1655

Although most of Bergen's historic hotels were destroyed during World War II, the Grand Terminus Hotel still stands in the central district. Opened in 1928 as a Lutheran temperance hostel, today it offers a more cosmopolitan charm. The neighborhood can be somewhat noisy, but the soft ambiance within compensates.

EATING OUT IN BERGEN

LYSTSTEDET BELLEVUE
Bellevuebakken 9
Tel: 47-5533-6999

The historic Bellevue, on a hillside overlooking Bergen's harbor, offers superb food and spectacular views. One of Norway's best restaurants.

BRYGGEN TRACTEURSTED
Bryggestredet 2
Tel: 47-5531-4046

Quite casual and popular with students is the Bryggen Tracteursted, near the SAS Radisson Hotel. It occupies one of the old Hanseatic League houses at the harbor's edge. Old beamed ceilings, sturdy wood furniture, and antique prints and maps.

The 130 guest rooms have pastel furnishings and tiled baths. Public areas are attractive with traditional woodworking and locally woven rugs. Wheelchair accessible. Doubles from $125, including breakfast.

SOLSTRAND HOTEL
30 kilometers (18 miles) south of Bergen
Tel: 47-56-57-1100, www.solstrand.com

A good hotel about an hour's drive from Bergen. It occupies a secluded position at the entrance of Hardanger fjord. 132 rooms. Doubles, $165.

MUSEUMS

Bergen has a number of museums. The Hanseatic League Museum and the Maritime Museum are outstanding. The Maritime Museum is located on the grounds of the university. Professionally staged exhibitions cover the history and development of Norwegian shipping from the Viking era through the Middle Ages into the 20th century. The Hanseatic Museum is housed in one of the oldest and best preserved wooden buildings in town. It shows how a Hanseatic merchant lived in the 18th century.

The Bergen Art Museum contains paintings by Norwegian artists of the last 150 years, as well as other European artists. It includes the Rasmus Meyers Collection, which focuses on Munch and Dahl. Small, but worthwhile.

Be sure to visit Troldhaugan, 13 kilometers (8 miles) south of Bergen. It was Edvard Grieg's home for 22 years and is preserved as a living museum, with the Edvard Grieg Museum, and the composer's house, cabin, and tomb. Troldsalen concert hall holds concerts and events throughout the year.

SHOPPING

Bergen has an abundance of shops selling the usual Norwegian specialties—handknit sweaters, silver and stainless dinnerware, glass and ceramics, and so forth—but much of it is inferior in quality to the selection available in Oslo. There are some better shops, however, including Prydkunst Hjertholm, with attractively displayed modern designs in pewter, textiles, and jewelry; Husfliden, with two shops featuring authentic houseware arts and crafts; and Glasmagasin, with a large supply of pottery and glassware.

LILLEHAMMER
The 1994 Winter Olympics put this delightful small town on the map.

COMFORT HOTEL HAMMER
Storgata 108
Tel: 47-61-26-3500

The Comfort Hotel Hammer is a charming establishment located downtown on the Storgata promenade. Its rooms are bright and colorful, and they include cable TV, writing desks, comfortable chairs, and showers. There's a cozy fireplace in the lobby. Ask for a room with a balcony overlooking Lake Mjosa, Norway's largest body of fresh water. The hotel also has a restaurant, a recreation center, and a sauna where cold tap beer is served. Doubles from $125; suites from $180.

INTER NOR LILLEHAMMER HOTEL
Turisthotellvn 27B
Tel: 47-61-28-6000

The best place to stay in Lillehammer is the Inter Nor Lillehammer Hotel. Set in a forested 3-hectare (8-acre) park, it was the host hotel for the 1994 Winter Olympics and is now a major convention and conference center as well as a sports-oriented establishment. Facilities include an indoor/outdoor swimming pool, a solarium, saunas, an

---

DINING IN LILLEHAMMER

SOLELHUSET
Tel: 61-2-26-9860

The most interesting restaurant in Norway is Solelhuset, at the farm of Kare and Torunn Toftum, in Lillehammer. A replica of a Viking pine log inn from 1100 A.D., this highly recommended spot was featured during Olympic telecasts to illustrate Viking customs. Guests can enjoy a drink around an open fireplace and then dine at long tables while seated on benches covered with reindeer furs. The medieval dinner is served on pita-like *halle* (barley) bread, and the main course is a combination of lamb, beef, pork, and mixed game, served with a soup of beans, white root, and onions. Dinner for two, with beer made from a Middle Ages recipe, about $60. Open year-round, 8 to 11 p.m.

TROLLSALEN RESTAURANT
Hunderfossen Familepark
Tel: 61-2-27-7222

Serving traditional Norwegian food, including the locally hunted favorites reindeer and *trollsteak* (ox), the atmospheric 130-seat restaurant is constructed of stone and wood indigenous to the area. It has a roaring fireplace and is decorated with huge troll sculptures.

exercise room, a mini-golf course, and a basketball court. The tastefully decorated 250 rooms have colorful bedspreads with matching draperies, cable TV, writing desks, minibars, and all the other customary amenities. There is also a comfortable lounge and a dining room with both a Norwegian buffet and an à la carte menu. Doubles from $180, suites from $270.

MOLLA HOTEL
Elvegaten 12
Tel: 47-61-26-9294, www.molla.ol.no

One of the city's most unusual accommodations, the Molla Hotel is built on the site of a former flour mill near the downtown area. There are 58 small rooms, cozily decorated with pine furniture, wrought-iron lamps, and rag rugs. The usual amenities are provided, and there is an exercise room. Restaurant Egon is located in the atmospheric building, and the adjoining terrace is a good place to enjoy a drink beside the stream. Toppen Bar, on the top floor, provides panoramic views of the city and countryside. Doubles from $135.

OSLO

Oslo, Norway's capital, is a city of great beauty, gentle people, and fine restaurants serving delicious reindeer steaks, roasts, and sausages. First-time visitors may be shocked by the prices, but the experience is memorable for better reasons than this.

Oslo is Norway's main gateway, an attractive port city with a population of about 480,000 and a rich cultural life. The heart of the city is compact, so choice hotels and most of the better restaurants and shops are clustered within walking distance. The busiest area is Karl Johans Gate, a promenade that extends from Oslo Sentralstasjon (central train station) to the Royal Palace. Nightlife centers around the promenade and the Aker Brygge wharf near City Hall, where the Nobel Peace Prize is awarded every December 10.

CLARION ROYAL CHRISTIANIA
Biskop Gunnerus Gate 3
Tel: 47-23-10-8000

The Clarion Royal Christiania, a comfortable hotel in the center of Oslo, was originally built for the 1952 Winter Olympics and was renovated in 1995. The heart of the hotel is a seven-story-high atrium with a huge Norwegian flag hanging over the Cafe Atrium, a popular meeting spot. Rooms are small by American standards but comfortable and tastefully decorated.

Bathrooms have shower/tub combinations, hair dryers, and heated floors. All the other customary amenities are also included. Ask for one of the three Governor or Lord Mayor suites, corner rooms on the eighth and nineth floors. The well-appointed recreation center includes a pool, Turkish and Finnish baths, and massage facilities. There are 451 rooms, including 60 suites. Doubles from $250, suites from $240.

GABELSHUS
Gabelsgate 16
Tel: 47-23-27-6500, www.gabelshus.no

Offering real Old-World charm, Gabelshus is situated in a

1912, ivy-covered mansion. The 44-room inn is dotted with antiques. Its restaurant offers solid Norwegian fare with a bit too much fanfare. A light lunch here is better than a formal dinner. Ground floor rooms are cramped, but they—and all the other guest accommodations—have been pleasantly decorated with summery fabrics. Best rooms have terraces. Wheelchair accessible. Doubles from $85; suites from $190, all including breakfast.

GRAND HOTEL
Karl Johansgate 31
Tel: 47-23-21-2000

The Grand Hotel, considered Oslo's finest, hosts the annual winner of the Nobel Peace Prize, and you can find the Nobel Suite on the first floor. Located on the promenade, the Grand is near the Parliament, the National Theater, and the Royal Palace. Since its opening in 1874, the hotel has been known for its high standards of comfort and luxury, and its staff for its professional service. Rooms are spacious and are decorated in styles that range from typically Scandinavian to Continental antique. Amenities include cable TV, in-room movies, trouser presses, hair dryers, minibars, and 24-hour room service. If you can't get the Nobel Suite, ask for a room with a balcony facing the park. There are 289 rooms, including 50 suites. Doubles from $260, suites from $570.

THE HOTEL CONTINENTAL
Stortingsgaten 24/26
Tel: 47-22-82-4000

Conveniently located midway between City Hall and the Royal Palace in central Oslo, the Hotel Continental has been owned and operated by members of the Brochmann family for four generations. A member of "The Leading Hotels of the World," the Continental covers an entire city block. With Old World charm, it maintains deluxe international standards. Rooms and suites are traditionally elegant with large comforters on the beds, writing desks, cozy chairs, minibars, and large bathrooms with shower/tub combinations. Ask for a junior suite facing the Royal Palace. The Royal Suite, with its wraparound windows, was originally furnished for Prince Philip of England. The hotel has 151 rooms, including 19 suites, and there are four restaurants and lounges. Annen Etage is an elegant dining room on the third floor. Doubles from $260, including a Norwegian breakfast.

SHOPPING

For shoppers, the best buys in Oslo are furs, hand-knit clothing, and handicraft items. Much of the selection is of top quality and is also in great demand, so don't expect bargains.

William Schmidt, Karl Johansgate 41, is famous for its sweaters, as well as gifts and souvenirs. Look for nice hand-carved wooden figures of well-known celebrities and statesmen.

For absolutely authentic knitwear, try Husfliden, the Norwegian Association for Home and Crafts, at Mollergaten 4. This charitable organization preserves handicraft traditions of Norwegian culture and offers by far the best choice of fabrics, woodenware, dolls, baskets, ceramics, weaving, knitting supplies, and the like.

Norway is fairly well known for its silver jewelry and stainless and pewter tableware, though the designs sometimes lack the freshness and imagination found in Danish work. Enamelware—brightly colored enamel-coated silver dishes and jewelry—is very popular. The top shops for gold and silver are David-Anderson, Karl Johansgate 20, and J. Tostrup, Karl Johansgate 25.

For antiques, try Kaare Berntsen, at Universitetsgaten 12. For glassware, Landsverk, Grensen 10, has a very large selection.

The Forum, a permanent exhibit sponsored by the Oslo Crafts and Industrial Association, has a large selection of well-designed ceramics, glassware, textiles, and furniture, all for sale. It's located at Rosenkrantzgate 7. More commercial, but with high standards, is Norway Designs, Stortingsgate 28/30.

For porcelain, your best choice is Porsgrunn Porselen, Karl Johannsgate 14.

You'll find rare books (many in English) and antique maps at N. W. Damm, Tollbugaten 25, and Borsuns Forlag og Antikvariat, Nansens Plass 2. For new books, especially guides and books on Norway, try Johan Grundt Tanum Bokhandel, Karl Johansgate 43. The shop also carries a complete stock of the excellent Cappelen sectional maps of Norway.

Finally, the Vika shopping mall, near the Continental Hotel; Aker Brygge, at the harbor; and Oslo City, across from the Central Station feature a wide variety of shops.

SIGHTSEEING

There are many intriguing points of interest in Oslo. Best known and not to be missed are Frogner Park and the museum complex at Bygdoy.

Frogner Park, 1.5 kilometers (1 mile) or so from the city center, is the setting for the impressive stone, bronze, and iron sculptures of Gustave Vigeland. This eccentric Norwegian was adept at powerful representations of the human condition in all its aspects. His studio, now the Vigeland Museum, is in the park as well.

Upon his death in 1944, Edvard Munch, Norway's most renowned modern artist and an important pioneer of expressionism, left 1,000 paintings, 4,500 drawings, and 18,000 prints—his personal collection of his own work—to the city of Oslo. The collection is now housed in the Munch Museum. Munch's haunting, silent figures and vibrantly colored landscapes have become virtual icons of contemporary angst.

The Sonja Henie–Niels Onstad Art Center, near the airport, includes work by such luminaries of modern art as Gris, Bonnard, Picasso, Miró, and Villon. The striking design of the building itself is as interesting as the art within. Miss Henie's ice-skating trophies are also on display there.

BYGDOY MUSEUMS

Bygdoy, a short, pleasant boat ride from the dock in front of City Hall, is Oslo's museum quarter. You can easily spend a full day visiting its attractions:

- The Folk Museum has a collection of everyday objects, furniture, and religious art. The complex includes a number of wooden buildings, among them a 12th-century stave church.

- The Viking Ship Museum features three graceful 1,000-year-old ships recovered from the Oslo fjord.

- Thor Heyerdahl's *Kon-Tiki.*

- Nansen and Amundsen's polar ship, *Fram.*

- The Maritime Museum.

NORWAY

Tucked under the awesome-looking Holmenkollen ski jump is the Ski Museum that, despite its modest size, is worth a look. Included are many old photographs, equipment ranging from the 2,500-year-old Ovrebo ski to the more familiar skis of the present day, sledging gear and other equipment used by the polar explorers Nansen and Amundsen, and other memorabilia.

Roald Amundsen's House is at Balerud, a 20-kilometer (12-mile) drive south of Oslo. Accessible by bus and open to the public, it overlooks the Bundefjord and is just as the discoverer of the South Pole left it. Notice the ship portholes in the bedroom. Nearby is a large bronze statue of Amundsen. The area is a popular spot for picnics and swimming.

The Resistance Museum tells the sobering story of the German occupation of Norway during World War II and of Norway's resistance movement throughout the war.

City Hall is where the Nobel Peace Prize is presented.

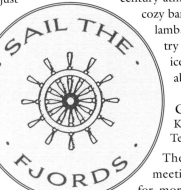

RESTAURANTS

ANNEN ETAGE AND THEATERCAFÉEN
Stortingsgaten 24-26
Tel: 47-22-82-4000

Annen Etage, in the Hotel Continental, is Oslo's grandest restaurant. The menu, which some call Norwegian cuisine with a French accent, features the standard seafood, veal, lamb, pork, and steak, as well as some wonderful game dishes—all very well prepared.

Try the filet of reindeer with morel sauce, or the breast of black grouse with red-wine sauce. Service is highly professional. Dinner for two, without wine, about $150. The Theatercaféen, also in the Continental, is one of the most famous cafés in the world. Dinner for two, without wine, about $75.

ENGEBRET CAFÉ
Bankplassen 1
Tel: 47-22-82-2525

A popular restaurant since 1857, this café maintains a 19th-century atmosphere in its 50-seat dining room and cozy bar. Norwegian cuisine, including seafood, lamb, and reindeer, is featured. For dessert, try the rhubarb soup and homemade vanilla ice cream. Dinner for two, without wine, about $100.

GRAND CAFÉ AND JULIUS FRITZER
Karl Johansgate 31
Tel: 47-23-21-2000, www.grand.no

The Grand Hotel's Grand Café, a meeting place for artists and intellectuals for more than a century, offers a variety of Norwegian and international dishes, and its buffet is the largest in Norway. Dinner for two, without wine, about $75.

The Julius Fritzer, also at the Grand, is the more sophisticated dining room. Named after the founder of the hotel, the restaurant serves a five-course daily menu based on seasonal fresh foods and has an extensive wine list. Dinner for two, without wine, about $150.

LE CANARD
President Harbitzgate 4
Tel: 47-22-54-3400, www.lecanard.com

One of Oslo's most exclusive and romantic restaurants is Le

Canard. Try the mussel soup and the salted duck with red wine. Service and cuisine are superb. Dinner for two, without wine, about $130.

MOLLA
Sagveien 21
Tel: 47-22-37-6519

Molla, an attractive restaurant on the outskirts of town (a short taxi ride), overlooks the Akerselve River and is housed in what was once an old mill that has been beautifully remodeled. It serves excellent food. Dinner for two, without wine, about $125. Call ahead.

PERNILLE
Johanne Dybwads plass 1

During the warm months, the most pleasant place in Oslo for coffee, sandwiches, beer and wine, or ice cream is Pernille, the outdoor café in front of the National Theater. Its central location makes it an ideal spot for people-watching or meeting friends.

NORTH FJORD

OLDEN FJORDHOTEL
Olden
Tel: 47-57-873-400, www.olden-hotel.no

The nicest place on the Nord Fjord is the Olden Fjordhotel, a bit west of Stryn. The establishment's featureless white facade belies its genteel, summery interior, with its card room and cozy bar. Most of the 60 rooms have terraces where breakfast can be served. Not far away is the Briksdal Glacier, a tilted wall hanging over a narrow valley. Even in summer months, there is fine skiing in the area. Wheelchair accessible. Doubles from $115, including breakfast; add $45 for half-pension.

GLOPPEN HOTELL
Sandane
Tel: 47-57-865-333, www.gloppenhotell.com

In Sandane, on the Nord Fjord's southern arm, the Gloppen Hotell has been offering rooms since 1866, when a local farmer, hard pressed to make something of his land, cleared a tract and built a hotel near an open stretch of water, hoping to attract summering Europeans. The gabled building holds 30 guest rooms and offers luxury amenities—really capacious bathtubs, for example. But this is not a tourist hotel; it derives most of its business from local weddings and fairs. There are noteworthy ancient petroglyphs just west of town. Doubles from $130.

GRAND ROYAL HOTEL
Kongensgate 62, Narvik
Tel: 47-76-941-500

The lunar landscape of the Lofoten Islands offers Europe's best birding and is home to some of Norway's finest stave churches. The Grand Royal Hotel, in the town of Narvik, 320 kilometers (200 miles) north of the Arctic Circle, is the best place to base yourself for a visit, despite the fact that it is a rather joyless establishment. Built in 1921, it was King Olav's favorite retreat, and, indeed, his portraits constitute just about all of the decorating. There are 119 moderately sized rooms, but the highlight of your stay may well be the dining room's excellent reindeer curry with apricots. Doubles from $75, including breakfast.

FJORD DAY CRUISES

www.skibladner.no
Tel: 61-14-4080

Just as fascinating and enjoyable as any fjord trip is a day cruise on the *Skibladner*, a completely authentic steam-powered sidewheeler that, since 1856, has been making the daily round-trip between Eidsvoll and Lillehammer on Lake Mjosa, Norway's largest inland body of water.

There are several stops along the way, and very good and full meals are served in the lovely Victorian dining room (complete with brass lamps hanging from the ceiling). Everything appears to be thoroughly original.

During the summer, the *Skibladner* departs each morning from Eidsvoll. The dock is a few steps from the railroad station, and the 8:45 train from Oslo gives just enough time for the connection. From Lillehammer, you can catch a train back to Oslo, or go on north as far as Trondheim.

HOTEL UNION OYE
Oye
Tel: 47-70-06-2100

On a tiny finger of the Starfjorden fjord, far from the call of ship or bus, the Hotel Union Oye is a welcoming Norse baronial inn offering 26 good, clean rooms. Kaiser Wilhelm II used the hotel to house his hunting parties each season, and Sir Arthur Conan Doyle was a guest (some of the staff will tell you his ghost is still hanging about). Ask for a room overlooking the 180-meter (600-foot) waterfall. The food is pleasant and hearty and is prepared with some aspirations to originality—although clam chutney seems a bit over the top. Wheelchair accessible. Doubles from $130, including breakfast. Set dinner for two, without wine, about $60.

KVIKNE'S HOTEL
Balholm, Balestrand
Tel: 47-57-69-1101, www.kviknes.no

Kvikne's Hotel has been offering hospitality on the edge of the world's longest fjord, the Sogne, only since 1913, although a hotel has stood at this crosswater since the 1750s. Of the several buildings that house the 110 guest rooms, the old chalet-style complex is nicest; you can even request Kaiser Wilhelm II's favorite room. On the other hand, there are several annexes where tour groups are usually warehoused. The nightly smorgasbord is a cut above most, if for no other reason than the variety of fish offered, 12 varieties of herring alone! Allow enough time to take the helicopter ride over the Jostedal Glacier. Doubles from $90, including breakfast; add $45 for half-pension.

VISNES HOTEL
Prestevegen 1, Stryn
Tel: 47-57-87-1087, www.visnes.no

On the Nord Fjord, where most of the lodging choices are

in spa-like establishments, the Visnes Hotel provides a welcome alternative. It's off the main tourist beat and offers no tourist attractions such as fjord cruises. But the 19 guest rooms are homey, embodying the Norwegian ethic of simplicity with their fresh flowers, crisp linens, and plain furniture. Spectacular vistas of waterfalls leaping from high cliffs lie a short drive from the hotel, and closer, in the town of Stryn, is a remarkable stave church. Doubles from $60, including breakfast. Dinner for two (smorgasbord), without wine, about $55.

NORWAY'S SOUTH COAST

If you plan to visit Norway in the summer, it's almost a necessity that you reserve hotel space well in advance. This is especially important in Oslo and Bergen. The traditional tourist season—June through September—is very short, and the hotel situation is always tight. Even quite ordinary places are usually booked solid through the summer.

Norway's South Coast has long been a favorite vacation shore for Scandinavians and has become popular with international travelers, thanks to an increase in good hotels. The resort area around Kristiansand has the best hotels.

CLASSIC HOTEL CALEDONIEN
Tel: 47-38-02-9100
A modern 12-story, 205-room facility overlooking the harbor. $175-$205.

INTER NOR ERNST PARK
Tel: 47-38-02-1400
An inn with 112 rooms in a traditional building dating from 1858. Doubles $120–$170.

BY TRAIN AND FERRY

www.raileurope.com or www.norway.com

It's easy to get to the South Coast by train from Oslo, or you can take a five-day tour from Oslo through Kristiansand to Stavanger, along a very interesting stretch of coast. The trip includes a cruise through Lyse Fjord to Pulpit Rock.

Drobak, a picturesque fishing village and artists' colony 35 kilometers (22 miles) south of Oslo, is worth a visit. The most enjoyable way to get there is via the M.S. *Prinsessen* ferry, which leaves from Aker Brygge and takes a little more than an hour.

En route, the ferry passes a number of islands that are the sites of many summer homes. You can also take a city

NORWAY'S CHEESES

Norway produces Gjetost, one of the strangest cheeses in the world—one that is an acquired taste, to say the least. Its sweet, aromatic flavor has been described by some as reminiscent of a dirty washcloth! Others sing its praises. The best is made from 100 percent goat's milk, although most varieties contain cow's milk as well. The goat's milk variety is called Ekta Gjetost.

Gammelost is a strong and aromatic, nearly brown, cheese. Traditionally it is soaked in gin and juniper berries. Norway's other principal cheeses are Jarlsberg, Nökkelost, and Ridder, which are local versions of Swiss Emmental, Dutch Leiden, and French St.-Paulin, respectively, but are not as good as their prototypes.

bus that makes the trip in 30 minutes. On the Oslofjord, Drobak has some interesting 18th- and 19th-century buildings, including fishermen's cottages decorated with ships' figureheads and a church built in 1776.

There are also many art galleries and shops. Be sure to stop at Det Gamle Bageri (The Old Bakery) for wine, cheese, and homemade bread. Its building was constructed in 1743 with log walls and beamed ceilings. Skip the Trollgarten, but don't miss Atleir G.H., where artists Gro Skaltveit and Haico Nitzche make and sell innovative ceramics and porcelain.

TRONDHEIM

Norway's third largest city, Trondheim, is on an ice-free fjord in an area of surprisingly attractive vegetation. Trondheim's Ringve Museum is worth seeing if you're interested in musical instruments. The late Victoria Bachke collected them from all over the world, and most are quite old. As a young girl in 1917, she fled the Russian Revolution, landing in Trondheim and eventually marrying Christian Anker Bachke, heir to Ringve Farm.

The farm had long been a principal employer and food source in the area. When Bachke died, he willed the farm to the Norwegian people with the provision that much of it be devoted to a museum depicting the history of music.

Victoria then began gathering ancient pianos, harpsichords, organs, and harps, obtaining most of them free of charge by use of her great charm, unceasing pressure, and beguiling Russian accent.

Later, more exotic instruments were acquired, including African tribal drums, a Japanese koto, gamelans from Java, and a large collection of music boxes. Tours in English are conducted mornings at 9:30.

DINING IN TRONDHEIM

BRYGGEN
Ovre Bakklander 66
Tel: 47-73-87-4242
Norwegian and French.

———— • ————

MONTE CRISTO
Prinsensgaten 38
Tel: 47-73-52-1880
International Norwegian cuisine.

———— • ————

HAVFRUEN FISKERESTAURANT
Kjemannsgaten 7
Tel: 47-73-87-4070
Specializing in fish.

THE BRITANNIA HOTEL
Dronningens Gate 5
Tel: 47-7380-0800
www.britannia.no

The Britannia was originally built for the 19th century's well-heeled English traveler. We describe it as either rich in Victorian tradition, or kitsch. Its exterior is a white wedding cake with cornice ornamentation.

Inside, there are 175 nicely renovated rooms, the quietest of which, facing an interior courtyard, also happen to be the smallest. There's a traditional pub as well as a Palm Garden where breakfast and lunch are served. Roast beef and Yorkshire pudding and steak and kidney pie are on the dinner menu, and while the food is not exceptional, it's all good fun. Doubles from $90, including breakfast.

LANDE'S FAMOUS LIST

I am indebted to TIME correspondents and colleagues, who have contributed to Lande's List over many years. Each is a tried and true selection.

ARGENTINA

BARILOCHE

LLAO LLAO RESORT
Tel: 54-29-4444-8530, www.llaollao.com

Llao Llao is a little piece of the Swiss Alps relocated in South America. Positioned spectacularly between two lakes, Nahuel Huapi and Moreno, the resort is within the Nahuel Huapi National Park. Surrounded by magnificent snow-capped mountains and forests, the lodge is fashioned from exotic native woods such as cypress, coigue, and arrayan in exposed beams and from the green stone of the region.

The Llao Llao rests comfortably within the inspiring natural beauty of the area and should not be missed when visiting Patagonia. The resort's German and Argentine restaurants are excellent and are know for their mouthwatering fondues.

BUENOS AIRES

ALVEAR PALACE HOTEL
Av. Alvear 1891
Tel: 54-11-4808-2100, www.alvearpalace.com

Located in the center of the exclusive La Recoleta district of Buenos Aires, close to business, shopping, and museums, the Alvear Palace Hotel is a venue popular with celebrities and heads of state. Built in 1932, the hotel has been completely renovated with the most up-to-date facilities, yet it retains its Old World feel and Louis XVI and Empire appointments, full of marble and statuary.

The guest accommodations, decorated in opulent blues and burgundies, could be at Versailles, with high ceilings, large windows draped in silk, and feather beds. Each room features personal butler service, Hermès de Paris toiletries, and the amenities you would expect in a hotel like this one.

Just five minutes from the financial district and surrounded by excellent restaurants, shops, and antique stores, the Alvear is one of the most elegant hotels in Buenos Aires.

CAESAR PARK
Posadas 1232
Tel: 54-11-4819-1100, www.lhw.com

Fine shops, museums, and restaurants are all available in the Recoleta district, the exclusive French neighborhood in Buenos Aires, and the stylish Caesar Park is a good choice for accommodations here. Situated across from the elegant Patio Bullrich shopping plaza, the hotel has 170 large rooms tastefully decorated with Empire furnishings, huge marble baths, and windows that open. Somewhat uncharacteristically for Argentina, the Caesar Park has designated nonsmoking floors. Cell phones are provided for guests' use. There are several good restaurants, along with a fitness center and indoor pool.

FOUR SEASONS HOTEL BUENOS AIRES
Posadas 1086/88
Tel: 54-11-4321-1200, www.fourseasons.com/buenosaires

Also in the city's fashionable and bustling La Recoleta district, the Four Seasons Hotel occupies an early 20th-century French mansion near the parks of Palermo and the best polo in the world. The hotel's modern comforts combine with the beauty of its gardens and pool to make for an enjoyable stay. The Four Seasons' outstanding Le Mistral restaurant has one of the best chefs in Argentina, and the Sunday Brunch in the Mansion is not to be missed.

SOFITEL BUENOS AIRES
Arroyo 841/849
Tel: 54-11-4131-0000, www.sofitelbuenosaires.com.ar

The Sofitel hotel, in a historic 1920s art deco building, has been redesigned and totally renovated. It is French boutique chic, with a striking library bar. The hotel, with 116 rooms and 28 suites, is situated in Retiro, one of the most elegant areas in the heart of the city, close to the financial district. There are six nonsmoking floors. Visit the Sofitel's Le Sud restaurant for French Mediterranean cuisine influenced by traditional recipes of the Provence region, or try its Café Arroyo, reminiscent of the traditional Buenos Aires cafés.

LOI SUITES RECOLETA
Vicente López 1955
Tel: 54-11-5777-8950, www.loisuites.com.ar/recoleta

This is a very reasonably priced and pleasant hotel in upscale Recoleta, home to so many shops, bars, cafés, and cultural attractions. The rooms are nicely decorated in soothing colors, and all have stereos, big-screen TVs, and microwave ovens. Enjoy a poolside breakfast and nightly happy hour.

AUSTRALIA

CAIRNS

PACIFIC INTERNATIONAL HOTEL ON THE ESPLANADE
Esplanade & Spence Street
Tel: 61-7-40-51-7888, www.pacifichotelcairns.com

This hotel is located on the Cairns waterfront near where the boats leave for trips to the Great Barrier Reef. A warm hotel created with care and a commitment to service, the Pacific International offers 174 rooms and suites, many with harbor views.

GREAT BARRIER REEF

LIZARD ISLAND RESORT
PMB 40 via Cairns
Tel: 61-2-8296-8010, www.lizardisland.com.au

Captain James Cook on his voyage of discovery in 1770 landed on Lizard Island as a way to escape from the Great Barrier Reef: He climbed the peak on the island to chart a safe course out to sea. Today, people come to Lizard Island Resort specifically to enjoy the Reef at its northernmost island resort. Lizard Island is a private paradise, with pretty cottages and white-sand beaches everywhere you look. One of Australia's premier resorts, Lizard Island offers great diving on the inner and outer reefs, as well as extraordinary food and sweeping coastal views from the broad veranda where dinner is one of Lizard's many great pleasures.

SILKY OAKS LODGE
Mossman Gorge 4871
Tel: 61-2-8296-8010, www.silkyoakslodge.com.au

While it's within easy reach of the Great Barrier Reef or Cape Tribulation, the Silky Oaks Lodge is all about the

THE GOLDEN KEYS

Hello Mr. Anson! Every wonder about those distinguished men who greet you and who stand sentry at the gateway of great hotels? Those who attend to your every wish? They are the men of the Golden Keys.

Rex Anson, in his smart black uniform and top hat, stands guard at the Hyatt Regency in Auckland, and is one of the nicest, most knowledgeable men I know. He reads the classics and has an encyclopedic knowledge of history.

Mr. Anson is a descendant of the navigator who brought Captain Cook to New Zealand, and he provides information, advice, and assistance to Hyatt guests in all manner of things, including hotel services, entertainment, restaurants, luggage, transport, and sightseeing. He also leads a team of assistant concierges, porters, commissionaires, and parking attendants. His position carries the responsibility of being a strategic contact for each guest.

As concierge, he fosters a team that is able to work together to provide the maximum level of service possible. His importance cannot be underestimated, for he develops strong interdepartmental relationships within the hotel. Developing a positive working relationship with guests, we rely upon him to have our needs met.

Anson has unquestionable integrity. He is well educated, often-quoting 19th-century literary figures, such as Charles Dickens and Jane Austin, Joseph Conrad and Mark Twain. Providing accurate and pertinent facts, drawn from an amazing font of knowledge and information, he serves as an ambassador for the hotel. He's usually the one to offer the first hello and last good-bye.

This Renaissance man told me the history of the role of the concierge. The idea started with a French concierge named Ferdinand Gillet, who worked at a small hotel in Paris and felt there was a need for the city's head porters to get to know each other so as to better serve their respective guests.

His initiative saw the foundation of the French Association of Les Clefs d'Or in October 1929. This French society developed and matured and had the foresight to realize that extending the concept of a friendly society of concierges beyond the borders of France would benefit hotels and guests. Gillet and his French associates expanded their society by forming a European association in Cannes in 1952. In 1953 at the San Remo Congress, the emblem of the crossed golden keys, to be worn on a member concierge's lapel, was adopted to identify members and to symbolize the opening of doors for travelers. This European association eventually became an International association in 1972 at the 20th Congress in Palma, Majorca.

The creation of Les Clefs d'Or established a group of professionals whose role is recognized by national and international travelers. There are 30 member countries worldwide with approximately 4,700 members. Concierge Anson represents the best.

Daintree Rainforest, the oldest living rain forest on Earth. Set on the edge of the Mossman Gorge within the rain forest, Silky Oaks is the best place to enjoy this exceptional wilderness in comfort.

Daintree's ultimate resort, Silky Oaks has the lodge itself, plus individual tree house accommodations that overlook a lagoon. If you can tear yourself away, you can also ride a scenic railway through the Barron Gorge or cruise along the Daintree River for different perspectives on nature's beauty.

MELBOURNE

PARK HYATT MELBOURNE
1 Parliament Square
Tel: 61-3-92-24-1234, www.melbourne.park.hyatt.com

The Park Hyatt Melbourne is an elegant, world-class hotel. It is located in one of Melbourne's most historic areas, opposite Saint Patrick's Cathedral, among beautiful Victorian-era buildings, and adjacent to Melbourne's delightful Fitzroy Gardens. The hotel's design and interior are distinctive, and the staff provides an exceptional level of personalized service. The Park Hyatt Melbourne is welcoming and cozy, a private haven that you will not leave without taking the memory with you.

LYALL HOTEL & SPA
14 Murphy Street, South Yarra Victoria
Tel: 61-3-98-68-8222, www.slh.com

Situated within the fashionable South Yarra area, the Lyall is undoubtedly the premium boutique hotel in Melbourne. It features attractive rooms and art galleries on every floor. The Lyall Spa is one of the country's best day spas and makes a great way to relax after a day of sightseeing in fascinating Melbourne and its environs.

OUTBACK

LONGITUDE 131°
Uluru, Northern Territory
Tel: 61-2-82-96-8010, www.longitude131.com.au

Considered by many to be one of the finest wilderness hotels in the world, Longitude 131° is deep in the heart of central Australia close to the boundary of the Uluru-Kata Tjuta National Park, with breathtaking views of Uluru (Ayers Rock). The accommodations consist of 15 luxury two-person tents, for a maximum occupancy of 30 people in the peace and solitude of this remote location. There is nowhere better to feel the spiritual wonder of this primeval world and its unique ecological wonders.

PORT FAIRY

OSCAR'S BOUTIQUE HOTEL
41 B Gipps Street
Tel: 61-3-55-68-3022, www.oscarswaterfront.com

A French Provincial boutique hotel in historic Port Fairy, Victoria, Oscar's is in a lovely waterfront setting right on the Moyne River. Breakfast is served on the veranda overlooking the sailing craft and fishing vessels of the local marina. Oscar's makes a great getaway in the colder months as well, with a roaring open fire in the grand drawing room, ideal for playing board games or reading a good book.

SYDNEY

OBSERVATORY HOTEL
89-113 Kent Street
Tel: 61-2-92-56-2222, www.observatoryhotel.com.au

The historic Rocks area is a good base for seeing Sydney, and the Observatory Hotel makes an excellent choice of

accommodations there. The Observatory provides every luxury found in a grand Australian home.

PARK HYATT SYDNEY
7 Hickson Road, The Rocks
Tel: 61-2-92-41-123, www.sydney.park.hyatt.com

Also located in the Rocks section of Sydney, the Park Hyatt Sydney has become the first choice of hotels for the sophisticated traveler. The boutique-style hotel is right on the waterfront of Sydney Harbor with spectacular views of the Opera House.

REGENT'S COURT
18 Springfield Ave, Potts Point
Tel: 61-2-93-58-1533, www.regentscourt.com.au

Built in 1926 as residences, this building was converted from apartments into a comfortable, stylish hotel that was once one of Sydney's best-kept secrets. The quiet location in Potts Point matches perfectly the intimate feel of this small boutique hotel. One of Regents Court's great delights is dining in the balmy garden setting on the rooftop, looking out at the lights of Sydney. The hotel has the elegance of many much more pricey accommodations.

SULLIVANS HOTEL SYDNEY
21 Oxford Street, Paddington, NSW
Tel: 61-2-93-61-0211, www.sullivans.com.au

Walking around the Paddington section is one of the great ways to spend a day in Sydney, exploring the winding streets, enjoying the village-like atmosphere, and taking advantage of the shopping and nightlife. Sullivans Hotel is ideally situated for investigating trendy Paddington and its plethora of boutiques, art galleries, and bars and restaurants. If you're lucky enough to be there on Saturday, don't miss Sydney's liveliest street market in Paddington.

AUSTRIA

HOTEL SACHER SALZBURG
Schwarzstrasse 5–7, Salzburg
Tel.: 43-66-28-8977, www.salzburg.sacher.com

The Hotel Sacher Salzburg is the city's Grand Hotel, with an impressive view of the Hohensalzburg fortress. It has been the very center of the city's social life since 1866 and has hosted members of reigning houses, aristocrats, scientists, poets, actors, and artists. New rooms and suites add character.

HOTEL GOLDENER HIRSCH
Getreidegasse 37, Salzburg
Tel: 43-66-28-0840, www.goldenerhirsch.com

With a history that stretches back at least to 1407, the Hotel Goldener Hirsch has been a part of Salzburg's illustrious life from the Baroque world to modern times. It was already 350 years old when Mozart was born nearby and is ideally situated for visiting his birthplace on Salzburg's main street and the city's other delights. The Goldener Hirsch is a personal hotel, rich in tradition.

HOTEL IMPERIAL
Kaerntner Ring 16, Vienna
Tel: 43-1-501-100, www.starwoodhotels.com

One of Vienna's most beloved venues, the Hotel Imperial is an architectural landmark that has been a center of the Viennese social scene for over a century. Originally built in 1873 as a Württemberg palace and later inaugurated as a hotel by Emperor Franz Joseph I, the Imperial still has five ceremonial palace halls in their original condition off the central rotunda. The opulent hotel, with its majestic entrance, exemplifies Vienna's own Ringstrasse style. There are 38 rooms and suites, each richly appointed with antique furniture and glorious works of art.

HOTEL PALAIS SCHWARZENBERG
Schwarzenbergplatz 9, Vienna
Tel: 43-1-798-45-15, www.palais-schwarzenberg.com

Built in the early 1700s, the Hotel Palais Schwarzenberg remarkably is still in the hands of the Schwarzenbergs, one of the last family-owned palaces in Vienna, and the personal touch shows. The Baroque hotel, set in a private park, has a grand entrance hall and five Baroque public rooms. The historic main building has 44 rooms and suites decorated with artworks and period furniture.

THE BAHAMAS

NASSAU

LYFORD CAY CLUB
New Providence Island
Tel: 242-362-4271

On the westernmost tip of New Providence Island is the private residential enclave known as Lyford Cay, a 400-hectare (1,000-acre) gated community of tropical beauty, with some of the highest hills on the island. The world-renowned Lyford Cay Club here was designed with a wide variety of family recreational and social activities in mind. A kilometer (half-mile) of powdery white sand beach provides the sea views you come to the Bahamas for, while the championship golf course, tennis courts, two yacht harbors and complete marina provide more active pursuits. There are guest rooms in the main clubhouse as well as separate cottages, and the variety of four-star restaurants, the manicured gardens, and the personal service are sure to make your stay enjoyable.

CAMBODIA

LA RÉSIDENCE D'ANGKOR
River Road, Siem Reap
Tel: 855-63-963-390, www.pansea.com

Angkor Wat, a UNESCO World Heritage site, is one of the most awe-inspiring manmade places on Earth, a mystical temple complex almost 1,000 years old surrounded by jungle. La Résidence d'Angkor lies just 10 minutes from this fabled lost city, providing an oasis of tranquility on the river in the heart of Siem Reap. The Khmer-style hotel provides all the comforts you might want after a day climbing over the ruins, including a beautiful tiled swimming pool and peaceful gardens.

CANADA

ALBERTA

Here, near Lake Louise, scenes for the movie *Dr. Zhivago* were filmed through a winter fantasy lens.

THE FAIRMONT BANFF SPRINGS
405 Spray Avenue, Banff
Tel: 403-762-2211, www.fairmont.com/banffsprings

The Banff Springs Hotel is the Grand Dame of the Canadian Rockies, built as a fairytale Scottish baronial castle by the Canadian Pacific Railway in the 1880s. There are few hotels in the world that can lay claim to a more magnificent setting than this, surrounded by stunning mountain views in every direction. If you're looking to combine skiing with some serious spa time, look no further. The Fairmont Banff Springs has a unique blend of opulence and seclusion, with championship golf courses,

NEWS FROM HEADQUARTERS

Tish Baldrige, former White House social secretary to First Lady Jacqueline Kennedy, once told me that her idea of roughing it was using a paper napkin.

Frette fanatics might agree with Tish. I think we all do from time to time. But I would trade the linen napkin for a paper one any day in exchange for intelligent service.

As a communications consultant for the luxury hospitality industry, I spend most of my professional time cocooned in luxury in the hotels and resorts I represent all over the world. Over the past five years I have seen the concept and expectations of sophisticated luxury travelers change dramatically. Obsequious service is annoying. Ostentatious presentations are passé. The endless "my pleasure" comments are cloying to a busy, sophisticated traveler. Genuine service and a sincere, expedient, intelligent response to requests is modern de rigueur.

The Plaza Athénée in New York made an indelible impression. I was staying there on September 11, 2001, and was with colleagues from Cannes when news of the attacks on the World Trade Center broke. The management of the hotel quickly came up with a plan to take care of us—advising us about safety precautions, transportation out of New York, and meal service. Their efficiency and caring, particularly to my colleagues from outside the United States, gave great solace.

The masters of the service universe in my opinion are the staffs of the Hotel de Crillon in Paris and the Hotel Martinez in Cannes. I've actually arrived at Charles de Gaulle airport on my way to the Crillon, telephoned the concierge, and by the time I'm in my room, my appointments are made, reservations are confirmed, and often a hairdresser is waiting for me.

The Hotel Martinez is another master. My friend Richard left his CD case on a flight to Nice. Miraculously, the hotel concierge retrieved it in two days.

My sister and I still laugh about an experience we had at the Gritti Palace in Venice. We had walked the city for hours, then flopped in our beds and ordered two Bellinis. When room service knocked at the door, we couldn't move. The next thing we knew, the waiter was graciously presenting our Bellinis bedside. Bellinis haven't tasted the same since.

For me it's these little memories that have made the biggest difference in my travels. I know I can get through that onerous immigration line and the wait at baggage claim, because in a short time I'll be experiencing the talents of some of the world's finest service professionals.

– Karon Cullen

Karon Cullen is the founder of Cullen International, luxury marketing and public relations consultants. www.karoncullen@aol.com

unparalleled skiing in the winter and hiking in the summer, classic cuisine, and Willow Stream, a world-class European-style spa.

THE FAIRMONT CHATEAU LAKE LOUISE
111 Lake Louise Drive, Lake Louise
Tel: 403-522-3511, www.fairmont.com/lakelouise

This sister hotel to the Fairmont Banff Springs started as the wilderness getaway from the Banff Springs, but in its magical site overlooking pristine Lake Louise, it quickly became every bit as popular as its older sister. Surrounded by the snowcapped Canadian Rockies and standing in front of a majestic glacier with the crystal-clear lake on its doorstep, this is as idyllic a spot as you can imagine to go hiking, canoeing, mountain biking, fly-fishing, horseback riding, skiing, or snowshoeing.

WHISTLER

THE WESTIN RESORT AND SPA
4090 Whistler Way, Tel: 604-905-5000
www.westinwhistler.com

Yet another spectacular ski-and-spa choice, this time in the more accessible Pacific Northwest, is the Westin Resort and Spa in Whistler, British Columbia. Located slopeside at the resorts of Whistler and Blackcomb, the gondolas are just steps away to take you to the top of the highest vertical rise in North America, whether for winter skiing or summer sightseeing. Whistler Village contains all the nightlife you'll need after hours, as well.

MONTREAL

CHÂTEAU VERSAILLES
1659 Sherbrooke Street
Tel: 514-933-8111, www.versailleshotels.com

Intimate and chic, the Château Versailles features 65 bedrooms and suites in an Old World atmosphere in exciting Montreal. Interior designer Patricia McClintock has brought in rich fabrics mixed with original antique elements, and contemporary art from Quebec artists is displayed everywhere, giving the place a private club feel.

HOTEL VOGUE
1425 Rue De La Montagne
Tel: 514-285-5555, www.loewshotels.com/hotels/montreal

The newly renovated Loews Hotel Vogue, anchoring the city's Golden Mile, has 142 spacious, blessedly quiet rooms that feature down comforters and are equipped with fax machines as well as the usual safe, umbrella, and robes. The huge, well-lit marble baths are fitted out with a TV above the whirlpool tub. Doubles from about $150.

CARIBBEAN

ANTIGUA

CARLISLE BAY
Old Road, St Mary's,
Tel: 268-484-0000, www.carlisle-bay.com

The Carlisle Bay on the stunning south coast of Antigua has 80 spacious suites all facing the Caribbean, fronted by an idyllic white sand beach. This exciting resort, a sister hotel to the award-winning One Aldwych in London, has tranquil interiors, two excellent restaurants, and superb service.

CURTAIN BLUFF
Morris Bay, Antigua
Tel: 268-462-8400, www.curtainbluff.com

Howard Hulford opened Curtain Bluff in Antigua more than 40 years ago, and it is still recognized as one of the best on the island. The newer beachfront junior suites are eye-catching. The open-air restaurant has first-rate Continental dining in a quietly posh private club ambience.

ST. BARTHÉLEMY

HOTEL GUANAHANI & SPA
Anse de Grand Cul de Sac
Tel: 590-590-27-6660, www.leguanahani.com

St. Bart's, in the French overseas department of Guadeloupe, is as exotic as it gets in the Caribbean, and the Guanahani is the perfect place to take it all in. A small, exclusive resort, the Guanahani and its 75 rooms and suites drape over the hills of Grand Cul de Sac, with the teal blue lagoon on one side and Marigot Bay and the ocean on the other. The distinctly West Indian–style rooms are available on either side. The lagoon-view rooms have white decor and terra-cotta floors, while the ocean-view rooms have hardwood furniture and parquet floors. Most suites have private swimming pools. The beachside Indigo restaurant is a wonderful vantage point and the food is delicious. The resort also features six hectares (15 acres) of gardens.

ST. MARTIN

LA SAMANNA
Baie Longue
Tel: 212-575-7030, www.lasamanna.com

The island of St. Martin/St. Maarten is unique in the Caribbean, half French, half Dutch. Thus, the distinct European flavor gives visitors an exciting escape from less exotic parts of the Caribbean. La Samanna is the place to stay here. Its Mediterranean villa-style architecture adds to the Old World charm of the island, with white stucco walls and terra-cotta rooftops, and every room is oceanfront. The colorful garden grounds are glorious.

ST. VINCENT & THE GRENADINES

THE COTTON HOUSE
Mustique
Tel: 784-456-4777 or 800-223-1108
www.cottonhouse.net

The Cotton House is located on a private island in St. Vincent and the Grenadines, the West Indies. With several beautiful beaches and protected coves for swimming or sunning, guests can forget about the outside world entirely here, which is why it's been a favorite destination of royalty and celebrities.

A creation of the famed London set designer Oliver Messel, the Cotton House is a West Indian plantation-style fantasy. The Great Room is a central focal point for the resort, with comfortable cabanas and bungalows surrounding it. From the hilltop pools you can see Endeavour Bay below, while the beautifully landscaped gardens on the other side trail down to L'Ansecoy Bay. Spend the day sailing, scuba diving or snorkeling, playing tennis, or horseback riding.

Dining at the Cotton House features Caribbean cuisine at its finest. The freshest ingredients are combined with the perfect wine, and you can savor the many signature dishes in an outdoor setting or in the intimate dining room.

PETIT ST. VINCENT RESORT
Petit St. Vincent
Tel: 954-963-7401, www.psvresort.com

Another picture-perfect islet in the unbelievably clear waters of the Caribbean, Petit St. Vincent is uninhabited except for the pampered guests at this resort. Surrounded by nearly three kilometers (two miles) of porcelain white sandy beaches, the accommodations consist of 22 luxurious cottages spread around the tiny piece of paradise. With swimming, snorkeling, sailing, diving, tennis, and seaside cocktail service, you won't even think about what's going on back home.

TURKS & CAICOS

PARROT CAY AND SHAMBHALA RETREAT
Providenciales
Tel: 649-946-7788, shambhala.como.bz

Shambhala is a Sanskrit word for "peace," and that's what you'll find at this Caribbean hideaway. The hotel, compliments of London interior designer Keith Hobbs, is exactly what you would hope for in this tropical locale, using traditional colonial decor and light, cool fabrics. Parrot Cay is ringed by more than five kilometers (three miles) of white sands beaches and crystal-blue waters.

CHILE

Chile has spectacular scenery everywhere, but I particularly love the land and sea journey from Chile's southern lake country all the way down to Patagonia's Torres del Paine National Park, taking in the snow-capped volcanic Andes and tiny villages along the way. At the Termas de Puyehue Hotel in the Lake District, guests can soak up the good life in the hot spring–fed pools while enjoying the stunning alpine views. At Torres del Paine, icebergs surround the most beautiful park in the world. Staying at the extraordinary Hotel Explora on an exquisite island that time has forgotten. Each day you can take a different excursion, returning each night to all the comforts of a fine European hotel.

The early explorers who discovered the Strait of Magellan christened this region "Patagonia" due to the enormous footprints they found in the snow. They were the tracks of the nomadic hunters who covered their feet with guanaco skins to protect themselves from the cold. Not just anyone can visit Patagonia. Here you can feel the silence, something that is increasingly rare. Patagonia is a place with areas that are untouched and unknown and others that are full of tradition.

PATAGONIA

PUYUHUAPI HOTEL & SPA
Patagonia, Chile
Tel: 56-2-225-6489, www.patagonia-connection.com

For a extraordinary getaway, what could be better than a lodge at the far reaches of the world that is accessible only by boat? Deep in the Ventisquero Sound, along the banks of Dorita Bay in Patagonia sits just such a place, the Puyuhuapi Hotel & Spa. You may have a hard time deciding between the energizing outdoor activities—nature hikes through the lush rain forest, fly-fishing in ice-cold mountain streams, mountain biking, or kayaking in the fjords—and the relaxing options closer to the hotel, such as soaking in one of the three natural hot spring pools or luxuriating in the spa in seawater, geothermal mineral waters, or glacier-melt water right from the waterfalls. But then, why not do both?

PATAGONIA EXPRESS
Tel: 305-388-6400, www.patagoniaexpress.com

Patagonia Express operates a modern catamaran that can take you on incredible one-, four-, or seven-day programs throughout Patagonia. One option in Chilean Patagonia consists of a combination of sailing through the southern channels of the Aysen region and lodging on shore where you can discover the immense, and until recently virtually inaccessible, landscapes of the Austral Highway area. The boat delves into a fantastic world of glaciers, icebergs, swollen rivers, and majestic fjords.

The catamaran was specially designed and built to operate in the waters of this region and offers safe and comfortable transportation. Its professional crew has vast experience in navigating through the region's fjords, so you can relax reclining in the wide lounge chairs on the first deck. Later the chefs onboard will prepare exquisite Chilean food, which you can enjoy in the bar-restaurant on the upper deck with delicious Chilean wines.

The major highlight of a Patagonia Express tour is amazing glacier in San Rafael Lagoon. The glacier, which flows from 3,000 meters (10,000 feet) up in the Andes, ends in the lagoon, calving ice into the water constantly. After entering the lagoon, you will be astounded by the falling ice from the glacier that scatters chunks of white and deep blue icebergs into the water; excursion boats can provide you with the opportunity for an even closer look at the process. You will never forget the experience.

HOTEL JOSE NOGUEIRA
Bories 959, Punta Arenas
Tel: 56-61-24-8840, www.hotelnogueira.com

The main town in Chilean Patagonia, Punta Arenas was the center of the country's shipping industry until the opening of the Panama Canal provided a cheaper and safer route than going through the Strait of Magellan. During its heyday, wealthy industrialists hired European craftsmen and imported luxurious materials to build magnificent Belle Epoque mansions, several of which today are museums and hotels. One of the most handsome is the Hotel Jose Nogueira, a 25-room property with a bar-restaurant located in a glassed-in winter garden. The best rooms are #311 and #312.

PUERTO MONTT

HOTEL Y CABAÑAS DEL LAGO
Klenner 195, Puerto Varas
Tel: 56-65-23-2291

The most enjoyable way to reach the Chilean lakes region of Patagonia is by catamaran from the dock at Llao Llao, a trip of several hours that requires portaging by bus through a national forest. Puerto Montt is a common stopover site, but Puerta Varas, a scenic town on Lake Llanquihue, is a more colorful choice. Here, the Hotel y Cabañas del Lago is an adequate choice offering 63 rooms and 21 cabins, all nicely appointed as well as a full range of hotel services, including a heated swimming pool. The best room is suite #500, facing the lake.

TORRES DEL PAINE

HOTEL EXPLORA
Tel: 56-2-206-6060, www.explora.com

The Torres del Paine National Park is a wondrous expanse of pristine mountains, lakes, rivers, and fjords, and the Hotel Explora is the perfect base from which to explore it. This is a remote part of the world. After flying all the way to Punta Arenas at the bottom of South America, it's another six-hour van ride to the park and the hotel. But when you get there, nature is all yours.

Built on the shore of Lake Pehoe, the hotel has 30 rooms, all but three facing the lake and the awesome twin peaks of the spectacular Cordillera Paine. Some suites (numbers 18, 19, 26, and 27) even have Jacuzzis and king-size beds, so you don't exactly need to rough it while you're on vacation.

Each day there is a choice of five guided excursions, ranging from moderately easy walks to difficult hikes. All are memorable, especially the trek across a wind-tossed suspension bridge over the world's third-largest ice field.

At the hotel, you'll find a spa, a lap pool, and an on-site masseuse, all of which help to relax those sore muscles after all that ambitious exercise. The food is good and plentiful; special dietary needs can be accommodated with advance notice. The park's climate is cool all year round, and it often rains, but don't let that discourage you. Bring hiking boots, layers of clothing, and raingear. Guests must book for a minimum of three nights, and advanced booking is absolutely necessary.

VALPARAISO

Hotel Brighton
Paseo Atkinson n°151-153, cerro Concepción
Tel: 56-32-22-3513 or 56-32-59-8802

On top of Valparaiso's tallest hill, Hotel Brighton Bed and Breakfast is a lovely yellow house that is one of the city's landmarks, visible from the beaches and much of the city. A funicular, the Ascensor Concepción, takes you 60 meters (200 feet) up to the hotel and its commanding view over this world-famous port. Small and appealing, with just five rooms, it provides a good restaurant and the chance to explore Pablo Neruda's poetic world. The hotel's breakfast area has furnishings in keeping with its turn-of-the-20th-century heritage, a Valparaiso where Oregon pine and oak were the basic building materials, chosen by owner Nelson Morgado, together with objects and artifacts brought by ship from England.

CHINA

BEIJING

Shangri-La China World Hotel
No. 1 Jianguomenwai Avenue
Tel: 86-10-65-05-2266, www.shangri-la.com

When visiting the capital of China, try the Shangri-La China World Hotel, which is centrally located in the heart of Beijing's diplomatic and business district. The hotel is large, with 716 rooms, but its service and standards are excellent, making it a top choice for businesspeople and government leaders to stay. Shangri-La's China World was fully renovated just two years ago and is located in the China World Trade Centre complex, which includes a shopping mall. The hotel's restaurants are highly praised.

SHANGHAI

Four Seasons Hotel Shanghai
500 Weihai Road
Tel: 86-21-62-56-8888, www.fourseasons.com/shanghai

In Shanghai, the Four Seasons will provide the top-flight level of service expected from Four Seasons hotels worldwide. It is well positioned in downtown Shanghai, a short distance from the shopping, entertainment, and business areas of Nanjing and Huaihai roads.

LUXURY HOTELS

While luxury endures and even transcends time, the concept of luxury has certainly changed. At The Leading Hotels of the World we've been taking care of the luxury traveler since our founding in 1928. The luxury traveler has always been the person most challenging to please. In short, this category is the most coddled and pampered class in the world.

But today's luxury travelers and luxury hotels have changed in appearance…inwardly and outwardly. From casual dress codes to the warm and friendly attitudes of staff in the most palatial of hotels, to the smaller properties that luxury guests gravitate to, not to mention their usage of the Internet and need for instant gratification, the look and attitude of luxury service and amenities has changed dramatically.

"Don't judge a book by its cover" is our mantra. Some of our most frequent guests are often the ones who look as if they have just climbed off the Alps, and indeed they may arrive at a Palace hotel weary and mussed after a four-day hike. They may check in at Villa d'Este in Italy in jeans, right off their private jet.

The look of hotels has changed, too. No one is surprised to find a hip bar in a classic hotel in the Plaza Athénée in Paris or at the Peninsula in Hong Kong. Dining options combine the grand Les Ambassadeurs at the Hotel de Crillon in Paris to the cutting edge decor of Carlisle Bay.

Gone is the frosty look from the concierge at the grandest hotel or the haughty waiter, the know-it-all sommelier in the Michelin three-star restaurant. Hotel staff must be friendly and warm without being obsequious, they must be engaging without being overfriendly.

The ambience of a luxury hotel can be Old World elegant highlighted by antiquities and fine art (such as the splendid Beau-Rivage Palace in Lausanne), classical in design but housing a modern art collection (such as the Merrion in Dublin), or crisply modern and elegantly hip with some of the best service in the world, such as One Aldwych in London.

Whatever the design, the hotel must provide instant gratification and fulfill all expectations. Today's luxury traveler looks for a private experience in a hotel, whether it has 400 or 40 rooms. Private butlers on private floors, personal concierges for certain suites, and personal private fitness rooms and treadmills on demand in rooms are the order of the day. They didn't exist 20 years ago. Luxury hotels are making their experiences for guests more intimate and more personal. Because experience is the new luxury, upscale travelers seek a sense of place, whether for a business or for a leisure trip.

— Paul McManus
CEO, Leading Hotels of the World, www.lhw.com

PEACE HOTEL
20 Nanjing Road
Tel: 86-21-63-21-6888, www.shanghaipeacehotel.com

While you can't beat the Four Seasons for service and efficiency, you can't beat the Peace Hotel for style and old-time romance. The building was originally built by the British in 1906, but the north building was constructed as a hotel in 1929 and considered the finest in Asia. The buildings still sport wonderful art deco features that make this Shanghai's most historic hotel. Try to get a room on the Bund, where the views are stunning. Dining options include the Dragon-Phoenix Room and Victoria Roof Garden; you can dance to big band music every night.

CUBA

HAVANA

THE HOTEL NACIONAL
Calles 21 y O
Tel: 53-7-33-3564, www.hotelnacionaldecuba.com

Havana was the place to be in the 1930s, and the Hotel Nacional, built in 1930, was the place to be in Havana. Perched on a bluff overlooking the sea, the hotel was patterned after the Breakers in Palm Beach, and it still has that palmy, art deco atmosphere. In the Vedado section, the hotel has 450 large and still reasonably attractive rooms, many with ocean views, recalling the Havana of old when the Hotel Nacional reigned over Havana's nightlife. It still offers a Las Vegas–style revue, complete with "feather ladies." There is a pool, of course, and a wonderful terrace with great views that's a tranquil spot for relaxing with a mojito, the delicious cocktail of rum, lime juice, soda, and fresh mint.

HOTEL COPACABANA
Calle 1ra. e/ 44 & 46, Playa
Tel: 53-7-24-1037

If the ocean is what you seek in Havana, try the Hotel Copacabana, located in the once upscale Miramar district in western Havana. Its location near Quinta Avenida makes it easy to reach in just a few minutes. This unusual hotel is almost part of the sea, and in fact it has a marvelous saltwater swimming pool built right into the sea. There's a freshwater pool as well. Built in 1957 and remodeled and expanded in 1992, the Copacabana is attractive and functional, with simple, pleasant rooms. It is fully equipped for all sports. The Copacabana's public spaces include the Brazilian-inspired Itapoa and Tucán restaurants, the Caipirinha snack bar, and the Ipanema discotheque.

CZECH REPUBLIC

PRAGUE

CARLO IV
Senovazne namesti 13
Tel. 420-224-59-3111. www.boscolohotels.com

Prague has bounced back from the Iron Curtain days and is once again one of the most vibrant and picturesque cities in Europe. In Prague's historical core is the glorious neo-classical palazzo of the Carlo IV, with its exquisite furnishings and artworks. Ornate and expressive, the hotel boasts both Old World touches of old wood and marble and contemporary features such as its business center and the Cigar Bar. There is an indoor swimming pool in elegant surroundings, and the hotel's service is of the highest standards.

EGYPT

CAIRO

HILTON CAIRO WORLD TRADE CENTER RESIDENCE
World Trade Center, Corniche al-Nil, Bulaq
Tel: 20-2-578-0444, www.hilton.com

If you want upscale in Cairo, try one of the 104 apartments at the World Trade Center Hilton Residence. With five or six rooms, including a full kitchen and two or three bedrooms, plus four bathrooms, you might be living better here than at home. Terraces look out over the city and the Nile. There are three more traditional Hilton hotels in Cairo as well.

FOUR SEASONS
35 Giza Street
Tel: 20-2-569-7581, www.fourseasons.com

The Four Seasons is tops in Cairo for efficiency and sophistication. The service is always top-notch. Choose from the Four Seasons Hotel Cairo at The First Residence on the west bank of the Nile with great views of the pyramids (that's what you're here for, isn't it?) or the relatively new and more modern Four Seasons Hotel Cairo at Nile Plaza.

WINDSOR HOTEL
19 Shar'a Alfi Bay
Tel: 20-25-91-5810, www.windsorcairo.com

Walking distance from the Nile and the matchless Egyptian Museum, the Windsor Hotel takes you back to the Agatha Christie days. Almost a century old and in business as a hotel since the 1930s—after having been a bathhouse and then an officers club for the British—the Windsor has many original features, yet doesn't lack modern services. It won't be hard to imagine why this has been a popular set for Hollywood movies in the past.

RED SEA

THE OBEROI SAHL HASHEESH
Hurghada
Tel: 20-65-344-0777, oberoihotels.com

Located on Egypt's beautiful Red Sea coast, legendary for its marine life and diving possibilities, but also wonderful for sun and sand, The Oberoi Sahl Hasheesh is an exclusive all-suite resort with a private 850-meter (half-mile) beach. Designed in contemporary Arabic style with graceful domes, arches, and columns. The restaurant is in a dramatic atrium with a fountain in the center and great ocean views. Eighteen suites have their private swimming pools, most of which are heated in the cooler months.

FRANCE

AFLOAT IN FRANCE
Orient-Express Trains & Cruises
10 Weybosset St, Suite 500
Providence, RI 02903
Tel: 401-351-7518
Venice Simplon-Orient-Express
Sea Containers House, 20 Upper Ground
London SE1 9PF
Tel: 08-45-(0)-77-2222, www.orient-express.com

One of the great ways to see Europe, especially France, is by barge. The country is crisscrossed with canals that allow access to many parts of the interior, and the views along the way are a lot better than those on the autopistes. This company operates five magnificent

péniche-hôtel barges that allow passengers to cruise past châteaux, fields, and forests in style. These are not little boats—they are luxurious floating apartments. To experience France's tranquil canals and rivers, from the beauty of the Midi and Provence to the majesty of Burgundy and Franche-Comté, step aboard one of these vessels and watch the passing countryside unfold through large windows or from out on deck.

FLEUR DE LYS

The owners claim this is the most impeccably appointed barge in the world, and they might be right. The barge carries up to six passengers in posh style, with three spacious suites and a stately salon with grand piano. It even has a heated plunge pool.

AMARYLLIS

This barge carries up to eight passengers on two decks. Each stateroom is decorated in a traditional style with a mixture of contemporary and antique Louis XVI and XV furniture. The vessel is fully air conditioned and has a heated plunge pool for relaxing.

THE HIRONDELLE

The *Hirondelle* is based in Burgundy and Franche-Comté and carries up to eight passengers through some of the most beautiful waterways in all of Europe: the Canal de Bourgogne, the Canal du Centre, the Canal du Rhône au Rhin, and the Saône River itself within sniffing distance of the grands crus vineyards.

THE ALOUETTE

This péniche-hôtel also cruises in Burgundy and Franche-Comté, allowing up to six passengers to delight in the sights of the tree-lined Canal du Midi.

THE NAPOLÉON

The fifth barge in this group cruises the Rhône River between the ancient Roman city of Arles and Tain l'Hermitage/Tournon in the celebrated Côte Rôtie of the northern Rhône, home to some of France's greatest wines. This is country that was such an inspiration to the likes of Matisse, Cézanne, and Van Gogh, and it will be an inspiration to you, too.

ALPES-MARITIMES

LE ST. PAUL HOTEL
86, rue Grande, 06570 Saint-Paul-de-Vence
Tel: 33-(0)-4-93-32-6525, www.relaischateaux.com/stpaul

Set in the heart of the famous medieval village of Saint-Paul-de-Vence, this XVIth century bourgeois home offers elegantly decorated rooms bathed in the scent of lavender. Choose between two dining rooms, one with a magnificent vaulted ceiling and frescos, the other set around a fountain. Alternatively, enjoy a romantic candlelit dinner on the flower-covered terrace, savoring Provençal cuisine beneath the stars.

AUBIGNY-SUR-NÈRE

CHÂTEAU DE LA VERRERIE
Oizon, D89
Tel: 33-(0)-248-81-5160, www.ila-chateau.com/verrerie

For a truly unforgettable immersion in Renaissance times, the Château de La Verrerie is everything you could imagine in a romanticized version of the French court. This breathtakingly handsome Renaissance castle with classic round turrets and pitched roofs sits alongside a lake and is surrounded by a large forest. Its history includes an alliance between the Scots and the French against the English. After the Stuarts of Scotland came to the aid of France's King

Charles VII in the 15th century and won the battle for him, the king rewarded them with La Verrerie.

Today, Count and Countess Béraud de Vogüé oversee this historical monument with gracious hospitality. The mansion has just 12 guest rooms, although each room here is the size of a small house. Each distinctly and individually

SMALL LUXURY HOTELS

Personalized service. Unique experiences. Luxurious rooms. Magnificent gastronomic fare. Local charm. Friendly staff. All of these phrases aptly describe what it is to be a member of Small Luxury Hotels of the World. Each member property of Small Luxury Hotels (SLH) is unique in its own right. Be it a European country house, an island retreat, a game lodge in Africa, or a city center hotel, all of the properties have their own personal charm and signature characteristics, while sharing a dedication to service and luxury that puts the guest first and creates a unique experience that goes far beyond just a place to stay. When searching for that perfect getaway, look for a hotel that will cater to your every need and still give you the privacy you desire. Among SLH you can find world-class accommodations high in the sky with modern technology or a beach bungalow lit only with candles. The choice is yours and the offerings abound. We look forward to welcoming you to one of our properties and having the staff serve you in whatever manner you choose.

— Brian Mills, Managing Director
www.slh.com

decorated room is comfortably equipped with period furniture but a modern bathroom.

The restaurant, La Maison d'Hélène, is in a charming 17th-century cottage in the park on the grounds. Its extensive menu is accompanied by wines from the nearby Sancerre and Loire Valley vineyards and the wood-burning fireplace is lit in season. Activities include horseback riding, tennis, cycling, and walking by the lake.

BAGNOLS

ROCCO FORTE CHÂTEAU DE BAGNOLS
Tel: 33-(0)-4-74-71-4000, www.bagnols.com

The Château de Bagnols is an impressive Burgundian castle nestled in the vineyards of Beaujolais near Lyons. First built in the 13th century and enlarged and improved many times over the following centuries, the castle was in serious disrepair when the current owners began its renovation in 1987. It is now more beautiful than it has ever been, and certainly more comfortable than its medieval occupants could have imagined. It is loaded with antique furniture and the decorative works were made by some of the world's finest craftsmen. No detail has been overlooked for the perfect experience of French countryside living.

BORDEAUX

CHÂTEAU CORDEILLAN-BAGES
Pauillac
Tel: 33-(0)-5-56-59-2424, www.relaischateaux.com

This 17th-century hotel is ideally suited for explorations of the most famous wineries in the world. Located in the commune of Pauillac in the very heart of the Médoc, three of the five first-growth Bordeaux châteaux are within bicycling distance of this converted historic Carthusian

monastery. The École du Bordeaux offers wine-tasting courses here. The hotel has 29 rooms, including four suites, and its restaurant prepares the perfect meals to match with a vintage Grand Vin, many of which are stored in the wine cave below.

BRIOLLAY

CHÂTEAU DE NOIRIEUX
26 route du Moulin
Tel: 33-(0)-02-41-42-5005, www.relaischateaux.com

This château in the Loire region with 18 rooms and one suite is typical of the beautiful country houses built by the nobility to escape the noise and bustle of Paris for a bit of peace among well-manicured gardens. Decorated in Louis XIII and Regency styles, this château has views across the river Loir, a tributary of the Loire itself. The restaurant serves meals on the terrace or in the garden, with seasonal dishes accompanied by fine Loire wines.

CANNES

HOTEL MARTINEZ
73 Boulevard la Croisette
Tel: 33-(0)-4-92-98-7300, www.hotel-martinez.com

One of the grandest hotels in one of the most fashionable cities on one of the most famous coastlines in the world. The French Riviera. Cannes. The Hotel Martinez. Its Penthouse, really a hotel within a hotel, has 11 luxurious junior suites and a four-bedroom penthouse suite, the largest and most expensive accommodation of its kind on the French Riviera. The hotel also features a Givenchy spa, the Michelin two-star restaurant La Palme d'Or, and a beachside restaurant.

CAP D'ANTIBES

HÔTEL DU CAP-EDEN-ROC
Boulevard Kennedy
Tel: 33-(0)-4-93-61-3901, www.edenroc-hotel.fr

"Stylish" wouldn't even begin to describe the Hôtel du Cap-Eden-Roc and its picture perfect setting overlooking the stunning blue sea. Opened as a hotel in 1870 in what was even then one of the most exclusive and desirable stretches of the Mediterranean, this graceful mansion at the tip of Cap d'Antibes became a mecca for the literati and glitterati by the Roaring '20s. F. Scott Fitzgerald immortalized the hotel, as the Hôtel des Étrangers, in *Tender Is the Night*. Other visitors of the day included Ernest Hemingway (of course), the Duke and Duchess of Windsor, Rudolph Valentino, and Marlene Dietrich. That parade of stars continues to this day, and it would be difficult to name a major movie star that hasn't stayed here.

The Hôtel du Cap is all about luxury, full of crystal chandeliers and polished marble. Each guest room has gilded mirrors, balconies, and terraces. The Eden Roc pavilion was built in 1914 with a smart English tearoom and private pool in a fairy tale-like setting carved out of the rocks. The property includes 10 hectares (25 acres) of ornamental gardens in as dazzling a site as anyone could desire.

CARCASSONNE

HÔTEL DE LA CITÉ
Place de l'Eglise
Tel: 33-(0)-4-68-71-9871, www.orient-express.com

While Carcassonne isn't exactly a medieval walled city—it's medieval, but the walls are a 19th-century reproduction—it *is* exactly what you wish every real medieval walled city still looked like. Standing high on a hill above the River Aude in

OF SPECIAL NOTE

EQUITOURS
10 Stalnaker Street, Dubois, Wyoming
Tel: 800-545-0019 or 307-455-3363
www.equitours.com

From Argentina to Zimbabwe, Equitours provides riding holidays all over the world. The eight-day Loire Valley ride in France is exceptional with rests at superb restaurants or picnics in historic landmarks during the day, and accommodations in a different chateau every night. In the centuries before the French Revolution, the Loire Valley was the place where French kings and aristocrats built their castles, magnificent structures with exquisite interiors. The countryside is beautifully arrayed with rivers and forests. The food and wine are justly famous, and you will have every opportunity to enjoy each meal with an appetite made keener by a day in the saddle.

EUROSTAR
www.raileurope.com

Smooth, modern, unbelievably convenient and hassle-free, the high-speed Eurostar from London to Paris has been carefully designed to relax passengers in an atmosphere of calm and comfort. Many feel so at ease they totally forget how fast they are traveling under the English Channel. The stylish, fully air-conditioned carriages have non-smoking cars, and each features clean, modern washrooms. The staff is handpicked to have pleasant personalities and is highly trained to provide exceptional customer care. Lunch and dinner are served.

southwest France, Carcassonne is an impressive monolith visible from far away. The Hôtel de la Cité, with its stone walls, wood paneling, and stained-glass windows, is set in its own glorious gardens right in the center of Carcassonne, situated between the 12th-century castle and the Gothic Basilica of Saint-Nazaire. The vineyards on the parched valley floor below produce Blanquette de Limoux, the oldest sparkling wine in the world.

LANDES

LES PRÉS D'EUGÉNIE OF MICHEL GUÉRARD
Eugénie-Les-Bains
Tel: 33-(0)-5-58-05-0607, www.relaischateaux.com

The elegant colonial hamlet of Eugénie-Les-Bains is named after the Empress Eugénie and the baths here that she loved. The agreeable village contained a small palace, a convent, an herb garden, and a restaurant among graceful magnolias and gardens of verbena. Today, the Prés d'Eugénie features 30 rooms and 10 suites, with two restaurants, the Grande Cuisine Gourmande and Auberge Ferme aux Grives. The ambience is restful surrounded by climbing roses and exotic fragrances.

NICE

LE PALAIS DE LA MEDITERRANÉE
15, Promenade des Anglais
Tel: 33-(0)-4-9-214-7700, www.lepalaisdelamediterranee.com

The Palais de la Mediterranée was built in the 1930s as a casino on the famous Promenade des Anglais that fronts the entire seafront of Nice. Now perfectly restored, it has elegant rooms overlooking the bay. The hotel has the only heated indoor/outdoor pool on the Cote d'Azur, giving it a longer season than most.

ONZAIN

DOMAINE DES HAUTS DE LOIRE
Route de Herbault
Tel: 33-(0)-02-54-20-7257, www.domainehautsloire.com

Beautifully sited in the Loire Valley between Blois and Amboise, this magnificent hunting lodge, built in 1860 by a famous publisher, is secluded in tranquil parkland. The 25 guest rooms and 11 suites have painted beam ceilings, and the restaurant is rich with French delicacies. Activities on the estate include tennis, bicycling, swimming in the outdoor pool, fishing in the lake, and walking through the 70 hectares (170 acres) of grounds. Nearby are many magnificent Loire castles and wineries.

PARIS

HÔTEL LE BRISTOL
112 rue du Faubourg Saint Honoré
Tel: 33-(0)-1-53-43-4325, www.hotel-bristol.com

The Hôtel le Bristol is found on Paris's elegant Faubourg St. Honoré, famous for its fashion boutiques, art galleries, and deluxe shops. Yet despite its central location, the hotel is housed within a vast garden that gives a rare bit of tranquility right in the heart of Paris. Each room offers a different decor, combining lavish chintz fabrics and 18th-century furnishings. The terraces that adjoin some of the rooms and suites overlook the garden or the sights of Paris. The impressive bathrooms are the city's largest with white Carrara marble throughout, accented with 18th-century paintings. But the prize of the Bristol is located on the sixth floor, where guests can take advantage of a swimming pool in the shape of a Spanish galleon, designed by the same naval architect who designed yachts for the Onassis and Niarchos families. The pool is situated under glass with views of Paris.

HÔTEL DE CRILLON
10, place de la Concorde
Tel: 33-(0)-1-44-71-1500, www.crillon.com

Paris has no shortage of luxury hotels, but few have the pedigree of the Crillon. Built for Louis XV in 1758, this legendary manse on the place de la Concorde couldn't be any more centrally located. Just north of the Seine in the bustling heart of Paris, many of the Crillon's rooms look out over the city's most famous plaza across the river to the Left Bank. The mansion was acquired by the Count de Crillon in 1788 and became a hotel in 1909. Its two facades on the place de la Concorde are one of the architectural masterpieces of the 18th century.

The Crillon is within walking distance of the Champs-Elysées, the Louvre, the Tuileries, and the Madeleine area. Inside, it is a masterpiece, and many of its famous suites have recently been redecorated. The restaurant, Les Ambassadeurs is opulent and justly renowned for its fabulous cuisine.

HÔTEL LANCASTER
7 Rue de Berri, Champs-Elysées
Tel: 33-(0)-1-40-76-4076, www.lhw.com

For a stay in a smaller townhouse hotel rather than one of the grand hotels, the Lancaster makes an excellent choice. It is located just off the Champs-Elysées boulevard, close to shopping and all the central sights of Paris. The exclusive Lancaster has 50 rooms, plus another 11 suites situated around courtyard garden. The service is impeccable, and the understated decor is filled with antiques and artworks like a distinguished private home.

HÔTEL MEURICE
228 Rue de Rivoli
Tel: 33-(0)-1-44-58-1010, www.meuricehotel.com

A little farther east, overlooking the Jardin des Tuileries, the

A GOOD PLACE TO STAY

Each Relais & Châteaux property brings to life the French "art de vivre" by gracefully melding traditional old-world charm with elegant surroundings and the renowned cuisine of the world's best chefs. During the past 50 years, Relais & Châteaux has set a standard for quality combined with a consistency that is unprecedented within the industry. Our charter of the five Cs (Courtesy, Charm, Character, Calm, Cuisine) ensures that every component of a guest's stay is attentively addressed. It is this unceasing quest for perfection that truly differentiates Relais & Châteaux properties from all others.

— Regis Bulot, Managing Director, Relais and Château, www.relaischateaux.com

Hotel Meurice is one of the finest hotels in Paris—and therefore in the world. It has the most comfortable beds in Europe, and each of the 160 flamboyantly elegant rooms is furnished with Persian carpets, marble mantelpieces, and ormolu clocks, as well as state-of-the-art amenities. The bathrooms, in white and gray Italian marble, are truly elaborate. The winter garden has a stunning Art Nouveau glass roof. At the Restaurant le Meurice, the decor of chandeliers and gilt-boiserie seems as precious as jewelry, with the food appropriately priced.

HÔTEL NAPOLEON
40, Avenue de Friedland
Tel: 33-(0)-1-56-68-4450, www.hotelnapoleonparis.com

Built at the turn of the 20th century, the Napoléon has long been a haunt of celebrities. Errol Flynn loved it, and Josephine Baker, the toast of Paris in the 1930s, stayed here. Situated near the Arc de Triomphe, the Napoléon is an art deco townhouse hotel, full of style and intimate grace. Some rooms have views of the Eiffel Tower.

HÔTEL DE VIGNY
911 rue Balzac
Tel: 33-(0)-1-42-99-8080, www.hoteldevigny.com

Also near the top of the Champs-Elysées, the de Vigny is a tasteful small hotel that allows a respite from the hustle and bustle of the city around you. There are just 26 guest rooms and 11 suites, each elegantly decorated for maximum comfort. The mahogany-paneled lounge with its roaring fire couldn't be any more welcome in the chillier months.

TREMOLAT

LA VIEUX LOGIS
Tel: 33-(0)-05-(0)53-22-8006, www.relaischateaux.com

La Vieux Logis is a 17th-century Carthusian monastery, flanked by annexes, surrounding lush gardens, a swimming pool, brooks, and weeping willows. The 25 guest rooms are sunny and elegant. Dine under the high ceiling of a former tobacco drying room or beneath the trees in the summer. Henry Miller, who knew a thing or two about enjoying life, came to spend a week here and stayed for a month.

VERSAILLES

TRIANON PALACE
1 Boulevard de la Reine
Tel: 33-(0)-1-30-84-5000
www.france.starwooddestinations.com

During the reign of the Sun King, Louis XIV, the palace at

Versailles was turned into the most magnificent residence on Earth in a location then far from Paris. The Trianon Palace hotel adjacent to the king's domain at Versailles, now just a few minutes west of Paris, is almost as grand, especially since its 2001 makeover. Just like the days when the court followed Louis out of the city to his palace, distinguished guests from royalty to the arts have made their way to the Trianon since it was built in 1910. You might as well do the same if you want to give Versailles and its surroundings the attention they deserve. The fabulous spa will soothe you after a day's sightseeing and the Michelin-starred restaurant, Les Trois Marches, will make you think you're dining in Louis's court.

FRENCH POLYNESIA

TAHITI

LE MERIDIEN TAHITI
Tamanu
Tel: 44-870-400-8440 or 1-800-543-4300
www.tahiti.lemeridien.com

Le Meridien Tahiti, which opened in 1998, is on the beach in the Punaauia region. The six-story main buildings have 138 rooms and suites, all with dramatic views of the amazing Tahitian lagoon. But if you want to get a little closer, why not stay in one of the 12 tropical bungalows, designed with an emphasis on natural materials and refreshing local colors, which actually sit on stilts over the lagoon itself? You can't get much closer to the beautiful blue South Pacific without getting wet.

BORA BORA

LE MERIDIEN BORA BORA
Tel: 68-9-60-5151, www.lemeridien.com

Bora Bora is the ultimate in tropical escapes, and Le Meridien Bora Bora is an ideal spot to make the most of your experience. Like its sister resort on Tahiti, this little slice of paradise opened in 1998, but there is no high-rise here—just bungalows, on the beach or over the water of the lagoon. The overwater accommodations have glass-bottom floors, so you can watch the fish without even getting out of bed. The hotel complex is on the southern point of Motu Piti Aau, a ten-kilometer-long (six-mile) islet on the coral reef.

BORA BORA LAGOON RESORT & SPA
Motu Toopua
Tel: 68-9-60-4000, www.boraboralagoon.com

This resort lets you stay right in the middle of Bora Bora's splendid lagoon on Motu Toopua, a 15-minute boat ride from the airport. On this gorgeous islet, accommodations choices include beach bungalows, overwater bungalows, and villas.

Another option, however, is to board one of Bora Bora Cruises' 70-meter (230-foot) motor yachts, *Ti'a Moana* or *Tu Moana,* for a seven-day, six-night cruise through the calm lagoons of Bora Bora and its leeward island neighbors—Huahine, Raiatea, and Taha'a—in the splendor of these luxurious custom-designed super-yachts. Imagine watching a vintage movie under the stars on a deserted island, followed by an elegant dinner on board with some of the best French cuisine available anywhere served on linen and china at tables in the waters of the lagoon, and a full breakfast when you wake up in the morning. These boutique cruises make it all possible.

FIJI

SAVUSAVA

JEAN MICHEL COUSTEAU FIJI ISLANDS RESORT
Vanua Levu
Tel: 61-3-98-150-379, www.fijiresort.com

Fiji Islands Resort is an all-inclusive destination on an exotic island in Fiji. Stay in an authentic thatched Fijian cottage or villa, with ocean or garden views, and spend your days sea kayaking or snorkeling or just enjoying the beautiful tropical beaches. Wellness programs include massage to invigorate body and soul. As you would expect at a resort carrying the Cousteau name, there is a full-time marine biologist on staff to give guests an introduction to the South Seas maritime environment. The open-air dining room features an 18-meter (60-foot) temple roof over your head.

GERMANY

BERLIN

HOTEL ADLON KEMPINSKI
Unter den Linden 77
Tel: 49-(0)-302-2610, www.hotel-adlon.de

Berlin's most renowned hotel, the Hotel Adlon is preparing to celebrate its 100th anniversary. In the early years of the 20th century, there was no better address in Germany than the Adlon, next to the world-famous Brandenburg Gate. The hotel lodged countless heads of state, royals, and world leaders. After the dark years of the war and the Iron Curtain, Berlin has come alive again, and the grand Hotel Adlon has been restored to its premier status.

The Hotel Adlon Kempinski now has about 400 rooms, with several excellent dining options, headed by the Quarré for Continental cuisine and the Lorenz Adlon restaurant for top-drawer fine dining.

MUNICH

BAYERISCHER HOF
Promenadeplatz 2-6
Tel: 49-892-1200, www.bayerischerhof.de

With more than 160 years of service in the heart of the old city of Munich, the Bayerischer Hof keeps a traditional and noble atmosphere. There are three restaurants, including the welcoming roof garden, where breakfast is served in view of the entire city. Rooms and public spaces are understated and elegant.

HOTEL VIER JAHRESZEITEN KEMPINSKI
Maximilianstrasse 17
Tel: 49-892-1250, www.kempinski-vierjahreszeiten.de

Located on the Maximilianstrasse with its exclusive shopping, lively theater district, and the Opera House, the Vier Jahreszeiten is a stately hotel. Built in 1852, the hotel has seen its share of Bavarian history. The service is renowned, and the solarium and pool with views over the city's rooftops is a delight.

GREAT BRITAIN

BATH

ROYAL CRESCENT HOTEL
16 Royal Crescent
Tel: 44-(0)-22-582-3333, www.royalcrescent.co.uk

At the center swerve of the monumental Royal Crescent, this Nash-converted house in Bath is an architectural treasure. The furnishings are consistent with the building's period elegance, and a Palladian villa in the garden provides extra lodging. If some bedrooms are on the small side, there are ample luxuries to compensate. The hotel's superb Pimpernel's restaurant wins consistent praise.

LONDON

DURLEY HOUSE
115 Sloan Street
Tel: 44-(0)-20-7235-5537, www.durleyhouse.com

Sloane Street is one of the best addresses in London, set in Knightsbridge, the world-famous shopping area that's home to Harvey Nichols and Harrod's and scores of boutiques. to is probably best in town. Durley House is a first-rate hotel in the middle of this posh neighborhood, yet with remarkable privacy. Anyone for a game of tennis? There are two tennis courts hidden away in the gardens here. A private park across the street, Cadogan Square, is open only to the people who live around the square and to guests at the Durley. Durley House has 11 suites, all individually designed and nicely furnished with antiques, and offers exceptional service.

THE SAVOY
The Strand, London
Tel: 44-(0)-207-836-4343, www.fairmont.com/savoy

This is one of the world's most famous hotels, and justifiably so. The guest rooms are simply perfect, particularly the art deco rooms. Some of the (more expensive) rooms look out toward the Thames and the rejuvenated South Bank. Since its opening in 1889, with César Ritz and Auguste Escoffier leading the staff, the Savoy has hosted everyone who was anyone. Royalty, opera stars, giants of industry, and artists galore have stayed in these rooms. The American Bar here was where the dry martini was invented, the Savoy Grill is freshly renovated and back up to speed. Another dining option, across the street, is the illustrious Simpsons-in-the-Strand.

CLARIDGE'S
Brook Street
Tel: 44-(0)-207-629-8860, www.theclaridgehotellondon.com

Claridge's is the second of the lofty tier of classy London hotels that includes the Savoy, the Berkeley, and the Connaught. Founded in 1812, Claridge's has been the choice for distinguished guests for almost two centuries. There are not enough superlatives to do justice to the rooms. Tessa Kennedy's Egyptian art deco suite was my mother's favorite. Each time she arrived at Claridge's, a Hungarian quartet in the Garden foyer would play Noel Coward's "A Room with a View," and I never knew if it was part of the fondness paid to her, or the elaborate tips she bestowed. The dining is superb here, especially at Gordon Ramsay's ethereal restaurant, but also in the art deco Reading Room.

DUKES HOTEL
35 St. James's Place,
Tel: 44-(0)-207-491-4840, www.dukeshotel.co.uk

Dukes is a classic stylish hotel on St. James's Place, occupying its own courtyard in an ultraquiet street between Mayfair and Green Park. The hotel makes it ideally situated for London's finest restaurants, most fashionable shops, exciting galleries, and West End Productions, with convenient links to the City and Canary Wharf.

Chic and intelligent, Dukes houses its own private and permanent art collection with both contemporary and antique works on canvas and in sculpture. Within this

classical framework, key modern features include wireless Internet connections in every room, plasma screen televisions, and rainforest showers. All suites have separate sitting rooms with private dining areas and the Penthouse suite has its own terrace.

The sophisticated Dukes Bar, the most "happening bar" in St James's, attracts a metropolitan crowd who go for great cocktails and the best dry martini in town.

THE BERKELEY
Wilton Place
Phone: 44-(0)-207-235-6000, www.berkeleyhotellondon.com

The original Berkeley was purchased by Richard D'Oyly Carte, owner of the D'Oyly Carte Opera Company and the Savoy, at the turn of the 20th century, but the current building was purpose-built in a new location in the 1970s. It maintains one of the highest reputations for service and comfort in London. Gordon Ramsay has a restaurant here, too, the Boxwood Café, but the spotlight here is on chef Marcus Wareing's Pétrus. At about 100 rooms, this is a more intimate atmosphere than many of the other first-class hotels in the city.

THE CONNAUGHT
Carlos Place, London
Tel: 44-(0)-207-499-7070, www.theconnaughthotellondon.com

If it's understated pampering you're after, there is no better option than the Connaught. This very upscale hotel is located in the center of Mayfair, near historic Grosvenor and Berkeley Square, a quiet, exclusive residential neighborhood. It's the preference of guests who want unparalleled service and every convenience while staying out of the limelight and hubbub of the busier commercial areas. It has the feel of a private residence, if you are accustomed to living in a fully staffed mansion. There are about 100 rooms, a quarter of them suites. The Connaught's premier restaurant here is Angela Hartnett's.

FOUR SEASONS HOTEL
Hamilton Place, Park Lane
Tel: 44-(0)-207-499-0888, www.fourseasons.com/london

Another Mayfair address of refined accommodations is that of the Four Seasons, overlooking Hyde Park. The roomy guest quarters are beautifully decorated and provide contemporary luxury in a convenient location. Lanes Restaurant has a sultry decor with views of the hotel's gardens and Hyde Park.

ONE ALDWYCH
1 Aldwych
Tel: 44-(0)-207-300-1000, www.onealdwych.com

Stylish modernist interiors, two excellent restaurants, friendly professional service, an original art collection, state-of-the-art technology, and an excellent location right in the middle of London's Covent Garden make One Aldwych an ever-popular venue. All rooms and suites have individually controlled air-conditioning, multiline facility with three telephones, international computer modem connections, wireless broadband internet access, satellite television, TV/movie systems, and CD players. Personalized direct facsimile and telephone numbers are available. Fresh fruit and flowers delivered daily. There is no better place to stay.

THE DORCHESTER
Park Lane
Tel: 44-(0)-207-629-8888, www.dorchesterhotel.com

The Dorchester offers the highest level of personalized service, with three members of staff per guest room, combined with discreet, friendly efficiency. Each room is

uniquely decorated in a comfortably lush English country house style. The Italian marble bathrooms deserve special mention, many with natural lighting, and all having the deepest bathtubs in London. Then there is the secret suite designed by the famed London set designer, Oliver Messel. Called The Harlequin suite, it has four bedrooms, four terraces and a sunken tub for four.

THE HALKIN
5 Halkin Street
Tel: 44-(0)-207-333-1000

Contemporary Italian design, with subtle Oriental influences. Each room has an all-marble bathroom with amenities; many offer a separate walk-in shower.

THE LANESBOROUGH
Hyde Park Corner
Tel: 44-(0)-207-259-5599, www.lanesborough.com

A European landmark of the St. Regis collection, the Lanesborough takes attention to detail to the limit. Each guest room has complimentary butler service and features an in-room personal computer with access to e-mail, the Internet, and video and music libraries.

THE STAFFORD HOTEL
St James's Place
Tel: 44-(0)-207-493-0111, www.thestaffordhotel.co.uk

The Stafford Hotel has the feel of a country house with a fashionable central London address. Near Green Park in glamorous St. James's, the hotel is just a few minutes' walk from busy Piccadilly, Buckingham Palace, and the Houses of Parliament. The entire hotel is furnished with period and antique pieces, while the staff ensures that your every need is seen to. The restaurant is outstanding, and the American Bar is inviting.

MAIDENHEAD

THE BELL AT HURLEY
High Street, Hurley, Berks
Tel: 44-(0)-1628-82-5881

If it's history you seek in Merry Old England, why not spend a night at what is reckoned to be the oldest inn in England? Built in 1135, Ye Olde Bell in Hurley dates from the days of the Normans. Take a stroll along the Thames river path before or after enjoying Sunday dinner with traditional roast beef and Yorkshire pudding from the trolley. The spacious rooms to overnight are appointed with English chintz. Henley-on-Thames is nearby if you're in town for the Henley Regatta.

THE NORTHERN BELLE

THE ORIENT EXPRESS OF THE NORTH
Tel: 800-524-2420

The *Northern Belle*, restoring the affluent "Belle" trains of the 1930s, is the first classic train of the new century. There are enjoyable day excursions and short breaks throughout Britain from major stations in the Midlands and the North of England.

Each Northern Belle carriage bears the name of a significant stately home. Furnished with commissioned designs, fabrics, and hand-rubbed paneling, the Belle has some of the most fashionable dining cars in the world. An exclusive Grand Tour of Great Britain is a weeklong journey throughout some of the most beautiful landscapes of the country to historic sites and classic hotels.

OXFORD

LE MANOIR AUX QUAT' SAISONS
Church Road, Great Milton
Tel: 44-(0)-1844-27-8881, www.manoir.com

A contemporary classic set in elegant gardens, this delightful manor in the Oxfordshire countryside has 32 rooms, each a unique example of the best in design and comfort, including 14 suites with antique furniture and canopy beds. All rooms are filled with quality art.

The Oxfordshire landscape provides a soft setting to savor magical cuisine, perfect for a summer evening. The kitchen is the realm of the amazing Chef Raymond Blanc, who cooks with the purest products and great skill; Blanc also runs his famous École de Cuisine here. Dishes to delight the palate are created from the freshest of foods, using as many organic products as possible and vegetables from the Manoir's garden when in season. There is a selective list of fine vintage wines, as well.

WINDSOR

STOKE PARK CLUB
Park Road, Stoke Poges, Bucks
Tel: 44-(0)-1753-71-7171, www.stokeparkclub.com

After a day exploring the fabulous castle and delightful towns of Windsor and Eton, a incomparable choice for spending a night away from London is to visit the nearby Stoke Park Club. This estate is a venerable one even by English standards, having initially been a Norman grant from William the Conqueror in 1066.

The mansion here was designed by James Wyatt, architect to George III, and built around the turn of the 19th century. The historic parkland around the estate was planned in part by the famous Capability Brown. Nowadays, the Stoke Park Club is renowned for its golf course, Stoke Poges, as much as its history. You may recognize the building and grounds when you see it: It was used as a set for not one but two James Bond movies—*Goldfinger* and *Tomorrow Never Dies.*

The accommodations here are regal. Many of the rooms open onto balconies for breakfast or evening drinks overlooking the hectares of parkland and historic gardens, and each bedroom and suite is individually designed with antiques, paintings, and original prints. The bathrooms have heated floors for those chilly English mornings.

GREECE

ATHENS

THE ANDROMEDA
22 Timoleontos Vassou, Off Plateia Mavili
Embassy District
Tel: 30-281-02-20088, www.ellada.net/andromeda

This small hotel is the most appealing place to stay in Athens. The guest rooms are nicely appointed. It is a very quiet hotel, which is blessed relief in teeming Athens. There are 30 rooms, including nine suites, plus apartments across the street.

CRETE

ELOUNDA BAY PALACE
Elounda
Tel: 30-284-10-67000, www.eloundabay.gr

Spanning 8 hectares (20 acres) of landscaped gardens on the northeast coast of the island of Crete, the Elounda Bay Palace is an idyllic Mediterranean retreat. The main hotel has lavish guest rooms and there are also bungalows waterside.

HONG KONG

KOWLOON

THE PENINSULA HONG KONG
Salisbury Road, Kowloon
Tel: 852-29-20-2888, www.hongkong.peninsula.com

Some of the world's grandest old hotels were built in the far-flung reaches of the British expatriate world, and the Peninsula Hong Kong is a member of that legendary group. Built in 1928, this Hong Kong landmark on Victoria Harbor has kept pace with time, consistently being ranked as one of the top hotels in the world.

The Peninsula is famed for its over-the-top service, as seen, for example, in its Rolls-Royce limousines and rooftop helipad to move guests around quickly and safely in crowded Hong Kong. The luxury of the rooms matches the service, and the dining is also first-rate, with Gaddi's and Felix being two of the best restaurants in the former colony and high tea a true delight.

INDIA

AGRA

THE OBEROI AMARVILAS
Taj East Gate Road
Tel: 91-56-22-23-1515, www.oberoiamarvilas.com

Practically in the shadow of arguably the world's most famous mausoleum, the Taj Mahal, the Oberoi Amarvilas is a modern homage to the good life. All 105 guest rooms and suites provide awesome vantage points for marveling at the beauty of the Taj Mahal. Verdant gardens, terraced lawns, fountains, reflecting pools, and pavilions complement the hotel's classic architecture.

GWALIOR

USHA KIRAN PALACE
Jayendraganj Lashkar
Tel: 91-75-12-44-4000, www.tajhotels.com

Rich in history, this 120-year-old palace played host to the King of England and is now a heritage hotel. Set in nine acres of beautifully landscaped lawns, this regal palace is outfitted with artistic stone carvings and delicate filigree work. Each of the palace's 36 rooms reflects local culture and intricate architecture.

JAIPUR

THE OBEROI RAJVILAS
Goner Road
Tel: 91-14-12-68-0101, www.oberoirajvilas.com

The Oberoi Rajvilas is the perfect way to experience the palatial treasures of Jaipur, the capital of Rajasthan. Set in a tranquil oasis of 13 hectares (32 acres) of beautiful gardens, pools, and fountains, the guest rooms are fit for a rajah. Teak four-poster beds in every deluxe room form a centerpiece for the spacious quarters. There are also 14 fully air-conditioned luxury tents, with teak floors, claw-foot tubs, and embroidered canopies. Two villas have their own private pools.

RAMBAGH PALACE
Bhawani Singh Road
Tel: 91-14-12-21-1919, www.tajhotels.com

Once the former residence of the Maharaja of Jaipur, Rambagh Palace now welcomes guests in 90 beautifully refurbished rooms overlooking fountains and landscaped gardens. Palace butlers provide personalized services for guests from the moment they arrive. Located near the walled Pink City, spectacular forts, and the unique shopping

bazaars of Jaipur, the Rambagh Palace holds the rich culture and history of Rajasthan's royalty.

JODHPUR

UMAID BHAWAN PALACE
Tel: 91-29-12-51-0101, www.tajhotels.com

High above the capital of Jodhpur, the Umaid Bhawan Palace is simply magnificent—a sprawling palace with a myriad of towers, turrets, and a huge peaked dome in the center. When it was the principal residence of the Jodhpur royal family, this honey-hued sandstone structure was one of the largest private residences in the world. It now hosts guests in a mere 30 luxury rooms and 15 suites. Umaid Bhawan Palace is a destination by itself, with its own private museum, two restaurants, bar, a majestic neoclassic ballroom, a smoking room, and a well-stocked library. Set in 10 hectares (26 acres) of lush gardens, this monolith offers its guest the use of an indoor subterranean pool, unique marbled squash courts, tennis courts, and a holistic spa, which provide rejuvenation for body, mind, and soul. You need to see it to believe it.

MUMBAI

THE TAJ MAHAL PALACE AND TOWER
Apollo Bunder
Tel: 91-22-56-65-3366, www.tajhotels.com

The Taj Mahal Palace and Tower has more than 100 years of Indian history and culture. Built in 1903, this 546-room hotel is an architectural masterpiece combining Moorish, Oriental, and Florentine styles into a grand confection. The hotel is a renowned landmark of the city of Mumbai, offering sweeping views of the Arabian Sea, yet located only minutes from the central business district of the city. Service is exquisite, and rooms are available in either the original Palace or the more modern Tower, all equipped with state-of-the art facilities.

UDAIPUR

THE OBEROI UDAIVILAS
Haridas Ji Ki Magri
Tel: 91-29-42-43-3300, www.oberoiudaivilas.com

Designed as a traditional Rajasthani palace, Udaivilas, sits on 12 hectares (30 acres) of landscaped gardens overlooking Lake Pichola. The 87 spacious guest rooms, many with uninterrupted views of the lake and the city palace, are elegantly appointed. The five suites have private swimming pools.

TAJ LAKE PALACE
Lake Pichola
Tel: 91-29-42-52-8800, www.tajhotels.com

Guests at Taj Lake Palace are pampered in luxury at this exquisite white marble palace that seems to float majestically on the quiet blue waters of Lake Pichola. Recently renovated, this 250-year-old palace offers modern conveniences and the latest technology in all of its 83 opulently decorated rooms and suites. Surrounded by a peaceful lake and set amid fairytale gardens and charming architecture, Taj Lake Palace may be the most romantic hotel in the world.

INDONESIA

BALI

The island of Bali is justly famed for its great natural beauty, but it's the unique culture and traditions, so unlike anything else in Indonesia or indeed the world, that make Bali exceptional. The island's main religion is Hindu—the only

place in Indonesia where this is the case—and this strongly influences the society in terms of their architecture, clothing, dance, and music. Bali is a truly captivating place to visit.

FOUR SEASONS RESORT BALI AT JIMBARAN BAY
Jimbaran, Denpasar
Tel: 62-361-70-1010, www.fourseasons.com/jimbaranbay

At Jimbaran Bay, the Four Seasons consists of a community of spacious and elegant private villas. Each villa has living, dining, sleeping, and bathing pavilions and enclosed gardens, and all have panoramic views of the bay. A sunset soak offers the opportunity to plunge into the cool waters of your personal pool followed by an outdoor shower. The inn offers a full spa, massages, and Indonesian herbal beauty treatments. Dining is available in a dramatic hilltop setting in two open-air covered lanais with views of the bay and the volcanoes in the distance.

THE FOUR SEASONS RESORT BALI AT SAYAN
Sayan, Ubud, Gianyar
Tel: 62-361-97-7577, www.fourseasons.com/sayan

In the treetops above Bali's sacred Ayung River are 18 two-room suites in the main building of the Four Seasons Resort and 42 outlying villas nestled in the jungle. Each light-filled villa has a private plunge pool surrounded by a large wooden deck. The baths and thatched-roof lounging pavilions provide the utmost in tranquility. The resort's open-air dining area juts out over the river, giving a heart-stopping view of the valley and people below. Lunch is served in the more casual poolside dining area in the valley itself.

JIMBARAN PURI BALI
Jalan Uluwatu, Jimbaran
Tel: 62-361-70-1605, www.pansea.com/bali

Walk along the famed soft white sands of Jimbaran Beach for as long as you want, and then make your way a short distance through tropical gardens to one of the 41 individual cottages on the grounds of the Jimbaran Puri Bali. Each cottage has a king-size bed, sunken bath, and a private courtyard and terrace.

THE LEGIAN
Jalan Laksmana, Seminyak Beach
Tel: 62-361-73-0622

The Legian is located in the fashionable district of Seminyak on yet another perfect stretch of white sandy beach. This all-suite luxury hotel offers 67 contemporary suites, each with its own secluded balcony looking out over the Indian Ocean.

NUSA DUA BEACH HOTEL & SPA
Kawasan Pariwisata Nusa Dua
Tel: 62-361-77-1210, www.nusaduahotel.com

The Nusa Dua Beach Hotel is an oceanfront property that combines the traditional artistic elements of Bali's rich culture with the latest in resort and spa facilities, all surrounded by rejuvenating pools and fountains and featuring palatial rooms.

JAVA

AMANJIWO
Borobudur, Central Java
Tel: 62-293-78-8333, www.amanjiwo.com

Blessed by mind-boggling tropical scenery and a dazzling array of cultural riches inherited from historic Buddhist and Islamic kingdoms, Central Java has long possessed the makings of a magnificent vacation spot. The ninth-century Borobudur Temple is the world's largest Buddhist structure, a huge step-pyramid on a hill with hundreds of Buddha statues looking out into the world.

Amanjiwo is a great base while visiting this ethereal site. The architecture of Amanjiwo enfolds Javanese history and culture, with a circular main building made of local limestone that has a domed center. Outward from this building radiate the 36 enchanting suites. The water gardens and swimming pool are magically relaxing.

On request, Amanjiwo can arrange private dawn tours of Borobudur. You enter the temple gates in darkness, climb the pyramid, and watch the sun rise over the distant volcanoes, slowly lighting up the rice terraces and coconut groves. No one could experience this without being profoundly moved.

IRELAND

CLARE

DROMOLAND CASTLE
Newmarketon Fergus, Co. Clare
Tel: 353-(0)-61-36-8144, www.dromoland.ie

Dromoland is one of Ireland's finest castle hotels. A Renaissance structure built in the 16th century, it was once the royal residence of the clan O'Brien. On the castle's 150-hectare (375-acre) estate, you can spend your time hunting, fishing, going horseback riding, golfing, playing tennis, or perhaps clay-pigeon shooting.

Each capacious guest room enjoys its own individual personality, decorated with period furniture and fresh-cut flowers from the garden, blending period decoration with modern amenities. The warming library bar looks out onto the 18th hole of the golf course and lake. There is afternoon tea in the drawing room, of course, and dinner in the grand dining salon, where you'll be surrounded by the flickering light of candelabras dancing against Palladian windows.

DUBLIN

THE MERRION HOTEL
Upper Merrion Street
Tel: 353-(0)-1-603-0600, www.merrionhotel.com

Dublin's first address in upscale accommodations, the Merrion is a set of four magnificent 18th-century Georgian town houses— the Duke of Wellington was born in one—in the very center of the city opposite the Government Buildings and not far from Trinity College. Shopping and dining opportunities abound nearby, not least the hotel's own Restaurant Patrick Guilbaud, possibly Dublin's best. The Merrion boasts historic gardens designed by Irish landscape artist Jim Reynolds, one of Ireland's largest private collections of art and antiques, and the Tethra Spa.

MAYO

ASHFORD CASTLE
Ashford, Co. Mayo
Tel: 353-(0)-94-954-6003, www.ashford.ie

A week of luxury in a grand old castle like Ashford gives you the feeling of how gracious life was for Irish aristocrats in better times. From here you can explore much of the West Coast of Ireland, immortalized by W. B. Yates. There are opportunities to ride in the mountains and valleys and along the Irish coast on horseback. Spectacular coastline, wide beaches, and fields of purple heather makes for an ideal riding tour.

Ashford Castle, a half-hour drive northeast of the city of Galway, dates back to 1228. Set on the shores of Lough Corrib, Ireland's second-largest lake, in the picturesque village of Cong, Ashford Castle was made famous more recently as the location of the 1951 Academy Award–winning film *The Quiet Man*. A world-class resort on a private 140-hectare (350-acre) estate, it was once the home of the Guinness family.

ISRAEL

JERUSALEM

THE KING DAVID
23 King David Street
Tel: 972-2-620-8888, www.danhotels.com

The King David is one of those hotels that is almost synonymous with its city—it is the first place that comes to mind when a head of state, CEO, or discerning visitor plans a stay in Jerusalem. The views over the Old City are unparalleled, especially at sunset as the last rays of the sun cast a glorious spotlight on the golden stone and the shadows stand out in sharp relief, but the panorama from the rooms facing the New City are not bad, either. All guest rooms are large, comfortable, and equipped with all the modern facilities in a traditional atmosphere. The King's Garden Restaurant has a lovely setting.

ITALY

AMALFI

HOTEL SANTA CATERINA
S.S. Amalfitana, 9
Tel: 39-089-87-1012, www.hotelsantacaterina.it

The road along the Amalfi Coast is one of the great drives in the world, clinging to the rugged cliffs with views that are nothing short of breathtaking. If you want to soak up the views without worrying about guard rails and hairpin turns, stay a while at the elegant Hotel Santa Caterina, built into the cliffs in a series of a natural terraces. The swimming pool and ocean bathing platform are at the bottom of the elevator, with a gymnasium above that and guest rooms spread out higher on the precipice, each with a private terrace. The suites are the most striking of all, each fully equipped with a Jacuzzi with hand-painted ceramic tiles.

BELLAGIO

GRAND HOTEL VILLA SERBELLONI
Via Roma, 1
Tel: 39-031-95-0216, www.villaserbelloni.com

With a prime location on Lake Como, considered Italy's most scenic lake, this former private villa hosted Leonardo da Vinci in 1493. The villa has all the grandeur the Renaissance pleasure palaces could offer, with high, ornately painted ceilings, elaborate parquet floors, frescoes, and tapestries everywhere. The gardens are placid and fragrant. It has been a hotel for more than 100 years, and during that time many other guests almost as famous as da Vinci—movie stars, presidents, prime ministers, and kings—have come here to be entranced by the region's splendor and the hotel's opulence. The Grand Hotel Villa Serbelloni is the only five-star hotel in Bellagio, that most famous resort on the promontory between two branches of Lake Como. Don't miss having lunch gazing out over the lake from the Terrazza Restaurant or taking a swim in the indoor "pool in the cave."

CERNOBBIO

VILLA D'ESTE
Via Regina, 40, Como
Tel. 39-031-3481, www.villadeste.it

Like Bellagio's Grand Hotel Villa Serbelloni, the Villa d'Este in Cernobbio is a Renaissance palazzo of the nobility on the shores of Lake Como that became a hotel in the late 19th century to cater to the modern aristocrats on the Italy

leg of their Grand Tour. Cernobbio is on the west side of the lake not far from the Swiss border, and its cobblestone streets lead right up to the villa's sculptured Renaissance gardens. Villa d'Este has 158 rooms in two buildings, both historic and both lakeside in four hectares (ten acres) of private grounds. Visitors are treated to a celebrated standard of service, including top-rated rooms, amenities, and cuisine. Dining options range from the formal and elegant Veranda Restaurant overlooking the lake to poolside at the sundeck.

FLORENCE

VILLA LA MASSA
Via della Massa, 24, Candeli
Tel: 39-055-62611, www.florenceby.com/villalamassa

Villa La Massa is the sister hotel of Cernobbio's Villa d'Este. It comprises three 16th-century villas built by influential aristocratic families in the days when the Medici ran Florence. They became the Villa La Massa luxury hotel in 1948. There are 37 guest rooms, each individually decorated with classic Tuscan antiques.

The villa is located outside of the city of Florence up the beautiful Arno River among verdant Tuscan hills and vineyards. It sits within a little Eden of gardens covering 10 hectares (25 acres). A hotel shuttle will carry guests back and forth to the center of Florence near the Ponte Vecchio, so you can have the solitude of the countryside or the vibrancy of the city as you choose.

VILLA SAN MICHELE
Via Doccia, 4
Tel: 39-055-567-8200, www.villasanmichele.com

The Villa San Michele started life in the 15th century as a Franciscan monastery. The simple façade was designed by none other than Michelangelo himself. It remained the property of the order until the 19th century, after which it became a private residence. After significant damage in World War II, the building was restored in stages and eventually opened as a hotel. There is still plenty of history embodied in the old monastery, though, including the 1642 "Last Supper" fresco by Ferrucci in the old refectory.

It now finds itself in one of the most fashionable residential areas of Florence, the hills of Fiesole, where cooling breezes make for magical summer evenings looking down at the Duomo and the lights of the great city, perhaps taking in one of the open-air concerts held here on the grounds.

The villa, which is listed among the Italian national trust monuments, has 26 tiled, terraced rooms with Jacuzzis. Trees surround a unique 25-meter (82-foot) outdoor heated pool overlooking ancient Florence.

MILAN

HOTEL PRINCIPE DI SAVOIA
Piazza della Repubblica, 17
Tel: 39-026-2301, www.hotelprincipedisavoia.com

The Piazza della Repubblica is the very heart of this bustling capital of business for Northern Italy, and the Hotel Principe di Savoia is in the prime spot on the piazza. The hotel's service, comfort, and privacy are well known. There is a fitness center and spa on the roof.

PORTOFINO

HOTEL SPLENDIDO
Salita Baratta, 16
Tel: 39-018-526-7801, www.hotelsplendido.com

One of the brightest jewels in Italy's crown is the city of

Portofino. Its achingly beautiful little harbor is everyone's dream of the Italian Riviera come true, and the Hotel Splendido has one of the best views of it from the hillside above the town. The building was originally a monastery, although it was abandoned in the 16th century due to the repeated raids by coastal pirates.

The revitalized ex-monastery opened as a hotel in the early 20th century, with the Duke of Windsor as one of its first guests. A long line of famous visitors has followed, and the hotel remains a popular spot with the jet-setters and savvy travelers. The pleasantly understated hostelry has 65 guest rooms, most of which have balconies or terraces from which you can see the hotel's gardens running down the slopes to the sea, with lavender and wild herbs growing thickly under ancient olive trees and clumps of bougainvillea. Behind the hotel are olive groves where virgin olive oil is pressed nightly in season.

The place to dine, naturally, is at the Terrazzo Restaurant, continuing to soak up the panorama below while enjoying the freshest fish in simple preparations, but the al fresco lunches at the Pool Restaurant are memorable as well.

SPLENDIDO MARE
Via Roma, 2
Tel: 39-018-526-7802, www.hotelsplendido.com

The Splendido Mare is a recent extension of the Hotel Splendido. While the Splendido offers wonderful views of the town of Portofino, the Splendido Mare offers a location in the heart of the village itself, and overlooking Portofino's famous piazzetta and waterfront. For those who want to be closer to the action, this is the better choice. And don't worry, the views of the harbor and the Castle of San Giorgio from the guest rooms are still fabulous.

The Chuflay Bar Restaurant at Splendido Mare has both indoor seating and al fresco dining on the terrace bordering the piazzetta, perfect for people-watching.

POSITANO

LE SIRENUSE
Via Colomb, 30
Tel: 39-089-87-5066, www.sireneuse.it

The distinguished Le Sirenuse, a unique deluxe hotel in an 18th-century villa, is centrally located on the steep hillside of Positano with one of the most impressive vantage points overlooking the Mediterranean. There is intense attention to detail throughout the hotel.

RAVELLO

HOTEL CARUSO
Piazza San Giovanni del Toro, 2
Tel: 39-089-85-8801

Ravello is another of the remarkable gems of the Amalfi Coast, but it is one of the most approachable. The town of Ravello sits high on a cliff-top perch with the deep blue sky above and the azure sea 300 meters (1,000 feet) below, and a few steps outside the stone lion–guarded gate of the hotel will bring you into the warren of narrow alleys of the town.

Lovers of sun, sea, fresh air, good food, and delicious wines have been coming here for centuries, and the Hotel Caruso is a part of Ravello's touristic history. The hotel was a favorite of the Bloomsbury Group, a group of intellectuals and bon vivants including Virginia Woolf and Lord Keynes, among others. Graham Greene and William Styron stayed here while working on, respectively, *The Third Man* and *Set This House on Fire,* and Gore Vidal wrote *Myra Breckinridge*

while staying in room 9. There are 50 other rooms available in this charming hotel, and almost all of them have sea views to perhaps inspire your next novel.

HOTEL RUFOLO
Via S. Francesco, 1
Tel: 39-089-85-7133, www.hotelrufolo.it

Another Ravello hotel with a literary history is the Rufolo. It was here that D. H. Lawrence, perhaps overcome by the sensuousness of the Amalfi Coast, began writing *Lady Chatterley's Lover*. The hotel is located right in the center of the town, adjacent to the historic Villa Rufolo, whose gardens play host to an annual music festival. The highlight of the season is generally the Wagner Festival, held in early July, when famous artists such as Zubin Mehta, Lorin Maazel, and Placido Domingo perform. The most unforgettable concerts are the ones held at dawn with the sun rising behind the orchestra.

HOTEL PALAZZO SASSO
Via S. Giovanni Del Toro, 28
Tel: 39-089-81-8181, www.palazzosasso.com

One of the most beautiful hotels on the Amalfi Coast, the Hotel Palazzo Sasso is a striking new deluxe hotel created out of a 12th-century Italian villa. There are 32 rooms and 11 suites in this glorious mansion with, of course, stunning views. The service is extravagant, and the hotel's terraced Rossellini restaurant has earned two Michelin stars.

ROME

HOTEL MAJESTIC
Via Veneto, 50
Tel: 39-064-21441, www.romeby.com/majestic

Built in 1889, the art deco Hotel Majestic is in the heart of the famed Via Veneto, the fashionable shopping district and one of the best addresses in the Eternal City. A fantasy of neoclassic elegance, the Hotel Majestic is within walking distance of the Spanish Steps and Villa Borghese Gardens. Its features include magnificent frescoed ceilings, distinctive antiques, and superb service. The hotel has about a hundred rooms, and there is a brand-new open-air terrace addition to its ever popular La Veranda Restaurant.

THE HASSLER
Piazza Trinità dei Monti, 6
Tel: 39-06-69-93 40, www.hotelhassler.com

The Hassler is a wonderful small hotel that is easily the best place to stay in Rome. The hotel has never been ostentatious and consequently is unknown to most travelers, but insiders have sworn by its standards of service and comfort for more than a century. The hotel pays careful attention to detail in order to make every guest's stay unforgettable. All the rooms and suites are tastefully decorated to the highest standards.

With a peerless location right at the top of the Spanish Steps, backed up to the Villa Borghese Gardens, the Hassler is quiet and isolated, yet is only a short walk away from some of the most exciting parts of Rome. The twin domes of the Trinità dei Monti Church dominate the view, echoed by other domes of various Roman churches, including the imposing dome of St. Peter's in the distance. Farther to the left, the Vittorio Emanuele II monument stands all lit up at night, and you can make out the dome of the Pantheon. The Hassler's rooftop restaurant, occupying one of the highest spots in the city center, is the ideal place to enjoy this panorama at leisure over an exquisite meal. Renowned Chef Francesco Apreda uses the freshest ingredients to make impressive creative Mediterranean cuisine.

The Hassler remains a traditional favorite with everyone from movie celebrities to journalists and authors (I had lunch while interviewing Federico Fellini and Marcello Mastroianni on my terrace). The rooms have the most breathtaking views of Rome from their own private rooftop terraces. This is a very special hotel.

SIENA

FONTEVERDE TERME AND HOTEL
Località Terme, 1, San Casciano dei Bagni
Tel: 39-057-85-7241, www.fonteverdespa.com

The Fonteverde Terme resort is an aristocratic residence in a beautiful part of Tuscany near Siena, surrounded by private parklands. It is located in the ancient spa town of San Casciano dei Bagni in the southern part of the famous Chianti wine region. There are lovely views over the valley and its vineyards, and the hotel features a lovingly restored 17th-century Medici portico. As you would expect, there is an avant-garde spa center with all the therapies and a wonderful naturally heated pool. A truly elegant atmosphere has been created by famous Italian interior decorators.

VENICE

HOTEL CIPRIANI
Giudecca 10
Tel: 39-041-520-7744, www.hotelcipriani.com

When you are one of a kind, you don't have to do much more. Under the leadership of Natale Rusponi, the legendary hotelier, The Hotel Cipriani was created to provide the very best Venetian hospitality, incorporating the most luxurious accommodations, the most attentive service, and the finest cuisine in an atmosphere of calm and seclusion.

THE COLLECTION

Rocco Forte Hotels, www.roccofortehotels.com

Sir Rocco Forte has collected special properties in Rome, London, Edinburgh, and Florence, and is still expanding. Each location is carefully considered, and his mission is to create the best hotel management teams to provide beautiful design and solid comfort. He feels that by concentrating on fewer and smaller hotels, he sets a standard for luxury. He is on the mark.

His father Lord Forte, a hard-working entrepreneur, came from Casalattico, Italy, which has been renamed Monteforte in his honor, to build an enterprise in the United Kingdom. Starting his first business selling Italian ices in 1934 in London, he became the largest caterer in the world with more than 400 restaurants and 800 hotels.

Rocco did not miss the target under his father's leadership, creating Rocco Forte Hotels a few years ago. He is personally involved in every detail of every hotel, and his sister, Olga Polizzi, designs each property. His goal is to establish a five-star hotel in major European Cities, always giving assurance for the best. Each hotel has its own identity, crafted to location, with emphasis on fine food and impeccable service. All rooms are spacious and furnishings are tasteful and comfortable. Most properties have well-designed spas.

His collection of hotels consistently wins major awards. We like Browns, London; Château de Bagnols, Beaujolais, France; Hotel Amigo, Brussels; St. David's Hotel & Spa, Cardiff, Wales; The Balmoral, Edinburgh; Hotel Savoy, Florence; The Lowry Hotel, Manchester, England; Hotel de Russie, Rome; and Hotel Astoria, St. Petersburg, Russia.

The Cipriani sits at the end of Giudecca Island, reached by a short motor launch ride from St. Mark's Square. The rooms and suites are elegant and have all the comforts you could ask for, with picture-postcard views of the lagoon, Venice, and the dramatic Basilica di San Giorgio.

Two 15th-century palazzi adjacent to the Cipriani have been opened as all-suite accommodations, with magnificent views looking toward Piazza San Marco. The entrancing flower gardens lead to the Palazzo Vendramin and Palazzetto Nani-Barbaro. Some of the newly opened suites are nothing short of princely, and so too is the regular clientele—people who desire the ultimate in privacy while staying at one of the most famous hotels in the world.

The Fortuny Restaurant at the Hotel Cipriani is world famous, and you will find no better meal in Venice. The surrounding countryside provides fresh produce to the kitchens of the Fortuny and the hotel's other restaurants.

BAUER IL PALAZZO
San Marco 1413
Tel: 39-041-520-7022, www.bauervenezia.com

From the most awesome vantage point in Venice, Il Palazzo is right there with Venice's finest shops, museums, and sights, just a short stroll from St. Mark's Square. Like most of the great Venice hotels, the normal arrival is at the private boat dock, in this case on the Grand Canal. Guests enter the hotel's lavish lobby, decorated in wood paneling and antique veneered Venetian panels, making a lasting first impression. Each of the hotel's guest rooms and suites is uniquely decorated with loving attention to detail. Many rooms feature balconies or terraces that provide amazing views of Venice, the Grand Canal, and St. Mark's.

More like a sophisticated home than a hotel, Il Palazzo at the Bauer is in fact a grand 18th-century mansion that has been converted into a luxurious boutique hotel with 75 rooms and suites, with tapestries, ormolu mirrors, and ornate carved stucco ceilings. Serving some of the finest cuisine in Venice, Chef Giovanni Ciresa prepares a delectable blend of innovative international and Mediterranean dishes at the hotel's restaurant, De Pisis, with a terrace set against the Grand Canal.

For one of the biggest splurges of your life, the Bauer will rent you the Palazzo Mocenigo, a recently restored landmark of Venice. Lord Byron stayed here, enjoying the palace's irresistible style and elegance and expansive courtyards. The five-bedroom, antique-filled national treasure is available for weekly rentals.

PENSIONE ACCADEMIA VILLA MARAVEGE
Fondamenta Bollani, Dorsoduro 1058
Tel: 39-041-523-7846, www.pensioneaccademia.it

Located in the Dorsoduro section of Venice, a somewhat quieter part of the city on the south side of the Grand Canal, the Pensione Accademia Villa Maravege is an oasis of calm in this dynamic city. It has two charming gardens where you can have breakfast or relax, but you are still next to the Grand Canal where you can quickly catch a water taxi or walk into the center of the action. Lord Byron also used to stay here. Until the 1930s this was the seat of the Russian consulate. The Accademia gallery, Venice's greatest art museum, is close by.

HOTEL GRITTI PALACE
Campo Santa Maria del Giglio
Tel: 39-041-79-4611, www.gritti.hotelinvenice.com

Another extravagant choice for lodging in Venice is the Hotel Gritti Palace, easily one of the most beautiful hotels in the world. Built for one of the dukes (doges) of Venice in the early 16th century and later serving as the Vatican

ambassador's residence in Venice, this palazzo was described by Hemingway as "the best hotel in a city of great hotels." The Gritti Palace's guest book reads like a Who's Who. There are 91 rooms, all of the very highest standards of comfort and amenities. The Club del Doge restaurant is remarkable.

JAPAN

TOKYO

HOTEL OKURA
2-10-4 Toranomon Minato-ku
Tel: 81-3-3582-0111, www.okura.com/tokyo

This hotel is a good choice for visiting professionals, given the array of customized services and amenities. Guest accommodations are fully equipped with advanced technology and communications capabilities, as well as the best in comfortable and elegant furnishings.

LAOS

LA RESIDENCE PHOU VAU
Luang Prabang
Tel: 856-71-21-2194

Luang Prabang, surrounded by mountains at the junction of the Mekong River and its tributary, the Khan, was the capital of the Lane Xang kingdom six centuries ago. The Lao culture began here, and Luang Prabang is consequently rich in this cultural heritage, with monasteries, monuments, and traditional costumes.

The spacious and extremely functional rooms of the Residence Phou Vau blend a decor of native woods, airy cottons, and shiny silks for a tranquil ambience. All have private balconies with vistas over the jungle to the distant mountains and the sedate town of Luang Prabang.

MALAYSIA

LANGKAWI

THE DATAI
Jalan Teluk Datai, Pulau Langkawi Kedah
Tel: 60-4-959-2500, www.thedatai.com

Here's a place to get away from it all—away from everything except comfort and fun. The Datai resort has villas in the rain forest on the island of Langkawi. Open-air covered walkways and paths connect the various areas. Red balau timber, black granite, and white marble make for a sleek design. There's a white-sand beach facing the Andaman Sea, where you can swim, dive, or sail. There's also an 18-hole golf course, a great spa, tennis, and all the ecoadventure hiking and biking you could ask for.

PANGKOR LAUT

PANGKOR LAUT RESORT
Tel: 877-757-5288, www.pangkorlautresort.com

This ideally unspoiled private island was once the exclusive playground of yellow pied hornbills and white-breasted sea eagles. Now a limited number of guests can share in its tranquility, seclusion, and natural beauty at the Pangkor Laut Resort. There is a choice of accommodations on the water, at the beach, or in a densely wooded hillside, each created to blend and complement the natural environment. The hillside rooms are nestled at the edge of the primeval rain forest that still covers most of the island.

Set in the middle of the Strait of Malacca, between Malaysia and Indonesia, Pangkor Laut takes a maximum of 250 guests at any one time. There is 400 staff, including 50 gardeners, to give attention to every botanical detail. The accommodations are spectacular. The sea villas are set on overwater walkways, while the hillside villas are lovely. Up an elevator to secluded jungle perches with great views are even more spacious accommodations. Room service and housekeeping are discreet, and the staff is friendly and unobtrusive. Different local fruit is provided each day—mangoes, water apples, and exquisite small bananas.

MALDIVES

The Maldives is an archipelago of 26 atolls and more than 1,000 beautiful islets in the Indian Ocean south of Sri Lanka. You are not likely to run into someone from the office here. What you are likely to find is the ultimate in tropical relaxation on some of the most beautiful white-sand beaches in the world.

NORTH MALÉ ATOLL

BANYAN TREE MALDIVES VABBINFARU
Vabbinfaru Island
Tel: 960-44-3147

The Banyan Tree is an extraordinary hotel taking up all of Vabbinfaru Island. There are a variety of villas spread about the island, some right on the beach, others a little more secluded. The diving and snorkeling here cannot be beat anywhere else on Earth.

SOUTH MALÉ ATOLL

TAJ EXOTICA RESORT & SPA
Emboodhu Finolhu
Tel: 960-44-2200, www.tajhotels.com

The Taj Exotica Resort and Spa is on one of the largest lagoons of the Maldives, and the resort's palm thatched villas are built entirely over water, with private sundecks that open out on the Indian Ocean. The beach villas have private plunge pools and their own courtyards with open air showers. At the far end of the island, is the spa, with a wide range of treatments and activities including yoga and tai chi.

MAURITIUS

FLIC-EN-FLAC

TAJ EXOTICA RESORT AND SPA
Wolmar
Tel: 23-0-403-1500, www.tajhotels.com

An exclusive refuge of solitude and luxury, the Taj Exotica Resort is spread over 11 scenic hectares (27 acres) facing the calm turquoise sea. No detail has been overlooked for this beautiful beachside hideaway, with interiors inspired by French Colonial, Indian, African, and Arabic design. Smartly decorated, the spacious private villas and suites have private pools, outdoor showers, open-air dining, and spectacular views of the blue waters of Tamarin Bay.

POINTE AUX PIMENTS

THE OBEROI MAURITIUS
Baie aux Tortues
Tel: 230-204-3600, www.oberoihotels.com

The Oberoi Mauritius features 73 exotic thatched-roof pavilions, each surrounded by lush gardens and with its own private swimming pool. As you would expect, every cottage has ocean views. There are 8 hectares (20 acres) of subtropical gardens and almost 1.5 kilometers (1 mile) of beachfront in a protected marine park. Other features include two large swimming pools, tennis courts, water sports, and a spa with a wide range of treatments.

ONE & ONLY LE SAINT GÉRAN
Belle Mare
Tel: 230-401-1688, www.saintgeran.com

The Indian Ocean is on one side and a coral sheltered lagoon on the other with kilometers of secluded white-sand beach. After a major remodeling in 1999, the hotel now offers 162 junior and ocean suites and a sumptuous Villa. All the suites are very roomy and comfortably decorated, with panoramic windows that let you see to the big blue horizon.

MEXICO

CABO SAN LUCAS

ESPERANZA
Punta Ballena
Tel: 52-624-145-6400, www.esperanzaresort.com

Outside Cabo San Lucas, at the very southern tip of Baja California, Esperanza is a private enclave where the desert meets the Gulf of California and the Pacific Ocean. All accommodations are in casitas arrayed on a gentle slope leading down to the beach. Each is appointed in authentic Mexican furnishings and with artwork and lavish amenities. The expansive terraces provide superb ocean views.

LAS VENTANAS AL PARAÍSO
Cabo San Lucas
Tel: 52-624-144-2800, www.lasventanas.com

Las Ventanas al Paraíso is a pampering place in the sun. This fabled Caroline Hunt hotel overlooks the Gulf of California with each view opening up to a "window to paradise." The infinity swimming pool is extraordinary.

Las Ventanas has a secluded ambience and unmatched service in a setting as warm and soothing as the Mexican sun. Panoramic views are framed by traditional Mexican art and architecture to create a Latin atmosphere that captures its ancient culture.

ONE & ONLY PALMILLA
Baja California Sur
Tel: 52-624-146-7000, www.palmilla.com

One and Only Palmilla has been serving sun worshippers for 50 years—it was a favorite retreat for Ernest Hemingway and Jean Harlow, for example—and it can now take pride in a major renovation from 2004. The resort features 172 casually elegant accommodations, all with ocean views, in the winter often including the sights of California gray whales enjoying their favorite wintering waters. Experience fine dining in two new restaurants, including C, created by the legendary Charlie Trotter.

CUERNAVACA

LAS MAÑANITAS
Ricardo Linares 107
Tel: 52-777-314-1466, www.lasmananitas.com.mx

Cuernavaca is a magnificent mountain town, which the Aztecs named the city of eternal spring. The elegant rooms at Las Mañanitas are decorated with beautiful Spanish colonial furniture and paintings by Mexico's finest artists.

The extensive grounds with their famous peacocks are lovely and the food at the hotel restaurant is the best in Cuernavaca. This is a very simpatico location from which to explore Mexico's ancient ruins.

PLAYA DEL CARMEN

THE ROYAL HIDEAWAY
Playacar, Lote Hotelero 6
Tel: 52-984-873-4500, www.royalhideaway.com

The Royal Hideaway Playacar is an all-inclusive resort in the heart of the Riviera Maya of the Yucatán. Luxurious guest rooms create a rich environment with stately wooden beds, fine linens, and splendid furnishings. Every effort is made to ensure the complete enjoyment of the guests.

ZIHUATANEJO

LA CASA QUE CANTA
Camino Escenico a Playa la Ropa
Tel: 52-755-555-7000, www.lacasaquecanta.com

A 24-suite hideaway above the sea on a coastal bluff over Zihuatanejo Bay on the Mexican Riviera, La Casa Que Canta ("The House That Sings") has consistently received accolades from world travelers for its dramatic multitiered architecture, small spa with original treatments (such as cactus extracts), and 11 pools. Adjacent to the resort is the elegant, four-suite (all with plunge pools) villa El Murmullo, with private butler, chef, and infinity pool. The hotel has two restaurants.

VILLA DEL SOL
Playa la Ropa
Tel: 52-755-555-5500, www.hotelvilladelsol.net

Zihuatanejo Bay has perhaps the most beautiful beach in Mexico. At the edge of the water lies the Villa del Sol. This is one of the most romantic getaways on the Mexican Riviera. The newest beachfront suites have plunge pools on their terraces.

MONACO

HOTEL METROPOLE MONTE-CARLO
4, avenue de la Madone
Tel: 377-93-15-1515, www.metropole.mc

Monaco may well be the most glamorous place on the planet, a grown-up fairy tale that's come to life. The Hotel Metropole, on the square in front of the world-famous Monte Carlo Casino, is owned by the Palace, so it doesn't get much glitzier than this. Recently refurbished in 2004, the Metropole combines the charm and grace of the romantic past with all the modern conveniences and superior service demanded in a world-class hotel. Matchless in the principality, there are a wealth of services, including gastronomic dining under the expert guidance of Joel Robuchon, and informal dining around the poolside and the penthouse terrace.

MOROCCO

MARRAKECH

LA MAMOUNIA
Avenue Bab Jdid
Tel: 212-44-38-8600, www.mamounia.com

This sophisticated hotel began with a vast garden just inside the ramparts, given to Prince Mamoun by his father as a wedding gift. The buildings went up in 1923 in a

WHAT MAKES THE BEST?

For me, the best is not just luxury. The best must combine an element of the unique, a special location, superlative food and wine, unusual cultural interest, and intelligent, nice guests who are interested in the pleasures of life. Orient-Express Hotels currently has 49 properties in 21 countries which all meet these criteria. Of course, they are luxurious as well.

My definition of luxury is above all pleasant and helpful staff, followed by comfortable beds in elegantly decorated rooms, large bathrooms with separate shower stalls and no spotlights on the top of your head, outdoor terraces when possible, large pools with depths of 2 meters/6.5 feet (not 1.2-meter pools for children or midgets), with quiet and relaxation even in a city center.

A luxury hotel should always have a garden even if it is on the roof, and the windows must open to get fresh air if desired. Decor should derive from the best of the local culture and history.

I always settle in with a wonderful regional drink: the caipirinha at the Copacabana Palace in Rio; the Pisco Sour at the Monasterio in Cuzco, Peru; the Margarita at Maroma in Mexico's Yucatan; a Planter's Punch at La Samanna in St. Martin; a Bellini at the Hotel Cipriani in Venice. Most of our properties are located in countries that have their own wines, and I ask our sommeliers to put the *Wine Spectator* rating beside each wine. My experience is that if you choose a wine with a rating of 90 or more you can never go wrong. Wines from my own vineyard in Tuscany, Capannelle (Solare, 50-50, Chardonnay, and Chianti Classico) are my favorite Italian ones and are rated more than 90.

Orient-Express Hotels does not own only hotels. The *Venice-Simplon-Orient-Express* train, the Road to Mandalay cruise ship in Burma, and Afloat in France canal barges in France are among the best travel experiences that move.

We own our own properties and are not just a brand name attached to someone else's hotel. Our general managers run them as their own businesses with minimal interference from head office. The result is "The Best."

— James B. Sherwood, Chairman,
Orient-Express Hotels Ltd. www.orient-express.com

blend of ornate Moroccan and art deco styles, the most beautiful colonial architecture in North Africa. It took on a legendary Kasbah cachet in the late 1920s, when dignitaries flocked here and it became Morocco's most prestigious and elegant hotel. Winston Churchill urged Franklin Roosevelt to come to Marrakech at the close of World War II's Casablanca Conference. Churchill set up his easel and painted on the grounds.

The Moroccan-cuisine restaurant, La Marocain, is a delight in its *Thousand and One Nights* setting, with an Andalusian band and belly dancers. There are four other restaurants, as well, including Marrakech l'Impériale for impeccable French haute cuisine and L'Orangeraie, a fascinating newly opened fusion restaurant.

MYANMAR

YANGON

THE GOVERNOR'S RESIDENCE
35 Taw Win Road
Tel: 95-1-22-9860, www.pansea.com/yangon.html

A small boutique hotel, the Governor's Residence, now part of the Orient-Express family, is located in a quiet, residential area in the embassy quarter of Yangon. Its architecture is spectacular, all Burmese teak in an ornate style, inside and out, sitting majestically above a lotus garden. Its spacious rooms are sumptuously decorated in tropical cottons and silks and have vantages over a private garden and free-form pool. There are 49 rooms Don't miss a visit to the Shwedagon Pagoda nearby, one of the world's great treasures.

NEW ZEALAND

AUCKLAND

HYATT REGENCY AUCKLAND
Princes Street and Waterloo Quadrant
Tel: 64-9-355-1234, auckland.regency.hyatt.com

New Zealand's largest city, Auckland is an aquatic wonderland. The Hyatt Regency sits in the middle of this city with superlative views of the Auckland harbor from rooms in the high-rise tower. The hotel has recently added 120 new rooms, including suites, one- and two-bedroom apartments, and penthouses, all with balconies.

THE HILTON
Princes Wharf, 147 Quay Street
Tel: 64-9-978-2000, www.hilton.com

The Hilton is at the end of Prince's Wharf, offering guests unobstructed views across Auckland's exquisite inner harbor and all those sails from most guest rooms, the stylish Bellini Cocktail Bar, and White, the hotel's restaurant, which is under the imaginative chef Geoffrey Scott. The nautical design of the lobby and public areas celebrate the maritime environment and set the mood of the hotel. Leisure facilities include an outdoor infinity swimming pool over the gulf. The hotel has about 160 rooms, all of which have balconies.

TAUPO

HUKA LODGE
Huka Falls Road
Tel: 64-7-378-5791, www.hukalodge.com

The cozy Huka Lodge is on the banks of the Waikato River,

upstream from Huka Falls in the center of the North Island. Some 70 years ago, it began as a simple fishing lodge. Today, the luxurious lodge lures anyone seeking one of the world's best retreats. The 20 guest rooms and suites are each set in a private setting around the native plants and trees of the gorgeous grounds. The bedrooms are ample and include a separate dressing room. A short distance away is the swiftly flowing river, where the fishing is just as good today as it was 70 years ago, here in arguably the best trout-fishing waters in all the world.

QUEENSTOWN

EICHARDT'S PRIVATE HOTEL
Marine Parade
Tel: 64-3-441-0450, www.eichardtshotel.co.nz

The South Island of New Zealand has some of the prettiest scenery on Earth, and Queenstown is especially well located to take advantage of all the island has to offer, from the heights of the Southern Alps to water sports on beautiful Lake Wakatipu to hiking, cycling, or horseback riding. Queenstown was New Zealand's largest city for many years during the gold rush. When the gold ran out, so did many of the people, but they left behind a perfect Victorian frontier town. Eichardt's Private Hotel is a landmark at the center of town that symbolizes the best those days had to offer.

Eichardt's has just five rooms, but they are all well-appointed and spacious suites with fireplaces, comfortable furniture, a separate dressing room and bathroom with generous bath and double vanity, and modern electronic conveniences. Each also captures astonishing lake and mountain views. The historic building is on the lakefront with all of Queenstown's cafés, bars, and restaurants a leisurely walk away.

WAIRARAPA

WHAREKAUHAU LODGE
Western Lake Road, Palliser Bay, Featherston
Tel: 64-6-307-7581, www.wharekauhau.co.nz

For the quintessential glimpse into country life in New Zealand, come to this 2,000-hectare (5,000-acre) working sheep ranch overlooking magnificent Palliser Bay southeast of the capital Wellington and near the very bottom of the North Island. Originally created by the innovative Shaw family, Wharekauhau includes ancient forests, pristine lakes, rolling pastures as far as the eye can see, and a wild and spectacular coast, so there is no shortage of activities and adventures to be had. Guests can choose from an overabundance of outdoor activities or simply idle their time away in splendid isolation. After aperitifs in the living room, everyone gathers together in the rustic yet somehow elegant dining room for terrific meals that always take advantage of whatever's in season locally, including local wines that are among the world's best. How many working farms have a *Wine Spectator* award for their cellar? Each special day ends in your own sumptuous cottage with built-in views of the magnificent ocean. What a way to get away from the rat race!

PERU

CUZCO

HOTEL MONASTERIO CUZCO
Calle Palacios 136, Plazoleta Nazarenas
Tel: 51-84-241-777, www.monasterio.orient-express.com

One of the wonders of the world lies high in the Andes that dominate Peru: Machu Picchu. The closest city is Cuzco,

three hours away by train. As it happens, Cuzco—the ancient Inca capital city 3,300 meters (11,000 feet) up in the Andes—is a fascinating destination as well, and the Hotel Monasterio in the heart of the city is the best place to stay while you're there. Cuzco itself sits in a valley that is overlooked by ancient ceremonial sites and is a showcase of Spanish colonial architecture. A 16th-century Spanish monastery, the hotel is only 10 minutes from the airport and a few minutes from the Plaza de Armas where Cuzco's cathedral and most important museums are located. It has 109 pleasant rooms plus suites, all a bit more comfortable than in the days of the monks. The Hotel Monasterio is affiliated with the Machu Picchu Sanctuary Lodge, the only hotel located within the very sanctuary of the Machu Picchu Inca citadel.

PORTUGAL

LISBON

THE LAPA PALACE
Rua do Pau de Bandeira
Tel: 351-21-394-9494, www.lapapalace.com

Occupying a noble building from the 1870s, the Lapa Palace is on a hilltop commanding a vista over the Tagus River. This former country house in the diplomatic Lapa district has entertained royalty and heads of state since it opened as a hotel a dozen years ago. The Palace Wing has dramatic rooms, individually decorated in different periods, each with balconies, marble accents, Jacuzzis, and other amenities. Also in the original palace is the Count of Valenças Suite, which is literally fit for a king. Ornate high ceilings, original palace furniture, and gold leaf decoration are just some of the features of this fifth-floor extravagance.

The newer Garden Wing is less exciting, but certainly pleasant enough, with views of terraced lawns, the pool, or the city and river. The third building, the Villa Lapa, has modern but luxurious rooms the size of apartments with the maximum of privacy.

THE PESTANA PALACE
Rua Jau, 54
Tel: 351-21-361-5600, www.pestana.com

For a central location in Lisbon, try the Pestana Palace. This mansion is just turning a century old, and it has all the grandeur of the patrician palaces of the day and has been registered as a national monument. With beautiful styling of Romantic revivalism, some French provincial, some Victoriana, and a little baroque, the impressive public spaces of the Pestana Palace are a riot of ornate fantasy. The lobby would not be out of place at Versailles, and the former grand ballroom has been converted into the Valle Flôr restaurant, serving exciting new Portuguese cuisine. Guests staying in one of the 190 rooms and suites can enjoy the indoor and outdoor pools, both magnificent, and the fine gardens surrounding the building with views of the Tagus River.

SETEAIS PALACE
R. Barbosa du Bocage, Sintra
Tel: 351-21-923-3200

A little ways outside Lisbon to the northwest sits the exceptional Seteais Palace. A Palladian palace converted into a hotel, much to the delight of travelers worldwide, this stately villa was built in the last quarter of the 18th century. Here, the Duke of Wellington signed the Convention of Sintra during the Peninsular War in 1808. Sintra itself has been declared a UNESCO World Heritage site, thanks to the important architecture of the many beautiful villas like the Seteais Palace. Nearby is the picturesque seaside towns

of Cascais and Estoril, together forming a classic turn-of-the-20th-century summer resort.

The interior of the Seteais Palace is notable for its spacious rooms decorated with exquisite French antiques, museum-quality patterned needlepoint carpets, and fresco paintings. Airy balcony rooms overlook the lovely formal gardens and have gracious period armoires and finely made Portuguese rugs. Delicious homemade breads and local wines are part of the whole delightful experience.

MADEIRA

REID'S PALACE HOTEL
Estrada Monumental 139, Funchal
Tel: 351-291-71-7171, www.reidspalace.com

Madeira is a jewel of an island in the Atlantic that has belonged to Portugal since the days when most sailing ships pulled in to load a few barrels of the local Madeira wine, a seemingly unique elixir that somehow magically improved after months in the hold of the ships rather than turning rancid.

Reid's Palace Hotel, from its vantage point on the cliffs above the paradisiacal Bay of Funchal, has seen its share of more modern ships stop to seek wine, provisions, or pure pleasure here since its opening in 1891. The hotel has itself become a destination since that time, as is indicated by the grand Winston Churchill and George Bernard Shaw suites, named after just two of the hotel's celebrated guests. Churchill spent a considerable amount of time here while working on his war memoirs and painting in later life. It is not hard to imagine those days in this timeless setting while enjoying one of the three pools or savoring a long, enticing meal under the stars in the Brisa do Mar restaurant.

RUSSIA

MOSCOW

THE METROPOL
Teatralny Proezd 1/4
Tel: 7-095-927-6000, www.metropol-moscow.ru

Moscow was renowned for beautiful, graceful architecture in the imperial days before the revolution, and the Metropol, built in 1905, is one of Moscow's most striking hotels. In the wake of the revolution, even the Bolsheviks couldn't resist the hotel's allure, as it was the site of several speeches by Lenin and of early meetings of the Central Committee. The Metropol was spared the fate of other grand buildings during the Soviet period by becoming one of the hotels specially designated for use by visiting foreigners. It is still one of the most luxurious hotels in Moscow.

The location is excellent for touring the capital city; it is just a short stroll to the Kremlin, Red Square, and the Bolshoi Theater. The Restaurant Metropol has fine dining under an atrium ceiling with a decor that is perfect for enjoying the finest in Russian cuisine, while those who prefer Continental cuisine may want to sample some Russian dishes at the Evropeisky.

ARARAT PARK HYATT MOSCOW
4 Neglinnaya Street
Tel: 7-095-783-1234, www.moscow.park.hyatt.com

Close to all the famous cultural and political attractions of central Moscow is the Ararat Park Hyatt Moscow. Somewhat nondescript and institutional on the outside, the interior is sleek and modern, with chrome and glass giving a space-age feel. Rooms are contemporary and comfortable.

LE ROYAL MERIDIEN NATIONAL
15/1 Mokhovaya Street
Tel: 7-095-258-7000, www.national.ru

Built in 1903, the Hotel National was designed by the Russian architect Alexander Ivanov. It stands in the very heart of Moscow, overlooking St. Basil's Cathedral. Each of the 194 rooms and 37 suites is individually designed and decorated.

ST. PETERSBURG

GRAND HOTEL EUROPE
Nevsky Prospekt, Mikhailovskaya Ulitsa 1/7
Tel: 7-812-329-6000, www.grand-hotel-europe.com

The Grand Hotel Europe dates back to 1824 and has the grace of a 19th-century St. Petersburg villa. It reopened as a hotel in the early post-Soviet days of 1991 and quickly became one of the first addresses for visitors to this glamorous former imperial capital. Located on Nevsky Prospekt, the great avenue of St. Petersburg, the hotel has well-appointed rooms and an efficient staff. It makes an ideal base for exploring the sights of St. Petersburg.

The hotel's restaurant is one of Russia's tops and is in the forefront of a revival of pre-Soviet culinary traditions, serving Russian and continental specialties. The guest rooms are crisp, clean, and elegant.

ROCCO FORTE HOTEL ASTORIA
39 Bolshaya Morskaya
Tel: 7-812-313-5757, www.roccofortehotels.com

Hotel Astoria, on the square opposite St. Isaac's Cathedral, is a few steps from the Hermitage and the Neva River. Its guest rooms and suites feature Russian antiques as well as contemporary pieces, and all the modern conveniences. The Davidov Restaurant serves excellent Russian and continental cuisine.

SEYCHELLES

BANYAN TREE SEYCHELLES
Anse Intendance Mahe
Tel: 248-38-3500, www.banyantree.com/seychelles

The Seychelles are an island paradise in the Indian Ocean, and the Banyan Tree Seychelles takes full advantage of the natural beauty, giving guests wonderful vistas of white-sand beaches, palm trees, and tropical forests from the resort's 36 glittering pool villas. Combining the best features of Seychellois architecture with contemporary comfort, the villas are graced by high ceilings, breezy verandas, private swimming pools, and spa pavilions on the ocean side. Saffron is the signature restaurant of Banyan Tree Seychelles, serving primarily Thai cuisine, complemented by additional dishes from a variety of Southeast Asian countries.

SINGAPORE

THE RITZ-CARLTON MILLENIA
7 Raffles Avenue
Tel: 65-6-337-8888, www.ritzcarlton.com/hotels/singapore

The Ritz-Carlton Millenia in Singapore is a high-rise hotel with 600 rooms that have unobstructed vistas of the landscape of Singapore or the seascape of Marina Bay. Its rooms, enormous by Singapore standards, all have raised beds to make gazing out at the sights that much easier. The hotel is renowned for its 4,200-piece art collection, scattered throughout the hotel, making it a living museum. The Ritz-Carlton anchors the new Marina Centre area.

RAFFLES HOTEL SINGAPORE
1 Beach Road
Tel: 65-63-37-1886, www.raffleshotel.com

Raffles Hotel is one of the most famous hotels in the world. After opening in Singapore in 1887, the hotel soon became the meeting point for expatriates and officials of the colonial government, and an essential layover point for any Westerners traveling through the Far East. Rudyard Kipling, Somerset Maugham, Douglas Fairbanks, Noel Coward, and Charlie Chaplin are just a few of the hundreds of luminaries who called the Raffles home for at least a short while, along with miscellaneous kings, maharajas, and sultans. It was declared a national monument on its centenary in 1987 and underwent a thorough makeover, reopening in the grand style of its youth in 1991. Each suite is spacious with overhead fans suspended below the 4.5-meter (15-foot) ceilings and timber floors covered with oriental carpets. There are 12 restaurants and bars, as well as the Raffles Culinary Academy.

THE REGENT SINGAPORE
One Cuscaden Road
Tel: 65-67-33-8888, www.regenthotels.com

Two days aren't long enough to enjoy the fabulous Regent. An attentive staff in uniform and white gloves is there at all hours to greet you. The light and airy atrium has glass elevators and rich, dark wood columns. Even if you arrive in the middle of the night, you will be brought light refreshments, a service of finger sandwiches and hot tea. The Regent Singapore is conveniently located near the Botanical Gardens and the exclusive shopping on Orchard Road.

SOUTH AFRICA

CAPE TOWN

ASHANTI LODGE
11 Hof Street, Gardens
Tel: 27-21-423-8721, www.ashanti.co.za

The Ashanti Lodge is an eclectic hostelry in vibrant Cape Town. It has a variety of accommodations from camping areas to rustic suites, located either in the main lodge building or two guesthouses nearby. Some of the rooms are huge, and most are around a swimming pool, perfect for an early morning wake-up dip.

SPAIN

In 1910 the Spanish government assigned the Marquis de la Vega Inclán the task of creating a hotel infrastructure that would house travelers and improve Spain's image abroad. King Alfonso XIII was very enthusiastic about the idea, and he personally chose hundreds of locations—designated "paradors"—that are clear examples of how hospitality can beautifully and seamlessly integrate with the restoration of castles, palaces, and convents. The project rescued from ruin numerous monuments that represent Spain's remarkable historical and cultural heritage.

All over Spain today you will find these amazing retreats and lodgings with up-to-date comforts and delicious meals. You can drive through Spain, especially the Pyrenees, parador to parador, and never be bored. For maps, addresses, locations, photographs, histories, and rates for all paradors, visit www.parador.es/english/index.jsp.

To mention just one parador out of the fantastic array of paradors available that illustrates how well historical and

artistic heritage combine in these treasures, I'll select Sos del Rey Católico.

PARADOR DE SOS DEL REY CATÓLICO
Sianz de Vicuña 1, Sos del Rey Católico
Tel: 34-948-88-8011

Located in the hinterlands south of San Sebastián on the road to Pamplona, this four-star hotel in the parador group is built in traditional Aragonese style. The parador is a centerpiece for the enchanting walled medieval town of Sos del Rey Católico, which has been declared a historical-artistic area. The town, with the Aragonese and Navarrese foothills of the Pyrenees part of the surrounding landscape, was the birthplace of many influential nobles and a Catholic king. A must see, must visit. In a word, spectacular.

BARCELONA

BARCELONA GRAN HOTEL LA FLORIDA
Crta. Vallvidrera al Tibidabo 83-89
Tel: 34-93-259-3000, www.hotellaflorida.com

The agreeable Gran Hotel La Florida, high atop Mount Tibidabo, with commanding panoramas over the city of Barcelona far below and the Mediterranean Sea beyond, opened in 1925. It has just been through a complete renovation, reopening in 2003, and is now better than ever. Many of the 74 rooms and suites offer private Jacuzzis and breathtaking panoramic views of Barcelona and the surrounding countryside. Extensive modern facilities, including high-tech conference facilities, fine dining in L'Orangerie restaurant, a generously equipped spa and beauty center, a Turkish bath, a sauna, and a rooftop infinity pool, make this hotel a winner.

HOTEL ARTS BARCELONA
Carrer de la Marina
Tel: 34-93-221-1000

The Hotel Arts, a Ritz-Carlton property, is waterside near the Olympic Port, providing wonderful views of the blue Mediterranean in one direction and the city, with the mountains as a backdrop, in the other. It is in a great position, so close to the waterfront, near Barcelona's finest shops and restaurants, and within walking distance of the Ramblas, but away from the noisiest parts of the city. The hotel is virtually a world of its own, with upscale rooms, suites, and apartments, the last category with personal butlers. There are three restaurants, one specializing in California cuisine, and an outdoor pool.

HOTEL PALACE BARCELONA
Gran Vía de les Corts Catalanes, 668
Tel: 34-93-510-11-30, www.ritz-barcelona.com

The Ramblas, the popular promenade for all-day and all-night shopping and partying, is a focal point in Barcelona, and the exemplary Hotel Palace (formerly known as the Hotel Ritz) has 120 comfortable rooms on a pleasant, tree-lined street nearby, convenient to the historic Gothic Quarter. Built in 1919, the Palace still has its Old World charm. The Cælis Restaurant has ceiling fans, white street lamps, and large patio doors leading to a flower-filled courtyard and fountain, which together give you the impression of being outdoors.

MADRID

HOTEL RITZ
Plaza de la Lealta, 5
Tel: 34-91-701-6767, www.ritz.es

The Ritz in Paris is, of course synonymous with the absolute

highest standards among hotels, and Spain's King Alfonso XIII decided he wanted one, too—and being a king, he got one. Designed and built under the personal supervision of the legendary hotelier César Ritz, Madrid's Hotel Ritz was inaugurated in 1910 and shares the same lofty pedestal with the Ritz hotels in Paris and London. The service is beyond compare, the accommodations are the ultimate in refined comfort, and the Goya Restaurant is one of the top places to dine in Madrid. Afternoon tea here is legend. The hotel is close to the world-class Prado, Thyssen-Bornemisza, and Reina Sofia museums.

MAJORCA

HOTEL LA RESIDENCIA
Son Canals
Tel: 34-971-63-9011, www.hotellaresidencia.com

On the magical island of Majorca in the Mediterranean, the Hotel La Residencia consists of two manor houses, dating from the 16th and 17th centuries, located in the enchanting mountainside village of Deià. Furnished with Spanish antiques, Majorcan fabrics, and a wealth of local art, the hotel is lovely. El Olivo restaurant is in an old building that once was an olive press. The ancient pressing stones still remain. Chef Guillermo Mendez and his team fashion consistently great dishes using fresh local fish and produce.

MARBELLA

MARBELLA CLUB HOTEL
Bulevar Principe Alfonso von Hohenlohe
Tel: 34-95-282-2211, www.marbellaclub.com

In this town of royal vacationers, live like a king—or at least a prince—in this former private residence of Prince Alfonso von Hohenlohe, now featuring 121 lavish rooms and suites. The resort is beachfront, naturally, and owns a lush 18-hole private golf course inland where the hazards include startling views of the Mediterranean, with Gibraltar and Africa on the horizon. The club's private gardens are a cool place to wander on a hot Andalusian day, perhaps followed by a swim in pool or ocean at the famous Beach Club.

SAN SABASTIÁN

HOTEL DE LONDRES Y DE INGLATERRA
Zubieta, 2
Tel: 34-943-44-0491, www.hlondres.com

The Hotel de Londres y de Inglaterra, built in the 19th century and recently renovated, is one of San Sebastián's most distinguished hotels. On the Playa de la Concha in the curve of the bay, it is a very pleasant hotel with a friendly and efficient staff, created—as one might expect from its name—in the style of an English seaside hotel where well-heeled Victorian travelers would feel right at home. The hotel retains some classic Old World details, such as a old elevator and the elegant grand breakfast room, but the rooms are modern enough and the bathrooms are full of marble.

SANTANDER

HOTEL REAL
Pérez Galdós, 28
Tel: 34-942-27-2550, www.hotelreal.com

In the early 20th century, the citizens of Santander decided to build the splendid Hotel Real as a way of luring the king and his court to spend the summer season vacationing in their city. It was completed in 1917 in the

THE BEST NEWSLETTER FOR TRAVELERS

PASSPORT NEWSLETTER
5315 N. Clark Street, Chicago, IL
www.passportnewsletter.com
Tel: 773-769-6760

The *Passport Newsletter* is the original "insider's" newsletter for travelers who want to know about the best in travel experiences. The print version of the *Passport Newsletter* has been published since 1965 and continues today with access to an extensive Internet Library for members.

By and large, subscribers are both knowledgeable and sophisticated in their travel preferences, and their interests focus on more unfamiliar or secluded places and on the special and little-known dining, accommodations, shopping, and cultural and adventure experiences. Regardless of their personal financial circumstances, they understand the importance of receiving full value-for-money, at all levels of spending.

The world's most experienced travelers have learned to trust the recommendations and opinions they get from the *Newsletter*. It accepts no advertising. It is not a travel agency and has no financial interests in any of the subjects it writes about. The reports are written by more than 50 seasoned journalists and writers stationed around the world, all of whom are encouraged to report freely what they observe.

A recent issue recommends the Sheraton Grand Laguna Phuket, in Thailand, a must-have new handbag at Jamin Puech in Paris, and London's great cheese shop, Neal's Dairy Yard.

neo-French style of the great European palaces and dedicated in honor of King Alfonso XIII. All spacious guest rooms, halls, and lounges have been redecorated.

SEVILLE

HOTEL ALFONSO XIII SEVILLE
San Fernando, 2
Tel: 34-95-491-7000, www.hotel-alfonsoxiii.com

Not satisfied with a single superlative hotel in Madrid, King Alfonso XIII commissioned a comparable one for Seville. The hotel opened in 1928 and was christened in the king's name, the Hotel Alfonso XIII. Ensconced in the center of graceful, seductive Seville along the Guadalquivir River, the Alfonso XIII is steps from the Reales Alcázares and Plaza de España. The architecture speaks of Andalusia, with its combination of Moorish, Castilian, and Baroque details, including marvelous dark wood pocket ceilings and colorful tile everywhere.

TORRENT

MAS DE TORRENT
Afores, s/n
Tel: 34-972-30-3292, www.mastorrent.com

A *mas* is the ancient Catalan word for a farmhouse, and indeed the main building of the Mas de Torrent is an 18th-century farmhouse that has been tastefully restored as a decadent hideout. Situated between Girona and the ever-inviting Costa Brava beaches, some 125 kilometers (75 miles) north of Barcelona, the Mas offers a swimming pool, tennis courts, and a restaurant whose cuisine is based on fresh products from the sea. The bungalows have a private garden. Contemporary paintings pay tribute to Picasso. Highly recommended.

SWEDEN

STOCKHOLM

GRAND HOTEL STOCKHOLM
Sodra Blasieholmshamnen 8
Tel: 46-8-679-3500, www.grandhotel.se

Since 1901, when the Nobel Prizes were first awarded until today, the laureates and their families have all been housed at the Grand Hotel Stockholm, which indicates its status as the best lodging in Stockholm and possibly in all Scandinavia. The hotel is a city landmark, rich in history and tradition and a premier destination for visitors who demand the best. Celebrated for its food, elegant surroundings, and gracious staff, the Grand Hotel offers guest rooms with glorious views of the harbor and royal palace.

THE LADY HAMILTON
Storkyrkobrinken 5
Tel: 46-8-506-4-0000, www.lady-hamilton.se

As delightful as its namesake, Lord Nelson's mistress, the Lady Hamilton is a 15th-century building. Swedish antiques fill the guest rooms and common areas. The breakfast room, furnished with captain's chairs, looks out onto the lively cobblestone street, and the subterranean sauna rooms, in whitewashed stone, provide a secluded fireplace and a chance to take a dip in the building's original medieval pool.

SWITZERLAND

GSTAAD

PALACE HOTEL
Tel: 41-33-748-5000, www.palace.ch

The famed Palace is on a hill above the village, with a breathtaking view of the surrounding mountains. A ten-minute walk takes you to the town center. For lunch and dinner, you can choose among five restaurants with national and international dishes.

LAUSANNE

BEAU-RIVAGE PALACE
Place du Port 17–19
Tel: 41-21-613-3333, www.brp.ch

Surrounded by hectares of private gardens on the shores of Lake Geneva, the Belle Époque Beau-Rivage Palace is one of the most revered hotels in Europe. Located in an elegant residential district of Lausanne, the magnificent property has for more than 140 years ranked as one of best properties in Switzerland.

LUGANO

HOTEL SPLENDIDE ROYAL
Riva Caccia, 7
Tel: 41-91-985-7711, www.splendide.ch

Overlooking the shoreline of one of the most enchanting lakes in Europe—Lago di Lugano—the Hotel Splendide Royal is located in a residential district of Lugano in the Italian-speaking Ticino section of Switzerland.

ST. MORITZ

BADRUTT'S PALACE HOTEL
Via Serlas, 27
Tel: 41-81-837-1000, www.badruttspalace.com

This celebrated landmark resort, in the heart of the legendary village of St. Moritz, offers breathtaking views over the lake to the Alps. It has terrific service in both winter and summer.

ZURICH

WIDDER HOTEL
Rennweg, 7
Tel: 41-1-224-2526, www.widderhotel.ch

Creatively fashioned from ten old townhouses, the Widder is a masterpiece of innovative restoration, with period architecture showcasing paintings and accessories. Superb rooftop terraces, and an exclusive library make for a home-like atmosphere.

THAILAND

BANGKOK

FOUR SEASONS HOTEL BANGKOK
155 Rajadamri Road
Tel: 66-2-250-1000, www.fourseasons.com/bangkok

With traditional Thai architecture, hand-painted silk ceilings, intricate artwork, an impressively scaled lobby, and glorious gardens, the Four Seasons Hotel Bangkok offers exquisite accommodations and gracious hospitality strategically located in the corporate, diplomatic, and shopping heart of Bangkok's bustling core.

THE ORIENTAL
48 Oriental Avenue
Tel: 66-2-659-9000, www.mandarinoriental.com

Since 1876 the Oriental Bangkok has been the first choice for royalty and heads of state when visiting the exotic and exciting city of Bangkok. Richly appointed, it is one of the great hotels of the world. On the Chao Phraya River, with gardens similar to Versailles, the Oriental Bangkok is a palace of indulgence. Rooms are exceptionally large, oases of Thai silks, cottons, and gleaming teak, and all have river views. On each floor a butler protects privacy and provides flawless service. There is also an extraordinary Thai cooking school, Thai cultural classes, and two swimming pools in rich tropical gardens. The historic Authors' Lounge is steeped in memories of such literary luminaries as Joseph Conrad and Somerset Maugham.

CHIANG MAI

REGENT FOUR SEASONS CHIANG MAI RESORT
Mae Rim, Samoeng Old Road
Tel: 66-53-29-8181, www.fourseasons.com

Nestled in the foothills of the misty Doi Suthep Mountains, a cluster of 67 Lanna-style pavilions is the starting point to explore northern Thailand and the famed golden triangle. From your pavilion in this Burmese-inspired, colonial-style setting, you can spend hours gazing out at the rice terraces and the mountains surrounding the beautiful Mae Rim Valley. But there's also elephant riding, hiking, tennis, golf, and hillside excursions available if you are so inclined. The restaurants—Sala Mae Rim, the resort's Thai restaurant; the Pool Terrace Restaurant and Bar; and the open-air Elephant Bar—terrace are all in dramatic settings.

PHUKET

AMANPURI
Pansea Beach
Tel: 66-76-324 333, www.amanpuri.com

On a headland overlooking the Andaman Sea, Amanpuri oozes with Thai style. Temple pavilion–inspired rooms interspersed throughout a coconut plantation are filled with fresh breezes and beautiful linens, treasured antiques, and tile floors. Paths lead to a shimmering swimming pool and the white sand of Pansea Beach. At both, the staff waits with towels and cool drinks. Dinner is often served on

Amanpuri's own beach with crystal and candlelight, while a fleet of yachts waits offshore.

BANYAN TREE PHUKET
33 Moo 4, Srisoonthorn Road
Tel: 66-76-324-374, www.banyantree.phuket.com

The Banyan Tree Phuket is a model of serenity. Its beautiful villas are decorated with exquisite Thai silks, teak furniture and floors, and out-of-this-world bathrooms, including al fresco sunken tubs. The Saffron restaurant has an incredibly varied and delicious menu.

LE MERIDIEN PHUKET BEACH RESORT
Phuket 83000
Tel: 66-7634-0480, www.phuket.com/meridien

A pearl in a tropical setting on the Andaman Sea on 16 hectares (40 acres) of tropical splendor, the Meridian Phuket has its own secluded beach, enticingly named Relax Bay. Within its lush green landscape, the resort offers tastefully appointed rooms, a wide range of facilities, an extensive choice of international cuisine, and of course a spa.

TURKEY

ISTANBUL

CIRAGAN PALACE HOTEL
Ciragan Caddesi 84, Istanbul
Tel: 90-212-326-4646, www.ciragan-palace.com

A true palace, home to the last of the Ottoman emperors, the hotel sits on a peak facing the Bosporus. Recently renovated and made even more lavish, this grand waterfront palace blends the European tradition with Turkish hospitality and a service standard almost beyond expectation. The handsome guest rooms are decorated with fine local textiles and have balconies and extravagant marble bathrooms. Its swimming pool parallels the bay, and the veranda restaurant overlooks the ships and ferries crossing the harbor.

UNITED ARAB EMIRATES

DUBAI

BURJ AL ARAB
Jumeirah Beach Road
Tel: 971-4-301-7777, www.burj-al-arab.com

Dubai has staked a claim to the world's center of modern architecture, and probably has more exciting new buildings per square kilometer than anywhere else on Earth. The Burj Al Arab is one of these architectural marvels: Shaped like a mainsail under a full gale, the billowing structure soars 321 meters (1,050 feet) above the Arabian Gulf in vivid homage to the region's seafaring traditions, symbolizing the very essence of Dubai. Rolls-Royce limousines, laptops and plasma TVs in every room, and private butlers give an idea of the level of service provided here. All guest rooms are two-floor suites with ocean views.

THE JUMEIRAH BEACH HOTEL
Jumeirah Beach Road
Tel: 971-4-348-0000, www.jumeiraheachhotel.com

Not to be outdone in the Dubai architectural derby, the Jumeirah Beach Hotel is designed with the profile of a giant ocean swell, a schooner under full sail—another tribute to the Arabian nautical heritage—or possibly a huge old-time roller coaster. Combining the latest technology

with a long-standing reputation of Arabian hospitality, the rooms are luxuriously appointed with mesmerizing panoramas of the Arabian Gulf; some have private balconies. There are also 19 even more extraordinary villas in an oasis within the hotel's gardens and more than a dozen places to dine on the property, with a wide range of cuisines to satisfy every taste.

UNITED STATES

ARIZONA

MII AMO,
525 Boynton Canyon Road, Sedona,
Tel: 928-203-8500, www.miiamo.com

Instead of going to a spa at your hotel, go to a hotel at your spa. Located on the grounds of Enchantment Resort in Sedona, Mii Amo has 14 guest rooms and two suites, providing extremely comfortable spaces, each with a fireplace and courtyard or balconies. The destination spa is the point here, however, and Mii Amo promotes healing through mind, body, and spiritual therapies. The complex, designed in tune with the Native American aesthetics and the natural surroundings, has indoor and outdoor treatment areas, indoor and outdoor pools, and the Mii Amo Café, where guests can choose family-style dining or mingling with other hedonists.

CALIFORNIA

BEVERLY HILLS

THE BEVERLY HILLS HOTEL AND BUNGALOWS
9641 Sunset Boulevard
Tel: 310-276-2251

Long a California legend, the Beverly Hills Hotel has beautiful guest rooms, lush gardens, exotic flowers, personalized service, and private walkways on five lush hectares (12 acres) in the center of Beverly Hills. The bungalows and the legendary Polo Lounge have been a favorite with movie stars and Hollywood executives for decades, and the hotel has one of the most celebrated power pools and cabanas in the world.

BIG SUR

POST RANCH INN
Highway 1
Tel: 831-667-2200, www.postranchinn.com

The Post Ranch Inn is a favorite with travelers who take to the road on one of the most dramatic and heart-pounding drives in the world—the Pacific Coast Highway, which outdoes itself in beauty in the Big Sur area. Nestled on the sea cliffs above the crashing surf of the Pacific, the Post Ranch Inn has local history and art, and soothing spa treatments, in an incredible setting. The resort's organic focus embraces the dramatic beauty of Big Sur's coastline, and the inn provides the ultimate getaway. From here you can explore the natural wonders on exciting hikes or take a short drive to the charming towns of Monterey and Carmel-by-the-Sea.

VENTANA INN & SPA
Tel: 831-667-2331, www.ventanainn.com

The Ventana Inn & Spa is an idyllic retreat where you can saturate your senses with the sights, smells, and sounds of the towering redwoods and an uninterrupted view of the rocky Pacific coastline. Take your choice of a room, suite, cottage, or house, all with natural splendor on full display. Ventana is on Highway 1, about 45 kilometers (28 miles) south of Carmel, 250 kilometers (150 miles) south of San

Francisco, and 500 kilometers (300 miles) north of Los Angeles. The award-winning Cielo restaurant is about as romantic a place to dine as there is.

HALF MOON BAY

THE RITZ-CARLTON
One Miramontes Point Road
Tel: 650-712-7000, www.ritzcarlton.com

Half Moon Bay makes a terrific day-trip from San Francisco, and since you're going to wish you could spend more time there, why not check in at the Ritz-Carlton? Set on an ocean bluff like some stately Scottish manor—only warmer—the golf and spa resort has two great seaside golf courses, overlooking 80 kilometers (50 miles) of coastline. Inside is warmth and comfort that will make you swear that San Francisco can't be just 45 minutes away.

LOS ANGELES

HOTEL BEL-AIR
701 Stone Canyon Road
Tel: 310-472-1211, www.hotelbelair.com

With 92 rooms, including 40 suites and a two-story red-tiled Mediterranean villa, the Hotel Bel-Air is located among the movie stars' homes and moguls' estates in this most exclusive residential area in the hills just west of Beverly Hills. The five-star hotel is set on 4.5 hectares (11 acres) of spectacular gardens, simply an oasis. Each of the guest rooms and suites at the Hotel Bel-Air is furnished with custom fabrics, exquisite furnishings, and luxurious Italian linens. All accommodations have fireplaces, private entrances, and tiled courtyards.

NAPA VALLEY

AUBERGE DU SOLEIL
180 Rutherford Hill Road, Rutherford
Tel: 707-963-1211, www.aubergedusoleil.com

What began as a French country restaurant inspired by a leading San Francisco restaurateur has become one of America's nicest small hotels. The Auberge du Soleil opened in 1981 as the Napa Valley's first fine-dining restaurant and the vision of French-born Claude Rouas, who sought to recreate a feeling of Provence in the premier wine region of California. Inspired by the picturesque hillside of olive trees and vineyards in Rutherford, the country cottages are welcoming, with romantic rooms and suites, each with a fireplace, a private terrace, and Mediterranean-inspired decor with original contemporary art. Of course, a prime reason for coming here is to savor the great restaurant, whose cuisine features the full splendor of the region's flavors and colors, accompanied by a selection of 500 California wines. Nearby are dozens of wineries, as well as hiking trails, hot air ballooning, and antique shops.

CALISTOGA RANCH
580 Lommel Road
Tel: 707-254-2800, www.calistogaranch.com

Up the valley in an area known for its geothermal springs and geysers, Calistoga Ranch is a 63-hectare (157-acre) luxury resort consisting of 46 individual guest lodges, one-bedroom suites with ample living space. The lodges have fireplaces, and some even have hot tubs on a private deck. Here you are halfway between the sophistication and excitement of the Napa wine region and the dramatic wilds of Northern California, with the utterly charming Wild West town of Calistoga nearby.

PEBBLE BEACH

Casa Palmero at Pebble Beach
1518 Cypress Drive
Tel: 831-647-7500, www.pebblebeach.com

Under an enchanting red-tiled roof and sporting rustic terra-cotta walls, this Tuscan-style estate sets exquisite standards for guest comfort and personal service in all 24 spacious rooms and suites. Casa Palmero, a hangout for owners Arnold Palmer, Clint Eastwood, and Peter Ueberroth when they are in town, is all about personal attention and privacy. Oh, and there's supposed to be some golf courses around, too.

The Lodge at Pebble Beach
1700 17-Mile Drive
Tel: 831-647-7500, www.pebblebeach.com

The Lodge at Pebble Beach, the second of three peerless golf resorts at world-famous Pebble Beach, has fine dining, inviting guest rooms, and outdoor pursuits ranging from tennis to equestrian and hiking trails to four championship golf courses, including the cypress-lined oceanside golf course that is such stuff as golfers' dreams are made of.

SANTA BARBARA

San Ysidro Ranch
San Ysidro Lane
Montecito, California 93108
Tel: 805-565-1700, www.sanysidroranch.com

Sooner or later all conversation in California turns to the land, and 150 kilometers (90 miles) northwest of Los Angeles, resting between the Santa Ynez Mountains to the north and the Pacific Ocean to the south, is Santa Barbara, where the L.A. sprawl stops. Beyond, spreading across the county, are some 40 land-grant ranchos such as Rancho San Julian, their vast estates unspoiled. At the San Ysidro Ranch, with cottages scattered along the expansive lawns and gardens high above the Pacific, guests find themselves at home with their names posted on their cottage doors. Each cottage is unique, and all are special.

Located in the Montecito foothills inland from Santa Barbara, just south of the green mountains of the broad Los Padres National Forest, the ranch has been a retreat to discriminating travelers for years. Suffice it to say that John and Jackie Kennedy honeymooned here, and Vivien Leigh and Laurence Olivier chose the site for their wedding. It's a magical spot.

The Four Seasons Resort
The Biltmore Santa Barbara
1260 Channel Drive
Tel: 805-969-2261
www.fourseasons.com/santabarbar

The Santa Barbara Biltmore is recognized as one of the most beautiful natural settings to be found anywhere in California. Part of this old hacienda is the Coral Casino Beach and Cabana Club, with an elegant tiled pool on the ocean. Red tile and graceful mission archways set the tone for this historic Spanish colonial estate with its many cottages. Guest rooms and private bungalows, lush botanical gardens, and ocean frontage make this a perfect base to scout out the nearby wineries, take a sailing trip to the Channel Islands, go horseback riding in the mountains, or take advantage of preferential tee times at several nearby golf clubs.

SAN FRANCISCO

CAMPTON PLACE HOTEL
340 Stockton Street
Tel: 415-781-5555

Campton Place Hotel, one of the smartest luxury hotels in San Francisco, recently completed a renovation to make you feel as comfortable in the hotel as you are at home. Set in the heart of trendy Union Square, this elegant, European-style hotel with one of the best restaurants in the country is minutes from Chinatown, the Financial District, theaters, entertainment, and shopping.

PARK HYATT SAN FRANCISCO
333 Battery Street
Tel: 415-392-1234, parksanfrancisco.hyatt.com

The Park Hyatt San Francisco is a great business hotel, located right in the Financial District, connected by landscaped pedestrian bridge to the historic Federal Reserve Building and the shops, entertainment, and cafés of dynamic Embarcadero Center. This regal hotel is near Chinatown and California Street cable cars, with access to Fisherman's Wharf and Ghirardelli Square.

FOUR SEASONS HOTEL SAN FRANCISCO
757 Market Street,
Tel: 415-633-3000, www.fourseasons.com/sanfrancisco

Set in an old Treasury Building in the Yerba Buena cultural district, two blocks from Union Square, the Financial District, and the Museum of Modern Art, the Four Seasons San Francisco is a savvy hotel with easy access to all that San Francisco offers. It also has a stunning pool.

THE SHERMAN HOUSE
2160 Green Street
Tel: 415-563-3600

Just minutes from Fisherman's Wharf stands a grand Victorian residence built in 1876 where Leander Sherman chose to welcome the greatest names in music, art, and literature. The splendor of Sherman House lives on, from its exquisite gardens to its great rooms, each individually styled with antiques, many with wonderful views of San Francisco Bay. Timothy Au offers imaginative menus with the finest seasonal ingredients. The Sherman House has eight rooms and six suites.

HOTEL REX
562 Sutter Street
Tel: 415-433-4434, www.thehotelrex.com

Between Nob Hill and Union Square, the Hotel Rex is a literary and stylish place with thousands of books lining the 1920s-style lobby. The proprietors even host book readings and round-table discussions in the lobby and in the small bistro, where California cuisine and local wines are served. Guest rooms are of a good size and have writing desks and lamps with whimsically painted shades.

MANDARIN ORIENTAL
222 Sansome Street
Tel: 415-276-9888, www.mandarinoriental.com

Situated amid the clouds in San Francisco's third tallest building, the Mandarin Oriental hotel is renowned for the beauty of its interiors, its seamless service, and the spectacular views of the city and the Bay with its graceful bridges. The plush rooms feature an Asian motif combined with every modern convenience. The hotel's Financial District address puts it within easy walking distance of Union Square.

National Parks of Tanzania

There are many outstanding national parks in Tanzania. Following is a description of some of them for the adventurous traveler. For more information visit www.kilimanjaro.com, www.africaguide.com, or www.tanzania.go.tz/n_parks.html.

ARUSHA NATIONAL PARK
Total Area Covered: 137 sq.km. (53 sq. mi.)
Best Time to Visit: To climb Mount Meru, June–February, although it may rain in November
Best views of Mount Kilimanjaro, December–February
Nearest Town: Arusha
Attractions: Momella, lakes, Ngurdoto Crater, Mount Meru, elephants, buffalo, Colobus monkeys, walking safaris
Accommodations: Momella Wildlife Lodge, Mount Meru Game Lodge, Tanzania Hotel, rest house, campsites

GOMBE NATIONAL PARK
Total Area Covered: 52 sq. km (20 sq. mi.)
Best Time to Visit: The chimps do not roam as far in the wet season so they may be easier to find, February–June, or November–mid-December
Better picture opportunities in the dry season, July–October and late December
Nearest Town: Kigoma
Attractions: Chimpanzee sanctuary, walking safaris

Accommodations: Hostel; camping on the beach is permitted

KATAVI NATIONAL PARK
Total Area Covered: 2,253 sq. km (869 sq. mi.)
Best Time to Visit: Dry season, May–October or mid-December–February
Nearest Town: Mpanda
Attractions: Buffalo, elephant, Masai zebra, gazelles
Accommodations: Katavi Luxury Tented Camp, rest houses, huts, and basic hotels

KILIMANJARO NATIONAL PARK
Travelers watching the sunrise from the 5,895-meter (19,341-foot) summit of Mount Kilimanjaro have been known to cry, hug their climbing companions, and breathlessly echo that the moment will be the most remembered in their lives. Through the switchback trails of the summit cone, sometimes smooth but often becoming relentlessly steep, your Tanzanian guide sings soft Swahili songs in the darkness to help you in a slow hypnotic rhythm of stepping and breathing, stepping and breathing. Near the top, where there are less options than at sea level, you come through a hypnotic fog taking in a few distant twinkling lights of Africa, past the Rebmann glacier, kilometers below. And below that, stunning

wildlife and animals in their natural habitat.

Total Area Covered: 756 sq. km (292 sq. mi.)

Best Time to Visit: Clearest and warmest conditions, December–February; also dry, though colder, July–September

Nearest Town: Marangu

Attractions: Mount Kilimanjaro, trekking, elephants, rhino, buffalo

Accommodations: Ashanti Lodge, Kilimanjaro National Park hostel, and campsites

LAKE MANYARA NATIONAL PARK

Total Area Covered: 325 sq. km (125 sq. mi.)

Best Time to Visit: For large mammals—dry season, July–October

For bird watching, the waterfalls, and canoeing—wet season, November–June

Nearest Town: Arusha

Attractions: Tree climbing lions, baboons, buffalo, zebra, hippo pools, hot springs

Accommodations: Lake Manyara Serena Safari Lodge, Lake Manyara Hotel, Kiruruma Tented Camp, campsites, and less expensive accommodations outside the park

MAHALA MOUNTAINS NATIONAL PARK

Total Area Covered: 1,577 sq. km (608 sq. mi.)

Best Time to Visit: For forest walks—dry season, May–October (although there is no problem in the light rains of late-October–November)

Nearest Town: Kigoma

Attractions: Chimpanzee, walking safaris, brush-tailed porcupine, guinea fowl, various species of primates, black and white Colobus monkey

Accommodations: Kasiha Guest House and campsites

MIKUMI NATIONAL PARK

Total Area Covered: 3,230 sq. km (1,246 sq. mi.)

Best Time to Visit: Accessible year-round

Nearest Town: Morogoro

Attractions: Mkata River flood plain, crocodile, hippo pool, zebra, buffalo, elephant, giraffe

Accommodations: Mikumi Wildlife Lodge, Mikumi Wildlife Tented Camp, campsites, and youth hostel

NGORONGORO CONSERVATION AREA

Total Area Covered: 8,288 sq. km (3,196 sq. mi.)

Best Time to Visit: Year-round

Nearest Town: Arusha

Attractions: Olduvai Gorge, the crater, predators, elephant, buffalo, flamingoes, black rhino

Accommodations: Sopa Lodge, Serena Lodge, Ngorongoro Wildlife Lodge, Rhino Lodge, and campsites

RUBONDO

Total Area Covered: 240 sq. km (93 sq. mi.)

Best Time to Visit: Dry season, June–August

For wildflowers and butterflies—wet season, November–March

For migratory birds, December–February

Nearest Town: Mwanza

Attractions: Walking safaris, diverse bird life, sitatunga, chimpanzee, and hippo

Accommodations: Limited accommodations in a double bungalow, luxury tented camp (Rubondo Island Camp)

RUAHA NATIONAL PARK

Total Area Covered: 13,000 sq. km (5,000 sq. mi.)

Best Time to Visit: For predators and large mammals—dry season, mid-May–December

For bird watching, lush scenery, and wildflowers—wet season, January–April

Nearest Town: Iringa

Attractions: Great Ruaha River, antelope, gazelle, elephant, hyena, zebra, lions; walking and driving safaris

Accommodations: Ruaha River Lodge, Ruaha Exclusive Tented Camp, Mwangusi Safari Camp, campsites, and self-catering bandas

GAME RESERVES

MKOMAZI GAME RESERVE

Total Area Covered: 3,600 sq. km (1,390 sq. mi.)

Best Time to Visit: June–October and January–March

Nearest Town: Tanga

Attractions: Dindera Dam, large mammals, walking safaris

Accommodations: Two campsites, The Elephant Motel, Luther Hostel, and Savanna Hotel

SAADANI GAME RESERVE

Total Area Covered: 300 sq. km (115 sq. mi.)

Best Time to Visit: During dry season

Nearest Town: Bagamoyo

Attractions: Old German fort and some German graves, lions, zebra, grey parrot, secretary birds, buffalo

Accommodations: Campsites; and a few beach hotels in Bagamoyo

SELOUS GAME RESERVE

Total Area Covered: 55,000 sq. km (21,000 sq. mi.)

Best Time to Visit: January–February and July–October; also during the dry season

Nearest Town: Iringa

Attractions: Elephant, buffalo, lions, black rhino; walking, diving, and fishing trips

Accommodations: Selous Safari Camp, Stiegles Gorge Safari Camp, Rufiji River Camp, Mbuyuni Safari Camp, among others, and several camping sites

UWANDA GAME RESERVE

Total Area Covered: 5,000 sq. km (1,900 sq. mi.)

Best Time to Visit: March–October

Nearest Town: Mbeya

Attractions: Antelope, localized puku, albino giraffes, zebra, crocodile

Accommodations: Camping area available

AMANI NATURE RESERVE

Attractions: Botanical gardens, several nature trails

Accommodation: About six camping sites

BIHARAMULO GAME RESERVE

Attractions: Vervet monkey, mongoose, and many more

Accommodations: No facilities.

NOB HILL LAMBOURNE
725 Pine Street
Tel: 415-433-2287, www.nobhilllambourne.com

A small, quiet hotel that takes pride in being a small, quiet hotel, the Nob Hill Lambourne is set apart and yet is close enough to walk to Union Square, the Powell Street cable car, or Grace Cathedral. The hotel's 20 guest rooms, including six suites, will pamper you like only a small, personally run boutique hotel can. The beds are so comfortable you may have a hard time making that morning boat for Alcatraz.

COLORADO

ASPEN

HOTEL JEROME
330 East Main Street
Tel: 970-920-1000, www.hoteljerome.com

A refurbished landmark hotel right in the midst of Aspen's glitz, the Hotel Jerome has 92 rooms and suites that have special features such as private-label beds and oversized tubs in the lavish bathrooms. Two fine-dining restaurants and two bars are welcome places for relaxation after of day of hiking or skiing.

FLORIDA

MIAMI

THE BENTLEY BEACH HOTEL
101 Ocean Drive
305-938-4600

Just opened in fall 2005 in the heart of South Beach's newest hot area, the Bentley Beach Hotel has 109 all-suite accommodations in a great beach setting. It is home to Flavin Restaurant and the only Caroli Spa located outside of Italy.

MANDARIN ORIENTAL, MIAMI
500 Brickell Key Drive
Tel: 305-913-8288, www.mandarinoriental.com

The Mandarin Oriental, Miami, is situated on exclusive Brickell Key, with spectacular views of Biscayne Bay and the downtown Miami skyline. Close to the financial district, yet retaining a resort feeling, the hotel is just minutes from South Beach and Coconut Grove, perfect for discriminating business and leisure travelers. The hotel provides levels of luxury and service that have made Mandarin Oriental legendary.

THE RITZ-CARLTON, SOUTH BEACH
1 Lincoln Road
Tel: 786-276-4000, www.ritzcarlton.com

Another landmark hotel in the city's historic art deco district on fashionable Lincoln Road, the Ritz-Carlton, South Beach, is right on the Atlantic beach. It has 376 guest rooms and an art collection worth more than two million dollars. The spa, La Maison de Beauté Carita, is the largest on Miami Beach and the only spa of its kind outside of Paris.

HAWAI'I

THE BIG ISLAND

MAUNA KEA BEACH HOTEL
62-100 Mauna Kea Beach Drive, Kohala Coast
Tel: 808-882-7222, www.maunakeabeachhotel.com

Located on stunning Kauna'oa Bay, possibly the Big Island's most picturesque beach, the world-renowned

Mauna Kea Beach Hotel is a beautiful base for endless days of water activities—swimming, snorkeling, scuba diving, sailing, kayaking, catamaran riding, whale watching, deep-sea fishing—followed by relaxing evenings at one of the hotel's restaurants or the Tuesday luau. After dinner, stroll out to Manta Ray Point to watch the graceful rays swim past. Founder Laurance Rockefeller's vast collection of museum-quality Asian and Pacific art is displayed about the walls and grounds of the resort.

Mauna Lani Bay Hotel and Bungalows
68-1400 Mauna Lani Drive, Kohala Coast
Tel: 808-885-6622, www.maunalani.com

One of the most exquisite hotels on the Big Island, Mauna Lani Bay Hotel and Bungalows is located in Mauna Lani Resort, 37 kilometers (23 miles) north of Kona International Airport. While the hotel consists of 350 guest rooms, 92 percent of which have ocean views, the best choices are the five individual bungalows, which offer guests exclusive privacy, including private swimming pools and round-the-clock butler service.

Four Seasons Resort Hualalai at Historic Ka'upulehu
100 Ka'upulehu Drive, Ka'upulehu-Kona
Tel: 808-325-8000, www.fourseasons.com/hualalai

Set on the otherworldly Kona-Kohala Coast, this tropical oasis captures the essence of Hawaii's golden age. It offers seclusion without isolation, a private Jack Nicklaus–designed golf course, and 243 bungalow-style guest rooms with lanais and some with outdoor lava rock showers. The sunset views from this part of the island are worth the trip by themselves.

KAUAI

Kauai Marriott Resort & Beach Club
Kalapaki Beach, 3610 Rice Street, Lihue
Tel: 808-245-5050, www.marriotthawaii.com/kauai

Kauai is the oldest of the major Hawaiian Islands and consequently has the most eroded and interesting mountains, all surrounded by pure white beaches and sapphire lagoons. The Kauai Marriott Resort has 345 rooms on a marvelous property of 320 hectares (800 acres) adjacent to Kalapaki Beach in Lihue.

LANA'I

The Lodge at Koele
Lana'i City
Tel: 808-565-7300, www.fourseasons.com/koele

Lana'i used to be of little interest to most tourists because of its lack of facilities and attractions, being essentially nothing more than a giant pineapple field. That's changed now with the development of outstanding resorts such as the Lodge at Koele. In a setting reminiscent of the plantation owner's home, set up in the highlands of the island's center, the 100 rooms and suites have beautiful hand-carved four-poster beds, ceiling fans, and in some cases fireplaces. Artworks by local artists decorate the facilities. There are two golf courses, one with ocean views. The hotel remains open in 2006 during a major renovation that promises even greater luxury.

The Manele Bay Hotel
Lana'i City
Tel: 808-565-7700, www.islandoflanai.com

Another top choice in Lana'i is the Manele Bay Hotel, set dramatically above amazing Hulopo'e Beach, probably the island's best beach. There's tennis, the Challenge at Manele golf course, and many other active pursuits, but you might prefer to let go with some sun time, a massage, and a leisurely meal. The hotel is graced by a priceless collection of ancient Hawaiian artifacts.

MAUI

HOTEL HANA-MAUI AT HANA RANCH
Hana
Tel: 1808-248-8211, www.hotelhanamaui.com

The Road to Hana is one of the great drives of the world, albeit not for the faint of heart. The 83-kilometers (52-mile) trip from the town of Pa'ia east to Hana along the old king's road takes from two hours to two-and-a-half hours, not counting stops or delays, although recent resurfacing of the road has helped a lot. When you arrive in Hana, you will finally know what the word "paradise" really means.

Having left the real world far behind, it is nice to know that paradise has good hotels, too. The legendary Hotel Hana-Maui has been a favorite for weddings, honeymoons, and romantic getaways for more than 50 years. As secluded and remote as this place is, don't be too surprised to see someone you know—or at least feel like you know because you've watched them on the TV or the big screen so many times. Luxury accommodations include a variety of sheltered cottages. There's also the ultra-extravagant Plantation Guest House, but that's probably where your "friend" is staying.

FOUR SEASONS RESORT MAUI AT WAILEA
3900 Wailea Alanui, Wailea
Tel: 808-874-8000, www.fourseasons.com/maui

A hotel for all four seasons. Ever-sunny Wailea features a perfect crescent of white sand, and the Four Seasons is in an ideal position on the bay, with a unique U-shaped design

BLUE HAWAIIAN HELICOPTERS

1 Kahului Airport Road, Hangar 105
Kahului, Maui, Hawaii 96732
Tel: 808-961-5600

Flying with Blue Hawaiian is the most exciting way to see Hawaii. Dave and Patti Chevalier came to Maui from Green Bay, Wisconsin. Dave, a former Vietnam scout pilot, found work flying tours for South Seas Helicopters; Patti taught high-school social studies. When South Seas was put up for sale, Dave and Patti risked everything to buy it.

At Blue Hawaiian, "Nothing but the very best" is not some casual slogan. Ever since they opened their doors in 1985, it's been a pledge, their promise, and their way of life. They have been awarded the FAA's coveted Diamond Certificate of Excellence every year since 1998. Being the only helicopter tour company in Hawaii operating a factory-authorized American Euro copter service center, Blue Hawaiian never stops innovating, never stops improving, never stops asking, "How can we do it even better?"

Blue Hawaiian Helicopters is the premier helicopter tour company in Hawaii, with a great safety record, flown by the best and most experienced helicopter pilots. The tour is a unique blend of cultural excursions to some of Hawaii's most remote and breathtakingly beautiful places.

You will explore deep valleys set in the rain forest of the ancient West Maui Mountains. Knife-edged ridges with mist-shrouded peaks separate the spectacular valleys. Waterfalls fall from towering cliffs into streams below. Then fly over Haleakala Crater and Hana's rain forest to the rugged shoreline of northeast Maui.

that allows almost all rooms to have ocean views. Expect Four Seasons service, of course, along with the comfort of the some of the largest rooms in the Islands, dining at Spago, and championship golf.

GRAND WAILEA RESORT HOTEL AND SPA
3850 Wailea Alanui, Wailea
Tel: 808-875-1234, www.grandwailea.com

Another marvelous resort on exquisite Wailea Bay is the Grand Wailea Resort Hotel and Spa. The hotel offers 780 rooms, including some 50 suites, on 16 hectares (40 acres) of tropical gardens. The water park area is unbelievable. The Grand Wailea Resort staff consistently has Hawaiian hospitality and aloha at its finest.

KAPALUA BAY HOTEL
One Bay Drive, Kapalua
Tel: 808-669-5656, www.kapaluabayhotel.com

On the west side of Maui, toward the end of the Lahaina road, is the Kapalua Resort with its world-famous golf courses and the picture-perfect Kapalua Bay. The Kapalua Bay Hotel is a luxury 191-room (plus 20 suites) hotel situated just above the bay, offering spectacular views of the ocean, with sensational sunsets over the neighboring islands Lana'i and Molokai. Low-rise deluxe accommodations feature oversized rooms and lanais, most overlooking the ocean. Choose from two restaurants, and don't miss breakfast on the open-air terrace under the banyan tree.

OAHU

SHERATON MOANA SURFRIDER
2365 Kalakaua Avenue, Honolulu
Tel: 808-922-3111, www.moanasurfrider.com

In 1901, the "First Lady of Waikiki" became the first true resort to rise on what quickly became the world's most famous beach. Today, restored to her original turn-of-the-20th-century grandeur, the oceanfront Sheraton Moana Surfrider is the perfect place to stay with the paradise of Waikiki Beach out one side and the haute shopping and nightlife of Honolulu's tourist mecca on the other. There are 793 rooms and suites on a scale that most modern hotels have forgotten about. Each room and breeze-swept veranda in the historic Banyan Wing has been restored to its original style with mahogany and koa wood.

IHILANI RESORT AND SPA
92-1001 Olani Street, Ko Olina
Tel: 808-679-0079, www.ihilani.com

The J. W. Marriott Ihilani is located in a new resort development on the southwest corner of Oahu in an area that used to be a royal playground. On the first of seven magnificent lagoon sites, the hotel overlooks the lagoons and one of the finest white-sand beaches in all of Hawaii. Its luxury suites include the Presidential Suite, the Beachfront Suite, and 34 others. The six deluxe spa rooms have private lanais with outdoor spas. There are two pools, four distinctive restaurants, world-class boutiques and spa, and a championship golf course on the resort.

HILTON HAWAIIAN VILLAGE
2005 Kalia Road, Honolulu
Tel: 808-949-4321, www.hiltonhawaiianvillage.com

Hilton Hawaiian Village Beach Resort and Spa is a superb Waikiki resort, offering the perfect mix of exceptional resort accommodations and classic Hawaiian hospitality, all nestled on nine beachfront hectares (22 acres) on the widest stretch of white sand on Waikiki. The complex is at the westernmost end of Waikiki, making it more convenient for venturing out of Waikiki to downtown Honolulu or

upcountry Oahu, while still being walking distance by beach or road to everything in exciting Waikiki itself.

HALEKULANI
2199 Kalia Road, Honolulu
Tel: 808-923-2311, www.halekulani.com

The Halekulani is another of the early Waikiki Beach hotels whose genial hospitality and flawless service have made this tropical paradise such a desirable vacation spot for nearly 100 years. The Halekulani's magnificent rooms and luxury suites are unsurpassed on the island and each has a lanai with wonderful views. Try the Vera Wang Suite for the ultimate in stylish comfort.

Each of Halekulani's three restaurants offers its own distinctive style, but La Mer stands out as one of the best places to dine in Hawaii, with one-of-a-kind dishes from Hawaii's freshest, most delectable ingredients. The House Without A Key is another choice for more relaxed dining, and it is renowned as one of the best places in Honolulu to watch the sunset, serenaded by live Hawaiian music.

MASSACHUSETTS

BOSTON

FIFTEEN BEACON
15 Beacon Street
Tel: 617-670-1500, www.xvbeacon.com

In a lovely 1903 Beaux Arts building in central Boston, Fifteen Beacon is a cozy hotel with Jeffersonian styling, guest rooms with working gas fireplaces and four-poster beds, and fresh flowers everywhere, yet contemporary in feel—the best of both worlds in Boston.

LENOX

WHEATLEIGH
Hawthorne Road
Tel: 413-637-0610, www.wheatleigh.com

In the beautiful Berkshire Mountains of western Massachusetts, the Wheatleigh is the quintessential New England getaway in high style, not a long drive from New York or Boston but light-years away in seclusion and fresh mountain air. The grand 1893 structure is patterned after a Florentine palazzo and is a perfect marriage of elegance and 21st-century comfort. With 9 hectares (22 acres) of grounds on a lake, the Wheatleigh has just completed a four-year renovation to bring it up to the highest standards. The hotel has just 19 rooms, including the unique Aviary—a tree house suite built in and around a century-old Norway spruce with its bedroom at treetop level.

NEW YORK

MANHATTAN

THE ST. REGIS HOTEL
Two East 55th Street at Fifth Avenue
Tel: 212-753-4500

The St. Regis Hotel is one of New York's best-known hotels, built in 1904 in Beaux Arts exuberance in midtown Manhattan. Step out the door onto Fifth Avenue, one of the most glamorous shopping districts in the world. The St. Regis has the poise of a grande dame with all the finest modern amenities. Its 256 guest rooms and suites are flamboyantly ornate, with Louis XVI–style furniture, crystal chandeliers suspended from high ceilings, and silk wall coverings.

FOUR SEASONS HOTEL
57 East 57th Street between Park and Madison Avenues
Tel: 212-758-5700, www.fourseasons.com/newyorkfs

Located on fashionable East 57th Street, the I.M. Pei–designed Four Seasons rises over Manhattan's premier shopping and business district, allowing sweeping views of Central Park from rooms on the upper floors. Some rooms and most suites have terraces with city or park views. The rooms are appointed in the homey feel of a classy Manhattan loft.

LE PARKER MERIDIEN
118 West 57th Street between Sixth and Seventh Avenues
Tel: 212-245-5000, www.parkermeridien.com

Le Parker Meridien is conveniently positioned for visiting Central Park, just two blocks north, or the Fifth Avenue shopping district two blocks east. Also nearby is the recently renovated Museum of Modern Art. The hotel is hip, moderne, and trendy, with 730 ergonomically inspired rooms and suites. The lobby has a three-story atrium with natural light, and the restaurant is home to the one thousand dollar caviar omelet.

THE LIBRARY HOTEL
299 Madison Avenue at 41st Street
Tel: 212-983-4500, www.libraryhotel.com

Its location near the New York City Public Library and the Pierpont Morgan Library inspired the bookish theme of this club-style hotel in a restored 1900 brick and terra-cotta building. The Library Hotel is has 60 plush guest rooms on ten floors themed to the ten major divisions of the Dewey Decimal System. Books and artwork abound and are matched with the floor's theme—Literature, Languages, or Math and Science, for example. The complimentary breakfast is served in the Reading Room, naturally, although presumably no one will berate you for talking.

THE LOWELL
28 East 63rd Street between Madison and Park Avenues
Tel: 212-838-1400, www.lowellhotel.com

For those looking for a home away from home, the Lowell provides a residential atmosphere on a quiet, tree-lined street just east of Central Park. The 47 individually decorated suites and 21 deluxe rooms have fireplaces, terraces, and fully equipped kitchens, making this a great location for visitors who will be spending more of their time in their rooms than in Times Square and want to feel at ease.

THE MARK
25 East 77th St. at Madison Avenue
Tel: 212-744-4300, www.themarkhotel.com

There aren't many better addresses. This classic European-style hotel is just off Central Park on the Upper East Side near the Museum Mile, including the Metropolitan Museum of Art, one of the greatest museums in the world. The Mark features excellent service, and it's wonderfully discreet.

HÔTEL PLAZA ATHÉNÉE
37 East 64th Street between Madison and Park Avenues
Tel: 212-734-9100, www.plaza-athenee.com

The Hôtel Plaza Athénée is another top-drawer, European-style hotel just a short walk from Central Park and well located for hitting the boutiques along Madison Avenue. Many suites have dining rooms, indoor terraces, and outdoor balconies.

SARANAC LAKE

THE POINT
P. O. Box 1327
Tel: 518-891-5674, thepointresort.com

In the days when high society was ranked by the number of mansions one owned and by the lavishness of the parties one could throw, the very wealthy of New York built mountain retreats in the Adirondacks where they could get away from it all—with all their servants and friends, that is. The area around Saranac Lake saw the construction of many of these so-called Great Camps in the late 1800s and early 1900s, and William Avery Rockefeller's was one of the finest. It is now open to all as the Point resort, with 11 distinctive guest quarters among four buildings on a four-hectare (ten-acre) peninsula stretching into Upper Saranac Lake.

The exterior of the Point is rustic log cabin style, although on a scale of the grand national park lodges. Inside, it's part woodsy hunting lodge, part palace. The main building contains the Great Hall, where guests gather to dine. The Eagle's Nest houses three guest rooms and a pub, while the Boathouse, constructed over the lake, has unique accommodations.

NORTH CAROLINA

THE FEARRINGTON HOUSE
2000 Fearrington Village Center, Pittsboro
Tel: 919-542-2121
www.fearringtonhouse.com

Just outside Chapel Hill, R. B. Fitch restored traditional Southern hospitality at this elegant country inn set amid floral gardens in the heart of a quaint Southern village. The attractive suites and guest rooms are each individually decorated with antique furniture, original artwork, and bouquets of fresh flowers. Experience exquisitely prepared regional cuisine by soft candlelight and enjoy poetry readings, wine tastings, and garden visits during your stay.

TEXAS

LAJITAS
Big Bend
Tel: 432-424-5000, www.lajitas.com

Far, far away from it all, in West Texas near Big Bend National Park, is the destination resort of Lajitas. Solitude in the 10,000-hectare (25,000-acre) private estate of land once traveled by the Comanche and Pancho Villa is the draw at Lajitas, where you can fill your lungs with some of the freshest air in the United States and enjoy desert vistas that seem to go on forever. This is far from the ranch days in the bunkhouse, however. Comfort is the byword, from the rooms to the spa, and nature is the reason for being here, whether seen from the 14th tee or the back of a sturdy Pinto.

UTAH

STEIN ERIKSEN LODGE
7700 Stein Way, Park City
Tel: 435-649-3700, www.steinlodge.com

A combination of moist Pacific lows, the Great Salt Lake, and cold temperatures bless the mountains above Salt Lake City with 12.7 meters (500 inches) of blue smoke powder snow each year. With only a limited number of skiers allowed on the mountain at Deer Valley Resort, the experience is a skier's dream. The Stein Eriksen Lodge here is the best place to stay while taking advantage of this great skiing, but it is also a year-round property where summer visitors can enjoy hiking and mountain biking on the slopes. Created in 1982 by Olympic gold medalist Stein Eriksen, the lodge was built

to rival the best mountain hotels in the world in terms of service and luxury. The luxury suites have gourmet kitchens, stone fireplaces, balconies, and sleep up to 18 people.

VIRGINIA

THE INN AT LITTLE WASHINGTON
Middle and Main Streets, Washington
Tel: 540-675-3800, www.theinnatlittlewashington.com

In the foothills of the Blue Ridge Mountains is a romantic village that was first surveyed by George Washington in 1749 and is today the home of one of America's most renowned country retreats. For two decades, Chef Patrick O'Connell and Reinhardt Lynch have treated guests to a festival of culinary wonders and exquisite hospitality. Each dish is a work of art, showcasing regional delights. Every extravagant guest room is a tribute to taste and comfort.

WASHINGTON, D.C.

HOTEL MONACO
700 F St., NW, Washington, DC 20004
Tel: 202-628-7177 or 800-6491201, www.monaco-dc.com

One of the newest luxury hotels in Washington's vibrant Penn Quarter, the Hotel Monaco is located in the 1839 National Landmark Tariff Building. Oriental carpets cover the floors of the Robert Mills-designed structure built originally to house the postal department. Convenient to theaters and the bustling arts scene, each room is distinctively decorated, taking advantage of the room's tall windows and 15-foot ceilings.

THE RITZ-CARLTON
1150 22nd Street, NW, Washington, DC 20036
Tel: 202-835-0500, www.ritzcarlton.com

Located just a few blocks from the White House in the Dupont Circle area and within walking distance of effervescent Georgetown, The Ritz-Carlton, continues to capture awards for its luxury setting and exceptional service. The rooms are decorated in the Ritz-Carlton version of American Colonial.

THE WILLARD INTERCONTINENTAL
1401 Pennsylvania Ave., NW
Washington, DC 20004
Tel: 202-628-9100, www.washington.intercontinental.com

Two blocks from the White House, the Willard hotel represents history in a town known for politics. As early as the 1860s, the Willard's lobby was christened the "center of Washington," and it was where Pres. Ulysses S. Grant first coined the term "lobbyist" to refer to those people who approached him as he relaxed there. President Lincoln held staff meetings in the same front lobby, and the Willard was the hotel he chose to stay in prior to his inauguration. Other Presidents from Taylor to Clinton have also used this historic location for meetings and relaxation. And it was here that the words to the "Battle Hymn of the Republic" were penned by Julia Ward Howe. Today, the Willard is still the place to overnight in Washington, especially if you can secure a room on the famed Pennsylvania Avenue side to watch an inaugural parade or the annual Fourth of July fireworks.

WEST VIRGINIA

THE GREENBRIER
300 W. Main Street, White Sulphur Springs
Tel: 304-536-1110, www.greenbrier.com

The Greenbrier is a world apart, completely self-contained in the scenic Allegheny Mountains of West Virginia yet

with every amenity one could desire. You might think this would be the ideal place to get away from the troubles of the world, and you would be right—at least the U.S. government thought so when it constructed an enormous top-secret A-bomb shelter under the wing of the main hotel that would have housed all the national leaders, including all of Congress, in the event of nuclear war. Fortunately, that oversized basement is now just a Cold War curiosity, to be visited on tours. With no fallout in the air, the Greenbrier can be better enjoyed above ground. Take advantage of the resort's 2,600 hectares (6,500 acres) to play golf on one of the three 18-hole courses, go hunting or fishing, or brush up on falconry skills. The healthful sulfur-laden water of White Sulphur Springs is the reason the first inn was built here in 1780, and guests can get the benefits from it at the spa. The Greenbrier has 803 guest accommodations, from rooms to estate houses, and throughout its 225-year history, these rooms have hosted 26 U.S. presidents or presidents-to-be.

WYOMING

AMANGANI
1535 North East Butte Road, Jackson, Wyoming
Tel: 307-734-7333 or 877-734-7333, www.amangani.com

Known for its lovely views and crisp clear air, Jackson Hole provides a haven from the work-a-day world, and the new Amangani Resort is a wonderful place to enjoy it. The decks outside the individual suites furnish a relaxing spot to enjoy views of the Teton Range and the Snake River, while recovering from a day's hike in Grand Teton National Park. Amenities include two exercise studios (for those who haven't climbed the peaks), steam rooms, and a 35-meter pool surrounded by mountains. For the winter outdoor enthusiast, the resort has a ski lodge at the nearby Jackson Hole Mountain Resort. Yoga and meditation classes, horseback riding, and flyfishing are among the other opportunities offered the guests.

RUSTY PARROT LODGE & SPA
175 North Jackson Street, Jackson Hole
Tel: 307-733-2000, www.rustyparrot.com

The natural splendor of Jackson Hole is unsurpassed, and the Rusty Parrot Lodge and Spa is another good place to stay while you soak it all in. Located a stone's throw from Jackson Town Square, the Rusty Parrot has top-rated accommodations, dining, and day spa. But Jackson is a place for the outdoors, so be sure to let the Rusty Parrot's concierges arrange for your daily activities, including wildlife safaris, whitewater rafting, and chuckwagon dinner shows, along with more modern pursuits such as golf, tennis, rock climbing, or cycling.

URUGUAY

FOUR SEASONS RESORT CARMELO
Ruta 21, km 262, Carmelo, Colonia
Tel: 598-542-9000, www.fourseasons.com/carmelo

The scenic riverbank of the Río de la Plata, a Pan-Asian temple-like spa, tasteful restaurants, championship golf, riding, and fishing—they're all here. A 1930 Buick sedan provides comfort that is pure Four Seasons. Just a ferry-crossing from Buenos Aires and a drive from Montevideo is Carmelo, where the accommodations and service are pure magic.

TRAVEL NOTES

TRAVEL NOTES

~INDEX~

INDEX

INDEX

INDEX

INDEX

INDEX

INDEX

INDEX

INDEX

Special Thanks & Acknowledgements

Outstanding appreciation to book designer Lisa Vaughn-Soraghan, whose extraordinary talents are seen on these pages.

To Rick Gerwitz, who created a cover and spreads for the catalog, and Mirko Ilic, whose design abilities are second to none.

—·—

And to editor Eugene Soraghan, who gave his time and talent.

Special appreciation also to Elizabeth Newhouse, Marianne Koszorus, Gary Colbert, and Cameron Zotter of National Geographic Books, and Jessica Papin and Michael Bourret of Dystel Goderich Literary Management.

—·—

And to Sheila Rice of Northstar Travel Media, who graciously provided copy, research, and access to company files.

To James Dunford Wood and Angelea Moore of Travel Intelligence UK for their staff of fine travel writers.

Our thanks also to photographers Eric Jacobson, for his tabletop photography, and to the talented Richard Barenholtz of New York and Michelle Strickland. All provided great images.

To Marie Cantlon, Maya Gottfried, and Jane Lahr, for their friendship, support, and love of design and the written word.

And Ken Petchenik, distinguished publisher and editor of the "Passport Newsletter," whose support, friendship, and research library made this book possible.

—·—

We are thankful to the following, a battalion of supporters for *The 10 Best of Everything*. Sincerest appreciation to each for their contributions.

Rob Robertson
Arnold Palmer
Frank Delaney
Pippa Isbell, Orient-Express
Nina Lora
Gabriela Knubis
Lori Lincoln

Lucy Powell, Air New Zealand
Lauren Kaufman, Spring-O'Brien
Jackie Mathews, Cunard Lines
Lucinda Morrison, The National Theater
London Pass
Lert Narongchaisakum, Tourist Authority of Thailand
Sarah Scoltock, Holland American Lines
Onie Chu, Three on The Bund, Shanghai
Doc Griffin
Teresa Delaney
David Rosenthal
Laura Font
Karen Winpenny, Hilton Hotels
Kristen Torrione, Spring-O'Brien
Elana Grossman
Anita Li, the Peninsula Hotel, Hong Kong
Jeffrey Raynor
Bea Wolfe, Passport Resorts
Country Walkers
Dr. Nancy Moss
Rege Ludwig
Vickie Legg
Anna Nash
Kathryn Malone
Myanmar International Airlines
Christopher Meigher
Pen Tudor

SPECIAL THANKS & ACKNOWLEDGEMENTS

Patrick Chourgnoz
Rory MacPherson
Sarah Johnson
Stephanie Platt
Fiona Duthie
Annika Bowman
The Rt. Hon. Victoria Thorneycroft
Lady Carla Thorneycroft
Sir John Ward
Sir David Landale
Mark Carlson, Star Clippers
Valerie Ramsey
Howard Rombough, One Aldwych Place, London
Lamey Chang
Mike Wong, Sansdisk
The Morgan Group
Brenda Rodricks, Versailles Hotels
Monica Helmer, Panasonic
Julie Gajcak, Ritz-Carlton
Karon Cullen
Dr. Carlos Sereday
Pablo Retamal
Bruno Trouble
Sundae May, American Airlines
Regent's Court Sydney
Sir Edmund Hillary
Paula McMahon
Campton Place, San Francisco
Michelle Lin, East Travel
Kristen Bergevin, The Phelps Group
Russell Burrows
George Deeb, iExplore.com
Ron Walters
Ken Davids, The Coffee Review

Sheila Donnelly
New Zealand Tourism Board
Tourism Board of Chile
Keoni Wagner, Hawaiian Airlines
Jana Czarnecki, Fox Global Communications
Kate Stingly
Malaysia Airlines
Bruce Good, Seabourn Cruise Lines
Gina Finocchiaro, Silversea Cruises
Crystal Cruises
Windstar Cruises
Jennifer Pearson, Cathay Pacific
Lori Lincoln, Shangri-La Hotels and Resorts
John Lampl, British Airways
Harriet Zois, The Hammond Group
Pam Carter, The Fairmont Group
Peter Sullivan
Anita Cotter, The Maybourne Group
Orient-Express
Meg Paynor, Murphy O'Brien, and the Peninsula Group
The Savoy Group
Mike Carpenter
Mark Carlson
Wyndham Carver
David Soskin

———·———

The authors have used information from their own files and researched thousands of candidates for the best from other sources. Selections, while subjective, are based on rigid criteria. We are very grateful for the cooperation of and contributions from hotels, airlines, cruise lines, and product manufacturers. We wish to credit and acknowledge the copy supplied by these companies for the book. In some instances, we have edited their materials and have listed telephone numbers and websites for more information.

And appreciation and thanks to a legion of TIME correspondents, colleagues, and contributors.

~Illustrations Credits & Text Contributors ~

ILLUSTRATIONS COURTESY OF:
Nathaniel Lande collection,
    vintage art throughout the book
Collection of David Levine 2
Pebble Beach Company 15
Argentine Polo Association 19, 31
Las Ventanas al Paraiso, A Rosewood
    Resort 25
National Park Service 34, 68
Equitours 37
Country Walkers 46
Boracay Island Tourism 51
Glass of Guinness, Guinness 66
Venice lion, The Rt. Hon. Victoria
    Thorneycroft 72
Pangkor Laut, Fox Global
    Communications 92
Savoy Hotel room, Fairmont
    Hotels 101
Yancy Hughes 108
Eric Jacobson Studio 123, 199, 201,
    210, 215, 220, 222, 223, 229,
    230, 237
Windstar Cruises 142
Visit London Image Bank 172
Richard Berenholtz 179, 180, 182
Peter Y. Sobolev 185
New South Wales Image Bank 197,
    198
Payard, courtesy of Alexandra Payard
    216, 218 (top)
Norman Love 218 (bottom)

Kathryn K. Russell 224
Haagen-Dazs 226
Orient-Express 43, 53, 61, 93, 113,
    133, 161 (courtesy Hotel
    Caruso)
Alain Dumas 151
Hotel Hassler Rome, courtesy Uta
    Wilmer 165, 167
Rome watercolor, Sir John Ward 166
Hotel Adlon 168
Hikmet Barutcugil 188
Istanbul mosques, courtesy Turkey
    Tourist Board 189
Hotel Crillon, courtesy Karon Cullen
    194
Nathaniel Lande 204
Virgil's Real Barbecue 212
The Ginger Man 232
Authors' photo, Michelle Strickland
    480

——·——

TEXT CONTRIBUTORS:
Tony Fins
Leslie Thomas
Stephen Lash
Orient-Express: the Road to
    Mandalay, Eastern Oriental
    Express, Simplon London-Venice,
    and Safari Lodges
James Sherwood

Paul McManus
SLH
Relais & Châteaux
The Lady Thorneycroft
Karon Cullen
Sheila Donnelly: Select hotels
Sheila Rice, Northstar Travel:
    Antarctica, Greece, Turkey, and
    Argentina. Copyrighted material
    provided by Northstar Travel
    Media, LLC. All rights reserved.
Starbucks Coffee Company
Ken Davids, The Coffee Review
Brian Mills, Small Luxury Hotels
Roger Bulot, Relais & Châteaux
Passport Newsletter: English Walking
    Tours, Teas, Cheese, and Beer,
    and accommodations in Greece
Rege Ludwig: best polo clubs
Pippa Isbell, Orient-Express
John Borthwick
Martin O'Brien
Frank Delaney
Bayard Fox
Bob Ellsasser
Peter Hayden
Luciano Pavarotti
Arnold Palmer
Doc Griffin
Sir John Ward
Fox Global Communications
Ken Petchenik

Nathaniel Lande was educated at Oxford University and earned his doctorate at Trinity College, Dublin. He is author of nine books including the highly acclaimed *Dispatches from the Front: A History of the American War Correspondent*, Oxford University Press.

He was creative director of the Magazine Group, TIME Incorporated; director of TIME World News Service; a founding director of TIME-Life Films; executive producer for both the CBS and NBC Television Networks; producer/director for Movies of the Week at CBS Television, Cinema Center Films, and Universal MCA.. His films and documentaries have won more than 20 international awards.

Lande has held appointments as professor to the School of Journalism and Communication at the University of North Carolina, Chapel Hill, and the Fuqua School of Business at Duke University, and as Distinguished Scholar to Trinity College, Dublin.

Wine and food expert Andrew Lande holds degrees from the University of California, Santa Cruz, and Trinity College, Dublin. He is co-author with Nathaniel Lande of *The Cigar Connoisseur* and co-writer of the award-winning A&E Biography special, "Bob Hope: America's Entertainer."

———•———

Books by the Authors

Mindstyles/Lifestyles
The Emotional Maintenance Manuel
Self-Health
Stages
The Moral Responsibility of the Press
Blueprinting
Dispatches from the Front
The Cigar Connoisseur, with Andrew Lande

Published by the National Geographic Society

A Nathaniel Lande Book
Copyright © 2006 Nathaniel Lande and Andrew Lande
All rights reserved. Reproduction of the whole or any part of the contents without permission is prohibited.

Library of Congress Cataloging-in-Publication Data
Lande, Nathaniel.
The 10 best of everything : passport to the best : an ultimate guide for travelers/
Nathaniel Lande, Andrew Lande.—1st ed.
    p. cm.
    ISBN 0-7922-5364-7
    1. Travel—Guidebooks. I. Title: Ten best of everything. II. Lande,Andrew. III. Title.

G153.4.L35 2006
910.2'02—dc22   2005043513

ISBN-10: 0-7922-5364-7
ISBN-13: 978-0-7922-5364-8

Founded in 1888, the National Geographic Society is one of the largest nonprofit scientific and educational organizations in the world. It reaches more than 285 million people worldwide each month through its official journal, NATIONAL GEOGRAPHIC, and its four other magazines; the National Geographic Channel; television documentaries; radio programs; films; books; videos and DVDs; maps; and interactive media. National Geographic has funded more than 8,000 scientific research projects and supports an education program combating geographic illiteracy.

For more information, please call 1-800-NGS LINE (647-5463) or write to the following address:

National Geographic Society
1145 17th Street N.W.
Washington, D.C. 20036-4688 U.S.A.

Log on to nationalgeographic.com; AOL Keyword: NatGeo

For information about special discounts for bulk purchases, please contact National Geographic Books Special Sales: ngspecsales@ngs.org

Printed in U.S.A.